ALL  THE  PARABLES  OF  THE  BIBLE

# ALL THE PARABLES
# OF THE BIBLE

A STUDY AND ANALYSIS OF THE MORE THAN 250 PARABLES IN SCRIPTURE

Including Those in the Old Testament, As Well As Those of Our Lord,
and Others, in the New Testament

by
DR. HERBERT LOCKYER. R.S.L., F.R.G.S.

*"Why speakest thou unto them in parables?"*
Matt. 13:10

ZONDERVAN
PUBLISHING HOUSE OF THE ZONDERVAN CORPORATION
GRAND RAPIDS, MICHIGAN 49506

Library of Congress Catalog Card Number 63-15746

| | | |
|---|---|---|
| First printing | | 1963 |
| Second printing | | 1964 |
| Third printing | | 1966 |
| Fourth printing | January | 1967 |
| Fifth printing | December | 1967 |
| Sixth printing | December | 1968 |
| Seventh printing | March | 1969 |
| Eighth printing | January | 1970 |
| Ninth printing | September | 1970 |
| Tenth printing | April | 1971 |
| Eleventh printing | November | 1971 |
| Twelfth printing | February | 1973 |
| Thirteenth printing | September | 1973 |

*Printed in the United States of America*

*Dedicated*
*to*
JAMES CORDINER, OF ABERDEEN
*A Great Defender of the Faith;*
*And to His Four Sons,*

JAMES, JR.
ALFRED,
NORMAN,
STEPHEN,

*All of Whom Are As Diligent*
*in the Cause of Christ.*

# CONTENTS

# INTRODUCTION

In the entire realm of literature there is no book so rich in its parabolic and allegoric material as the Bible. Where, for instance, can we find parables, emblems or figures of speech, comparable to those of the prophets of old, including Jesus, the greatest of them all, employed as they addressed themselves to those of their time? Knowing the power and the fascination of pictorial speech, they used it to great effect in their oral ministry. As we shall discover in our study of such a subject, Bible parables, especially those of the Lord Jesus, are the choicest examples of figurative speech employed to express and enforce Divine truths.

Already in a previous volume, *All the Miracles of the Bible,* we have drawn attention to the differences between *Miracles*—which are parables in *works;* and *Parables,* which are miracles in *words.* There is nothing of the miraculous in parables, which, in the main, are natural and inevitable, and illustrate grace and judgment. Miracles display power and mercy. Westcott, in his study on *The Gospels,* tells us parables and miracles "are exactly correlative to each other; in the one we see the personality and power of the Worker, and in the other the generality and constancy of the Work; . . . in the one we are led to regard the manifoldness of Providence, and in the other to recognize the instructive of the Universe."

In a discussion of the various aspects of the development and demonstration of the parabolic method as found in the Bible, it is interesting to note how many writers on such a theme, pay tribute to the comprehensive survey Trench gives us in his *Notes on the Parables.* Dr. Cosmo Gordon Lang, for example, in the *Preface* of his most helpful volume on *The Parables of Jesus,* tells us that Trench's great work was the only one he consulted as he

prepared his own book. "It would be mere presumption to attempt to write anything on the subject of the Parables," says Bishop Lang, "without using the guidance of Archbishop Trench's scholarship and insight." Other expositors of *the Parables,* including myself, are equal in their confession of indebtedness to Trench. For the guidance of preachers and students we set forth necessary introductory material under the following sections:

## The Maturity of the Parabolic Method

While the use of parables was a unique feature of the popular teaching of Jesus for, "without a parable spake He not unto them," He did not invent this form of teaching. Parables go back to antiquity. While Jesus contributed His unique parables to religious literature, and raised such a method of teaching to its highest level, He was cognizant of the antiquity of this method of presenting truth. In the age and country in which Christ appeared, parables were a common and popular method of instruction, for both parables and fables were popular among the people of the East. Dr. Salmond, in his handbook on *The Parables of Our Lord,* reminds us in the paragraph dealing with "The Charm of Figurative Speech," that speech of this kind had —

> A special attraction for the peoples of the East, with whom the imagination is quicker and more active than the logical faculty. The great family of nations known as the Semitic, to which the Hebrews, together with the Arabs, the Syrians, the Babylonians, and other remarkable races belong, has shown a particular genius and liking for it.

The ancient status of this common mode of expression is proved by its abundant use in different forms in the

9

Old Testament. The first recorded parable in the form of a fable, is that of the trees choosing for themselves a king, an exposition of which follows (Judges 9). Jotham used this fable in order to convince the inhabitants of Shechem of the folly of having elected so vile a man as Abimelech for their King. The parables and similes of the Old Testament outlined in this section prove how common was the parabolic method of instruction. For an understanding of the way Jewish writers of old used the visible world to illustrate the spiritual realm, the reader is referred to the most interesting chapter Trench has on "Other Parables Besides Those in the Scriptures." In a footnote, Jewish Cabbalists are quoted as saying that "the heavenly light never descends without a veil . . . It is impossible that the Divine ray can shine upon us unless it be shrouded with a diversity of sacred coverings."

Because of His infinity, God had to condescend to those things with which man was familiar in order to convey to man's finite mind the sublime revelation of His will. Thus bare precepts were clothed with parables and similitudes. Hillel and Shammai were the most illustrious teachers by parables before the time of Christ. After Him was Meir, with whom tradition says the power of inventing parables notably declined. The fig-tree of the Jewish people was withered and could put forth no more fruit.

When our Lord appeared among men as a Teacher He took possession of the *parable* and honored it by making it His own, by using it as the vehicle for the highest truth of all. Knowing how Jewish teachers illustrated their doctrines by the help of parables and comparisons, Christ adopted these old forms and gave them a newness of spirit, as He proclaimed the transcendent glory and excellency of His teaching. After Him, the parabolic method was seldom used by the apostles. There are no parables in *The Acts,* but as we shall indicate when we reach the New Testament, *The Epistles* and *The Revelation* contain striking examples of divine truth clothed in human garb.

While *The Apocrypha* makes full use of figurative language, there are no parables in the *Apocryphal Gospels.* Among the early fathers of the Christian Church, there were one or two who constructed parables as the media of expression. Trench gives us a selection of these early Church writers whose writings were rich in similitudes. Among samples Trench quotes is this one from the writings of Ephraem Syrus—

> Two men set out for a certain city, which lay some thirty furlongs off. And when they had now accomplished two or three furlongs, they came upon a place by the roadside, where were woods and shady trees, and streams of water, and therein much delight. As they gazed at all these, one of the two wayfarers, eagerly bending his course to the city of his desires, passed by the place as one that races; but the other first halted to gaze, and then stayed there. Later on, when he began to wish to issue beyond the shade of the trees, he feared the heat, and thus staying still longer in the spot, and at the same time delighted and absorbed with its pleasantries, was surprised by one of the wild beasts which haunt the wood, and was seized and carried off to its cave. His companion, who had not neglected his journey, neither suffered himself to be stayed by the beauty of the trees, made his way straight to the city.

A comparison of these parables with those in the Bible makes them somewhat tame and puerile. As we shall later on prove, the parables of Jesus are superb in their aptness, conciseness, beauty and appeal. Although He did not create the parabolic type of teaching, He certainly endowed it with high originality and gave it a deeper spiritual import and dimensions hitherto unknown.

## The Meaning of the Term — Parable

Although we are apt to confine the significance of the word *parable* to the complete parables of our Lord as found in the first three Gospels, actually the word itself has a flexibility of use, covering different phases of figurative language, such as similitudes, comparisons, sayings, proverbs and the like.

In the Old Testament the Hebrew word for "parable" is *Māshāl,* meaning proverb, similitude, parable. In a wide range of use this word "covers several forms of picturesque and suggestive speech — all those forms in which ideas are presented in the robes of imagery. As its applications are thus varied, it is variously translated in our English version." The root idea of *māshāl* is "to be like," and often refers to "the sentences constructed in parableism," so characteristic of Hebrew poetry. The word is never used in the narrow technical sense of its counterpart in the New Testament.

It is used of the figurative discourse of Balaam.

> "He took up his *parable"* (Numbers 23:7,18; 24:3,15).

It is used of short, pithy, proverbial sayings.

> "Therefore it became a *proverb,*
> Is Saul also among the prophets?" (I Samuel 10:12)

Salmond remarks that "in this sense it is used of the maxims of wisdom which are contained in the book that is distinctively known as *Proverbs,*" these maxims being given in large measure in the form of comparisons, as when it is said —

> "Treasures of wickedness profit nothing, but righteousness delivereth from death" (10:2).

*Māshāl* is the word used for *Proverbs* in 1:1; 10:1, and in the phrase,

> "So is a parable in the mouth of fools" (26:7,9; see I Kings 4:32).

It is used of Job's sentences of ethical wisdom.

> "Job continued his parable" ( 27:1; 29:1).

It is used of a dark saying, enigmatical utterances, riddles.

> "I will open my dark saying upon the harp" (Psalm 49:4).
> "I will utter dark sayings of old" (78:2).

It is used to represent a figure or allegory.

> "Speak a parable unto the house of Israel" (Numbers 17:2; 24:3).

C. W. Emmet in Hastings' *Dictionary of the Gospels* remarks that "there are five passages in the Old Testament which are generally quoted as representing the nearest approach to 'parables' in the technical sense. It is noticeable that in none of them is the word used; as we have seen, where we have the word, we do not really have the thing; in the same way, where we have the thing, we do not find the word."

The parables of Nathan (II Samuel 12:1-4), and Joab (II Samuel 14:6) are somewhat similar, having a natural story with a forceful application. The first parable is parallel to that of "The Two Debtors," and Joab's parable calls to mind the parable of the Prodigal Son.

The Parable of the Wounded Prophet (I Kings 20:39) is helped out by a piece of acting. "In all three parables," says Emmet, "the object is to convey the actual truth of the story, and by the unguarded comments of the listener to convict him out of his own mouth. The method has perhaps in the last two cases a suspicion of trickery and was not employed by our Lord; the application of the parable of the Wicked Husbandman (Matthew 21:33) was obvious from the first in the light of Isaiah 5:1-6."

The Parable of Jehovah's Vineyard (Isaiah 5:1-7) is a true parable, though only slightly developed, and illustrates the relation between a parable and a metaphor. The border-line between parable and allegory is narrow (Psalm 80:8).

The Parable of the Plowman (Isaiah 28:24-28) gives us a comparison between the natural and spiritual world, but no story. Thus the Old Testament makes a wide use of parable, showing sometimes alike in spirit, form, and language, a remarkable resemblance to the parables of the New Testament. Our exposition of Old Testament Parables will reveal that they fall into three classes —

> *Story-Parables,* of which that of the Trees is an instance (Judges 9:7-15);
>
> *Sermon-Parables,* as found in the Vineyard (Isaiah 5:1-7);
>
> *Symbol-Parables,* as illustrated by the Two Sticks (Ezekiel 37: 15-22).

In the New Testament the word "parable" takes on a varying meaning and form and is not confined to those lengthened narratives in the *Gospels* we know as Christ's parables. There are two Greek words rendered by the one English term "parable." The more common term is *parabolē,* occurring 48 times in the synoptic gospels, but nowhere defined for us. Its meaning is taken for granted, being taken over from the Septuagint which usually gives the Hebrew word for "parable" as *parabolē.*

Two prominent ideas are suggested by the root meaning of this first word, namely, "to represent or to stand for something"; "likeness or resemblance." This Greek word implies "beside" or "to throw or cast," suggesting nearness for the purpose of comparison for likeness or difference. A "similitude" or "the placing of one thing by the side of another." One writer says that an aspect of the original word signifies to rule or govern, as a prince whose righteous precepts and commands his people ought to obey.

The other word used for "parable" is *paroimia,* meaning an "adage, dark saying, wayside saying, a proverb, a presentation deviating from the usual means of speaking." This word is almost peculiar to John, who uses it four times (John 16:6-18,25; 15:1-18). John never uses the first word *parabolē,* the only one employed by Matthew, Mark and Luke. *Paroimia* used in the Septuagint, as well as by John, indicates a proverb or parable, "being drawn from common objects and incidents, was available and meant for public use.

What was once said in any particular case could always be repeated under similar circumstances."

Flexibility in the use of the term "parable" is seen in its application to terse, proverbial sayings —

> "Doubtless ye will say unto me this *parable,* Physician, heal thyself" (Luke 4:23.r.v.).
>
> "He spake a parable unto them" (Luke 6:39; 14:7).

It is also used of comparisons or illustrative statements which have no narrative in them. For instance, the blind leading the blind: "Declare this parable unto us" (Matthew 15:15; Luke 6:39). Then there is the fact of the fig-tree and its evident sign: "Now learn the parable of the fig-tree" (Matthew 24:32,33). Christ's words about the things that defile are referred to as a "parable": "His disciples asked him concerning the parable" (Luke 7:1-23). In our English version the Greek word *"parabolē"* is rendered *figure*: "Which was a figure (parable) for the time then present" (Hebrews 9:9). "He received him in a figure (parable)" (Hebrews 11:19).

So many of our Lord's figurative sayings contain the germ of a parable. Parables, so-called, are simply extended similes or illustrations. Think of the embryonic parable: "Can the blind lead the blind?" (Luke 6:39). Fairbairn says that we have only to work on this brief hint and we have the perfect story. "Two blind men are seen leading each other along the road, and, after struggling for a time with the difficulties of doing so, both fall into the ditch by the wayside." In these terse, illustrative sayings of Jesus we have the substance, although not the form of the parable. In the incidents described a common aspect of life is employed for the illustration of higher truth.

With the foregoing understanding of the terms used we are ready to answer the question, "What exactly is a parable?" What it is *not* will be seen when we have examined the nature of a parable. "The constant use of a word, meaning *resemblance* both in the Hebrew and in Greek, makes it evident that an essential feature of the parable lay in the bringing together of two different things so that the one helped to explain and to emphasize the other." A study of Christ's parables convinces us that they are something more than a mere felicitous illustration of truth He expounded. A parable has been described as "an outward symbol of an inward reality." Further "its power is in harmony which it brings out between the natural and the spiritual world." Bond, in *The Master Teacher,* explains a parable as being "a rhetorical figure that translates through contrast and similitude the natural facts and laws into terms of the spiritual life." A narrative true to nature or to life, is used for the purpose of conveying spiritual truth to the mind of the hearer. The Sunday school scholar was near the mark when she gave her explanation of a parable as being "an earthly story with a heavenly meaning."

The parables display a pre-ordained harmony between things spiritual and things material. Material objects are used to express spiritual truths and reveal that nature is more than it seems. Nature is a book of symbols — a fact Tertullian had in mind when he wrote, "All things in Nature are prophetic outlines of Divine operations, God not merely speaking parables but doing them." Charles Kingsley re-echoes such a sentiment in this paragraph: "This earthly world which we do see is an exact picture and pattern of the spiritual and heavenly world which we do not see."

Paul's statement on the visible world of God instructing us in the mysteries of faith and the duties of morality reads: "The invisible things of God, since the creation of the world, are clearly seen, being perceived through the things that are made" (Romans 1:20).

Other testimonies to the fact that when the Bible and nature are put side by side they are seen to be counterpartal, are legion in number. Lisco, whose most instructive work, *On The Parables,* is particularly valuable for its quotations from the great divines of the Reformation, in connection with each parable, says of the physical typifying the higher moral world, "Both kingdoms develop themselves according to the same laws; Jesus' parables are not mere illustrations, but internal analogies, nature becoming a witness for the spiritual world; whatever is found in the earthly exists also in the heavenly kingdom." When we come to examine the Parables of Jesus we shall discover them to be earthly in form, heavenly in spirit, and answering to the parabolic character of His own manifestation.

That nature was intended by God to represent truths, and relationships spiritual in nature and eternal in duration is what Lord Bacon had in mind when he wrote that, "Truth and Nature differ only as seal and print." Thomas Carlyle in *Sartor Resartus* agrees and says, "All visible things are emblems. What thou seest is not there on its own account; matter only exists to represent some idea and body it forth."

Archbishop Trench, whose outstanding *Notes on the Parables* cannot be too highly praised, reminds us that "Analogies assist to make the truth intelligible . . . Analogies from the natural world . . . are arguments, and may be called as witnesses, the world of Nature being throughout a witness for the world of spirit, proceeding from the same hand, growing from the same root, and being constituted for the same end. All lovers of truth readily acknowledge these mysterious harmonies, and the force of arguments derived from them. To them, the things on earth are copies of the things in Heaven."

From the gifted pen of a true Christian seer, Dr. John Pulsford, we cull the following contribution from his *Loyalty to Christ:* "Parables are not forced illustrations, but rather mirrors of spiritual things. Heaven and Earth are the work of the One God. All natural effects hold on to their spiritual causes, and their spiritual causes hold on to them. Spiritual worlds and natural worlds cohere, as inner and outer."

Sufficient has been said on this matter of analogies existing between God's works in nature and providence, and His operations in grace. A fitting conclusion to this marked correspondence in many of the parables is that given by William M. Taylor in his *Parables of Our Saviour.* "The world of Nature came at first form, and is still sustained by, the hand of Him who formed the human soul; and the administration of Providence is carried on by Him who gave to us the revelation of His will in the Sacred Scriptures, and provided for us salvation through His Son. We may expect, therefore, to find a principle of unity running through all these three departments of His administration; and a knowledge of His operations in any one of them may be helpful to us in our investigation of the others."

As the general word used for "parable" signifies to set side by side, and conveys the idea of comparison, a parable is literally a placing beside or comparison of earthly truths with heavenly truths, or a similitude, an illustration of one subject to another. Parables prove that the external is the mirror in which we may behold the internal and the spiritual, as Milton indicates in the lines:

> What if earth
> Be but the shadow of Heaven and things therein,
> Each to the other like, more than on earth is thought.

## The Manifold Phases of Figurative Speech

The figures of speech the Bible employs are variegated, and it takes them all to illustrate deep, divine truths. As we are apt to clump these figurative expressions together, failing to distinguish one from the other, each form,

we feel, is worthy of careful consideration. Benjamin Keach in his ancient and somewhat cumbersome work on *The Metaphors* has an introductory dissertation of the distinction of each figure of speech. There is also Dr. A. T. Pierson's chapter on "Biblical Figures of Speech." The reader is strongly urged to read Trench's scholarly treatment *On the Definition of the Parable,* in which he differentiates between parables, allegories, fables, proverbs and myths.

SIMILITUDE. The word *simile means like* or resembling and is illustrated for us in *The Psalm of the Two Men:* "He shall be *like* a tree planted by the rivers of water . . . The ungodly . . . are *like* the chaff which the wind driveth away" (Psalm 1:3,4).

The *simile* differs from a *metaphor* in that it merely states resemblance, while a *metaphor* boldly transfers the representation, as we can see by placing these passages together: "All flesh is as grass, and all the glory of man as the flower of the field. The grass withereth, and the flower thereof falleth away" (Isaiah 40:6,7). "All flesh is grass, and all the goodliness therefore is as the flower of the field" (I Peter 1:24).

In a *similitude,* the mind rests simply upon the points of agreement between two things that are compared and experiences that pleasure which is always afforded by the discovery of resemblance between things that differ. Dr. A. T. Pierson remarks that — "a parable proper is, in Scripture usage, a similitude, usually put in narrative form, or used in connection with some incident." Parables and similitudes are akin.

PROVERB. While the germs of a parable may appear in some of the short proverbs, dark prophetic utterances, and engimatic maxims of the Bible (I Samuel 10:12; Psalm 78:2; Proverbs 1:6; Matthew 24:32; Luke 4:23), yet it is distinct from the recognized proverb, which is usually brief, deals with less lofty subjects, and does not concern itself with telling a story. *The Apocrypha* groups parables and proverbs together: "The countries marvelled at thee for thy proverbs and parables . . . He will seek out the secrets of grave sentences, and be conversant in dark parables" (Ecclesiasticus 47:17; 39:3).

Although *parable* and *proverb* are interchangeable in the New Testament, yet as Trench points out, "the so-called *proverbs* of John's *gospel* claim much closer affinity to the parable than to the proverb, being in fact allegories: thus Christ's setting forth of His relations to His people under those of a shepherd to his sheep, is termed a *proverb,* though our translators, holding fast to the sense rather than to the letter, have rendered it a *parable* (John 10:6; see 16:25,29). It is easy to account for this interchange of words. Partly it arose from one word in Hebrew signifying both parable and proverb." (Compare Proverbs 1:1 with I Samuel 10:12; Ezekiel 18:2). Generally speaking, a *proverb* is a wise, wayside saying, a trite expression, an adage.

METAPHOR. The Bible is rich in its metaphorical language. A metaphor distinctly affirms that one thing *is* another thing. The word itself comes from two Greek words meaning to *carry over*. One object is equated with another object. Here are two examples of the use of *Metaphors:*

"The Lord God is a sun and a shield" (Psalm 84:11).
"He is my refuge and my fortress" (Psalm 91:2).

Thus, as can be seen, *metaphor is a* word familiar to us "in the region of sensible experience and denoting some object possessed of particular properties, is transferred to another object belonging to a more elevated region in order that the former may impart to us a fuller and livelier idea of the properties which the latter ought to possess." In the above passages all that are suggested by the sun, a shield, a refuge, a fortress, are transferred to the Lord. The sun, for example, is the source of light, heat and power. The life of earth depends upon the properties of the sun.

Therefore the Lord as a Sun, is the Source of all life.

In John's gospel there are no parables, strictly speaking, but rather a series of arrestive metaphors such as:

"I am the good shepherd" (John 16:11).
"I am the true vine" (John 15:1).
"I am the door" (John 10:7).
"I am the bread of life" (John 6:35).
"I am the way, the truth, the life" (John 14:6), etc.

ALLEGORY. It is not easy to draw a distinction between *parable* and *allegory*. The latter is not an extended metaphor. *Allegory differs from metaphor* in that no transference of qualities and properties takes place. Both parables and metaphors cover phrases and sentences, and serve to open and explain some hidden truth which cannot be as easily understood if not so draped. In Fairbairn's article on "parables" in his renowned *Bible Encyclopaedia,* he says that, "The allegory corresponds strictly to what is involved in the derivation of the word. It is the teaching of one thing by another thing, of a second by a first; a similarity of properties is supposed to exist, a like course of events to be traceable in both; but the first does not pass off in the second; the two remain distinct. Viewed in this light, allegory, in its widest sense, may be regarded as a genus, of which the fable, the parable, and what we commonly call allegory, are species."

An *allegory,* explains Dr. Graham Scroggie, ". . . is a statement of supposed facts which admits of a literal interpretation, and yet requires or justly admits a moral or figurative one." Allegories are distinct from Parables in that there is less of the hidden and mysterious. Allegories interpret themselves and in them "the person or thing that is to be illustrated by some natural object is identified at once with the object," says Dr. Salmond. "So when our Lord speaks the great allegory of the Vine and the Husbandman and the Branches, under

which He instructs His disciples in the truth of their relation to Himself and to God, He begins by saying that He *is* Himself the true Vine, and that His Father is the Husbandman" (John 15:1).

For a thorough understanding of the figures of speech mentioned in the Bible, the reader is directed to the exhaustive work on the subject by Dr. E. W. Bullinger which, without doubt, is the most monumental study of all times on the pictorial method the Bible employs. Dr. Bullinger reminds us that great controversy has raged over the exact significance and definition of an *allegory* and then goes on to elaborate on the fact that similes, metaphors and allegories are all based upon comparison.

> *Simile* is comparison by *resemblance.*
>
> *Metaphor* is comparison by *Representation.*
>
> *Allegory* is comparison by *Implication.*

In the first, comparison is *stated;* in the *second,* it is *substituted;* in the third, it is *implied. Allegory* thus differs from *parable,* for a *parable* is a continued simile. While the allegory *represents,* or *implies* that the one thing is the other.

One distinctly described *Allegory* is given by Paul: "Abraham had two sons, the one by a bondmaid, the other by a free woman. But he who was of the bondwoman was born after the flesh; but he of the freewoman was by promise. Which things are an *allegory"* (which things teach or tell us something beyond what is said — see Galatians 4:22,24). Bullinger goes on to prove that an allegory *may* sometimes be fictitious, but Galatians 4 shows us that a true history may be allegorized (that is, be shown to have further teaching in that which actually took place), *without detracting from the truth of the history.* Allegory is always stated in the *past* tense and *never in the future.* Allegory is thus distinguished from prophecy. The *allegory* brings out other teaching out of

past events, while the *prophecy* tells us events that are yet to come and means exactly what is said.

Hillyer Straton, in *A Guide to the Parables of Jesus,* remarks that "the allegory is description in code. It personifies abstract things; it does not set one thing beside another but makes a substitution of one for the other. Every point in the allegory becomes important." Dr. Straton then goes on to cite the most famous allegory of all literatures, *Pilgrim's Progress,* in which John Bunyan used his remarkably fertile imagination to drive home the truth of the Christian pilgrimage.

FABLE. A *fable* is a fictitious narrative intended to illustrate some maxim or truth (See Judges 9:8-15; II Kings 14:9). The primary mission of fables is to enforce a prudential maxim. The *fable,* used sparingly in Scripture, is far removed from a *parable,* although the one may sometimes resemble the other in outward aspect. Comparing any of Aesop's *fables,* with any of our Lord's parables, one realizes that fables are of a lower kind of figurative speech and deal with less elevated subjects. They are of the earth and look to common life and business. Their function is to convey lessons of practical prudential wisdom and inculcate the virtues of prudence, industry, patience and self-control. They also expose evil as folly rather than as sin, and hold up faults to ridicule, vices to contempt or scorn or fear. This is why fables take great liberties with fancy, endowing plants and animals with human faculties making them reason and speak. Parables, however, move in the higher, spiritual sphere and never descend to mockery or satire. Dealing with the truths of God, parables are correspondingly lofty, with illustrations true to reality — never monstrous or unnatural. In a parable, there is nothing contrary to the truth of Nature. Fairbairn says that, "The parable has a nobler end. . . . The parable might take the place of the fable, but not the fable of the parable." For information of the *mythic* narrative, the

reader is asked to refer to Trench's paragraph, *The Mythus.*

TYPE. This means *stamp* or *impress,* and has the force of *copy* or *pattern* (I Corinthians 10:1-10,11, "ensamples," margin "types"). Parables join the types on the one side, and miracles on the other. All the figures of speech the Bible employs are links in a chain so inseparably united that they can only be severed at the expense of some of the links. The many types in the Bible form an independent and fascinating study.

PARABLE. While we have already dealt with the nature of a *parable,* we return to it by way of summary. In a *parable,* an image is borrowed from the visible world and is accompanied by a truth from the invisible or spiritual world. Parables are the bearers, the channels of spiritual truth and doctrine. What must be emphasized is that parables do not run on all fours. In some, there are great disparities, some aspect we cannot apply spiritually. They are always related to the territory of the possible and the true.

Speeches and sentences, full of spiritual wisdom and truth, are called *parables* for two reasons:

1. Because they carry conviction and divine authority.
2. Because they are as touchstones of truth — they are rules, and therefore ought to rule.

A parable has been defined as, "A beautiful image of a beautiful mind." A parable is also the juxta-position of two things differing in most points, but agreeing in some. "Miracles," says Dr. A. T. Pierson, "teach us of the *forces* of Creation; the Parables, of the *forms* of Creation. When a parable is predictive and prophetic, it is always in allegorical dress, when preceptive and didactic, actual and historical."

"Distinguished both from *similitude* and *metaphor,* and regarded as a species of allegory," Fairbairn says, "the Parable may be said to be a story which, either true, or possessing all the appearance of truth, exhibits in the sphere of natural life a process parallel to one which exists in the ideal and spiritual world." The story of the Prodigal Son may have been a history of literal facts. Parables are "Apples of gold in pictures (frames) of silver."

# The Merit of Parabolic Instruction

Teaching by parable serves many useful ends and possesses distinct advantages. Its merit or worth, as an instrument of teaching, lies in its being at once, a test of character, with that which, as a penalty or blessing, is adapted to it. Smith in his *Dictionary of the Bible* says that, "Parables sometimes withdraw the light from those who love darkness. They protect the truth which they enshrine from the mockery of the scoffer. They leave something with the careless which may be interpreted and understood afterwards. They reveal, on the other hand, seekers after truth." Parables may be listened to, and their meaning received, yet the listeners may never care to ask what is the actual meaning.

Among the many advantages, proving the profitableness of parabolical Scripture, mention can be made of the following:

1. Parables attract, and when fully understood are sure to be remembered. They are a great help to memory. We are more apt to remember illustrations or stories, than other things delivered in a sermon. Parables are called to remembrance long after the main substance of the sermon is forgotten.

2. Parables greatly help the mind and thinking faculty. Their meaning must be studied. They are like a golden mine, and we must dig and search with all diligence if we would discover the true vein. The parabolic method arouses thought. "The Great Teacher Himself knew that He could not teach His hearers unless He made them teach themselves. He must reach their own

minds and get *them* to work with His. The *form* of the parable would attract all; but only the thoughtful could read its meaning." The meaning could not be found without thinking. The parables therefore both attracted and sifted the crowd.

3. Parables stir up, or excite the affections, and awaken consciences, as when hell in a parable is set up as a furnace of fire, and conscience by a gnawing worm.

4. Parables arrest and hold attention. Listening to Jesus as He spake His parable, the listeners were enthralled and said, "Never man spake as this Man." He *must* make the people listen to Him — and they did! How wonderfully, He would swiftly and spontaneously use the suggestions of the moment, and thus catch and keep the attention of those around Him!

5. Parables preserve the truth. Writing on this particular merit, Cosmo Lang says, "What men think out for themselves they never forget; the exercise of their mind makes it their own. Moreover the language of symbols — expressed in what is seen by the eye or pictured by the imagination — is more powerful and enduring in its effects than the language of mere abstract words. It conveys and brings back to the mind the inner meaning with swiftness and sureness; it carries with it a wealth of suggestion and association. And mere words are constantly changing their meaning, whereas the symbols of life and nature, such as our Lord used in His parables, are as abiding as Nature and Life themselves."

Commenting on the parables in Matthew 13, Finis Dake in his popular *Annotated Reference Bible* gives us seven beneficial reasons for using parables:

1. To reveal truth in interesting form and create more interest (Matthew 13:10-11,16).

2. To make known new truths to interested hearers (Matthew 13:11-12, 16-17).

3. To make known mysteries by comparison with things already known (Matthew 13:11).

4. To conceal truth from disinterested hearers and rebels at heart (Matthew 13:11-15).

5. To add truth to those who love it and want more of it (Matthew 13:12).

6. To take away from those who hate and do not want it (Matthew 13:12).

7. To fulfil prophecy (Matthew 13:14-17, 35).

## The Mission of a Parable

Closely allied to the merits of the parabolic form of teaching, are its motives and mission. What are the functions or objects of a parable? We have touched upon the drawing power, but why did Christ use such a method? He employed it to enlighten, exhort and edify. In the *Preface* to his illuminating *Lectures on Our Lord's Parables,* Dr. John Cumming says that —

*Prophecy* is the cartoon of the future, which events fill in.

*Miracles* are the fore-acts of the future, done on a small present scale.

*Parables* are foreshadows of the future, projected on the sacred page.

All three grow every day in radiance, in interest, in value. Soon the light of a Meridian Sun will overflow them all. May we be found ready! By it, He sought to commend to men's understandings and hearts the spiritual truths of His kingdom. Adopting a method that was recognized by Jewish teachers, Christ attracted the mind and conciliated attention. Men had to be won and the parable was a ready means of securing this, and He was superb in the use of it.

Jesus adopted the parabolic form of teaching whether addressing His disciples or those like the Pharisees who were His foes in order to convince the one group and condemn the other. The question of the disciples, "Why speakest thou in parables?" Matthew 13:10, is answered by Jesus in the following five verses. Jesus opened His mouth and spake in parables because of their diversified character and degree of spiritual and moral perception in His hearers (Matthew 13:35) "Therefore I speak to them in parables." *Therefore* implies, as Lisco expresses it, "Because the instruction so often given to them in plain language has proved of no avail to them, I shall now try, through means of figures and similitudes, if I can lead them to reflect, and to move them to carefulness for their salvation." Alas, such was the stupid insensibility of the religious leaders, but their minds failed to comprehend the deep, spiritual truths Jesus so forcibly illustrated in parabolic fashion! Those leaders, likewise, failed to realize that parables are the appropriate instructors of those who are possessed by the Word of God, and teach and value the things belonging to everlasting peace.

## The Misinterpretation and True Interpretation of Parables

At the outset attention must be drawn to this fundamental principle, namely, that a parable must be regarded as a whole, and as illustrating and emphasizing some important central truth or obligation or principle in the divine government, and which the different parts of the Parable only serve in some respect to open out and develop. It is imperative to ascertain the real scope and object of the Parable.

Further, it is necessary to carefully investigate and note the connection of a Parable with its context and attendant circumstances in order to arrive at as precise an approach as possible to the truth that the parable unfolds. Says Lisco: "When a parable is expounded and applied, we must first of all consider its connection with what precedes and follows, and determine accordingly, before everything else, its prominent idea. Until, through repeated

attentive consideration of the circumstances and subject, this central point and kernel of the parable has been discovered and set forth in the most precise and determinate manner, we need not meddle with the import of particular parts, for these can only be seen in their true light when contemplated from that central point."

The main scope or design of a parable can be gathered, either from the more general or more particular exposition of it, or else from the speaker's main and principal design, which can usually be gathered from the preface of it, or else from its conclusion. For instance, note what precedes and succeeds the parables of the Vineyard, and of The Rich Man. On this matter a perusal of Ada R. Habershon's chapter on "The Setting of the Parables" will repay the reader.

Much has been written on the interpretation of parables. As far as their misinterpretation is concerned, the parables have suffered much. Let us take *misinterpretation* first. What abuse there has been in the use of parables! How guilty many have been of an artificial application of certain parables, and of forcing more from them than their authors ever dreamed of! There are two extremes to be avoided in the interpretation of parables. One extreme is to make *too much* of them — The other to make *too little* of them. Cumming, in his *Lectures,* puts the double fault this way:

There are two great errors in interpreting the parables: one consists in screwing meaning out of every part, as if there were nothing subsidiary at all; and the other in regarding much of the parable as mere subsidiary, and to be regarded as mere drapery. The first is very objectionable, for the parable and its truth are not, as has been said, two perfect planes that touch at all points, but rather, a plane and a sphere touching at great points. Each parable embosoms a grand design, which is prominent at chief and highest, and this ought to be kept constantly in view in interpreting all the subsidiary touches in the Bible.

The second plan sees too little meaning in the parable; it regards much as merely intended to make up a tale, other parts to be mere connecting links, and some parts as rather marring than bringing out the end and object of the parable. This last mode destroys much of the riches of Scripture. Every part of the parable, like every text of the Bible, has its meaning and its importance. A perfect portrait has no parts that do not contribute to the general effect, and through every part life so glows and shines, so much so, that the absence of the minutest part would be a deficiency.

For a more exhaustive treatment of the *pros* and *cons* of interpretation the student is urged to read *The Interpretation of Parables* in Trench's incomparable work, *The Parables of Our Lord,* and "Methods of Interpretation" in Ada Habershon's volume, *The Study of Parables.* Trench says, referring to the above extremes, that exaggerations have characterized both sides. "The advocates of interpretation in gross and not in detail have been too easily satisfied with their favourite maxim. Every comparison must halt somewhere." Trench gives us a saying from Theophylact, "A parable, if it be maintained in all its points, is no longer a parable, but the very thing which occasions it."

As for the other extreme of interpretation, "There lies the danger of an ingenious trifling with the Word of God, a danger, too, lest the interpreter's delight in the exercise of this ingenuity, with the admiration of it on the part of others, may not put somewhat out of sight that the sanctification of the heart through the truth is the main purpose of all Scripture."

Many of the Early Fathers, endeavoring to allegorise both Old and New Testament passages, went to great extremes. Whether they were wrong in thinking there was a meaning in all things, has been a matter of dispute for centuries.

Augustine is an outstanding example of those who pressed parables to teach something plainly outside their limits. Dealing with the traditional teaching of the church (treating parables as allegories, in which each term stood as a cryptogram for an idea, so

that the whole had to be de-coded term by term), C. H. Dodd in *The Parables of the Kingdom* cites Augustine's interpretation of the Parable of the Good Samaritan . . .

By *the certain man who went down from Jerusalem to Jericho*—Adam himself is meant:

*Jerusalem* is the heavenly city of peace, from whose blessedness Adam fell:

*Jericho* means the moon, and signifies our mortality, because it is born, waxes, wanes, and dies;

*Thieves* are the devil and his angels.

*Who stripped him,* namely of his immortality;

*And beat him,* by persuading him to sin;

*And left him half dead,* because in so far as man can understand and know God, he lives, but in so far as he is wasted and oppressed by sin, he is dead; he is therefore called *half-dead.*

*The Priest and Levite* who saw him and passed by, signify the priesthood and ministry of the Old Testament, which could profit nothing for salvation.

*Samaritan* means guardian, and therefore the Lord Himself is signified by this name.

*The Binding of the Wounds* is the restraint of sin.

*Oil* is the comfort of good hope;

*Wine* is the exhortation to work with fervent spirit.

*The Beast* is the flesh in which He deigned to come to us.

*Set upon the beast* is belief in the incarnation of Christ.

*The Inn* is the Church, where travellers are refreshed on their return from pilgrimage to their heavenly country.

*The Morrow* is after the Resurrection of the Lord.

*The Two Pence* are either the two precepts of love, or the promise of this life and of that which is to come.

*The Innkeeper* is the Apostle Paul.

Archbishop Trench follows the main lines of Augustine with even more ingenious elaboration. Another instance of this phase of interpretation is seen in the Reformed and Roman Catholic interpreters who found a tremendous significance in the oil in the Parable of the Virgins. With one the oil was faith, without which the maids could not be admitted into the wedding festivities — with the other it was work, which according to this view was equally necessary. Much was also made of the women as *virgins,* and in the equal division of the term. So, as Hillyer H. Straton expresses it, "Your interpretation depended upon the point where you were; you paid your money and you took your choice. Now we know that Jesus was driving home one point, and that was preparedness."

Further illustrations of this method of unwarranted interpretation is seen in the Story of the Unjust Steward as being the history of the apostasy of Satan, and The Pearl of Great Price, a description of the Church of Geneva. Trench relates the instance of Faustus Socinus who argued from the Parable of the Unmerciful Servant, that as the king pardoned his servant merely on his petition (Matthew 18:32), and not on the score of any satisfaction made, or any mediator intervening, we may from this conclude that in the same way, and without requiring sacrifice or intercessor, God will pardon sinners simply on the ground of their prayers. With such an application before us we agree with Jerome's observation of those who "twist to their own will a contrary Scripture."

As each parable is charged with its own lesson, which should safeguard us from trying to find some distinct and special significance in each of its circumstances and descriptive teaching, it is necessary to discover the underlying purpose of the parable. Dr. Graham Scroggie tells us how we can be delivered from any artificial, unnatural or mistaken ingenuity in dealing with parables. Care should be taken in studying them to distinguish between *interpretation* and *application.* "One interpretation, many ap-plications," can be an entirely unwarranted distinction, for if the application is designed by the Holy Spirit, it *too* can become an interpretation. Alas, often applications are made which can scarcely be called interpretations! "All the Bible is *for* us, but it is not all *about* us. Interpretation is limited by the original intent of the parable, and this intent is determined by occasion and circumstance; but application is not limited, for the way in which it can help us is in its meaning for us. Interpretation is *dispensational* and *prophetic.* Application is *moral* and *practical.* The principles of interpretation can be learned from the two parables which Christ Himself has interpreted" (Matthew 13:18-23, 36-43). As far as His parables as a whole are concerned it may be difficult to assess how far He means us to interpret any parable apart from its general, main scope. If we are honest and sincere in our quest for truth, we can rely upon the Holy Spirit to take of the things of Christ and reveal them unto us (I Corinthians 2:11,13).

As we look for actuality in the features of a parable, it is as well to bear in mind that in most cases the true parable has only one major point. "We cannot maintain, however, that all Christ's parables have only one point, for Jesus was an artist who was interested in communicating truth, not in maintaining a certain form." C. H. Dodd agrees with this important principle of interpretation: "The typical parable, whether it be a simple metaphor, or a more elaborate similitude, or a full-length story, presents one single point of comparison. The details are not intended to have independent significance. In an allegory, on the other hand, each detail is a separate metaphor, with a significance of its own." Dodd then cites one or two illustrations of this principle, among them the Parable of the Sower: "The wayside and the birds, the thorns and the stony ground are not cryptograms for persecution, the deceitfulness of riches, and so forth. They are there to conjure up a picture of the vast amount of wasted labour which the farmer must face, and so to bring into relief the satisfaction that the harvest gives, in spite of all."

In her chapter on "The Method of Interpretation," Ada Habershon in *The Study of the Parables,* takes the view that we "may be certain that each detail (of the above parable) had a meaning, and may be quite prepared to find that some of them had several. . . . No single explanation will exhaust the meaning of the simplest parable which our divine Lord spoke, and if we recognize this, we shall also be prepared to gather from them 'great spoil of every kind.' The safest way to handle a parable is to search out the leading thought or principle idea round which as centre the subordinate parts must group themselves. The main idea must not be frittered away on a too wire-drawn extension of accessories even though they may have a spiritual significance. The parables are not to be handled as if they were a storehouse of texts. Each parable must be seen with its own distinctive peculiarity, and any analogies made must be real, not imaginary, and subordinate to the main lesson of the parable."

Other aspects of interpretation fully dealt with by Fausset's *Bible Encyclopaedia* are:

1. The Parable in its mere outward form must be well understood (e.g., the relation of love between the Eastern shepherd and sheep).
2. The context also introducing the parable, as Luke 15:1, 2, is the starting point of the three parables in the chapter.
3. Traits which, if literally interpreted, would contradict Scripture, are colouring, e.g. the number of the wise virgins and the foolish being equal (Matthew 7:13,14).

In his chapter on *The Place and Province of Parables,* Dr. A. T. Pierson says: "Biblical Parables are narratives, either of fact or fiction, used to convey moral and spiritual truth and instruction. They may be historical, ethical and allegorical, all at the same time; but, if the higher meaning is lost or obscured in the lower, the spiritual in the literal, their main purpose and purport are missed. Commonly, some hint of its true interpretation accompanies each parable. The central lesson is the main matter of interest; the rest may be non-essential and subordinate, like drapery and scenery in a drama."

## The Multiformity of the Parables

What variety and diversity are represented in Bible parables! Truly, they are unique for their descriptive imagery. Under the guidance of the Holy Spirit, the writers of the Bible ransacked every realm for fitting vehicles of expressing divine truth. And it takes them all to illustrate the matchless wonder of God's Word, which is radiant in its wealth of parabolic material. The summary Dr. Graham Scroggie gives of New Testament parables we herewith take and extend to describe the scope of Bible parables as a whole. As we come to our exposition of these parables reference will be made to the particular realm they represent.

1. The Spiritual Realm.
   Parables associated with heaven, hell, cherubs, angels.
2. Natural Phenomena.
   Parables connected with the sun, light, lightning, earthquakes, fire, clouds, storm, rain.
3. Animate Nature.
   Parables related to creatures — horses, beasts, lions, eagles, camels, oxen, sheep, lambs, wolves, asses, foxes, swine, dogs, goats, fish, birds, serpents.
   Parables illustrated by plants and trees, thorns, thistles, figs, olives, sycamore, almonds, grapes, reeds, lilies, anise, mint, vine, cedar, bramble cummin.

Parables symbolized by metals —
gold, silver, brass, iron, tin.
4. Human Life. The range of parabolic illustrations is very wide.
*Physical*—flesh, blood, eye, ear,
hands, feet—hunger, thirst, sleep,
sickness, laughing, weeping, death.
*Domestic*—houses, lamps, seats,
food, oven, cooking, bread, salt—
birth, mothers, wives, sisters, brothers, children, service, marriage,
treasures.
*Pastoral*—fields, valleys, shepherds,
sheep, husbandmen, soil, seed, tillage, sowing, growth, harvest, vineyards.

*Commercial*—fishermen, tailor,
builder, merchant, business bushel,
talents, money, debts.
*Civil*—slavery, robbery, violence,
judgment, punishment, taxes.
*Social*—marriage, hospitality, feasts,
journeyings, salutations.
*Religious*—tabernacle, temple, alms,
tithes, fastings, prayer, sabbath.
The succeeding pages will serve to
show that Bible parables are superb
illustrative comparisons telling out the
divine story. They can be defined as
"narratives expressly imagined for the
purpose of representing a religious
truth in pictorial figure."

# SECTION ONE — OLD TESTAMENT PARABLES

# SECTION ONE — OLD TESTAMENT PARABLES

It is to be regretted that almost all reference books dealing with the parables, concentrate upon those spoken by our Lord, and neglect what the rest of the Bible — apart from the four gospels — holds for us in figurative language. One has searched in vain for a study volume expounding Old Testament Parables, of which there are many. G. H. Lang in *The Parabolic Teaching of Scripture* devotes five pages to the subject. The fullest treatment of Old Testament parables that I know of is that by A London Minister, on *Miracles and Parables of the Old Testament,* first published in 1890 and now re-issued by the Baker Book House, Grand Rapids, U.S.A. Certainly some of the Bible Dictionaries carry a synopsis of the parabolic teaching of the Old Testament, where the uniform word *Māshāl* is used with a wide range of meaning. Although, as we have already hinted, there are only five passages which are thought to represent the nearest approach to "Parable," in the technical sense, commencing with Nathan's parable, yet, as the following studies will prove, the Old Testament is rich in its use of parabolic illustrations.

Perhaps the most exhaustive and illuminating treatment of Old Testament symbolism is that by Ada Habershon in her most instructive volume on *The Study of the Parables,* a brief condensation of which we have endeavored to give. The One who spake "many things in parables" is the same One who inspired "holy men of old" to write the Old Testament, and we can therefore expect to trace the same mind running through them all. Many of the parables, types and visions of the Old Testament illustrate and throw light on those in the New Testament, proving the marvelous unity of Scripture. Those to whom our Lord addressed His parables had some perception of typical teaching underlying the Levitical ritual and discerned a spiritual significance in the ceremonies commanded.

The manna of Deuteronomy 8 would occur to the Jews, when Jesus spoke of Himself as "The Manna" in John 6, and of the fact that man could not live by bread alone in Matthew 4.

The building on a rock would send the thoughts of Christ's hearers back to The Song of Moses where God is spoken of as the Rock (Deuteronomy 32:1).

The Parable of the Wicked Husbandmen would recall the Parable of the Vineyard, in almost identical language in Isaiah 5. Compare also Isaiah 27; 2, 3 with John 15.

The feasts of Leviticus 23 should be carefully studied with the parables of Matthew 13. There are many analogies between the yearly festivals and the group parables.

The Law of Clean and Unclean Animals (Leviticus 11; Deuteronomy 14) took on deeper significance when Peter saw that sheet let down from heaven.

The figure of a house to be pulled down finds an echo in the New Testament (Jeremiah 33:7; Ezekiel 36:36 with Acts 15:15-17; Romans 11:1,2).

The instruction regarding lost sheep forms a beautiful supplement to the Parable of the Saviour (Deuteronomy 22:1-3 with Luke 15).

Many incidents in the life of Joseph are illustrative of our Lord's life and reign.

The story of Naboth's vineyard reminds us of the vineyard in the Parable of the Wicked Husbandmen portrayed by Jesus.

The Parable of the Unjust Judge is

akin to the experience of the woman of Shunem (II Kings 8) who cried unto the king for her house and her land.

The purchase of a field (Jeremiah 32) suggests the Parable of the Hidden Treasure (Matthew 13).

The parabolic clothing of Joshua (Zechariah 3) can be placed along-side the Parable of the Prodigal Son (Luke 15).

Zechariah's vision of the ephah corresponds in many ways to the Parable of the Leaven.

As for the symbolism of the Psalms, Psalm 78:2 can be linked with Matthew 13:34, 35; Psalm 1 with Matthew 24:45-51, and Psalm 2 is that of the Wicked Husbandmen. Psalm 23 is precious when placed alongside of John 10. Psalm 45, describing the bride and her beautiful apparel, has a counterpart in the Marriage of the Lamb (Revelation 19). Psalm 19, where the bridegroom comes out of his chamber and rejoices as a strong man to run a race, suggests the Incarnation and the Return of our Lord.

The most beautiful of all parables is that of the little City in Ecclesiastes 9:13-17, a picture of the world, attacked by Satan but delivered by the Lord Jesus. It is interesting to note in the books of Proverbs and Ecclesiastes many verses which contain the same symbolical language as the parables of our Lord. Compare Proverbs 12:7; 14:11; 24:3 with Matthew 7 and I Corinthians 3. The closing verses in Proverbs 4 remind us of several of the Lord's parables, especially that in which He taught the disciples that defilement arises, not from what goes *into* the mouth as food, but from what comes *out* of the heart and mouth in speech. Amongst the words of Solomon are references to sowing and reaping. Compare Proverbs 11:24 with II Corinthians 9:6; Proverbs 11:18 and 22:8 with Galatians 6:7; Proverbs 11:4, 28 with the Parable of the Rich Man in Luke 16; Proverbs 12:12 with John 15; Proverbs 28:19 with the Prodigal Son; Proverbs 13:7 describes Him who sold all that He had that He might purchase the field and the pearl.

Apart from actual and borderline Parables, there are hundreds of phrases, verses, and words of a parabolic nature. One could profitably dwell upon the many titles of God in the Old Testament, like "A Little Sanctuary," "Fortress," "Mother" etc., indicating the spiritual significance of such figures of speech. It is to be hoped that the following instances will stimulate further study in this most absorbing aspect of Bible truth.

# PARABLES IN THE HISTORICAL BOOKS

## The Parable of Mount Moriah

(Genesis 22; Hebrews 11:17-19)

The Holy Spirit is our authority for calling the incident of Abraham's offering up of Isaac, a parable. The inspired writer to *The Hebrews* says that after Abraham's act of obedience — "He received him in a figure" (11:19). The word used for "figure" here is the same one used of "parable" in the gospels. The R.V. renders it, "Received him in a parable." The placing of Isaac upon the altar was a parabolic representation of death — the parable being in action instead of words —and his deliverance was therefore a parabolic representation of resurrection. The figurative accomplishment of the deed passes to the historical narrative— "he was in the act of offering." This phrase, and the fact that Abraham believed God was able to raise up Isaac from the dead, reveal the greatness of the sacrifice Abraham was called to make. It is interesting to note that

Isaac is the only one in Scripture, apart from Christ, to be spoken of as "only begotten son" (Genesis 22:2; Hebrews 11:17).

Faith gave Abraham power to act upon the divine command even when Isaac must be slain. Up to Abraham's time no one had ever been raised from the dead, but the father of faith, believing the promise of God, had the confidence that his son, once slain, could be raised again. Thus when Isaac was on the altar, in the very shadow of death, Abraham received him back to life again, by God's grace. When Abraham said to his servants, "We will come again to you" (Genesis 22:5), he spoke the language of faith. The patriarch never doubted the almightiness of God.

What an impressive parable the whole narrative is of the offering up of God's only begotten Son, who was freely "delivered up for us all" (Romans 8:32) and who was received from the dead by His Father (I Timothy 3:16)! One point of difference, however, in this acted parable is the fact that although Isaac was offered up by Abraham, he was yet spared. The ram, caught in the thicket became Isaac's substitute and was slain in his stead. But Christ was smitten of God and afflicted. God gave His only begotten Son to die for our sin. We should have died, but Christ, as the sacrificed Ram, was sacrificed as our Substitute. He died for the sin of a lost world.

Another message for our hearts is that of readiness to do the will of God. Paul would have us know that the great quality of true service is the willing mind, "If there be first a willing mind, it is accepted according to that a man hath, and not according to that he hath not" (I Corinthians 8:12). Abraham went a long way and suffered much heart-anguish to do the will of God. Once he received the divine command, Abraham manifested a deliberate readiness to fulfil it. Too many of us go so far in obedience and then stop short like Mark whom Paul refused to take on

his missionary journey (Acts 15:28). Abraham stands out magnificently as one who went as far as God would let him go.

# The Parable of the Tabernacle
(Hebrews 9:1-10; Exodus 25-31)

Here again, the Holy Spirit is our authority for affirming that the Tabernacle which Moses reared in the wilderness was a parable of a more glorious heritage. "The Holy Spirit this signifying . . . the first tabernacle . . . was a *figure* (Greek, parable) for the time then present" (Hebrews 9:8, 9).

The parabolic pictures or objects associated with all the services and furniture of the Tabernacle are a most fruitful line of study. In a most remarkable way the Sacrifices, offerings, feasts and construction of the Tabernacle, illustrate the Person and Work of the Redeemer, as well as the privileges and blessings of the redeemed. The wonderful ninth chapter of Hebrews is the Holy Spirit's exposition of the Tabernacle, which presents a grand picture of the complete work of Christ for the believer and also of the whole life of the believer in Christ.

For the student desiring to understand the symbolic significance of all associated with the Tabernacle, there is an extensive library of expositions from which to choose. Some expositors have let fancy run away with them in their interpretation of some of the minor features of the temporary erection in the wilderness. Dr. A. T. Pierson wisely said, "No one can claim infallibility in interpreting these parabolic pictures and objects, the very beauty of this form of teaching being in part that it admits of ever-increasing clearness of vision and accuracy of insight, as our life and character approach nearer to final perfection. But we are sure that there is here a wealth of meaning yet unexplored and unsuspected by even the children of God, and which only the ages to come will fully unveil and reveal."

The main feature of the Tabernacle was its three-fold division—a trinity in unity:

> *The Outer Court,* with its Brazen Altar of Sacrifice, and the Laver.
>
> *The Inner Court,* or Holy Place, with its Table of Shew Bread, The Golden Candlesticks, The Altar of Incense.
>
> *The Innermost Court,* or Holy of Holies, with its Ark of the Covenant surmounted by the Mercy Seat.

It does not require much imagination to see in these pronounced features a parable of the work of Christ set forth in order, from His vicarious sacrifice on the cross, the advent of the regenerating and sanctifying Spirit, throughout His whole career as The Light of the World, The Bread of Life, The Intercessor within the veil in the presence of God for us.

The Tabernacle may also be regarded as a parable illustrating how the believer may draw near to God in Christ.

*The Outer Court* suggests two conditions—remission of sins through the atoning blood and regeneration of spirit through the Word of God and the Holy Spirit—the *terms* of communion.

*The Inner Court* illustrates the three *forms* of communion—a living light of testimony; the systematic consecration of substance; a habitual life of prayer.

*The Innermost Court* portrays the final *goal* and *ideal* of communion, when "perpetual obedience is like an unbroken tablet of law, the beauty of the Lord our God is upon us, and all His attributes and our affections and activities are in perfect harmony." For a fuller treatment of this fascinating aspect of Bible study the reader is directed to the chapter on *Old Testament Symbolism* in Ada Habershon's volume on *The Study of Parables.*

This gifted writer has also a small volume, *Studies on the Tabernacle,* which contains many clear, biblical outlines showing how the arrangements and details of the Tabernacle were a "shadow of good things to come" and "patterns of things in the heavens" (Hebrews 10:1; 9:23; Colossians 2:17; John 5:45).

## The Parables of Balaam
### (Numbers 22; 23:7, 18; 24:3, 15, 20-23)

Of the eighteen appearances of the English word "parable" in the Old Testament, six are found in connection with Balaam's pronouncements. George H. Lang remarks that "the prophetic utterances of Balaam are called *parables.* They are such because facts and projects connected with Israel are set forth by comparisons. These are drawn chiefly from non-human realms." Strange though it may seem, the prophetic parables of this worthless prophet are among the noblest and most distinct in Old Testament Scriptures. In their range they "bear testimony to the calling of Israel to be the chosen people of Jehovah," says Fairbairn, "and to the blessings which were in store for them, and which no enchantment, or curse, or force, could take from them, to the rise of the Star out of Jacob, and to the destruction of all His enemies."

What was the background of Balaam of Pethor, and how did he come to be associated with King Balak? Balaam was a man who practised *divination,* which comprised those arts of folly and deception that have ever abounded in idolatrous countries. That he was also a *covetous* man is clear from the statement that "the rewards of divination" were in his hands and of those of his confederates. Balaam "loved the *wages* of unrighteousness." It was to this man that Balak came for information. The Israelites, pursuing their journey to

Canaan, pitched their tents in the most fertile parts of Arabia. Alarmed at the numbers and prowess of the Israelites, who had recently conquered King Og of Bashan, the Moabites feared lest they also should become a prey. Balak, therefore, sent to the neighboring Midianites and consulted with their princes but the knowledge he received was heavy with doom.

That God uses the best material He can find when need arises, even though such material is adverse to His holy nature, is seen here in that He used a false prophet to utter divinely-inspired parables, which are to be regarded as the direct expression of God's love and purpose toward His people. God said to Balaam, "Go with the men: but only the word that I shall speak unto thee, that shalt thou speak." Meeting Balak, directed by God, Balaam said, "Lo, I am come unto thee: have I now any power at all to say anything? the word that God putteth in my mouth, that shall I speak." When upbraided by Balak, King of Moab, for blessing Israel, Balaam replied, "Must I not take heed to speak that which the Lord hath put in my mouth . . . then shall I curse whom the Lord hath not cursed? or how shall I defy whom the Lord hath not defied?"

Thus compelled to utter what he would have gladly suppressed, Balaam broke out in a strain of most beautiful and impassioned parabolic poetry and foretold the eminent blessing of the people he was hired to curse. The parables of Balaam may be easily distinguished.

In the first parable, the leading thought is that of separation unto God for the fulfilment of His purpose: "The people shall dwell alone, and shall not be reckoned among the nations" (Numbers 23:9).

This divine choice of Israel was the basis of all God's claims upon them and the reason for all the peculiar rites and institutions, divinely provided, for the people to observe, for God had said: "I am the Lord your God, which have separated you from other people. Ye shall therefore put difference between clean beasts and unclean. . . . Ye shall be holy unto me; for I the Lord am holy, and have severed you from other people, that ye should be mine" (Leviticus 20:24-26).

There is also the fulfilment of the long-formed purpose when God "set the bound of the people according to the number of the children of Israel" (Deuteronomy 32:8). In this parable dealing with the separation of Israel, an illustration is drawn from the *soil* beneath our feet. "Who can count the dust of Jacob?" (Numbers 23:10). We here have a reference to the numerical vastness of Abraham's descendants, earlier spoken of as *sand* and *stars* (Genesis 22:17). Some expositors see in the *dust* and *sand* a figurative description of Israel, the earthly descendants of Abraham, and in the *stars,* a symbolic reference to the Church of God, the spiritual heavenly descendants of Abraham. But as George H. Lang says, "This is a warning against a fanciful treatment of parables and symbols, for three times Moses uses the symbol of *stars* of the earthly Israel" (Deuteronomy 1:10; 10:22; 28:62; I Chronicles 27:23).

This much is evident, the same separating and sovereign choice of God forms the ground of the Christian's calling in this age of Grace. We were "called to be saints," that is, *separated ones.* We were "chosen in Christ before the foundation of the world." We were "saved and called with a holy calling . . . according to his own purpose and grace, given us in Christ from before the world began." These and other characteristic descriptions are of those who compose the true Chruch. Separated from the World, we are to live as strangers and pilgrims while in it.

The next parable emphasizes the

*justification* of the people *separated.*
The progression in Balaam's parabolic
pronouncements and predictions is indicated by the five-fold phrase, "He
took up his parable." Having chosen
Israel, God could not go back upon
His choice, so He met Balaam and
put this word in his mouth for Balak;
"God is not a man that he should lie;
neither the son of man, that he should
repent: hath he said, and shall he not
do it? or hath he spoken, and shall he
not make it good? . . . He hath not
beheld iniquity in Jacob, neither hath
he seen perversion in Israel: the Lord
his God is with him, and the shout of
a king is among them" (Numbers
23:18). The history of the chosen
people shows that there *was* iniquity
of which the true Jacob was painfully
conscious; and there was such per-
verseness in Israel that the heathen
world around wondered at it. But the
marvel is that the eye of God looked
upon His people in the light that
streamed from His own grace, across
the blood of the sacrificial offerings
presented in their behalf, and on to
the atoning death of His well-beloved
Son.

Nature again contributes to Balaam's inspired parabolic instruction,
for God is described as having "the
strength of an unicorn," while Israel
is depicted as having the strength of
the wild ox and the terribleness of
the lion, and lioness (Numbers 23:22,
24; 24:8-9). As those justified freely
by His grace, justified by the blood of
Jesus, justified by faith, and therefore
justified from all things we Christians,
too, have a strength not our own. Our
strength is in the grace of Christ Jesus
our Lord (II Timothy 2:1).

The third parable Balaam uttered declares fruitfulness for God, as the
necessary result of separation unto
Him and justification before Him. How
beautifully expressive is the inspired delineation of God's chosen people! "How
goodly are thy tents, O Jacob, and thy
tabernacles, O Israel! As the valleys are

they spread forth, as goodness by the
river's side, as the trees of lign aloes
which the Lord hath planted, and as
cedar trees beside the waters" (Numbers 24:3-14). The figurative speech
Balaam employed forms a study in itself.
A ruler from Heaven is referred to as a
*star* (Numbers 24:17 with Revelation
2:28; 22:16). A *sceptre,* the common
symbol of royalty, describes the powerful sovereignty of Israel's Messiah.
A *bird's nest set in a rock* distinguishes the security of the Kenites
(Numbers 24:21). *Ships* from the coast
of Chittim were prophetic of Alexander's victories (Numbers 24:24).

Although disappointed, God had
yet every right to expect fruit from
His people in the wilderness. Had He
not chosen, redeemed, and blessed
them, and made them His own peculiar treasure? How much more does
He expect from us who have been
bought with the precious blood of His
dear Son? Do we not glorify Him
when we bear much fruit? (John
15:8). Are we not exhorted to be
filled with the fruits of righteousness?
(Philippians 1:11). Is it not intensely
practical to be separated unto God and
justified by grace before Him? Should
not our privileged position result in
being fruitful in every good work?
(Colossians 1:10).

Is it not fitting that the next parable
looks forward to the Second Advent
of Christ? A crown of victory is to
adorn the brow of Him who called,
separated, justified, and blessed His
people. "I shall see him, but not now:
I shall behold him, but not nigh: there
shall come a Star out of Jacob, and
a Sceptre shall arise out of Israel"
(Numbers 24:17). One commentator
writes, "The Star refers to His first
Advent, the Sceptre to His second
Advent; and as the false prophet
would not see Him as his Saviour, he
pronounces his own doom." It is the
time of judgment for the ungodly, for
—"Out of Jacob shall come he that
shall have dominion, and shall destroy

him that remaineth of the city." The destruction shall be sweeping and terrible, therefore Balaam—"Took up his parable, and said, Alas, who shall live when God doeth this?" (Numbers 24:23).

## The Parable of the Trees
(Judges 9:7-15)

This parable spoken by Jotham, youngest son of Gideon and the lone survivor of the massacre of his seventy brothers by another brother, Abimelech, to the men of Shechem, is another parabolic prophecy, seeing it was fulfilled. Abimelech, Gideon's bastard son, aspired to be king and persuaded the men of Shechem to murder all but one of the seventy legitimate sons of his father and appoint him their king. Jotham, who had escaped, delivered himself of his parable to king and people from Mount Gerizim, and then fled for his life.

Many scholars disallow the parabolic nature of Jotham's utterance. For instance, Dr. E. W. Bullinger in *Figures of Speech* says, "This is not a parable, because there is no similitude by which one thing is likened unto another . . . Where trees or animals speak and reason we have *Fable;* and if the Fable is explained then we have *Allegory.* But for the explanation, 'Ye have made Abimelech king' 9:16, which renders it *Allegory,* we should have *Fable.*" Dr. A. T. Pierson refers to it as, "the first and oldest allegory in Scripture . . . One of the most beautiful of all the fables or apologues in the whole range of literature." Professor Salmond likewise speaks of it as a "genuine example of the fable . . . the grotesque and improbable elements which unfit it for serving as an instrument for the expression of the highest religious truth."

Ellicott comments, "As in this chapter we have the first Israelite 'king' and the first massacre of brethren, so here we have the first fable. Fables are extremely popular in the East,

where they are often current under the name of the slave-philosopher, Lokman, the counterpart of the Greek Aesop . . . A 'fable' is a fanciful story to inculcate prudential morality." With other expositors, however, the present writer inclines toward the parabolic aspect of Jotham's appeal who, as Stanley says, "spoke like the bard of English ode." Lang thinks of it as a *parable* and makes these three observations:

1. The material of a parable may be real, as trees are actual objects.
2. The use made of the material may be wholly fanciful; as when trees were pictured holding a conclave, proposing to elect a king, invite low growing trees — the olive, fig, vine, bramble — to wave to and fro over the far loftier trees, as the cedar.
3. The purely fanciful details may correspond accurately to the men who are to be instructed, and to their doings . . . The cedar tree was a tall and lofty one, so were the men of Shechem strong enough to carry out the horrible massacre.

A further word is necessary as to the difference between *interpretation* and *application.* The former has to do with the matter in hand, namely, the relation between Israel and Abimelech, and is historical and local. The latter is dispensational and prophetic. As to the direct *interpretation* of Jotham's parable: the various trees are represented as seeking a king, and successively apply to the olive, the fig-tree the vine, and lastly to the bramble. By these trees desiring a king we have a figurative presentation of the Shechemites, who were discontent with God's direct government and yearned for a visible, titular head such as surrounding, heathen nations had. The slain sons of Gibeon are compared with Abimelech, as good trees are with the bramble. The word translated *rule over* implies, to float about, and includes the idea of restlessness and insecurity. Keil and Delitzsch in their Old Testament studies comment that "Wherever the Lord does not found the monarchy, or the king himself does not lay the foundations of his government in the grace of God, he is never anything but a tree, moving about above other trees without a firm root in a fruitful soil, utterly unable to bear fruit to the glory of God and the good of men. The words of the briar, 'Trust in my shadow,' contain a deep irony, the truth of which the Shechemites were very soon to discover."

Then, as we are to see, the national life of Israel is portrayed under the similitude of the trees cited in the parable, each of which possessed properties making it peculiarly valuable to the people of the East. Much could be said as to the individuality of each tree, the life of each being distinct from every other. While all trees derive their sustenance from the same soil, yet each tree takes from the soil that which is fitted to its own nature and necessary for the production of its own fruit and use. Then the trees are different in respect to their size and form and worth. Each tree has its own glory. Strong trees shelter and protect weaker ones from intense heat and furious storms (see Daniel 4:20, 22; Isaiah 32:1).

*The Olive Tree* is one of the most valuable of trees. Oliveyards were numerous in Palestine. Winifred Walker in her beautifully illustrated book, *All the Plants of the Bible,* says that "a full-sized tree yields a half ton of oil yearly." This oil supplied artificial light (Exodus 27:20), and was used as food, being found as an ingredient in the *Meat Offering.* Its fruit was also eaten, and its wood was used for building purposes (I Kings 7:23,31,32). Olive leaves were a symbol of peace.

*The Fig Tree,* famed for its sweetness, was also highly prized. Its fruit was widely consumed and its widespreading branches provided grateful shelter (I Samuel 25:18). Adam and Eve used fig-leaves to cover their nakedness (Genesis 3:6,7). Figs are the first fruits recorded in the Bible.

*The Vine* was likewise held in great esteem because of its immense cluster of grapes producing the wine—a great source of wealth in Palestine (Numbers 13:23). "Wine that cheereth the heart of God and man." To sit under one's own fig-tree and vine was a proverbial expression, denoting peace and prosperity (Micah 4:4).

*The Cedar,* greatest of all Bible trees, was renowned for its remarkable height —"often one hundred and twenty feet tall and forty feet in girth." Because of the quality of its wood, it was used in building of Solomon's Temple and Palace. Lofty and strong, the Cedars symbolized the men of Shechem who were strong enough to carry out their horrible massacre of Gideon's sons. Lang makes the application: "As a burning bramble might set on fire a forest of cedars, or as a burning cedar would cause the destruction of all the brambles around it, so could Abimelech and the men of Shechem prove destructive of each other and inflict on one another the due reward of their common ingratitude and violence."

*The Bramble* is a powerful bush-like plant flourishing in any soil. It produces no fruit of any value, and the tree, as such, is useless as a means of shelter. Its wood is used by the natives for fuel. Dr. A. T. Pierson reminds us that the "bramble is the *Buckthorn* or *Rammus,* and that "fire coming out of the bramble, refers to its inflammable character being easily set in a blaze and rapidly burning." The application is only too obvious. The nobler Gideon and his worthy sons had declined the proffered kingdom, but this baseborn and vile Abimelech had accepted it and would prove like an irritating thorn bush to his subjects and a fierce destroyer, his course ending like the burning thorn bush in the mutual reign of himself and them (Judges 9:16-20). The fire "coming out" of the bramble can refer to the fact that fire is often originated among dry bushes by the friction of the branches, thus forming an apt emblem of the war of passions which often destroys combinations of wicked men.

While Jotham's skilful use of imagery captured the attention of the men of Shechem and acted as a mirror to reflect their own criminal folly, such a reflection did not result in repentance for their wickedness. The Shechemites did not pass sentence on themselves as David did after listening to Nathan's moving parable, or as many of the hearers of the parables of Jesus did (Matthew 21:14). Effective eloquence is that which moves the heart to action. The hearers of Jotham's parable of the trees still suffered Abimelech to rule over them for three years.

For ourselves this lesson is obvious: "Sweet contentment with one's appointed sphere, and the privilege of being of service to God and man in the place where God has put us; and the vanity of the lust of mere promotion." Then as the olive tree, fig tree, the vine and the bramble are often used in a typical sense of Israel, a brief reference to such an application might prove profitable:

*The Olive Tree* speaks of Israel's covenant privileges and blessings (Romans 11:17-25). It is rightly named the first "king" of the trees because being evergreen it speaks of God's enduring covenant made with Abraham, before Israel came into being. In Jotham's parable the olive tree is characterized by *fatness,* and by its use both God and man were honored (Exodus 27:20-21; Leviticus 2:1). Israel's privileges (fatness) are found in Romans 3:2 and 9:4-5. No other nation was ever so blessed of God as Israel.

Israel's failure is seen in that some of the branches are broken off and wild branches grafted into their places. The Gentiles are enjoying some of the privileges and blessings of the olive tree. Chief among the blessings granted to Israel was the gift of the Word of God and the Son of God. Today regenerated Gentiles are preaching the Son of God and dispensing the Word of God to Israel. But her restoration is seen in the fatness in that day when "all Israel shall be saved . . . If the fall of them be the riches of the World . . . how much more their fulness."

*The fig tree* speaks of Israel's national privileges (Matthew 21:18-20; 24:32-33; Mark 11:12-14; Luke 13:6-8).

That which characterized the fig tree was sweetness and good fruit. God planted Israel, His fig tree; but the fruit was corrupt, and instead of sweetness there was bitterness. So it was when our Lord came to Israel, for His own (people) received Him not. In bitterness they branded Him as devil possessed and "held a council against Him, how they might destroy Him." It is the same today for Israel still rejects her Messiah and is bitter against Him. David Baron says, "I have known personally most amiable, and, as men, lovable characters among the Jews; but immediately the name 'Jesus' was mentioned, a change came over their countenances, and they would fall into a passion of anger . . . clenching their fists, gnashing their teeth, and spitting on the ground at the very mention of the name."

Israel's failure is seen in the withering away of the fig tree (Matthew 21:19-20). Our Lord came seeking fruit and when He found none, He cursed the fruitless tree, and it withered away. In the parable in Luke the tree is cut down. This has been Israel's condition nationally for centuries. She is dried up, with no king, no flag, and no home. She is the tail instead of the promised head of the nations.

Israel's restoration is seen in the green shoots on the fig tree. When our Lord cursed the tree He said, "Let no fruit grow on thee henceforth *unto the age.*" These last words tell us that the fig tree is destined to sprout and bear fruit again. "Now learn the parable of the fig tree; when his branch is yet tender, and putteth forth leaves, ye know that summer is nigh. . . . "So likewise ye, when ye see these things come to pass, know ye that the kingdom of God is nigh at hand" (Matthew 24:32; Luke 21:30).

*The Vine* symbolizes Israel's spiritual privileges (Isaiah 5:1-7; Psalm 80:9-19; Ezekiel 15; John 15).

That which characterized the vine was wine, which cheered both God and man. Wine is God's chosen symbol for joy. When Israel found their wine vats full to overflowing it was proof positive that the blessing of God was upon them to the full·and overflowing, and of course there was joy under His approval, and God Himself had joy in the drink offering of His people.

Israel's failure is seen in the wasted, devoured vine, and the vineyard trodden down. God brought the vine out of Egypt, planted it in a prepared place, did everything for it; but the vine failed, so the hedges were taken away, and the vineyard is desolate. There is no wine.

Israel's restoration is seen in the day of God's visitation. "O God of Hosts: look down from heaven, and behold, and visit this vine; and the vineyard which Thy right hand hath planted. Turn us again, O Lord God of Hosts, cause thy face to shine; and we shall be saved" (Psalm 80). That visitation will be in the Person of the Son of God, for all spiritual blessings are bound up in Him, and from henceforth Israel will find them only through the True Vine.

*The Bramble,* the meanest and most worthless of trees, is fit only to be burned. The bramble was willing to reign over them. All the trees were willing to have it so. This is prophetic of that day when Israel shall be ruled by the Anti-christ. The bramble is a thorny tree, and thorns symbolize the curse of sin.

When the bramble comes he will say, "Come and put your trust in my shadow." When our blessed Lord was here He said to them, "Come unto Me"; and they cried, "We will not have this man to reign over us. . . . Away with Him! . . . Crucify Him!" But when this one comes, they will receive him and enter into a covenant with him, and put their trust in his shadow.

A fire shall come out of the bramble and devour them. That is prophetic of the great tribulation, the time of Jacob's trouble. But the bramble itself shall be burned and destroyed (Judges 9:20). This will be at the coming of our Lord (II Thessalonians 2:8). And then shall the fatness, the sweetnesses, and the cheer of the trees bless Israel and make her a blessing, through the One who died on the cursed tree.

## The Parable of the Ewe Lamb
### (II Samuel 12:1-4)

This skilfully conceived parable which Nathan used to convict David of his grievous sin illustrates the effectiveness of word-painting. Such a parable of reproof is treated more as a *fable* than a *parable* by some writers. This we know, the telling of the touching story of the ewe lamb awoke the better nature of King David. Had Nathan the prophet gone into David's palace and directly and immediately denounced his guilt, and pronounced the punishment due to his sin, it is questionable whether David would have listened to Nathan. The bald, naked approach might have angered the king and kept him from repentance. He might have answered the prophet in the words of Hazael, "Is thy servant a dog that he should do this great thing?"

But by the employment of the parabolic method, Nathan exposed the terrible sin of David and drew from him the ejaculation, *I have sinned,* which was the germ of the entire fifty-first Psalm and the beginning of a penitence which was as sincere as the transgression had been aggravated. Nathan's skill in concealing the real application of his parable reminds us of Christ's Parable of the Vineyard and the Wicked Husbandmen, and in practical application to the heart and conscience it never has been surpassed (Mark 12:1-12). The two general features of the parable before us are the *favor* and the *forgiveness* of God.

1. *The Favor of God.* Although David had sinned, in the first place, before God (Psalm 51:4), God took the first step in the restoration of His sinning servant to divine favor through repentance. Thus we read, "The Lord sent Nathan." While the prophet was doubtless cognizant of the King's sin, he did not go to him until sent from *above.* David had fallen into a horrible pit and only divine grace could rescue and restore him. How wise it was of God to choose Nathan as His mouthpiece! Did he not have David's confidence and had he not been the bearer of good tidings to David? (II Samuel 7:1-19). The feeling for each other disarmed David's suspicion and prepared him to listen attentively to Nathan's moving story. When we stray from the pathway of obedience to God's will, He has His own ways and means of restoring us to His gracious favor (Psalms 23:3; 40:2).

A further evidence of God's desire to deliver David from the miry clay can be gathered from the incomparable story He inspired Nathan to relate to David who, because of his shepherd-heart, would be moved by it. As we examine this matchless parable we are, first of all, impressed with the "the two men in one city." In one respect they were equal, fellow-men and fellow-citizens. By the "two men" we understand David and Uriah who although they were level on the common ground of humanity, and both subject to the laws of God, were yet different.

David was by birth a member of the highly-favored nation God had so signally blessed and became its great king.

Uriah was a subject of the king, and, by choice, a citizen of the city where David lived and reigned.

As to their qualities, David and Uriah were as "two men in one city," for both were fearless, courageous and valiant men. From his youth, David had been noted for his bravery; and Uriah the Hittite was a man of like spirit. Part of David's dark crime was that he used Uriah's bravery to bring about his death.

The contrasts in the two men portrayed by Nathan are likewise conspicuous. Dwelling "in one city," they were poles apart in position and privilege—"the one rich and the other poor." God had graciously endowed David with much wealth. What prosperity was his! Yet such divine favor can prove to be a perilous gift. "Wealth means power to gratify one's desires, and to execute one's will." We have the adage that "Money speaks." David's position as a wealthy potentate then, made it possible for him to indulge his unlawful appetites.

The "poor" man was Uriah, a soldier in the king's army, and therefore obliged to submit to his sovereign's will. Yet with his less exalted position, Uriah was nobler in his actions than his king. Such inequality only aggravated David's foul crime.

Nathan's parable presents a further contrast: "The rich man had exceeding many flocks and herds: but the poor man had nothing save one little ewe lamb." David, as a king, and a rich one, had many wives, but Uriah was no polygamist—he had but one wife, to whom he gave all his love. As the rich man in the parable could not estimate his poor neighbor's affection for his only small lamb, so David was a stranger to the pure, undivided love for one woman. What a striking contrast there is between the lawless passion of David and the pure, deep love of Uriah! As "A London Minister" expresses it in *Miracles and Parables of the Old Testament,* "The river which keeps within its channel is a blessing to the country through which it flows; but the same river, when it bursts its banks and overflows the land, becomes a means of desolation and destruction. So is it with lawful affection, and lawless passion."

As the parable unfolded and David heard of "the rich man" taking "the poor man's lamb" and killing it to feed a traveler, "David's anger was greatly kindled" and he vowed to kill the rich man capable of such a heartless, pitiless deed. Ellicott remarks at this point, "David's generous impulses had not been extinguished by his sin, nor his warm sense of justice; his naturally quick temper (I Samuel 25: 13,22,23) at once roused his indignation to the utmost." But how crestfallen he was when he discovered that in planning Uriah's murder, he was the one killing the poor man's lamb.

Boldly and suddenly, Nathan applied his parable to David's aroused conscience and said, "Thou art the man." David, tenderly sensible of what the poor man was supposed to suffer in having his ewe-lamb made a dish at his rich neighbor's table, was now made conscious of how much the injured Uriah must have suffered in the seduction of his much-loved wife.

1. *The Forgiveness of God.* Guilty of a great crime, David became conscious of the need of a great confession, which, as soon as he saw himself in the parable, he made. "I have sinned against the Lord." Nathan's reply was immediate, "The Lord also hath put away thy sin, thou shalt not die." But although David's sin was forgiven, and out of his experience he wrote Psalms 32 and 51, many of its consequences remained. "The sword shall never depart from thine house." Can we not read a wealth of meaning in David's word, "He restoreth my soul"? If we, as believers have sinned, no matter how heinous our sin, the promise is that, "if we confess our sin, he is faithful and just to forgive us our sins and

to cleanse us from all unrighteousness." David passed condemnation upon himself as unreservedly as he had passed sentence upon the rich man in the parable, and with a sorrow, deep and lasting, enjoyed once again the smile of God.

# The Parable of the Two Sons
## (II Samuel 14:1-24)

It is interesting to compare and contrast the parable of the woman of Tekoa with that of the parable of the ewe-lamb just considered. Again, David is the recipient of the parable. The one of the ewe-lamb was uttered by Nathan, the inspired prophet; the one of the two sons was spoken by a clever woman at the instigation of Joab who was "wily and politic and unscrupulous," and well able "to read human character and discern human motives through a very small crevice."

Nathan's parable was intended as a scorching condemnation of David's double sin of seduction and murder; the Tekoan's parable was full of guile and flattery. The former was based on the divine principles of truth, righteousness and justice, and was delivered in all solemnity; the latter was a mixture of truth and falsehood, and of incorrect conclusions about God. The woman Joab suborned to tell the parable he had contrived was destitute of any real, deep feeling, and was guilty of a theatrical sentimentality. Hers was an impressive show. Then, too, the objective of each parable differed. Nathan's parable was calculated to convict David of his sin and to induce true repentance; the woman's parable had as its end the promotion of Joab's schemes of self-interest and self-preservation.

1. *The Setting of the Parable.* The feigned story of an "obscure and humble woman, of an obscure village in Israel, almost three thousand years ago" was attentively listened to by David because he felt it had its parallel

in his own history. Although God had given David rest from his enemies, he was still subdued by the recollection of his grievous fall, and in the sins and crimes of his sons he heard the sad echo of his own transgressions. His harp, so often his solace, was on the willow tree. Absalom, his much-loved son, had been in exile for three years because of the murder of his brother Amnon, who had ravished Tamar, full sister to Absalom, and half-sister to Amnon. In spite of the sin of his son, lonely David yearned for Absalom. "The soul of King David longed to go forth unto Absalom."

In his volume of vivid biographical sermons, Clarence E. Macartney, dealing with *The Woman of Tekoa* graphically describes the conflict David experienced at this time. There was David the King, the administrator of justice, and David the father longing for his criminal son.

"David the king, upholder of the law, is saying, 'Absalom, you are a murderer. You treacherously slew your own brother. You dipped your hand in the blood of Amnon. You have broken the law of God and the law of man. Absalom, remain in exile. Never see my face again.' "

But David the father is speaking in a far different manner. What David the father is saying is this: "Absalom, come home. Without thee the feast is tasteless; without thee my harp is tuneless; without thee the palace halls are cheerless; without thee the pomp and circumstance of war is but an empty show. Thou hast slain thy brother: yet with all thy faults I love thee still. Absalom, my son, my son, come home." Thus passed the days, the weeks, the months, and the years.

2. *The Substance of the Parable.* Discerning David's personal desire to bring Absalom back, though justice constrained the king to severity, Joab, the captain of the host, and David's counselor and friend, knew that there was only one cure for the grief which

was causing David to be unfit for his kingly duties. He conceived the idea of the parable because he knew a woman could tell it better than a man. Evidently the woman from Tekoa had wisdom, tact and eloquence, and the parable was purposely made not to parallel too closely the case of Absalom. So adorning the garments of grief and affliction, the woman told the story put into her mouth by Joab. Macartney says of this story that, "it is one of the four or five great speeches of the Bible . . . Nowhere in the Bible is there, in so short a space, a passage which has in it such beautiful metaphors, such pathos and eloquence."

The cry of a woman in evident grief, touched the kind and sympathetic heart of David, and telling her to rise, he asked, "What aileth thee?" Then she told her moving tale of her two sons, striving together in a field, and how one killed the other. Because of this murder, the rest of her family arose and demanded that she deliver the living son up to death for the killing of his brother. As she pled for the safety of her supposed son, David was stirred and told the woman to go home for her request would be granted. "There shall not one hair of thy son fall to the earth."

Having crushed the outer defenses of David's heart, the woman, as instructed by crafty Joab, moved against the inner defenses of the King's heart, and with incomparable grace, tact and humility, presented the plea for Absalom's return and safety, even though he had murdered his brother, Amnon. David penetrated the woman's disguise and detected the stratagem of Joab. "Is not the hand of Joab with thee in all this?" The woman readily confessed that the whole scheme was Joab's. David then sent for Joab and commanded him to "bring the young man Absalom again." And so the banished son returned.

But although Absalom was recalled there was no immediate family reconciliation. David forbade Absalom to see his face, and evils arose as the result of this half-measure of a return. It was to be another two years before father and son met face to face. Irritated by his father's action, Absalom conceived the idea of a conspiracy to overthrow David and take his throne. As for David himself, was he not reaping a sorrowful harvest of his own sin which included the crime of both his sons? Amnon had been guilty of seduction, Absalom of murder, both of which are seen in David's treatment of Bathsheba and Uriah. It may be that the consciousness of his double sin made David weak in purpose. Had he punished his son Amnon as he deserved, there would have been no need to banish Absalom. Alas, David was bitterly conscious that he was reaping what he had sown, and that his sons were but treading in his steps.

3. *The Spiritual Significance of the Parable.* A thousand years before Christ died on the cross to bring exiles back to God, the woman of Tekoa had a glimpse of a divine truth, even though she mis-applied it and perverted it to a bad purpose. "He also deviseth means that His banished should not be expelled from Him." What a mighty Gospel this woman unwittingly preached! God does not take instant vengeance but "waits to be gracious." Sin banished man from God but He devised means to bring the sinner home. What means did He devise? Why, the Incarnation, Death and Resurrection of His own beloved Son! God loved a world of lost sinners and His heart went out to the banished ones who, when they return, are not half-heartedly received as David received his prodigal son, Absalom. Once the sinner turns to God, the reconciliation is complete and the returning, believing one is at one with God, fully accepted in the Beloved.

The Parable of the Two Sons which Jesus told in Luke 15, is the New Testament counterpart of Joab's Parable of Two Sons. The father had lost one of his sons, who became a prodigal in a far country, but his love followed the wayward boy who, on his return, was accorded a full welcome and received the complete, unreserved blessing of his father and the privileges of sonship. God's plan of forgiveness and restoration went further than that of Joab's. David sent his captain to bring Absalom home. The Father-heart of God constrained Him to send His only begotten Son to die for sin, so that sinners could be fully reconciled unto Him. Amazing grace!

## The Parable of the Wounded Prophet
(I Kings 20:35-43)

The parable before us is an example of those in the prophetical writings where parabolic *action* accompanies the words (Jeremiah 27:2; Ezekiel 12:7). These *Action Parables* must have made a deep impression on those who saw and heard them.

According to Josephus, "the certain man" who acted this parable, was Micaiah, the son of Imlah. Evidently he was a representative of a prophetic school. The slaying by a lion recalls the death of the disobedient prophet by a lion in a previous chapter (13:24). The design of the parable was to make Ahab condemn himself. A similar aspect of condemnation featured the last two parables we considered. This parable, however, did not excite any compunction of conscience in Ahab, but elicited the characteristic sullenness of displeasure he later displayed (21:4).

The prophet claimed divine inspiration for his utterance which would have constituted the request of a madman had it not have been "the word of the Lord." As Lange remarks in his well-known *Commentary,* "The penalty inflicted on the man who would not obey the prophet's command, proves beyond a doubt that the demand was accompanied with a statement of reason, and an appeal to the word of Jehovah." As it was essential not only for the application of the parable to be hidden from the one receiving it, but also for the teller of the parable to be unrecognized, there was assumed the disguise of the ash-covered face. As the angler seeks to conceal both his person and his hook by bait, so here, as in the case of Nathan, the hook of intention was hidden. Ahab had no respect for Jehovah's messengers, and so the one confronting him had to be disguised as a wounded man in order to bring upon this disobedient king the passing of a sentence of condemnation upon himself.

As to the significance of this parable, while it is not very clear in all its details, this much is indisputable as Lange suggests, "that the young man who had gone out into battle is the representative of Ahab, and the man entrusted to his keeping but allowed to escape through carelessness, was the representative of Benhadad. Israel had just endured a hard, bloody fight, and had carried off the promised victory; but now, in the person of Benhadad it had let the arch-enemy, whom God had given into their hands, go free and unpunished."

Several lessons can be drawn from this parable. The prophet in the narrative was ruled by the Word of God and had to suffer for obeying it: Obedience to the Lord sometimes leads us along a painful path. Those who go against divine truth bring condemnation on their heads. Ahab's sentence upon the man of God was executed upon himself. He was paid back in his own coin. Then in the solemn charge which the man who turned aside from the battle made to the prophet, there is a further truth to glean. "He brought a man unto him and said, Keep this man." The courage and sacrifice of the heroic are never in vain. Christ sacrificed Himself that the prey might be taken from the mighty and captives delivered, and He did not die in vain, as myriads of redeemed souls in heaven and on earth can testify.

Further, is not the king's lack of intention and attention rebuked in the words, "As thy servant was busy here and there, he was gone"? Do we stand condemned in the matter of negligent watchfulness? The man who effected the escape in the parable was gone. May we be saved from neglecting our solemn charge! Many of us are far too busy here and there on errands of minor importance, and allow a more solemn charge to escape us. We need more *concentration* as well as *consecration* — more *attention* with *intention*.

## The Parable of Micaiah
### (I Kings 22:13-28)

The prophet Micaiah, who is here found addressing Zedekiah, was not a man to prostitute his calling. He did not contribute to the superstitious idea that believing the inspiration of prophets came from God, such inspiration could yet be directed as the prophets deemed best, and that accordingly they could be bribed, or beguiled, or coerced to prophesy smooth things. Micaiah was a true disciple of Elijah and his stern reply proved him to be an enemy of corruption.

Micaiah's prophetic parable, couched in impressive metaphor and symbolic vision, is akin to that of Job's description of Satan's intercourse with the Lord (1:6-12). Ellicott says that the one idea to be conveyed by the parable "is the delusion of the false prophets by a spirit of evil, as a judgment of God on Ahab's sin, and on their degradation of the prophetic office. The imagery is borrowed from the occasion. It is obviously drawn from the analogy of a royal court, where, as in the case before Micaiah's eyes, the king seeks counsel against his enemies."

## The Parable of the Thistle and the Cedar
### (II Kings 14:8-14)

Spoken by Jehoash to Amaziah, this parable takes us back to the tree and animal realms, and recalls the pithy parable of Jotham (Judges 9:8-15). The background of the parable was the reduction of Edom. Amaziah, King of Judah, was elated over subduing the Edomites, slaying ten thousand men, and concluded that he should be equally successful against the most formidable foes of the armies of Israel. But Amaziah learned that his first success was only a relative one. Making the mistake of undervaluing the military might of his opponent, Amaziah met with defeat. Then came his insolent challenge to Jehoash, "Come, let us look one another in the face."

The two metaphors taken from nature are *The Cedar* and *The Thistle,* and convey Jehoash's sense of superiority as he reproved Amaziah. *The Cedar,* the slow-growing and long-lived tree used for sacrificial duty in the Temple, represented the strength of Israel. *The Thistle,* identified by Ellicott as the bramble or briar, or blackthorn, is a weedy plant with spines and thorns, and of no value, and as used by Jehoash conveyed his contempt for his rival in forcible terms. "The cedar of a thousand years could not be uprooted or removed by the strongest earthly power, while the thistle of yesterday was at the mercy of the first beast of the forest who passed by that way."

Then we have an illustration taken from the domestic realm. "Give thy daughter to my son to wife." It was an oriental custom that the man, asking the daughter of another in marriage, was expected to be his equal in rank, otherwise the request was regarded as an insult. Skilfully, Jehoash shows that the proposal of the thistle to the cedar was akin to a poor man asking a rich man for permission to marry his daughter. Thus, "the fate of the thistle sets forth what would be the result of the self-esteem of the King of Judah if he did not take the advice which is the application of the whole, 'Tarry at home for why shouldest thou meddle to thine hurt.' "

The parable, then, was a true picture of the character of Amaziah who, unfortunately, was not willing to see his own picture. Deformed characters have no desire to see themselves reflected in a faithful mirror. The matchless parables of Jesus often failed to gain the approbation of His hearers on this account. Amaziah's pride and insolence were his undoing. Had he been content with his conquest of Edom, he would then have been spared the humiliation of defeat at the hands of Jehoash, King of Israel. The kernel of the parable is that, "Pride goeth before destruction, and a haughty spirit before a fall" (Proverbs 16:18).

## The Parable of Job
### (27:1; 29:1)

While Job's eight answers to his friends cover chapters 26 to 31, and are full of arrestive, symbolic speech, actually the section contains no actual parable, although twice over the word is used in Job's dialogue. The component parts of his first *Parable,* as Job calls his reply, can be easily discerned in the chapters cited:

1. His determination not to renounce his righteousness, 27:2-6.

2. His own estimate of the fate of the wicked, 27:7-23.

3. His magnificent estimate of the nature of wisdom, 28.

4. His comparison of his former life with that of his present experience, 29-30. How Job recounts wistfully his past happiness!

5. His final declaration of his innocence and irreproachable conduct, 31. In this chapter we have one grand confession of uprightness.

The word Job used for "Parable" in connection with his eloquent speeches was *Māshāl,* meaning *similitude,* the same term used of Balaam's prophecies (see also Psalms 49:4; 78:2). The above term is also used in a wide, vague sense, embracing prophetic as well as proverbial poetry (Numbers 21:27).

## The Parable of the Vine Out of Egypt

(Psalm 80)

Actually, this great Psalm presents a multiplication of arrestive figures of speech. For instance, we have:

1. The beautiful, familiar metaphor of the Shepherd, one of the special designations of the Lord used in connection with Israel, and of the Church (Genesis 48:15; 49:24; John 10:11).

2. The Bread of Tears (Psalm 80:5). What trials and tribulations, sorrows and strife God's people had endured.

3. The Vine (Psalm 80:8-11) is used as an emblem of Israel — an emblem so "natural and apt that we do not wonder to find it repeated again and again in the Old Testament, and adopted in the New" (Genesis 49:22; John 15:1). Israel was brought out of Egypt and planted in Canaan and her shadow covered the mountains, and her branches unto the river, which describes the boundaries of the land of Promise, from the sea to the river of Euphrates.

4. The Cedars (Psalm 80:10). The boughs of the Vine are likened unto "goodly cedars" or, as the margin has it, *cedars of God*. The prosperity of Israel resembled the luxuriance of the most magnificent of all forest trees.

5. The Boar Out of the Wood (Psalm 80:12). This is the only reference to the *wild boar* in the Bible, and is used to illustrate the ravaging power of an oppressor of Israel, just as the *crocodile* is used of Egypt, and the *lion* of Assyria, etc. But God was well able to protect His own against all destructive forces (Psalm 80:14-19).

> Protect what Thy right hand hath planted, The branch which Thou hast made strong for Thyself; Let Thy hand be over the man of Thy right hand, Over the son of man whom thou hast made strong for Thyself.

Here we have "a fine instance of the mode in which the thought can pass naturally from the figurative to the literal." This parabolic Psalm ends with a fine gradation in the style of address to God, with the refrain reaching its full tone, expressive of completest trust. In spite of permitted trials, God knows how to preserve and deliver His own, as Whittier suggests in the lines —

> God's ways seem dark, but soon or late They touch the shining hills of day. The evil cannot brook delay; The good can well afford to wait.

# THE PARABLES OF SOLOMON

*The Apocrypha* agrees with the acknowledged fact among ancient Jews that Solomon wrote in Parables. Of him we read: "Thy soul covered the whole earth, and thou filledst it with dark parables. Thy name went far into the islands; and for thy peace thou wast beloved. The countries marvelled at thee for thy songs, and proverbs, and parables, and interpretations" (Ecclesiastes 47:15, 17). We have only to read the books Solomon penned — *Proverbs, Ecclesiastes, Song of Solomon*—to realize how able the King was to express himself in such a rich, varied parabolic fashion. And as Habershon says, "In the light of the New Testament some of Solomon's parables are no longer dark, for we can see in them prophecies of the greater than Solomon." Dr. R. K. Harrison, in his *History of Old Testament Times,* says that "Solomon was a person of great intellectual ability who became legendary at a comparatively early age. He was credited with a great many poetic compositions, and was particularly adept at crystallising the manifold aspects of life in the form of literary proverbs."

## The Parable of Uselessness
### (Proverbs 26:7)

The Book of Proverbs is unique for its employment of parabolic illustrations. How loaded the book is with illustrations, metaphors and figures, taken from every realm! Habershon's chapter on this fact is illuminating. Among some of the parabolic gems this writer enumerates is that of the Parable of the Houses with and without a foundation (9:1; 24:3,27; see 12:7; 14:11). How suggestive these passages are of Matthew 7:24-29 and I Corinthians 3:11-15. The seemingly strong house of the one is not so secure as the fragile tent of the other.

The solemn passage about those treating an invitation to the feast with contempt (Proverbs 1:24-27), should be compared with our Lord's parable regarding the refusal of bidden guests to a lavish feast (Matthew 22).

The paragraph about humility in the presence of royalty and of the great (Proverbs 25:6,7) is almost identical to what our Lord had to say about those coveting high places having to take lower ones. In His adaptation of Solomon's parabolic exhortation, our Lord points to His own example (Luke 14:10; Matthew 20:25; see I John 2:28).

The power of a righteous king to scatter evil (20:8) may be placed alongside of the effect of our Lord's reign when He sets up His throne (Matthew 25:30-46). A look from His righteous eyes will be sufficient to make those speechless who are destitute of the wedding garment.

The proverb, "the king's favour is toward a wise servant," finds an echo in the parables where the servants show their wisdom by faithfulness in trading, diligence in serving, and constancy to watching. In Proverbs 8:34 the Lord Himself is speaking about the watching one just as He did in the gospels, "Blessed is the man that heareth me, watching daily at my gates, waiting at the posts of my doors."

In his description of the path of the wicked, and how it can be avoided (Proverbs 4:20-27), Solomon uses language akin to that of our Lord's parables in which He taught His disciples that defilement arises, not from what goes *into* the mouth as food, but from what comes *out* of the heart and mouth in speech. "The importance of keeping the heart with all diligence is the central thought in Solomon's sevenfold chain of precepts. They divide themselves into two groups, the first three showing how the Word reaches the *heart* through the *ear* and *eye,* and then four teaching that the heart governs the walk. "Did not our Lord Himself teach that, 'Out of the abundance of the heart the mouth speaketh'?"

Further, Solomon uses a good deal of figurative speech about sowing and reaping (Proverbs 11:18,24; 22:8; Ecclesiastes 11:6), all of which may be placed alongside of the Parable of the Sower, and also that which Paul wrote about the same theme (II Corinthians 9:6; Galatians 6:7).

*The Parable of the Rich Man* (Luke 16:19-31) is an expansion of the proverb, "Riches profit not in the day of wrath. . . . He that trusteth in his riches shall fall" (Proverbs 11:4,28).

Phrases like, "The righteous shall flourish as a branch" and "The root of the righteous yieldeth fruit" (Proverbs 11:28; 12:12), take on fresh meaning when compared with John 15. Then "He that followeth after vain persons shall have poverty enough" (Proverbs 28:19), sums up the experience of the Prodigal Son. As for Proverbs 13:7, the same describes Him who sold all that He had that He might purchase the field and the pearl. This is the only time the word *parable* is found in Proverbs, although in a broad sense the word is sometimes used of a proverb. Here Solomon says, "The legs hang down from a lame man, and so is a parable in the mouth of fools," implying that the spiritually blind can make no more use of a parable for guidance, than can a lame man use his crippled legs. Is this not what Jesus had in mind when He said to His disciples, "Unto you it is given to know the mysteries of the kingdom of God: but to others in parables; that seeing they might not see, and hearing they might not understand" (Luke 8:10)?

There is also *The Parable of the Poor Wise Man,* which the Revised Version makes more plain (Ecclesiastes 4:13-16). While the exact historical association of this brief parable may be difficult to determine, it is easily seen that in the "old and foolish king" Solomon gave us a self-portrait. In the application of the parable, Ada Habershon says that "the poor wise youth is evidently the Lord Himself . . . 'Out of prison he cometh to reign,' or 'came forth to be king.' Surely this looks forward to a greater than Solomon. 'Yea, even in His kingdom He was born poor.' Solomon considers the kingdom of the second, that is 'to stand up in his stead.' He contemplates the number of his subjects, 'There was no end of all the people.' Is this a prophecy of our Lord's rejection, a hint of the long centuries after His incarnation, when men shall not have learnt to rejoice in Him?" Solomon's Psalm (Psalm 72) tells of that glad day when all nations shall call the Lord *blessed.*

# The Parable of Eating and Drinking

(Ecclesiastes 5:18-20)

In this brief parable, Solomon the Preacher returns to the conclusion at which he had arrived (See 2:24; 3:12, 22). The sum of the parable seems to be that "in the enjoyment of God's gifts Solomon does not think much of the sorrows or brevity of life." Is there not a double significance in this striking parable about eating and drinking? What Solomon wrote about applies to spiritual food as well as to natural food. A good, healthy, natural or spiritual appetite is a

gift of God, and something for which to be grateful: Whether for body or soul, a good appetite denotes health and promotes health. How can we have physical desire for food, or spiritual vigor for the Word of God, if our appetite is poor?

Continuing his parable, Solomon goes on to show that loss of appetite is an evil disease (Ecclesiastes 6:1-2). The inability to eat food, even when there is plenty at our disposal, can result in serious physical effects. Does not this fact have its counterpart in the spiritual life? Through lack of appetite for God and His Word, many professed Christians fail to "grow in grace and in the knowledge of the Lord." And it is not hard to detect their lean, starved condition. Linked to this parable is another miniature to be found in "the race is not to the swift . . . neither yet bread to the wise" (Ecclesiastes 9:11). Mere fleshly wisdom can never find food in the Word. All truth is revelation.

# The Parable of the Little City

(Ecclesiastes 9:13-18)

Futile attempts have been made to find a historic reference in this delightful parable, but as Ellicott remarks, "What is here told is so like the story of the deliverance of Abel-beth-Maachah by a wise woman, whose name, nevertheless, has not been preserved (II Samuel 20), that we cannot even be sure that the writer had any other real history in his mind." That it is the most beautiful of all Solomon's parables, is taken for granted by students of figurative speech.

Every word of this parable is full of significance. "There was a little city, and a few men within it; and there came a great king against it, besieged it, and built great bulwarks against it: now there was found in it a poor wise man, and he by his wisdom delivered the city; yet no man remembered that same poor man." The application of the parable is obvious, as Habershon indicates. The world is attacked by Satan, but delivered by the Lord Jesus Christ. The contrast between the figures and forces is marked. A "poor wise man" — "a great king." Then we have "a little city" and "great bulwarks." It would seem that such a small city with so few men to garrison it, had no hope of survival with a strong king determined to capture the city. Yet the mighty monarch was defeated by an insignificant poor man who evidently was stronger than the king, proving, as Solomon says that, "Wisdom is better than strength."

How suggestive the whole narrative is of Christ, and of the great deliverance He wrought for souls beseiged by sin! The description of the treatment meted out to the poor wise men is prophetic. We read that his "wisdom was despised, and his words were not heard." Is this not a forecast of Him who came as the One, despised and unesteemed (Isaiah 53:3)? As for the city's ingratitude in failing to remember this same poor man, does not the same prefigure the base ingratitude of those who never pause to think of all Jesus endured on their behalf? Rich, for their sakes, He became poor; and this poor Man who was born in a stable, and who, when He died, had nothing to leave, by His infinite wisdom and grace displayed by His death and resurrection overcame the monarch of hell and provided, thereby, a blood-bought emancipation for all sin-imprisoned souls.

This One made a request of His own before He left "the little city" which His presence had sanctified. Ordaining the Feast of Remembrance He said, "This do in remembrance of Me." And whenever we take the bread and the wine in our hands, with loving grateful hearts we remember the Poor Man, who through His poverty has made us so rich. Hallelujah, what a Saviour!

# The Parable of the Beloved and His Lover
(Song of Solomon)

Before we leave the appealing, allegorical style of Solomon, space must be given to his "Song of Songs" as his last book is called. Psalm 45 is most naturally compared with *The Song of Solomon*, seeing both have marriage for their theme. This Psalm is called "A Song of Loves." This Marriage Song foreshadows the Marriage of the Lamb John describes (Revelation 19:2,9). There have been those who have questioned the right of this piece of secular literature being bound up with the sacred, seeing there is not a single line of religious or spiritual sentiment. In Solomon's *Song* there is no divine name and no mention of any sacred rite or ordinance whatever. Yet, as Bunsen in his study on *The Song of Solomon* expressed it, "There would be something wanting in the Bible, if there was not found there an expression of the deepest and the strongest of all human feelings." *The Song of Solomon* is a valuable contribution to the Bible in that it teaches that the passion of love is ennobling according as it partakes of the moral sentiment. Then the beautiful idyll expressing as it does, the union and communion existing between the lovers in the book, is parabolic of the precious bond existing between the heavenly Beloved and His Bride. "I am my Beloved's and my Beloved's mine."

Solomon's prophetic poem ends with two short verses that compress all that has been over and over again related under different metaphors, namely, the wooing and the wedding of two happy hearts. "Make haste, my beloved." Is this not the plea of our hearts as we think of our absent Lover? But we have the hope that before long He will come over the mountains of spices to claim His Bride.

# THE PARABLES OF ISAIAH

## The Parable of the Master's Crib

### (Isaiah 1:2-9)

The prophetical writings, as we shall discover, are renowned for their graphic, figurative speech. Those great prophets were patriots, and as preachers of righteousness and judgment knew how to use natural forces to illustrate their messages. They turned most frequently to wind and sea, to thunderstorms and earthquakes, the symbols most fit for their stirring themes. Gentler scenes of the land of Israel are also reflected in their writings. God's bounty is likened unto "a vineyard in a very fruitful hill" (Isaiah 5:1). Practical Micah speaks of "showers upon the grass" (5:7). Jeremiah, acquainted with the habits of the birds in his homeland, uses bird-illustrations with great effect (8:7; 17:11). References to, and application of, hills, cedars, pasture lands, flocks, cloud, fire are too numerous to collate.

The highly parabolic and prophetic nature of *The Prophets,* along with their distinctive spiritual values, causes them to rank with the world's best literature. Out of the writings of these voices of God one could construct a panorama of Canaan, the much coveted land. "To the Hebrews, the blood of their sires and the associations of a historic past had sanctified the soil of Canaan. . . . Canaan was doubly dear and doubly sacred to Israel because it was a gift of their God, and a sign and token of His favour. Their land and their faith were one and unseparable." This is one reason why we find the land so vividly portrayed. Robert Browning wrote of the land under whose blue skies his happiest years were spent:

"Open my heart and you will see
Graved inside of it—*Italy."*

We have only to read what the prophets had to say of their plentiful land to know that with no less fervor they could say that in their hearts was graven — *Canaan.*

Among the prophets, Isaiah is conspicuous for his use of illustrious language. Ellicott says of this great poet-prophet of Israel that, "the Proverbs of Solomon then, as always, prominent in Jewish education, furnished him with an ethical and philosophical vocabulary (11:1,3; 33:5-6), and with the method of parabolic teaching (28:23-29), and taught him to lay the foundations of morality in the fear of the Lord." Isaiah displayed a remarkable versatility in his choice of parallelisms, pictures and parables to illustrate and enforce his message. That he had a great flair for the use of the symbolic can be seen even in the giving of names to his children. A writer of genius with the passing years, the prophet enlarged his vocabulary, varied his phraseology and style according to the occasion, or the intensity of his emotion. Before us is the first of Isaiah's forceful figures of speech in which the prophet uses the parable value of contrast between the behavior of Israel toward God and the common sentiment of family relationship — even the grateful instincts of the beasts of burden.

Isaiah opens his great indictment of Israel for their ingratitude and iniquity by calling upon the universe to listen to it. "Hear, O heavens, and give ear, O earth" (1:2). He then likens God's children to those who grew up under a loving father's care, of whom filial love and respect were expected, but who rebelled against their father's control. Appealing, figurative language is then used to emphasize the utter disobedience and degradation of a divinely blessed people. Beasts have instincts and know and obey their masters, but Israel would not acknowledge the laws of Jehovah. If man's ingratitude to man produces widespread sorrow, man's ingratitude to God causes deep grief in the divine heart.

47

In graphic colors, Isaiah paints the several stages of the growth of evil in the nation of which he was part. The people first of all forsook the Lord, then spurned Him, and then openly apostatised. How opposite to the divine nature the people had become! *The Holy One of Israel* is the Divine name which Isaiah delighted in using (it occurs some 30 times in his prophecy) because it was a name gathering up in itself all the ideas of consecration, purity and holiness. Israel was meant to be "a holy Nation," reflecting the holiness of "The Holy One," but she sank in corruption. The prophet then goes on to depict how sin, as the deadly epidemic, spreads and results in a dreadful disastrous disease. "From the sole of the foot even unto the head there is no soundness in it." The description of rottenness (Isaiah 1:5-6) is "one of the natural parables of ethics, and reminds us of Plato's description of the souls of tyrants as being full of ulcerous sores."

From this point on, Isaiah piles similitude upon similitude. It would form a profitable separate study to gather out all the metaphors, similitudes and parabolic sayings the prophet employs. While prophecy is conspicuous in his dramatic book, the prophecies, as well as his visions, carry a parabolic aspect. For instance, sins are described as being *scarlet,* but yet those who sin can be made as *white as snow* (1:18). Two images describe the degenerating of the rulers to whose neglect the disorder of which Isaiah speaks was due. "Thy *silver* is become *dross,* thy *wine* mixed with *water"* (Isaiah 1:22). This symbolic language is resumed later on, "I will purge away thy dross, and take away all thy tin" (Isaiah 1:25). God, the great Refiner, can purify debased metal (Malachi 3:2,3). Sin *withers* and also *burns* (Isaiah 1:30,31). "In the manifested glory of Jehovah men were to find, as a traveller finds in his tent, a protection against all forms of danger, against the scorching heat of noon, and against the pelting storm" (4:5-6).

A study of Isaiah's versatility of expression leads us to agree with Driver in his masterly volume on *Isaiah* that his "poetical genius is superb." The prophet's unique style marked the climax of Hebrew literary art. Jerome likens this Old Testament bard and orator to Demosthenes. For brilliancy of imagery, Isaiah had no superior, not even a rival. "Every word from him stirs and strikes the mark. Beauty and strength are characteristic of his entire book. He is a perfect artist in words." For the reader's fuller study we group together some of the features which Dr. George N. Robinson deals with in his most helpful handbook on *The Book of Isaiah.*

1. No other Old Testament writer uses so many beautiful picturesque illustrations (5:1-7; 12:3; 28:23-29; 32:2).

2. Epigrams and metaphors, particularly of flood, storm and sound. (1:13; 5:18-22; 8:8; 10:22; 28:17, 20; 30:28,30).

3. Interrogation and dialogue (10:8; 6:8).

4. Antithesis and alliteration (1:18; 3:24; 17:10,12).

5. Hyperbole and Parable (2:7; 5:17; 28:23-29).

6. Paranomesia, or play on words (5:7; 7:9).

7. He is also famous for his vocabulary and richness of synonyms. Ezekiel uses 1525 words; Jeremiah 1653; the Psalmist, 2170; Isaiah *2186.*

8. He frequently elaborates his messages in rhythmic or poetic style 12:1-6; 25:1-5; 26:1-12; 38:10-20; 42:1-4; 49:1-9; 50:4-9; 52:13-53; 12:60-62; 65:5-24.

9. In several instances Isaiah slips into elegiac rhythm: for example, in 37:22-29, there is a taunting poem on Sennacherib, and in 14:4-21, another on the King of Babylon.

Without doubt, the book of this major prophet stands out as a masterpiece of Hebrew literature.

# The Parable of the Vineyard

(Isaiah 5:1-7)

One or two necessary introductory thoughts emerge for our consideration as we approach this beautiful parable of the Vineyard which stands closely related both to what precedes and to that which follows. Actually, Isaiah gives us two parables in one — the first of tender care without response and the second of inexorable judgment with appeal or appeasement. Everything possible had been done to assist the fertility of the vineyard, to ensure the development of its latent possibilities. But such care bestowed upon the vineyard was in vain. Israel, the Vine, had rejected the Vine-dresser's attention and consequently became a worthless tangle — a wild weed-ridden plant. The first fact is that —

*Isaiah Was Pre-eminently a Prophet.* From the moment of his divine call and commission, he regarded prophecy as his life's work, and with noteworthy alacrity, he responded to what he knew from the outset would be a task of fruitless warning and judgment (6:9-13). The theme about which all his prophecies revolve is "Judah and Jerusalem" (1:1). This "universal prophet of Israel" frequently interspersed his prophecies with history as occasion required (Isaiah 7:20,36-39). "No prophet of the Old Testament," says Robinson, "combined more perfectly than Isaiah earthly vision and sagacity, courage and conviction, versatility of gifts with singleness of purpose on the one hand, a love of righteousness and a keen appreciation of Jehovah's majesty and holiness, on the other." This was why he was able to cast his prophetic teaching in parabolic form. Parables were used to foretell events of history yet to come to pass. As the time of the fulfilment of prophecy draws nigh, the meaning of what was obscure grows plainer, the outline fills up, until the complete development of that which was foretold enables us to understand clearly all that was wrapped in the garment of the parable. Another fact that emerges in our study of parabolic language is that —

*Parables Go in Pairs.* Isaiah's parable of the vineyard closely resembles our Lord's parable of the husbandman (Matthew 21:33). Remarkably alike in some details, both parables contain a prophecy of the fate of the Jewish nation, which is still in process of fulfilment. As a diligent student of the Old Testament, and with a mind saturated with its imagery, our Lord might have had Isaiah's vineyard parable before Him as He uttered His own parable on a similar theme. Many writers have dealt upon this dual aspect of the parables, particularly Habershon, whose section in the *Appendix* of her volume deals with the comparison and contrast of double parables, especially those of the New Testament. A further feature, to which we have already drawn attention, must be stressed, namely —

## Parables Usually Have One Main Lesson to Teach

Here in Isaiah's Parable of the Vineyard, while many details are given to describe the adequate care the owner of the vineyard bestowed upon it, not every detail has separate significance. Each detail should not be forced to teach a distinct lesson. As Lang puts it, "Parables are like pictures, in that they require details to make up the general picture but without each detail having of necessity a special and separate lesson." The sole purpose of a vineyard is to produce fruit. This Israel had failed to do.

When Jehovah looked for His vineyard to bring forth grapes, it brought forth wild grapes; and when He looked for justice, behold bloodshed, and for righteousness, behold a cry of wrong. With a play on words (5:7), Isaiah goes on to give us a few specimens of "wild grapes" or sins of the nation, as Robinson indicates:

1. Insatiable greed; but their crop will only be a tenth of the seed sown (5:8-10).
2. Dissipation and disregard of the Word and work of Jehovah; but carnival and carousing will end in captivity (5:11-17).
3. Daring defiance of Jehovah, and wilful contempt of the prophet's denunciations, boldly displayed by their challenging "the day of Jehovah" to come (5:18,19).
4. Hypocrisy and dissimulation, confusion or moral distinctions (5:20).
5. Political self-conceit, which scorns to submit to God's correction (5:21).
6. Misdirected power, heroic at wine-drinking, but cowering before a bride in avenging wrong (5:22-23).

Punishment for such transgression was to be the withdrawal of divine protection and provision. National vitality was to be sapped, and thieves were to rob the people and wild beasts devour them as Assyria and Babylon did in Israel. From such deserved divine judgment there would be no escape (Isaiah 5:24-30). The parable, then, was a prophecy of the coming chastisement of the Jewish people by the Assyrians and Nebuchadnezzar, the details of which follow in chapters seven and eight. The full meaning of the parable, however, could not be apprehended until the events foretold had become facts of history.

As to the significance of the figure of a vineyard, with each family being a plant, and each individual a branch thereof, we note —

*The Position.* Care was displayed in the selection of the place in which the vineyard was found. It was on a "fruitful hill," which is illustrative of the abundant natural advantages of Canaan, the land Israel came to possess.

*The Provision.* Provision for protection is seen in the "fences," a figure of speech, describing the natural position of Canaan, and of the character of the country which made invasion from without most difficult.

*The Preservation.* When God is said to "gather out the stones thereof," the preservation of His people from subjugation is meant. He expelled the idolatrous nations of Canaan lest they should turn away Israel from following him.

*The Privilege.* God spoke of the vineyard as His "choicest vine," an expression referring to Abraham, to whom God made over the land of Canaan by solemn covenant, so that he was the original vine, from whom sprang the house of Israel, the Vineyard of the Lord. The expression also describes God's estimation of Israel when first established in Israel.

*The Punishment.* As the nature of sin is degeneration, the good vine became a wild vine and distasteful to the owner, and must be discarded. The formal, lifeless, hypocritical profession of Israel became offensive to God. Unfruitfulness was the nation's transgression, and barrenness became its punishment. God took away the hedges from His Vineyard, meaning that He withdrew the special privileges from His people and allowed them to sink to the level of surrounding nations. The nation had broken its fences first by its idolatry and neglect of divine laws. Thus they became as "children of the Ethiopians," as depicted by Amos (9:7). But God will not utterly forget His people. A glorious future awaits His *Vineyard,* as Isaiah so graphically prophesies.

This latter thought is brought out clearly by Robinson who says that "Isaiah lived in the future of Israel's theology, whereas Paul correlated the teachings of the past. *Prediction* is the very essence and core of Isaiah's entire message. His verb tenses are *predominantly futures* and *prophetic perfects.* Isaiah was pre-eminently a *prophet of the future.* With unparalleled suddenness he repeatedly leaps from despair to hope, from threat to promise, from the actual to the ideal. . . . The book of Isaiah is *the gospel before the Gospel.*"

## The Parable of Comfort
(Isaiah 28:23-29)

This is one of the great chapters of Isaiah's book and introduces us to a series of Six Woes (chapters 28-33). The prophet was certainly one of *Woe*, six of which may be found in chapter 5. In chapter 6, he was a woe for himself: "Woe is me." Here, Isaiah begins by calling upon the people to have ears for a parable he does not interpret apart from the fact that God's judgments are always proportionate to man's offence.

Ellicott says that "the idea that lies at the root of this parable is like that of Matthew 16:2-4, that men fail to apply in discerning the signs of the times the wisdom which they practice or recognise in the common phenomena of nature and the tillage of the soil. As that tillage presents widely varied processes, differing with each kind of grass, so the sowing and the threshing of God's spiritual husbandry presents a like diversity of operations. What that diversity indicates in detail the prophet proceeds to show with what may again be called a Dante-like minuteness." God's judgments were not to be arbitrary. The methods employed by peasants in agriculture are a parable of God's purpose in disciplining His own. "The husbandman does not plow and harrow his field the whole year round; he plows and harrows that he may sow and reap.

So God will not punish forever; a glorious future awaits the redeemed." Isaiah, the Prophet of Hope, assured those who listened to his "Woes" that as the husbandman does not thresh all kinds of grain with equal severity — no more will He discipline His people beyond their deserts. Is this not indeed a comforting truth?

We could fain linger over Isaiah's use of parabolic and metaphoric language. There is, for example, his wonderful fortieth chapter, so full of arrestive similes in which he describes the eternal majesty and glorious power of Jehovah who "holds the Water in His hand, weighs the mountains in scales, counts the nations as a drop of a bucket, sits on the circle of the earth, tells the number of the stars, is never weary, and is able to cause His people to mount up with wings as eagles. We trust we have said sufficient to whet the appetite of the reader for a fuller study of Isaiah's picturesque style. As for the writer, he leaves Isaiah with the feeling expressed by Valeton who describes the prophet in his work on *The Prophecies of Isaiah:* "Never perhaps has there been another prophet like Isaiah, who stood with his head in the clouds and his feet on solid earth, with his heart in the things of Eternity and with mouth and hand in the things of time, with his spirit in the eternal counsel of God and his body in a very definite moment of history."

# THE PARABLES OF JEREMIAH

Like Isaiah, Jeremiah prophesied chiefly to the kingdom of Judah, and his message to the people, couched in appealing symbolic language, was a repeated announcement that God had rejected the nation because of its backsliding and sin. Jeremiah was also commanded to prophesy concerning the Captivity as being the divine will for the

people who were called upon to reject all worldly alliances, especially with Egypt to whom the leaders turned for help against the Assyrians. Such a pertinent ministry made the prophet extremely unpopular, and he was constantly persecuted for his courageous utterances.

It is because of the close similarity existing between Jeremiah and Jesus, that the prophet has a fascination for the saints of God. Both were men of sorrow and acquainted with grief. Each came to his own, and his own received him not; each endured hours of rejection, desolation and forsakenness. Of all Old Testament Prophets, Jeremiah seems to have had the hardest lot of suffering. There was no sorrow like unto his sorrow (Lamentations 1:12; 3:1). He is popularly known as "The Weeping Prophet" and was portrayed by Michaelangelo, as brooding, with downcast eyes, in sorrowful meditation. Jeremiah had the grace and gift of tears. Possessed of an ascetic temperament, he was "devout, sensitive, easily depressed and made self-distrustful, kindling all too easily into a bitter and angry indignation." The pages of his prophecy are stained with his tears.

We know more of Jeremiah's personal history than any of the other prophets. Of him it has been said, that "more than any other of the goodly fellowship of the prophets, his whole life is before us as in an open scroll." Called in tender years to serve the Lord, Jeremiah felt keenly his condition when he said, "I am a child," referring, doubtless, to his age. He was conscious of his youthfulness and weakness in view of the enormity of his great and solemn task. He also declared that he could not speak, meaning that he lacked eloquence, yet speaking was the very ministry to which he had been called. Commenting on Jeremiah's consciousness of deficient speech, Dr. F. B. Meyer says: "The best speakers for God are frequently they who are least gifted with human eloquence; for if that be richly present — the mighty power of moving men — there is an imminent peril of relying on it, and attributing the results of its magnetic spell. God cannot give His glory to another. He may not share His praise with men. He dare not expose His servants to the temptation of sacrificing to their own net or trusting their own ability."

Alas, some are too big for God to use,

since they incline to take all glory to themselves! It is to those like Jeremiah, who are weak and as nothing in their own eyes, that the Lord chooses to perform exploits for Him (Judges 6:11-16; Isaiah 6:5; I Corinthians 1:27,28). Jeremiah's lips were yielded to God, and although he was not as eloquent as Isaiah and seraphic as Ezekiel, yet timid and shrinking as he was, and conscious of his utter helplessness, God laid hold of him and used him as His chosen organ to proclaim the divine message to his corrupt and degenerate age. Naturally diffident in his weakness, Jeremiah was made strong in the Lord (II Corinthians 12:9,10). There were occasions when before the Lord he shrank from the tasks assigned him, yet when he actually faced the people, he was full of courage. God touched the lips of the prophet, that purified and empowered, they were able to deliver those truths put into his mouth to utter.

Being immersed in the law and literature of Israel greatly helped Jeremiah's style in the presentation of the message of God. The Alphabetic Psalms (9, 25, 34, 37, 111, 112, 119, 145) helped to shape the style of the alphabetic structure of the *Lamentations*. Familiarity with the best part of Isaiah's prophecy also contributed to Jeremiah's vividness of imagery. In some places, it would seem as if Jeremiah copies some of Isaiah's parabolic illustrations. A reading of the book of Jeremiah impresses one with this feature, namely, that his style corresponded to his character. He was peculiarly marked by pathos and sympathy with the wretched, as his Lamentations indicate. The whole series of his parables and elegies had but one object, to express sorrow for his country so fallen and miserable because of its sin. Phrase is heaped upon phrase, and repetitions abound, as Jeremiah expresses his affected feelings. The Jews so venerated him that they believed he would rise from the dead and be the forerunner of the Messiah (Matthew 16:14).

# The Parable of the Almond Rod and Seething Pot

(Jeremiah 1:11-19)

Ellicott says of the figurative speech in this chapter, "As before, we have the element of ecstasy and visions, symbols not selected by the prophet, and yet, we may believe, adapted to his previous training, and to the bent and, as it were, genius of his character. The poetry of the symbols is of exquisite beauty."

The double parable before us was for the eye and the ear, and suggests some of our Lord's parables. One writer comments that "in the Institution of the Lord's Supper and in the Master's washing of His disciples' feet, we have parables appealing to the mind through the eye instead of through the ear, and both of them of such a character as to be more deeply impressive than any words setting forth the same truths. When Christ washed the feet of the Apostles He *acted* a parable, and we have many instances in the Old Testament of the Prophets being commanded to *act* parables." In the Supper of Remembrance the *action* is not so prominent; but it may be termed a parable in visions, inasmuch as it foretold to the apostles, and sets forth to us "The Lord's Death" by a symbol (I Corinthians 11:26).

The vision Jeremiah had in this opening chapter of his Prophecy was parabolic, and contains *one thought* in different stages of development. The change of metaphor from *agriculture* to *architecture* will be noted. We read of "rooting up" and "pulling down" and "building," implying restoration on the basis of repentance. The prophet's predictions were primarily denunciatory, thus the destruction of the nations is put first and with a greater variety of terms than their restoration.

*A Rod of an Almond Tree.* In contrast to the previous words of terror, yet in harmony with the message of hope, Jeremiah sees the almond bough, with its bright pink blossoms flowering in January and bearing fruit in March, and its pale green leaves, the token of an early spring, rising out of the dreariness of winter. The name Jeremiah uses for the almond-tree, which is poetical and not common as a name, makes the symbol more expressive. It means, "the wakeful tree," or "the watcher," or the tree "that hastens to awake," because it awakes out of its wintry sleep earlier than other trees. By this parable, God indicated the *early* execution of His purpose. "I will hasten my word to perform it" (Jeremiah 1:12). Jeremiah plays upon the name *almond,* meaning "watcher," for *hasten* is literally "watching." The judgments pronounced upon the Hebrew nation were nearing their fulfilment (Amos 8:2).

*A Seething Pot.* In this parabolic illustration, the prophet sets forth the darker side of his ministry. In a vision, Jeremiah saw a large metal cauldron on a great pile of burning wood, boiling and steaming, with its face turned *from the north,* and so on the point of emptying out its scalding contents toward the south. Here we have the instrumentality of how another divine word was to be performed. The boiling was made possible by reason of the flame under the pot kept brisk by blowing — an oriental symbol of a raging war. Trouble was coming from the north. "The pot in the north rested on one side, its mouth being about to pour forth its contents southwards, namely, on Judea."

The Jews are said to be like a boiling pot, indicating that God permitted them to be cast like flesh in a pot and boiled and boiled until they were reduced to almost nothing. First, God used the gentle chastisement of the rod (Romans 2:4), but this was without result. He resorted to the severer chastisement of boiling (Exodus 20:5; Psalm 7:12; Hebrews 10:31). Chastisement increased in severity with the increase of national sin. What a strong contrast there is between the vernal beauty of the almond bough and the boiling pot, the latter being illustrative of the terrors Israel could expect from the regions north of their country, namely, Assyria and Chaldaea (Micah 3:12).

The chapter ends with Jeremiah being described as a defended city: iron pillar, brazen walls. These images of strength heaped one upon another assured the prophet of the presence and the protection of the One who had commissioned him to witness in His name. The repeated calls to courage were necessary for Jeremiah's constitutional timidity (See I Timothy 4:12; 6:13; II Timothy 2:3).

## The Parable of the Marred Girdle
### (Jeremiah 13:1-11)

Ellicott discounts any parabolic significance of this and other figurative presentations of truth. "There are absolutely no grounds whatever for looking upon the girdle as a vision or a parable, any more than there are for looking on the symbolic use of the 'potter's earthen bottle' (19:1), or the 'bonds and yokes' (27:2), or on Isaiah's walking 'naked and barefoot' (Isaiah 20:2)." But, using the term *parable* in its widest sense, it is clearly evident that what Jeremiah was commanded to do was another *acted* parable of God's dealings with His rejected people. The above figurative acts not only existed in the mind of Jeremiah, as part of an inward vision; they also materialized into an outward performance.

The opening phrase of the parable, "Thus saith the Lord unto *me,*" reveals the divine method of revelation, namely, that of teaching men by man. God placed His treasure in earthen vessels that all the glory may be His. Those whom He chose and chooses to convey His message to men are "men of like passions" (Acts 14:15; II Corinthians 4:7). Further, those who are called to instruct others are sometimes permitted to suffer for the truth they declare. Jeremiah had to buy and actually wear the girdle until it almost stank, and journeying to the Euphrates, hide it in a rock.

The prophet had to exhaust the full meaning of the girdle before discarding it. Later on, the apostles suffered for the name they preached.

*The Linen Girdle.* This particular part of Jeremiah's priestly dress (Exodus 28:40; Leviticus 16:4), was significant in the interpretation of the parabolic act. Being *white,* the color reminded the Israelites of the holy character they were expected to bear, as "a holy nation" (Exodus 19:6; Revelation 19:8). Israel, as the girdle of Jehovah, had been chosen for consecrated purposes. The "getting" or "purchasing" of the girdle was also a reminder to the people that they had been redeemed or purchased by God.

*Put It on Thy Loins.* This further act denoted close intimacy wherewith Jehovah had joined both Israel and Judah to Himself (13:1,2,11). They were intended to be "a people near unto the Lord." The girdle was also an ornamental part of the priests' oriental dress. "For glory and for beauty" (Exodus 18:40). In like manner, Israel had been chosen to glorify the Lord before the nations of the earth (Jeremiah 13:11). Is not our chief end to glorify God? Then as the girdle, bracing up the body of the wearer, increased his strength, so Israel was designed to be a power for God as she witnessed in His name.

*Put It Not in Water.* Priests of old were never allowed to forget their holy calling. Along with clean hearts there had to be clean bodies, thus the frequent Levitical washings both of body and garments. The exceptional prohibition here signified the moral filth of Israel who had become like the literal filth of a garment worn constantly next to the skin without being washed. The longer Jeremiah wore the girdle without washing, the worse it became. The unwashed girdle, then, signified the absence of the "clean water" of repentance (Ezekiel 36:25. See Zechariah 3:3).

*Hide It in a Hole of the Rock.* Because of their corrupt, unrepentant condition, the people were to be confined in rock-like prisons (13:17). Woven to serve a noble end, the rotting, marred girdle was to be placed in a hole of a rock, discarded as being unfit to fulfil its purpose. So Israel, failing in her holy and honorable mission, became captive. As a girdle in a rock she was exposed to the evil influences of surrounding godless nations she could not resist.

*After Many Days . . . the Girdle Was Marred.* The interval may have been seventy days — "adequate symbol of the seventy years' exile which the act of placing the girdle by Euphrates represented (see 13:18-22; Hosea 3:3). The girdle stained, decayed, worthless, was a parable of the state of Judah after the exile, stripped of all its outward greatness, losing the place which it had once occupied among the nations of the earth." *Though the dignity of Judah and Jerusalem has been great, yet will I mar it.* Time was allowed for the girdle to become unfit for use, "good for nothing," symbolizing how the Jews were corrupted by surrounding heathen idolatries, and ceasing to function as witnesses for God, were cast away as a marred, spoiled, useless girdle. How solemn is the lesson of this parable for your heart and mine! "If the salt have lost his savour . . . it is henceforth good for nothing" (Matthew 5:13).

## The Parable of the Wine Bottle

(Jeremiah 13:12-14)

Bottles in the East were usually made of animal skins and held liquids of all kinds. The bottle in this parable, however, was an earthen jar or flagon, the potter's vessel (Lamentations 4:2; Isaiah 30:14), an anticipation of future imagery (see Jeremiah 19:1,10; 25:15). As Jeremiah spake the parable, it was not understood by those who heard it. The significance of the parable is that as wine intoxicates the drinkers, so God's wrath and judgments were to reduce His wayward people to that state of helpless distraction causing them to

rush on to their own ruin. "Drunken, but not with wine" (Isaiah 29:9), impotence and confusion like that of drunkenness would overtake the people (25:15; 49:12; see Isaiah 51:17,22; 63:6).

The prophet was commanded to proclaim to "*all* the inhabitants of this land," his dark saying which half in astonishment and half in mockery they were to reject, "Do we not know this? What need we to hear it from a prophet's lips?" Indiscriminately of rank *all* were to be dashed as a vessel because there had been no mourning or humbling over sin (see Psalm 2:9; Revelation 2:27). The falling kingdom was to crash, and all bonds keeping society together would break. National pride, Judah's besetting sin (Jeremiah 13:9), was ruined, as the marred girdle and the broken jar vividly portray. The humiliation suffered should have resulted in the people giving glory to the Lord their God, but guilt was not confessed. What sorrow was Jeremiah's as he saw the Lord's flock carried away to captivity!

Two expressive figures of speech are used to describe the terrible exile of a disobedient and degraded people.

1. *The Ethiopian and the Leopard.* Habit can become second nature. The persistent sin of Judah was too deeply ingrained to be capable of spontaneous reformation. As the dark-skinned Cushite could not change the color of his skin, or the leopard eradicate its spots, so it was impossible for the degenerate Jews to alter their inveterate habits of sin. So fixed were they in their evil ways, nothing remained but the infliction of the most extreme punishment which came to them when scattered abroad.

2. *The Wind-Blown Stubble.* By *stubble* we are to understand, "the stalks of the corn left in the field by the reaper." Such broken straw was liable to be carried away by the first gale (Isaiah 40:24; 41:2). Wilderness winds have full sweep, not being broken by any obstacle. The solemn application of this simile is that punishment would answer

to the perversity of the people. "As their sin had been perpetrated in the most public places, so God declared that He would expose them to the most open contempt of other nations" (Lamentations 1:8). Perhaps the irretrievable finality of judgment is softened by the question, "Wilt thou be made clean, and if so when?" While Jeremiah appears to deny the possibility of one so long hardened in sin becoming *soon* cleansed, yet there was the lingering hope that the leopard might change its spots. "There is nothing too hard for thee" (Jeremiah 32:17; see Luke 18:27; I John 1:7).

## The Parable of the Potter and the Clay
### (Jeremiah 18:1-10)

Jeremiah was first directed to learn the lesson, as he watched the potter at his wheel, of God's dealing with the nations of the world. The parable was continued when the prophet was sent to the valley of Ben-Hinnom, to warn both king and people of the destruction about to overtake them. As the potter dashed his vessels to pieces, they were to be condemned as worthless (Jeremiah 19). The figure of the Potter had been already used of God's creative work (Isaiah 29:16; 45:9; 64:8). Much of Jeremiah's figurative speech is a reflection of Isaiah's.

What impressed both Isaiah (29:16; 45:9) and Jeremiah (18:4,6), was the absolute dominance of the will of the potter over his clay, and the mystery and marvel of his creative skill. After watching the potter, Jeremiah declared to the Jews that they were, notwithstanding all their boasted strength, as fragile as clay, and as subject to the will of God as was the clay to the potter's will. All their privileges and position were of divine ordering that they might become vessels unto honor. But in the process of formation they resisted the will and power of the heavenly Potter. What must not be lost sight of is the fact that "the whole tenor of this parable, as

well as the known character of God, is *against* the conclusion that He had any pleasure in the degenerate character of Israel, or could possibly have put forth any power which would lead to such a result." The marred vessel was not the potter's fault. Some foreign substance in the clay frustrated his efforts and ruined his work.

The parable before us is one of deeds, not words, for we have no recorded conversation between the prophet and the potter. As Jeremiah stood and watched a work being created on the wheel, through what he *saw,* he heard God *speak.* At once, he discerned the symbolic significance of the potter and the clay although the potter himself saw nothing parabolic about his task. Jeremiah, however, saw the sermon in the marred vessel and so carried his challenge to the nation, frustrating the divine purpose. "Can I not do with you, O House of Israel, as this potter?"

None of the Old Testament parables has a more direct and personal and withal, a more general appeal to us than this of the potter. While its original interpretation concerned Israel in its current state, it has a wider application. Old Testament prophets were first of all messengers to their own times — *forthtellers,* before functioning as *foretellers* or messengers to succeeding generations. The parable of the potter and the clay, therefore, *was* all about God and *Israel.* It *is* all about God and *ourselves.*

God, however, is the God of the second chance, as Jeremiah learned as he watched the potter take the disappointing clay and fashion it again into a pleasing vessel. What a parable this is of God's dealings both with men and nations! (Romans 9:21; II Timothy 2:20). Is He not able to remake characters, lives, and hopes? Is yours a marred life through the resistance of God's moulding hands? Well, as His, you are still in His hands (John 10:28, 29), and He waits to re-make you, even as He will re-fashion Israel into a vessel of great honor when He returns to usher in His reign. Then, as never before, Israel will be His glory. So long as we lie as submissive clay in His hands, we have nothing to fear. Though we are weak and worthless in ourselves, He is able to mould us into vessels of honor meet for His use. How apt are the closing verses of Browning's poem on "Rabbi Ben-Ezra" in *Men and Women*

> But I need Thee, as then,
> Thee God, who wouldest men;
> And since, not even while the whirl was worst,
> Did I — to the wheel of life,
> With shapes and colours rife,
> Bound dizzily—mistake my end, to slake Thy thirst.
> So take and use Thy work!
> Amend what flaws may lurk,
> What strain o' the stuff, what warpings past the aim!
> My times are in Thy hand:
> Perfect the cup as planned!
> Let age approve of youth, and death complete the same.

# The Parable of the Broken Bottle

(Jeremiah 19:1-13)

This further *acted* parable must not be confused with the one just considered even though Jeremiah may have taken the bottle from the same potter's house. This dramatized parable represents the darker side of the previous parable of the potter. The conspicuous difference between these two parables indicates the hopelessness of the nation's condition and position.

In the Parable of the Potter there is the thought of *Construction*. The clay, although marred, was still soft and capable of being re-shaped into a desired form. So he "made it again."

In the Parable of the Bottle, the evident theme is that of *Destruction*. Israel was so confirmed in sin and rebellion that she seemed to be beyond any hope of recovery. Here the clay is baked and hardened. Any re-moulding was impossible, and being unfit for its designed use, there was no other course but to destroy it. What a solemn, striking symbol of Israel's obduracy which resulted in the breaking up of her nationality, polity and religious system!

*The Ancients,* both of the people and the priests, were the Elders and Representatives of the civil and ecclesiastical rulers, and were therefore called to witness the acted parable and prophecy of all that they held most precious (19:10; Isaiah 8:1,2). "God deals with nations in and by their representatives." Afterwards, the Jews could not plead ignorance of a prophecy their *ancients* had received.

It is somewhat significant that the scene of guilt was chosen as the scene of divine denunciation against Israel. The very place where they looked for help from their idols was to be the scene of their own slaughter. The Valley of Hinnom was where the most abominable form of idolatry was practiced. Topheth was the center of sacrifices to Molech (II Kings 23:10) — human sacrifices to which Israel became addicted. Thus, the place of degradation was to witness retribution and destruction, just as later, Jerusalem where Christ was crucified became the place of terrible destruction.

As for the breaking of the bottle in the sight of men, such a parabolic act emphasizes the divine right and power to break men and nations in pieces like a potter's vessel (Psalm 2:9). The familiar imagery expressed God's absolute sovereignty (Jeremiah 18:6; Romans 9:20,21). The tragic phrase, "cannot be made whole again," depicts Israel's doom. God, as the Divine Potter, *breaks* what cannot be restored. Jeremiah foretold the breaking up and scattering of Israel as a privileged *Nation* — a prophecy completely fulfilled by the Romans. The terrible woes in this chapter were the *choice* of Israel, and the penalty for the rejection of God had to be paid.

While a bottle or potter's vessel cannot be restored, a new one may be made of the same material, so there is, happily for Israel, a depth of divine compassion

Jeremiah's parable does not fail to present. God gathered up the fragments from the heap of rubbish and raised up a new Jewish seed — not identical with the destroyed rebels whose doom the prophet pronounced, but the substitution of another generation in their stead. Paul teaches that the scattered fragments are to be united and Israel fashioned into a vessel of great honour (Romans 11).

# The Parable of the Two Baskets of Figs
## (Jeremiah 24:1-10)

Chapters 22 through 24 relate to the same period, namely, the reign of Zedekiah, after the first capture of Jerusalem and the captivity of its chief inhabitants, and form the setting for Jeremiah's symbolic vision (see Amos 7:1,4,7; 8:1; Zechariah 1:8; 2:1). If the baskets of figs were actually seen, then we have an illustration in this parable of the prophet-poet's power of finding parables in all things — "Sermons in stones, and books in running brooks." But because Jeremiah begins this parable with the words: "The Lord shewed me," we conclude that the prophet received a special interposition of God. His bodily eyes saw the potter and his wheel, but it was to his spiritual eyes that the vision of the figs came. In a state of consciousness and responsibility Jeremiah received the divine message for Zedekiah.

### Very Good Figs

One basket carried good, first ripe figs. These "summer fruits," or "hasty fruit before the summer" (Isaiah 28:4; Hosea 9:10; Micah 7:1), were treated as a choice delicacy. In the day of national calamity two distinct groups were found — the good and the bad. The "very good figs" represented the captives who had been taken to the land of the Chaldeans. From them in the future God would restore His own. Daniel, Ezekiel, and the three Hebrew youths, and Jeconiah (Jehoiachin) were among the *good* figs (Jeremiah 12:15). How this parable-prophecy must have encouraged the despairing exiles! It also was designed to reprove the people who had escaped captivity and who prided themselves as being superior to those carried away to Babylon and abused the forebearance of God (52:31-34).

### Very Naughty Figs

*Naughty* is an old English word meaning "worthless," and was frequently used of things and of persons. Plutarch speaks of men "fighting on *naughty* ground," while Shakespeare in *Merchant of Venice* has the line — "So shines a good deed in a *naughty* world." Today, when we speak of a child as being *naughty* we imply something different from that of worthlessness.

But in the basket of worthless figs, so bad that they could not be eaten, we have symbolized the captives of Zedekiah and those rebellious, refractory and obstinate Jews who remained with him. These were those upon whom divine judgment was to fall (Jeremiah 24:8-11). The terms *good* and *bad* are used, not in an absolute, but a comparative sense and as a rejoinder to the punishment of the latter. The former were regarded with favor by God, which is the significance of the divine *acknowledgement,* about which Jeremiah speaks (24:5). God looked upon the exiles in Babylon as one looks on good figs favorably, and over-ruled their captivity "for their good." By their removal to Babylon, God saved them from the calamities which befell the rest of the nation and led them to repentance and the betterment of their condition (II Kings 25:27-30).

The return from the Babylonian captivity and restoration to God is the result of the chastening effect of bondage, and is a type of the full, complete restoration of the Jewish people. Then, at the coming of the Messiah, they will be as a nation born again in a day. Then, having turned to God with their whole heart, all His people will be a basket of very good figs. Lange's *Commentary* offers this application, "The prisoners and broken-hearted are like good figs, well-pleasing to God because —

1. They know the Lord and turn to Him.
2. He is their God and they are His people.

Those who dwell proudly and securely are displeasing to God, and like bad figs because —

1. They live on in foolish blindness.
2. They challenge the judgment of God."

This Parable of the Good and Bad Figs can be profitably compared with our Lord's Parable of the Wheat and the Tares.

Jeremiah was a "good fig," a true prophet, but false prophets, "bad figs," endeavored to influence the captives and those in Jerusalem, and the remainder of Jeremiah's divinely inspired message to Zedekiah denied the authority and inspiration of the false teachers and the accuracy of the God-given vision of the baskets of figs.

## The Parable of the Cup of Fury
### (Jeremiah 25:15-38)

This solemn chapter is taken up with the Prophecy of the Seventy Years Captivity, the destruction of Babylon, and of all nations oppressing the Jews. The reason for Judah's judgment was her persistent sin. In spite of repeated divine calls to repentance, she failed to hearken to God and found herself conquered by Babylon and taken into captivity. Then we have the prophecy of Babylon's judgment after the seventy years' captivity by a confederacy of nations and kings. Looking further ahead, Jeremiah foretold the inescapable judgment to fall upon all nations, when divine punishment would go forth from nation to nation, until a great tempest would be raised from the uttermost parts of the earth, with the severest strokes falling upon the kings and rulers. In this prophecy Zedekiah detects the inevitable doom threatening himself and Jerusalem.

We are not to take "the wine cup" in a literal sense, as if Jeremiah offered an actual goblet of wine to the ambassadors of the nations named and assembled at Jerusalem. Such a "cup" describes what God revealed to the prophet's mind concerning His righteous judgments. The wine cup symbolized stupefying punishment (Jeremiah 13: 12,13; 49:12; 51:7). As we have already indicated, Jeremiah often embodies the parabolic language of Isaiah in his prophecies (Lamentations 4:21 with Isaiah 51:17-22; see Job 21:20; Psalm 75:8; Revelation 16:19; 18:6).

Nations, drinking of the wine cup of fury, would be "moved and be mad," meaning they are to reel as those drunk with wine. Ellicott says that, "the words describe what history has often witnessed, the panic-terror of lesser nations before the onward march of a great conqueror — they are as if stricken with a drunken madness, and their despair or their resistance is equally infatuated. The imagery is one familiar in earlier prophets" (Psalm 60:5; Ezekiel 23:21; Habakkuk 2:16).

The phrase, "If they refuse to take the cup" (Jeremiah 25:28), seems to suggest that no effort to escape destruction will avail. "If I spared not mine own elect on account of sin, much less will I spare you" (Ezekiel 9:6; Obadiah 6; Luke 23:31; I Peter 4:17). The consummation of divine fury upon a godless, guilty world will be experienced in the Great Tribulation, when the vials of God's wrath will be emptied out upon the earth (Revelation 6:16; 14:10,19; 16:19 etc.)

Jeremiah concludes this chapter with a reference to the rulers and kings falling like a "pleasant vessel," or vessel of desire. They were to become broken and useless. Coniah was once idolized by the Jews, and Jeremiah speaking for them, expresses astonishment at one from whom so much had been expected but had been so utterly cast aside (Jeremiah 22:28; Psalm 31:12; Hosea 8:8). What a solemn lesson this holds for your heart and mine!

## The Parable of Bonds and Yokes

(Jeremiah 27, 28)

We group these two chapters together, seeing both of them are taken up with "Bonds and Yokes," or as one expositor expresses the phrase, *Bands and Bars.* Chapter 27 speaks of the futility of resisting Nebuchadnezzar's dominion. Jeremiah having shown by his vision of the baskets of figs the punishment determined against Judah by Babylon, now announces the divine aspect and attitude in this matter. The prophet was commanded to make bonds and yokes, wearing one of each himself, while the rest were sent to the ambassadors of the kings desiring to have the King of Judah confederate with them. Zedekiah and the rest are urged to yield because the captivity was the divine plans for reformation. "Bring your necks under the yoke of the King of Babylon . . . and live" (Jeremiah 27:12,13). But the people rejected God's plan and the advice of Jeremiah and suffered accordingly (Jeremiah 39:6-8).

Chapter 28, as well as 29, contain prophecies akin to those of previous chapters and have to do with the direct relations between Jeremiah, the true prophet, and the false prophets against whom Jeremiah had so solemnly warned Zedekiah. Hananiah falsely prophesied that God would break the Babylonian yoke in two years, and broke yokes to signify the breaking of the captor's yokes. Jeremiah was commanded by God to contradict Hananiah's prophecy and declare that yokes of iron would succeed those of wood, and that Hananiah would die, as he did after the imposition of the more severe bondage.

*Bonds.* It was by means of these thongs that the yoke was made fast to the beast of burden.

*Yokes.* Usually a yoke was a carved piece of wood attached at both ends to the two yokes on the necks of a pair of oxen, so as to connect them. Their being in the plural signifies that Jeremiah was to wear one himself and give the others to the messengers (Jeremiah 27:3; 28:10,12).

How the command came to Jeremiah we are not told. The prophet simply says, "Thus saith the Lord to me." Ellicott suggests that Jeremiah received a vivid symbolic prediction similar to that which Isaiah received when he was called upon to walk "naked and barefoot" (Isaiah 20:2). Parabolically, Jeremiah was to think of himself at once as a captive slave and a beast of burden in order to emphasize the coming grievous subjugation of the people (see Acts 21:11). It is clearly evident, however, that Jeremiah obeyed the divine command quite literally (Jeremiah 28:10).

Hananiah's self-inspired action in taking Jeremiah's yoke from his neck and breaking it was impious audacity and a demonstration that God would not fulfil His solemn word. Because Hananiah, who professed to be a prophet of peace, had broken the symbol of servitude, he declared that same would be the pledge of the destruction of the hateful bondage the yoke represented.

The substitution of "yokes of iron" (see Deuteronomy 28:48) for "yokes of wood," indicate and illustrate the truth that when light affliction is not freely accepted, heavier affliction is permitted (Jeremiah 28:13,14). False prophets urged the Jews to rebel and throw off the comparatively easy yoke of Babylon. In doing so, they only brought upon themselves the more severe yoke imposed by Nebuchadnezzar. "It is better to take up a light cross in our way, than to pull a heavier one on our heads. We may escape destroying providences by submitting to humbling providences. Spiritually, we contrast the easy yoke of Christ with the yoke of bondage of the law" (Matthew 11:28-31; Acts 15:10; Galatians 5:1). Accepting God's righteous judgment on our sin, affliction becomes beneficial and salutary. More extreme judgment overtakes us if, after condemnation, we continue in sin (I Corinthians 11:31). Had the Jews submitted to their deserved captivity it would have cured them of their idolatry. Resisting their bondage *killed* them.

> Count each affliction, whether light or grave,
> God's messenger sent down to thee, do thou
> With courtesy receive Him, rise and bow,
> And ere His shadow pass thy threshold, crave
> Permission first His heavenly feet to lave,
> Then lay before Him all thou hast, allow
> No cloud of passion to usurp thy brow,
> Nor mar thy hospitality.
> The love-tale
> Infected Zion's daughters with like heat;
> Whose wanton passions in the sacred porch
> Ezekiel saw.

## The Parable of the Hidden Stones

(Jeremiah 43:8-13)

Jeremiah's courage in the face of the rejection of his divinely inspired messages is magnificent. Evidently he knew that in spite of warnings, his people would go down into Egypt and die there by the sword, famine and pestilence. The accuracy of his message was immediately manifest, and all passed over into Egypt, Jeremiah included, where he continued his ministry of denunciation and warning. Had he not declared the utter folly of trying to escape from the decreed judgment of God?

We have another of those impressive *action-parables*. Jeremiah was instructed of God to take great stones and hide them in the clay in the brick-kiln at the entry of Pharaoh's palace, in the sight of the men of Judah. How significant this parabolic act was to those whose minds were open to the reception of the divine implication of the act. The prophet's prediction is all the more vivid as we remember that he set the stones in mortar or cement, and then concealed them with a fresh coat of mortar. As we are seeing, these symbolic acts are common to Scripture (Jeremiah 19:10; 27:2; Ezekiel 12:7, etc.). The king was to sit upon the stones Jeremiah hid, "not merely in regal pomp, but in the character of an avenger executing the wrath of Jehovah against the rebellion." The visible symbol of the king seated on the stones signified that the throne of Nebuchadnezzar would be raised on the downfall of Pharaoh's reign.

To the Jews, *stones* were familiar as historic and prophetic symbols. They conveyed to posterity some accomplished fact, and predicted facts to be accomplished. Jacob and Laban erected a heap of stones (Genesis 31). There were the twelve memorial stones Joshua placed at Jordan (Joshua 4:3,6,9,21). The two and a half tribes built a stone altar on the banks of Jordan (Joshua 22). All the time a cairn of stones stood, their message was transmitted from generation to generation. This was the ancient way of preserving archives.

As the stones were taken from the soil of Egypt they could remind Israel of the bondage of their fathers, and of how God had delivered them with His "outstretched arm and mighty hand." The stones buried in a brick-kiln must have brought to mind the bondage and persecution of their ancestors, and of how God made the ashes of the brick-kiln, the instrument of retribution to the Egyptian oppressors (Exodus 9:8). The burial of the stones symbolized the past and present condition of the Jews, buried under the oppressive tyranny of heathen domination. Those stones, with their past, present and prospective significance, were intended to induce the wayward Jews to seek help and protection where alone they could be found, namely, in Him to whom His people were ever as the apple of His eye. Is it not also significant, as we think of those stones, that tradition affirms that Jeremiah was stoned to death by his own countrymen at Tahpanhes?

# THE PARABLES OF EZEKIEL

We know nothing of the personal history of seraphic Ezekiel apart from what can be gathered from the book bearing his name, and from the circumstances of the times in which he lived. He is not mentioned in any other Old Testament book, and his writings are never directly quoted in the New Testament. That much of Ezekiel's imagery is to be found in the book of Revelation is a fact we shall deal with when we come to the Bible's last book.

His name, Ezekiel, meaning, *God will strengthen,* was singularly appropriate to his life and labors. The repeated phrase, "The hand of the Lord was upon me" (Ezekiel 1:3; 8:1; 37:1; 40:1), reveals how conscious Ezekiel was of his divine commission and empowerment. Although a captive, he lived in his own house by the river Chebar and for well over 22 years served God and the people (Ezekiel 1:2; 3:15). An impression of the Divine glory resulted in Ezekiel's call to service (Ezekiel 1:1,3). His oft repeated expression, "a rebellious house," suggests that his message was sometimes contemptuously rejected (Ezekiel 3:7). Called often to rebuke the people, they refused to take his words to heart (Ezekiel 33:30-33). Yet there were those among his fellow-captives who regarded him as a true prophet and who came to his house for counsel (Ezekiel 8:1; 14:1; 20:1). He was a pastor as well as a prophet for he both watched over souls and fearlessly proclaimed God's message.

Ezekiel, carried away captive to Babylon with King Jehoiachin (1:2 with 33:21), in the eighth year of Nebuchadnezzar's reign, was married. When his wife died suddenly about the ninth year of his captivity (24:1, 16,17), he was forbidden to mourn for her. Thus the exiled prophet was left in solitude to bear the great trials of his prophetic life.

His life, especially the first part of it, was one of much trial. He had to contend against great difficulties in the midst of abounding evil, and he died without being able to see the full result of his untiring and faithful labors. Hengstenberg, in his monumental *Christology of the Old Testament,* says of Ezekiel: "He was a spiritual Samson, who, with a strong arm, seized the pillars of the temple of the idols, and dashed it to the ground; an energetic, gigantic nature who was thereby suited effectually to counteract the Babylonish spirit of the times, which loved to manifest itself in violent, gigantic, grotesque forms: One who stood alone, but was yet equal to a hundred scholars of the Prophets."

Being a man of outstanding character, Ezekiel commanded attention. "His moral courage was impressive (3:8); he ever acted as 'a man under authority,' accepting an unpleasant commission and adhering to it in spite of speedy and constant suffering (3:14,18; 33:7). When he sighed, it was at God's bidding" (21:6,7). Distinctly a prophet, he had to do with the *inward* concerns of the divine kingdom. *Penetration* describes the quality of his prophecies for he was able to speak to Israel *through* the exiles, and *through* Israel to men of all nationalities and of all times. Power was likewise his to see through all prevailing conditions the foundations and principles of eternal verities. Throughout his prophecies the note of hope rings clear and jubilant. Says Dr. Campbell Morgan in his *Message of Ezekiel:* "In all probability Jeremiah's prophecies of hope were the inspiration of Ezekiel's, but it may be that the absence of tears and lamentations in the messages of Ezekiel was due to the fact that his vision of God, and His processes, and His ultimate victory was clearer than that of Jeremiah."

It was quaint George Herbert who sang:

> A man that looks on glass,
> On it may stay his eye,
> Or if he pleaseth through it pass,
> And thus to heaven espy.

"Ezekiel saw the glass, but he saw through it. Accurately observing the temporal, he as surely perceived beyond it the eternal. He was sensitively conscious of the material, but supremely conscious of the spiritual."

Ezekiel was also a *priest* — "a priest in prophet's garb." He speaks of himself as a "priest, the son of Bazi" (Ezekiel 1:3), and the consciousness of his Aaronic heritage colored his mission and messages. "Every inch a Churchman," a strong ecclesiastical character pervades and gives tone to his prophecies. Thoughts and principles of the priesthood controlled his conduct (Ezekiel 4:14) and enriched his vigorous ministry and reached fruition in his detailed description of the Temple at the end of his book. "As a priest, when sent into exile, his service was but transferred from the visible temple at Jerusalem to the spiritual temple in Chaldea." Unable to undertake the official priestly work, Ezekiel exercised a vital prophetic and pastoral ministry.

The parabolic and symbolic style of the prophet characterizes his oral and written messages. Designedly, he spoke in parables in order to awaken the attention of the people to the real import of his message. "They say of me, Doth he not speak parables?" (Ezekiel 20:49). Doubtless he was influenced by the garb of Jeremiah's prophecies. Ezekiel is referred to as "the prolongation of the voice of Jeremiah," and the influence of the latter upon the former is evident. While a study of the two prophets reveals an inner harmony of truth existing between them, yet in natural character they were widely opposite. "Jeremiah was plaintive, sensitive to a fault, and tender; Ezekiel was abrupt, unbending, firmly unflinching, with priestly zeal against gainsayers. His dealing with prevalent corruption was as severe as was that of Jeremiah," says Campbell Morgan, "and his messages of judgment were equally stern. He never resorted to tears as did Jeremiah, but his vision of the ultimate deliverance of the people by the triumph of Jehovah was even clearer."

As to Ezekiel's style, repetitions abound, not for ornament, but for force and weight. Where repetitions occur in Scripture, divine emphasis is implied. "I, Jehovah, have spoken"; "They shall know that I am Jehovah." These phrases are used 56 times. "Thus saith the Lord," is a familiar introduction to Ezekiel's prophecies and implies the prophet's call to declare God's will, and to assert His authority. Ezekiel's favorite word for idols is used some 58 times. His book abounds in imagery and at times we have a mixture of the figurative and the literal (31:17). Poetical parallelisms were used to stimulate the dormant minds of the Jews. Ezekiel saw clearly the matters before him and described them in expressive figures (Ezekiel 29:3; 34:1-19; 37:1-14). There is also a genuine lyric force in his dirges (27:26-32; 32:17-32; 34:25-31). Nowhere in the Bible have we such forcible language concerning sin as here in Ezekiel. Fairbairn, in his study, *On Ezekiel,* says of the apparent obscurity of some of his symbols: "The darkness inseparably connected with our prophet's delight in the use of parable and symbol was, when rightly contemplated, by no means at variance with his great design as a prophet. His primary object was impression — to rouse and stimulate, to awaken spiritual thoughts and feelings in the depth of the soul, and bring it back to a living confidence and faith in God. And for this, while great plainness and force of speech were necessary, mysterious symbols and striking parabolical delineations were also fitted to be of service. Accordingly, while Ezekiel often addresses the people in the simplest language of admonition or of promise, he also abounds in the most elaborate visions (1:8; 9; 37; 40-48), and symbolical actions (4; 5; 12); and has also similitudes (15; 33; 35) and parables (17) and prolonged allegories (23); while in his denunciations, as of Egypt (29-32), he sometimes rises to the height of the most bold and effective poetry."

After such an introduction we are now prepared to consider the inspired parabolic instruction of Ezekiel, who always strived after a concrete representation of abstract thoughts. Having a rich fancy, he was yet possessed of deep emotions and ever before his mind was the accomplishment of a definite practical result.

## The Parable of the Living Creatures
### (Ezekiel 1:1-28)

While there is an element of mystery associated with this first parable of Ezekiel, such an involved vision suggests a deep sense of manifestation. Campbell Morgan reminds us that "The key word to the vision is *likeness*. Likeness means that which reveals something else. The root idea of the Hebrew word is comparison. Its suggestion is exactly that of the Greek word which we translate *parable*. I do not say the root significance is the same, but the suggestion is identical. A parable is something placed by the side of, in order to explain. It is a picture intended to interpret something, which apart from it might not be clearly understood. This is the keynote to the vision. It was a likeness, a similitude, a parable, a picture. Jeremiah did not see what no man has seen, but he saw a vision of Jehovah in the form of a likeness."

What Ezekiel saw began on earth and ended in heaven with a Man-occupied throne. The stately and wonderful language the prophet used clothed the supreme and central verity of four living ones constituting "a revelation or manifestation of the infinite mystery of the Being who occupied the throne above the firmament — which vision also constituted the reason of Ezekiel's hope." There are three aspects of this vision of the Highest Intelligence worthy of note before we come to examine it in detail.

1. Because of His infinity, God had to clothe the revelation of Himself in language or in forms within the reach of our finite comprehension. This is why He clothes unseen and eternal realities in the raiment of seen and temporal things. Ezekiel struggled to portray that which necessarily exceeds the power of human language, hence, his repetitions and obscurity of detail. "All similar descriptions of divine manifestations," says Ellicott, "are marked more or less strongly by the same characteristics" (see Exodus 24:9,10; Isaiah 6:1-4; Daniel 7:9,10; Revelation 1:12-20; 4:2-6).

2. Ezekiel's parabolic vision includes all forms of divine manifestation up to his time. Enumerating these we have —

*The Fire,* which appeared to Abraham, to Moses, to Israel at Sinai.

*The Whirlwind,* out of which God spoke to Job, and which rent the mountains before Elijah.

*The Rainbow,* which was the sign of God's covenant with Noah.

*The Cloud of Glory,* such as had often rested on the Tabernacle and the Temple.

*The Theophanic,* or *Human Form* in which the Judge of all the earth appeared to Abraham. Now we have a new symbol —

*The Wheels of Beryl,* "full of eyes" and "so high that they were dreadful."

3. There are four expressions used of the revelation of God granted to Ezekiel, the first three of which describe what was presented from without to assure the prophet of the reality of the revelation. The fourth expression related to Ezekiel's internal fitness to receive the revelation.

*The Heavens Were Opened* (Ezekiel 1:1; see Matthew 3:16; Acts 7:56; 10:11; Revelation 19:11). Opened heavens imply God's favorable approach to man. Reversely, when the heavens are closed man is shut off from divine access and supply.

*The Visions of God* (Ezekiel 1:1; see margin of Genesis 10:9; Psalm

36:6; 80:10; Jonah 3:3; Acts 7:20). What Ezekiel had was no trance, no hallucination, but divine visions, or manifestations of God, which God Himself provided (Ezekiel 8:3; 40:2).

*The Word of Jehovah* (Ezekiel 1:3; 24:24). Only in these two instances does Ezekiel mention his own name, and as he does, it is as the recipient of a divinely imparted communication. *Came expressly* means "came certainly," with the fullest proof of reality. The oft-repeated phrase, "The Word of the Lord," carries with it the force of divine inspiration (I Thessalonians 4:11).

*The Hand of the Lord was upon me.* (Ezekiel 1:3; 3:22; 37:1; see I Kings 18:46; Daniel 8:15; 10:15; Revelation 1:17). The Lord, by His mighty touch, strengthened Ezekiel for the high and arduous ministry of communicating aright the divine revelation received.

We now come to examine the constituent features of the prophet's vision of the glory of the Lord occupying the rest of the chapter.

1. *A Whirlwind came out of the north* (Ezekiel 1:4; see Jeremiah 1:14, 15; 4:6; 6:1). Ezekiel learned from Jeremiah that the whirlwind was emblematic of God's righteous judgments (Jeremiah 22:19; 25:32). Coming out of the *north* has a double significance. The *north* was thought to be the seat of divine power (Isaiah 14:13,14). Then it was from the *north,* that is, from Assyria and Chaldea, that hostile forces invaded Judah.

2. *A Great Cloud.* The phrase in this fourth verse may be read, "A whirlwind out of the north brought on a great cloud." Ezekiel knew that the cloud was the symbol of divine manifestation and how at Sinai, it represented the hiding-place of divine majesty (Exodus 19:9-16). The *cloud* was all the human eye could bear to see.

3. *A Fire Infolding Itself* (Ezekiel 1:4; Exodus 9:24). The Bible elsewhere reminds us that *fire* is expressive of divine holiness. "Our God is consuming fire" (Hebrews 12:29). *Fire*

lays hold on whatever surrounds it, and drawing it to itself, devours it. Terrific thunderstorms are accompanied by large black clouds which are often illuminated by flashes of lightning. Such a natural appearance is in the prophet's phrase, "there was a brightness about it."

4. *Out of the Midst of the Fire . . . the Color of Amber* (Ezekiel 1:4,27; 8:2). The word for *color* is "eye," and *amber,* found only in Ezekiel, is generally recognized as meaning some form of bright metal, either glowing in its molten state or as fire or polished brass (Ezekiel 1:7; Revelation 1:15), burnished and glowing in the light of the "infolding flame." So we have "superadded to the first appearance of the natural phenomenon, a glowing eye or center to the cloud, shining out even from the midst of the fire."

5. *The Four Living Creatures* (Ezekiel 1:5-26). From the center of the fiery cloud there appeared these symbolic but not actually existing creatures. In his God-given vision, Ezekiel saw these creatures having a strange variety of details, but each having a general human form. It may prove helpful if we take the details separately:

*They Were Creatures. Beasts* is a mistranslation. One had "the face of a man," and *man* cannot be termed a "beast." Later on, Ezekiel identified these "creatures" as the *cherubim* (Ezekiel 10:15,20; 41:18-20), a detail we shall consider more fully when we reach this chapter. Generally speaking, the *Cherubim* represent "the immediate presence of the God of Holiness." Having "the figure of a man," then, these living creatures presented the appearance of a human body in all points not otherwise specified. They had "hands," "faces," and their "feet" were *straight,* or standing upright. The anonymous author of *Miracles and Parables of the Old Testament* wrote, over seventy years ago, "There is no necessity for regarding the cherubic forms as symbolical of *any one order* of created beings exclusively; but rather they seem to be designed to *embrace and unite all the orders of holy intelligences, whether angels or men,* and to be significant of *moral and intellectual properties, whatever order of beings may possess them."* In this connection, the repeated word "likeness" is not without significance. What came out of the fiery cloud looked like, but were not actually, the creatures portrayed.

*They Were "Living" Creatures.* Again and again this prominent characteristic is cited (Ezekiel 1:5,13,14,15,19,21; Revelation 4:6, etc.) These were no mere phantasies but alive and vibrant, with life most closely connected with the Source of all life, "the living God," whose throne was above the heads of these *"living* creatures" (Ezekiel 1:26).

*They Had Four Faces.* Each of the four creatures had *four* faces (Ezekiel 1:6). The Cherubim in the Tabernacle and in the Temple appear to have had only a *single* face; those later described by Ezekiel appear with *two* faces (41:18, 19); the four living creatures John describes were each different from the other (Revelation 4:7). But here (Ezekiel 1:6,10), the four faces are combined in each one of the cherubim. Of this central symbolism on the earth Campbell Morgan comments: "Each creature faced in four directions, each face suggesting a differing idea by the differing symbolism of a man, a lion, an ox, an eagle. Moreover, these four were so placed at the four corners of a square that the face of a man looked every way, the face of a lion looked every way, the face of an ox looked every way, and the face of an eagle looked every way. Thus in the unity of the four the same truths were suggested as in the unity of each. Each had four faces, and the whole square had the same fourfold revelation."

*Four* is the number of the earth, so we have the four quarters of *N*orth, *E*ast, *S*outh, *W*est — the first letters spelling NEWS. A *newspaper* brings us information from these four corners of the world. Further, the four faces represent a manifold variety and a remarkable distribution of gifts and properties combined for one design, each face being the symbol of different qualities of mind and character.

*The Face of a Man. Man* is the noblest of the four mentioned and is the ideal model after which they are fashioned (Ezekiel 1:10; 10:14). The Man-Face is the sign of *intelligence* and *wisdom.* Man is the head of the whole animal creation. "The man was the symbol of manifestation .... Manifestation suggested the unveiling of life at its best, and *man* was the symbol man."

*The Face of a Lion.* As the lion is king of wild beasts, we here have the symbol of supremacy. "Supremacy suggested kingship, and the lion was the symbol of the king." The lion is also the established type of *power* and *courage.*

*The Face of an Ox.* The Ox is the recognized head of domestic animals and symbolizes *service, persevering effort, strength* and *patience.* "Service suggested sacrifice, and the ox was the symbol of the servant."

*The Face of an Eagle.* The Eagle is the undisputed Sovereign of the birds, and is "the emblem of what is *ardent,* and *penetrating,* and *elevating, is moral sublimity and devotion."* In another light, "the eagle is the symbol of mystery, and mystery suggests the unfathomable, and the eagle was the symbol of deity."

From the Early Fathers on, Bible expositors have seen in these four faces an inspired presentation of Christ in the Four Gospels. Is He not the One combining all excellencies?

> In Matthew we have His supremacy as *King.*
> In Mark we have His sacrificial service as *Servant.*
> In Luke we have His perfect manifestation as *Man.*
> In John we have His infinite and unfathomable mystery as *God.*

Other details which have parabolic significance are as follows:

*Each One Had Four Wings.* Motion, swiftness in the execution of God's purpose, are suggested by the wings, two of which were joined together (Ezekiel 1:6, 11) implying that all moved in harmony and by a common impulse. The other two wings covered their bodies expressing reverence (See Isaiah 6:2).

*Each One Had Straight Feet.* "Each of their legs was a straight leg," that is without any bend, such as we have at the knee. Being straight they were equally fitted, not only for stability but also for motion in any direction. As to "the sole of their feet" being "like the sole of a calf's foot," this implies that the part of the foot resting on the ground "was not like the human foot, formed to move forward only, but was solid and round like the sole of a calf's foot." Sparkling like the color of burnished brass, is a detail adding to the general brilliancy and magnificence of the vision.

*Each One Had Hands Under Their Wings.* These human-looking hands representing *action* were hid under the wings. *Wings* and *hands!* What an interesting combination! Wings suggest *worship* — hands, *work.* The wings, however, covered the hands, indicating that in the life of a believer the spiritual and the secular are one, and that the spiritual should ever pervade the secular. The daily round and the common task should glorify God, as well as the prayer-chamber.

*Each One Went Straight Forward.* They turned not, like Asahel, when they went. Having "four faces," the creatures looked in all directions, and having round feet made it equally easy for them to move in any way. Whichever way they wished to go, they could still go "straight forward." They never deviated from the divinely-prescribed course. What a lesson for our wayward hearts to ponder!

*Each One Had the Appearance of Fire . . . Lamp.* The prophet was not guilty of *tautology* in the use of "likeness" and "appearance." The former expresses the general form — the latter,

the particular aspect. *Coals of fire* (torches or lightnings) can denote the intensely pure and burning purities of God consuming everything alien to His holy will. Lightning out of the fire going up and down and the living creatures running and returning, indicating splendor and speed, express many precious truths. There is the marvelous vigor of God's Spirit in all His movements, never resting, never wearied. The bright fire is symbolic of divine holiness and glory. Lightning out of the fire can suggest the solemn thought that as God's righteousness was to cause the bolt of His wrath to fall on Jerusalem, so will it ultimately overtake a guilty earth.

*Each One Had Four Wheels.* Wheels of vast proportions are now added to the Cherubim implying that gigantic and terrible energy was to characterize the manifestations of the God of Israel. Resistless might was now to appear in His dealings, all forming a perfectly harmonious action controlled by one supreme will. Several truths can be gathered from the additional and peculiar symbolism before us.

First, these wheels of great height were upon the earth (Ezekiel 1:15), then connected with the throne above (Ezekiel 1:26). The wheels also had the lustre of gold, in keeping with the frequent mention of fire and brilliant light in the vision. Then there was a wheel in a wheel. When we use the phrase, "There are wheels within wheels," we describe a situation having an element of mystery, as well as involvement. Such a wheel as Ezekiel describes would be impossible of mechanical construction and is used only in a parabolic sense. One wheel was at right angles with the other, and their motion was inexplicable — "they went upon their four sides," that is, in four directions.

The rings, *felloes* or *circumferences,* of the wheels were "full of eyes" (see Revelation 4:8, "full of eyes within"). Multiplicity of eyes (Ezekiel 1:18; 10:12) symbolizes God's perfect knowledge of all His works and the absolute wisdom of all His doings (II Chronicles 16:9). Jamieson has this interesting comment on this detail: "We have here symbolized *the plentitude of intelligent life,* the eye being the window through which 'the spirit of the living creatures' in the wheels (1:20) looks forth (Zechariah 4:10). As the wheels signify the providence of God, so the eyes imply that He sees all the circumstances of each case, and does nothing by blind impulse."

Summarizing the message of the mystery and movements of the wheels which are made round to go around, we know that Ezekiel saw the Lord in the midst of the strange revolving wheels of procedure, and the resistless energy of which he spoke as the Spirit. Since they are constructed to move, *motion* is the normal condition of wheels — *rest* is the exception. As we think of God's laws of providence and of nature, we realize that constant motion is their order. In the history of nations and of individuals, one event constantly succeeds another. "In the order and general movements of the universe there is *constant revolution, ceaseless progression,* perfect regularity and undeviating harmony amidst all that may seem involved and complicated. As His own Interpreter, God ultimately makes all things plain." The impressive lesson of the machinery of the wheels, then, is the representation of the system of physical and material agencies and of the entire course of the physical world united with the intellectual and moral agencies symbolized in the living creatures, all under the control of the Throne above, and existing for the glory of its Divine Occupant.

Finally, we have the three specific aspects of divine glory as seen by Ezekiel in his vision, namely: the Voice, the Throne, the Rainbow.

*The Voice.* As "noise" may be translated voices, "the voice of the wing"; "the voice of great waters"; "the voice of speech"; "a voice from the firmament" convey something of the idea of the awesomeness of "the voice of the Almighty." As His voice was heard, the living creatures, overwhelmed by its majestic tones, became reverently silent. "The mighty sounds of their goings were hushed, and their wings fell motionless, all in the attitude of reverential attention."

*The Throne.* The Godhead now appears in the likeness of enthroned humanity. "The appearance of a man above upon it" (Exodus 24:10). The glowing descriptions of the throne with its "appearance of a sapphire stone"; "colour of amber"; "the appearance of fire" combine to extol the glory, holiness, power and sovereignty of the One occupying the Throne. "If in the prophecies of Isaiah we saw the Throne with its fundamental principles," says Campbell Morgan, "and in those of Jeremiah we discovered the activities of the One who occupies the Throne; in those of Ezekiel we have the unveiling of the nature of God."

Do we not have here a hint or prelude of the Incarnation of God the Son, who as the Son of God became the Son of Man that He might make of the sons of men, the sons of God? Christ is not only the Representative of "the fulness of the Godhead" (Colossians 2:9); He is likewise the embodied Representative of humanity. Is it not good news to know that the Throne is filled by One who appears as a "man" and as a "Saviour," and who, when He returns to earth, will function as the "Judge" (Revelation 19:11-16)? The deep secret of Ezekiel's hope was the consciousness of the Throne and of the principles of government applied by Him who, as the God-Man, acts on behalf of both God and Man.

*The Rainbow.* "The bow . . . in . . . rain" recalls the rainbow God produced as the symbol of the sure covenant of His mercy to His children which He could ever remember amidst judgments on the wicked (Revelations 4:3; 10:1). Added to the attributes of His terrible majesty described by Ezekiel were those of mercy and loving-kindness. Brightness as well as terror surround the Throne. "The bow in the cloud of rain" is not merely a reference to the ordinary natural phenomenon of a rainbow, but distinctly connects Ezekiel's vision with the gracious promise of Genesis 9:13.

Finding himself bathed in the glory of the Lord, what else could the prophet do but fall upon his face and be silent as the Voice spake? The immediate, glorious manifestation of the Divine always leaves man overpowered and hushed (Ezekiel 3:23-25; Isaiah 6:5; Daniel 8:17; Luke 5:8; 8:37; Acts 9:4; Revelation 1:17). Here, also, is our spiritual attitude as we enter on any active work for God. In Ezekiel's first vision, God gathered in this initial revelation of Himself the substance of all that was to occupy the prophetic agency of the prophet, as was finally done in the glorious vision John had in the Revelation of Jesus Christ.

As to the general significance of Ezekiel's parabolic vision, Ellicott draws attention to the fact that it was seen four times by Ezekiel in various connections with his life-work.

1. When called to exercise the prophetic office (1:1-28).

2. When sent to proclaim judgments upon a sinful people and to foretell the destruction of Jerusalem and the Temple (3:23, etc.).

3. When, a year and a half later, he sees the same vision, while he is made to understand the evils and abomination wrought in the Temple, and also the future restoration of the Temple (11:23).

4. When he saw the presence of the Lord re-enter and fill His house with His glory (43:3-5).

## The Parable of the Eaten Roll

### (Ezekiel 2; 3)

These two chapters, which should be read as one, are taken up with the call of Ezekiel to his office and with instructions for his work. The designation, "son of man," is applied over ninety times to Ezekiel, only once to Daniel (3:17), but not to any other prophet. Christ was known by the same title seeing He came as the Representative Man. The Spirit entered the prophet, and receiving the strengthening command, "Stand upon thy feet," he was equipped to deliver a message of judgment to God's rebellious people. How Ezekiel needed divine preparation and encouragement to act as spokesman for the Lord to the hard-hearted and perverse nation of Israel, which eleven times over is referred to as a "house of rebellion"!

Ancient books were made up in the form of a roll, and written on within and without, that is, on the face and the back. Usually the parchment was written only on its *inside* when rolled up. But this one was full of God's message of impending woes. It was written also on the back. Figuratively, Ezekiel was commanded to *eat* this roll. There was no *literal* eating, just as there is no literal eating of Christ's flesh and literal drinking of His blood as Romanists erroneously teach. The figurative language before us implies that Ezekiel must receive the judgment-message into his heart and be thoroughly possessed by what was being communicated to him (See Jeremiah 15:16; John 6:53-58; Revelation 10:9-10). He was to digest with his mind, and the unsavory contents of the message was to become, as it were, a part of himself, so as to impart the message more vividly to his hearers.

The double and diverse effect of this appropriation is given by the prophet. What he ate was in his mouth as "honey for sweetness" yet because as "bitterness" (2:3,14), Ezekiel was first to *eat* then to *speak*. How futile it is for a preacher to *speak* without *eating*. Says Jamieson, "God's messenger must first inwardly appropriate God's truth himself, before he speaks it to others." The outward symbolic action coming from the inward, spiritual vision made the prophetic statement more impressive.

"Honey for sweetness." The first impression Ezekiel experienced as the result of his prophetic mission was one of delight. "I delight to do Thy will," True, the message he had to deliver was a painful one, yet by making God's will his will, the prophet rejoiced in such a high privilege of bearing such a message to the people. "The fact that God would be glorified was his greatest pleasure."

"I went in bitterness." Glad that he was called upon to be God's mouthpiece, Ezekiel was sad on account of the impending calamities he was commissioned to announce. "The hand of the Lord was strong upon me," suggests the divine powerful impulse urging the prophet, not to consider his feelings whether glad or sad, but to deliver the God-given prophecy (Ezekiel 3:14; See Jeremiah 15;16; 20:7-18; Revelation 10:10). "The command of the Lord was sweet, its performance bitter." Thus there was the mixture of delight yet of sorrow as Ezekiel realized the task laid upon him. But God's Word was as a burning fire within and he could not refrain, which is surely an experience through which every faithful messenger in God's name is obliged, more or less fully, to pass.

The chapter ends with Ezekiel becoming dumb-like when the time actually came to deliver his sweet-sour message. Because the people refused to listen to him, his tongue seemed to cleave to the roof of his mouth. Yet he was promised all necessary speech at the right moment. "I will open thy mouth." As to the result of a God-prompted message, some would hear, others refuse to hear. It was the response the Master experienced, and one every God-sent messenger likewise experiences (Revelation 22:11).

## The Parable of the Decorated Tile
### (Ezekiel 4:1-17)

The whole of this chapter is taken up with symbolic acts related to the severity of the coming siege of Jerusalem. Bricks with painted signs, often two feet long by one foot in breadth, abound in the ruins of Babylon. Soft and plastic clay was made into tiles and cuneiform inscriptions traced upon them. Then, when baked in the sun, the object or lettering sketched upon the tile was permanently preserved. Many examples of Babylonian art in this direction may be seen in almost any national museum. Whether Ezekiel actually drew a picture of Jerusalem depicting the process of the siege, on a soft tile, or describes a symbolic act, is a matter on which authorities disagree. The same is true of all the actions referred to in this parabolic vision of Jerusalem's coming plight.

Urging the prophet to raise fortifications for protection against the siege, God instructed His messenger to take an iron pan, or flat plate, and set it as a wall between himself and the city. Kiel, in his study on *Ezekiel* says that — "The iron pan, erected as a wall, is to represent neither the wall of the city nor the enemy's rampart, for this was already depicted on the brick; but it signifies a firm impregnable wall of partition, which the prophet as the messenger and representative of God raises between himself and the beleagured city." Ezekiel, then, in God's stead, represents "the wall of separation between him and the people as one of iron, and the Chaldean investing army, His instrument of separating them from him, as one impossible to burst through."

Then we have the further parabolic act of Ezekiel lying on his left side for 390 days, then on his right side for 40 days, symbolizing thereby, the bearing of the iniquity of a corresponding number of years, prophesying against Jerusalem during the whole period. "It was a long and tedious process of bearing the iniquity of the house of the Lord in the sense of confessing it, and so revealing the reason for the siege and the judgment." To bear the iniquity of any one (Numbers 14:34) is a Biblical expression denoting the suffering of punishment due to sin. By lying on his left side, the prophet acted out the way the people would endure divine judgment upon their sins. The significance of the *left* side is seen in the fact that it was "the Oriental habit to look to the East when describing the points of the compass, and the northern kingdom was therefore on the left." This is why "the house of Israel" is distinguished from "the house of Judah," which answered to "the right side" (4:6), the more honorable side.

Further symbolic acts were the set face and the uncovered arm. *Set thy face* is a common Scripture term for steadfastness of purpose (Leviticus 17:16; 26:17; II Chronicles 20:3). As a favorite phrase of Ezekiel's (15:7; 20:46, etc.), it implies the steadfastness of purpose to be exercised "towards the siege of Jerusalem." There would be no relenting; divine judgment would overtake the city as decreed.

"Thine arm shall be uncovered." This action would make a vivid impression. The long Oriental garment usually covering the arms would prevent readiness for action (Isaiah 52:10). Then suiting his words to his actions, Ezekiel prophesied against the city. As for the "bands" upon the prophet, preventing him from turning from the left to the right side until the siege was over, Ellicott's comment is illuminating at this point. "This is a fresh feature of the unrelenting character of the judgment foretold: God's power should interpose to keep the prophet to his work. Not only pity, but even human weakness and weariness should be excluded from interfering. The prophet is spoken of as besieging the city, because he is doing so in figure."

Then the hardness of the siege is graphically described. Instead of the simple flour used for delicate cakes (Genesis 18:6), the Jews were to have a coarse mixture of six different kinds of grain, such as the poorest would eat. Grains, from the best to the worst, were to be mixed in one vessel — a violation of the spirit of the Law (Leviticus 19:19; Deuteronomy 22:9) — symbolizing thereby the straitness of the siege and the stern necessity laid upon the sufferers. The food was to be cooked in such a way as to indicate uncleanness. Dietary laws regarding clean and unclean food would not be observed (Hosea 9:3,4). Lack of bread and water to supply their physical needs would afflict the inhabitants of the city (Ezekiel 4:11; 16:17; see Lamentations 1:2; 2:11,12), intensifying thereby, the desolation accompanying the judgment against Jerusalem. Eating bread by weight, and drinking water by measure, speak of the terrible scarcity prevailing during a time of famine. Because of the continued sins of the people, extreme suffering and distress were to be theirs. No wonder they were "astonied one with another," a phrase implying the stupefied look of despairing want.

# The Parable of the Shaved Head and Beard
## (Ezekiel 5:1-17)

The Prophet's abundant use of parabolic acts claims our prayerful and careful attention. No other writer resorted so often to the parabolic method of instruction as Ezekiel. Closely connected with the previous chapter, the present chapter records, with fresh symbolism, the intensification of the denunciation of judgment upon the Jews. Severer judgments than the Egyptian afflictions were to come upon the people for their sins.

The "sharp knife" and "a barber's razor" signify any sharp cutting instrument such as a sword and is here used to symbolize the sword of the foe (Isaiah 7:20). A sword, then, sharpened as a barber's razor, was to be used for cutting off the prophet's hair and beard. As the representative of the Jews, the sword was to come upon his "head," the shaving of which was a sign of severe and humiliating treatment, especially in the case of a priest (II Samuel 10:4,5). *Hair* being the token of consecration, the priests were expressly forbidden by law to shave either the head or the beard (Leviticus 21:5). The shaving of both head and beard was to signify a most desolating judgment.

The shorn hair had to be weighed and divided into three parts. The first part was to be burned in the midst of the city at the expiration of the siege; the second part was to be smitten with the sword round about the city; the third part was to be scattered to the wind. The meaning of the parable is given at length by Ezekiel, a third part of the people was to die by *pestilence* in the midst of the city; a third part would die by the *sword;* a third part would be scattered to the winds. This happened to the remnant. A few hairs had to be gathered and bound in the prophet's skirt, and some of them were to be cast into the fire. The few escaping the severe judgments did not escape a fiery ideal (Jeremiah 41:12; 44:14). In better days, God had assured His people that the hairs of the head were numbered, a proof of divine care and provision. Now cut off from God and separated from His presence, bald heads betokened the withdrawal of divine bounty and protection.

Summarizing the symbolic acts of this chapter and the previous one, *The Biblical Expositor* says that these acts must have attracted a circle of curious spectators to whom Ezekiel explained their significance: "It is not Babylon and its fall that he has portrayed, but the well-deserved and irrevocable judgment upon unholy Jerusalem. Instead of being the center from which salvation might radiate to the nations, it has outdone the heathen in wickedness. Therefore God will no longer spare or have pity. Its punishment will be so severe because it has trodden under foot the greatest gifts of God's favour."

# The Parable of the Image of Jealousy

(Ezekiel 8:1-18)

After the symbolism ending with Ezekiel 5:4, the prophet, in chapters 6

and 7 utters, for the first time, his prophecies in plain language. His style changes from prose to the more ordinary form of prophetic utterance in parallelisms, which constitutes the distinctive picture of Hebrew poetry. Here in chapter 8, Ezekiel resumes the parabolic method with his fresh series of prophecies. The most striking writer of all the prophets, Ezekiel exhibits a force and energy in his denunciations which can find no parallel. His frequent repetitions present before the view of the reader the very judgments which he predicts.

Because the captives in Babylon complained that God had dealt hardly with them (Ezekiel 8:15), God granted Ezekiel a vision of what was being transacted in the Temple at Jerusalem, in spite of the terrible judgments inflicted upon them. Idolatry was being practised, in all its most hateful and abominable forms, even by priests and elders, men who ought to have exerted their authority to repress idolatry. As the prophet sat in his house, he felt the pressure of the divine hand upon him and saw an appearance as of fire. The Elders sat before the prophet to listen to the cause and process of deserved judgment. Present, at the giving of the prophecy, these leaders were left without excuse. It would seem as if there were four phases in the divine exposure of hidden idolatry.

1. Transported "in a vision by the Spirit of God," to Jerusalem, Ezekiel beheld the glory of God in the court of the Temple, and in the dazzling light of such glory he also saw the darkest recesses of his people's unfaithfulness (Isaiah 6). Wherever he looked, he saw the perversity of the human heart ever guilty of exchanging the glory of the immortal God for images (Romans 1:23). At the entrance of the inner court of the house of God, Ezekiel saw "the image of jealousy" provoking God to a righteous jealousy (Deuteronomy 32:21; Exodus 20:4,5). Ezekiel is told by God that this was the reason He had departed from the sanctuary. God cannot brook a rival

(Ezekiel 8:5,6; Deuteronomy 4:23,24).

2. Then the prophet was bidden to dig a hole in the wall, and coming to a door he discovered, to his horror, the elders of Israel burning incense before creeping things, abominable beasts and idols (8:7-12). They thought they could escape detection, but the Lord penetrates all chambers of darkness. Nothing is hid from Him. Incense to idols is the stench of iniquity and obnoxious to God. Those religious leaders had departed so far from conscious fellowship with God as to imagine that He had forsaken the earth, and that therefore they were not seen. On such a sin Jamieson has this pertinent paragraph, "How awfully it aggravates the national sin, that the seventy, once admitted to the Lord's secret council (Psalm 25:14), should now 'in the dark' enter 'the secret' of the wicked (Genesis 49:6), those judicially bound to suppress idolatry being the ringleaders of it!"

3. The depravity of the women of Israel, weeping for Tammuz, was next seen by the prophet (Ezekiel 8:13,14). Tammuz was the popular Babylonian god of vegetation and fertility. "Part of the ceremony devoted to insuring a return of the growing season consisted in mourning over Tammuz who in the barren time of the year was said to have died. In their folly, the women of Israel served a pagan god instead of a living God, the God of Israel." How apt are Milton's lines on the weeping for Tammuz —

> The love-tale
> Infected Zion's daughters with like heat;
> Whose wanton passions in the sacred porch
> Ezekiel saw.

4. Finally Ezekiel sees twenty-five men with their backs turned toward the Temple, worshiping the Sun (Ezekiel 8:15-18). Israel's idolatry was not merely "an outward deviation in form or the result of popular ignorance. It is a deliberate and complete turning from God as if the entire priesthood with the high priest at their head stood with their backs to the Holy of Holies and gave their full devotion to the heathen sun

god" (I Chronicles 24:5-19; II Chronicles 36:14). In spite of the loud crying of the people, God proceeded with judgment, as chapters 9 through to 11 show. The destroying weapon of divine justice was in the hands of appointed executioners smiting the wicked idolaters of Jerusalem (see Exodus 12:23; II Samuel 24; II Kings 19).

# The Parable of the Man With the Ink-Horn
### (Ezekiel 9; 10)

The same continuous vision of the prophet is before us. Previous chapters deal with the exposure of Israel's sin, now we have its consequent punishment, with the addition of the sealing of the faithful. A remarkable feature in these chapters is the fact of divine discrimination in judgment. In the parable of the enlarged vision given to Ezekiel there are distinguishable features. For instance, we have:

1. *The Man With the Ink-Horn.* Among the six men from the higher gate of the city was one who was not armed with a sword, but with a writer's inkhorn. His dress of "fine linen" marked his office as being distinct from the six officers of vengeance. Worn by the high priest, white linen symbolized purity (Leviticus 16:4). At the girdle of this priest-like person was an "ink-horn," a small case containing pens, ink, and knife, commonly worn by an Oriental scribe. No clue as to the identity of the man with the ink-horn is given. "He is simply a necessity of the vision," says Ellicott, "an angelic messenger, to mark out those whose faithfulness to God amid the surrounding evil exempts them from the common doom" (see Revelation 7:3). Some expositors see in this person a figure of the High Priest in heaven whose peculiarly assigned task is *Salvation* and who bears His ink-horn in order to "mark" His elect, and to write their names in His book of life (Exodus 12:7; Revelation 7:3; 9:4; 13:8-11,17; 20:4).

2. *The Mark Upon the Foreheads* (Ezekiel 9:4). The glory of God having departed from the center of the Temple to the threshold of the house, the six armed men pass through the city to slay its inhabitants, but the man with the ink-horn went first, setting a mark on the foreheads of those who mourned the abominations exposed and denounced. As the six men followed, slaying all the unmarked people, the marked ones who mourned the cause and terrible process of judgment were spared.

Such symbolic marking is common to Scripture (Exodus 12:7,13; 28:36; Revelation 7:3; 9:4; 14:1) and was necessary to the guidance of angelic and human executors of God's commands. In the vision of judgment, so appalling to Ezekiel that he cried out in intercession only to be answered that such judgment was irrevocable, no regard was paid to birth or position. Only the marked, who had kept themselves from national evil and who mourned over it, were graciously spared from slaughter. Being marked upon their foreheads (the most conspicuous part of the person) meant that their claim to safety would be manifested to all (Jeremiah 15:11; 39:11-18; Revelation 13:16; 14:1,9). In times of retribution, God is a respecter of persons. But that it is only in *character* that He is a respecter of persons is evident from the solemn fact that the terrible judgment depicted began at the Sanctuary (9:6). God never spared the angels that sinned, even though they were *angels*.

3. *The Vision of a Throne* (Ezekiel 10:1-22). The man with the ink-horn who had passed through the city setting a mark on the sighing and crying men, is now found obeying the command to pass in between the whirling wheels and gather coals of fire in his hand and scatter them over the city. The Cherubim, already seen by Ezekiel, re-appear as a sign of the return of the glory of the Lord. Here the Cherubim are viewed as being closely associated with the process of judgment which Ezekiel goes on to describe. The man who gathered fire and scattered it over Jerusalem, went into the midst of the wheels, and the visible glory of Jehovah as it departed from the threshold is now mingled with the wheels and the Cherubim. The whole purpose of this vision was to make clear that the Lord, enthroned above the Cherubim, was executing His just judgments through the Babylonians. Israel stood condemned before the Lord who, because He cannot tolerate the spurning of His Mercy, commanded all His power in heaven and earth to punish the base ingratitude of those He had so signally blessed. The vision reveals in true perspective the black guilt of Israel and its dire consequence.

# The Parable of the Cauldron and the Flesh

(Ezekiel 11:1-25)

In some miraculous way, the prophet is lifted by the Spirit and brought to the last gate, the place from which the Divine glory had departed, to witness in the presence of such glory, a new scene of destruction. The prophet saw a conclave of twenty-five men presided over by the princes of the people who had met to devise iniquity which consisted of plotting against the King of Babylon. These men felt they were safe in the city, but Ezekiel, divinely instructed, denounced them for their folly and declared God's vengeance against them.

The figure of the *Cauldron* is used to illustrate the divine fiat that these men would die because of their sin. Even as Ezekiel prophesied, one of the princes perished. Deluded, the leaders felt that they themselves were safe within the city's walls as meat is protected from fire in a cauldron. But the prophet, as the divine spokesman, declared that Jerusalem was a cauldron only in the sense that it was filled with the slain. There was to be no hiding place from the invaders. Dragged from their homes, the leaders would suffer judgment.

Much encouragement is offered the faithful remnant in exile from Jerusalem. Denied the worship of its much-loved Temple, He would be as "a little sanctuary" unto them. God also promised them that He would restore them to their land, and that once they were morally and spiritually cleansed, restored privileges would be theirs.

## The Parable of the Removal
(Ezekiel 12:1-28)

We have now come to a second series of parabolic actions and words of doom which take us to the end of chapter 14. Alas, these further signs did not shatter the unholy pride of those who thought they were unconquerable! In sight of the people, Ezekiel was commanded to act out the part of an exile going forth from his own house and country, preparing "stuff for removing," and carrying it from place to place. What the prophet portrayed was the rebellious house of Israel with the prince at its head leaving all behind but "an exile's baggage, and setting out into the night of exile." The King, Zedekiah, would be taken captive to Babylon but he would not see it. Blinded, he was to die in the unseen land of his captors (Jeremiah 39:4-7; 52:4-11; II Kings 25:1-7).

Ezekiel was charged to give the people another ocular demonstration conveyed by a word-painting of actions, namely that of eating and drinking his bread and water with fear and carefulness and by such a sign to foretell the desolations about to fall on Jerusalem, when its inhabitants would have scanty provisions, common to a time of siege. This chapter closes with two distinct messages from the Lord (21-25; 26-28), both of which were designed to meet the objection that the long-promised prophecies of judgment would not be fulfilled until some far distant future. Two proverbs indicate the failure of prophecy and the postponement of its fulfilment to some distant time. But Ezekiel was charged to announce the imminence of the divine visitation and the fulfilment of every word that had been spoken. Sinners, experiencing the patience, forbearance and long-suffering, hide in a false refuge if they believe that God will not execute His word regarding their ultimate doom, if they linger and die in their sin (see Ecclesiastes 8:11; Amos 6:3; Matthew 24:43; I Thessalonians 5:3; II Peter 3:4). In his next chapter, Ezekiel denounces false prophets and prophetesses who by their uninspired messages had given the people a false sense of security, which the prophet likened to a wall built with untempered mortar, and against which Jehovah would proceed as a stormy wind, in fury sweeping it down with those who built it (Ezekiel 13:10-16). The false prophetesses, not mentioned elsewhere in the Old Testament, come in for special mention and particular judgment (Ezekiel 13:17-23). God's severe dealings with all such false messengers and worshipers will create wonder (Ezekiel 14:7-8).

## The Parable of the Vine Branch
(Ezekiel 15:1-8)

Here we have another evidence of Ezekiel's debt to the previous great prophets, for his Parable of the Vine Branch supplements Isaiah's Parable of the Vineyard (5:1-7). Ezekiel, dwelling upon the natural condition of Israel, declares that as a vine tree she has proved useless and cannot be turned to any good account. In the magnificent parable occupying this chapter, he expresses in stronger terms than ever before used, the sin of Israel (3-34), her rejection (35-52), and her final restoration (53-63). The enormity of the nation's sin is adduced from the fact that Israel had no original claim upon God's favor, nor anything to make her attractive. She is now exposed for what she really is, a repulsive foundling (3-5). Yet in His pity, God saved her and cared for her (6, 7), and when of age, entered into a covenant with and greatly blessed her (8-14). Alas, she proved utterly unfaithful to her covenant, an unfaithful wife, wanton beyond all precedent and therefore worthy of punishment (15-63).

This parable before us, then, teaches us the end of Israel's existence as a Nation. God had created and chosen her with gladness (Psalm 105:45), but in spite of all His care and toil, the Vine failed to produce fruit. Like another tree, this one had *foliage* but no *fruit* (Luke 13:6-9). As a vine is worthless except for its fruit, so Israel was of less worth to the world than the heathen nations surrounding her. In consequence of this apparent worthlessness, Israel must be destroyed as a Nation. The Divine Husbandman had no alternative but to allow the flame of retribution to consume the fruitless Vine (See II Kings 15:29; 23:30,35). As an empty Vine, Israel had brought forth fruit to herself (Hosea 10:1), but living to herself she became universally despised.

Does not this parable teach, in a very strict manner, that when God chooses us as branches of the Vine that He expects us to bring forth fruit to His glory? Is this not the truth embodied in the parabolic sayings and actions of John the Baptist and of our Lord (Matthew 21:33-41; Mark 11:12-14)? Blessed of God with the highest privileges, may we never be guilty of disappointing Him. May grace be ours to be fruitful in all good works!

# The Parable of the Faithless Wife
## (Ezekiel 16:1-63)

In a way, this parable is linked to the previous one in which the prophet proved that Israel, failing to fulfil her purpose as a chosen Nation, was charred and consumed by divine judgments. Having failed to respond to the goodness and grace of God, Ezekiel now employs the parable of a lewd wife to illustrate

the reason of deserved punishment. Israel was fruitless because faithless, and her sin was outrageous. It is not a pleasant picture Ezekiel draws. At great length he describes how black, putrid and offensive is sin to God. Jerusalem is arraigned on account of her abominations and Ezekiel depicts them under the figure of that spiritual adultery and harlotry, Hosea also so graphically and powerfully sets forth.

An approach to the parable before us shows that the material of parables may be real or fictitious, and borrowed from nature or from human life. The vine is nature, the adulteress from human life. Lang remarks that to grasp the meanings of the composite picture Ezekiel gives us is "a valuable education in the study of Parables. . . . To discern the history and prophecy declared in this allegory is to hold a key to the past, present, and future as seen by God, and so to understand the chief parts of the Old Testament as the background and basis of the New Testament."

Ezekiel is not content in this parable to use here and there a metaphorical expression; he occupies the whole of the long chapter in drawing a parallel between an adulteress and the Jewish people, and his series of pictures gives great force to his reproofs. The whole history of Israel is set forth in this way:

1. *The Girl-Child* (1-5). As an infant she was exposed and cast out to die, which is figurative of the precarious situation of the new settlement founded by an Amorite and a Hittite. The origin of Israel was of the land of the Canaanite, with an Amorite as her father and a Hittite as her mother. Because of her close association with her heathen neighbors, she had no natural endowments to entitle her to her position as God's chosen people, and no beauty to commend her or innate strength to exist. She was as an abandoned, forsaken child (16:1-14).

2. *The Passer-By* (6-7). Is there not a tender, moving description here of God finding the cast-out one and nur-

turing her? How God cared for and reared Israel! This picture of God stooping down and lifting her from ignoble extinction is full of beauty. Did He not make Israel the object of His special concern so that she became renowned for her "beauty and splendour" which He had bestowed upon her? God also decreed that Jerusalem should become both His and her center on the earth.

3. *The Husband* (8-14). Reaching maturity, the chosen girl became the wife of her Benefactor, who bestowed on her every possible ornament and luxury. In the character of a Husband, He loaded her with benefits which made her the admiration and the envy of all who beheld her. Because of her glorious state the renown of her "went forth among the nations" — all of which is a parable of Israel's lowly origin in Canaan, God's care of her in Egypt and deliverance therefrom right on until her prosperity in the days of David and Solomon.

4. *The Adulteress* (15-25). The parable now takes a tragic turn for instead of requiting her husband with the love, honor and fidelity becoming her, this richly endowed wife abandons herself to open prostitution. Trusting in her beauty and possessions she turned to harlotry and in an ungrateful and unfaithful way transferred her husband's wealth to her false lovers. She became guilty of seducing and attracting them like a common harlot, as well as yielding to the temptations of her paramours. Gifts, lavished upon her in love by her husband, became the means of prosecuting her evil course. This stark realism reveals the "abominations" and despicable history of Israel. Exalted from nothing to eminence among the Nations, Israel rejected Jehovah for false gods, and plunging into the depths of iniquity, prostituted the gifts of God to her base desires. Because of her licentious and infamous conduct Israel had compelled God to put her away and withdraw from her those advantages He had bestowed upon her.

5. *The False Lovers* (35-43). Because of the terrible sin of this adulteress, her punishment would be severe. Israel's iniquity was intensified by her political alliances with those foreign nations whose heathenism she had copied (26-34). Her paramours were the Egyptians and the Assyrians she had bribed for political help showing thereby her distrust of God as the Source of her protection and provision. These false lovers turned against Israel and became her destroyers, and in terrible vengeance stripped her of her vaunted possessions and exposed her to shame. Ezekiel had not minced words in describing Israel's failure and folly, and now he announces her punishment in similar shocking terms. "To Ezekiel the destruction of Jerusalem was already an accomplished fact. When it actually is an event of history, the irony of human folly became manifest: God destroys the pride of men by the very idols of their desires."

6. *The Two Sisters* (44-49). While the three cities, Jerusalem, Samaria and Sodom are described as *sisters,* and all guilty of "adultery" and of apostasy from the true God, Ezekiel introduces two sister nations at this point as supporting characters in the drama of his parable. All three *sisters* were of the same spiritual parentage, but the guilt of one — Jerusalem — was greater and more heinous in that she had professed to set a standard for her *sisters,* whereas she had been more abominable than they. "Sin is measured in direct ratio to the grace it spurns. Sodom and Samaria had never been so highly honoured and enriched by God as Jerusalem. But apostate Samaria and heathen Sodom had been swept away in God's fury, therefore, could Jerusalem's day of judgment be long delayed? The two sisters, then, enter the story to reveal Jerusalem's sin in its proper perspective of blackest guilt and to add lustre to God's mercy."

7. *The Restoration of the Wife* (60-63). Although all three *sisters* are por-

trayed as profiting from the severe penalty of their sin, and repenting, are restored, the last movement in this shameful parable is that in which the prophet foretells the restoration of the sinning wife by God's remembrance of the Covenant and re-establishment of it (Jeremiah 31; Hebrews 8:6-13). Grace reigns through righteousness on the part of the injured *husband*. Where the sin of apostasy (Samaria), the sin of pride (Sodom), the sin of unfaithfulness (Jerusalem) abounded, grace much more abounds (Romans 5:20). Once judgment has served its purpose, God stands ready to restore to fellowship the repentant one (Romans 11:32).

## The Parable of the Great Eagle

(Ezekiel 17:1-24)

Commanded by God, Ezekiel put forth a riddle in parabolic form to illustrate God's sovereignty over nations and men. Four kings and their kingdoms make up the parable in this chapter. Each king possessed points of contrast to all the others, yet had someing common with the rest. As Two Eagles, The Vine and The Branches form parts of the parable, let us try to understand their setting and significance.

In spite of the exposure of her crimes and of pronounced judgment on same, Israel, "the rebellious house," refused to be warned. "Israel was sure that the Babylonian threat could be averted by playing the game of international power politics. She would be saved by breaking her agreement with the Babylonian King Nebuchadnezzar, and allying herself with Egypt which was challenging Babylonian world supremacy." The purpose of the parable we are now considering was to expose the delusion of such a false hope and to show that the sure promises of God may only be realized in the restoration of the House of David.

1. The first king, likened unto a great eagle, was the Babylonian ruler, Nebu-chadnezzar, who took off the top of the cedar, another king, Jehoiachin of Judah, and brought him to the city of merchants, Babylon (Jeremiah 22:23; 48:40; 49:22). The seed of the land was carried away and planted in fruitful soil, where it became a spreading vine. Nebuchadnezzar, the first great eagle, was full of strength and ruled over many nations, expressed in the length of his wing and the variety of the colors of his feathers.

2. The second king and also second great eagle was Pharaoh, King of Egypt, whose length of wing and strength were not so great as that of the first eagle. By this time Egypt had passed the zenith of her power. Decay was apparent. Her dominion was not so extensive as that of Babylon. It was toward this second great eagle that Judah, the vine, bent her roots, that he might water it. This treacherous act was denounced by God who declared that the vine should be plucked up by the roots and be withered by the east wind.

3. The third king was Mattaniah, Nebuchadnezzar re-named *Zedekiah*. Made king in the place of Jeconiah, his uncle, Zedekiah, the vassal king of Judah, was the vine of low stature planted by the first eagle, Nebuchadnezzar, who suffered Zedekiah to enjoy all the rights and honors of royalty, not as an independent sovereign, but only as tributary to Nebuchadnezzar. Such a gratuitous act on the King of Babylon's part, brought Zedekiah under the strongest obligations to fulfil all conditions of subjection confirmed by a solemn oath.

But Zedekiah sought the covering of the second great eagle, Egypt, and earned the punishment of God. Unmindful of his oath, Zedekiah sought Egypt's aid, thinking that he could be delivered from a disgraceful vassalage and experience a sovereignty independent and free. This treachery is depicted in the parable under the image of a twig, cropped off a lofty cedar by a great eagle and planted as a low spreading vine, a good stock yet inferior to the parent stock. Dissatisfied with its state, the vine spread its roots toward another great eagle in the hope of greater eminence and fertility. But for such a violation irreparable ruin came to the vine.

4. The fourth king is the One of divine choice whose kingdom is yet future, who is to be a descendant of the kings of Judah. This King is to be greater than the greatest of all previous kings. Under the figure of "a young and tender twig" planted "in the mountain of Israel," and growing into "a goodly cedar," the establishment of Christ's Kingdom is foretold (Isaiah 11:1-12). This glorious Kingdom will never be subverted but will be an everlasting monument of truth and power. Divine government is to be established over all nations and operate through all their operations. The concluding promise of the parable is that from the line of David, "the high cedar," the Divine Ruler will come and when He does, He will dwarf all other powers, "the trees of the field," and under his reign all men will be safe with their needs supplied (Luke 2:67-75).

## The Parable of the Lioness and Her Whelps
(Ezekiel 19:1-9)

In this beautifully poetic and parabolic dirge, Ezekiel mourns the downfall of the Kingdom of Israel as an accomplished fact. The bereaved lioness is Israel; the captive Jehoahaz was the first young lion (II Kings 23:31-33) and Jehoiachin the second young lion (II Kings 24:8-16). The captivities and calamities were not accidents of history, but God-appointed as punishment for Israel's surrender of her unique character, and for the folly of wanting to be like other nations.

These two princes of Judah are spoken of as *lions,* not because of a lion-like courage and nobility of nature they possessed (Genesis 49:9), but because

of their lawless and ungovernable indulgence in their own selfish desires and disregard of any will besides their own. These two young lions, eager in the pursuit of prey, followed the same wilful course and met a similar end. The figure of the lion is a frequent one in the Bible being used in different ways (Numbers 23:24; 24:9 etc.).

## The Parable of the Vine With Strong Rods
(Ezekiel 19:10-14)

This chapter closes a long series of prophecies and consists of a moving lament over the fall of the royal family of Israel and over her utter desolation as a Nation, and hopelessness of any escape from divine judgment. The parable itself is an extension of the Parables of the Vineyard already dealt with (see Isaiah 5:1-7; Ezekiel 15:1-8). This parable also reveals the wide range of Ezekiel's vocabulary. What variety of expression was his! With great aptness he passes from lions to vines.

The exact significance of the unique phrase, "The vine is the blood," is difficult to decide. It is certainly not the same as "the vine of low stature" we thought of in a previous parable (Ezekiel 17:6). Here we have a strong, conspicuous and goodly vine. The phrase has been expressed in this way, "Thy mother is like a vine living in the blood," that is, in the life of her children, or "planted when thou wast in thy blood — in thy very infancy — when thou hadst just come from the womb, and hadn't yet the blood washed from thee" (Ezekiel 16:6). Calvin translates the phrase, "In the blood of thy grapes," meaning, in her full strength, as the red wine is the strength of the grape (Genesis 49:11).

This we do know that the vine, chief of the fruit-bearing trees, is here used by the prophet as an emblem of the royal house of Judah as a whole. Her favored position is noted: "she planted by the waters" thereby having every advantage of growth and fruition responsible for the power and glory of her early monarchs. Mention of the former royal dignity contrasts sadly with the present degradation of the royal house of David (19:13). The lamentation of the prophet is, "Fire is gone out of the rod of her branches, which hath devoured her fruit," a reference to Zedekiah's folly and its tragic consequences (Ezekiel 17). We are given a description of the nation as it had been, a vine having "thick branches" symbolic of the numbers and resources of the people, and as it will be when Christ's Kingdom fills the whole earth (Psalm 110:2; Isaiah 11:1). The "thick branches," however, were *plucked up,* not gradually withered — parabolic of the *sudden* upturning of the people in their national judgment, which should have produced repentance.

By the *strong rods* we understand those stronger branches representing the royal sceptres of Israel's Kings, the authority of rulers being indispensable to the well-being of a people. Says Lang, "Part of the punishment of rebellion is that the people are left unguided and unprotected." The singular, "a rod," doubtless refers to the last king, Zedekiah, who brought utter ruin to himself and to the people. The breaking and withering of the rods indicates the nation's terrible calamity when deprived of rulers. These are days when all the nations are in need of "strong rods," rulers who are righteous and able to rule. Fire *out of the rod* is figurative of the kindling of God's wrath upon the people because of their sin and folly. "The anger of the Lord" against Judah is given as the cause why Zedekiah was permitted to rebel against Babylon (II Kings 24:20; Judges 9:15). Campbell Morgan's comment is, "Plucked up in fury, her strong rulers ceased and out of her rods went forth a fire that destroyed. That is to say, Judah's final destruction had come through those having rule over her, and the reference undoubtedly was to Zedekiah."

# The Parable of the Two Sisters
(Ezekiel 23:1-49)

Chapters 20, 21, 22, give us a further glimpse into the apostasy and deserved judgment of the nation, whose elders were more entertained than instructed by Ezekiel's vivid parables (20:45-49). They still thought they were entitled to God's favor as His chosen ones without removing the abomination of idolatry. Thus in further symbolic language Ezekiel describes the certainty of judgment about to overtake them even though they had been God's privileged people. Destruction, like an unquenchable fire, would overtake them. The sword would devour them (20:45; 21:32). In "The Song of the Sword" (21:8-17), the prophet indicates the slaughter impossible to resist. Ezekiel was to sigh "with a breaking heart and bitter grief," to impress upon his sceptical hearers that the sword would certainly cut down all the inhabitants (21:1-7). The prophet sees the fire of divine wrath poured out upon all classes of society because of total corruption. Princes, prophets, priests and people all alike are to be caught up in the holocaust of God's wrath.

The final parables relate the doom of the nation, the first of which is the allegory of the two sisters, *Aholah* and *Aholibah.* God's rejection of His chosen people is again portrayed as a breaking of the sacred ties of wedlock (see chapter 16). First of all, let us consider the identity of these two lewd sisters in the parable.

*Aholah,* or Oholah, meaning, *Her own tent,* intimating that the worship at Samaria, the capital of the Northern Kingdom, was self-invented and never sanctioned by God. On the contrary, this self-conceived worship was the object of divine abhorrence. The northern tribes, seceding at Solomon's death, established their own tent or sanctuary. Samaria, represented by *Aholah,* was more corrupt than her sister. She played the harlot to Assyria and Egypt by rejecting the promises of God and seeking security in the armed strength of her neighbors' false gods. "She became famous," or more correctly "notorious." The conquest of Samaria made her a byword among the nations.

Samaria is also charged in the parable with being first in transgression (Ezekiel 23:5-10). Her nearness to Syria, closely associated with the Assyrians, contributed to her early apostasy, which began with calf-worship under Jeroboam (28:3; I Kings 12:28). She is called *the elder,* or greater, because she preceded Judah in her apostasy and its punishment. The prophet sees Samaria as having been destroyed. "Charged with her unfaithfulness in her alliance with the Assyrians in that she allowed herself to be seduced by their wealth and their strength, from her loyalty to Jehovah," the prophet reminds her of her former confederacy with Judah. Because of her double sin, she was suffered to be taken captive by the Assyrians who suppressed her.

*Aholibah,* or Oholibah, means "My tent in her," and implies that Judah still retained the sanctuary of the Lord, at Jerusalem, her capital. The Bethel worship of Samaria was of her own devising and not God-appointed. On the other hand, the temple worship of Jerusalem was expressly instituted by God who *dwelt* there, setting His tabernacle among the people as His dwelling place (Exodus 25:8; Leviticus 16:11,12; Psalm 76:2). But Aholibah, like her sister, Aholah, played the harlot. The Lord said of her, "Why gaddest thou about so much to change thy way?" (Jeremiah 2:36). She did not know her own mind for first she doted on the Assyrians (Ezekiel 23:12), and again she fell for the Chaldeans (23:16). Then her mind was alienated from them (26:17). Sharing Aholah's sin, Aholibah must likewise share her fate (23:11-35). She represented Jerusalem which must drink "the sister's cup, a cup of horror and desolation" (23:33). Because she had forgotten God and cast Him behind her back, horror and desolation were to be her portion (23:35).

The two sisters were of one mother, implying that Israel and Judah were originally one nation, born from the same ancestress, Sarah. But both sisters in their early history were guilty of idolatry (Joshua 24:14; Ezekiel 26:6-8). Even in their youth when receiving extraordinary favors from God, their hearts were set on other gods (16:6). Now both are included in divine judgment. The sins of both Israel and Judah are enumerated and because of their common sin, they are involved in common punishment. *All women* means "all nations." The judgments falling upon Israel and Judah were to be for all time a conspicuous monument of God's righteous severity. In terrible language Ezekiel describes the wickedness of alliances formed with surrounding nations and of the righteousness of the judgment upon the adulteresses. "Under the figure of the Hebrew method of dealing with the sin of adultery, namely, stoning, the prophet describes an assembly against Jerusalem and Samaria, carrying out this judgment, and destroying the people utterly." Guilt and punishment merge into a single picture (Ezekiel 23:36-49). The wages of sin are paid to the sisters in full. Not only were they stoned and slain, but their children and their habitations were doomed (Ezekiel 23:43). "The story of Aholah and Aholibah delineates the tragic irony of man's sin," says *The Biblical Expositor.* "Just as Samaria's and Jerusalem's paramours are their executioners so sin has within it the sting of death."

Because Israel and Judah changed their true God for false gods, they were severely punished and remain thereby a warning to both nations and men. The buried "cities of the plain" still speak of God's judgment to the world; and Samaria and Jerusalem have been preachers of righteousness for ages. The tragedy is that the nations are slow to learn that they can only be happy and prosperous if the true God is their Lord.

## The Parable of the Boiling Cauldron
### (Ezekiel 24:1-4)

In this final prophecy in this division of his book, Ezekiel connects his divine mission with the events of his time. On the exact day that Nebuchadnezzar came against Jerusalem, the fact was revealed to Ezekiel in Chaldea, and he was commanded to declare that the hour of Jerusalem's judgment had struck by the Parable of the Cauldron. Here we have a specific parable, not a parabolic action, but simply a parable spoken to the people in language describing action.

Jerusalem had been described as a *cauldron* (Ezekiel 11:3), and in a proverb of the self-confidence of the people who followed their own spirit rather than the Spirit of God. "The city is the cauldron and we be the flesh." The boastful language of Israel was about to become true in history and experience, but in a different sense from what the people had intended. Because the city was well-fortified it was compared to an iron cauldron, and the city's inhabitants felt they were secure from attack from without as the flesh within the vessel is safe from the fire outside. Alas, the people would not believe how they were to be boiled! In effect, Ezekiel in his parable is saying, "Your proverb shall prove awfully true, but in a different sense from what you intend. So far from the city forming an iron cauldron-like defence from the fire, it shall be as a cauldron set on fire, and the people as so many pieces of meat subjected to boiling heat" (Jeremiah 50:13).

The prophet, then, applies the parable of the boiling cauldron directly, declaring that Jerusalem was indeed a cauldron. He turns to their own figure of security and uses it against them making it indicate not safety as they thought but judgment. Precise language is used to describe the destruction of the city and its citizens.

"Every good piece . . . choice bones." Here the prophet depicts the most distinguished of the people. They are not bare bones but "choice" bones *in* a pot with flesh adhering to them.

"Bones under the pot." By these particular bones we have those destitute of any flesh and used as fuel under the pot. These bones answer to the poorest who suffer first and are put out of pain sooner than the rich who endure what answers to the slower process of boiling.

"Burn . . . bones . . . scum." The word *scum* occurs five times and is not found elsewhere. Probably it means "rust," implying that Jerusalem was as a cauldron corroded with rust and so fit for destruction. Then by the poisonous scum we have symbolized the people's all pervading wickedness. The scum was not the poor of the city, but poor and rich alike who had wallowed in the filth of sin.

"Bring it out piece by piece." The refuse alike with the choice was doomed to destruction, the contents of the pot, the flesh, drawn out in process of judgment. The city and its people were not to be destroyed all at the same time but in a series of attacks. All classes shared the same fate but "piece by piece." The hot terrors of the siege were endured, and a worse experience came with the victors dragging them out of the city.

"No lot" was cast to determine who should be saved from judgment; all alike were punished irrespective of rank, age, or sex.

"Blood . . . top of rock . . . " The people were to be exposed and their judgment conspicuous to all. *"Blood* is the consummation of all sin and presupposes every other form of guilt. God purposely let the people so shamelessly pour the blood on the bare rock that it might more loudly and openly cry for vengeance from on high and that the connection between the guilt and the punishment might be the more palpable." Jamieson goes on to say, "The blood of Abel, though the ground received it, still 'cries to heaven for vengeance' (Genesis 4:10,11), much more blood shamelessly exposed on the bare rock."

"Set her blood." Israel was to be paid back in kind. Openly shedding blood, her blood shall openly be shed (Matthew 7:2).

"The pile for the fire." The line illustrates the hostile materials used for the city's destruction.

"Spice it well." What an ironic touch! The beseigers were to delight in the sufferings of their victims, as if sitting down to a savory, well-seasoned meal.

"Brass . . . burn." It was not enough for the contents of the pot to be destroyed, the pot itself infected by scum must also be destroyed. Its spots of rust would not yield to cleansing (Ezekiel 24:12,13). The very house infected with leprosy had to be consumed (Leviticus 14:34-35).

"She hath wearied me out with lies." In spite of God's efforts to purify His people, they would not respond to His gracious overtures, so He had to allow judgment to fall upon them for their determined and deliberate wickedness. Through His prophets, the law with its promises, privileges and threats, He had tried to bind the people to Himself but all gracious interpositions were of no avail. Thus, they were left to their own course and to take its final consequences. Patient and longsuffering, God now comes to judge and cannot go back, spare, or repent (24:14).

## The Parable of the Prophet's Wife

(Ezekiel 24:15-24)

This touching parable is an instance of the combination of the literal and symbolic. Hengstenberg, however, disagrees with the literalness of the death of Ezekiel's wife. "If the first symbolic action of the chapter belongs to the department of the inner, the same holds good obviously of the second. A wife of Ezekiel has no more actually died than he is actually set on a cauldron. The thought, in verses 16 and 17, is not that the existing public misfortune is so great, that the pain of the undivided at the heaviest personal loss is thereby overpowered, but that the prophet merely prefigures a future state of the people. He is the type of the nation, and the wife the counterpart of all that was dear and precious to the people — namely, the Temple, in which all else was included. They shall not weep for the downfall of it, because they shall be wholly taken up with the pain of their own misery."

But the reading of verse 18 is explicit: "At even my wife died; and I did in the morning as I was commanded." The whole setting of the parable confirms that the prophet's wife actually died. As God's watchman, Ezekiel is a sad and lonely figure, and this one glimpse into his private life is one of stark tragedy. With the divine announcement of his wife's death there was the prohibition of the usual signs of mourning. The desire or delight of his eyes, his wife, was to be suddenly taken from the prophet, and the subordination of his whole life to his prophetic office is vividly portrayed as the narrative of his dear one's death. The phrase, "The desire of thine eyes," indicates how deeply he loved his wife who was to be snatched from him at a stroke (Deuteronomy 33:9).

In the removal of "the desire of his eyes," we have symbolized the sanctuary in which the Jews so much gloried as well as the Jews themselves pictured as the wife of Jehovah (Psalm 27:4; Ezekiel 24:31). Their crowning calamity was acted out in the death of Ezekiel's wife. She was dear to him, and the "beautiful house, where their fathers had praised Jehovah" (Isaiah 54:11), was dear to every devoted Jew. But a divine visitation was to take away the sanctuary, the desire of their eyes, and the worshipers themselves along with the Temple would lay in the dust as Ezekiel's wife (24:21-24).

"Take away . . . with a stroke." This phrase indicates the suddenness of his wife's death, and must have been overwhelming for Ezekiel. Yet his self-control is enhanced in that, in spite of a most trying experience, all individual feeling is made to yield to the higher claims of God. All through his life, personal feelings had been submerged in the performance of his unappreciated task, and now with priestly prostration of every affection before God's will, there is no external manifestation of grief. Ezekiel was comforted in the knowledge that his bitter experience was to convey a prophetical lesson to his doomed people (Ezekiel 24:15-25).

"Forbear to cry." The prophet was to lament in silence and to refrain from customary mourning rites. His sorrow was not forbidden but the loud public expression of it, typical of the lack of regret over the universality of the ruin of Jerusalem.

"Make no mourning for the dead." Priests were expressly allowed to mourn for their nearest relations (Leviticus 21:2,3), but priestly Ezekiel is here made an exception, figurative of Jerusalem's death over which there would be no mourning as is usual at a death (Jeremiah 16:5-7). Hair was not to be cut, as was usual at such a time (Leviticus 21:2,3,10), and the prophet's shoes had to be kept on his feet. To go barefoot was an ordinary sign of mourning (I Samuel 15:30; Isaiah 20:2). The covering of the lower part of the face, another sign (Micah 3:7), was forbidden Ezekiel in his sorrow.

The people perceived that the prophet's strange conduct had a parabolic significance for themselves and so asked, "Wilt thou not tell us what these things are to us? (Ezekiel 24:19). Their curiosity was aroused in the unusual actions of Ezekiel who, replying to their question, announced the destruction of the beloved Temple, and that in the depth of sorrow and trouble at its fall

there would be no outward show of mourning. Ezekiel obeyed the divine command which came to him on the heels of the foregoing parable of *The Cauldron* (24:18), and his tragic loss was to play a part in his public ministry. It was a "sign" to his fellow exiles that Jehovah was about to visit His people with a punishment so terrible that they would not be able to find relief in mourning or weeping. Ezekiel was told that when news of the fall of the city was brought to him the silence of his personal grief would be broken and his lips opened to declare with assurance the unalterable Word of God. Ellicott remarks that "after the judgment was made known to the prophet, there came a marked change in his utterances, and from that time his general tone is far more cheering and consolatory."

## The Parable of the Anointed Cherub
### (Ezekiel 28:1-19)

Two prophecies constitute this chapter. The first and larger one we are to consider was against the Prince of Tyre, the briefer prophecy was against Zidon (Ezekiel 28:20-26). Of the whole prophecy, so full of the most varied and striking imagery, Ellicott says, "There is no other passage in Scripture where there is such detailed and peculiar irony. It brings out most powerfully the impiety of all ambition, and the vanity of all greatness, which seeks its foundations and support elsewhere than in the power and goodness of the Eternal."

The prophecy on the King of Tyre falls into three sections: His Deification (2-5), His Doom (6-10), His Destruction (11-19). The Prince who was deifying himself was the reigning King, *Ithobah,* whose name implies a close association with Baal, the Phoenician supreme god, whose representative he was. This proud sovereign, like others, suffered from "the insanity of prosperity" seen in the folly of Sennacherib (II Kings 18:33-35) and in Nebuchadnezzar, the then living monarch of Babylon, to whom this prophecy carried a solemn warning (Daniel 3:15; 4:30), and also in Pharaoh (Ezekiel 29:3) and Herod (Acts 12:21-23). Ithobah, like Oriental monarchs of his time, and later Roman emperors, actually claimed for himself religious homage. The language used of him also shows that he suffered from a proud sense of elevation and self-sufficiency. Like some modern dictators, Ithobah was conspicuous for his inordinate pride, begotten of great prosperity, which he attributed to his own power and wisdom instead of its true source, the true and only God. How forcibly he was reminded that in spite of his vaunted deity he was only mortal!

The proud King of Tyre felt that as God sat enthroned in His heavenly citadel exempt from any harm, so he was secure in an impregnable stronghold, immune from danger. But how hollow was his boast. After all, he only ruled over a small isle of the sea, which was in God's sight "a very little thing" (Isaiah 40:15). His sceptre held sway over merchant-princes who, like ants, spent their days in gathering and hoarding riches for the King. With a fortune and a fleet superior to any other kingdom at that time, Ithobah felt he was secure from any threat of invasion and in the insolence of fancied security and the pride of possessions said, "*I am a God.*" But he was to learn to his sorrow that the God to whom "the nations are as a drop of a bucket" had the power to bring the princes of the earth to nothing and to make the judges of the earth as vanity (Isaiah 40:15,23). The greatness of Tyre's prosperity was the cause of her pride, and hence "the foundation of her fall."

In his overweening opinion of himself, the King felt that he had a wisdom superior to Daniel's, who was famed for his heavenly wisdom in the great Chaldean Empire (Daniel 1:20; 2:48; 4:18). How ironically Ezekiel rebuked the King for presuming to have such exalted wisdom! But his weakness and foolishness in contrast to the power and

wisdom of God is strongly emphasized in the phrase, "Yet thou art man, in the land of Him that slayeth thee." Because he had allowed the pride of his heart to deceive him, and had entertained thoughts and purposes fitting only to the Supreme Being, Ezekiel took up his lament over the King of Tyre, and declared that because of his pride he would be cast down in the presence of kings, and for the multitude of his iniquities would be burnt to ashes.

Ezekiel's ironic reference to the King of Tyre as an "anointed cherub" harks back to the Cherubim overshadowing the mercy-seat. Ithobah, a demi-god in his own esteem, extended his protection over the interests of Tyre and became a type of the pretensions of the coming Antichrist who will endeavor to ape God (Daniel 7:25; 11:36,37; II Thessalonians 2:4; Revelation 13:6). Regarding the remarkable description the prophet gives us of the King of Tyre, it is most likely that from "his height of inspired vision he saw behind the actual prince the awful personality of Satan, whose instrument Ithobah was, and who will possess and inspire the Antichrist. In his message addressed both to Ithobah and the evil force behind him, Ezekiel declares Satan's involvement in the overthrow of Tyre, and how in the midst of desolation God will be glorified. The reader is directed to Scofield's footnote to this chapter.

Zidon, or Sidon, closely associated with Tyre, its offshoot, in its idolatry will not escape punishment for her sins. It was Zidon's heathen worship that polluted Israel more than Tyre's form of idolatry. These nations were to vanish, in order that there be no more "a pricking brier to the House of Israel." Amid the destruction of Tyre and Zidon, the prophet has a brief word concerning the ultimate restoration of Israel, God's faithful, scattered ones would be gathered and set apart in the midst of the nations, dwelling securely with those surrounding them knowing that Jehovah was their God (Ezekiel 28:20-26).

# The Parable of the Cedar in Lebanon

(Ezekiel 31:1-18)

In chapter 29, the prophet begins a series of seven prophecies against Egypt, Israel's principal foe.

The First Prophecy was against Pharaoh and all Egypt (chapter 29).

The Second Prophecy was brief, foretelling that the instrument of judgment would be Nebuchadnezzar, and that the capture of Egypt would be his wage for the defeat of Tyre (29).

The Third Prophecy describes the process by which Nebuchadnezzar would accomplish God's judicial purpose (30).

The Fourth Prophecy was directed against the power of Pharaoh, whose arm would be broken (30).

The Fifth Prophecy was directed against the greatness of Pharaoh (31).

The Sixth Prophecy is taken up with a lamentation for Pharaoh whose doom is vividly described (32).

The Seventh Prophecy consisted of a wail for the multitudes of Egypt whose descent to death is described in terrible and awe-inspiring language (32).

It is the fifth of these prophecies we are concerned with in *The Parable of the Cedar*. Here again we have the combination of the literal and symbolic. It was Ezekiel's custom occasionally to interrupt a parable by literal utterances (Ezekiel 31:11,14-16). The form of a parable whereby a kingdom is represented as a tree was considered in chapter 17 (see also Daniel 4). A tree seems to have been a Chaldean mode of representation. Addressing himself to Pharaoh and his hosts, Ezekiel asks, "Whom art thou like in thy greatness?" In reply, the greatness of Assyria is described, a description proud Pharaoh applied to himself. But Egypt, like Assyria, was to lose its prominence as an empire in the world. As the haughty King of the Assyrians was conquered by the Chaldeans, so Pharaoh and Egypt were to share the same fate.

This parable, like that of the previous one concerning the King of Tyre, merges the historical with the figurative, and is made of history, symbol and arguments. The significance of several phrases in the parable should be noted. First of all, *Lebanon* is specially mentioned because it was here that the most famous cedars grew in their greatest perfection. Although we have already dealt with some of the facts of the cedar tree, which is one of the grandest products of the vegetable world, it is used here in a different way. Because of its magnificent, stately appearance, overtopping all other trees, it was appropriately selected to symbolize the surpassing glory of the King of Assyria. As no tree equals the cedar in its height, symmetry and bulk, so none could compare with the Assyrian monarch. The long boughs of the cedar affording shelter for "all the fowls of heaven," sets forth the extent of the Assyrian's dominion.

"Sending out her roots to the little rivers" is a figurative way of describing the various surrounding and subordinate nations which nourished the great stream of Assyrian prosperity and helped to swell the power and wealth of the empire. "The garden of God" refers to the traditional site of Eden which was within the bounds of the Assyrian Empire. "The mighty one of the heathen" was the Chaldean monarch, Nubapolassar. "The trees of the field" represent the subordinate potentates, who are dismayed or "faint" at the fall of Assyria (Ezekiel 26:13,18). But the mighty tree was hewn down, and its bare and lifeless trunk became the resting place of birds and beasts — a graphic description of the overthrow of Assyria, the crash of which affected all surrounding nations. "To whom art thou thus like?" The whole prophetic parable is brought to a climax in this question. Egypt, like Assyria in glory, shall be like her in the experience of the judgments of God. Jamieson comments, "The lesson on a gigantic scale of Eden-like privileges abased to pride and sin by the Assyrians, as in the case of the first man in Eden, ending in ruin, was to be repeated in Egypt's case. For the unchangeable God governs the world on the same unchangeable principles . . . . retribution in kind (28:10). Pharaoh's end shall be the same humiliating one as I have depicted the Assyrian's to have been. 'This is Pharaoh'— *this is* demonstrative, as if he were pointing with the finger to Pharaoh lying prostrate, a spectacle to all, as on the shore of the Red Sea" (Exodus 14:30,31). The direct application of these figures to Pharaoh closed Ezekiel's fifth prophecy.

# The Parable of the Unfaithful Shepherds
## (Ezekiel 34:1-31)

The parabolic prophecy in this chapter opens with an indictment of the rapacious rulers of Israel, likened unto false shepherds who ruled "with force and cruelty," whose sin was that of exploiting the sheep instead of feeding them. "My sheep became a prey" (Ezekiel 35:1-10). After the fulfilment of divine judgment in the destruction of Jerusalem, Ezekiel, although he has denunciations of the oppressors and enemies of Israel, becomes more consolatory, and his prophecies are full of rich promises for God's afflicted people. Thus, in the chapter before us, the prophet announces that God will deliver His people out of the hands of selfish and evil rulers who have oppressed them, and will Himself provide for and protect them. As a whole, the chapter may be treated as an amplification of Jeremiah's short prophecy (Jeremiah 23:1-8). The three discernible divisions of the chapter are:

1. *The Promise of Judgment on Unfaithful Shepherds* (1-10). By "shepherds" we are to understand not prophets, or priests, but *rulers* who sought in their government their own selfish ends, and not the good of those they ruled. These rulers stood in the same relation to those they governed as shepherds to

their flocks, and this portion is heavy with indictment because of their unworthiness (See I Kings 22:17; Matthew 9:36). They lacked the essential qualifications of true rulers. Their self-indulgence led to negligence of the sheep. "Woe to the shepherds of Israel that do feed themselves." The diseased were not cared for, the lost were not sought. Further, the leaders of Israel thus described were "fat and strong" themselves but were guilty of cruelty toward those for whom they should have cared. Ahab's treatment of Naboth has been repeated so often. "Not content with appropriating to their own use the goods of others, they from mere wantonness spoiled what they did not use, so as to be of no use to the owners" (Ezekiel 35:18, 19). The result of the negative and positive transgressions of Israel's rulers was the Captivity and then the scattering of the sheep. The Ten Tribes became wanderers in the land of Assyria, and the people of Judah were dispersed in Babylon and Egypt, separated from the few remaining in their own desolated land. Yet though they were so widely scattered, the Omniscient One knew where every one of His sheep were.

2. *The Promise of Divine Care for the Flock* (11-22). The removal of the false shepherds was a necessary preliminary to the raising up of a divine deliverer. "I will deliver My flock from their mouth." Here we have the interposition of God on behalf of His people Israel (Jeremiah 23:1; Zechariah 11:17). Because of the general profligacy of her kings and rulers, and daring abuse of their power and influence and unholy gratification, God undertakes the office which the rulers had so grievously perverted, namely, the guardianship of the flock. This divine oversight is described in language full of beauty. "I Myself, even I will search . . . and seek . . . and deliver . . . and bring out . . . and gather them . . . bring them in . . . and feed them . . . and cause them to lie down . . . and bind up . . . and strengthen."

God declares that He would not only deliver, but govern. "I will feed them in judgment," meaning that His discrimination and administration would be manifest. He would prevent the strong from treading down the pasture to the injury of the weak. Rich oppressors would be judged, and the humble poor, enriched.

3. *The Promise of David's Appointment As His Shepherd* (23-31). David was raised up by divine appointment, not only as Israel's good and beneficent ruler, but as the head of the Theocracy and the Ancestor of our Lord after the flesh. David typified the gracious and glorious Shepherd who was to perfectly realize the purpose of God. In the fullness of time, great David's greater Son appeared as the Good Shepherd giving His life for the sheep, but through the rejection of Him by the Jewish rulers, the people of Israel became scattered more widely and terribly than before.

After severely reproving the negligence of those appointed to watch over the flock, God promises to raise up a Shepherd, a plant of renown, who would faithfully discharge all His duties and execute the trust reposed in Him (Ezekiel 34:2-16;23,24). The term *shepherd* was appropriate for David as a "ruler," who was a type of the true David (Ezekiel 34:22,23). David was taken from being a shepherd for the office of a king. His new office, like that of a shepherd for his flock, was to guard and provide for his people (II Samuel 5:2; Psalm 78:70,71). "Shepherd means *King,* rather than religious instructor," says Jamieson, "in this preeminently Christ was the true David, who was the *Shepherd King* (Luke 1:32,33). Messiah is called 'David' in Isaiah 55:3,4; Jeremiah 30:9; Hosea 3:5." This great chapter closes with the tender assurance that God's chosen people will be His flock and that He will be their God (Ezekiel 34:31). This Shepherd King is to establish His Kingdom, and under His rule there will be peace, provision and protection. Divine resources, well able to care for the needs of all, and divine care and vigilance without intermission, will be experienced by His flock.

# The Parable of the Valley of Dry Bones
## (Ezekiel 37:1-14)

The previous chapter provides us with the prediction and method of Israel's ultimate restoration. God's people are to be gathered out of all countries and cleansed inwardly and spiritually, enabled to renew their witness to surrounding nations about God's character and truth. Israel's land is to be restored to prosperity for the Lord's own sake and made like a garden of God. This present chapter continues the same consolatory promise of restoration. God's ancient people had become like dry bones, but raised to new life, and with the two divided kingdoms reunited, God's sanctuary is to be established among them forever.

The first parable of this chapter is taken up with Ezekiel's symbolic vision of the restoration to national life of a people scattered and in a hopeless condition. In the weird and amazing spectacle of the valley of dry bones, we hear the moving of the wind over the separated bones, then watch them come together and clothed with sinew, flesh and skin, stand up as a living army. All of which is parabolic of Israel as a re-made race and nation. What a glorious resurrection awaits those about whom Ezekiel prophesied! In order to appreciate, however, such a glorious revival, let us look at Israel's present hopelessness.

"The valley . . . full of bones." These bare bones were not heaped together but thickly strewn over the face of the plain — figurative of the scattering of the people and of their desolation and slaughter by invading forces. These dismembered bones were also "very dry," meaning that life had long since left them. The marrowless bones had become bleached by long exposure to the atmosphere — parabolic of the dry, barren spiritual condition of Israel because of her sin and ensuing bitter captivities.

"Can these bones live?" Humanly speaking, they could not. There was no hope of a national restoration apart from divine omnipotence. "O Lord, thou knowest." The prophet knew, and the people receiving his prophecy were made to realize, that "what is impossible with man is possible with God." So speaking on His behalf, Ezekiel prophesied upon the bones, meaning that the scattered and still rebellious people were to listen to the message of their future, literal resurrection. As Ezekiel prophesied, there was "a noise," that is, a mutual collision as the bones came together and were clothed with sinew, flesh and skin. But the dry and scattered bones brought together made only unsightly corpses. They needed *life*.

"Breathe upon these slain that they may live." By the power of God's creative word, life came into the assembled bodies and there stood up "an exceeding great army." As God had formed man of dust from the ground and breathed into his nostrils the breath of life, making him a living soul (Genesis 2:7), so Israel was commanded to believe that the same God would open their graves, and bring them into the land of Israel (Ezekiel 37:12). The teaching, then, of this vivid parable is that "a revived Israel is that earthly clay out of which God will call into being the people of His eternal Kingdom."

# The Parable of the Two Sticks

## (Ezekiel 37:15-28)

In this further parabolic prophecy which has a close connection with the one of *The Bones*, Ezekiel is told to perform a symbolic act and explain its meaning to the people. Commenting on the two parables in this chapter, Ellicott says: "In the former, under the figure of the revival of the dry bones, God had set forth His power to accomplish the promise He had made of the spiritual resurrection of Israel; in the latter, He adds to this specific declaration of what had been before only implied, that the two long severed nations of Israel shall be re-united and prosperous under the rule of the future David . . . These promises prepare the way for the prophecy of the great and final attack (38, 39), and then the overthrow of all their enemies by the power of God."

Ezekiel was instructed to take two sticks and inscribe on them for Judah and for Joseph, and for the whole house of Israel. These sticks were to be joined together, becoming one stick in his hand. The two sticks represented the two kingdoms. After the death of Solomon the united Kingdom was severed, ten tribes siding with Jeroboam and becoming known as *The House of Israel,* two tribes remaining with Rehoboam, Solomon's successor, and known as *The House of Judah.* As he spoke of *sticks,* the prophet may have had in mind the tribal rod of which Moses speaks (Numbers 17:2, 6-9). Doubtless the two separate pieces of wood were so shaped that when held together, they appeared as one — a parable, or prophecy, in action of the brotherly union which is to unite the ten tribes and the two tribes into one indissoluble nation under the one covenant-King. All previous divisions are to cease, and with the unification of Israel there will come the consolidation of national interests. In spite of powerful opposition from her enemies (Ezekiel 38,39), God's promise of restoration and unification will not be thwarted. His Word cannot fail of fulfilment. God will hide His face from His people no more forever.

Of chapters 38, 39, describing as they do the complete triumph of Israel's anointed King, Fairbairn says, "This is a *prophetical* parable in which every trait in the delineation is full of important meaning, only couched in the language of a symbolical representation."

## The Parable of the Measuring Reed
(Ezekiel 40:1-5; 41:19,20; 43:1-19)

Chapters 40 through 48 of Ezekiel's prophecies form "the weightiest in the book, presenting us with a carefully elaborated sketch of the polity of re-patriated Israel, as in an ecclesiastical organization, rather than as a nation." Thus we have a detailed account of the Temple and its services and worship in this continuous prophecy of a distinctly marked character. Much has been written on whether the prophecy of the Temple with its minute detail, careful measurements and various ordinances is to be taken literally, or as a parable of a Temple, ideal in its character. The prophecy was uttered when Solomon's Temple lay in ashes, and the land was desolate. Afterwards the Temple was re-built and the Jews re-established in Palestine, but what Ezekiel here depicts is yet in the future. As to the *pros* and *cons* of a literal or symbolical interpretation of all related to the Temple and the new and remarkable division of the land, the reader is referred to the full discussion given to this subject in Elli-cott's *Preliminary Note* on these concluding chapters of Ezekiel.

As to the difficulties generally associated with this portion they may be all *seeming*, not real. "Faith accepts God's Word as it is," says Jamieson, "waits for the event, sure that it will clear up all such difficulties. Perhaps, as some think, the beau-ideal of a sacred commonwealth is given according to the then existing pattern of temple-services, which would be the imagery most familiar to the prophet and his hearers at the time."

The hand of the Lord brought the prophet to a high mountain in Israel where he saw the man with a measuring reed in his hand. A characteristic definiteness in details is seen in *a line of flax* used for longer measurements, and *a measuring reed* for shorter measures. If what Ezekiel saw was a parable-pattern

of "a coming spiritual society, possessing a real unity, inhabited by a Divine presence, resting on the Divine name," then several precious thoughts emerge. First of all, the measurements here given took an angel of God to measure. The Temple of Solomon was measured and made by human hands, but the Temple in Ezekiel's vision is beyond human reckoning. The habitation of God (Ephesians 2:20,21) will consist of a multitude "no *name* can number" (Revelation 7:9).

Then the great variety of materials, each kind being adapted to serve a special purpose in the Temple, is figurative of the characteristics of unity and diversity in the living Temple of God. The Temple here measured was a perfect square, and such buildings are most firm, secure and enduring. Is it not so with the Temple built upon Christ the chief corner-stone? (Ephesians 2:20; Matthew 16:13). Further, the perfect Temple Ezekiel saw in his vision was remarkable for its beauty, symbolic of the glorious Temple of His body, beautiful and glorious.

## The Parable of the Rising Waters
(Ezekiel 47:1-12)

The wonderful symbolic river Ezekiel beheld came from the sanctuary and proceeded under its threshold, past the altar and outward in steadily increasing stream. God had returned to dwell among His people before the stream of life issued forth (Ezekiel 43:7-9). The river in John's vision had its source in "the throne of God and of the Lamb" (Revelation 22:17). As the self-sustaining One, the Lord is the only well of Living Water (John 4:14). He is "the fountain of life" (Psalm 36:9), and His living Temple can drink of "the river of His pleasures" (Psalm 36:8). "Messiah is the temple and the door; from His pierced side flow the living waters, ever increasing, both in the individual believer and in the heart." Out of Him, flows rivers of living water (John 7:37-39).

The main point in the parable before us is the description of the rapid augmentation from a petty trickle into a torrent, not by the influx of side-streams, but by its own self-supply from the sacred miraculous source in the sanctuary. The man with his measuring line noted the steadily swelling stream — a thousand cubits beyond its emergence, the stream was ankle deep, a thousand farther it reached the knees, a thousand farther the loins were covered, and a thousand farther there were waters to swim in. Of the increase of Messiah's government there is to be no end (Isaiah 9:7; Zechariah 14:89; Joel 3:8). For our hearts we have this application: "Searching into the deep things of God, we find some easy to understand, as the water up to the ankles; others more difficult, which require a deeper search, as the waters up to the knees or loins; others beyond our reach, of which we can only adore the depth" (Romans 11:33). The measuring of the sanctuary waters, first small in appearance then unfolding itself in ever-richer fulness is in contrast to the streams of worldly enterprise whose water is still and stagnant (Job 6:15-20; Isaiah 58:11)

Because the waters from the sanctuary were clean and flowing, everything lived wherever they flowed. Being *living* waters they functioned as *healing* waters. The "desert" is a fitting symbol of the barrenness of ungodliness, of a world estranged from God (Psalm 107:5; Isaiah 35:6). But the living waters from above can transform any Dead Sea, if there is an inlet and outlet. If a Dead Sea refuses the healing waters then "its mire and its marches are not healed" (Ezekiel 47:11). An application is not hard to seek. Those unreached by the healing waters of the Gospel through their negligence, earthly-mindedness or rejection, are to be given over to their own bitterness and barrenness and remain as an example to others in deserved punishment (Peter 2:6; Revelation 22:11).

Then the flowing waters, becoming wider and deeper as they rise, are a fit parable of the growth of the Church which began with a few at Pentecost and is now a mighty river. The rising waters also symbolize the progressive spiritual life of the true believer, which is meant to become deeper with the passing days. At the beginning of a new life in Christ, little is known of the fruitful, invigorating work of the life-giving Spirit, but as we journey on with Him we come to experience the fulness of the blessing of the Gospel He makes possible for the obedient heart. Evidences of the Holy Spirit as a life-giving River are numerous (Isaiah 44:3; Ezekiel 36:25-27; Zechariah 13:1: John 7:37-39).

# THE PARABLES OF DANIEL

All the facts of Daniel's personal history are to be found in the Book bearing the great prophet's name. Of royal birth, he was taken as a youth to Babylon as a captive by Nebuchadnezzar in the fourth year of Jehoiakim, and was engaged in prophetic activity lasting over seventy years. He lived in an age when the spirit of prophecy was extant. Ezekiel mentions Daniel's wisdom and hints at his prevailing intercession (Ezekiel 14:14; 28:3). Because of the eminent position he attained, his unique prophetic ministry, and his sustained character, Daniel rendered valuable aid to his fellow-Jews, both in and outside exile.

Living chiefly under the Babylonian Empire, Daniel manifests an intimate acquaintance with the life and times of

Babylon. As a true prophet he was cognizant of three classes of magicians operating in Babylon (Daniel 2:2). He knew the magician's phraseology, *dissolving of doubts,* and their theology, which recognized "gods whose dwelling is not with flesh" (Daniel 2:11; 5:12). He was familiar with Babylonian dress and punishments (Daniel 2:5; 3:6,21). These and other details reveal an author living in Babylon.

It will help to provide a background for our review of Daniel's parabolic visions if we remember that over a long period he witnessed the marvelous and rapid growth of the Babylonian Empire under Nebuchadnezzar. Daniel also watched "the gradual decay of this mighty Empire after the decease of its founder; he saw the final collapse of it, and witnessed the first beginning of Persian supremacy, under which, as well as during the short period that a Median viceroy presided over Babylonia, he probably maintained the high position which he had filled during his younger days."

The writings of Daniel are "apocalyptic rather than predictive," says Ellicott. "He presents the future in a series of enigmatic pictures rather than in enigmatic language . . . . The object of the Book of Daniel is:

1. To supply a missing link in the chain of the continuity of revelation.

2. To support Israel amidst the doubts and fears occasioned by the Exile.

3. To reveal to a polytheistic nation the eternal power of the One true God."

The prominent characteristics of this man of God, Bengel called "the politician, chronologer and historian among the prophets," are varied. Political experience under successive dynasties of great world powers, coupled with natural qualifications, and added supernatural spiritual insight, enabled him to interpret prophecy. We also note his:

Personal purity and self-restraint amidst the world's corrupting luxuries (Daniel 1:8-16; see Hebrews 11:25; Genesis 39:9).

Faithfulness to God at all costs, and fearless witnessing for God before great men (Daniel 5:17-23).

Refusal to be bribed by lucre and unawed by threats (Daniel 6:10,11).

Single-minded patriotism which with burning prayers interceded for his chastened countrymen (Daniel 9).

Intimate communion with God, so that, like the beloved disciple and apocalyptic seer of the New Testament, John, Daniel is called "a man greatly beloved," and this twice, by the angel of the Lord (Ezekiel 9:23; 10:11). Divinely instructed, he received the exact disclosure of the Messiah's advent, the seventy weeks of years, and the successive events down to the Lord's final advent for the deliverance of His people. Thus, in every way, Daniel is an illustration of how God fits His organs for His work.

Auberlen, in his study on *Daniel,* compares the prophet with Joseph: "one at the beginning, the other at the end of the Jewish history of revelation; both representatives of God and His people at heathen courts; both interpreters of the dim presentiments of truth, expressed in God-sent dreams, and therefore raised to honour by the powers of the world; so representing Israel's calling to a royal priesthood among the nations; and types of Christ, the true Israel, and of Israel's destination to be a light to lighten the whole Gentile world, as Romans 11:12,15 foretells. As Achilles at the beginning, and Alexander at the end, of Grecian history are the mirrors of the whole life of the Hellenic people, so Joseph and Daniel of Israel."

## The Parable of the Great Image
(Daniel 2:31-45)

This remarkable chapter, so full of historical prophetic import, has two clear divisions, namely —

The Revelation of the Image (31-36)
The Interpretation of the Image (37-45).

Usually strong-willed men, who ruthlessly reach the pinnacle of power, are afflicted with insomnia, and Nebuchadnezzar was no exception. Restless, he dreamed, but on waking failed to recall his dream. Evidently fearful over what had passed through his mind, and desperate for tranquility, he sought the aid of his magicians, astrologers, and soothsayers in the interpretation of his dream. The unreasonable demand of the despot was that the recognized wise men first reconstruct the dream he had forgotten and then give its significance. Was this to be a test case to discover whether the magicians were lying and corrupt?

The wise men insisted that what the King asked for was utterly impossible (Daniel 2:10,11), but he vowed that they would all be slain if they failed to recall and interpret the dream (Daniel 2:12,13). Daniel, learning what was planned, gathered his three friends together for a time of prayer for a key to the "secret." In answer to the fervent prayers of the holy quartette, the revelation and interpretation of the dream was given to Daniel, whose prayer of praise is "one of the most beautiful and lyrical expressions of the wisdom of God in Holy Writ." (See Daniel 2:20-23.) The dramatic demonstration of Daniel's power to interpret dreams shows that he had not innate, inherent ability to do so. All that was necessary came to Daniel as a revelation from God.

Seeking out Arioch, who had been ordered to slay all the wise men, Daniel pleaded for a stay of execution and also for an interview with the tyrannical King (Daniel 24-25). Unashamedly, Daniel tells the King that as God alone was able to reveal secrets, the secret dream was unfolded, not by any wisdom of his own, but by a divine revelation (2:28). Daniel then proceeded to describe one of the greatest apocalyptic visions ever given to man. Nebuchadnezzar must have been enthralled as he listened to Daniel re-construct the dream and then outline the commencement, continuation and consummation of Gentile history and dominion. The metal colossus, parts of which were made up of different materials, symbolized four successive kingdoms, and the final rule of God's King, "the stone that smote the image became a great mountain, and filled the earth" (Daniel 2:35).

Daniel's interpretation is most fascinating. The *Colossus* symbolized the unity and historical succession of four world kingdoms. Because the head was of gold, and the feet of iron and clay, the image was top-heavy and destined to crash.

*The First Kingdom* was Babylon, as Daniel declared when, in interpreting the dream, he said to Nebuchadnezzar, *"Thou* art this head of gold" (Daniel 2:38). This first great Empire existed from 604-538 B.C. Gold fittingly represents the absolute autocracy of Nebuchadnezzar, whose power was supreme. "Whom he would he slew" (Daniel 5:19).

*The Second Kingdom* was Medo-Persian, existing from 539 to 333 B.C. Inferior to the previous Empire, the Medo-Persian Empire is illustrated by the chest of *silver*. This was a monarchy dependent upon the support of an hereditary aristocracy, a Monarchical oligarchy in which nobles were equal to the King in all but office, and a system in which the King could by no means do as he willed (Daniel 6:12-16; Esther 8:3-12).

*The Third Kingdom* was the Grecian Empire continuing from 490 to 146 B.C. This Empire, founded by Alexander the Great, continued through his successors in Syria and Egypt and remained as one kingdom in spite of confused reigns. Greece is symbolized by the belly of *brass*. The government of Alexander was a monarchy supported by a military aristocracy that was as weak as the aspirations of its leaders.

*The Fourth Kingdom* was Rome, in existence from 27 B.C. to 455 A.D. This last earthly Empire was ruled by the Caesars, nominally elected by the people, and had a senate which was supposed to counsel and control them. These Roman Emperors wore no crown, but only the laurel crown of a successful commander. Rome is pictured for us in the thighs and legs of *iron,* so descriptive of an Empire, metallic and coherent. *Iron* signifies "strength," and Rome had a strength greater than other kingdoms, and has retained its original iron might, or democratic imperialism.

*The Two Legs* of the image represent the separation of the Roman Empire into the Eastern and Western divisions, with the Greek Church in the first division, and the Papal Church in the second.

*The Ten Toes* of *iron* and *clay,* suggest the fragile combination, resulting when the iron of Rome was mixed with the clay of popular will. An absolute monarchy degenerates into an autocratic democracy. This is the form of government largely existing today. We live under the divisions of the Roman Empire which began over 1400 years ago, and which at the time of Christ's return shall be definitely *ten* (Revelation 17:12). The degeneration of world kingdoms is represented in the diminishing value of the metals used. Silver is worth less than gold — brass less than silver — iron less than brass — clay less than iron, this latter being more perishable and more easily corroded or rusted than brass, silver or gold. The basic substance of each is *dust,* and dust must return to dust. All that failed in the hand of man is to pass away, and that which is kept in God's hand shall be introduced.

*The Fifth Kingdom.* After the process of deterioration there is the emergence and establishment of a new order represented by "a stone cut out of a mountain" crushing the feet of the Colossus and tumbling it. None can doubt that this is a parable of the Messianic Kingdom, whose rule is to encompass the whole earth. Christ is the *Stone* able to grind men and nations to powder (Matthew 21:44). "In the days of those kings," means those represented by the *ten toes,* ruling at the end of the Gentile Age. Gentile dominion was a gradual process, passing from head to feet. But the *Stone* is not to fill the earth by degrees. Suddenly and swiftly, Christ, the King of kings, will come and usher in His universal reign. Some mistakenly hold that this Fifth Kingdom is a spiritual one — The Church. But this last Kingdom will be as literal as the four earthly kingdoms we have considered. The Church is not here to destroy any earthly kingdom but to extend her influence as a spiritual kingdom. As with the four metals, so with the *Stone* which is also made up of solidified dust. But what a difference! Christ took upon Himself the likeness of our flesh, and some of humanity's dust, glorified, in the wonder of heaven, and nothing can withstand the might of dust mingled with deity. World-kingdoms destitute of God must end in dust, and as we journey on to Christ's millennial reign the less enduring and the more worthless are the mere kingdoms of this world.

The result of the recall and interpretation of Nebuchadnezzar's dream by Daniel, was his advancement to high position (Daniel 2:46-49). Convinced of the reality of Heaven's revelation, the King prostrated himself before Daniel and confessed to the power of God. But Nebuchadnezzar only recognized Him as a "God of *gods"* — head of multiple deities. The pagan tyrant did not accept Him as the only *true* and living God. Humiliation was necessary to bring this about, as we are to see.

# The Parable of the Great Tree
## (Daniel 4:1-37)

While this chapter opens with a doxology, the godly and courageous witness of Daniel and his three Hebrew companions doubtless brought Nebuchadnezzar an appreciative understanding of God's great power, but the King was loathe to recognize his obligation to God, who vouchsafed him another parabolic dream. This time he remembers and describes his dream which was of a great tree, lofty and flourishing. Suddenly it is cut down at the order of the heavenly watcher and destroyed. Its fruit was scattered, its branches no longer afforded a shelter for birds and beasts. All that remained was a miserable stump. This parabolic vision, similar to the Parable of the Great Cedar (Ezekiel 31:3-17) in its implication, supplies a few additional features.

Nebuchadnezzar, after reciting to Daniel the dream his magicians were unable to interpret, received from the prophet (who now had a Babylonian name, *Belteshazzar*) its divine interpretation. Daniel, astonished as he saw the application of the dream to the dreamer himself, "commenced his interpretation with the courteous address, expressive of his sense of the calamity about to fall on the King. Nevertheless, in loyalty to truth he interpreted its meaning to the King, and appealed to him to turn from his sin and show mercy to the poor in order that his tranquility might be lengthened."

Daniel explained that the great tree was a symbol of the King himself, that its strength and fruitfulness illustrated his wealth and power, that its being cut down indicated a break in his sovereign power. The position of the tree, "in the midst of the earth," set forth Babylonian unlimited growth in every direction. Ancient Orientals loved to illustrate the growth of human greatness and power by the figure of a growing or fallen tree. Birds and beasts gathering together under the tree was a figurative way of describing the varied people united under the sceptre of Nebuchadnezzar.

Disaster did not fall upon Nebuchadnezzar all at once. A year later as the King, disobeying the appeal of Daniel, walked in his pride, boasting that he had built the great city, Babylon, by his own power and for his own glory, judgment fell. A voice from heaven told the haughty King that the kingdom he boasted of would be taken from him and Daniel's prophecy would be fulfilled. It is thus that, after the manner of dreams, the figure changes from a *tree* (a vegetable organism clinging to the ground) to a *beast*, an animal organism, which, "while naturally capable of unimpeded motion and of an individual and independent participation in life, is for the present forcibly restrained. The fetters of iron and brass symbolize the chains of darkness and coarse bestiality in which the mind of the King was held during an extended period."

As with Herod, so with Nebuchadnezzar, as he vaunted his pride he was immediately stricken. In the grip of lunacy known as *lycanthropy,* the deposed King imagined himself an animal and acted like one. He was driven out from among men to dwell and eat with the beasts of the field. In the mercy of God, after a while the King's reason returned, and with his restored mind, he sought to honor God. This time, divine judgment seemed to have a salutary effect, for the King understood the true meaning of God's power. Restored to his kingdom he praised the King of Heaven, whose works are true and whose ways are judgment. Nebuchadnezzar had learned the lesson of humility and that the God most high was able to abase those who walked in pride. Judgment was necessary discipline for the proud potentate. Now the figure of the stump, which had indicated his later return to power, is fulfilled.

The lessons from this parable for our own hearts are clearly evident. Undue fleshly pride often results in degradation. Vain-glory and self-exaltation bring their own disaster. Pride and arrogant self-confidence are an offense against God and merit His judgment. Then, when chastisement has produced a right state of heart before God, there returns the token of His favor. Further, praise to

God proves that affliction has not been in vain. Nebuchadnezzar passed through a painful and humiliating experience, but it resulted in bringing him to the feet of the Eternal God. As the sin of pride is one of the most common to man, and one which God hates most, may He in His mercy keep us meek and lowly in spirit!

## The Parable of the Mystic Handwriting

### (Daniel 5:1-31)

It has been said that, "All we learn from history is that we do not learn from history." How true this is in the story of Belshazzar who succeeded his father, Nebuchadnezzar, as king! While we have no details of Belshazzar, he stands revealed in this chapter as a man of profligate habits. The graphic picture provided by Daniel gives us an estimation of the character of a son who failed to learn from the folly and degradation of his father. The carousal reveals the man and was the occasion of the final manifestation of the sin of Belshazzar, desecrating the golden vessels taken from the House of God at Jerusalem. Belshazzar and his lords after an evening of licentious revelry were suddenly smitten with consternation by a mystic hand writing on the plaster of the wall of the King's palace, the message of his doom and that of his kingdom.

Belshazzar, pale and shaken by the dramatic and strange appearance of the hand, called for his wise men to interpret the writing, just as his father had requested them to interpret his dreams. Human wisdom, however, can never interpret a divine message. The worldly wise men were baffled by the writing. The Queen, however, remembered Daniel, gifted in the interpretation of dreams, and he was brought before the King who promised Daniel great gifts if he could read the mysterious writing of the wall. Full of dignity and heroic loyalty to God, Daniel, with clear, inci-

sive words, declined all the profferred gifts, and then charged the King with his terrible guilt and announced his tragic end. The prophet declared God to be the Sovereign Lord, seated high over the thrones of earth and about to end the Babylonian Empire and divide it among the Medes and Persians.

Thus, as *The Biblical Expositor* expresses it: "Another world power had struggled to the top, become profligate, was judged by God, destroyed and replaced. Were we to put the successive kingdoms of this world on a graph, we would see again and again parallel lines representing early energy, mounting prosperity, crest of power and the downward plunge to oblivion. Years or centuries may be involved in the process so often repeated in history. Sometimes the downward descent is swift, as in the case of Belshazzar; sometimes slow, involving centuries of decline, as in the case of the Roman Empire, but the direction and the end are the same."

## The Parable of the Four Beasts

### (Daniel 7:1-28)

Daniel's vision of the four beasts which came up from the sea, another parable of pictorial power and grace, was given to the prophet some 48 years after Nebuchadnezzar's dream of world dominion. In his vision, Daniel was standing on the shore of the *Great Sea* (the Mediterranean Sea) from which the four Kingdoms of Babylon, Medo-Persian, Greece and Rome arose. Out of the sea *four great beasts* came up in succession. We here have an extension of Nebuchadnezzar's dream.

In the *Great Image* we have Gentile dominion in its intelligent, well proportioned might. While the Empire possessed differing substance, strength and character, they yet had one form. Now in the *Four Beasts* we have another side presented, namely, the terrific wasting power of world empires, symbolized by brute force. Let us see how these two aspects agree. Godlessness and worldly ambition resulting in the natural fruits of cruelty and crime, are vividly portrayed by the *Kingdoms* and the *Beasts* — the former were regarded according to their *external* political aspects; the latter are represented as being the mind of God as to their *moral* features. The first vision is made up of images taken from the inanimate sphere — here we have images taken from the animate sphere.

*The Sea.* This is a fit symbol of a restless humanity. The Bible pictures world-powers rising out of the agitations of the political *sea* (Jeremiah 46:7,8; Luke 21:25; Revelation 13:1; 17:25; 21:1). The *sea* can be *treacherous,* and treachery has played a large part in the emergence of world-kingdoms. *Restlessness* also characterizes the sea, and the history of nations is one of constant change. The sea can be *destructive,* and the succeeding empires Daniel saw were destructive rather than constructive forces in the world. "The four winds" answering to "the four beasts" are parabolic of several conflicts in the four quarters or directions of the World.

*The Beasts.* In general, the four beasts are analogous to the four great Empires in Nebuchadnezzar's dream, the characteristics of which were animal rather than human. This is why these Empires of the parabolic vision are symbolized by beasts of prey noted for strength and cruelty. No animal of a gentle, peaceful nature is mentioned, suggesting the entire absence of those traits in kingdoms without godliness.

*The Lion With Eagle's Wings.* As Daniel watched he saw the lion lifted up from the earth and made to stand upon its feet as a man, and "a man's heart was given to it" (Daniel 7:6). In the British Museum may be seen colossal stone lions with the wings of an eagle and the head of a man taken from Babylonian and Assyrian ruins in 1850 A.D. This *beast* corresponds to the First World Kingdom — Babylon and to its King, who in his madness imagined himself for a season to be a beast (Daniel 4:16,34). The Lion is the king of beasts, and the Eagle, the king of birds which figuratively, represents the Royalty of "the Head of Gold," and the Eagle-like swiftness of Nebuchadnezzar's armies. By "the plucking of the wings" we can understand the beastly insanity of Nebuchadnezzar (Daniel 4:20-27).

*The Bear With Three Ribs.* This beast devoured flesh (Daniel 7:5) and appropriately indicates the Medo-Persian Empire which quickly devoured Babylonia, Libya and Egypt. After the lion, the bear is strongest, and known for its voracity. Lacking the agility and majesty of the lion, the bear, awkward in its movements, overcomes its victims by brute force and sheer strength. Thus the Medo-Persian Empire, ponderous in its movements, gained its victories not by bravery and skill, but by vast masses of troops able to "devour much flesh." By the three ribs we understand the three kingdoms of Babylon, Libya and Egypt which formed a "Triple Alliance" to check Medo-Persian power, but were all destroyed by it.

*The Leopard With Wings and Heads.* The third beast "like a leopard, which had upon the back of it four wings of a fowl . . . also four heads" (7:6), is usually identified as the Grecian Empire, which struck swiftly and engulfed the known world with astonishing and unforgettable rapidity. The "leopard," the most agile and graceful of creatures, had speed assisted by "wings." Alexander the Great, with small but well-equipped and brave armies, moved with great celerity and in ten years overthrew the unwieldy armies of Persia, and subdued the civilized world. "Four" being the number of earth, may denote the four quarters of the earth over which Alexander, who died having no more worlds to conquer, extended his kingdom. As for "the four heads," these stand for the four kingdoms into which the Grecian Empire was divided by the generals:

namely, Egypt, Syria, Thrace and Macedonia. The *Leopard* corresponds to the belly and hips of the Image.

*The Great Beast With Ten Horns.* Unlike any other beast Daniel had ever seen or heard about, this one "was dreadful and terrible, and strong exceedingly, and it had great iron teeth . . . ten horns." In the iron teeth, corresponding to the iron legs, and the ten horns, to the ten toes of the Image, it is not hard to see Daniel's further description of Rome, the fourth World Kingdom. Among the ten horns was a "little horn" arising that pulled out three of the original ten horns by the roots. Looking closely at this "little horn," Daniel discovered that it had "eyes like the eyes of a man, and the mouth of a man speaking great things" (Daniel 7:7,8). Such an aspect greatly troubled and mystified Daniel, and suggests the tremendous arrogance and presumption of the anti-Christ as he wars against the saints of the most high during the Great Tribulation.

As with the metals forming the Image, so here with the Beasts there is degeneration — gold to iron; lion to a nondescript monster. The *Metals* provide us with man's estimation of world kingdoms — the concentration of wealth, majesty and power. The *Beasts* give us God's view — the succession of rapacious wild beasts devouring one another.

*The Ancient of Days.* What a different scene is before us in the heavenly King overcoming all earthly potentates, and the inauguration of His kingdom of peace and righteousness. Because God is eternal, He is patient, and His will be the last word, and when He speaks in judgment, woe be to the godless rulers of earth. Daniel provides us with a scene symbolic of the throne of judgment (Daniel 7:9-14). How glorious is the Ancient of Days in His white garment, His white hair, His throne of flame and surrounding majesty! The Book is opened and the end of earthly kingdoms follows. To God's King is given a Kingdom including all people,

nations and tongues willing to serve Him. He is on His way to clear up the mess of earth, for which the nations are responsible, and when He appears as "the Prince of the kings of the earth," His Kingdom will be sure, peaceful, beneficial, indestructible and eternal. Compare this scene with the one John received (Revelation 5:6-10).

Worldly kingdoms arise out of the earth, but "the Son of Man came with clouds of heaven" (Daniel 7:13,14). "Ye are from beneath," He said, but "I am from above" (John 8:23). Thus, a kingdom not of this world is to possess the world. "Thine is the kingdom" — an everlasting kingdom.

Intimately associated with the Second and Third Kingdoms, is the further vision granted to Daniel in which we have a close-up of the Medo-Persian and the Grecian Empires. So we come to —

## The Parable of the Ram and the Goat
### (Daniel 8:1-25)

Daniel saw a ram with two horns pushing northward, westward and southward. Nothing could stand before the one thus illustrated. Whatever he willed was accomplished (Daniel 8:4). As Daniel watched, a he-goat attacked the ram and overcame him and magnified himself. Four horns appeared out of one from which came another, which grew until it had broken down the sanctuary. As Daniel pondered the vision and sought to understand a situation that greatly troubled him (Daniel 7:8), a divine interpretation was granted unto him.

The Ram symbolized the united power of Medo-Persia, and the rough He-Goat was the King of Greece, against whom a fierce force would arise and succeed him but who would be ultimately broken without hand. While the reader will find a fuller treatment of this fascinating aspect of Gentile History in the writer's *All the Kings and Queens of the Bible,* a brief summary of the significance of these two further Beasts will suffice at this point.

*The Ram* stood for the Medo-Persian Empire, and its "two horns," the two Kings, Darius and Cyrus. One horn was higher than the other, and the higher came last.

*The He-Goat* represented the Grecian Empire: the "Great Horn" between its eyes, the first King, Alexander the Great; and the "four horns," the four kingdoms into which Greece was divided, namely, Macedonia, Thrace, Syria and Egypt, which four became absorbed in the Roman Empire.

As Daniel considered the vision of the Ram, he saw the He-Goat come from the West unmolested and noticed the "notable horn" between its eyes and moved with anger, attack the Ram and stamp upon it. The He-Goat waxed great, but its "great horn" was broken off and the "four notable horns" waxed exceedingly great toward the South, the East, and toward Palestine, "the pleasant land" (Daniel 8:5). A *Goat* was the symbol of Macedonia, and was found on its coins. Legend has it that Caremus, first King of Macedon, was led to his capital, Edessa, by a herd of goats. *Edessa* originally meant "the goat city." In like manner Persian coins displayed a Ram's head and a *Ram* was looked upon as the guardian spirit of Persia.

It was revealed to Daniel that the "Two Horns" of the Ram, the "Two Shoulders" of the Bear, the "Two Horns" of the Great Image, represented the same thing, namely the double kingdom of Medo-Persia. The "Four Horns" coming up in the place of the "Great Horn" correspond to the "Four Heads" of the Third Wild Beast, the Leopard. So the He-Goat, the Leopard (the Belly and Thighs of the Image) all stood for the Grecian Empire, and its fourfold divisions among the generals of Alexander the Great. What must not be forgotten is that Daniel's revelation was progressive, each new vision throwing light on previous visions. For instance, the Ram pushing in a three-fold direction threw light upon the Bear crunching "three ribs" in its mouth, parabolic of the subjugation of Lydia to the west, Babylon to the north, and Egypt to the South.

Daniel saw a "little horn" come up on one of the "four horns," and Gabriel explained to the prophet the significance of the symbol. The passage describing the "little horn" in his role as tyrant and desecrater of the Temple probably found fulfilment in Antiochus Epiphanes. We may also have here a parable of the Tribulation Era, when the Antichrist will seek to exercise world-wide dominion (Daniel 8:22-27). Such a tremendous revelation of coming events so overcame Daniel that he fainted and was sick for many days.

# THE PARABLES OF HOSEA, MICAH, HABAKKUK

Apart from his great personal tragedy, we know little regarding Hosea's background. He was the son of Beeri, of Isaachar. Born in Bethshemesh, he was a native of the Northern Kingdom. He began his ministry in the last years of Jeroboam II, was contemporary with King Uzziah, and prophesied about the same time as Isaiah and Amos. The quartette known as "The Eight Century Prophets": Amos, Hosea, Isaiah and Micah, were mighty men of God whose combined contribution to Old Testament Prophecies would be difficult to exaggerate. These four prophet-evangelists were "God's immortal challenge to sin and immorality and idolatry and paganism. They brought His deathless Word of warning and denunciation and doom. With that stern word they pronounced the divine promise of hope and salvation and victory."

There are evident traces of Hosea's influence on Isaiah, Jeremiah and Ezekiel, and "he is probably the only prophet of the Kingdom of Israel whose oracles have come down to us in complete and literary form," says Ellicott, "bearing in their very language traces of the dialect of Northern Palestine." Hosea is placed first in the list of Minor Prophets because of "the length, vivid earnestness, and patriotism of his prophecies, as well as their resemblance to those of the greater prophets." The major influence of this minor prophet may be seen in the way later prophets stamp with their inspired sanction, Hosea's prophecies (Isaiah 5:13; 9:12, 13; 11:12,13; Zephaniah 1:3; Jeremiah 4:3); and also by the many New Testament references to Hosea's ministry (Matthew 2:15; 9:13; Luke 23:30; Romans 9:25,26; I Corinthians 15:4, 55; I Peter 2:10; Revelation 6:16).

The times in which Hosea lived necessitated the strong, compassionate voice of one who would not shrink from driving home the Lord's message of coming judgment and disaster, and that these calamities would result in certain doom. In a most appealing summary *The Biblical Expositor* comments: "All through his long ministry he waded through anarchy, revolt, bloodshed, feuds, immoral behaviour, broken homes, class hatreds, corrupt courts, extravagance, drunkenness, slavery and shallow religious observance. Idolatry and ignorance and godless indulgence combined to make an intolerable burden. Priests had failed and were lined up with bandits and racket bands. Worship was formal, professional, and meaningless. It was a pathetic situation. How could God look with favour on such people? How could a spiritual prophet hope to do anything with such godless people?

Kings and priests and princes were all against him. He had no help from his own home. Sin and selfishness and greed and paganism mocked him at every turn. His was a hopeless task".

But whom God calls He equips. With the "Go ye," there is always the "Lo, I am with you." Thus, out went Hosea as God's anointed messenger to a sinful people with the message of grace as well as judgment. Essentially this strangely poetic and deeply spiritual, highly sensitive soul with "lightning flashing from his tear-dimmed eyes," was an evangelist whose form of preaching was personal and persuasive. He pleaded for decisions, as he reminded the people that their ugly sins cried out for repentance and confession. What pathos is in the appeal, "O Israel, return unto the Lord, thy God" (Hosea 14:1).

Hosea appears as "a man of emotion rather than of logic, a poet rather than a preacher," in his pleadings, the keynote of which is love, outraged love. And a reading of his book reveals the wealth of resource by which his pleadings were enforced. Says one writer dealing with Hosea's rapidity of transition from one form of speech to another, "The language of the prophet resembles a garland of divers flowers; images are woven to images, similes strung to similes, metaphors ranged on metaphors."

## The Parable of the Faithless Wife

### (Hosea 1; 2; 3)

Much has been written regarding the marriage of Hosea and Gomer, the daughter of Diablain. Is this event to be interpreted as a prophetic vision, an allegory, a parable of a divine truth, and therefore not an actual historical event, or is the account of Gomer strictly literal? With Ellicott we maintain the view that marriage and its issues are not merely allegory, but historic fact which was responsible for the ever-recurring grief of Hosea's sorrow-stricken heart.

The most reasonable interpretation of the marriage is that Gomer was not actually an adulterous, unchaste woman at the time of her marriage to Hosea, but that she became unfaithful in prostitution after her marriage. Such domestic misery of a faithless, unclean wife was permitted by God to serve as a parable of the way He had suffered from the sins of His people all the way along from their deliverance from Egypt. What a long history of unfaithfulness to God Israel had! Hosea suffered untold agony over his unworthy wife, yet he loved her with an unquenchable devotion, and came to understand and proclaim God's love for His faithless people. Out of the depth of his own anguish, "with flaming heart and impassioned tongue, Hosea went among the people with the burning evangelistic challenge to tell of the amazing grace of God." Was his loving appeal in vain? The brighter, final note in the Book (Hosea 14; II Kings 17:2) seems to indicate that in the worldly heart of King Hoshea a change had been wrought by the exhortations of the prophet; and that also Israel had experienced the forgiving, restoring quickening grace of God.

While Hosea's central theme was that of Israel's unfaithfulness to Jehovah, such unfaithfulness seems to fall into two clearly marked aspects.

### 1. There was unfaithfulness in political relations

All through Hosea's prophecy divine judgment is pronounced upon Israel for her alliance with, and dependence upon, surrounding powerful heathen nations. Unholy alliances had been made with Assyria and Egypt, and to the mind of Hosea all this policy of subservience to foreign Empires was in flagrant violation of the old theocratic principle. To the mind of the prophet political affiliations for the sake of expediency constituted a treacherous abandonment of Israel's God, and so with scathing, figurative words, Hosea denounced the unfaithfulness of Ephraim (singled out as the dominant tribe, yet the whole nation was involved) to Jehovah, the Lord of Hosts, Leader of Israel's armies and the Supreme Protector of their soil. So we have these descriptive similes:

Ephraim is as a "silly dove" hovering between Egypt and Assyria for help (Hosea 5:10; 7:11). "A covenant is made with Assyria and oil is carried to Egypt" (Hosea 11:1). "Strangers have devoured his strength, and he knoweth it not" (Hosea 7:9). The purpose of Hosea's stern denunciation was to lead Israel back to faithful dependence on the God of Jacob, and returning in penitence to Him, to confess; "Ashur shall not save us" (Hosea 14:1-3).

### 2. There was unfaithfulness shown in idolatry

There are various metaphors used in the Bible to represent God's association with, and care of, His people: but the most sacred and endearing of them all is that of a marriage covenant, expressions of which abound. Jeremiah has whole chapters devoted to Israel as an adulterous wife, invited to be reconciled to her Divine Husband (Jeremiah 3:1,14, etc.). Hosea likewise employs the similar parable, with the addition of an adulterous wife as a visible sign to the Jewish nation of their unfaithfulness. Idolatrous sensuality and excess prevailed. The worship of the true God had been degraded into calf-worship and then to the Baal-worship of the Canaanites. Such idolatry was regarded by Hosea and other prophets as treachery to the pure and Holy God of Israel. This form of *spiritual* idolatry consisted in a loving and serving of the creature more than the Creator. Hence covetousness and sensuality are spoken of under that term (Romans 1:25; Colossians 3:5; Philippians 3:19).

But God was loathe to let His people remain in their unfaithfulness, and Hosea's unchangeable love for his prodigal wife was a reflection of God's unchangeable love for His wayward people and of His desire to take back His "wife of whoredoms." In declaring His purpose to redeem the people from their idolatries, God said that He would hedge up their way with thorns, and alluring them, provide for them a door of hope. "I will call them my people" (Romans 9:24-26). The response that gladdened the divine heart may be found in the words, "We will follow after other lovers" no more, but "will return to our first Husband" (Hosea 2:5; Isaiah 26:13). Hosea in passionate tones endeavored to awake a yearning for the old and privileged covenant-relations with the God who had brought His people out of Egypt.

*The Parabolic Germs.* It would be a profitable exercise to tabulate the expressive figures of speech so numerous in *Hosea.* These *miniature* parables are the art of brevity, and "brevity causes obscurity, the obscurity being designed of the Holy Spirit to call forth prayerful study." A beauty peculiar to Hebrew poetry and many prophetic writings is that of the amplification of important truths with figurative illustrations and sublime metaphors explained by simple declarations. Thus if Israel follows the Lord, He will be to her "as the latter and former rain upon the earth" (Hosea 6:3). The return of showers after drought illustrates the refreshing and fructifying grace of God. "Your goodness is as a morning cloud, and as the early dew it goeth away" (Hosea 6:4). We are here taught man's instability and the forbearance of God.

We think of these further parabolic sentences: "Ephraim is a cake not turned . . . Grey hairs are here and there" (Hosea 7:8,9). "A cake not turned" means it was burned up on the one side, and doughy on the other and fitly represented Israel, cold and indifferent in their relationship to God, yet excessively ardent in their pursuit of other objects displeasing to God. "Grey hairs" point to the causes and symptoms of spiritual decay. "They have sown the wind, and they shall reap the whirlwind"

(8:7), illustrates how misery and disaster are the inevitable consequences of sin. "Israel is an empty vine" (10:1) describes the fruitlessness of a life when self is the principle, the measures and the end of our actions. We are only fruitful in the best sense as we abide in Him, who is the True Vine (John 15).

As for the fruits of God's favor, what beautiful imagery Hosea uses to describe them. Imagination cannot conceive a richer display of divine blessings, vouchsafed both to Israel and to the Church, found in the last chapter of Hosea.

"I will be as the dew": God's communications are often as silent as they are sublime. "Dew distils silently and almost imperceptibly on the ground, yet it insinuates itself into the plants on which it falls, and thus maintains their vegetative powers." God's visits to His people are secret, as He seeks to cheer and revive their fainting spirits.

"He shall grow as the lily." Growth, beauty, fragrance and fertility are expressed in the mixed metaphors of this verse (14:5-7). The lily, quick of growth, has a beauty all its own. "The olive-tree" is renowned for its manifold uses. "Smell of Lebanon" refers to its odoriferous vines and lofty cedars symbolic of the fragrance and strength of a life lived in the will of God.

"Revive as corn . . . grow as vine," are expressly emblems of the fruitfulness of those who dwell under His shadow.

"I am like a green fir-tree" (Hosea 14:8). With its remarkably thick shade, which cannot be penetrated either by sun or rain, the fir-tree afforded a safe retreat from the rays of the meridian sun, and also from the violence of the impending tempest — parabolic of our secure hiding-place in Him from whom our fruit is found.

In conclusion, then, the book of Hosea has "three permanent values. They are its unveilings of *Sins,* of *Judgment,* and of *Love.*"

*Of Sin.* In chapters 4 to 7, we see how a holy God suffers as He looks down upon the foul sin of Israel. Sin is intolerable in the presence of His august holiness. Sin saps the vital juices — physical, mental and spiritual — until a mere shell is left. Sin "cuts the optic nerve of the soul," and also hurts the holy, loving heart of God.

*Of Judgment.* A just and holy God must bring severe judgment (chapters 8 to 10). "Love spurned called for judgment. Deliberate breaking away from the covenant vows made retribution inevitable." So in stern language, Hosea told the people that they would "reap the whirlwind" because of their unprecedented faithlessness. Israel's judgment was inevitable and necessary.

*Of Love.* What amazing love and grace are proclaimed by Hosea! "How shall I give thee up, Ephraim? His past, present and prospective love are fully described. As a loving God, He will provide restoration, healing, forgiveness, and full salvation. Unfailing in his own love, in spite of his wife's treachery, Hosea's heart-cry is that of a champion human lover representing the champion Lover of all times seeking His own." Love wins through and gains the victory (chapters 11 to 14). Through all the failure of Israel there may be heard the music of the love of Jehovah.

As Micah is one of the four "Eight Century Prophets," we can glance at his use of the word *parable* in his brief yet weighty prophecy. "In that day shall one take up a parable against you, and lament with a doleful lamentation" (Hosea 2:4). Here the prophet is saying, in effect, "The enemies shall repeat in mockery the doleful lamentations with which you bewail your pitiable state."

Isaiah and Micah have a remarkable similarity of style, and the same power of graphic description. Micah, however, is more tense, and gives the telling touches which in Isaiah's utterances expand into long bursts of sustained elo-quence. As with other prophets, Micah knew how to use apt, parabolic language.

## The Parable of Mockery
(Micah 2)

In this chapter with its denouncement of sin and declaration of deserved judgment, Micah uses a gradation of terms, to make the deliberate character of the people's transgression: "In the night they *formed* the plan, they *thought it out* upon their beds and *carried it out* into execution in the morning." The same gradual intercourse with the wicked, reaching a tragic culmination is found in the first Psalm. *Walking* with the ungodly leads to *standing* among sinners, and at last *sitting* habitually in the seat of the scornful. What sorrow and shame Israel would have been spared if only she had watched the first step in her departure from God.

## The Parable of Derision
(Habakkuk 2:6-20)

This derisive song is similar to the previous references (Isaiah 14:4; Micah 2:4), continuing to the end of the chapter in a symmetrical whole, consisting of five stanzas —the first three being made up of three verses each; the fourth, of four verses, and the fifth of two verses. Each stanza has its own subject, and all except the last begin with *Woe,* and all have a closing verse introduced with "for," "because," or "but." Habakkuk's style, particularly in his vision of divine interposition, framed as a lyrical poem, changes with the subject. "Terseness gives way to florid eloquence, sentenious denunciation to an exuberance of ornate description."

In the denunciatory parable, put into the mouths of the invader's victims, these are the *Woes* to be noted:

Woe on the reckless rapacity which has spared neither life nor property (Habakkuk 2:6-8).

Woe on the aggrandisement of the new dynasty by force and cunning (Habakkuk 2:9-11).

Woe on the extension of Babylon by oppression and enforced labour (Habakkuk 2:12-14).

Woe on the cruel invader who has made the world drink of the cup of wrath (Habakkuk 2:15-17).

Woe on him who neglects Jehovah to worship dumb idols of his own making (Habakkuk 2:18-20).

"The book of Habakkuk," says Campbell Morgan, "is the story of a believer's conflict of faith, and of the ultimate triumph of faith." Like the book of Jonah, this book relates the story of a personal experience, and ends, not with a wail, but with a song. Habakkuk does not end as he began, with inquiry, but with affirmation. The prophet starts by saying that amid all violence and cruelty God is silent and does nothing, but a mighty change takes place and he ends by rejoicing in the God of his salvation. "When Habakkuk looked at his circumstances he was perplexed. When he waited for God and listened to God, he sang" — and what a song of triumph.

For though the fig tree shall not blossom
Neither shall fruit be in the vines:
The labour of the olive shall fail,
And the fields shall yield no meat;
The flock shall be cut off from the fold,
And there shall be no herd in the stalls;
Yet I will rejoice in the Lord,
I will joy in the God of my salvation.

# THE PARABLES OF ZECHARIAH AND MALACHI

The prophet Zechariah, son of Berechiah, was born in the latter years of the Babylonian Captivity. Berechaiah died when Zechariah was but a child and he was reared by his grandfather, Iddo, who accompanied Zerubbabel, Judah's Prince, and Joshua, the high priest, back to their desolated country (Ezra 2:1,2; Nehemiah 12:4). Probably like Ezekiel, Zechariah was priest as well as prophet. Therefore, a priestly birth suits the sacerdotal character of his prophecies (6:13). He was one of the three prophets of the Restoration, the other two being Haggai and Malachi. Haggai and Zechariah labored at the beginning of this period and Malachi at its close. This triad of Prophets complete the Old Testament with their faces turned toward the sunrise even though darkness still brooded deep over their contemporaries. Thus, one thought seems to pervade the prophecy of Zechariah: he is pre-eminently the Prophet, as Peter is the Apostle, of Hope.

A perusal of the book of Zechariah reveals how intimately acquainted its writer was with the writings of other prophets. There is a Jewish saying to the effect that "the spirit of Jeremiah dwelt in Zechariah." For a full treatment of this profitable aspect of Zechariah, the reader is referred to the tabulation of the prophet's use of the works of other prophets in Ellicott's *Introduction to Zechariah*. In itself, Zechariah's book "possesses a grandeur of scope, and a wealth of spiritual wisdom. At once profound and spectacular, it should bring to the Christians not only new insight, but also sure comforts in the midst of a bewildered generation."

The book of Zechariah has been described as the Apocalypse of the Old Testament. An apocalypse means the removal of something that hides, an unveiling, and Zechariah was a great unveiler of "the pervasive power and the persistent purpose of Jehovah" and of truths obscured by the prevalent conditions of adversity. The three general sections of the book are —

1. Symbolic (1-6)
2. Didactic (7-8)
3. Prophetic (9-14) ·

As to Zechariah's style, while it changes, it always accords with the subject. Critics affirm that the book must have been composed by two or more writers because of its differing style. But Ellicott answers this criticism effectively by saying that there is no reason in the nature of things why God should not at one time reveal His will to a prophet in visions, and at another time by other means. "We consider that the high-flown poetic language and imagery and deep prophetic insight of its latter chapters are just such as might have been expected, in his later years, from one who in his youth, saw and related the mysterious series of visions contained in the former portion . . . . The seer, who even in his youth was found worthy of such mysterious revelations, had spent many years in communion with God, and meditation on the promises revealed by 'the former prophets' — the deep things of God — seems only in accordance with our experience of the workings of Divine Providence that he should, in after life, become the recipient of the stupendous revelations contained in the concluding chapters."

Notable for his graphic, vivid power of expression, Zechariah, like Ezekiel and Daniel, delights in symbols, allegories and visions of angels ministering before Jehovah and executing His commands on earth. As we come to consider the parabolic significance of Zechariah's prophecy, we shall discover the threefold conviction of the prophet, namely:

1. Jehovah reveals His will to those able to receive it.

2. Jehovah calls men back to Himself, and provides the way for their coming.

3. Jehovah promises that if they will return, He will return to them, and He does so in the power and might of His own Holy Spirit.

## The Parable of the Horses and Myrtle Trees
### (Zechariah 1:8-17)

The introduction of the book (1:1-7) is made up of a warning based on the previous warnings of Haggai (Haggai

1:4-8). Zechariah received a command to exhort the people to avoid the sorrows and judgments that had overtaken their fathers, and through sincere repentance prepare themselves to receive visions of a glory yet to be revealed. The repeated phrase, "Came the word of the Lord" (Zechariah 1:1,7), fitly used of the prophet's nocturnal visions, implies a divine revelation the substance of which was conveyed to Zechariah by the Angel of the Lord. Examining the component parts of the ecstatic vision Zechariah received when fully awake, although it was night (Zechariah 1:8; 4:1), we have —

1. *The Horses.* These horses are described as being *red, speckled* or bay, and *white* — colors most commonly found among horses, and which John adopted and gave a special significance (Revelation 6). Interpretations of these colors differ. Some writers suppose they represent the land and nations to which the riders had been sent, or denote the three imperial Kingdoms of Babylon, Medo-Persia and Greece, or were connected with the various missions which the rider had to perform, in the East (red), in the North (brown or black: Zechariah 6), in the West (gray), in the South (dark-red). Further, red horses suggest war and bloodshed; pale-gray horses — hunger, famine and pestilence; white horses, conquest, times of complete prosperity, the Jewish people experienced. Halley remarks, "This vision of the horses means that the whole world was at rest under the iron hand of the Persian Empire, whose King, Darius, was favorably disposed toward the Jews, and decreed that the Temple should be built."

2. *The Rider.* The "man" riding the "red horse" and standing "among the myrtle trees" is the same heavenly being described as "my Lord" and as "the angel of the Lord." It was the office of this angel-interpreter, and also angel-intercessor, to explain the significance of the parabolic vision (Zechariah 1:18; 2:3; 4:1,4,5; 5:5-10; 6:4), and who is

often referred to simply as *he*. Charles Simeon identifies this rider as the Lord Jesus Christ, The Angel of the Covenant, who often appeared in Old Testament times in human form. This is the same person, Simeon says, who is later referred to as "the Man, that was Jehovah's fellow," or equal (Zechariah 13:7). Fausset refers to this angel who knows Jehovah's will, intercedes with Jehovah for Israel, and of whom Jehovah speaks (Zechariah 1:9), as "The Angel of Jehovah — The Second Person in the Godhead."

The messenger of Jehovah announces that after walking to and fro through the earth he found it at rest. This secure rest is the interceding Angel's plea for the desolate Temple and Judah, and calls forth Jehovah's great jealousy for Zion, so that He returns to her with mercies and with judgments on her heathen oppressor (Zechariah 1:14-17; Haggai 2:20-23). How different is the counterworking of Satan who "walks to and fro upon the earth" (Job 1:7), to hurt the saints and rob them of peace!

3. *The Myrtles. Myrtles,* not mentioned before the Babylonian Captivity, Nehemiah 8:15 (Esther's name Hadassah means "Myrtle"), represent the then depressed Jewish Church. Other interpretations are that the myrtles are symbols of the pious, or the Theocracy, or the land of Judah. The myrtles *in the hollow* represent the Lord's people in a low and debased state into which they had fallen. "The myrtle," says F. B. Meyer in his volume on *Zechariah,* "was significant of the return of the exiles from the lands of the north, and its humble beauty was an appropriate symbol of the depressed condition of the people, who could no longer be compared to the spread-cedar, or the deeply rooted oak, but were like the myrtle, which, though gracious and evergreen, is nevertheless an inconspicuous and unassuming plant."

A word of caution is necessary as we endeavor to interpret the various aspects of a vision or a parable. "We must not

expect to find something in the interpretation to correspond with each detail of the figurative representation: the setting must not be confounded with the gem." What is the "gem" of the parable before us? The people were conscious of the shady place but were not conscious of the Heavenly Watcher, even though He was unveiled. In the parable we have "a picture of Israel as she long has been, and still is, outcast from privilege and position, yet never forgotten by Jehovah, who declares His determination ultimately to return to her with mercies, and to restore her to favour."

Then let the World forbear their rage,
  The Church renounce her fear;
Israel must live through every age,
  And be the Almighty's care.

## The Parable of Horns and Smiths
### (Zechariah 1:18-21)

The second vision was full of consolation for the people to whom Zechariah ministered. "The good and comfortable words of the previous chapter are continued, like the long-drawn-out sweetness of a lullaby." The small group of returned exiles was filled with alarm as they thought of the mighty world-empires surrounding them. How could they cope with these powerful forces? This parable of the four horns supplies the answer.

*The horn* is the symbol of power and hostility and here represents the pride and power of the ravager and oppressor of the flock. Daniel speaks of the horn which made war with the saints, and overcame them. *Four,* reminding us of the cardinal points of the compass, indicate the heathen nations which destroyed the national unity of the Jews when they took them captive. There were foes all around determined to resist any renewal of national life — Chaldaea, Assyria and Samaria on the *north;* Egypt and Arabia on the *south;* Philistia on the west; Amnon and Moab on the *east.* Beyond these nations we can see the four great Gentile Monarchies which occupied, and still occupy, "The Time of the Gentiles" (Daniel 8:8; Haggai 2:6).

*The four carpenters* were four smiths or workmen, well able to deal with the *four horns*. These *smiths* (R.V.) symbolize instruments of Divine power for the destruction of alien power and the redemption of God's people. They were His destroyers of the nations seeking to destroy Judah and Israel. For Babylon, the carpenter, or smith, was Cyrus: for Persia, Alexander; for Greece, the Roman; for Rome, the Gaul. Very different from each other, very ruthless and unsparing — but very well adapted for their work.

This parable, then, has a way of saying that the ultimate overthrow of the enemies of the purpose of God is ensured. If in the previous parable, the chosen people were in a shady place, cast out, without influence or power among the nations, in this second parable we have the assurance of the deliverance from all oppression. God reigns, even when His people are temporarily vanquished. Commenting on this passage (Zechariah 1:20,21) C. H. Spurgeon says: "He who wants to open an oyster must not use a razor; for some works there needs less of daintiness and more of force; Providence does not find clerks or architects or gentlemen, to cut off horns, but carpenters. The work needs a man who, when he has work to do, puts his whole strength into it, and beats away with his hammer, or cuts through the wood that lies before him with might and main. Let us not fear for the cause of God; when the horns become too troublesome, the carpenter will be forthcoming to fray them."

In every age God has found His appropriate instruments of power: Martin Luther, Hugh Latimer, John Wesley, George Whitefield, D. L. Moody, Billy Graham. When the predestined hour strikes, God knows where His workmen are!

# The Parable of the Measuring Line
## (Zechariah 2:1-13)

It is natural enough for us to dream of what occupies our waking thoughts. Jerusalem was a city of blackened and broken walls and heaps of ruin. But national pride was aroused and surveyors would be active mapping out new streets and walls. The young man with his measuring line was therefore a fitting embodiment of the new spirit characterizing the Nation bent on rebuilding the ancient city. This third vision describes the prophetic realization of the fulfilment of the promise, "A line shall be stretched forth upon Jerusalem" (Zechariah 1:16). The *man* with the measuring line was not an *angel* as in a previous passage (Zechariah 1:8). This *man* had no message to deliver or mission to perform. He is a mere figure in the vision and was implicitly rebuked for his action. Some have supposed "this young man" to refer to Zechariah himself. Fausset says that he can be thought of as the Messiah, the coming Restorer (Ezekiel 40:3; 41:42).

The city's boundaries were not measurable, seeing its population was to spill over into the country (Zechariah 2:4). There was to be no limiting wall. The safety of a wide-open city was to consist in divine protection without, and divine indwelling within (Zechariah 2:5). Thus everyone was exhorted to hasten their return to the city whose safety and sanctity are in God alone (Zechariah 2:6-13).

"I, saith the Lord, will be unto her a wall of fire round about, And will be the glory in the midst of her."

Amid all their troubles and chastisements, God had not forgotten His people, and here He promises to shield them. "The unseen but almighty presence of God would be a bulwark on which all the powers of earth and hell would break to their own undoing." How safe we are in Him who has said that no weapon formed against us shall prosper!

Dr. F. B. Meyer says that this chapter closes with three appeals:
1. An appeal to the Exiles (vv. 6, 7).
2. An appeal to Zion (v. 10).
3. An appeal to all Flesh (v. 13).

## The Parable of Joshua the Priest
### (Zechariah 3; 6:9-15)

The three parable-visions already considered deal principally with the material side of Israel's tribulation and restoration. We now come to the first of five further visions, pre-eminently associated with Israel's moral and spiritual influence. The *Joshua* whom Zechariah saw was the then actual high priest, standing before the angel of the Lord but clothed in filthy garments. At Joshua's right hand stood Satan, his adversary, pleading against the cause which Joshua represented. But his filthy garments were removed and substituted for a fair mitre and rich apparel.

Those filthy garments symbolized the Nation's sins, as well as those of the high priest himself (Isaiah 4:4; 64:5). The change of garments pictures the restoration by moral cleansing to priestly position and function of access to God and meditation. The removal of sin is guaranteed, and the promise of still greater glory through *The Branch,* that is, The Messiah, is given (Zechariah 3:4,8; 13:1). From Ezra we learn that Joshua, or Jeshua, and 4,289 priests were among the exiles who returned with Zerubbabel from Babylon, and whose plight is described by Malachi. As a whole, the priests despised God's name. Without scruple they offered forbidden blemished offerings. The table of the Lord was polluted, and the routine of the Levitical service was a weariness. They turned aside from the Law and caused the people to disobey it (Malachi 2:5,6,9; Ezekiel 22:26).

Then it would seem as if the regulations for the maintenance of the priest-hood by the people had been neglected, seeing they lacked the robes, vessels and proper equipment required for the stately services of the House of God. Therefore, under such conditions, there was great propriety in Zechariah's vision of Joshua, the high priest, and his fellows. There was no mitre on Joshua's head, no insignia of his exalted office on his person, no clean, well-kept robes to clothe him. But Joshua and his fellow-priests, we are told, "are a sign." Parabolically, they represent all those who are priests unto God, called "to offer up spiritual sacrifices acceptable to God by Jesus Christ" (I Peter 2:5). As priests, are our garments clean?

Another person is introduced to us in the vision. While engaged in his priestly duties, Joshua felt as a criminal before the Angel, as the great Adversary accused him. Satan tried to accuse Joshua because of his attire of filthy garments. But the Lord rebuked Satan, and He is the only One qualified to do so. "Who shall lay anything to the charge of God's elect?" Joshua, the representative of the people both in guilt and in the pardon and promise, was a brand plucked from the fire, and all plucked out of the fire by God may never be cast back again into the fire by Satan.

Upon Joshua was laid a stone having "seven eyes" (Zechariah 3:9) which can represent "the seven spirits" (Revelation 1:4), or the all-embracing, and here, special providence of God (Zechariah 4:10). Ellicott remarks that "the expression, 'to put eyes upon,' is used in Jeremiah 39:12; 40:4, in the sense 'to protect,' 'to take care of.'" Christ is *The Stone* (Psalm 118:12; Isaiah 28:16; I Corinthians 3:11; I Peter 6:7), and as such a living Stone, not only attracts the eyes of His people (Zechariah 4:10; I Timothy 3:16), but emits from Himself all illumination. Contrast the "little horn" with "the eyes of a man" (Daniel 7:8). The close of the chapter is bright with the promise of Israel's birth as a nation in one day. When the Messiah, the coming

"Branch," in David's House is seen as the piercéd One, then full restoration will be experienced (Zechariah 13:1-9).

## The Parable of the Golden Candlestick

(Zechariah 4:1-14)

How fittingly this vision follows the previous one! In chapter 3 we have a parable setting forth the need and ground of cleansing and forgiveness. In this present chapter, we are taught that such restoration cannot be made effectual unless it is followed by constant supplies of the oil of the Spirit. As we look at Zechariah's visionary candlestick we find it differs from the actual one in the Tabernacle and the Temple in that it has "a bowl," "pipes," "olive trees," on each side of it, and two "golden spouts."

Continuing our study of Old Testament visions, it must be borne in mind that like the Parables of the New Testament they give a shadowy presentation of important truths. Frequently the full significance cannot be seen, yet invariably a clue is given us, whereby we may discern the true import of the vision or parable. Not infrequently an explanation is given by God Himself. We must content ourselves with an understanding of their main scope, without struggling to master every particular they contain. As Simeon puts it: "As in the Parables, there will be sometimes found circumstances, the precise drift of which is not easy to be explained: but an attention to the main scope of the whole will keep us from ever deviating far from the true interpretation."

A case in point is the vision before us which appears to be of difficult interpretation and perhaps to those who received the vision from Zechariah, somewhat inexplicable. But the design of this parable-vision is summarized for us in the words, "This is the word of the Lord unto Zerubbabel, saying, Not by might, nor by power, but by my Spirit, saith the Lord of Hosts"

(Zechariah 4:6). This declaration of the chief design of the vision, namely, that all is of God, reflects no inconsiderable light on every part of it. With this thought in mind, let us look at some of its parts.

*Gold.* We read of a candlestick, or lamp "all of gold," of "golden pipes" and "golden oil." Reckoned as the most precious metal, "gold" holds first place among the metals, and as used here indicates the worth, both to God and the World, of Israel as a witness to truth. As a Nation, God meant her to be all pure in doctrine and practice, precious and indestructible (Psalm 45:13). Alas, she allowed her gold to become as dross! God designed Israel and the Church to function as golden light-bearers, and therefore at once precious and luminous. Both are His peculiar inheritance, their members His jewels acquired by an immeasurable ransom and thus fitly symbolized as made of solid gold.

*The Candlestick.* The idea of this candlestick, or lampstand, or chandelier, was borrowed from the Tabernacle (Exodus 25:31; 27:21). The golden candlestick was placed in the Holy Place of the Tabernacle and of the Temple "before the Lord, as an everlasting statute for their generations on behalf of the children of Israel." The sanctuary *in which* the light shone before the Lord, was to be the center *from which* the same light was to shine before men. The mission of a candle, or lamp, is to shine for the benefit of others. The seven-branched candlestick flanked by two olive trees represents their light-bearing qualities, and both Israel and the Church were created by God to shine amid the darkness of the world, fed from a source outside themselves.

*The Oil.* Throughout Scripture, *oil* is an eloquent symbol of the fullness of the Holy Spirit, who alone is responsible for the out-shining of Christian character. In Him there is an inexhaustible supply of power and illumination. The direct application of oil in this parable is that it illustrates the anointing so necessary for cooperation with God in service. The Spirit would be communicated to Israel through King and Priest, and thus would shine in the darkness surrounding her.

*The Seven Lamps and the Seven Pipes.* The seven lamps, or branches, are in keeping with the pattern-candlestick of the Tabernacle, which were united in one stem (Exodus 25:32). In John's "candlestick" (Revelation 1:12), the seven branches are separate. "The Gentile Churches will not realize their unity till the Jewish Church as the stem unites all the lamps in one candlestick (Romans 11:16-24)." *Seven* being the number of perfection, here signifies perfection of united witness. John speaks of the "seven lamps," as "the seven Spirits of God" (Revelation 4:5). There are not seven distinct Holy Spirits — only One, who has a seven-fold, united manifestation (Isaiah 11:1-3).

"The seven pipes" were feeding tubes, seven apiece from the bowl to each lamp. Seven and seven, or forty-nine in all. "The greater the number of oil-feeding pipes, the brighter the light of the lamp." This aspect of the parable indicates the unlimited nature of the supply of oil. How inexhaustible is the supply of the Spirit, whose grace is ever sufficient.

*My Spirit.* The angel revealing the parable to the prophet, interpreted it as Zechariah asked, "What are these, my Lord?" and learned that all associated with the golden candlestick was a para-bolic-prophecy. Zerubbabel, whose mission it was to complete the restoration of the Temple, was told that it would not be by any merit or strength of his own or of Israel, but only by the Spirit of the Lord of Hosts that the "dead bones" of Israel would live, and the people be placed in their own land. Future restoration can only be effected by divine power (Hosea 1:7,11; Micah 4:11-13; Ezekiel 37:11-14). The un-

failing sources of oil assure the future temple's spiritual abundances (Zechariah 4:11-14). The reality of the new Temple will be the Spirit, and all obstacles in building it are removed by Him under whose supervision it stands (4:7-10).

"The great mountains" is figurative of the colossal difficulties created by the neighboring powers, besetting the building of the Temple (Matthew 21:21), but Zerubbabel was assured that he would be able to make the mountain a plain. Thus the King shouted a prayer of triumph, "Grace, grace unto it," meaning, May God's grace or favor rest on the House forever! Zerubbabel was thus exhorted not to despise the day of small things by keeping his eyes on the grandeur of the goal. Every mountain in his way must yield. Fausset suggests that antitypically, "the destroying mountain," Antichrist (Jeremiah 51:25; Daniel 2:34,35; Matthew 21:44; Isaiah 40:4; 49:11) must give place to "the stone cut out of the mountain without hands." Because of the *Oil,* the all-sufficient Source of life, God's small beginnings issue in great results. The law of the spiritual kingdom begins with the small and ends with the great. Israel began with one man, Abraham, but became a mighty nation. From the 125 gathered in the upper chamber at Jerusalem there developed the countless myriads forming the Church of the Living God.

*The Seven Eyes of the Lord.* What perfection of vision is His, from whom nothing is hid. God's eye was upon Zerubbabel in his task. The providential care of the Lord would be his (Zechariah 3:9), and because His providence extends over the whole earth, He was able to make all things and all nations work together for the good of His chosen people, Israel (Romans 8:28). Because God's eye was upon Zerubbabel and his work, he could expect God to support him with His favor.

*The Two Olive Trees . . . Branches.* Two important features are now incidentally introduced for the first time — the olive branches, or bunch of fruits on each olive-tree, and "the two golden pipes" or "spouts." What is implied is that on "each side of the golden bowl at the top of the candlestick was a golden spout turned upwards, into which the two clusters of olives poured their oil spontaneously, and from which the oil flowed into the bowl, and thence through the forty-nine pipes to the seven lamps." "The gold" stands for pure bright oil, gold-like liquor. "Out of themselves." Does not this phrase imply that ordinances and ministers are only channels of grace, not the grace itself? "The supply comes not from a dead resorvoir of oil, but through the olive trees fed by God" (Psalm 52:8; Romans 12:1). Man's power by itself can neither retard nor advance God's work. The real motive-power is God's mighty Spirit.

Lange in his *Commentary* suggests that these living trees from which oil was conveyed through tubes to feed the lamp represent the Kingship and Priesthood of the Lord Jesus Christ. By His sacrifice He procured the measureless grace of the Holy Spirit, and by His enthronement at the Father's right hand He has power to shed down the life-giving influence in mighty streams. The oil of grace cannot fail, just because the Lord Jesus is an eternal Priest and an eternal King. Other writers, applying the symbol of the candlestick to the Church of God, say that as the olive-tree is the producer of oil, so the dispensations of God in the Bible are the only sources from which divine truth is derived to men in perfect purity. Hence, the olive trees are fit symbols of the dispensations of the Law and the Gospel. As for "the pipes," they are the ordinances of religion, by which means continual supplies of oil are imparted to the Church, that her light may never be extinguished. The direct application of the two olive-trees and branches is associated with Joshua the High Priest, especially prominent in

chapter 3, and Zerubbabel the King, prominent in this chapter.

*The Two Anointed Ones.* The margin has this interesting interpretation— "two sons of oil" (Isaiah 5:1). Joshua, the religious ruler, and Zerubbabel, the civil ruler, must first be anointed with grace themselves, so as to be the instruments of furnishing it to others (I John 2:20,27). The imagery is carried over into the vision of the two witnesses (Revelation 11). Joshua and Zerubbabel "stand by the Lord of the whole earth" as God's appointed instruments, and through whom He causes His Spirit to flow to His people. In the preceding parable, Joshua, the *religious head* of the nation, was purified and accepted by God for service. Here, Zerubbabel, the *civil head,* receives the assurance of God's assistance in his work. In the last verse of this chapter the anointed priest and the anointed prince are mentioned together to indicate that by their joint efforts the prosperity of the Nation is to be brought about, a forecast of Him who, as God's anointed Priest and King, is coming to complete God's purpose for Israel, the Church and the world.

## The Parable of the Flying Scroll
### (Zechariah 5:1-4)

While there is something in favor of the view that the three parables in this chapter are essentially in three dissolving views, we deem it profitable to consider them separately. Once again Zechariah profits through the ministry of the angel-interpreter. The form of the flying scroll in the air is similar to the vision Ezekiel had (Ezekiel 2:9, 10). Comparing the visions of this chapter with previous ones, we note a change of emphasis. Those just considered were calculated to inspire joy, confidence and hope. But from sunshine we go to storm. The sweet assurance of divine forgiveness and help in chapters 3 and 4, gives way to judgment, sharp and terrible, with no ray of light to illuminate the darkness. From the *goodness* of God we go to His *severity;* from His long-suffering to His indignation, wrath and anguish (Romans 2:4-9).

The giant, dressed-skin, unrolled wallmap which Zechariah saw was *flying,* implying, perhaps, the swiftness of the execution of the portrayed judgment. The dimensions of the roll are impressive — 30 feet long and 15 feet wide — corresponding to the same measurements of the holy place of the Tabernacle, reared in the Wilderness, and also of the porch of Solomon's Temple. As the dimensions of the roll, or scroll, are parabolical, "we may regard them as indicating that the measure of the sanctuary is the measure of sin: that is, the sinner must not say, 'I am not worse than my neighbour,' but should measure his conduct by the standard of divine holiness" (Leviticus 11:44; Matthew 5:48).

Inscribed on each side of the scroll, slowly floating in mid-heaven, were the solemn curses of the Law—against the thief for stealing (the second command), and against the false swearer for perjury (the first command). Passing over the whole earth, or land of Israel, the flying roll was to remove sin by destroying sinners and their possessions. Having been instructed that God was prepared to be as a wall of fire about His people, and their glory in their midst, they are now made to realize what a solemn thing it was to have such a Holy, August Being near them who was as determined to purge out those who transgressed His Law, as He was to defend His people against their foes.

God's curse against sin, then, is before us in symbol, and it is His purpose to extirpate the fraudulent and perjurers (Malachi 3:5-8; Matthew 13:10). The effect of such a curse is presented in graphic, parabolic form. The roll, in its movement, hovered over and then settled down upon certain houses. It made no difference whether the houses were ornate and occupied by reputedly respectable people; the flying roll, directed in its movements by God, made no mistakes. The house it settled down upon indicated that its master was either a thief or a liar, and must be destroyed. Then the angel-interpreter describes those divine dealings with the house of those singled out, "It shall abide in the midst of his house, and shall consume it, with the timber thereof, and the stones thereof." The moment the curse-marked roll settled down on a house, its whole fabric commenced to rot. Similar destruction overtook the house of the leper. "There is a plague spread in the house; it is a fretting leprosy, it is unclean." The arrestive command, "Bring it forth, saith the Lord of Hosts," means to come forth from His holy presence — from His treasure house where all pre-ordained events are stored up. "Is it not laid up in store with me, and sealed up among my treasures? To me belongeth vengeance and recompence . . . the things that shall come upon them make haste" (Deuteronomy 32:34,35).

In his *Exposition of the Whole Bible,* Dr. G. Campbell Morgan gives us this excellent summary of the first parable in Zechariah 5: "The vision of the flying roll represents the principle of the law as it will be administered by Israel when she fulfills the true ideal. It must be considered as a sequence following the realization of those preceding. Israel, cleansed and anointed by the Spirit, becomes again a moral standard and influence among the peoples. The law is a curse on evil in action and in speech, not merely pronounced, but active. Thus while Israel in realization is to stand as priest, mediating, and as light-bearer, illuminating, she is also to affirm and apply the principle of law in the World."

# The Parable of the Woman and the Ephah

(Zechariah 5:5-11)

This further vision is closely allied to the previous one. After the application of the Law, we have a description of the results of such an enforcement. The flying roll and the flying ephah can be taken as *one* vision. The first prepares the way for what is carried out in the second. Emerging from the invisible into the visible, the angel-interpreter answers the question of the prophet, "What is it?" Zechariah's eyes saw "the ephah" and could easily identify it as such. What he wanted to know was its parabolic significance, which was what the angelic interpreter supplied.

We here have a more graphic symbol of the discovery and removal of sin. Those who had been revealed as being guilty of theft and perjury also made the *ephah* to represent falsification of measure, and the instrument of defrauding was to be made the instrument of their punishment. The *Ephah,* symbol of commerce, was a measuring basket slightly lighter than a bushel, and represented seven and a half gallons. "This is their resemblance." The Jews, known at that time as traders and constantly handling the Hebrew dry measure, were made to see themselves pictured by the ephah and the woman. "As in an ephah separated grains are all collected together, so will the individual sinners over the whole length and breadth of the land be brought into one confused heap" (Matthew 13:30).

The next features, namely: the woman sitting in the midst of the ephah and held down by a heavy leaden lid, develop the teaching of the parable and provide a climax. First, two classes of sinners are spoken of: thieves and perjurers. Then they are heaped into an indistinguishable mass. Now they are described as *one* woman, the personification of wickedness. How apt we are to place the leaden weight on the top of the ephah containing wickedness! Well, we may be successful in hiding sin from those nearest to us, but nothing is secret as far as God is concerned. "She was cast out of the midst of the ephah." The principle of wickedness, finding its last vantage ground in commerce, must be removed.

Further details are introduced to give greater distinctness to the parable. Zechariah saw two women with wind in their stork-like wings: Sin is personified by a *woman,* and the agents employed to punish and remove sin are consistent with the image — *women.* *Two* were necessary because one was not able to carry such a heavy load. As there were "two anointed ones" standing by the Lord as His ministers (Zechariah 4:14), so we have two winged women ready to execute His purposes. There may be a prophetical hint here of the coming Branch who will be able to remove man's sins in one day (Zechariah 3:8-9). This Branch, brought into the world by a woman without the agency of man, provided by His death a perfect remedy for sin.

These *two women* are viewed in different ways. Some writers see in them representatives of the Assyrians and Babylonians, God's instruments of removal, who carried away idolatry in the persons, respectively, of Israel and Judah. Others see in these two women who bore the ephah to the land of Shinar, the two-fold aspect of the colossal system characterizing Mystery Babylon in "The Great Tribulation," namely, its religious and its civil power (Revelation 17:3-5).

*Wings* denote velocity. The *stork* is a migratory bird with long, wide wings, and would have no difficulty covering the distance between Jerusalem and Babylon. *Wind* helps the rapid motion of wings, so the woman and the ephah are carried away, as far as the two women with stork-like wings can carry them. Thus God banishes sin from Israel (Isaiah 2:18; 4:4). Being "lifted up between heaven and earth" implies open execution of the judgment before the eyes of all. Wickedness may appear to be entrenched, but once God arises, it is not long in being removed. So as F. B. Meyer says, "Be encouraged by this vision! Lift up your eyes and see the stork-like wings, with favouring breeze bearing them forward as they speed to perform God's behest. If only you are willing, God will certainly free and deliver you."

The ephah was borne to a house in the land of Shinar — the place where mankind first organized a rebellion against God (Genesis 12:2). It was also the land of Jewish captivity. Babylonia, the capital of God-oppressed world-kingdoms, represents in general the seat of irreligion. "Set . . . upon her own base." Wickedness is to be fixed in its proper place. Cast out of Judah, wickedness shall for ever dwell with the antichristian apostates, of whom Babylon is the type, reaping the deserved fruit of their sin: Habershon suggests that the vision of the ephah corresponds in many ways with the Parable of the Leaven, and that "it represents the end of apostate Christendom, and the Parable of Matthew 13, the beginning of corrupt Christendom. The leaven of Matthew prepares for the 'wickedness' of Zechariah, for the evil permeates the kingdom of heaven in its earthward aspect, makes possible, and leads up to, the seeming triumph of Satan's counterfeit kingdom." The spirit of lawlessness, finding its own vantage ground, "is restricted in its operations and is compelled to occupy its own house in its own land on its own basis." But ultimately there will be no more sin.

## The Parable of the Four War Chariots
### (Zechariah 6:1-8)

Actually, this vision is an extension of the truth embodied in the previous vision of the Horns and Smiths (Zechariah 1:18-21), and provides us with a parable of protection and deliverance. Here we have "the final revelation of the method of the restored order. In the day of restoration the administrative forces of righteousness will be spiritual." Taking the vision as it came to Zechariah, we have, first of all, a repetition of the number —

*Four.* As already indicated, this is the earth-number referring to the four quarters of the horizon. The number may also mean universal judgments over-taking the four world-kingdoms of Daniel.

*Chariots.* These symbolize messengers of God's judgments patrolling the earth, executing the decrees of God upon Israel's enemies. Receiving orders from the Lord of heaven and earth, they fulfil their mission. Chariots were associated with war and so with judgment. Jamieson says of them that they "symbolise the various dispensations of Providence towards the Gentile nations which had been more or less brought into contact with Judea: especially in punishing Babylon . . . Chariots are the various changes wrought in nations, which, as swift heralds, announce to us what before we knew not."

*Two Mountains.* The four chariots went out from two mountains of brass. By the "two mountains" we can understand the Mount of Olives and Mount Zion, between which lies the Valley of Jehoshaphat, where the *Lord judges* (meaning of *Jehoshaphat*) the nations (Zechariah 2:10; Joel 3:2). The "two" may also correspond to the "two olive trees" (Zechariah 4:3), or to the "two horns" employed to execute God's purpose to punish the nations (Daniel 8:3,4). Represented as being of *brass* gives us a further evidence of judgment. Brass was the metal among the ancients signifying hard solidity and was figurative of the immovable and resistless firmness of God's people (Jeremiah 1:18), also of the immovable firmness of God's dwelling place, and where He has founded His kingdom. In turn we have the Four Horses, the color of which stand for the commission their hurrying drivers bore to the different nations, which before that time had ravaged God's people.

*Red Horses.* By "red" we understand "bay" (Zechariah 1:8; 6:7), or "powerful." The chariot, with its bay horse, went to and fro in the earth, on a general mission of patrol and defense. These strong horses complete the task already in part executed by the other three chariots who have stilled Babylon, Medo-Persia and Greece, namely, to punish finally the last great foe of Israel, the final form assumed by the fourth World-kingdom, Rome, which is to continue down to the second advent of Christ. Thus, these horses with their chariots "walk to and fro through the earth" counterworking Satan's "going to and fro in the earth" (Job 1:7; II Thessalonians 2:8,9; I Timothy 4:1), in connection with the last awful development of the fourth world-kingdom. Their "fleetness" is needed to counteract his restless activity; their *red* color implies the final great carnage (Ezekiel 39; Revelation 19:17-21).

*Black Horses.* "Black" is associated with defeat, despair, sorrow, famine, death (Revelation 6:5,6). It would seem as if both the *black* and the *white* horses went into the north country, where there were two powers to overcome — the remnant of the old Asshur, and Babylon and Medo-Persia. Theirs was a greater cruelty and guilt in respect to Judea. These "black horses" went to the "north country," or Babylon (Zechariah 1:15; 2:6). Primarily, they represent the terrible desolation with which Darius visited the nations in the fifth year of his reign (two years after this prophecy) for revolting.

*White Horses.* These symbolize the joyous victories and successes of a conquering people, before whom Babylon was laid low in the dust, a prophecy fulfilled in the rise of the third great world-wide Grecian Empire, under Alexander the Great.

*Grizzled Horses.* These piebald horses represent mixed experiences, partly disaster and partly prosperity, which would befall Egypt on the southern frontier of the Holy Land. Egypt was a long-standing foe of God's ancient people. A grizzled, or the four, *mixed* dispensations, though various in character to the Gentile nations, portended alike good to Israel.

*Four Spirits.* The "four chariots" were interpreted as being "the four spirits of the heavens" by the angel-interpreter. "Winds" are symbolic of the working of God's Spirit (Psalm 104:4; Jeremiah 49:36; Daniel 7:21; John 3:8). From Scripture we learn that heavenly spirits "stand before Jehovah" to receive His commands in heaven, and proceed with chariot speed to execute them on the four quarters of the earth (I Kings 22:19; II Kings 6:17; Job 2:1; Psalms 68:17; 104:4). All the revolutions in the World, says Calvin, are from the Spirit of God, and are, as it were, His messengers or spirits.

*Quieted my spirit.* Ellicott says that "spirit" is used in the sense of "wrath" (Judges 8:3). "To quiet wrath" (Ezekiel 5:12,13; 16:42; 24:13). God's anger is at rest (Ecclesiastes 10:4). Babylon alone of the four great world-kingdoms had in Zechariah's time been finally punished; therefore in its case alone does God now say His anger is satisfied; the others had as yet to expiate their sin; the fourth has still to do so.

The parable as a whole is comforting for our hearts because it clearly teaches that when sin is put away, God constitutes Himself our gracious Keeper. Once we are right with Him, tongues rising in judgment against us are condemned. No weapons turned against us can prosper. Safe within the precincts of God's Almighty guardianship, we can "dwell securely in the wilderness, and sleep in the woods."

## The Parable of the Crowns
(Zechariah 6:9-15)

In this further vision Zechariah is distinctly charged to observe an impressive parabolic ceremony. From Babylon.

where the best part of the Jewish nation still remained, a trio of Jews, Heddai, or Helem (Zechariah 6:14), Tobijah, and Jedaiah came to Jerusalem, bringing a present of gold and silver. This deputation was received and entertained by Josiah, or Hen, the son of Zephaniah. Zechariah was commanded to take the gold and silver and commission skilled workmen to fashion them into a crown, or crowns. Then there came the coronation, when the crown was placed on the fair mitre already set upon the high priest's head.

Ordinarily, the high priest did not wear a royal crown (II Samuel 12:30). The Levitical priesthood did not allow the same person to wear at once the crown of a king and the mitre of a high priest (Psalm 110:4; Hebrews 5:10). The two offices of king and priest, the sacerdotal and regal, were always kept jealously apart. When Uzziah as *king* attempted to undertake the ministry of a priest by burning incense upon the altar, he was smitten with leprosy. But here, in our parable, the crown was placed upon the mitre, a symbolic act, illustrating the combination of the two offices in the same individual. The divinely commissioned prophet makes it clear that the true priesthood and kingship are to be conferred on the Messiah, on whose head many crowns are to rest, one surmounting the other (Revelation 19:12)

The phrase, "the same day," is suggestive. As soon as the gifts of gold and silver were received, they were fashioned into a crown. No time was to be lost. In the double crown made from the gifts and set on Joshua's head, we have typified the gathering in of Israel's outcasts to Messiah hereafter, who shall then be recognized as the true King and Priest. Zechariah speaks of Him as a *man,* "Behold the Man." Pilate also unconsciously spoke of Jesus in this way (John 19:5). But the sense here is, "Behold in Joshua a remarkable shadowing forth of Messiah." Not being of the royal line of David, Joshua could not be

crowned as a king. Thus it was not for his own sake that he was crowned, but only in his *representative* character.

Before we pass on to consider Christ as Priest and King, let us think of Him as *The Branch* — a favorite designation of Him who was of David's royal line (Zechariah 3:3; Isaiah 4:2; Jeremiah 23:5; 33:15; Luke 1:78). His was a lowly and unlikely origin. He was a root out of dry ground (Isaiah 53:2). For thirty years He was unknown except as the reputed son of a carpenter. Some commentators speak of Him sprouting up from His place as meaning, a place peculiar to Him: not merely from Bethlehem of Nazareth, but by His own power, without man's aid, in His miraculous conception. Because men see Him only as a Branch, they reject Him. "The idea in a Branch is that Christ's glory is growing, not yet fully manifested as a full-grown tree. In the Millennium, He will be as a full-grown tree with multitudes sitting under His shadow with great delight, and finding His fruit sweet to their taste."

Halley says, "The 'Branch' was to be of Zerubbabel's (David's) family, the kingly line. But here Joshua, the Priest, is crowned, and is represented as the 'Branch' sitting on the throne of David (6:12-13), a symbolic merging of the two offices of King and Priest in the Coming Messiah." Two expressive phrases indicate the royal rule and priestly atonement of Christ, "He shall sit and rule upon His throne: He shall be a Priest upon His throne."

## PRIEST

Presently, He is our Great High Priest, interceding on our behalf (Hebrews 9:11; 10:21, etc.). As our merciful and faithful priest, appointed in things pertaining to God, He offered Himself as the Sacrifice for our sins, and ever lives to plead His efficacious blood on our behalf.

## KING

Although the Priest, Christ has ever been a King in His own right. He was born a King (Matthew 2:2). He came as "the King eternal." But His manifestation as the King of kings is yet future (Revelation 15:3; 17:14; 19:16). While on earth He was attested as "King of the Jews." Actually, then, in heaven, He is our Priest-King of whom Melchizedek is a type — "King of Salem, and Priest of the Most High God." Do we think sufficiently of Christ in this dual aspect? Is He our Prince as well as our Saviour? As Priest, Jesus pleads the merit of His precious blood; as King, He exercises His risen, glorified power on our behalf. As Priest, He pacifies the guilty conscience; as King, He sends thrills of His own victorious life into our spirits. As Priest, He brings us nigh to God; as King, He treads out enemies under His feet. He sits as Priest and King upon His throne. Because of His intrinsic dignity and finished mediatorial work He *sits*. When He returns to earth as its rightful Lord and King, then blessings will abound.

Between the two offices of Priest and King, there is a "counsel of peace." What exactly is implied by the prophet's phrase, "between them both"? Campbell Morgan says it means, "the resulting peace would accrue from the union of the kingly and priestly functions in the One Person." There is no conflict between the priestly and the regal. "Joshua and Zerubbabel," Jamieson comments, "the religious and civil authorities co-operating in the temple typify the *peace,* or harmonious union, *between* both the kingly and priestly offices. The kingly majesty shall not depress the priestly dignity, nor the priestly dignity the kingly majesty."

In His priestly office, Christ atones; in His kingly office He imparts the benefit of that atonement. No matter how meritorious the death of Christ as a sacrifice, such a sacrifice would not have availed on our behalf had He not risen again from the dead and ascended on high. We must never lose sight of the fundamental truth that men can only be saved as they accept by faith the death

*and* resurrection of Christ (Romans 10:9-10).

Twice over, it is affirmed that this Priest-King is to build the Temple of God. The crown, or crowns, which Joshua wore during the coronation ceremony were retained for a memorial in the Temple of the Lord, a memorial of the three donors who had formed the deputation and of Joshua's coronation, and to remind all of the Messiah, the promised anti-typical King-Priest. To the small band of returned exiles, who with sad hearts gaped upon their temple site strewn with ruins, the prophecy of Zechariah, as to the re-building of the temple must have come as a great stimulus.

The necessity of "obedience" must be noted. The completion of the re-building would be accomplished, if the Jews diligently on their part obeyed the Lord, which, alas, they failed to do. Further, disobedience and unbelief did not set aside God's gracious purpose as to Messiah's coming. The message before us is that His glory as Priest-King of Israel shall not be manifested to the Jews till they turn to Him with obedient penitence. Meantime, as a Nation, the Jews are cast away as "branches" until they be "grafted" in again on the Branch, and their own olive tree (Matthew 23:39; Romans 11:16-24). Presently, the spiritual Temple is rising by the Spirit, the Master Builder responsible for "God's Building" which is composed of regenerated Jews and Gentiles (See Zechariah 9:16-17).

# The Parable of Beauty and Bands
## (Zechariah 11:1-17)

This highly symbolic chapter describes some terrible visitation coming from the North, to distress and spoil the people. Because of the mixture of metaphors, expositors are not agreed as to whether the "shepherds" referred to are heathen or native rulers. If the chapter is read alongside of chapter 13, it presents remarkable foreshadowings of the Messiah's ministry among His flock to the chosen people, as well as among those other sheep which He spoke about (John 10:16). The first three verses describe a frightful storm sweeping down even the mighty cedars of Lebanon. Israel's doom is twice spoken of as "the flock of the slaughter."

Who were these three false shepherds the prophet describes? They are explained as being the Babylonian, Medo-Persian, and Macedonian Empires, each of which in turn exploited the Jews. Other interpretations of the three shepherds cut off in a month — the period being symbolical (Ezekiel 4:4-6; Daniel 9:24-27) — are the three Syro-Grecian Kings, Antiochus Epiphanes, Antiochus Eupator, and Demetrius I. Pusey in his commentary on *Zechariah* suggests that the three unpitying shepherds were "the priests, the judges and the lawyers" who, having delivered to the cross the Saviour, were all taken away, or cut off, in one month, Nisan A.D. 33.

In this second section of his prophecy (Zechariah 11:4-14), Zechariah in an acted parable describes divine judgment overtaking the hirelings who care nothing for the sheep. Ezekiel, as we have seen, wonderfully depicts the two kinds of shepherds: those that think only of themselves, and not the sheep: others that make the welfare of the sheep their first concern (Ezekiel 34). What a picture of Israel's history is etched for us! The seven-fold description of their condition under unfaithful shepherds is cited. They had become diseased, sick, broken, driven away, lost, scattered, wanderers (Ezekiel 34:4-6). But both Ezekiel and Zechariah forecast the time when Israel once more will be "the sheep of His pasture." When Christ was on earth, He saw the multitudes as "sheep having no shepherd," but when He returns to earth as the Messiah, He will search out, feed, and cause to lie down, His presently scattered sheep (Ezekiel 34:11-16). "The total fulfilment of the

entire prophecy (Zechariah 11), in view of its universal application, must lie at the end of time. In the vision, the past and the future, the Last Days, go hand in hand."

Acting as God's representative, Zechariah said, "I will feed the flock of slaughter, verily the poor of the flock" (11:7). Then the prophet performed a parabolic action, figuring thereby God's treatment of His people. They were to be fed in a strange way, with two staves, one called *Beauty* and the other *Bands,* both of which were broken, symbolizing the breaking of the Divine Covenant. These two staves set forth the gentle and wise rule of the shepherd — a club to beat back the beasts of prey: the crook, with which to reclaim any sheep entangled in a thicket or pit. To David, the rod and the staff represented God's perpetual attitude toward His sheep (Psalm 23).

*Beauty.* This first stick means "grace," suggestive of God's abundant grace or favor (Psalm 90:17). As a Nation, the Jews experienced peculiar *excellency* above other nations (Deuteronomy 4:7). They were the recipients of God's special manifestations (Psalm 147:19-20). For them, the glory of the temple was "the beauty of holiness" (Psalm 29:2; 90:17; II Chronicles 20:21).

The breaking of this first staff intimated that because of their sin, favors would be withdrawn from the people. The cutting asunder of the *Beauty* staff implied the setting aside of the outward excellencies and favors of the Jews as God's people. Through the centuries this solemn prophecy has been fulfilled in the scattering, persecution and martyrdom of millions of Jews.

*Bands.* The name of this second stick actually means *binders,* as the margin expresses it. The same is used of confederate *companies* (Psalm 119:61). The people of the East in making a confederacy, or union, often tie a cord or band as a symbol of the bond, and untie it when they dissolve the union. As used by Zechariah, *bands* signify the bond of brotherhood between Judah and Israel. The Divine Shepherd sought to join both sections of the nation in the *bonds* of a common faith and common laws, but they resisted His efforts (Zechariah 11:14).

God broke this stick, illustrating thereby a just retribution upon those with whom He had made a covenant. The nation was broken up into various parties, manifesting themselves in a terrible manner after Christ's rejection. The ruin of the privileged people was accelerated in the Roman war. The prophet foresaw this Roman victory as the result of their abandonment of the true Shepherd. The blessing of fraternal unity which Israel originally enjoyed by the favor of God is still withheld. But the day is coming when all Israel will be as one. Although presently scattered, the Jews are still His sheep, awaiting the re-gathering (Isaiah 40:9-11).

The divinely raised up shepherd and the idol shepherd provide a contrast in character. The first was the One who came as the Good Shepherd, but whom a false shepherd, sold for thirty pieces of silver. The *idol,* or useless shepherd, may refer to some ruler among the Jews themselves, who, after spoiling them, destroyed them (Daniel 9:27; 11:30-38). Fausset sees in this vain shepherd, the idolatrous and blasphemous claims of the Antichrist, who, in the Great Tribulation will seek to destroy the flock (II Thessalonians 2:4,8; Daniel 11:36; Revelation 13:5-6). But God's sword is to descend on His "arm," that is, on the instrument of tyranny toward the sheep (II Thessalonians 2:8).

As we leave Zechariah's parables, attention should be drawn to the three significant appellations the prophet uses of the Good Shepherd, who became the Great Shepherd, and is to return as the Chief Shepherd. He is referred to as *Shepherd, Man, Fellow.*

As the *Shepherd,* Jesus was wounded in the house of His friends, and then smitten by God (Zechariah 13:6-7). His *friends* were His own kinsmen who received Him not and sought His death. When the sword symbol of judicial power, the highest exercise of which is to take away the life of the condemned, (Psalm 17:3; Romans 13:4) awoke against Him, the stroke was God's act. He permitted the One He called, "*My* shepherd," to be judicially smitten for our sins (Isaiah 42:1; 53:4; 59:16).

As the *Man,* "a mighty man," one peculiar man in his noble ideal, we are introduced to His sinless humanity. Christ was made like unto us in all points, sin excepted. How we praise and adore Him as the Man, Christ Jesus.

As the *Fellow,* or associate, we have a further glimpse of Him. He was God's Fellow, or Equal, the One with whom He had had unbroken fellowship from the dateless past. Yet through grace, the Divine-Human, smitten Shepherd is *my* Fellow. Has He not made His abode with us, and does He not desire His own to be fully associated with Him in all His ways?

The book of Zechariah, then, is precious to the Christian, seeing it teems with Messianic flashes, mentioning literally many details of the life and labors of Christ. Among these foregleams we have:

His Atoning Death for the Removal of Sin (3:8-9; 13:1).

His Work as Builder of the House of God (6:12).

His Universal Reign as King and Priest (6:13; 9:10).

His Triumphal Entry into Jerusalem (9:9; Matthew 21:5; John 12:15).

His Betrayal by Judas (11:12; Matthew 27:9-10).

His Unmistakable Deity (12:8).

His Pierced Hands (12:10; 13:6; John 19:37).

His Death As the Good Shepherd (13:7; Matthew 26:31; Mark 14:27).

# The Parable of Christ's Advent

(Malachi 3:1-3,17; 4:2)

In keeping with Zechariah's prophecies of our Lord, we should consider those of Malachi, another prophet of the Restoration, and the last mentioned of the noble roll of Old Testament Spirit-inspired Prophets (I Peter 1:11). The Bible tells us nothing about the personal history of Malachi. From his prophecy, it would seem as if Malachi's mission was one of reformation following up the Restoration. "We should regard him as Nehemiah's coadjutor in his second reformation." As for his small book, it is made up of continual rebuke from beginning to end. As we look at it, it has the appearance of one single address, but as Ellicott expresses it, "Probably it is but a systematically arranged epitome of the various oral addresses of the prophet." Roughly there are six discernible sections, all more or less intimately connected with one another.

1. Rebuke of Israel for gross ingratitude (1:1-5)
2. Rebuke of, and decree against the priests (1:6-2:9)
3. Rebuke of the people for marrying and divorcing (2:10-16)
4. Rebuke of sceptics, and prophecy of Messiah (2:17-3:5)
5. Rebuke of people for withholding titles and offerings (3:6-12)
6. Rebuke of formalists and sceptics. References to Christ, Moses, and Elijah (3:13-4:6)

As to Malachi's style of writing, it lacks the poetic imagery of the writings of some of the other prophets. Yet the parabolic or symbolic element is not lacking. "When for the moment he removes his gaze from the dark present to look back on the glorious past, or to foretell the events of a more glorious future, he rises to a high degree of poetic diction" (Malachi 2:5,6; 3:1-5; 4:1-6). Malachi's scathing rebukes were delivered in artistic, yet trenchant terms, and at the same time forcible to a degree.

Nägelsbach, in his study of *Malachi* has this beautiful description of the prophet: "He is like a late evening which closes a long day, but he is at the same time the morning twilight, which bears in its womb a glorious day."

As Malachi's reformation and prophetic mission ended, there came a silence of some four hundred years, before another prophetic voice was heard, namely, John the Baptist, who came in the spirit and power of Elijah, as the messenger to prepare the way for the Messenger of the Covenant.

In this, our concluding study of Old Testament Parables, let us look at the parabolic references to Christ, with which Malachi provides us:

1. *The Messenger of the Covenant* (3:1).

Two messengers are referred to in this verse, one human, the other heavenly. Here Malachi reveals his fondness of making use of a word which carried with it a covert reference to his own name, which means *angelic,* or *my messenger.* The prophet calls the priest, the angel or messenger of the Lord (Malachi 2:7). The messenger sent of the Lord is the same one Isaiah prophesied of, who would prepare the way of the Lord in the wilderness (Isaiah 40:3). "From the nature of his mission, this messenger is proved to be identical with the 'Elijah' of chapter 4:3. These words had their first, if not their perfect fulfilment in John the Baptist" (Matthew 17:12).

The Messenger of the Covenant is a more august Person. He is the Lord, appearing suddenly in His temple, the One sent by the Lord of Hosts, God Himself. In the fulness of time Christ came as the *Messenger* of the Covenant, which His people had corrupted (Malachi 2:8), the ancient Covenant made with Abraham and Isaac (Isaiah 63:9; Galatians 4:16-17), the new Covenant embracing all (Jeremiah 31:31; Revelation 6:16, 17). As the Messenger, Christ's mission covers His two advents. As the Son of God, He was manifested in the flesh and came to His Temple (Luke 2:35), but was not recognized as the heaven-sent Messenger by the official upholders of the ancient Covenant (Matthew 21:12; 28:13).

How faithful Christ was as *The Messenger!* Truly, He was the Lord's messenger having the Lord's message! (Haggai 1:13). He never flattered the theocratic nation's prejudices, but subjected His hearers to the fiery test of His heart-searching messages (Matthew 3:10-12). And because the religious leaders were stung by His words, they never rested until they saw Him crucified. Thus He died, not for *doing* things, but for *saying* things. His *words,* not His *works,* sent Him to His bitter cross. Are we, as heralds, as faithful as Jesus was in His declaration of God-given words? (John 17).

2. *The Refiner and Purifier of Silver* (3:2,3).

In this figurative way we are reminded of the Lord's purging, sanctifying ministry. By the "Sons of Levi" we understand the priests, the sons and successors of Aaron (Exodus 6:16-20). Judgment must begin at the house of God (Jeremiah 25:29; Ezekiel 9:6; I Peter 4:17). "The process of refining and separating the godly from the ungodly beginning during Christ's stay on earth, going on ever since, and about to continue till the final separation (Matthew 3:12; 25:31-46). The refining process, whereby a third of the Jews is refined as silver of its dross, whilst two-thirds perish, is described" (Isaiah 1:25; Zechariah 13:8,9).

The three-fold attitude of the Refiner is full of parabolic teaching. First of all, we note that he sits: "He shall sit."

Because of the preciousness of the commodity he works with, the silversmith is in no hurry in the purification of the silver. He *sits* before the crucible, eyes fixed on the molten metal. Care is taken not to have the fire too hot. How long does he sit? He remains seated until his image is reflected in the glowing mass. Then, and not till then, he knows the silver is ready to be moulded.

"As a Refiner." This process is distinct from that of purifying, although the one is bound up with the other. Through the action of the fire the dross is separated from the silver which in its original condition as ore in the earth was impregnated with dross. But in the crucible, the separation process goes on, and the fierce heat changing the hard silver into a fluid, forces the dross out and up to the surface.

"As a Purifier." The silversmith functions as a *refiner* when, as he sits at the crucible watching both the fire and the metal, he uses a ladle to constantly skim the surface of the liquid metal as the dross appears. When *all* the dross has been separated and removed, then in the surface of the pure silver he can see his face.

Is it not in this two-fold way the Lord works, not only with the sons of Levi who, although the ministers of God needed purging of their depravity, but with us all? With patient love and unflinching justice He purifies His own. Untiringly He seeks to reveal and remove our sin. The purer the silver, the hotter the fire. Some of the greatest saints have been the most sorely tried. We may shrink from the furnace of trial, but our heavenly Refiner knows how to temper the fire. And, no matter what progress He makes in our sanctification, we shall not be thoroughly free from the dross of iniquity until we awake in His likeness. Then His face will be reflected in the silver, for we shall be like Him, and as His jewels, flash with a brilliance not our own. In that day we shall be His peculiar treasure, His special possession (Malachi 3:17; Exodus 19:5; Deuteronomy 7:6; 14:3; 26:18; Psalm 135:4; Titus 2:14; I Peter 2:9; see Ecclesiastes 2:8).

3. *The Sun of Righteousness with healing in His wings* (Malachi 4:2). All who fear the Lord, think upon His name, speak about Him among themselves (5:16), are those qualified to see the Lord in all His radiant glory. *The Sun* is the source of earth's light, life and

heat. The Moon simply reflects rays borrowed from the sun. The Lord God is the *Sun,* the Source of all supply. His true Church is the *Moon* reflecting His light (Revelation 12:1). Christ as *The Sun* gladdens the righteous (II Samuel 23:4; Psalm 84:11; Luke 1:78; John 1:9; 8:12; Ephesians 5:14). The full meridian splendor of our Sun will be manifested at His coming (II Peter 1:9).

But the qualifying term, "righteousness," must not be neglected. With the advent of the reign of righteousness, all outward unrighteousness will be scorched and wither away. Then the righteous shall by His righteousness "shine as the Sun in the Kingdom of the Father" (Matthew 13:43). Then we have this beautiful touch, "With healing in His wings" — wings being figurative for *rays. Wings* themselves imply the *winged swiftness* with which He will appear for the relief of His people (Malachi 3:1). But what healing for all of humanity's sores will be in the beams of this Sun when He appears (Psalm 103:3; Isaiah 50:10; 57:19). Then the curse upon the earth will be removed (Malachi 4:6). Are you not happy that the Bible ends on a different note to that of the end of the Old Testament? (Revelation 22:20,21).

Now that we have reached the end of our study of the Old Testament section, it is to be hoped that the reader has profited by the coverage offered. It may be felt that much more might have been cited on Old Testament Symbolism, which with New Testament figurative speech, presents striking proof of the marvelous unity of Scripture. The Levitical laws and institutions and ceremonials, such as the feasts, are laden with symbolic import. Old Testament characters, like Joseph, have a parabolic significance, as do the incidents relative to Israel's wilderness experiences. As we have already suggested, a perusal of Habershon's chapter on *Old Testament Symbolism* will serve as a guide to those who seek a fuller understanding of such a fascinating study. It is because the writer knows of no volume dealing with parabolic teaching in Scripture as a whole, that he believes this Old Testament section, unique in its conception, will prove of great value to all students of the sacred Word.

# SECTION TWO — NEW TESTAMENT PARABLES

# SECTION TWO — NEW TESTAMENT PARABLES

In contrast to the scarcity of expositional works on parabolical instruction in the Old Testament as a whole, the New Testament offers us a treasure house of spiritual wealth. For instance, alongside of *one* solitary volume, dealing more or less fully with Old Testament parables, I had before me, for reference, some *fifty* volumes on New Testament parables. Doubtless this more popular field of exposition is accounted for by the parables, parable germs, similes and figurative speech which abound in the New Testament.

However, the majority of volumes dealing with the parabolic element in the New Testament concentrate upon the parables uttered by our Lord, which are dealt with in varying numbers from twenty-five to seventy. It is felt by many writers that parables, in the stricter sense of this term in Christian Theology, number about thirty, which number Trench takes as being a fair and convenient summary. Thus, most expositors follow Trench in their individual treatment of this number. But as we shall find, thirty by no means offers a complete list of our Lord's fully-formed parables. Almost His entire oral ministry was cast in parabolic form. His was a unique aptness for figurative speech. Many of His sayings were cast in this mould. "Without a parable spake He not unto them."

Further, almost all published works on New Testament *Parables* concentrate upon those in the four gospels and state nothing regarding the presence of the symbolical in the epistles and the book of Revelation, all of which make a valuable contribution to the general scope of parabolic teaching in the Bible. Both Paul and John, doubtless inspired by Christ's genius in His use of parable, simile and metaphor, expressed truth in similar forms, as we hope to prove. We readily concede with William Arnot that — "As the Lord's people in ancient time dwelt alone, and were not reckoned among the nations, the Lord's parabolic teaching stands apart by itself, and cannot with propriety be associated with other specimens of metaphorical teaching. Logically, as well as spiritually, it is true, that 'never man spake like this man.' "

## Parables As Preaching Potential

The concluding chapter in Hillyer H. Straton's *Guide to the Parables of Jesus* deals with "Preaching and Teaching Parables," and is a chapter of practical value to all who minister the Word of Life. Says Dr. Straton, "Parables have always been a rich source for preaching but never more so than when we see them in their own milieu and do as Jesus did: make the parable speak to the situation that confronted him. . . . Men do not forget what Jesus said, because He was wise enough to couch it in a form that is the easiest and most surely recalled — that of the story. The modern preacher will do well to emulate Him. Men of the pulpit who most effectively have moved multitudes to make the Christian decision in all areas of life have been almost without exception those who have illuminated their message with what we today call effective illustrations. In the time of our Lord the illustrative method was the method of the parable."

Drs. William M. Taylor, and Charles E. Jefferson, who in turn gained distinction as pastors of the Broadway Tabernacle, New York, were wont every Sunday to preach one expository sermon and one topical sermon. Both preached on *The Parables,* and their sermons are embodied in *The Parables of Our Saviour* by the former preacher, and in *The Parables of Jesus* by the latter pastor. No wise preacher will neglect the same aspect of biblical material. He will find as he studies the methods of the Master Preacher that His parables reflected His attitude toward life, and that His was the same world in which men live and suffer and are tempted today. Then men were sordid in their ambitions, ignorant of religion, oppressed by social customs, and sinners under divine wrath, but they touched the heart of the Preacher. He never grouped men *en masse*. To Him, each poor unfortunate person appealed to His sympathy and help. His parables reveal His love for the individual, poor, ignorant and sinning, but competent to be saved.

A striking illustration of how the preacher can apply Christ's parables to modern life and living can be found in Dr. William Ward Ayer's small, compact study all preachers should possess, *Christ's Parables Today*. Here are Dr. Ayer's adaptations of the Parables to present day needs and situations. Christ's parables give the answer to many of our modern Christian problems.

*Christ's Pessimism Concerning the Present Age*
  The Parables of The Sower, The Wheat and The Tares, The Mustard Seed, and The Leaven.

*Christ's Optimism Concerning the Present Age*
  The Parables of The Treasure, The Pearl and The Dragnet.

*Shall the Church Trouble Itself With Society's Problems?*
  The Parable of The Good Samaritan.

*Handling God's Invested Wealth*
  The Parable of The Talents

*Riches Coupled With Folly*
  The Parable of The Rich Fool

*Wages and Hours*
  The Parable of The Laborer In The Vineyard

*Standing in a Crisis*
  The Parable of The House Built on a Rock

*Are You the Prodigal's Brother?*
  The Parable of The Prodigal Son
*Who Loves God The More?*
  The Parable of The Two Debtors
*How Prayer Prevails*
  The Parables of The Friend at Midnight and The Unjust Judge.

Dr. George A. Buttrick in *The Parables of Jesus* echoes a similar application. "In every age the parables prove their startling modernity. They are more recent than today's newspaper; for a newspaper follows the fashion, and a fashion because it has become a fashion has begun to die. The parables utter the eternal verities by which all fashions, the shifting moods of an indifferent society, are judged. They are as recent as present breathing, as vivid in their tang as the 'now' of immediate experience." The preacher, therefore, must handle the Parables for they are "spirit and they are life."

As the preacher uses the parables he will discover how fitting they are as the media of doctrinal teaching. As Arnot expresses it, "The parable is one of the many forms in which the innate analogy between the *material* and the *moral* may be, and has been practically applied." Arnot goes on to quote a foreign author: "The parable is not only something intermediate between history and doctrine; it is both history and doctrine — at once historical doctrine and doctrinal history. Hence its unchanging, ever fresh and younger charm. Yes, the parable is nature's own language in the human heart; hence its universal intelligibility, its, so to speak, permanent sweet scent, its healing balsam, its mighty power to win one to come again and to hear. In short, the parable is the voice of the people, and hence also the voice of God."

Parables must be studied in connection with the fuller exposition of divine truth, which Christ taught and inspired His apostles to teach. Pictorial illustrations and the more direct doctrinal statements of the Bible should go together for reciprocal elucidation and support. An instance of the use of the parables in this way is found in F. B. Drysdale's most profitable treatise, *Holiness in the Parables,* in which he shows that *Scriptural Holiness* impregnates the parables. Of this holiness, this most spiritual writer says,

It breathes in the Prophecy,
Thunders in the Law,
Murmurs in the Narrative,
Whispers in the Promises,
Supplicates in the Prayers,
Sparkles in the Poetry,
Resounds in the Songs,
Speaks in the Types,
Glows in the Imagery,
Voices in the Language,
Burns in the Spirit,
Challenges in the Parables.

*Parables on Prayer* give the preacher another theme upon which to dwell. Take, for example, the general teaching on this subject in Luke's gospel, which is the *Gospel* of *Prayer* and *Praise* and is therefore appropriate as being interwoven with examples of prayer running through narrative and parable. There are three contrasting parables on Prayer.

There is the prayer-parable directed against those who trusted in themselves and despised others (Luke 18:1-9). Here, our Lord teaches us that humility is the true spirit which should animate us as we approach Him. What a contrast He presented between the proud and self-righteous Pharisee and the humble and penitent Publican. "Both men went to the same place, at the same time, for the same purpose; both adopted the customary Jewish attitude of standing, both addressed God, and both spoke of themselves; but here all comparison and similarity ends." Wm. C. Procter goes on to say, "There was a striking contrast in the *manner* of their prayers, and a still more striking contrast in their *matter*. Then the result of their prayers was also correspondingly different."

There is the prayer-parable of the churlish friend in contrast to the kind, beneficent friend (Luke 11:5-10). God is the Friend who loveth at all times and sticketh closer than a brother (Proverbs 17:17; 18:24). The churlish friend, aroused from his slumbers, gave ungraciously enough, but all the more bountifully to avoid being troubled with a repetition of requests for bread. How different the Lord is who urges us to ask, seek and knock, and who in response "giveth to all men liberally, and upbraideth not" (James 1:5). He even delights in the frequency and fervency of His people's prayers.

There is the prayer-parable of the unjust judge (Luke 13:1-8) who had been appointed for the special purpose of hearing the cause of the poor and the oppressed, redressing their wrong, and relieving their wants (Deuteronomy 16:18-20; II Chronicles 19:5-7; Psalm 82:2-4). But our Lord depicts for us a judge who prostituted his position for he is represented as one who feared not God, neither regarded man. This unworthy judge turned a deaf ear to the needy widow. Poor woman, she was too poor to bribe him and too weak to compel him; but at last her importunity prevailed, and the judge granted her request, "lest she wear me out by her continual coming." How different "the judge of all the earth" is! (Genesis 18:25). There is no fear of Him perverting justice or failing to give the poor and the needy His special care (Job 8:3; 34:10,12; Psalms 10:14,18; 68:5). He is never weary with our prayers. Alas, we often weary Him with our sins!

Habershon tabulates examples of prayer in the parables in this way:

| | |
|---|---|
| Importunate prayer for others | — The Friend |
| A prayer that was no prayer | — The Pharisee |
| A justifying prayer | — The Publican |
| Asking amiss | — The Prodigal |
| A prayer composed but never uttered | — The Prodigal |

No prayer                      — The Elder
                                 Brother
Prayers that were too— Dives, False
late                           Professors,
                               The Foolish
                               Virgins.

Thus a number of parables illustrate different truths about prayer. Some are uttered in order to teach men how and when to pray; and others give examples of prayer — right and wrong prayers, earnest prayers and unavailing prayers.

Preachers will also find another large group of parables illustrating *Christian service,* with lessons varied and comprehensive. For instance, service must be rendered *in all places*: the Sower must sow in all parts of the field; the Messengers sent forth with the King's invitation must visit town and country, calling guests from the highways and hedges, streets and lanes of the city. Service is also necessary for *all sorts of people.* Travelers, beggars, lame and blind must be invited to the feast: the Steward must look after the needs of the whole household; the Light must shine for all to see. Service must be given *at all times:* the Faithful Servant must labor day and night and thus be ready for the Master's return; there must be labor at the eleventh hour as earlier in the day. Service is likewise associated with *all kinds of gifts:* the Man with the One Talent is expected to double it as those who have more talents; the Master has left to everyone his task. Service must be rendered to *the right Master:* the Husbandmen must do the work of the Vineyard well; the Wicked Laborers either keep the fruit of the vine for themselves, or neglect the vines.

Thus the immense diversity of service is represented by many parables and similes. We work for the same Master but the work is varied in character as this list reveals:

> *The Servant* scatters the Master's seed.
> *The Messenger* carries out His command.

*The Steward* looks after His property and household.
*The Porter* watches at His gate.
*The Husbandman* cares for His vine.
*The Trader* invests His money.
*The Reaper* gathers His harvest.
*The Field Laborer* ploughs His field.
*The Farm Laborer* feeds His herds.
*The Indoor Servant* serves in His house.
*The Outdoor Servant* serves in field, farm, city, vineyard and palace.

All service inspired by the Master will be rewarded according to His sovereign grace (Luke 12:37; 17:7-10).

Further subjects, taught in the parables and awaiting the preacher's treatment, are the *Word of God.* The purpose of the Parable of the Two Builders is that of *doing* the Word as well as *hearing* it. The Seed sown is God's Word. Several parables deal with a wrong attitude toward the Word. Much can be garnered for pulpit ministry from the results of hearing and doing, of hearing and understanding, of hearing and receiving, of hearing and keeping: also judgment upon rejecting, disobeying, neglecting and making light of the Word of God.

Then *joy* is another theme that may be dealt with. The parables reveal the secret of true joy. We have the Lord's joy as the Seeker and Finder (Matthew 13; Luke 15). There is joy over the fruitful branches (John 15); joy experienced by Sowers and Reapers alike (John 4:36-38); joy at the Bridegroom's voice; the Joy of the Lord; joy of the Angels.

A further perusal of the parables will reveal that three of them are connected with *Money,* or *Intrusted Goods* or *Property.* The Parable of *The Talents* shows that although distributions are unequal, if the use of same is equal, the reward will be equal (Matthew 25:14). The Parable of *The Pounds* proves that, where or so far as the distribution is equal, if the improvement is unequal, the measure of reward accords therewith (Luke 19:12-27). The Parable of *The Pence* carries the lesson that, where the opportunity has been lacking, if used when offered, the reward will be according to the fidelity in the use of such a given opportunity (Matthew 20:1-16). Together, these "three parables present God's method in distributing responsibility and reward for service; but, in each case the teaching is somewhat different, all together giving the complete truth."

Preaching from the parables will also include lessons on the subjects of —

*Consistency of Teaching and Practice* from the minor parables of New Cloth on Old Garment, New Wine and Old Bottles, Old and New Wine, Blind Leaders of the Blind, and Strong Man Keeping his Palace.

*The Need of Heart Purity* taught by the parables of The Empty House and Seven Demons, Things That Defile, and The Leaven of the Pharisees.

*The Duty of Vigilance* is illustrated by the parables of The Fig Tree and Summer and in The Porter Commanded to Watch. Of the thirty parables of our Lord (the number Trench, Arnot and others ascribe) about half are concerned with *Judgment* and present various phases of the Final Assize; the other half exhibit some aspect of *Love* and *Grace*.

As it may assist those who proclaim the Sacred Oracles to have a suggested list of themes which the Master Preacher Himself represented in figurative forms, we herewith append an interesting table:

| PRECEPTS | PARABLES | PORTIONS |
|---|---|---|
| The Gospel sent from God to save man | The Sower | Matthew 13:3 |
| Vindication of God's mercy | Lost Silver and Sheep | Luke 15:1 |
| Christ a sufferer | Jonah; broken bread | Matthew 12:39; Luke 22:19 |
| Christ the life and support of the Church | Woman in travail | John 16:21; John 12:24 |
|  | Grain in ground; Rock; Vine | Matthew 16:18; John 15:1 |
| Christ a Saviour | Temple; Water; Bread | John 2:19; 4:14; 6:35 |
|  | Door; Shepherd; Light | John 10:7, 13 |
|  | Physician; Serpent of Brass | Matthew 9; John 3 |
|  | The Resurrection and Life | John 11:25 |
| Christ in heaven | New wine; Providing mansions | Matthew 26; John 14 |
| The Church a blessing | Light of the World; Salt | Matthew 5 |
| The Church imperfect | Tares | Matthew 13 |
| The Church transferred | Unfaithful steward | Matthew 21 |
| The Church will become universal | Mustard seed | Matthew 13 |
| Satan dispossessed | Strong man armed | Matthew 12 |
| Man a sinner | The Sick | Matthew 9 |
| The Gospel rejected by impenitence, un- | The Two Sons | Matthew 21 |
| belief, compromise, and superficial faith | Two Masters | Matthew 6 |
|  | Seed on bad ground | Matthew 13 |
|  | The Ploughman | Luke 9 |
| Convictions lost | The Unclean Spirit | Matthew 12 |
| Invitations rejected | The Great Supper | Luke 14 |
| Hypocrisy, Ostentation | Sounding the trumpet | Matthew 6 |
| Hypocrisy, Censoriousness | Mote and Beam; Gnat and | Matthew 7; 23 |
|  | Camel; Cup and Platter |  |
| Hypocrisy, Scrupulousness, False and in- | Whited Tomb; Covered Grave | Matthew 23 |
| jurious pretensions |  |  |
| False teachers | Wolves in sheepskins; Blind | Matthew 7; 15 |
|  | leaders |  |
| Receiving the Gospel | Seed in good ground | Matthew 13 |
| Receiving great and difficult change | New birth; Strait gate | John 3; Luke 13 |
| Receiving forethought exercised | Laying up treasures; Builders | Matthew 6; 7 |
| Receiving forethought exercised | Housekeeper forewarned | Luke 12 |
| Receiving forethought exercised | King going to war, etc.; Unjust | Luke 14; 16 |
|  | Steward |  |
| Prizing the Salvation of God | The hidden treasure; the pearl | Matthew 13 |
| Returning home | The Lost Son | Luke 15 |
| Relationship of believer to Christ | The family of Christ | Matthew 12 |
| The service of Christ easy | The Yoke | Matthew 11 |
| Piety, progressive | The Leaven; Growing plant | Matthew 13; Mark 4 |
| Branches of piety: Humility | The Hired Labourers | Luke 17 |
| Branches of piety: Humility | The Humble Guest; Pharisee | Luke 14; 18 |
|  | and Publican |  |
| Love, self denial | Two Debtors; Offending Hand | Luke 7; Matthew 6 |
| Forgiveness, simplicity | Relentless Servant; the Sound | Matthew 18; 6 |
|  | Eye |  |
| Kindness | Good Samaritan; Benevolent | Luke 10; 14 |
|  | Host |  |
| Trust in Providence | Birds and Lilies | Matthew 6 |

| PRECEPTS | PARABLES | PORTIONS |
|---|---|---|
| Prayer importunate | The Friend; the Importunate Widow | Luke 11; 18 |
| Prudence and good sense | The Pearls: New Cloth and Wine | Matthew 7; 9 |
| Prudence and good sense | The Children of the Bride-chamber | Matthew 7; 9 |
| Confessors and martyrs | Sheep among Wolves; the Husbandman | Matthew 9; 22 |
| True ministers wanted | Instructed Scribe; Harvest | Matthew 10; 13 |
| Principles of action | The Tree recognized | Luke 6 |
| Actions betray character | Good and Bad Tree | Matthew 7 |
| Signs of the times | The Tree; the Lightning | Matthew 24 |
| World unreasonable | Children in Market-Place | Matthew 11 |
| Death ends probation | Dives and Lazarus; Rich Fool | Luke 16; 12 |
| Judgment, certainty of | Ax at root; Deluge | Matthew 3; 24 |
| Judgment, certainty of | Servant rioting | Matthew 24 |
| Judgment, day of discrimination | Drag-net; Sheep and Goats | Matthew 13; 25 |
| Judgment, day of discrimination | The Fan; Wedding Garment | Matthew 3; 22 |
| Judgment, day of discrimination | The Ten Virgins | Matthew 25 |
| Judgment, dreadful account | The Barren Figtree | Luke 13 |
| Judgment, dreadful account | The Buried Talent | Matthew 25 |
| Retribution; or rewards proportioned to merit | The Absent King | Luke 19 |

## Parables As Portraiture

A conspicuous feature of the parables is the portrait of Christ's character and work with which they provide us. Almost all of them describe Him in one or another of His various relationships. Habershon's chapter on *The Lord's Portrait of Himself in the Parables* is a most valuable contribution to the subject. This gifted teacher of the Word shows how many divine attributes are illustrated in the parables:

His *grace* and *mercy* in the Parable of the Debtors

His *patience* in the Parables of the Lost Sheep and Growing Seed

His *compassion* in the Parables of the Good Samaritan and the Debtors

His *power* and *majesty* in the Parables of the Pounds and Two Kings

His *greatness* and *liberality* in the Parable of the Marriage Supper

His *love* in the Parables of the Treasure, the Pearl, the Prodigal

His *care* in the Parables of the True Vine and the Good Shepherd

His *tenderness* and *pity* in the Parable of the Lost Sheep

His *longsuffering* in the Parables of the Husbandman and the Fig-tree

His *sovereignty* in the Parable of the Labourers in the Vineyard

His *strength* in the Parable of the Strong Man

His *faithfulness* in the Parable of the Good Shepherd

The following list, indicating the various relationships under which the Lord describes Himself and His Father, likewise suggests one way in which the parables naturally group themselves, and how one parable may represent different truths:

| PORTRAITS | PARABLES | PORTIONS |
|---|---|---|
| A King | The King and His Servants | Matthew 18:23-35 |
| A King | The Marriage Feast | Matthew 22:1-14 |
| A King | The Two Kings | Luke 14:31,32 |
| A Nobleman | The Pounds | Luke 19:12-27 |
| A Bridegroom | The Marriage Feast | Matthew 22:1-14 |
| A Bridegroom | The Ten Virgins | Matthew 25:1-13 |
| A Bridegroom | The Returning Bridegroom | Luke 12:35-48 |
| A Bridegroom | The Present Bridegroom | Matthew 9:15; Mark 2:19,20; Luke 5:34,35 |
| A Creditor | The Two Debtors | Luke 7:40-50 |
| A Creditor | The King and His Servants | Matthew 18:23-35 |
| A Judge | The Unjust Steward | Luke 16:1-13 |
| A Judge | The Adversary | Matthew 5:25,26; Luke 12:58,59 |
| A Judge | The Unjust Judge | Luke 18:1-8 |
| A Master | The Talents | Matthew 25:14-30 |
| A Master | The Pounds | Luke 19:12-27 |
| A Master | The Absent Lord | Luke 12:35-48 |
| A Master | The King and His Servants | Matthew 18:23-35 |
| A Master | The Marriage Feast | Matthew 22:1-14 |
| A Master | The Man on a Journey | Mark 13:32-37 |
| A Master | The Unjust Steward | Luke 16:1-13 |
| A Master | The Field Labourers | Luke 17:7-10 |

| PORTRAITS | PORTIONS | PARABLES |
|---|---|---|
| A Host | The Marriage Feast | Matthew 22:1-14 |
| A Host | The Great Supper | Luke 14:16-24 |
| A Sower | The Sower | Matthew 13:3-23; Mark 4:1-20; Luke 8:5-15 |
| A Sower | The Tares | Matthew 13:24-30; 36-43 |
| A Sower | The Mustard-Seed | Matthew 13:31,32 |
| A Sower | The Growing Seed | Mark 4:26-29 |
| An Owner of a vineyard | The Labourers | Matthew 20:1-16 |
| An Owner of a vineyard | The Father and His Sons | Matthew 21:28-31 |
| An Owner of a vineyard | The Wicked Husbandman | Matthew 21:33-46; Mark 12:1-12; Luke 20:9-19 |
| An Owner of a vineyard | The Fig-tree | Luke 13:6-9 |
| A Husbandman | The Fig-tree | Luke 13:6-9 |
| A Husbandman | The True Vine | John 15:1-8 |
| A Planter of trees | The Plants | Matthew 15:13 |
| A Shepherd | The Lost Sheep | Luke 15:3-7; Matthew 18:11-14 |
| A Shepherd | The Sheep in a Pit | Matthew 12:11,12 |
| A Shepherd | The Good Shepherd | John 10:1-30 |
| A Father | The Prodigal Son | Luke 15:11-32 |
| A Father | The Father and his Sons | Matthew 21:28-31 |
| A Samaritan | The Good Samaritan | Luke 10:30-37 |
| A Finder of Treasure | The Hidden Treasure | Matthew 13:44 |
| A Merchantman | The Pearl of Great Price | Matthew 13:45,46 |
| A Physician | The Physician | Matthew 9:12,13; Mark 2:17; Luke 5:31,32 |
| A Conqueror | The Strong Man | Matthew 12:25-29; Mark 3:27; Luke 11:17-22 |
| A Builder | "On this Rock" | Matthew 16:18 |
| A Rock | "On this Rock" | Matthew 16:18 |
| A Rock | The House on the Rock | Matthew 7:24-29; Luke 6:46-49 |
| A Corner Stone | The Husbandman | Matthew 21:42-44; Mark 12:10,11; Luke 20:17,18 |
| A Cloud and Shower | The Cloud | Matthew 16:1-4; Luke 12:54-56 |
| A Corn of Wheat | The Corn of Wheat | John 12:24 |

Then the parables present portraits of saints and sinners. Figures of speech are used to describe men in a corresponding variety of ways, sometimes associated with the saints, sometimes with sinners; sometimes of friends, sometimes of foes. While the following list is not complete, nevertheless it will serve as a guide to the use of figurative speech in the Bible.

| PORTRAITS | PARABLES | PORTIONS |
|---|---|---|
| As debtors | The Two Debtors | Luke 7:40-50 |
| As debtors | The King and his Servants | Matthew 18:23-35 |
| As debtors | The Adversary | Matthew 5:25,26; Luke 12:58,59 |
| As sons | The Two Sons | Matthew 21:28-31 |
| As sons | The Prodigal | Luke 15:11-32 |
| As guests | The Marriage Feast | Matthew 22:2-14 |
| As guests | The Great Supper | Luke 14:16-24 |
| As travelers | The Good Samaritan | Luke 10:30-37 |
| As travelers | The Blind Leaders of the Blind | Matthew 15:14 |
| As travelers | The Strait Gate | Matthew 7:13,14; Luke 13:24 |
| As virgins | The Ten Virgins | Matthew 25:1-13 |
| As keepers of a vineyard | The Husbandmen | Matthew 21:33-46; Mark 12:1-12; Luke 20:9-16 |
| As servants | The Talents | Matthew 25:14-30 |
| As servants | The Pounds | Luke 19:12-27 |
| As servants | The Absent Lord | Mark 13:34-37 |
| As servants | The Absent Lord | Luke 12:35-48 |
| As servants | The Marriage Feast | Matthew 22:1-14 |
| As servants | The Labourers in the Vineyard | Matthew 20:1-16 |
| As servants | The Field Labourers | Luke 17:7-10 |
| As servants | The Faithful Steward | Luke 12:42 |
| As servants | The Unjust Steward | Luke 16:1-13 |
| As a Householder | The Householder | Matthew 13:52 |
| As a rich man | The Rich Man and His Barns | Luke 12:16-21 |
| As a rich man and a beggar | The Rich Man and Lazarus | Luke 16:19-31 |
| As a king | The Two Kings | Luke 14:31,32 |
| As worshippers | The Pharisee and the Publican | Luke 18:9-14 |
| As builders | The Corner Stone | Matthew 22:42-44; Mark 12:10,11; Luke 20:17,18 |
| As builders | Houses on Rock and Sand | Matthew 7:24-29; Luke 6:46-49 |
| As builders | The Tower | Luke 14:28-30 |
| As dwelling-places | The Strong Man | Matthew 12:29; Mark 3:27; Luke 11:21,22 |
| As dwelling-places | The Unclean Spirit | Matthew 12:43-45; Luke 11:24-26 |
| As good and bad soil | The Sower | Matthew 13:3-23; Mark 4:3-20; Luke 8:5-15 |
| As good seed | The Growing Seed | Mark 4:26-29 |
| As wheat | The Corn of Wheat | John 12:24 |
| As wheat and tares | The Tares | Matthew 13:24-30; 36-43 |

| PORTRAITS | PORTIONS | PARABLES |
|---|---|---|
| As wheat and chaff | (By John the Baptist) | Matthew 3:12; Luke 3:17 |
| As plants | . . . | Matthew 15:13 |
| As trees | . . . | Matthew 7:16-20; Luke 4:43,44; Matthew 12:33 |
| As branches | The True Vine | John 15:1-8 |
| As a fig-tree | The Fig-tree | Luke 13:6-9 |
| As sheep | The Good Shepherd | John 10:1-30 |
| As sheep | The Lost Sheep | Luke 15:4-7; Matthew 18:12,13 |
| As sheep | The Sheep in a Pit | Matthew 12:11,12 |
| As sheep | The Sheep and the Goats | Matthew 25:31-46 |
| As fish | The Drag Net | Matthew 13:47-50 |
| As a piece of silver | The Lost Silver | Luke 15:8-10 |
| As a treasure | The Hidden Treasure | Matthew 13:44 |
| As a pearl | The Pearl of Great Price | Matthew 13:45,46 |
| As lights | The City Set on a Hill | Matthew 5:14 |
| As lights | The Candle | Matthew 4:15; Mark 4:21; Luke 8:16 |
| As salt | . . . | Matthew 5:13 |

Perhaps the most practical way of dealing with the parables is to read them for our own heart's sake. Although so many of them are full of prophetic teaching and are, as we have just seen, profiles of the Saviour and also of saints and sinners, it is most profitable to treat a parable as a mirror, reflecting what is lacking or unnecessary in our personal life. Applied to the individual for the development of Christian character and service, the parables become a most valuable media of revelation and encouragement. From such a repository of truth we can learn much for our personal enlightenment and edification. G. H. Hubbard in his treatise on *The Parables* says, "The value of a parable does not depend upon the new and varied truth that we are able to extort from it, but upon our progressive and practical application of its simple truth to our daily life." For instance, in reading the Parable of the Lighted Candle, one sees a portrait of himself as Christ means him to be, namely, a light shining, not in a secret place, but in an open, dark world. This parable forces the reader to ask the question of his or her own heart, "Am I a radiant Christian?"

## Parables According to Plan

Among expositors of the parables there is infinite variety as to their classification. Principal Salmond in his *Parables of Our Lord* says, "It is a question of great interest whether there is any such connection of principle, occasion, or subject in our Lord's parables as makes it possible to arrange them in groups. Many attempts have been made

to classify them according to likeness of subject or intention."

A Swiss scholar divides Christ's parables thus:

1. Those referring to the Kingdom of God in its preparatory existence under the Old Testament economy
2. Those referring to its realization in the Church, or in the new dispensation in its foundation and consummation
3. Those referring to the life of individual members in the Church

A similar plan divides the parables into these three classes:

1. Those treating of Messiah's reign in its origin and its progress, given about the middle of His ministry
2. Those treating of Messiah's Reign in its Consummation, given toward the close of His ministry
3. Intermediate Parables, given by Luke (13-19), and treating mainly of the individual

Siegfried Goebel's plan of the parables is:

1. The First Series of Parables at Capernaum
2. The Later Parables According to Luke
3. The Parables of the Last Period

Bauer arranges the parables in three divisions:

1) Dogmatic, 2) Moral, 3) Historic.

Still another plan groups the Parables thus:

1. *Theocratic* or *Didactic* parables, by which are meant those spoken by Jesus, as *Rabbi* or *Master* with disciples to instruct and train, and

including those in Matthew 13, with some others.

2. *Evangelic* parables, or parables of *grace,* those spoken by Jesus in the character of *Evangelist* preaching the Gospel to the poor, and including mainly those recorded by Luke.

3. *Prophetic* or *judicial* parables, those spoken by Jesus as *prophet* proclaiming the great truths of the moral government and judgment of God, including those like The Wicked Husbandman (Matthew 21:33-41) and The Barren Fig-tree (Luke 13:6-9).

Arnot speaks of insurmountable difficulties attending any attempt at rigid classification of the parables. Butterick's wise comment on any prescribed plan is worthy of note: "It is largely individual taste that must determine the arrangement of the parables. Any division will be open to attack, for a parable may have so many aspects of truth that it will leap over any fence of classification by which we may endeavor to confine it."

The chronological plan, if same could be determined, might be the best, but such a chronological order in which the parables were spoken is unknown. Matthew and Mark, for instance, arrange the parables each to subserve his own purpose. Thus, the *kingdom* parables of Matthew 13, and the three parables of Luke 15, with the words "lost and found" as their motif, illustrate the point.

As many of the reported parables are introduced with the phrase, "The Kingdom of God is like" (an introductory formula enabling us to apply these parables), it is certain that Jesus made use of these parables to illustrate what Mark calls "The mystery of the Kingdom of God" (Mark 4:11). Each of these parables contained some characteristic, or presented some feature of His Kingdom, which was not of this world, and therefore intensely distasteful to the carnal Jews of Christ's time.

The majority of expositors associate the parables with the Kingdom the King proclaimed. Some arrange them in two groups:

1. Parables dealing with the nature and development of the Kingdom of God
2. Parables dealing with the right conduct of members of the Kingdom

For the most part a three-fold plan is preferred:

1. Those which describe the Kingdom of Heaven as a divine force
2. Those which describe it as a Church founded by the divine forces of the Word of God
3. Those which describe the members of the kingdom in their disposition, walk and destiny.

The most complete and satisfactory plan of the parables we have encountered is that given by George A. Butterick in his most illuminating treatise published by Harper and Brothers, *The Parables of Jesus.* Of his grouping, Dr. Butterick says, "The arrangement suggested in this book is an attempt, undoubtedly vulnerable, to arrange the parables in approximate natural sequence . . . That the attempt is very fallible no one is more clearly aware than the author, who would be well content if his work should prove only one of those hidden stones which make the foundation of a bridge." Dr. Hillyer H. Straton, who in his volume on *A Guide to the Parables of Jesus* recognizes his indebtedness to Dr. Butterick's work, follows a plan closely resembling that of Dr. Butterick which is herewith cited:

# I. Parables of the Early Ministry

THE GOOD NEWS OF THE KINGDOM OF GOD

    I. THE CONFLICT OF NEW AND OLD

        a. The Parable of the Children of the Bridechamber

        b. The Parable of the New Patch and the Old Garment

## II. Parables of the Later Ministry

## III. Parables of the Passion Week

# THE PARABLES OF JOHN THE BAPTIST

The great importance of the coming and the ministry of John the Baptist cannot be too strongly emphasized. Dr. Campbell-Morgan in *The Crises of the Christ* remarks, "How important the personality of John was considered is seen by the manner in which Luke introduces him. One Roman Emperor, one Roman Governor, three Tetrarchs, and two High Priests are all made use of to mark the hour in which the Word came to John" (Luke 3:1). The pregnant phrase, *until John,* indicates that the advent of Christ's forerunner marked the beginning of a new era. With his appearance the former dispensation characterized by law and prophecy gave place to the present age notable for the proclamation of good tidings. Is it not to the Baptist that we are primarily indebted for practically all the major articles of the Christian faith? Are not the truths he published the foundation stones and pillars on which major Christian doctrine was subsequently built? Was it not John who first gave us the intimation of the pre-existence of Jesus in the statement, "For He was *before* me" (John 1:15; 3:28-31)? Further, it was John who first described Christ as "the Lamb of God" (John 1:29,36), thereby declaring His atoning work. Then John testified to Christ's deity in an equally surpassing phrase, "The Son of God" (John 1:34; 3:28-31). John preceded the Apostles and Christ Himself in the proclamation of the major doctrines of our faith, namely, The Deity, The Atonement, The Kingdom, Sin, Repentance, Baptism and the Confession of Faith. All these and other truths find their foreshadowing in the revelation granted to John.

The inclusive theme of both John and Christ was the two-aspect of the prophesied Kingdom which the prophets of old directed men's minds. "The God of the heavens shall set up a kingdom" (Daniel 2:44). All the prophets could do was to prophesy such a coming event. It was John's privilege to announce, "The kingdom of the heavens has drawn near" (Matthew 3:2). The two aspects and periods of this Kingdom, presented in many parabolic forms, were its outward feature in human affairs, and its inward aspect as a spiritual rule in the hearts of men — with the former waiting upon the realization of the latter. From John's day on, this dual aspect is before us in the rest of the New Testament. Thus it is doubtful whether any other Bible figure has exercised so unique an influence over the thought of Christendom as that of the Baptist. It is because he was first in the new, or transitional era, and first in importance, that John's ministry must be studied.

That Christ set His divine seal upon His forerunner is clearly evident from the ways He described John:

> "There is not a greater prophet than he" (Luke 7:28)
> "He is much more than a prophet"
> "He was a burning and a shining light"

Of no other individual have we such an intriguing narrative. For instance:

> God in His wisdom ordained that his conception should be supernatural (Luke 1:18)
>
> There were specific prophecies concerning his life and work (Luke 1:15-17; 76-9)
>
> His Spirit-filled father was authorized to describe his activities (Luke 1:76-79)
>
> Strict instructions were given as to his upbringing (Luke 1:80)
>
> His very name was divinely chosen for him (Luke 1:63)
>
> Items of his daily food and his clothing are given (Matthew 3:4; Mark 1:6).
>
> His period of effective service was short, possibly only six months.
>
> The Jewish rulers feared him and his words (John 22-23)
>
> His fame caused Herod to tremble (Matthew 14:2)
>
> Although martyred, his influence lived on (Matthew 16:13,14)

The baptism epic at Jordan wondrously transformed both the man and his ministry. After meeting Jesus face to face, John felt he was unworthy even to stoop down and touch Christ's sandal lace (Matthew 3:11). The scene at Jordan, when Christ received the benediction of heaven, made an indelible impression on John's mind, and the ensuing interview with Jesus influenced John and his message (John 1:26,27, 30). For such a message the Baptist

claimed divine authority, "He that *sent* me . . . *said* unto me." God appeared unto many Old Testament worthies from Abraham onward. But in what form He appeared to John we are not told. This we do know that he was conscious of a direct personal charge as a divinely ordained messenger and harbinger of Christ.

What presently concerns us is the dramatic, parabolic garb of John's affirmations. For some four hundred years the heavens had been silent, and suddenly John appears, and surpassing all previous prophets in the grasp of the superb majesty of his message, links himself on to Isaiah and Malachi as the fulfiller of their prophecies. His orders were explicit as is evident from the imagery he used to announce them. The double, striking pictures John employed, are worthy of reflection and understanding.

# The Parable of Valleys and Mountains
### (Luke 3:4-6; Isaiah 40:3)

John was fiercely opposed to the Jewish isolationist-view that, although the Jews were a privileged people, salvation was only for them. "*All* flesh," said John, "shall see the salvation of God." To Gentiles, as well as to Jews, there was to be granted repentance unto life (Acts 11:18). Thus in his pictorial proclamation, John envisaged a world under the King's control, not a favored nation. The Lamb of God who was to die, would, by His death, bear away the sin of the *world*. Knowing all about the terrible danger of the nation he represented, and the need of the world as a whole, John's call to repent was urgent, impetuous. All obstacles must be removed. Nothing must impede the journey of the King or block the march of God. Let us, then, examine the parabolic instruction regarding the straightness of the way (Matthew 3:3).

*Every valley shall be filled.* It is significant in no small degree that the first big obstacle John refers to is the unfilled valley, not the mountain. These unfilled valleys make it difficult for the King to reach us. What is the message behind the metaphorical language John uses? What may rationally be thought to be meant by valleys, mountains, hills, crooked things and rough ways? In dealing with symbolic and parabolic Scriptures we must not forget that parables may not run on all fours. In some parables there are disparities. For example, when Christ's coming is compared to a *thief,* He will not come as a godless thief unrighteously to rob and steal. Care must be taken not to strain incidentals of a parable beyond the analogy of faith.

The filling up of valleys can imply what God is willing to accomplish for poor, undone sinners who, like valleys, lay low under despondency of spirit. John's call to repentance meant that through God's free-grace, sinners could be taken from the dunghill and placed among princes. Under the curse, mankind is in low estate. Dead in sin, sinners are down and cannot rise. But God is able to raise the fallen. There is a sense in which *despair* can be a deep valley, but despair of any sufficiency in ourselves, of any worth, power, and strength of our own, is a holy despair. Such a valley of humility and self-abasement must never be filled up. Self-exaltation is abhorrent to God. "No flesh must glory in His presence" (I Corinthians 1:29). Valleys are filled up, or exalted when, as old Benjamin Keach puts it, sinners are lifted up:

"From a state of wrath to a state of grace

From a state of death to a state of life

From a state of condemnation to a state of justification.

From God's fearful curse, or curse of the law, to be blessed with all spiritual blessings in heavenly things in Jesus Christ.

From being the children of Satan, or children of wrath; to become the children of God, sons and daughters of God.

From under Satan's power, into the kingdom of God's dear Son

From being obnoxious to the wrath of God in hell, into heirship of eternal life, and eternal glory in Heaven."

The practical question is, Are there any unfilled valleys in your life and mine? How many souls has God *lost* because of these unfilled valleys?

*Every mountain and hill shall be brought low.* This further figure John uses probes even more deeply. What were these obstructions deliberately blocking the way of God? These mountains and hills had a definite application to the Pharisees of John's day. In their pride and superciliousness the Pharisees and lawyers "rejected the counsel of God against themselves," or "frustrated the counsel of God," as the margin has it (Luke 7:30). Pride has ever been the great obstacle in the path of God to human hearts. It seems almost incredible that man *can* obstruct God's efforts. "Strict and stern watch must be enforced against all forms of pride, arrogance, class spirit, haughtiness, snobbery and the superior air."

The haughtiness of the Pharisees is expressed in the confession of one of them, "God, I thank thee, I am not as other men." They boasted of their own righteousness, being ignorant of divine righteousness (Romans 10:3). Thinking themselves righteous, they despised others (Luke 18:9). Then they felt themselves to be like mountains in respect to their legal privileges as God's covenant people (John 8:33). They also boasted that they alone had the key of knowledge, and were therefore the *only* teachers and masters in Israel. But theirs was a carnal confidence (Romans 2:17-21), and the lofty thought of themselves had to be brought low (Isaiah 2:11-14). John's dynamic ministry brought down the mighty from their seat. Humiliation is the only way to exaltation (I Corinthians 1:26,27; Matthew 11:35; Philippians 2:9).

But there are other applications we can make of the mountains and hills. The Jews had to learn that they must be put on the same level with the Gentiles and made fellow-heirs to the same grace. Did not Christ, by His death, take away the legal covenant and covenant privileges, and make it possible for all who believe to be *one* in Him?

Then our personal sins and iniquities may appear to be mountainous, reaching up to heaven, calling for wrath and divine vengeance. But glory to God such a mountain can be leveled and thrown into the sea (Micah 7:19). What a mountain of guilt was ours! Yet it was brought low in our repentance, faith and justification (I Peter 2:24).

Proud monarchs may appear as mountains. "Who art thou, great mountain. Before Zerubbabel, thou shalt become a plain" (Zechariah 4:7). God knows how to divest the haughtiest monarch of all his power and kingdom, because it is by Him kings rule and should therefore live and act humbly. What shameful, humiliating ends proud, tyrannical dictators like Adolph Hitler and Benito Mussolini had!

*Mountains* may also apply to Satan and his evil hosts who, originally exalted on high, endeavored to be as God, but were deposed and exercised their diabolical reign over mankind. These satanic powers still rule in the children of disobedience. But Christ by His death and resurrection brought down these "cursed mountains and high hills," meaning that He divested them of all their power, rule and authority. It was for this purpose Christ was manifested (I John 3:8). He it was who spoiled these principalities and powers and triumphed over them (Colossians 2:15). Satan is under His feet. "By death He hath destroyed death, and him that hath the power of death" (Hebrews 2:14,15).

Other mountains and hills that must be leveled are those lofty imaginations and high thoughts magnifying themselves against the knowledge of God (II Corinthians 10). Wealth and wisdom make carnal men proud and haughty, and raised to a lofty pinnacle, the less fortunate are despised. Lowliness and humbleness of spirit receive God's commendation. "Let the brother of high degree rejoice, in that he is made low" (James 1:9,10). If the poorest saint has more grace, is most like Christ, he is lifted up higher than another who is rich in the world but who has not attained the degrees of humility. "When men are cast down, then thou shalt say, There is a lifting up; and he will save the humble person" (Job 22:29).

*The crooked things shall be made straight.* The religious hierarchy which John the Baptist encountered were crooked in many ways. Their road was not quite straight, therefore God could not travel to them. They were crooked as to their interpretation of the Law, the strict rule of which was, "He that doeth these things shall live in them." But the Scribes and Pharisees had a righteousness that was not even, or in a straight line, with the Law of God. As Benjamin Keach expresses it, "They were crooked, sometimes short on one hand, and wide on the other. For in many things they did not what the Law required, and in other things they did what the Law forbade, or commanded not; yet they thought their opinions and lives were more straight and even than others, when indeed they were more crooked." Christ came that their crooked opinions, principles and practices might be made straight, and those who believed were set straight, both in faith and practice by Him.

*Crooked things* may likewise apply to those ways of worship which Christ never instituted or appointed. All pretended ordinances not in accordance with the New Testament rule for worship, and administration of such ordinances, are crooked ways and must be made to conform to the divine rule.

Then there is crookedness of life and living. The will and Word of God form the only rule of life. Sin means missing the mark, erring from the divine line and plumb, transgression against God's Law; and so sinful ways are crooked ways. When Paul declared that the carnal mind is not "subject to the law of God, neither indeed can be" (Romans 8:7), he meant that as sinners we were born crooked and become more crooked by practice. It is Christ alone by the power of His Spirit who can make every part of our life lie straight and even with the divine will.

*Rough ways shall be made smooth.* It may seem a far cry from *mountains* to *rough ways,* but they all come within John's vision and are conceived by him as definite obstacles, causing the march of the King (in His haste to reach the souls of men) to slow up. Boulders, rough stones all partake of a hindering character and must be removed, so that the King will be unimpeded in His progress. Of old, God commanded the stumbling-blocks to be taken out of the way (Isaiah 57:14). He meant the way to Him to be smooth, plain, and easy, but the Pharisees were guilty of placing many obstacles in the way of man to God and of God to man. Is there not a pertinent message for our hearts in the call to make the rough places smooth? There may be nothing wrong in life — no valley to be filled up, no mountain to be razed, no crookedness to deal with. We are saved and well-established in the Christian life, yet we may have a roughness of disposition, a brusqueness which repels and makes approach difficult. Without thought, our words hurt and bruise. There is a sternness of manner, a forbidding unattractive something about us that prevents the King reaching others. Life lacks smoothness. There are bumps on the road. May the Lord, as the Restorer of paths, take from us those rough, obstructing features, so injurious to an effective witness!

The chief design in the leveling of mountains, the exalting of valleys, the straightening of crooked corners, and the smoothing out of rough roads is that all flesh might see the salvation of God and witness the revelation of His glory — the Glory of His love, justice, holiness, truth, grace and power. Christ came into the world to manifest the glorious attributes of the blessed Trinity.

# The Parable of Axes and Trees
## (Matthew 3:10)

Those who listened to John speak of sin in terms difficult to parallel must have thought of the stern language of Elijah and of other Old Testament prophets. Here the parabolic language of the Baptist is graphic and alarming for "the axe laid unto the *root* of the trees" is a sentence, indicating that the trees were already trembling to their farthest wings. Since the trees are condemned as fruitless, judgment begins to fall and would last till completed. One old commentator says of John the Baptist, "His ministry did burn as an oven, and left the Pharisees neither the root of Abraham's covenant, nor the branches of their own good works; he cutteth them off from the covenant of Abraham, and by cutting them off from the root, he leaveth them no ground to trust to."

The *root* of which John speaks, is that part on which the tree and branches stand and grow, and is parabolic of Abraham and of the covenant God made with him. It was this root or foundation to which the Jewish leaders laid claim when John confronted them. "We be Abraham's seed." By the *tree* we understand the seed of the stock of Abraham, according to the flesh. But, alas, the Jewish people became an "evil and corrupt tree" (Matthew 7:17) and must therefore be cut down. By the *axe* felling the tree, we have symbolized for us the instruments God used to deal with those who in spite of their Abrahamic rights and privileges, were fruitless trees (Psalm 17:14). God's Word, sharper than a two-edged sword, was the axe He used to hew down "the rotten, fruitless tree." "I have slain them by the words of My mouth" (Hosea 6:5). His truth is either a savor of life unto life, or of death unto death (II Corinthians 2:16). But in this fact we rest and rejoice that the axe is in the hands of a just God. In these days so conspicuous for much that is fruitless and rotten, God desires to make us His battle-axe and weapon of war (Jeremiah 51:20,24). Christ, the Stone cut of the mountains, is to be God's Axe to destroy the opposing powers standing in the way of the establishment of His Kingdom (Daniel 3:34, 44).

## The Parable of the Vipers and Their Offspring

(Matthew 3:7; Luke 3:7)

Such a condemnation does not make pleasant reading. What a figure of speech to use of men, and religious men at that — VIPERS! But as John used the phrase, "a generation of vipers," he was well aware of the innate hopeless character of those who tried to thwart the coming of the Kingdom. Hypocrisy was their cancerous root, and the only hope of their removal was a surgical operation, seeing they would not be warned to flee from coming wrath. In spite of their claim to be the offspring of a godly progenitor, John calls them the offspring of vipers. Says G. H. Lang, "They inherited a vicious spirit entirely useless, eminently dangerous, capable only of causing pain and death. They were the true descendants of their forefathers described by Isaiah (59:1-8)." How this term *vipers* must have stung those Scribes and Pharisees to the quick as they came to see John baptize! As *vipers* they were more related to that old serpent, the devil, than to Abraham.

## The Parable of the Fan and Winnowing

(Matthew 3:12)

This parabolic saying left no doubt on the minds of those who heard it as to what was impending. The Eastern mind would understand this picture of harvest time, with reapers winnowing the gathered wheat. With his shovel, the reaper throws against the steady, strong wind all that lies on the heap before him, wheat and chaff alike. The wheat being the heaviest falls back at or near the same spot, but the chaff being light is blown around on the threshing floor. The process of separation completed, the wheat is removed to the garner, and the useless chaff is set on fire. In order to appreciate the full significance of the expressive simile before us, let us look at it in sequence:

"Whose fan is in his hand" — the same divine hand wielded the axe. For the reaper, this fan was the instrument he used to cleanse or purge his wheat from the chaff and evil seeds. He engaged in this fanning process on his knees, tossing up and shaking to and fro wheat and chaff together, the action separating the one from the other. The fan Christ uses to purge His floor is His separating Word. "Now are ye clean through the Word I have spoken unto you" (John 15:3). Another fan is divine providence which often cleanses the wheat of its chaff. The Holy Spirit is another fan purging out the chaff of corruption (I Corinthians 6:11). Often persecution is another fan purifying the hearts of God's people (Matthew 13:20, 21).

*"He will thoroughly purge his floor."* By "his floor" John implied the Jewish people — a great heap, a mighty floor. On that floor little else but chaff could be found, for God's people had become a profane and ungodly generation. True, a little wheat could be found on His floor — sincere, godly souls like John's parents, or Simeon and Anna, who waited for Christ to come. The old floor, the ancient Jewish church, has gone. On the new floor of the Church of the living God, wheat made up of regenerated Jews and Gentiles may be found. "Gather his wheat into his garner." Wheat is a choice grain, the best grain, and it symbolizes that which Satan tried

to sift in Peter. True believers are likened unto wheat, because they are God's choice treasure (Psalm 16:3). Sometimes His spiritual wheat finds it hard to get rid of the clinging chaff. "When I would do good, evil is present with me" (Romans 7:21-24). The flailing of the wheat is necessary for its purification. Too often, we resist the flail in His hand as He seeks to remove inner corruption. When the wheat is thoroughly cleansed, the reaper brings it into his "garner" or a reaper where the wheat heaped up is safe and secure and may be carefully looked after. The Lord has a two-fold garner for His choice wheat. There is His Church appointed and prepared to receive His redeemed people. Provided for His spiritual wheat, chaff and tares are often found in it. Then Heaven may be looked upon as His other garner which will contain nothing but pure wheat. "There shall in no wise enter into it any thing that defileth" (Revelation 21:27).

"The chaff He will burn up with unquenchable fire." The religious yet unspiritual religious leaders receiving John's pointed message formed the chaff. Later on, Jesus called them "hypocrites" and worthless as chaff to Him. "What is the chaff unto the wheat, saith the Lord?" (Jeremiah 23:28). Chaff is light and airy and easily carried this way and the other by a slight wind. It was thus with the Scribes and Pharisees who made a show of religion but who, like chaff, lacked weight and substance. Chaff is the husks of wheat, and the religious professors of John's day had only the husks or shell of truth. They were taken up with the external part of religion rather than with its inner reality.

"Burning with unquenchable fire" is a dreadful figure of speech. This one fierce flash lights up the doom of the finally impenitent. It symbolizes the just wrath of God which is often compared to fire in the Bible (Psalm 8:8; 82:46; 90:3; Nahum 1:7). Wood, hay, stubble, chaff, are fit fuel for fire to sieze upon (Nahum 1:10). Divine wrath is like

fire — intolerable. How fearful the condition of those who fall under the just wrath and vengeance of God! A godless world needs to be reminded that the heavenly Reaper is coming and with His fan in His hand will purge the earth of its worthless chaff and gather its wheat into His millennial garner. "Thy kingdom come."

## The Parable of the Lamb and Its Load
### (John 1:29-36)

In the central theme of his witness, namely, the personality of the Lord Jesus Christ, John uses three expressive terms to describe Him: The Lamb of God, The Son of God, and The Bridegroom, and of all presentations of Christ to a ruined and lost world, these three have never been superceded. They indicate the Father's thought concerning the all-embracing work of His Son, and they came to the Baptist directly from God. "This is He of whom I spake." "This I have seen, and I have become a witness that He is the Son of God" (John 1:33, 34). The trinity of truth resident in these three designations is apparent: His atoning work as the Divine Lamb; His Deity as the Son of God; His advent for His own as the Bridegroom.

Twice over John speaks of Jesus as *the Lamb of God,* a description as unfathomable in its depth as it is crystal clear in its simplicity. Apart from the twenty-seven references to the figure of the Lamb in the *Book of Revelation,* it seldom occurs elsewhere in Scripture (Acts 8:32; Isaiah 53:7; I Peter 1:19). Dr. G. Campbell Morgan reminds us that, "the first time in the Bible when the word 'Lamb' is found is in connection with the sacrifice of Isaac . . . Coming up from the long gone centuries is heard the plaintive cry of the lad about to be bound on the altar, but 'where is the lamb for a burnt offering?' The first time that word occurs in the New Testament is where the last messenger of the great nation that had sprung from the loins of Abraham, through Isaac, announced to the multitudes of the children of Abraham, 'Behold the Lamb of God.' This is no mere accident. It is part of the great proof of the unity of the book. The Old Testament asks the question, 'Where is the Lamb?' The New Testament answers, 'Behold the Lamb.' "

In the fulness of time Christ came as God's Lamb, the sacrificial Lamb led to the slaughter. No wonder John calls us to "Behold" Him who came as God's gift to a sinful world, and as the expression of His heart's love. He was the Lamb without spot or blemish, and the innocent One, more innocent than any child, more loving, more gentle, and by the constraint of His love, more helpless than any other could be. What else can we do but join the constant refrain John the Apostle has given us: "Worthy is the Lamb that was slain" (Revelation 4:11; 5:2,9,12).

> Worthy the Lamb that died, they cry,
> To be exalted thus;
> Worthy the Lamb, our lips reply,
> For He was slain for us.

But the Baptist, in endeavoring to describe the indescribable not only reveals *who* bore the sin away, but *how* it was borne away. The tragic term, "sin," fully and adequately encompasses the problem of all time and all peoples. It is not *sins,* the fruit, but *sin,* the root, a word indicating a wrong state of mind or soul — sin, in its totality, covering and including all sins of every description, condition, and clime, excluding none. Then John's symbol indicates that God considers "sin" primarily as a "load or burden." He *bore* our sins in His own body on the tree. Then the divine method of removing the unbearable load is implied in the Baptist's message that "transformed him from the last of the prophets into the first and premier evangelist of Christendom." The load was lifted, carried, borne, taken away. The original for *beareth* means "to raise, lift up, take away, remove," and is so used twenty-five times in the New Testament. This, then, was John's conception of the coming atoning work of the One whose way

he prepared, namely, the taking away of the sinner's iniquity. Why continue being "heavy-laden" (Matthew 11:28), when He bore the load?

## The Parable of the Bridegroom and His Friends
### (John 3:29,30)

While it is true that to John, Christ's redemptive work takes priority, he yet had by divine revelation a wonderful insight into the character of the Messiah. He knew that He was *The Christ* although while in prison he seems to be offended with Him. Despair must have gripped the Baptist's heart when he asked, "Look we for *another?*" How consoling is His message, "Blessed is he, whosoever shall not be *offended* in me" (Matthew 11:6). John "did no miracle," but learning of the miraculous ministry of Jesus must have assured him of His Deity.

Here he speaks of Him as the *Bridegroom* and of himself as His "friend" rejoicing over the sound of the Bridegroom's voice. Is not this glimpse of the One of whom John said, "He must increase," a foregleam of the teaching of Paul and of John? Before the historical birth of the Church, John spoke of all those accepting Christ as His Bride. But who are the "friends" of the Bridegroom? Are they not the vast host of believers *before* the death of the Lamb, including John himself who accepted Him as the Sent-One of God? Did not Jesus say, "He that is least in the kingdom of heaven is greater than he"? (Matthew 11:11). The *greatness* here is positional, not moral. John announced the Kingdom, but it did not then come. John was martyred; the Kingdom was rejected, and the King crucified. Certainly John the Baptist, along with all the saints before him, will be in heaven, but not as part of the Bride brought into being as the result of the death of the Lamb.

The part of "the friend" was to seek for the bride and bring her to the bridegroom, as Abraham's servant sought out Rebekah and brought her to Isaac. Later on, Paul applied to himself the same appealing figure of a servant of God. Did he not cause the Corinthians to fall in love with Christ, and then present them to Him as *a pure virgin* (II Corin-thians 11:2,3)? Thus as Lang says, "As to service, John and Paul are 'friends of the bridegroom,' to bring the bride to Christ. As to position, they will be part of the company afterward shown as the heavenly Bride" (Revelation 19:7,8; 21:9).

# THE PARABLES OF OUR LORD

Jesus steps before us in the *Four Gospels* as the Master of Parables because He is the Master of Life. As Butterick so beautifully expresses it, "The parables are the characteristic messages of Jesus (Mark 4:34). They are His most remarkable message; for pictures are still etched in recollection when a homily has become a blur. They are His most persuasive message; a prosier teaching might not break our stubborn will, but the sight of the father running to welcome his wayward son leaves us defenseless utterly."

The parables of Jesus stand alone and defy comparison. *Aesop's Fables* and *The Canterbury Tales of Chaucer* pale into insignificance alongside the matchless stories of Him who remains the "unrivalled Teller of stories." If, as Hillyer Straton contends, that "one of the interesting things about the parabolic form of literature is its rarity, good parables are few and far between," our Lord certainly had no lack in this direction. None could, or can, vie with Him whose perception was so instant, His imagination so rich, and His discrimination so true. "From the standpoint of their reality to life the parables of Jesus are unsurpassed." His was the ability to employ every form and variety of figurative speech, from its simplest form to its widest elaboration.

Regarding the parables and similes, more or less expanded and more or less explained, while some thirty parables are cited as being actual parables, over one hundred figures of speech occur. As our Lord doubtless used many more, it is impossible to know how many parables He uttered. All of His discourses, so highly figurative, constitute beautiful and impressive exhibitions of truth. As already indicated, all His miracles have a hidden parabolic meaning, just as parables have a deeper than their literal significance. His parabolic teachings are generally introduced formerly by the phrase, "He spake a parable." Occasionally, the imagery of a parable is implied in a parabolic saying, not so called.

In our survey of Old Testament parables we saw that many of them had a plain meaning, but that in others it was not so. For example, in the Parable of the Ewe Lamb, David did not see the application till he had himself judged the culprit. Ahab and the escaped captive is another instance. These Old Testament symbols were intended to strike home an intended lesson by portraying in an objective way the stated evil. As some parables necessitate an expositor, Jesus acted thus and explained the meaning of some of His parables privately to His disciples for it was given unto them to know "the mysteries of the Kingdom" (Matthew 13:11). Other of His parables, however, were so pointed that they were understood even by His foes, which doubtless was His intention — they were laid bare in His presence.

Butterick suggests that our Lord's

gift of parabolic presentation found early use. "The life of His day poured through golden gateways into the city of His soul, there to be changed by a divine alchemy into matchless parables . . . If only we could have heard the stories He told in the Syrian dusk to the younger children in Mary's cottage!" It is evident from a study of His known parables that those thirty hidden years in Nazareth brought Him in contact with all kinds of people. He was intimately associated with human life, as well as with the political order of His time. Thus, when He entered upon His public ministry the "motley array of characters" He had encountered and vivid scenery He knew so well were "wrought into unforgettable stories — each parable with lines as sharp as an etching."

As to the order in which Christ's parables should be studied, attempts have been made to set them forth in chronological order. This is a difficult task, however, because of the uncertainty when several of them were delivered. Then, again, they have been grouped together, as we have indicated, around various themes. Here the student can compare the systematic order of the parables with the tables given by Butterick and Straton. Many of the kindom-parables have been classified according to the moral lessons they enforced. Thus Pierson groups them in this way:

*Five* specially set forth the divine character and attributes

*Eight,* the history of the Kingdom in this present age

*Nine,* the responsibility of stewardship

*Nine* more, the importance of obedience as a habit of heart

*Six,* the beauty of forgiveness and unselfish love

*Four,* the need of perpetual watchfulness

*Three,* the importance of consistency in teaching and conduct

*Three* others, of humility and importunity in prayer

*One,* of humility in all relations to God

Feeling that it is more profitable for the preacher and reader to consider all the parables and parabolic illustrations of Jesus as recorded in the *four gospels* in the sequence in which they occur, we are now to journey from Matthew to John accordingly. There are those expositors who divide the parables into two groups—those commonly regarded as parables, as, for instance, The Sower; and illustrations or figures of speech having a parabolic value. The latter are what we might call minor parables, parables of second rank and not so full and prominent as those which are usually included in the first list. As will be seen, we brought parables and parable-germs together, and set them forth as they appear in the sacred record of Him into whose lips, grace was poured.

## The Parable of Fish and Fishers
### (Matthew 4:19; Mark 1:17; Luke 5:10)

When a parable occurs in more than one gospel, it is essential to compare the corresponding records. The parable before us, as with almost all the parables, teaches us that in the spiritual world there are counterparts to all that is legitimate in the natural world. In spite of the fact that our Lord spent a large part of His ministry around the borders of the Sea of Galilee and that the majority of His apostolate were fishermen, it seems singular that so little use was made of parables upon fishery. As Jesus entered upon His brief yet wonderful task, He realized the necessity of those who would be able to imbibe His message and continue His ministry after His ascension, as well as accompany Him in His journeyings while among men. For His original band of followers and associates, He did not go to any rabbinical school or center of learning but called humble fishermen to leave their nets and follow Him. "I will make you fishers of men." Thus they were raised from a lower to a higher fishing, as David was called from feeding sheep to a higher feeding (Psalm 78:70-72).

The response of the quartette of fishermen to the call of Christ was immediate, for they left their nets, ships and relatives to accompany Christ. Now they were to ply the gospel net in the sea of the world, and land souls on the shores of salvation. We can imagine how Peter, "The Big Fisherman" who became the spokesman of the apostolic band, entered into the significance of the Master's parabolic use of fishers and fish. Fish on the Galilean Sea were caught alive but quickly died when taken from their natural element. Now, these whom Jesus called were to catch men who were *dead* — dead in trespasses and sins — and once in the gospel net they would begin to live spiritually.

Expert fishermen lay down three rules for successful fishing, which must be observed by all who fish for the souls of men:

> The first rule is — *Keep yourself out of sight.*
>
> The second rule is — *Keep yourself further out of sight.*
>
> The third rule is — *Keep yourself still further out of sight.*

Soul-winners must learn that they cannot make much of Christ and of themselves at the same time. If a fisherman casts his shadow over the water where the fish are, he cannot expect to catch them. In like manner, the shadow of self is disastrous to the art of winning souls. When Dr. J. H. Jowett was about to speak at a large gathering, an earnest brother prayed, "We thank Thee, O Lord, for Thy dear servant, and for the work he is doing. We thank Thee for sending him to speak to us. Now, Lord, blot him out, blot him out."

Then, for fishermen, bait is an all-important item, and through practice the fisherman comes to learn what bait to use to attract different kinds of fish. Fishers of men must likewise be able to bait the hook. A curious view expressed by the Early Fathers was that the cross was the hook and Christ the bait by which the Almighty captured the devil. Such a figure of speech may seem grotesque, but with all reverence we can say that Christ, as the Bible reveals Him, is always the right kind of bait to catch men. John Bunyan in parabolic language expressed it thus: "Grace and glory are the bait of the Gospel; milk and honey was the bait that drew six hundred thousand out of Egypt." No matter what difficulties sinners may present when being dealt with by the soul-winner, who is efficient in the Word of God, he will know that Scripture bait to use to meet any problem.

As this calling of Peter, Andrew, James and John is sometimes confused with two other sea accounts, a word is necessary as to the difference between them. The *call* in John 1:35-42 was not the same as here in Matthew 4:18-22, for the following reasons:

1. The former was given while Jesus was yet in Judea — the latter, after His return to Galilee.

2. In the former Andrew solicits an interview with Christ — in the latter, Christ calls Andrew.

3. In the former Andrew having been called, with an unnamed disciple, who was clearly the beloved disciple (John 1:40), goes and fetches Peter his brother to Christ, who then calls him — in the latter, Andrew and Peter are called together.

4. In the former John is called along with Andrew, after having at their own request had an interview with Jesus; no mention being made of James, whose call, if it then took place, would not likely have been passed over by his own brother — in the former John is called along with James his brother.

Then we have a further *call* in Luke 5:1-11, which is also different from the one in Matthew 4:18-22. In the former a miracle was performed; in the latter, there is no miracle save the miracle of grace as exhibited in the taking of fallible men by the infallible Christ to be His co-workers. In the former, all four are called together; in the latter, the four are called, separately, in pairs. In the former, the nets have been used for a miraculous haul; in the latter, the one pair are casting their net, the others are mending theirs. In the former, we have an advanced stage of our Lord's earthly ministry and some popular enthusiasm. In the latter, there had been no public appearance in Galilee, hence, the lack of multitudes lying upon Him. While walking alone by the shores of the lake, Jesus accosts two pairs of fishermen, and calls them to be fashioned into soul-winners. "Follow Me, and I will *make* you." There are no self-made Christians or Christian workers in Christ's service, they are all *Christ made*.

## The Parable of Salt and Its Savour
(Matthew 5:13; Mark 9:50; Luke 14:34,35)

This parable (along with the next we shall consider on *Light*) form a parallel pair seeing that they both deal with Christian witness and influence. *Salt* arrests corruption; *Light* dispels darkness. There is a distinction and difference, yet the figures merge into one thought, "Salt of the earth . . . light of the world." "That both are needed is a revelation of the moral and spiritual state of the world." Our Lord had given utterances to those wonderful, authoritative Beautitudes of His; now He proceeds to illustrate the influences the subjects of His Kingdom must exert.

*Salt* — what is it? Dr. G. Campbell Morgan dealing with its value says, "Salt is not antiseptic, but aseptic. *Antiseptic* is something which is against poison and which tends to its cure. *Aseptic* is something which is devoid of

poison in itself. Salt never cures corruption. It prevents the spread of corruption. If meat is tainted and corrupt, salt will not make it untainted and pure. But salt in its neighbourhood will prevent the spread of corruption to that which otherwise would become tainted." The meaning of the parable is evident. The Lord expects His own to function as a moral, spiritual influence, preventing the spread of sin's corruptive forces. Living near to Him, the Source of untainted holiness, we are to give goodness its opportunity. He alone can deal with the corruption, but as His *salt* we are to hold in check all that is antagonistic to His holy nature and will.

Although salt is beneficial, it can lose its savour or "tang," as the Scotch express it. Once this pungent power goes, the salt is "good for nothing," as Jesus, who often mentioned *salt* in His figurative utterances, stated. Naturalists tell us that if salt, which has lost its savour, is thrown out upon fields, it will cause barrenness. While saints can never lose their *soul,* they can lose their *savour*. They can become unsavoury in life, and exhibit decay in grace and piety. And savourless, their influence is lost over an unsavoury world. Christians who put up with the corruption around them add to the festering corruption of humanity. May grace be ours to have a life, as well as lips, always with grace seasoned with salt! (Colossians 4:6). Lot should have been the salt of Sodom, but somehow his "salt" lost its saline, preservative property. As for Lot's wife, for not being savoury, or for looking back, seeing Sodom was in her heart, she was turned into a pillar of salt, as a warning against identification with the world.

## The Parable of Light and a City
(Matthew 5:14-16)

In this portion, our Lord employs two figures of speech as He continues to illustrate the influence His own should exert in the world. "A lamp . . . on a stand." "A city set on a hill." The city, built on an eminent position, is seen by many eyes over a wide area and represents illumination of vast distances. Here we have our corporate relationship and responsibility. As "the City of God" (Revelation 21:1-3), the Church must be bound together in love, friendship and service in the reaching of those in darkness in the regions beyond.

Then we have the figure of a shining lamp illuminating all within the home and the world. All the loving, obedient subjects of the King are to radiate a spiritual revelation to all around. A light shows us the way to be trodden; and by life and example Christians are to show the way back to God. There is no contradiction between *salt* and *light*. Both symbols refer to a moral quality of things. The world is corrupt and its iniquity needs the saints as salt. The world is also blind and dark, and its ignorance requires the saints as lights.

*Light* is of a three-fold nature: natural, artificial, and spiritual. The light of the sun is natural; that of a lamp, artificial; that of the Word and of those who believe it, is spiritual. "The light of the glorious gospel" (II Corinthians 4:4,6; Psalm 119:105). The word Christ used to describe His own is not "lights" as the A.V. has it, but *luminaries* (Philippians 2:15). How wonderful it is of the Master to give us the distinctive title He appropriates to Himself. "I am the Light of the World" (John 1:4,9; 3:19; 8:12; 9:5; 12:35, 36). His is no borrowed, reflected light. As the Eternal Son, His is an eternal, uncreated light. Not only does He give light to the Gentiles (Malachi 4:2), He *is* Light. The moon is a luminary, but has no light of its own. What it receives from the sun, it reflects on the world. As luminaries, we have no light of our own. "What hast thou, thou didst not receive?" As His disciples we can only shine with His light. In virtue

of being His, and having the Spirit of Light indwelling us, and having the same mind as Christ, we function as burning and shining lights in our day (John 5:35).

A lamp or candle is a dark body and can give no light until it is lighted. Likewise we can give no light until we have received divine grace and enlightenment from the Spirit of God. Once lighted, we are to shine and not hide our light under a bushel or a bed. If the bushel represents trade, commerce, work, and the bed, rest and ease, then we must be careful lest our business or leisure occupy too much of our thought and time and dim the light of our witness thereby. Alexander Maclaren once said, "No man lights a lamp and puts it under a bushel. If he did, what would happen? Either the bushel would put out the light, or the light would set the bushel on fire!" Surely, this is at the heart of our Lord's teaching here.

Once again comparing the figures of *salt* and *light,* expressing as they do the dual function of Christians, namely, their sanctifying and enlightening influence on others, there is a distinction to note. "Salt operates *internally,* in the mass with which it comes in contact: the sunlight operates *externally,* irradiating all that it reaches," says Fausset. "Hence Christians are warily styled 'the salt of the *earth*' — with reference to the masses of mankind with whom they are expected to mix; but 'the light of the *world*' — with reference to the vast and variegated surface which feels its fructifying and gladdening radiance." Thus our Lord ends with the exhortation to let our light shine, a light reflected in good works and resulting in the glory of God. Can we say that our lives as "lights" are helping to glorify the Father for His redeeming and transforming power; and that by our sanctified and enlightened hearts we are impressing those around, at home and abroad, with the reality of His redemptive and transforming grace and power?

## The Parables of Moths and Thieves

(Matthew 6:19-20)

Actually, in this, a further double parable, there are three illustrations: The moth, rust, and thieves, each with its own distinctive feature. Our Lord was not guilty of mixing metaphors. All three merge into one lesson, namely, the utter futility of an earth-centered life. The same truth is made more impressive in this three-fold parable. We are not to hoard up our treasures on earth, but provide a "treasure in the heavens that faileth not" (Luke 12:23).

The first illustration of the "moth" is associated with one form of Eastern wealth, the costly garments of rich material, often embroidered with gold and silver, and liable to be consumed by clothes-moths. James refers to moth-eaten garments (5:2; Job 13:28; 27:16; Isaiah 50:9; 51:8).

The second figure of speech is "rust," which like the moth can render things worthless. The reference here is not confined to the corroding, or eating into, of precious metals the Easterners were proud of, but to the decay which eats into and corrodes all the perishable treasures of earth. It is suggested by Lang that the moth and the rust illustrate the outward and inward phases of destruction, but both moths and rust, once they settle upon an object, gradually eat their way from the exterior to the interior.

The third simile, "thieves," is another instance of our Lord's use of finely sarcastic language in warning those who are not rich toward God and who are proud of their earthly accumulations. To the Easterner, who kept his treasure underground and who was ever aware of the possibility of thieves digging in, the figure of speech would be readily understood. Moths and rust attack perishable things, but thieves seek the imperishable treasures. Taken together, then, these three swift, silent robbers of wealth describe the folly of amassing earthly possessions for their own sake. Our Lord exhorts us to lay up treasures in heaven where moths or rust can't destroy nor thieves break through and steal.

The unassailable treasures we are to store up above are equivalent to those "good works" of which our Lord speaks (Luke 12:33), and the character formed by them which follows us into the unseen world, and which are not subject to the process of decay (Revelation 14:13). If "rich in good works" (I Timothy 6:18), and "rich in faith" (James 2:5), and partakers of "unsearchable riches" (Ephesians 3:8,16), then where our treasure is, there will our heart be also. Said Martin Luther, "What a man loves, that is his God." The Master goes on to say that we cannot serve God *and* mammon, "mammon" meaning riches. It must be God *or* mammon. Ellicott's comment is: "Men may try to persuade themselves that they will have a treasure on earth and a treasure in heaven also, but in the long-run, one or the other will assert its claim to be *the* treasure, and will claim the no longer divided allegiance of the earth."

A word of explanation is necessary about our Lord's command, "Lay not up for yourselves treasures upon earth." "Laying up" is not in itself sinful. Does not Paul enjoin honest industry and sagacious enterprise? (II Corinthians 12:14). If treasures come our way they are to be used, not only merely for our own pleasure and profit, but for the good of others. Treasures on earth, if scattered for God's glory, become treasures in heaven.

In showing that our Lord is condemning worldliness, Richard Glover in his *Commentary on Matthew* has this impressive summary of the Master's teaching at this point: "The visible treasure has great and obvious attractions. Jewish wealth lay chiefly in garments, in gold and in jewels; ours, in land, houses, shares. The Saviour appeals to them to fix not their hearts on the visible wealth of earth, whose perishableness He vividly suggests; for those who do so are at the mercy of things *as insignificant as the* 'moth,' *as subtle as the* 'rust,' *as numerous as* 'thieves' *ready to* 'break through and steal.' *He builds too low who builds beneath the skies.* The perishable can never be a portion of the soul's regard. If no other destroyers come against us *old age is a sort of moth* which impairs, and *disease is a sort of rust* which lessens our enjoyment of earthly treasures, and *death is a thief* which breaks through and steals all we have that belongs to earth. Aspire to higher things, even *treasures in heaven* — to immortal possessions of the immortal soul."

# The Parable of Single and Evil Eyes

(Matthew 6:22-24)

To prevent exhausting ourselves upon earthly pursuits our Lord follows on with additional parabolic illustrations full of profound practical wisdom. As the Creator and Lord of the body, He knows all about the intricate mechanism of its members and here uses the figure of the "eye" to great effect as He enforces the necessity for singleness of motive in life. Paul was a man with a single eye, a man of one purpose and passion. "This one thing I do." The teaching of the parable before us is that of singleness of aim, looking right at an object, as opposed to having two ends in view (Proverbs 4:25-27). If double-minded, then we are unstable in all our ways (James 1:8). Thus our Lord ends the section we are considering with the positive pronouncement, "Ye cannot serve God and mammon."

Dealing with the importance of accurate powers of perception, enabling us to discern the true value of things, Jesus said that the eye is the *lamp,* not the *light,* of the body. Do we realize sufficiently the value and marvel of our physical eyes? Without them the world is as dark as if it were sunless. Blind or dim eyes leave every organ embarrassed and unguided. Further, if there be no light, the eyes are useless. "The light is not in the eye, but the eye is the means of interpreting and applying the light. The eye is that which regulates the motions of the body." While it is wonderful to know that those who are denied their sight experience a sharpening of other senses, the sightless are the first to admit that the natural order is that the eye is the lamp in which the light shines.

In His illustration of the *single* and the *evil* eye, Jesus sets forth the contraries of each other, to mean respectively a *good,* clear-seeing eye, and a *faulty* or blind eye. With marvelous scientific accuracy, He uses two distinct words to describe the condition of the eye which is the great faculty whose clearness determines the well-being of every other faculty. The word for "single" is *aplous,* meaning "single-folded" or "without a fold," an eye having no complications within itself. Dr. Campbell Morgan quotes the definition of an oculist on what is known as *astigmatism:* "An astigmatism is a structural defect of the eye so that the rays of light do not converge to a point in the retina."

There is a "fold" within the eye, something is out of place or complicated and therefore the eye is not "single." So Jesus applies such an optical defect to our spiritual vision. If the eye of the soul is not folded over, nothing out of place, then everything is seen in the right perspective. As we look with good, sound eyes, and walking in the light see objects clearly, so the single and persistent desire to serve and please God in everything will make our whole character consistent and bright.

By way of contrast Jesus uses the word evil, or *poneros,* meaning, "evil in influence, distempered." An *evil* eye is a *bad* eye and implies "not merely an obliquity, but that there is a *squint.*" Such an eye sees things double, and such an eye, spiritually, exercises an evil influence upon the one possessing it, and upon others. Says Jesus, the evil eye results in the whole body being "full of darkness." Because there is not the unification of life at the center everything is out of focus. If the inner eye is faulty all is dark, and "how great is that darkness." At the heart, then, of Christ's illustration of the *single* or *evil* eye is the truth that as "a vitiated eye, or an eye that looks not straight and full at its object, sees nothing as it is, so a mind and heart divided between heaven and earth is all dark." Distorted and double purposes or aims impair our attitude toward God and life. Our Lord goes on to apply this solemn truth in what He says about the impossibility of serving two masters, God and mammon.

## The Parable of Birds and Lilies
### (Matthew 6:25-34)

That Christ was a lover of Nature is borne out in His illustrations taken from the world He created and which He used so effectively in His ethical teaching. The *Therefore* commencing this portion, connecting it with the previous section, impresses upon us two great lessons:

1. The service of mammon always involves us in anxiety.
2. All anxiety is in itself a service of mammon.

All fear and corroding care is an evidence of the lack of faith in the sovereignty and sufficiency of God. Because of His care and provision all anxiety is superfluous. What we said about the right and wrong aspect of "laying up treasures" is applicable here where Jesus speaks of taking no thought about our material needs. To those saintly scholars who gave us the incomparable Authorized Version of the Bible, the word "thought" meant *anxiety* and so suitably represents the Greek term which means "anxious concern," or "distracting care." As there is a legitimate saving for a "rainy day," so here our Lord is not forbidding proper interest in the necessities of life, but an over-anxious solicitude, or carking care, regarding same.

*Thought* or forethought about temporal things is required by the Bible and by common sense.

Our *life* is more than *meat,* says Jesus. Does this not imply that as God has given us the greater gift of life, can we not trust Him to give us the lesser gifts to maintain that life? Surely, He who gave life is able to maintain it while it animates the body! Then, the body is more than raiment, which can include a house to surround the body as well as raiment to clothe it. Doubtless the pointed question had a definite appeal to "a people who reckoned their garments, not less than their money, as part of their capital, and often expended on them the labour of many weeks or months" (see verse 20 and James 5:2).

*The Birds of the air.* All birds familiar to Galilee, and well-known to Jesus, like turtle doves, wood pigeons and finches, were spoken of as being cared for by the Creator. The exclamation, *Behold,* implies the necessity of observing well and considering so as to learn wisdom from the parallel and parable (Luke 12:24). Martin Luther, in his homily on *The Sparrow,* reckoned that a sparrow will eat a bushel of corn in twelve months. Not endowed by the heavenly Father with a capacity for thinking, planning, laying in store such a quantity of corn, little birds would perish if it were not for divine provision. They are not able to take thought of the morrow, so God feeds them without work or worry.

Because we are of more value than many sparrows, we are more worthy of God's care. Redeemed by the blood of His beloved Son, we can trust His wisdom and love to order all things well for the highest as for the meanest of His creatures. We are nobler and dearer to God than His dumb creatures, which, void of human reason, are incapable of sowing, reaping and storing. And as He miraculously fed and sustained the Israelites for almost forty years during their wilderness journeyings, He is able to provide us with all that is necessary.

"The Lilies of the field" refers to the *huleh* lily of Palestine, renowned for its colors from brilliant scarlet to a fine deep purple, and one of the most gorgeous of flowers. Perhaps as our Lord spoke, the birds were nestling in the trees, and around Him in the fields there were the lilies surpassing all artificial human grandeur. If these flowers growing wild in great beauty and profusion were more exquisitely clothed than any monarch, and that without anxiety on their part, why may we not trust the universal processes of Providence to distribute to all who believe, the things exactly required?

Thus, in this parabolic form Jesus rebukes worry as being disastrous to ourselves, and dishonoring to God. As our heavenly Father, He knows what things we have need of, even before we ask Him for such. We are guilty of being "little-faithed ones" (Matthew 8:26; 14:31; 16:8), if we fail to believe in His loving thought and provision. Anxiety is unnecessary, seeing our necessity is known to Him. The admirable, practical maxim, "Sufficient unto the day is the evil thereof," indicates that every day brings its own cares; and to anticipate them with anxiety is only to double them. With a fine touch of satire Jesus says that worry does not get us anywhere, nor bring us anything.

Worry cannot add one cubit to our stature. The R. V. gives "age" for stature and the playful irony is that worry cannot help us to live longer. If anything, worry shortens life. While the prolongation of life depends upon the necessaries of food and covering, the length of our days is in the hands of Him, who is our beneficent, unfailing Provider. May grace be ours to trust Him who feeds, even the sparrows, and who clothes the transient life of the grass of the field with such beauty, to care for our immortal beings! Lack of faith in His ability to undertake for us strikes Him as an unfathomable mystery (Mark 6:6). Let us not grieve His tender heart with the unreasonableness of unbelief.

# The Parable of the Mote and the Beam
(Matthew 7:1-5)

Richard Glover reminds us that from "the more special theme of the inwardness of true life, the Saviour passes, in this section (7:1-12), to corrections, encouragements, and warnings of which we stand in need." We may classify its lessons and say that He points out —

A Fault
A Neglected Privilege
A Forgotten Duty

While the double parable before us is curiously allied to the following one of dogs and swine, we are taking each pair separately. The four figures of speech are co-joined seeing they concern the one subject our Lord was illustrating, namely that of the principles that are to actuate us in the exercise of judgment. Both "doubles" are in the same possibility of action and activity in life. When our Lord said, "Judge not that ye be not judged," He was protesting against that kind of judgment that condemned. Discrimination is necessary and is enjoined by Christ's use of the mote and the beam, and shows us that we may use judgment wrongfully: the dogs and swine show how judgment, although terrible in application, must be exercised. If we judge, it must not be according to appearance, but a righteous judgment based on the exercise of the power of distinction and discrimination. It is thus that the Judge of all the earth judges. What is the true significance of the startling figures of *the mote* and *the beam?*

1. *The Mote.* Here we have a small splinter, a little chip off the beam, a tiny object. Ellicott comments that the Greek noun translated here means a "stalk" or "twig," rather than one of the fine particles of dust floating in the sun to which we attach the word, "mote." A like illustration was familiar to the Jews and is found in the proverbs and satires of every country teaching men about being keen-sighted as to the faults of others

and blind to their own shortcomings. Personal faults require the careful scrutiny which we never give them. Robert Burns gave us a precious truth in the couplet:

"Oh, wad some Power the giftie gie us,
  To see ourselves as others see us!"

2. *The Beam.* This word implies a massive piece of timber, a joint which could hardly go into the head, much less into the eye. A beam in the eye becomes almost grotesque by its bigness, while the mote, because it is so small as not to be seen, yet causes suffering. What is this *beam?* Dr. Campbell Morgan says that it is "not a vulgar sin. The man guilty of a great sin is never critical of a man who has committed a little sin." A man may see a mote in his brother's eye, something wrong in the life that ought not to be there. He should not be blind, however, to the beam in his own eye, a greater fault than that he discerns in his brother's life.

With gravity, our Lord is warning us against the great fault of *censoriousness,* often treated as a failing rather than a sin. This sin of the spirit is worse than a sin of the flesh. "There is no sin so blasting, so blighting, so damning, as the spirit of censorious judgment of another man . . . . Censoriousness dwells upon the mote and criticizes the brother. That censoriousness is a beam that is blinding the man." If we approach a brother with a mote in his eye in the spirit of love and not in the spirit of censorious condemnation, God will judge us in the same way. From our Lord's teaching we gather that:

1. The fault-finding always have the faults they rebuke. "You can always tell a man's weaknesses by noting his antipathies . . . . The wasp complains of other people's stings . . . . Your form of fault may differ from the form which offends you, but in substance *you have the faults you dislike.*"

2. The fault-finding may have the faults they rebuke in others, in greater measure in themselves. Such a form of fault-finding is usually marked by hypocrisy, an assertion of freedom from faults generally and especially from the fault we name. Those who judge thus should set about the necessary tasks of curing their own faults rather than trying to cure others' faults.

3. We should judge no man unless it be a duty so to do, and if we do, we must judge the offence not the offended, confining our judgment to the earthly side of the fault, and leave the relation of the one judged to God, who sees the heart, and knows all about the ignorance and infirmities which may extenuate the sinfulness of others. If we have to correct others let it be not by harsh reproof, but by example, lowliness, love and prayer. "Heaven is the world of love," says Glover, "and love is fitness for it and the essence of it. Unlovely harshness is meetness for the inheritance of perdition. Cherish the character that would be at home in heaven."

# The Parable of Dogs and Swine

(Matthew 7:6)

This brief, parabolic illustration describes the opposite extreme of the truth just considered. We are to guard against the folly of ignoring palpable evil and treating it in the same way as we do the good. Truth is not to be forced upon rebels who reject it, and holy things are not to be given to fault-finders, mote-hunters and evil-speakers. After His utterance of the previous parabolic illustration, Jesus somewhat sharply and suddenly insists upon the necessity of discrimination. "If there is to be no hindering beam that prevents us from removing the mote, there is to be no blindness that prevents us from seeing corruption that is hopeless and helpless."

DOGS. Our Lord here refers to savage and snarling dogs, dogs that turn and bite the hand feeding them. Eastern dogs are wilder and more gregarious than our domesticated animals, and feeding on carrion and garbage, are coarser and fiercer than dogs in the West. It was these Jesus had in mind when He used them to describe coarse haters of truth. Ellicott remarks that the first part of the verse before us points to "the flesh which has been offered for sacrifice, 'the holy thing' of Leviticus 22:6,7,10,16, of which no unclean person or stranger, and no unclean beast was to eat. To give that holy flesh to dogs would have seemed to the devout Israelite the greatest of all profanations. Our Lord teaches us that there is a little risk of desecration in dealing with the yet holier treasure of divine truth."

Christ's use of the simile of savage dogs reminds us that there are testimonies we instinctively withhold when confronted by those who utterly despise them. We are forbidden to countenance the prostitution of holy things. Peter, who listened to this parable germ, ended one of his Letters writing of some people who, like dogs, return to their vomit, and as sows, wallow in the mire.

SWINE. Under the Mosaic Law, *swine* were considered as unclean and therefore unfit for human consumption. Thus "dogs" and the "swine" symbolize distinct forms of evil. The former represent ferocity (Philemon 3:2; Revelation 22:15), and the latter, impurity (Psalm 80:13). As "pearls" were reckoned to be the costliest of all jewels (Matthew 13:45; I Timothy 2:9), they came to symbolize the preciousness of truth. Can we not imagine the disappointment and consequent rage of the swine at finding that what they took for grain was only pearls? How apt a figure this is of those who are impure and coarse, and incapable of appreciating the priceless jewels of our Christian faith! These are they, Christ says, to whom we have no right to give the treasure of our pearls. These are those who, after hearing the Word, are worse than they were before. The double parable at this point forbids the offering of the sacred ordinances to the unregenerate. It is the Church's solemn responsibility to guard her most holy treasures. "In past history she gave over her sacred deposits to dogs, and cast her

pearls before swine when she admitted government within her borders by pagan nations. She does it today whenever she compromises with the sacred things of her faith."

A word of warning is necessary regarding the setting down of *all* our neighbors as dogs and swine, and excusing ourselves from the endeavor to help them spiritually. We must not forget the previous teaching about judging with the harshest judgment. Says Ellicott, "In thinking of the dogs and swine as representing not men and women as such, but the passions of this kind or that which make them brutish. So long as they identify themselves with these passions, we must deal cautiously and wisely with them . . . We need, it might be added, to be on our guard against the brute element in ourselves not less than in others. We may desecrate the holiest truths by dealing with them in the spirit of irreverence, or passion, or may cynically jest with our own truest and noblest impulses."

## The Parable of Stones and Serpents

(Matthew 7:7-12)

While the transition from previous similes to those we are now to consider may appear abrupt, the sequence of thought is suggestive. Where may we find the necessary wisdom and courage for the enjoined discernment and discrimination taught by the single and evil eye, dogs and swine? The answer is, in prayer to the Father. The illustrations used are full of contrast: the loaf and the stone; the fish and the serpent. Their appearance at this point in the King's manifesto indicates that among the code of laws, prayer is a necessity, if we are to judge, act and live aright.

In describing the explicit, universal pledge that if we come to God in faith, asking explicitly for those things in harmony with His will, Jesus used three simple yet great words on the matter: ask, seek, knock. The first letter of each word, A-S-K, suggests that prayer means asking God for what we need. Why did Jesus use these words? Was He simply repeating the formula of prayer in different forms, to prevent the possibility of mistake, and embolden us to obey His command? By His use of the trio of words was He prescribing prayer as an increasing urgency, and implying different degrees of intensity? Richard Glover indicates another and deeper reason for the different forms of precept: "If a child wants anything of a parent, what is his process? If mother is near and visible, he simply *asks*. If she is not near and visible, he *seeks* her, and having found her, he then asks. If, finding her, he finds her inaccessible, within her chamber, unwilling to be disturbed, he *knocks* till he gains her attention and consent. All suppliants at the throne of grace know something of all these three experiences."

Our Lord gives us the triple assurance that if we ask, we shall receive, if we seek, we shall find; if we knock, the door shall be opened unto us. Fausset says, "We *ask* for what we *wish;* we *seek* for what we *miss;* we *knock* for that from which we feel ourselves *shut out."* Asking for *bread* we do not receive a *stone,* which is round and smooth as a loaf or cake, much in use then, only to mock us. Asking for a *fish* we do not receive a serpent, something alike in form to a fish but which does not have the serpent's sting. We must ask for good things according to the divine will." If earthly fathers give good things to their children in response to their plea, will not our loving heavenly Father above bestow upon us the better gifts of the Spirit? God always gives us the best. He never offers us stones or serpents, even if in our ignorance we ask for them.

An important phrase in our Lord's teaching on prayer is, "For *every one* that asketh receiveth." No suppliant leaves the Throne of Grace unanswered. Perhaps his prayer is not answered at the time, or in the way or form he expects. *No* as well as *yes* may be an answer. Paul prayed three times for the removal

of his thorn, and his prayer was answered in the form of grace to endure his thorn. For a thorough treatment of answered and unanswered prayer, the reader is referred to the author's volume on *All the Prayers of the Bible.*

A summary of Christ's teaching (7:1-12) about the judgment of others, fault-finding, mote-hunting, dispensing holy things and the urgency of prayer is given in the so-called *Golden Rule:* "Therefore all things whatsoever ye would that men should do to you, do ye even so to them: for this is the law and the prophets."

# The Parable of Two Gates and Two Ways
(Matthew 7:13,14)

In His ethical teaching, our Lord comes to the realm of application and illustrates the two opposite ways of life's pilgrimage by the use of gates and roads. With the figurative teaching of the chapter before us we come to the conclusion of the Sermon on the Mount, and to its effect on all those who face it. The response to its teaching is seen in the two opposite classes herewith described by Christ: the many refusing each ethical teaching and consequently bent upon following the path of ease and self-indulgence; and the few, accepting the truth, seeking eternal safety above everything else, whatever the cost.

The solemn truth unfolded before us is that there are only two ways for humanity to choose: the way of the righteous; the way of the ungodly (Psalm 1). The world may think there are three kinds of people; *good, bad, neutral,* but the Bible knows of only two kinds; sinners and saved sinners. We are either *black* or *white.* There is no *grey.* There is no debatable, or no man's land. We are either "in Christ" or "without Christ," travelers to heaven or hell. And the blessed truth of Scripture is that "the Lord knoweth them that are His."

*Two Gates.* Familiar as He would be with the gates of a nearby city set on a hill, Christ uses the figure with great effect. There was the *wide* gate. The entrance to the two ways is called *strait* (Luke 13:24-27). Scripture notes the reasons for this entrance (Deuteronomy 30:15; I Kings 18:21; II Peter 2:2,5). *Wide* alludes to "the careless sinful way of life of the wicked, intimating that it is easier to be revengeful and covetous; to take advantage of another to enrich self rather than walk according to the golden rule." The name of this wide gate is *self*—one's own desires, proud thoughts, our own righteousness, our own chosen and darling sins, our own plan and will. Being *wide,* this gate is easily entered.

The other gate is called *strait,* being hardly wide enough to admit one at all. This description of the entrance and gate indicate the difficulty of the first right step toward God. One must triumph over all natural inclinations. Repentant sinners must *strive* to enter this narrow gate (Luke 13:24). If the name over the wide gate is *self,* the one over the strait gate is *Christ.*

> "Christ trusted, to the neglect and humiliation and crucifixion of Self;
> Christ sought with repentance and godly sorrow;
> Christ followed at any hazard and to any martyrdom — no honor and no friend but Christ."

The *strait* gate alludes to a strict observance of the Golden Rule, previously enunciated by our Lord (7:12).

*Two Ways.* The nature of the *ways* corresponds to the *gates.* Entering the gate is a matter of consciousness, freedom and choice; and thereafter life, here and hereafter, is fashioned by such a choice. How solemn a thought it is that our destiny depends not upon a fate, but on a personal choice! The *wide* gate leads to the *broad* way. On such a way there is plenty of room for the sinner and his sin. This way recommends itself to the majority because of the ease and naturalness with which it is trodden and the plentiful company of travelers found thereon. But this apparently primrose path tends ever downward. The world's ease and comfort and good-natured carelessness are in the *wide* way.

The strait gate leads to the *narrow* way, leading, as it were, "through a gorge between precipitous rocks which nearly meet, haunted by dangers and enemies, chosen by comparatively few." The narrow gate and a straitened way prohibit the breadth of license. Many things have to be left outside the narrow gate. Yet though we must walk according to the straitness of God's law, the way leads to a glorious breadth of life. As we walk along this way we find it widening, broadening and expanding with new breadth and views and glory. Another aspect of this phase of Christ's parabolic illustration is that He Himself is *The Way* over which we must travel (John 14:6), as well as *The Gate* through which we enter (John 10:7). *Through* Him and *in* Him is obtainable holiness and eternal life.

*Two Companies.* What an impressive difference there is between the numbers on the respective ways. Through the wide gate on to the broad way "many" pass. A life, permitting the indulgences of preferences, leaving self-will free, and requiring neither surrender nor sacrifice, allures more followers than the narrower way of full abandonment to the claims of Christ. The tragic fact is that there are millions upon millions more people serving the devil, than the Saviour who died for them. The pilgrim on the broad way never lacks for suitable company. Reversely, on the narrow way there are "few" pilgrims. "Few there be that find it." A life of separation from sin and unto God is not a popular one. Ellicott quotes an allegory known as *The Tablet of Cebes,* the disciple of Socrates: "Seest thou not a certain small door, and a pathway before the door, in no way crowded, but few, very few, go in thereat? This is the way that leadeth to true discipline." Ellicott goes on to say that the contrast between the *many* and the *few* runs through all our Lord's teaching. "He comes to 'save the world,' and yet those whom He chooses out of the world are but as a 'little flock.' Well, if there are few pilgrims on the road leading from *The City of Destruction* to *The Celestial City,* those on this unpopular way have the very best of company in Him who said, 'Lo, I am with you alway even unto the end.' With Him, as our fellow-traveller, we are thrice blessed."

Although the one gate is narrow, yet it is wide enough for all who choose to enter. Few, however, find the gate with its pillars of Repentance and Faith. The majority may complain of the straitness of the way of surrender and service, but if the gate at the outset were wider than the gate at the end, it would only permit delusion and prevent salvation. Is not the breadth of the gate and way fixed by the necessity of things? What the majority of sinners must learn is that without repentance and regeneration, bliss here and hereafter is impossible. Further, they wait in vain if they expect the strait gate to get broader.

> Broad is the way that leads to death
> And thousands walk together;
> But wisdom shows a narrow path,
> With here and there a traveller.

*Two Destinies:* Our Lord makes it clear that while we are all travelers to eternity, there are two ends or stopping places. Probably the most solemn statement the world has heard since its creation, yet one the vast majority allow to pass unheeded is, "Broad is the way that leadeth to destruction." *Destruction!* What does this terrible word mean? Certainly it does not represent annihilation or cessation of existence, for whether saved or lost, we are to live on forever. Actually, the word means waste, or the loss of all that is precious to existence. For the sinner, choosing the broad gate and way, and who dies in his sin, there is the death of peace and of expectancy. Once, at the end of the broad way, and in a lost eternity, the sinner's position is irretrievable. Campbell Morgan says that the word *destruction* literally means

"narrowing limitation, confinement, imprisonment; until everything is brought to an end under crushing pressure." No matter how the sinner thinks he may end his way, Christ's warning word for him is *destruction*.

But for those who accept the despised narrow way what a blessed end awaits them — *life;* life, in all its glorious fulness; a life without sin and sorrow; life in the Paradise of Life; life in the presence of God and of Christ for all eternity. Although few find this way of life and few are found *on* it, it is to be hoped that the reader is among the number who consciously, deliberately and unequivocally have chosen the narrow way, the end of which is everlasting life.

## The Parable of Sheep and Wolves
(Matthew 7:15)

There is a vital connection between this double figure and the one just considered. How is the narrow way to be found? Who are the authorized guides? Are they not those divinely inspired teachers? Here, our Lord is warning against those counterfeit guides (Acts 5:39), who are traitors to their trust. These false prophets are like wolves disguising themselves as sheep in order to gain entrance into the fold (John 10:12; Acts 20:29). Probably, there is an allusion here to the "rough garments," the "sheep-skins and goat-skins," worn by false prophets of the hermit or ascetic type (Hebrew 11:37).

A prophet may teach a perfectly correct doctrine, but if his life is adverse to his teaching, he is a ravening wolf, one whose influence is destructive. We are not to be deceived by outward appearance. On the other hand, the prophet or teacher may come as an authorized expounder of the mind of God yet be a false guide (II Peter 2:1,2; I John 4:1). He may have a bland, gentle, plausible exterior (as many modernistic preachers have) and persuade us that the gate is not strait nor the way narrow, and that to teach so is illiberal and bigoted. Is this not what the false prophets of old tried to do? (Ezekiel 13:1-10,22). Are these not those Paul describes as being bent on devouring the flocks for their own ends? (II Corinthians 11:2,3,13-15).

It is not always easy to detect the false prophet in sheep's clothing. Like Balaam, he may have marvelous insight; and like Simon Magus, do wonders; or, like Satan, seem "an angel of light." But the Master gives us a test, "Ye shall know them by their fruits." Here He merges His figures of speech. If *false* prophets, then they are corrupt trees and cannot bring forth good fruit. What is the influence of a pastor or teacher on you? If it endears the Saviour to you, deepens your penitence and gratitude, heightens your spiritual aspirations, intensifies your desire for God, your spiritual guide is a safe one — follow him as he seeks to follow his heavenly Guide.

# The Parable of Thorns and Thistles
### (Matthew 7:16-20)

*Evil* fruit cannot grow from a *good* tree. "This test of the practical influence of any doctrines on the life is one which all can apply and is the surest test of truth which any can use." If a tree is corrupt, that is, rotten or decayed at the core, it cannot produce good fruit. Wrong thinking leads to wrong living. Falseness in teaching, or in the teacher, will sooner or later show itself in his life, and becomes thereby a teacher whose guidance we cannot follow. "Their fruits," refers to the practical effect of their teaching. Grapes cannot be gathered from thorns, or any kind of prickly fruit; and figs cannot come from thistles. Every tree bears its *own* fruit. For our own hearts the teaching is obvious: we reap what we sow (Galatians 6:7).

If we are obedient to the will of the Father, then power is ours to distinguish, so far as we need distinguish, truth from error, human teaching from the divine. Obedience is the final test

of everything. "Do, and thou shalt know." As the Father is the Husbandman, He can transform the thorn into the fir tree, and the briar into the myrtle tree. Bad-natured trees may be changed by divine power and mercy into good trees, the planting of the Lord. Thistles may blossom into roses fit for the bosom of the King of kings. But if bad trees persist in being bad, then they are hewn down and cast into the fire.

# The Parable of the Two Houses
### (Matthew 7:21-28)

In this section of our Lord's discourse He testifies to His own deity, "Lord, Lord" (Matthew 7:21; John 13:13), and as such demands our implicit obedience. Profession, without possession, will bar the professors from Christ's recognition, both now and at His coming. Of this we are certain, He does *know* His own (II Timothy 2:19). Then bringing His discourse to a close Jesus said, "Therefore whosoever heareth these sayings of mine, and doeth them, I will liken him unto a wise man." He then goes on to describe what this obedient, shrewd and prudent man does. He builds his house, his whole life, on the rocks of true discipleship, or genuine subjection to Christ. The disobedient build differently.

*The Rock Foundation.* Is not the Rock on which we build, Christ Himself? "Upon the rock," that is, upon His Deity to which Peter confessed, "I will build My Church" (Matthew 16:13; Deuteronomy 32; Psalm 18:2, 46: I Corinthians 3:10,11; Psalm 46:1, 2). This Psalm has been called *The Song of the House on the Rock,* which had no fear when the storms come. By the parable before us Christ teaches the importance of *doing* as well as *hearing.* In His description of the two builders, He made it clear that they were judged, not by the care which they took in building their houses, but by the foundation on which they stood. In a striking fashion, He illustrated the importance of foundation in building life. If we desire to build more stately mansions for the soul, the foundations must be carefully selected.

The interpretation of the parable, doubtless suggested by surrounding architecture, is related to "the general fabric of an outwardly religious life," a life resting on, and rooted in, all that the Lord is in Himself. It is only in personal union with Christ the Rock that we can find the stability of wall without which even our firmest purposes are as shifting sand. We are eternally secure if built on that "foundation which God hath laid in Zion" (Isaiah 28:16). Luke describes the wise builder as "digging deep, and laying his foundation on a rock" (Luke 6:48). Dear old Benjamin Keach says of the significance of digging deep, "The soul of a believer digs deep into the nature of God, to find out what righteousness will comfort and suit with the righteousness and infinite holiness of God."

*The Sand Foundation.* Christ had knowledge of the fact that strangers coming to Galilee to build would be attracted to a ready-prepared level surface of sand rather than upon the hard and rugged rock near by. But when the seasonal floods came, he was left with nothing but a heap of ruins. What does a sandy foundation represent? Does it not denote a loose foundation, an empty profession and mere external religion? Ellicott comments that "sand" answers to "the shifting, uncertain feelings which are with some men (the 'foolish' ones of the parable) the only ground on which they act — love of praise, respect for custom, and the like." The second house, even though most impressive, is without foundation, and therefore doomed to destruction. What a searching distinction our Lord portrays! How perilous it is for men whose resolves do not rest upon God's help sought in prayer, whose joys do not rest in God's heart trusted, whose confidence rests not on God's presence revealed, whose virtues have no root, goodness no

motive, hope no ground! The house of such a one merely hangs together and may fall at any moment. The Pharisees of Christ's time built their hopes on external blessings and privileges, "We have Abraham to our father" (Luke 3:8; John 8:33). But their hearts were estranged from the Rock of their salvation, and Christ had to tell them that the devil, and not Abraham, was their father.

*The Builders.* In the "wise" and the "foolish" builders, our Lord describes two classes under the natural image of the building of an house. From His vivid picture we take it that both houses looked attractive and substantial, but the comparative stability of both is set forth. As the respective houses went up, the materials used and actual buildings were correct, and both houses looked erect, firm and strong.

What is life but a "building up of character, habits, memories, expectations, of powers or weaknesses; like stone on stone, we add one thing to another in building the house of life. Our desire is that what we build should be secure." Good people, who are not the Lord's, appear to build well, and feel that their house is well and wisely built on money, friends, health, successful methods in business — all of which are commendable in themselves, but disastrous without a "rock" foundation. But there are others who build their house differently, "by daily adding to their powers of service, their knowledge of God, their victories over faults, their joys and hopes, till their life becomes a palace fit for God."

*The Testing Elements.* Eastern monsoons, floods and hurricanes do great damage to seemingly strong houses and destroy those less strongly built — a fact our Lord used to great effect. "Rain descended." Jesus compares the testing times, terrific in their strain, to the concurrent forces of a rainstorm threatening the roof of the house. How the whistling, howling rains, when they descend, create fear! "The floods came," and these tempestuous torrents can undermine the walls. "The winds blew," and these sweeping, hurricane-like winds threaten the sides of the house.

These combined natural forces remind us that summer suns are not always shining. Whether we are "wise" or "foolish," strain comes to all, in afflictions, disappointments, losses, temptations, fears, and in thoughts of dying and of the life beyond. Says Ellicott, "The *wind,* the *rain,* the *floods* hardly admit, unless by an unreal minuteness, of individual interpretation, but represent collectively the violences of persecution, of suffering, of temptations without, beneath which all but the life which rests on the true foundation necessarily gives way."

A dramatic touch is added to the disaster overtaking the house built on a foundation of sand — "Great was the fall of it." In this pitiful phrase Christ warns us to avoid a similar fate. How this imagery of terrible ruin must have impressed the audience accustomed to the fierceness of an Eastern tempest, and the suddenness and completeness with which it sweeps everything unsteady before it! No wonder when Jesus had finished His parabolic discourse, the people were astonished at the uniqueness and authoritativeness of His sayings. "The consciousness of Divine authority, as Lawgiver, Expounder, and Judge, so beamed through His teaching, that the Scribes' teaching could not but appear drivelling in such a light." The Scribes were retailers merely of what others had said. When we speak what we know from heart-experience then like the Master we, too, speak with authority.

Foolish builders should heed the warning of Jesus and build anew on a solid foundation, even on Himself (I Corinthians 3:11). Ere a final, irretrievable loss overtakes them they will be wise to recognize their utter helplessness apart from grace, and build on the only sure foundation of penitence and faith in God's redemptive provisions.

# The Parable of Foxes and Birds
(Matthew 8:18-22)

The Scribe, or rabbi, to whom we are introduced was one of the few of his order who came to believe in and follow Christ. His was the desire to join the fishermen-apostles as Christ's disciple. Doubtless His preaching had gripped the scribe's heart, and in a moment of enthusiasm and impulse, he declared his willingness to follow Jesus wherever He went. But Jesus tested the reality of the scribe's decision as to whether he was willing for the sacrifice that following the Master entailed. Observing the growing popularity of Jesus, perhaps the scribe felt it would be a good thing "to jump on the bandwagon." He was warned, however, as to what whole-hearted consecration really meant. Endeavoring to destroy any illusions the scribe may have had, Jesus referred to His own homelessness, even in Capernaum.

As for Him, He had no certain dwelling-place. The foxes were not without their holes, nor the birds of the air their nests, but for Him there was the constant dependence upon the hospitality of others, and a borrowed pillow for His head. There were times when even this hospitality failed and Jesus slept out under the Syrian skies. "Every man went to his own home, Jesus went to the mount of Olives." There was no one with decency enough to offer Jesus a bed. He had to retire to the sacred mount where, with the darkness of the night to cover Him, He spent the lonely hours in fellowship with His Father. Such was a part of His humiliation on our behalf. It is to be hoped that the scribe counted the cost of true discipleship and weighed well the real nature and strength of attachment to Christ. It would seem as if the scribe was not willing for the spiritual solitude and impoverishment full allegiance involved.

The second would-be disciple is a little more difficult to understand. If the scribe is presented as a rash or precipitate disciple, this second man appears as a procrastinating and entangled disciple. Because, at first sight, the man's cause for delay seems most reasonable, we may marvel at Christ's apparently sharp reply. Various interpretations have been given of the man's request and Christ's response. With Richard Glover, we feel that it is inconceivable that this man left the dead body of his father to listen to Christ's preaching and neglected all preparations for interment. He could not, in the nature of things, be free for such engagements as listening to Christ's preaching in such circumstances.

The only view, then, "which appears to be consistent with the conditions of the case is that which supposes the man's father aged, but not dead nor dying; and the man professing a filial piety which constrains him to wait with his father, to comfort his age, and after death perform for him the last duties of filial service. If the father were already dead, he had died that day, and the burial would have followed within a few hours of death . . . He is, therefore, like many who would be missionaries 'but for an aged mother,' or those who will do a great work, only not yet. The heart being more in the delaying and the excuse than in the intent.'

But the same Christ, who deferred the hasty scribe, here spurs the delaying disciple. *Follow Me!* The unquickened can bury dead bodies. His disciples, by divine empowerment, can give life to dead souls. "The *sharp* words of Christ have more of love in them than the pleasant words of the world. It is to be hoped that both of these men were delivered from their personal dangerous weakness by Christ's faithful Word."

# The Parable of the Physician and the Bridegroom

(Matthew 9:10-15)

There is a vital connection between the question of the Pharisees, "Why eateth your Master with publicans and sinners?" and that of the disciples of John, "Why do we and the Pharisees fast oft, but thy disciples fast not?" There is a companionship with sinners which confirms them in their sin — this must be avoided. There is a companionship with sinners that lifts them out of their sin — this was the type of companionship here, and is a type to cherish. A closer walk with God should result in a closer walk with sinners, in order to win them for God.

The failure of the multiplication of Pharisaic rules was, that the more they developed, the larger grew the number of those neglecting them, and the wider their separation from their more strict brethren. One strict rule was not only not to eat with, but not to buy from those neglecting the traditions. But Jesus broke through all rules by feasting with publicans or despised tax-gatherers, and sinners. Matthew's great feast, in which Jesus participated, was doubtless a farewell feast to old friends and neighbors before he entered on his new calling as a disciple of Christ. As tax-gatherers were treated with contempt, and looked upon as sinners, the Pharisees would never think of entering the house of a sinner. Shocked, the Pharisees asked the disciples, "Why eateth your Master with publicans and sinners?" Jesus replied with a gem of a parable germ: "They that are whole need not a physician, but they that are sick." Luke, as a doctor gives the Master's reply a more professional touch: "They that are in health" (Luke 5).

This was not the first time Jesus had referred to His redeeming work as the Great Physician (Luke 4:23). He here rebukes the questioning Pharisees by reminding them that the claims of "mercy" were higher than those of the ceremonial law. In a somewhat cynical way He told the Pharisees that He had not come to call the "righteous" (which was their own estimate of themselves) but sinners to repentance. The Pharisees deemed themselves whole, therefore Christ's mission was not to them.

As a Physician, His place was near to the neediest. Have not myriads of broken hearts and sin-sick souls found consolation in Christ's matchless saying? The "righteous," like those miserable self-satisfied Pharisees, are sent "empty away."

But Jesus was not only censured by the separatist Pharisees, the disciples of John were also perturbed over Christ's association with sinners. John the Baptist, the austere Apostle of the Wilderness, shunned eating and drinking at feasts, and his followers, perhaps influenced by the Pharisees, asked Jesus the question, "Why do we and the Pharisees fast oft, but thy disciples fast not?" So the Master was questioned for going against the conventional way of acting.

Ellicott observes that the followers of the Baptist continued during Christ's ministry to form a separate body (Matthew 11:2; 14:12), and that they obeyed the rules the Baptist had given them, more or less after the pattern of the Pharisees. But they were not as hypocritical as the Pharisees, and were therefore answered without the sternness marking Christ's reply to the Pharisees.

The parabolic illustration of the Bridegroom gains full significance when we connect it with John the Baptist's testimony to Jesus as "The Bridegroom" (John 3:29). He taught the people that the coming of the Bridegroom would be the fulfilment of his joy. There is no rebuke for John's disciples as for the Pharisees, only a loving explanation. The tenor of our Lord's language suggests that He looked upon the feast in Matthew's house as a *wedding-feast,* which in a spiritual sense it was, seeing it celebrated Matthew's union with Christ. Was not the transformed taxgatherer another "married to Christ" (Romans 7:3,4)? The consummation of such a wedding-feast will be realized when the cry is raised, "Behold, the Bridegroom cometh" (Matthew 25:6; Revelation 19:10).

Christ's presence at the feast, and His parabolic illustrations at this point, demonstrate the entire absence of those ascetic practices which the Pharisees deemed to be the essence of religion. His first miracle contributed to the happiness of the wedding party at the marriage in Cana (John 2). Here He uses the figure of an Oriental marriage, with ceremonies, merriment and festivity lasting for seven days, to illustrate His rejection of the Pharisaical asceticism of His time. The taunt thrown at Him was that He came eating and drinking with sinners (Luke 15:1).

By the sons of the bride chamber we are to understand guests invited to the wedding. But Christ's disciples were at once the guests of that feast *individually;* and *collectively* they formed the beginning of the *Ecclesia,* or His Bride whom He had come to make His own (Matthew 22:2; Ephesians 5:25-27; Revelation 19:7; 21:2). Applying the illustration of the Bridegroom to Himself, Jesus said that the reason why His disciples did not fast was because He was with them. With Him in the midst what else could they be but joyful?

But He reminded His own that He would be taken from them, or lifted and caught up, a prophecy of His coming death, Resurrection and Ascension. All the time the disciples had the Master's bodily presence all fear and doubt were far away. But after Calvary they would mourn, as the episode on the Emmaus Road proves (Luke 24:21). Left alone, in a hostile world, that early band found *fasting* to be natural and therefore proper. Yet what triumphs were theirs. Later on, He said to them, "Ye therefore have sorrow but I will see you again, and your heart shall rejoice, and your joy no one taketh from you." True, we do not have the bodily presence of our heavenly Bridegroom with us to complete our joy, nevertheless He is not absent and never has been since His victory over death. Have we not His royal promise, "I will never leave you, nor forsake you" (Hebrews

13:5)? Ascetic practices are not necessary to demonstrate our loyalty to Him. United to Him and loving Him, we seek to live as unto Him, awaiting that blissful moment when we shall see His face as our Bridegroom, and sit down with Him at His marriage feast.

## The Parable of Old Garments and Old Bottles
### (Matthew 9:16-17)

Speaking to the same people, with a reference to the same people with whose policies He had no sympathy, Jesus used the figures of mended garments and wine skins, in order to make plain His teaching of the nature of the Kingdom. "To those who objected to the merriment of His disciples He replied that the very merriment was inevitable while He was with them; and the whole system He was creating, was not something crowded into the old, but was something new." Ellicott suggests that there is a closer connection between the parabolic illustrations used here than at first appears: "The wedding-feast suggested the idea of the wedding-garment, and of the wine which belonged to its joy. We may even go a step further and believe that the very dress of those who sat at meat in Matthew's house, coming as they did from the lower and less decently-habited classes, made the illustration all the more palpable and vivid. How could those worn garments be made meet for wedding-guests? Would it be enough to sew on a patch of new cloth where the old was wearing into holes? Not so He answers here; not so He answers again when He implicitly makes the king who gives the feast the giver also of the garment" (Matthew 22:2).

The *bottles* of which Jesus spoke were "wineskins," seeing animal skins or hides were shaped into the form of a living animal and used as bottles. No one would think of putting new wine into an old skin, one already stretched to the utmost. "Wine intended to ferment would burst any bottle, whether new or old. Unfermented wine must be put into new bottles. Wine, when fermentation is complete, can be put into any bottle, whether new or old, without harming the bottle, and without harm to the wine." Dry with age, and liable to crack, old skins would be unable to resist the pressure of fermenting liquor. So new wine required new skins.

The interpretation of this part of the parable is not hard to seek. Christ virtually abrogates the old Levitical Law and offers a charter of a new freedom. To force His new teachings into the old formulae would bring decomposition and ruin. To take His truth and try to press it into some other form than His, would be to make it deteriorate, as unfermented wine. The new energies and gifts of the Spirit, given on the Day of Pentecost, are likened unto new wine (Acts 2:13). The Pharisees of old, however, persisted in believing that the old wine of the Law was better (Luke 5:39).

The same principle applies to sewing new cloth on to old, frayed garments. Mending, of course, is usual, as every mother knows. But here the normal mode of repair does not apply. The old garment of our sinful, selfish life cannot be mended. Christ excludes any repair work. It must be regeneration, or the production of a new garment or creation. By "new cloth" we are to understand a piece of unshrunken cloth, cloth that has not passed through the fuller's hands, new and undressed, in its freshness and strongest state. Because such a piece of cloth agrees not with the worn out garment to patch it on to such would, on the first strain, tear the cloth around it, and result in a worse rent.

Did not Christ teach that life must not be a mixture, resulting from following two opposing principles? Did He not illustrate singleness of principle and motive which Paul later on emphasized when he said, "To me to live is Christ"? We must be simple and single in all our motives. We cannot serve two masters (have two strings to our bow, trust for salvation in Christ and in our own works, mix law and grace, follow the world and Christ at the same time). If the "new wine" represents the inner aspect of the Christian life, then the "new cloth" illustrates its outward life and conversation. Belief is reflected in behavior. The old garment is the common life of sinful men — the new garment is the life of holiness, which the new man in Christ wears. In the narrative, *fasting* of which the Pharisees made much, was an old garment, for which a piece of new cloth was useless. The whole system Jesus came to create was not something to be crowded into an old order, but was something new. Therefore He could not crowd into an outworn formula the new truths He came to teach. Is it not blessed to know that His transforming ministry will continue till old things are passed away, and all things are become new?

## The Parable of the Sheep and the Harvest

(Matthew 9:36-38)

What contradictory figures of speech are here brought together: a flock of scattered, shepherdless, starved, dying sheep and a plenteous harvest. Yet, combined, these figures illustrate the mission of the Master, and the task of those following Him. What constituted the plenteous harvest Jesus spoke about? Was it not the multitude of lost souls Isaiah wrote about as being sheep going astray, every one to his own way (Isaiah 53:6)? Our Lord's combined parabolic illustrations, then, are indicative of His own conception of His mission, and of His desire to have co-laborers to assist Him as the compassionate Shepherd and as the Lord of the Harvest.

The introduction to this section is full of instruction. As an itinerant preacher, Jesus taught in the villages as well as the cities. Preachers who only yearn for the largest crowds, prostitute their gift. The Master was at home, preaching and healing no matter where He went, whether in the synagogue, or out among the people. Looking out on the multitudes, He was moved with compassion. He came as the Good Shepherd, but the crowds around Him were as sheep without a shepherd. "The eye with which a man looks on the crowd will tell you what he is." Some look on crowds with contempt, some with knavish speculation as to what they can make out of the simplicity of those forming the crowd.

As the sympathetic eyes of Jesus looked on the multitude, He saw them as sheep, worn out, too weary to go further, abandoned and neglected. The Redeemer's compassion was moved, says Faussett, "By their pitiable condition as wearied and crouching under bodily fatigue, a vast disorganized mass, being but a faint picture of their wretchedness as the victims of Pharisaic guidance; their souls uncared for, yet drawn after and hanging upon Him."

The tender Shepherd pitied their bodily weariness and still more, their spiritual unrest and despair, and looked upon them as a plenteous harvest waiting to be gathered into God's garner. "Then saith He to His disciples." It was not enough for Him to be moved with compassion. He craved the sympathy and prayer of His disciples. He desired them to feel and pray as He did, as fellow-laborers. "The harvest truly is plenteous," He said, suggesting that there was not only a multitude to reach, but that among them were many *ripe souls* ready for salvation, those who only needed a little labor from the true harvester to gather them in. The phrase regarding the plentiful harvest is "the first occurrence in the record of the first three Gospels of the figure which was afterwards to be expanded into the two Parables of the Sower and the Tares, and to reappear in the visions of the Apocalypse" (Revelation 14:14-19).

But as the eye of Jesus rested immediately on the Jewish field, and saw it widening into the vast field of the world, teeming with souls to be gathered unto Him (Matthew 13:38), He sighed and said, "But the labourers are few." Those divinely called and qualified to gather in the lost were never more needed than they are today. In Christ's day, the Pharisees and Scribes, supposedly the shepherds of souls, were numbered by the thousands, but soulwinners were so few. How was the number of those with a passion for souls to be increased? Only by *prayer.* "Pray ye," not organize, nor educate, but *pray,* for God alone can make gospel laborers ready and willing to be *thrust* forth, as the phrase, "sent forth," means. He is "the Lord of the Harvest," the One supplying the seed for sowing, the sowers and the harvest. Are we among the number thrust out with constraints of love and of necessity, and overcoming love of ease and of money, fear of failure, and opposition of others, blessed by God as harvest-gatherers?

# The Parable of Sheep and Wolves
## (Matthew 10:1-28)

This section is taken up with the apostolic commission, and how the Apostles were to live and act. Antagonism and suffering were to be expected. The Master's sufferings would be theirs, but fearing God they had no reason to fear what men might do unto them. Sending the first disciples on their mission, Jesus not only gave them the assurance of protection and provision, but reminded them of their responsibility as His delegates and witnesses. He employed a three-fold figure to describe their attitude: sheep among wolves, wise as serpents, harmless as doves — strange description of missionaries and ministers!

"I send you forth." The *I* here is emphatic, implying that Christ holds up Himself as "the Fountain of the gospel ministry, as He is also the Great Bur-

den of it." How does He send His disciples forth?

"As sheep in the midst of wolves." He had just described the lost multitudes as shepherdless "sheep," now He speaks of His own as "sheep" who will find themselves among those with whom their lot will be cast as witnesses, as a pack of destructive wolves. Wolves hardly seem convertible. Yet among these waiting to turn on and rend His sent-ones, they will be as defenseless sheep willing to die for Christ, and that the lost might be saved. To Christ, the "wolves" were those who had preyed upon those who were weak, wounding and fleecing them, as the Pharisees had. These "wolves" are the same He described as hating and killing His witnesses for His name's sake. But with prophesied conflict, suffering and death, there was the promise of victory and sovereignty. Persecutors may surround His flock as hungry and raging wolves, He would be their Defense. To be left exposed, ready to be made a prey of (John 10:12), as sheep to wolves, was startling enough; but that the sheep should be *sent* among wolves must have sounded strange indeed. No wonder this section and announcement begins with the exclamation, Behold! "Be ye therefore as wise as serpents, and as harmless as doves." What a wonderful combination! Because they were to be as sheep among wolves it would be imperative for His representatives to manifest certain characteristics. They were to have the wisdom, not the poisonous capacity, of the serpent; and the harmlessness, not helplessness, of the dove. "Alone," says Fausset, "the wisdom of the serpent is mere cunning, and the harmlessness of the dove little better than weakness; but in combination, the wisdom of the serpent would save them from unnecessary exposure to danger; the harmlessness of the dove, from sinful expedients to escape it. In the apostolic age of Christianity, how harmoniously were these qualities displayed! Instead of the fanatical thirst for martyrdom, to which a later age gave birth, there was a manly combination of unflinching zeal and calm discretion, before which nothing was able to stand."

Those who serve the Lord best, are "harmless only as they are wise, and wise when they are harmless. Any man going out upon the Master's business who lacks wisdom, is not harmless. Any man going out is not wise unless he is harmless." In a hostile world then, as sheep facing wolves eager to destroy them, His workers, if called upon to shepherd the sheep and to fight the wolves, must seek to catch men with "guile" (II Corinthians 12:16), and yet be not only supremely guileful but absolutely guileless. The Holy Spirit, who came upon Jesus "like a dove," is the only One who can reconcile the contradictory qualities suggested by "serpents" and "doves."

No matter what experiences overtake the heralds of the King, the grace of endurance must be theirs. Alas, too many give up in the good fight of faith! Christ called His disciples to a life of service and suffering. The tragedy is that throughout the ages Christians generally have preferred living lives of ease and comfort.

## The Parable of Sparrows and Hairs
### (Matthew 10:29-31)

In describing God's providential care for His witnesses in a world of sin and hate, it would seem as if metaphors are again mixed. *Sparrows* and the *hairs* of our head. Yet both prove that if chance reigned, or evil was supreme, then the witness of sent-ones would be hopeless and vain. But they labor with hope because God is Master over all and is well able to protect and provide.

"Two sparrows . . . more value than many sparrows"

Common Syrian sparrows, similar to those to which we are accustomed, were so cheap that two of them could be bought for a "farthing," one of the smallest Roman coins. Luke speaks of "five sparrows for two farthings" (12:6), meaning that the purchaser taking two farthing's worth, had the fifth one thrown in — of such small value were sparrows. Yet God's eye was on the odd sparrow. Jesus said that when a sparrow falls and dies, that it dies upon the bosom of God. Does not this exquisite figure teach God's tender care of His messengers when out as sheep among wolves? To Him, they are of greater value than many sparrows. "Was ever language of such simplicity felt to carry such weight as this does? But here lies much of the charm and power of our Lord's teaching."

How comforting and encouraging it is to know that the same loving interest extended to God's smallest creatures, covers His dear people. Without His consent, not one sparrow falls, whether struck with a stone or attacked by larger birds of prey. In like manner, the apostles were made to realize that the omnipotent God would watch over them and undertake for them in all things. And how they came to prove this!

"The very hairs of your head are all numbered"

No one, apart from an almost bald man, knows the number of hairs in his own head. We are told that on a normal head there are six or seven hundred on a square inch of skin of the head, and reckon there are usually from about thirty thousand to fifty thousand on a head. Does not this striking figure of speech convey the natural expression of the thought that even the incidents of life that seem most trivial are in very deed working together for the good of those who love God? At no moment of his life is a Christian uncared for by his Father above. As He knows and notes precisely how many hairs are on the head (I Samuel 14:15; Luke 21:18; Acts 27:34), so He watches over us better than we can watch over ourselves. Those Jesus commissioned were bidden to remember that at every turn of their life and labors, God would be present, ready and certain to succor and deliver.

## The Parable of Swords and Foes

(Matthew 10:32-38)

While the unashamed confession of Christ is the great duty of all He calls to follow and serve Him, He here reminds us that such confession is still necessary even though it proves disturbing. We here light upon one of those hard and apparently contradictory sayings of our Lord. Was not His birth heralded as bringing "peace on earth"? Did He not say, "In Me . . . peace" and is He not our Peace? Is He not portrayed as "the Prince of Peace"? Yes, all this is true. But it is likewise true that He cannot give His great heavenly peace till He has disturbed our low, and at times, our false earthly peace.

This seeming paradox was intended to prepare the disciples for the strife and division their true witness would entail. Was it not revealed to the mother of our Lord that, "a sword would pass through her own soul also" (Luke 2:35)? Now He illustrates the effect His work and witness, and also that of His children, would produce. The figure of the sword meant that His cause would be division, even to the breaking up of households, but that amid all separations His own must be loyal to Him. Because His truth would be contrary to all the impulses of the human soul, inevitably divisions would arise. There would come "deadly opposition between eternally hostile principles, penetrating into and rending asunder dearest ties." He who alone can fashion true households, yet wields a sword and divides households.

When Jesus spoke of foes of one's own household, had He in mind His own brothers according to the flesh, who had not yet believed in Him? This we do know that the treason of Judas against Jesus was an extension of the Psalmist's complaint (Psalm 41:9; 55:12-14; see Micah 7:6; John 13:18). Often in a home there arises the necessity of a choice between Christ and the nearest relations. This is the severe test a Jew or Roman Catholic often has to face when stepping out for Christ. Such obedience to the higher, supernatural calling, no matter what cost is involved, constitutes the cross to which Jesus referred. The disciples knew what it was for their Master to take up His cross, and they came to experience what it was to endure ignominy, suffering and death for His dear sake. Our cross is not the daily burdens or irritations coming upon us, but a preparedness to go forth even to crucifixion. The pith of our Lord's paradoxical maxim about losing life to find it is summed up for us in the couplet:

"The life of self is death,
The death of self is life."

All those who pass "a sentence of death on themselves," or who accept Christ at whatever cost, are assured that the reward of such discipleship is great. There is the reward of the dignity of ambassadorship, we will witness before, and the promise and prospect of a glorious reward when Jesus appears to judge every man's service of what sort it is.

## The Parable of the Reed and the Soft Clothing

(Matthew 11:1-15)

We have already dealt with John the Baptist's witness to Christ; here we have Christ's witness to John who, although the greatest of the prophets, felt the ways of Providence to be mysterious. Hearing of Christ's miraculous works while he was in prison, John was perplexed over the Master's apparent neglect of him while he was suffering for righteousness sake. John expected Christ to use the *fan* of judgment, the *axe* of retribution and the *fire* to consume, but the works he heard of were those of mercy, not of judgment. But like a wise man, John took his doubts about Christ to Christ *Himself* and was not long in being relieved of his doubt and difficulty. The marvels John heard about ended his darkness and gave him light at eventide. Out John went to die triumphant as a martyr for truth's sake.

Christ is silent about Himself, but speaks simply and naturally in symbolic fashion about the greatness of John; and He asked and answered successively three questions about His forerunner:

"A reed shaken with the wind?" What impression had the people gathered of John when, as a lone voice, he cried in the wilderness? Did they see one who vacillated, who was swayed this way or that by every blast of popular feeling? No, something altogether different. The rushes growing upon the banks of Jordan were the symbol of weakness. Although growing some twenty feet in height, these rushes or reeds were slender and weak, and being unstable, were easily agitated and swayed by winds sweeping across the valley. There might have been those who, contrasting the grand faith of John's preaching with the halting doubt of his question to Christ, "Art Thou He that should come, or do we look for another?" felt he was more of a reed shaken by the wind. But Jesus, in His own gracious way, did not answer John's question of doubt. He knew him to be more of a solid oak than a weak reed.

"A man clothed in soft raiment?" Had John been a favorite at Herod's court, he would not have been chained in the king's prison. Dr. Campbell Morgan tells us that "soft raiment was the emblem of enervation. Writing to the Corinthians Paul used that word which is here rendered, 'soft raiment,' *effeminate,* and that undoubtedly was its meaning. Jesus used two Greek words in which the letters are exactly the same, differently arranged. A reed — *kalamos.* A man in soft raiment — *malakos.* Had they gone out to see a *kalamos,* or a *malakos;* a reed blown about by every breeze, or an enervated man, a man in soft raiment?"

Jesus went on to explain that wearers of soft raiment were to be found in kings' houses, or palaces, and not in a prison where John was. Thus with satire Jesus proved that John was not a man in whose life there was a prostitution of virility for personal pleasure. He was no effeminate dilettante, hanging on at the courts of kings for the gratification of lusts. John was no popularity-hunter. So with great dignity Jesus defended John from the possibility of misunderstanding. "We gather therefore that there are two characteristics that disqualify any man for prophetic work. What are they? Weakness that yields to every passing wind that blows, or such self-indulgence as can be expressed only when they wear soft raiment."

"A prophet?" Continuing His defense of John, Jesus declared him to be the greatest of the prophets and the greatest of men. At the moment John was in despair at his useless life, Jesus was crowning his name with loftiest honor. How kind and gracious He is! When the people went out to see John in the wilderness, they were not disappointed, for they saw and heard a prophet. Why think less worthily of him now? Even in his suffering, John was still the divinely commissioned messenger of the Lord who was raised up to prepare His way. Jesus bestowed upon John a still greater honor. He named him *My Messenger* and called him *Elijah,* on the ground that he came in "the spiritual power of Elijah," and wrought, like the prophet, a great spiritual awakening in Israel (Luke 1:17). John had prepared the way for Christ into human hearts more than any previous messenger had done. Then our Lord tells us who have ears to hear, to listen to all that He had said regarding John, and to give heed to these lessons:

The greatest of saints may have seasons of darkness.

If Christ does not deliver us *from* adversity, He will sustain us *in* it.
None can appreciate the value of a faithful witness like the Lord.
We have a mighty, violent force in the Gospel, if we will use it.
The message we proclaim is greater than that of John's, seeing we live on the Calvary and Resurrection side.

## The Parable of a
## Generation and of Children
(Matthew 11:16,17)

From the defense of the character of John, Jesus passes to describe the character of the age in which both John and Jesus found themselves. The Lord of Nature who could find sermons in lilies and birds now finds a text in children at their games. "The surly child who will not play at any game, and blames another for it, is the figure under which Christ sets forth the people round about Him." His homely illustration fittingly portrayed the unreasonableness of His age, which was therefore unable to appreciate and receive His message.

At the back of Christ's use of the common amusements of an Eastern city, is the way the children played at weddings and funerals. How often He had witnessed the childish representation of wedding festivities and funeral pomp. The children would play their pipes and expect others to dance; they would beat their breasts in lamentation and expect others to weep. They were peeved if the other children would not join them in the juvenile imitations of the joyous and mournful scenes of life. It was in this way Jesus likened the capricious evil generation in which John and He lived.

One interpretation of the parabolic illustration is the fact that the antagonistic Jews were loud in their complaints against John the Baptist because he would not share their self-indulgent mirth; bitter against Jesus because He would not live according to the rules of their hypocritical austerity. Another explanation is that our Lord and John invited others to mourning and mirth respectively, but they were repelled by their sullen fellows. The unreasonableness of the people has been paraphrased thus by Campbell Morgan: "You will not mourn to John's wailing, and you will not dance to My piping. John came with the stern, hard, ascetic and profoundly necessary message, calling men to repentance, and you say he has a demon, and you will not listen. I have come with such humanness that men say of Me, I am a gluttonous Man, and a winebibber, a friend of publicans and sinners." It was an age that would not mourn to John's wailing, or dance to Jesus' piping. Or to reverse the order, John would not dance to their piping, and Jesus would not mourn to their wailing. The people were like a group of children who did not know their own mind. The stern, severe note of John was denounced as being the utterance of a demon-possessed man; the tender, joyful message of Jesus was rejected because it lacked the ascetic note (Proverbs 27:7). No wonder Jesus ended this particular conversation by saying that "Wisdom is justified by her works, or children." True wisdom knows "the necessity for the real reason of mourning, and the true inspiration of dancing, and she is justified in her methods as they are presented to men." There is great concurrence of the children of wisdom in the acceptance of both sides of truth in obeying the call to repentance and faith in the Saviour.

## The Parable of
## Sheep and a Pit
(Matthew 12:10-13)

In this chapter we have a renewal of the Sabbath Day dispute in which the Pharisees were constantly involving Jesus. But He had suggested that the letter of every law of outward action is sometimes with propriety broken, if the spirit of it is kept, and that obedience to higher laws gives some relief from lower ones. Here again we have Jesus entering a synagogue on a Sabbath Day, where the Pharisees waited to convict Him of Sabbath-breaking because the penalty of such an offense was death. The presence of the man with a palsied arm favored the Pharisees, who knew only too well that Jesus could not look on disease without relieving it. For a full treatment of the miracle He performed, and its complications, the reader is referred to the writer's volume on *All the Miracles of the Bible.*

In reply to the question the Pharisees asked Jesus, He replied with two questions designed to expose the dishonesty of their traditionalism. Constantly He flung Himself against the bondage of traditionalism because it overlay the Law of God. Tradition had been heaped upon tradition, binding the people with intolerable burdens. The first question was direct and personal: "What man shall there be among you, that shall have one sheep, and if it fall into a pit on the sabbath day, will he not lay hold on it, and lift it out?"

Many of the Pharisees, if they had seen a sheep in a pit, would not have stopped to draw it out, but had it been their *own* sheep, they would have rescued it. This is the point of our Lord's illustration. "Which of *you*, having one of your own sheep fallen into a pit, would you not pull it out on the Sabbath?" How this question exposed their inconsistency and hypocrisy. What simple yet unanswerable questions Jesus could ask! Each Pharisee convicted by the question knew that instinctively, without consulting the Law, he would extricate the sheep from a pit, for such an act was regarded as lawful, even by the more rigid Scribes. Some worked out the compromise that the sheep was not to be pulled out of the pit till the Sabbath was over, but in the meantime it was lawful to supply it with fodder.

Familiar as the Pharisees were with the Old Testament maxim that "a righteous man regardeth the life of his beast" (Proverbs 12:10), Christ's appeal was resistless, for they knew that they would instinctively rescue a sheep from suffering or death, even on the Sabbath. Thus, most skilfully, He prepared the way for His second question: "How much then is a man better than a sheep?" Christ's critics were silenced by the startling alternative, "Is it lawful on the sabbath days . . . to save life or to destroy it?" (Mark 3:4; Luke 6:8,9). If the Pharisees could and would rescue

their property, man, as God's property, was of more value than many sheep and therefore had a higher right to be rescued, especially when the man was sorely afflicted as the one Jesus healed. Was not the palsied man, as all men, immortal, made of God, and thus better than a sheep?

By healing the palsied man, Jesus proclaimed that mercy is the best Sabbath-keeping. Says Richard Glover, "We should not shock anyone's religious scruples when truth or duty do not require it; but when they require it, we ought to do so." In defiance of the carping Pharisees, Jesus healed the sufferer, and in doing so, endangered His own life, for His foes took counsel as to their next step. As for the healed man, he was one of a great multitude that found release and blessing in God's sanctuary.

## The Parable of the Tree and Fruit
### (Matthew 12:33-35)

In returning to the symbol which He had already used in His ethical manifesto, Jesus seeks to illustrate the dishonesty of His foes and enforce His claims against opposition. How could any honest mind attribute good to an evil source? How could His victory over Satan come from complicity with Satan? What Christ asked for was honest judgment. Accept the fact that both the *tree* and *fruit* are *good,* or both *tree* and *fruit* are *evil,* but do not believe that the tree is bad and its fruit good. But the dishonesty of the Pharisees was the *treasure* of evil in their hearts. How could they promote good as evil, or evil as good?

Revealing the venomous malignity of the hearts of His enemies, Jesus utters a solemn warning about their words developing into great crimes damning their souls. *Idle,* as used by Christ, implies that words can be mischievous as well as needless. The words of the Pharisees formed no innocent jest. They were the index of their graceless hearts and would rise up to condemn them at the Day of Judgment. Applying the truth to the

Pharisees, Jesus asked, "How can ye, being evil, speak good things?" He wanted them to apply His illustration of the tree and its fruit to Himself and His work. "He appealed to these men to test Him, and to find out the secret of His ability, by the things at which they were looking, the things done, by the fruit produced." Calling good, evil, or ascribing divine work to Satan, constituted the unforgivable sin, (the blasphemy against the Holy Spirit,) the Inspirer of the works and words of Jesus.

## The Parable of Jonah and the Queen
### (Matthew 12:38-42)

Immediately after a great miracle had been wrought, certain of the Pharisees sought a sign from Heaven. Spiritually blind, they failed to see that what they asked for was before them. What they needed was not *light,* but *sight,* for Christ was in Himself the great Sign. But blind to truth, they did not grasp the significance of either His works or character. Having attributed His miracle-working power to the devil, they now asked Jesus for a sign from heaven (Luke 11:16) where they thought the devil could not reach with his beguiling arts. But Christ replied that only the evil and adulterous seek after signs.

While those who were blind to Christ's deity and Messiahship could not have a sign which would convey belief, they can and will have a sign, overwhelming them with dismay — the Resurrection of Jesus, after they had slain Him, would be the dread sign to convince them. To illustrate His death and resurrection, Jesus used the historic sign of Jonah, the sign the Pharisees already had in their own literature, and which now Jesus applies to Himself. Three days and three nights in the belly of a great fish was a sign to Nineveh — and such a mystic sign of a man coming back from the dead, produced repentance in Nineveh, and suspended its judgment for a hundred years. The death, burial, and resurrection of Jesus would

likewise be a sign establishing His claims as the Son of God, and also the divinity of His mission. Earlier, He was asked for a sign and said, "Destroy this temple (His body), and in three days I will raise it up."

The essential faults of the evil and adulterous generation were denounced by Jesus, who likewise proved it to be condemned by the Ninevites who repented at the preaching of Jonah, but who were not moved to repentance at the call of a Greater than Jonah. Then Jesus cited the Queen from the South of Arabia, who risked much to see and hear Solomon, but here were these Pharisees, blind to the fact that a Greater than Solomon was in their midst. They heard Him speak as never man spake, yet they only listened to catch some word with which to slay Him. The Queen of Sheba praised Solomon for his wisdom and bestowed upon him rich gifts. Those to whom the Saviour came, however, saw no beauty in Him that they might desire Him, and despised, rejected, slighted, slandered, and slew Him.

## The Parable of the Empty House and Eight Spirits
### (Matthew 12:43-45)

By "this wicked generation" we are to understand Israel as a whole, who was like a man out of whom an evil spirit had been cast, without goodness "taking its place." "The evil spirit of idolatry had been cast out after the Babylonian Captivity, but true faith in, and love to God, did not fill the void. It remained from the days of Ezra *empty and swept,* and *garnished* itself with the conceit of superiority to all other lands. The devil ejected would return with greater force and invade successfully his lost abode, and the people would sink into worse sin than even their idolatry had been."

Both John the Baptist and Jesus had exercised a cleansing, purifying and exorcising ministry. But Israel was still like a tenantless house, swept and garnished by divine teaching, but not possessed. One evil master had been dispossessed but because the house still lacked a new possessor, the empty house was the opportunity for the re-entry of the demon, and seven more like him, making the last condition of the house worse than the first.

For our generation the lesson is evident. No one is safe whose life is empty. Doing no harm is a condition that will not continue unless we take to doing good. A man may try to clean up his life and expel bad habits, but *reformation* without regeneration is of no avail. We must try to sweep society and garnish it and improve the environment of men, but if they fail to admit a new Master in their life, reformation will only prepare the way for worse desolation. Being and doing good can only be effectual when inspired by Him who is the Fount of Goodness.

## The Parabolic Scheme of Matthew Thirteen

Before dealing individually with the parables forming this great chapter, it is vitally important to consider the chapter as a whole, seeing it contains Christ's explanation of His use of the parabolic method of instruction. "Chronologically in the ministry of Jesus the record in this chapter marks a stage in that ministry when our Lord turned largely to the parabolic method when dealing with the multitudes, employing it also with His own disciples."

Surveying the eight parables of the chapter we find in them "the King's own view of His Kingdom as to its history in the age which He had then initiated. These parables, pictures, stories, reveal His view of the Kingdom, not in its eternal and abiding sense, but in its history in the age which He had initiated by His coming into the world." As much has been written about the group of *seven* parables in this chapter, it is necessary to point out that it contains *eight* parables, all delivered on the same occasion, though not as one set discourse. Here is the way some ex-

positors try to group the first seven parables to the neglect of the eighth one, which is a most important parable as a fitting climax to the parabolic teaching of the chapter.

Fausset speaks of the parables as being "Seven in number, and it is not a little remarkable that while this is the *sacred number,* the first *four* of them were spoken to the mixed multitude, while the remaining *three* were spoken to the *twelve* in private — these divisions, *four* and *three,* being themselves notable in the symbolic arithmetic of Scripture. Another thing remarkable in the structure of these parables is, that while the first of the *seven* — that of the Sower — is of the nature of an Introduction to the whole, the remaining Six consist of three pairs — the Second and Seventh, the Third and Fourth, and the Fifth and Sixth, corresponding to each other; each pair setting forth the same general truths, but with a certain diversity of aspect. All this can hardly be accidental." Thus the eighth parable has no place in Fausset's scheme.

Akin to this incomplete grouping of this chapter's parables is that dealing with *seven* as one of the perfect numbers of Scripture. This number denotes *completeness* (Psalm 12:6; Revelation 11:4). Four of the parables spoken to the multitude exhibit, not only the aspect of the Kingdom to the outside world — the number four, when used typically, is the number of the earth (Ezekiel 37:9; Daniel 7:2,3; Matthew 24:31; Revelation 7:9 etc.). It also shows the working of "the mystery of iniquity," and the actual extent to which the evil one is permitted to go, in his opposition to the truth of God in this dispensation. The remaining three parables — the number *three,* when viewed symbolically signifying, not only heavenly things (Genesis 18:2,9,13; Numbers 6:25-27; Isaiah 6:3; I Corinthians 13:13 etc.), but the fulness of testimony (Deuteronomy 19:15; II Corinthians 13:1), were spoken to the disciples themselves, in the house after

Jesus had sent the multitudes away. These *three* show in the *inner* aspect of His subject.

Other writers, dealing only with seven of our Lord's parables in Matthew thirteen, try to use them in parallel form, with the seven Beatitudes of the Sermon on the Mount. While such a comparison may prove profitable, and a few coincidences are obvious, this line of observation should be jealously kept subordinate to the primary substantial lesson which each parable contains.

Arnot, who does not refer to the eighth parable in his volume dealing with thirty parables of our Lord, groups the seven in his logical arrangement, representing the Kingdom of God in different aspects. The *first* pair exhibit the *relations* of the Kingdom to the several classes of intelligent creatures with which, as adversaries or subjects, it comes into contact: the *second* pair exhibit the *progress* of the Kingdom from small beginnings to a glorious issue: the *third* pair exhibit the *preciousness* of the Kingdom, in comparison with all other objects of desire: and the remaining *one* teaches that the good and evil which intermingle on earth will be completely and finally separated in the great day. Here is Arnot's outline:

I. RELATIONS
{
1. *The Sower;* the relation of the kingdom to different *classes of men.*
2. *The Tares;* the relation of the kingdom to *the wicked one.*
}

II. PROGRESS
{
1. *The Mustard-seed;* the progress of the kingdom under the idea of *a living growth.*
2. *The Leaven;* the progress of the kingdom under the idea of *a contagious* outspread.
}

III. PRECIOUSNESS
{
1. *The Hid Treasure;* the preciousness of the kingdom under the idea of *discovering what was* hid.
2. *The Goodly Pearl;* the preciousness of the kingdom under the idea of *closing with what is offered.*
}

IV. SEPARATION
{
*The Draw-net;* the separation between good and evil in the great day.
}

Arthur W. Pink in his small treatise on *The Prophetic Parables of Matthew Thirteen* deals only with the first seven, ignoring completely the eighth parable on *The Scribe and Householder.* Trench, in his standard work, *Notes on the Parables,* likewise omits any treatment of this eighth parable. He speaks of "the relation in which the seven parables recorded in the thirteenth chapter of Matthew, stand to one another."

Then there are those writers who, in an ingenious fashion connect the first seven parables of Matthew 13 with the Seven Churches of Asia (Revelation 2; 3). While there may be a parallel between these two "sevens," the prudent preacher will guard against an attempt to trace it too minutely. Habershon has a full discussion on the parallels between The Seven Parables and The Seven Churches.

> *Ephesus,* noted for Patience — The Sower bearing fruit with patience.
> *Smyrna,* "Jews and are not" — The Darnel Parable.
> *Pergamos* — "Satan's seat" — The Mustard Tree Parable.
> *Thyatira* — Jezebel. The Woman and Leaven Parable.
> *Sardis* — Name lives yet dead. Treasure Hidden in Field.
> *Philadelphia*—"I have loved thee." Pearl of Great Price.
> *Laodicea.* Spued out. Good Gathered, Bad Cast Away Parable.

The renowned expositor, Lange, sees in the series of seven Parables, the subsquent historical development of the Christian Church. Briefly, this is his contention: "We . . . trace in the parable of the sower a picture of the Apostolic Age; the parable of the tares, the ancient Catholic Church springing up in the midst of heresies; the parable of the mustard tree resorted to by birds of the air as if it had been a tree, and loaded with their nests, a representation of the outward church as established under Constantine the Great; the leaven that is mixed among the three measures of meal, the pervading and transforming influence of Christianity in the mediaeval Church among the barbarous races of Europe; the treasure in the field, the period of the Reformation; the pearl, the contrast between Christianity and the acquisition of modern culture and secularism; the draw net, a picture of the closing judgment."

We fail to understand why so many expositors do not see that the chapter before us contains eight parables, with "the first — *The Sower,* and the eighth –– *The Householder* as the key parables, the one introducing and the other concluding the whole series; one anticipative and the other reflective, looking on and looking back." While the first seven parables are likened to "seven notes in a scale, yet an eighth is required to make the octave repeating the first note in another key, so after the seven parables, there is an eighth which completes the group." After the first series of four parables we read, "All these spake Jesus unto the multitude in parables" (Matthew 13:34); at the end of the eighth parable we have the phrase, "When Jesus had finished these parables (all eight of them) He departed thence" (13:53).

When Jesus finished the first seven parables, He said to His disciples, "Have ye understood these things?" They replied, "Yes." Their comprehension made it possible for Jesus to utter one more parable revealing the responsibility of the disciples as scribes instructed in the Kingdom of Heaven, to bring forth from such a treasure, "things new and old." The first four parables were given to the multitudes as they thronged the shore, where the Master's pulpit was a boat. The last four parables were spoken to the disciples in the house.

Without any preparation on the part of the hearers for the subject to be treated, Jesus commenced His discourse and continued it in parabolic form following one parable with another, in no connected way. The parables are merely linked with phrases like, "Another parable set He before them," or "spake unto them," or "the kingdom of Heaven is like," or "likened to." The longest parable in the eight is the first, namely, *The Sower,* which carries with it an explanation. A few moments would suffice for the recital of this parable. Jesus teaches us by the simplicity and shortness of His parables that brevity is the soul of wit, and simplicity is the body of an illustration. His method is in sharp and singular contrast to the involved and lengthy style of some preachers and expositors, as, for example, the tremendously involved and wordy exposition of Benjamin Keach on *The Parables* and *The Metaphors.*

As we enter upon a study of the thirty or more accepted complete parables of our Lord, we shall discover how near to life He lived. Farmers must have been thrilled as they listened to His pictures of agricultural life. Home-life offered another favorite source of figures of speech. Merchants heard the commercial world illustrated and translated in terms of spiritual values. Civic duties and social life were also vividly portrayed. The world of nature, the birds and flowers, supplied Him with analogues for the spiritual realities. The majority of Christ's parables were suggested, as we shall presently discover, by the fitting occasion and thus "preserve a naturalness and a vitality that invite admiration but discourage limitation."

While we have discoursed upon many of Christ's parabolic illustrations in the first twelve chapters of Matthew, the word *parable* occurs for the first time in the New Testament in the announcement, "He spake many things unto them in parables" (Matthew 13:3). From the question of the disciples, "Why speaketh he unto them in parables?" (Matthew 13:10), we gather that the parables were a new form of teaching to them. Thereafter the term *parable* implies the fuller form of the narrative embracing facts natural and probable in themselves. "The prominence given in the first three gospels to *The Parable of the Sower,* shows how deep an impression it made on the minds of men, and so far justified the choice of this method of teaching by the Divine Master."

## The Parable of the Sower and the Seed

(Matthew 13:3-23)

As this parable is also given with slight variations in Mark (4:3-9, 14-26) and in Luke (8:4-15), it is necessary, as we have previously indicated, to compare and contrast parallel references to a parable. In this way we gather a complete picture of what our Lord taught about *The Kingdom of Heaven,* which implies, not the glorified state of the future life, but "that presently existing spiritual community of which Christ is the Head, and which is composed of those whose hearts and lives are subject to Him as the Sovereign." *The Sermon on the Mount* dealt with the same theme, and the *parables* before us may be regarded as an illustrative appendix to that matchless sermon. In the *Sermon,* Jesus treated the subject abstractly and impersonally. In the *parables,* He used familiar figures for its illustration and has special reference to the different effects produced by its presentation, on men of different dispositions. In the *Sermon,* Christ was mainly retrospective; in His *parables* He is almost entirely prospective, as He unfolds the manner of the progress of His Kingdom, and the nature of its consummation. This is why the *Sermon* and the *parables* should be studied together.

Approaching a particular study of our Lord's Parables, one can appreciate the decision Dr. C. G. Lang made as he came to prepare his volume on *The Parables of Jesus,* dealing with sixteen

of these parables: "It would be mere presumption to attempt to write anything on the subject of the parables without using the guidance of Archbishop Trench's scholarship and insight, but I have thought it best not to consult any other commentaries." Alas, before me are over sixty published books dealing with *The Parables* in varying number, and it is no mean task to wade through them all in order to discover what light each writer throws upon each parable!

In *The Sower,* which Jesus gave as a type of all the rest of His parables, and concerning which He laid down the reasons which led Him to choose this way of reaching the hearts and consciences of His hearers, it is easy to imagine the scene of its telling. Dean Stanley in *Sinai and Palestine* gives us a beautiful description of "The Plain of Gennesaret," which elucidates the setting of this first parable. Jesus was in a boat on the blue waters of the lake, and before Him, on the fringe of the bright yellow sand, stood the crowd of eager listeners. Raising His eyes, Jesus happened to notice a sower on the slope of a hill behind the beach, scattering his seed, the birds flying around and behind him. Instinctively, with swift, vivid reality, He thought of His own immediate situation. There He was sowing the seed of the Word, and His disciples were to follow Him in preaching and teaching the Gospel; and thus the parable of the sower was born.

The three constituent elements of this parable are: the sower, the seed and the soils. Hillyer H. Straton speaks of "the rule of three" in folk tales. "In the nursery tale there are three bowls of porridge, three chairs, and three bears. These same factors operate in the parables. . . . Three types of response in the parable of the talents, three travelers on the Jericho Road, three kinds of soil, and three rates of growth." Dr. Straton also shows that "the rule of the two" also operates in some of the Parables: the two sons, the two debtors, the Pharisee and the Publican, etc.

*The Sower.* Goebel objects to this as a title for the parable and prefers calling it *Divers Soils.* "The thought is not that of a certain individual sower, who did so and so in distinction from others, and who fared so and so. . . . In the sequel, the person of the sower is left out of sight. The narrative speaks simply of the fate of the seed sown, the different kinds of soil on which it fell, and the corresponding effect it produced. . . . The parable is named after the sowing, which is the subject, and not after a particular person supposed to be treated of." But surely the sower is not incidental to the parable because without him there could have been no sowing and no fruit. Who, then, was Jesus illustrating when He said, "Behold, the sower went forth to sow"? *The sower* is a generic, denoting, not a certain individual but a class or company. The language implies any typical sower. We must not overlook the fact, however, that our Lord directs attention to the *sower* in the words, "Hear ye therefore the parable of *the sower"* (Matthew 13:18). Surely He knew how to choose the most fitting title, not only for this parable, but for all of His matchless parables.

Jesus used a double exclamation in introducing the sower, "Behold"; "Hearken" (Mark 4:3). "Behold" was designed to arrest attention and was a call to ponder carefully what follows. "Hearken," indicated that our Lord was about to communicate something of unusual importance. The disciples and those to whom Jesus spake this parable were bidden to look and learn. Truths profoundly suggestive and instructive were about to be uttered. Before we try to identify the sower, a word is necessary regarding his inconspicuousness. Scarcely anything at all is revealed in the parable about him, beyond the simple fact that he actually sowed the seed. As we already hinted the emphasis in the parable is upon the seed, and the various kinds of soil and the obstacles to, and conditions of, fruitfulness. The personality of the sower and the method of sowing are of secondary importance. *The sower* is adaptable, suggesting differing interpretations.

*God* likens Himself to a sower. "I will sow the house of Israel and the house of Judah with the seed of man, and with the seed of the beast" (Jeremiah 31:27). What a persistent and abundant Sower He is! Both in the natural and the spiritual realms, God works majestically alone, and as the Sower, is untiring in His task. He knows full well that although much seed falls by the wayside, ultimately a great harvest will be His when "the kingdoms of this world will become the kingdoms of our Lord and of His Christ."

*Christ* is also the Sower. The Master likens and announces Himself as *The Sower.* Did He not come forth from "the storehouse of infinite beneficence and wisdom and life, to sow this earth with living seeds of truth and holiness and joy — seeds of the Law that shall produce conviction, and seeds of the Gospel that shall produce responsive gratitude and joy and love"? Did He not appear as the Great Teacher, the Divine Apostle of the Gospel? In the next parable Jesus speaks of Himself as "the Son of Man . . . that soweth the good seed." Others before Him had acted as sowers, sowing beside all waters, but Jesus above all others knew how to string parables like pearls on the thread of His discourses, and the saving truths He scattered have enriched the world. Thus in *the sower,* Jesus presents a true emblem and image of Himself (Matthew 13:37). Such a title befits Him. In a footnote Butterick says, "If the parable is autobiographical the immediate reference would be to Jesus. Wellhausen goes so far as to say, Jesus is not so much teaching here as reflecting aloud upon the results of His teaching."

*The Holy Spirit* is a sower. He it is who inspires sowers of the seed, and waters the sown seed. "The Spirit, like the wind, blows where He lists, and every breath of that Divine Spirit is a word of God," says C. G. Lang. "The language in which He speaks is manifold, unexpected, all-pervading as Himself. Sowing to the Spirit, we know what it is to have our spirit touched and aroused to scatter the seed. Since Christ, the Divine Sower, ascended on high, by the agency of His Spirit He has ever since continued His ministry through His redeemed children in whom He acts by His Spirit."

*Every Christian* should be a sower. In commissioning His own, Christ spoke of the hearts of men as the field, and His Gospel as the seed to be cast everywhere. "Go ye, and make disciples from among all nations" (Matthew 28:19,20; Mark 16:20). What He began to teach, His Apostles continued teaching (Acts 1:1). Knowing that he was Christ's representative as a sower, Paul could say, "Christ speaketh in me" (II Corinthians 13:3). The Apostle regarded his whole ministry as a sowing of spiritual things (I Corinthians 9:11). From the time of his remarkable conversion, Paul knew that he was a chosen vessel for sowing the precious seed of the Gospel into human hearts wherever an opening should appear among Jews and Gentiles (Acts 9:15).

It is also the privilege and obligation of all who are Christ's to function as sowers. We were saved to serve and sow. Alas, in comparison to the vastness of the field, the sowers are few! Our heavenly Father, the Husbandman, exhorts us to pray that He would send forth more sowers into His field. *All,* not merely preachers and teachers, may be sowers. As Arthur Pink says, "A little child may drop a seed as effectively as a man; the wind may carry it, and accomplish as much as though an angel had planted it." To each and all of His redeemed children the Lord has this promise, "He who goeth forth and

weepeth, bearing precious seed, shall doubtless come again with rejoicing bringing his sheaves with him."

The greatest service any Christian can render is sowing the good seed of the Word by life, lip and literature. Words and works are seeds to drop in the soil of hearts. Shakespeare wrote of a man of thoughtful wisdom:

"His plausive words
He scattered them not in ears, but
    grafted them
To grow there and to bear."

While all ministers of the Word, called by the Spirit, and qualified by grace and talents, have a solemn responsibility as sowers, yet all Christian parents, Sunday school teachers, lay preachers, and tract distributors share the same responsibility. Each of us must realize that life or death, heaven or hell, may depend upon our personal sowing of the good seed of the Gospel.

The sower, no matter who he or she may be, must be *judicious,* praying for appropriate seasons and sphere for the sowing; *diligent,* laboring as one who must give an account for sowing; *persevering,* sowing in season and out of season; *devoted,* yielded heartily, entirely and sincerely to this greatest of all tasks. Everyone bringing the divine Word to bear upon men must give heed to the wise words of Alexander Maclaren that — "Fruitfulness is the aim of the sower, and the test of the reception of the seed. If there be no fruit, manifestly there has been no real understanding of the Word. A touchstone, that, which will produce surprising results in detecting spurious Christianity, if it be honestly applied." But sowers, especially preachers of the Word, must learn from the parable before us that much of their labor is hard and sometimes fruitless from a human standpoint. It may seem as if much of their work is wasted. "Some hearers will never grasp the truth effectively at all," writes Dr. C. H. Dodd. "Others will be discouraged by difficulties, beguiled by prosperity. Yet the preacher may be sure that in the end there will be results from his labours" (Psalm 126:6).

Further, all the sower has to do is to *sow*. It is beyond his power to make the seed grow. If all who witness for the Saviour were responsible for the effect of the Gospel upon the hearts of men, theirs would be a sorry plight indeed. The word Mark uses of the seed growing secretly, "of itself" (4:26-29), is *automate,* from which we have "automatically." The one object and obligation of the sower is to *sow,* leaving the Holy Spirit to make well-prepared ground open as a thousand mouths to take in the seed, and to fructify same. The word *sown* in the explanation of the parable ("that which was sown" — not *received*), implies the perfect identity and incorporation of the seed with those that receive it. For the former we are responsible, but not for the latter.

*The Seed.* The seed to be sown is described in a two-fold way, namely, "The word of the kingdom" (Matthew 13:19), "The word of God" (Matthew 5:19; Luke 8:11). *All* the seed must be sown. The whole counsel of God must be presented. To Paul, "preaching the kingdom" was equivalent to "testifying of the grace of God" (Acts 20:24,25) and "teaching the things concerning the Lord Jesus Christ" (Acts 28:31). Pre-eminently, the full Gospel is *seed,* that is, "the most vital form of matter, that which transmutes its own nature, earth, sap, sunshine, and changes these dead things into living beauty." As to the nature of the seed we sow, it is spoken of as being "living" and "incorruptible" (I Peter 1:22-25); powerful and soul saving (Romans 1:16; 10:17); heavenly and divine (Isaiah 55:10,11); immutable and everlasting (Isaiah 40:8); engrafted and able to save (James 1:17, 18,21).

As "the Word of God" is the seed, and Christ came as "the Word of God" (John 1:1), He Himself is the Seed. The Written Word testifies of Him who came as the Living Word (John 5:39). The Bible is "the Word" because it is full of Christ who came as such. Those who receive the seed of the Word come to "live," not because they believe the Bible truth presented. They have life through His name (John 20:30,31). The seed we sow, then, is not only *from* Christ — it *is* Christ. Arnot expresses it, "The seed of the kingdom is Himself the King. Nor is there any inconsistency in representing Christ as the Seed while He was in the first instance also the *Sower.* Most certainly He preached the Saviour, and also was the Saviour whom He preached. The incident in the synagogue at Nazareth (Luke 4:16-22) is a remarkably distinct example of Christ being at once the Sower and the Seed. . . . The Saviour preached the Saviour, Himself the Sower and Himself the Seed."

*The Soils.* The different soils to which the parable calls attention are its outstanding features. Attention is focused not on the sower or his seed, but on the soil and its reaction to the seed sown. Here we come to the importance of this parable, an importance we cannot exaggerate. Jesus said of it, "Know ye not this parable? and how shall you know all parables?" (Mark 4:13). The seed sown in all *four* soils was the same, but what a marked difference. It is this that makes it the *key* parable and it is so, "Because it deals comprehensively with the fundamental truth, namely the proclamation of the Gospel to sinners. Other parables deal with subsequent truths, and would not be understood without this one. Let us then call it *The Parable of the Soils,* and understand that these soils are different states of heart and their reaction to the Gospel. Which of them represents *you?*"

1. *The Wayside Hearer,* or the hearer with the *closed* mind. This type receives the seed by the ear, but no life ensues. The seed is *on* the surface but not *in*. We have here represented those hard-surfaced souls who are destitute of spiritual perception. Such may be re-

ligious and be regular at church but the truth received never fills the soul with fearful grandeur. The truth is "trodden down" by "the wheel of traffic and the wheel of pleasure." It takes no hold because the heart is like a highway; the surface is hard and nothing can make an impression on it. The seed cannot penetrate and germinate; therefore the "birds," agencies of "the wicked one," snatch it away. The truth takes *no hold,* the hard crust of thoughtlessness hinders reception. When once the Word is understood and received in faith, it is beyond Satan's reach.

2. *The Stony Ground Hearer,* or the hearer with an *emotional* mind. In this instance, the seed is received but does not take root. The seed is *on* and *in* but not *down.* Here we have the easily excited and enthusiastic people well known to those who preach the Gospel, whose hold of it is only superficial, and whose faith is thin-surfaced. Such people do not know what it is to be born again of the incorruptible seed. "The root of the matter" is not in them. Impressions are transitory, and when temptations and persecution arise, they quickly backslide. Depth of faith, surrender and character are lacking. It is not without significance that the superficial character is connected with the hard heart. If the first class represent those who take *no hold,* this next class in the gradation stands for those who take a superficial hold. Says Wm. M. Taylor in his *Parables of Our Saviour,* "Violent emotion is a sign of shallowness, and never lasts; but the tender heart disposes to moral thoughtfulness, and where that is, the feeling is permanent." The *stony* place was where there was only a shallow layer of earth, beneath which was hard, unimpressible rock. Churches have too many of these *stony* hearts. What a blessing they would be, if only they had depth!

3. *The Thorny Ground Hearer,* or the hearer with the *wandering* mind. Here the seed takes root but bears no fruit. The seed is *on, in* and *down* but

does not come *up.* It is *choked* and *typifies* the pre-occupied people. The truth takes hold, but the hold is disputed by a trio of antagonists. Forces in opposition to the nature of the seed are permitted to exist.

*The Cares of This World.* An anxious, unrelaxing attention to the business of this present life chokes the seed. A score of interests, legitimate in their place, are allowed to dominate one's life, with religion as just another department of the already highly departmental life. Pre-occupied professed Christians permit spiritual impressions to come to nothing because of their submission to dissipating influences; petty trifling distractions fill the heart with paltry solicitudes and mean anxieties. These people, like Martha, "cumbered with much serving," miss the joy and privilege of sitting at the Master's feet.

*The Deceitfulness of Riches.* What is here implied are those riches accruing as the fruit of worldly care and anxiety. Christ did not say that wealthy Christians bear no fruit but that they do not bring forth fruit to perfection (Luke 8:14). "How hardly shall they that *trust* in riches enter into the kingdom of heaven." F. W. Robertson comments, "Christ does not say the divided heart has no religion, but that it is a dwarfed, stunted, feeble religion."

*The Lusts of Other Things.* This phrase may be translated as "The pleasures of this life." Enjoyments, innocent in themselves, in which worldly prosperity enables one to indulge, smother the seed. So much of time is taken up for pleasure that only the dregs remain for spiritual things. In the early stages of Christian profession there was growth and the *promise* of fruit, but other considerations prevented the fruit from ripening. May the good Lord deliver us from becoming engrossed with earth and earthly things resulting in the neglect of the great realities of the soul and eternity. The Rich Young Ruler wanted his great possessions *and* eternal life. But it had to be Christ *or* his possessions, not both. No man can serve *two* masters.

4. *The Good Ground Hearer,* or the hearer with the stedfast, understanding mind. Because there was deep root in this instance, there was much fruit. The seed was *on, in, down* and *up*. The seed had taken full hold. It had entered the whole soul, filling mind, heart, conscience and will. The Word being received, understood and yielded to, produces faith binding to Christ, and service glorifying to God and beneficial to others. This last soil is reverse to the previous three. Therein the seed takes root, does not quickly lose the moisture and so sap and vigor are giving life to the growing plant. William Ward Ayer says that "the good-ground hearers present the optimistic side of this pessimistic parable."

The seed bears fruit just in proportion as it is allowed to possess the "honest and good heart" (Luke 8:15). If the seed brings forth fruit with "patience" or continuance "enduring to the end" in contrast with those in whom the Word is "choked," then the seed sown achieves its mission. How are we to interpret the different degrees of fruitfulness mentioned by Jesus? Fausset expresses the difference thus: "The *thirty fold* is designed to express the *lowest* degree of fruitfulness; the *sixty fold,* the *intermediate* degree of fruitfulness; the *hundred fold,* the *highest* degree. As 'a hundred fold,' though not unexampled (Genesis 26:12), is a rare return in the natural husbandry, so the highest degrees of spiritual fruitfulness are too seldom witnessed." Lisco observes, "As the degrees of hearing without fruit were three-fold, so also the abundance of fruit is three-fold. To him that hath is given." Cummings comments, "It is a well-known fact, that three-fifths of the seed sown in every country does not grow into the harvest; and according to this parable, three-fourths of the audience received the seed, but altogether in vain." The practical question is, What amount of in-

crease is your life and mine yielding? Are we giving back thirty fold, a fair return; sixty fold, more heartening to the Sower than the former; or a hundred fold, a striking, wonderful and God-honoring return that is actually the fulness of the blessing of the Gospel of Christ?

We must not lose sight of the fundamental and universal character of the Master's warning, "He that hath ears to hear, let him hear." As we read the parable we must strive not only to be fruitful, but to abound therein to the glory of God. We must give heed to the indispensable characteristics of profitable hearing, and of the blessed advantages of receiving, understanding and obeying the Word. From the parable we learn:

> The greatness of the privilege of those who sow the seed, and of those who receive it.
>
> The individual responsibility for improving those privileges.
>
> The terrible doom of those who hear to no profit (Hebrews 3:4.)
>
> The final results of those who keep on sowing the seed.

As we conclude our meditation on the *Parable of the Sower,* a further word is necessary regarding our Lord's explanation of same (Matthew 13:10-17). His profoundest truth is given in parabolic germ, and the parables "disclose truth exactly in the degree in which men can admit it; hiding it from those who would abuse it, imparting it to those who would obey it." A parable revealed truth to those accepting and appreciating it —— concealing it from those resenting and abusing it. Goebel says, "The parable, it is supposed, is meant to do two things, namely, to reveal the truth to the receptive, and to conceal it from the unreceptive." Thus, parables serve the double and opposite purpose of *revealing* and *concealing*. "The mysteries of the kingdom" are "presented to those who know and relish them, though in never so small a degree, in a new and attractive light; but to those who are insensible to spiritual things yielding only, as so many tales, some temporary entertainment." With the disciples we, too, are thrice blessed, if our ears and eyes voluntarily and gladly open to receive the Light Divine.

## The Parable of the Tares and the Wheat

### (Matthew 13:24-30; 36-43)

With a slightly different aspect this parable teaches the same truth as the previous parable. Here we have the mixed character of the Kingdom and the final and absolute separation of all men into two classes. Again, in this further exquisite parable, the Great Preacher Himself, with characteristic, charming simplicity and clarity, expounds the significance of His teaching. In the *Parable of the Sower,* "the seed is the word of God" (Luke 8:11). But those who received that word into their hearts and proved it to be the transforming Word, are now "children of the kingdom," as James expresses it, "Of His own will begat He us with the word of truth" (1:18).

This parable presents the problem of evil. The fact of the mingling of the evil with the good is a condition of things confronting us in all grades of society, all forms of government, in the home and in the church. No matter how we may legislate or separate, seeds of corruption seem to find lodging and grow to noxious weeds in good fields. The real and the counterfeit are ever with us. Good and evil are inextricably interwoven in our human society. Even Reinhold Neibuhr says, "The creative and destructive elements in anxiety are so mixed that to purge even moral achievement of sin is not so easy as moralists imagine."

In the *Parable of the Soils,* there was *one* sower, *one* kind of seed, and six results. In the *Parable of the Tares and Wheat* there are *two* sowers, *two* kinds of seed, and *two* harvests: one of the good, the other, bad. In the first parable there are *four* kinds of soil; here the fourth kind, the good soil is before us with no reference to the wayside rocky place or thorny soil. "The field" is not divided into four unequal parts, yet each of the four soils of the previous parable may be found throughout the whole field. The good ground is not separated and by itself in the field but is "interspersed with other soils over the whole field." This is an important feature to note in the interpretation of the parable before us.

*The Field.* What are we to understand by *The Field* yielding both wheat and tares? Some expositors have assumed because of the reference to "wheat" that our Lord taught the field to represent the Church or Christendom. Dr. E. H. Kirk says, "This parable is a prophetic declaration that the Church of Christ on earth should be an imperfect body. The visible Church, or the Church as a body organized on earth has two kinds of imperfection; the personal defects of the regenerated, and the membership of unregenerated persons. These imperfections have, in every age, awakened a sincere zeal: and caused also an unenlightened, and even an impure zeal, to engage in the work of purification. The design of this parable is to enlighten and modify the former; and to strip the latter of its plausible argument." Fausset likewise affirms that the tares are sown with the wheat, or "deposited within the territory of the visible Church." Arthur Pink also distinguishes the field as the religious world.

Jesus distinctly taught that "the field is the *world*" — "his field" (13:24,38). He here claims proprietorship. We do not deny the lamentable fact that in the realm of Christian profession there are tares *and* wheat; *all* within the true Church, the Church of the living God, form the good seed, the wheat, but in Christendom a mixture of "the sons of God" and "sons of the evil one" can be found. Note the expressions, *His field, Thy field,* which assert that the Master is the Owner, Lord, Husbandman of this world of man. "The earth is the Lord's and the fulness thereof." This field, then, is the sphere of human habitation in the world God loved (John 3:16), and in which the enemy catches away the good seed, and also sows tares.

*The Two Sowers.* The audience receiving this further parable was the same as before, namely, the crowd assembled on the shore, as well as the disciples in the boat. To these, Jesus described the two sowers, so different in character and purpose. First, there was the "man" revealed as the "householder" (Matthew 13:24,27), and as "the Son of Man" (Matthew 13:37). In the previous parable "the sower" stands for all proclaimers of the Gospel, even Jesus Himself. Here, "the sower" is Jesus only. As the Creator, He made man upright, created him in His own likeness, that is, planted within him holy principles and aspirations. The other sower is referred to as "his enemy," "an enemy," "the wicked one," "the devil" (Matthew 13:25,28,38,39). It was not long before Satan sowed tares in God's wheat, Adam and Eve. The word Jesus used for His enemy was *diabolos,* the traducer, the liar, the one who is against all that is true, high and noble. Note the emphasis here, "*His* enemy" that is, Christ's enemy. Christ has ever been the object of the devil's malice (Matthew 4:1-11). A trinity of good and a trinity of evil stand opposed to one another: The *Father* and the *world* (I John 2:15, 16); the *Spirit* and the *Flesh* (Galatians 5:17); *Christ* and Satan (Genesis 3:15). His enemy sowed in a field that was not *his*. In spite of prevailing evil in the world, it is still Christ's world, and when He returns to it as "the Prince of the kings of the earth," it will be a purer world in which to live.

The cunning of the enemy is seen in his action of sowing his tares among the wheat while the servants slept. We cannot take this to mean a lack of watchfulness on their part and that therefore they were to blame for the mixed field.

Doubtless it was night time and the ordinary sleeping time for the field workers and watchers. Rather are we given an insight into the cowardly nature of the devil, in choosing the darkness for his diabolical work. Evil is sown secretly, and the devil's dupes love darkness because their deeds are evil. Thus the sleeping servants are not merely the dress, or color of the parable.

*The Two Products.* The Son of Man sows *wheat* in His field and "his enemy" sows tares "among the wheat." This diabolical being would not think of sowing the wicked among the wicked. He sows the wicked among the good, and the two together constitute Christendom. What are we to understand by the figurative products in the parable? Let us take, first of all:

*The Tares.* The devil's action was motivated by pure malice, for tares, like weeds, have never been a marketable product. More accurately "tares" are "darnel," a seed scarcely distinguishable from wheat seed (and not until it is sprung up can the difference be detected). "Tares" are not what we understand by the term but some noxious form of plant, or wild corn, and poisonous as food. *Tares!* So vigilant and unresting an enemy as Satan has so many of them to sow; tares of fleshly wisdom, of pride, of procrastination, of sin. And because, as Thomson in *Land and the Book* informs us, "the closest scrutiny will often fail to detect the difference between tares and wheat when both are less developed, we have an insight into Satan's subtle working." His method is *opposition by imitation* as Dr. Scroggie puts it. The bad are sown among the good, and the difference is not always discernible. Many who are not the Lord's yet resemble those who are: they go to church, pray, read the Bible like Christians, but are, alas, Christless.

Richard Glover in his *Commentary on Matthew* informs us that sowing tares among wheat was "a form of revenge, happily rare, but one against which laws were made in Rome, and still occasionally practiced in all lands. The mischief aimed at was the poisoning of some of the wheat, necessitating great labour to get rid of it, and the lingering presence for years of some seeds of mischief. How wicked men become when they give way to revenge! Dean Alford had once a field belonging to him sown with wild mustard by a foe who disliked him." The devil, then, is revengeful and malicious.

But in His interpretation of the parable Jesus says that the "tares" are "the children of the wicked one" (13:38), not plants but *persons*. What differences of nature are suggested by the phrases, *children of the kingdom* and *children of the wicked one*. The latter do not draw their origin from the wicked one, but many mould their character by his promptings, and are thus called his children (John 8:44). These are the ones whom Satan sows among "the children of the kingdom."

*The Wheat*. "The good seed," "the wheat," "the children of the kingdom" are equivalent terms. In the previous parable, "the seed" was the word of the kingdom, here, "the good seed" is the product of that precious word received, understood and obeyed, namely, those who through such become "children of the kingdom." The Son of Man, as the Sower or Householder sows only good seed: lives transformed by, and embodying the word of truth. It is the Redeemer's purpose to sow His redeemed ones in this world of sin and misery in order that there may be fruit for His glory and satisfaction for His travailed soul. This is why He has sown *you* where you live and labor. As one bought with a price and born of His Spirit, and a new creation in Him and an heir of eternal life, He expects you to bear fruit in the corner of the field of this world, in which He sowed you.

*The Two Questions*. The servants of the Householder or Owner of the field, asked Him two general questions: "Sir, didst thou sow good seed in thy field — from whence hath it tares? . . .

Wilt thou then that we go and gather them up?" The first question is in two parts, with the first part acknowledging that the field was the Householder's, and that He had done the sowing, and that He had sown only *good* seed.

The earth is the Lord's. He also originated and first spread the Gospel, and nothing but the Gospel. But the second part of the first question brings us to the deepest of all mysteries, namely, the origin of evil and its continuance in the world. This problem of the parable is as old as the human race. Why was the Serpent allowed to enter Paradise? Why was Judas permitted to be counted among the Twelve? Why was the early church almost wrecked by false brethren? Why does God allow the sin and sorrow blighting His world today? Jesus said, "An enemy hath done this." But why is the enemy so active, after almost two millenniums of Christianity, sowing more tares than ever in God's field? This is one of the mysteries to be revealed. Presently, as "Christians we should be mainly concerned with victory over evil rather than a full explanation of it."

The second question, "Wilt thou then that we go and gather them (the tares) up?" suggests that the servants were eager to rid the field of its noxious weeds at once. The Householder's reply is in two parts. First of all, He refers to the growth of the wheat and the darnel. In its unripe condition the wheat and the darnel looked alike, and to try and destroy the one, would mean destroying the other. The separation of the one or the other would be beyond the wisdom of the servants. The second part of the answer is taken up with the final harvest. "Let both grow until the harvest." Not forever will the good seed and the tares be intermingled. The time of separation will come, when angels, and not men, will secure the wheat and burn the tares.

*The Two Harvests*. Describing the time of harvest, Jesus said that the reapers will be able to distinguish between wheat and tares, and that the separation between them will be effected in this way: "Gather ye together first the tares, and bind them in bundles to burn them . . . Gather the wheat into my barn." Such a harvest of destruction for tares is to take place at "the end of this world." First of all, let us deal with the destruction of the tares which are to be bound up in bundles. As the gathering together of the tares into bundles takes place *in* the field, it is interesting to watch how this process of binding the tares into bundles is proceeding with amazing rapidity. Never was there a day like ours for combines and amalgamations. We see it in the *commercial* world, in which private interests are being eliminated. Trusts, syndicates, unions and corporations dominate industry and commerce. In the *social* world, we never had so many clubs, guilds, fraternities and organizations. In the *political* world, we have United Nations, Commonwealths and Common Markets. Communism is forging many nations into one block and avowed atheistic countries want to live in peaceful co-existence with professedly Christian nations. In the *religious* world, the bundling together is prominent. Protestants, Roman Catholics and Jews fraternize, and *ecumenicity* is their prominent gospel. One wonders if the Divine Command has gone forth, "Gather the tares in bundles."

After the gathering and binding of the weeds, there comes their destruction by fire. The time of such a harvest is appointed: "God hath appointed a day in which he will judge the world" (Acts 17:31). The course of human history, then, is set toward judgment. "The time of moral assessment and award is approaching with all the precision of moral machinery, and none will escape the last Grand Assize." As to the *time* the reapers obey the summons of the Householder to deal with the tares, Jesus said it would be at "the end of the world," or *age* — the end of the Gentile age when Christ returns to earth as King and gathers out from His Kingdom all things that cause stumbling (Revelation 16:14, 16). The final judgment of all the wicked will take place at the Great White Throne, which is to witness the ratification of God's judgment upon Satan, evil angels, and all who died outside of Christ.

"Burned in the fire" is a most solemn phrase. As the "tares" symbolize all lost souls, we cannot make light of their future after such a declared fate. Jesus affirmed the utter destruction of the tares. The "furnace of fire" and "wailing and gnashing of teeth" describe the horrors of Hell, and of the final abode of the wicked, the Lake of Fire. Such terrific strength of language is dreadful to contemplate. Fausset says that "the *casting* or *flinging* are expressive of indignation, abhorrence and contempt (Psalm 9:17; Daniel 12:2): 'the furnace of fire' denotes the fierceness of the torment: the 'wailing' signifies the anguish this causes: while 'the gnashing of teeth' is a graphic way of expressing the despair in which its remedilessness issues (Matthew 8:12)." The doom of the wicked will be fearful (Revelation 20:11). What Jesus said about the bundles burning was not mere parable drapery, but a solemn revelation and declaration of fate (Hebrews 2:1-4).

But what a different harvest awaits the wheat, which is to be gathered into the divine barn. There will be no tares in *that* barn, just as there will be no wheat in the furnace of fire. The question is, When will the gathering of the wheat of the Son of Man take place? When Jesus returns to the air then there will be gathered out all His wheat from the field of this world. What a gathering of the ransomed that will be! (I Thessalonians 4:15-17). Is not His Father's House the *Barn* He will gather us into? (John 14:1-3). His chosen gathered from "the four winds" (Matthew 24:30,31), are to be with Him where He is. What a glorious destination awaits the righteous, who are to shine as the stars forever. Exaltation and blessedness are to be theirs throughout eternity (Matthew 13:43; 25:24)! They have been called to God's eternal glory in Christ (I Peter 5:10; II Peter 1:1-11). A ravishing prospect is the portion of all who have been saved by grace (Daniel 12:1-3; Acts 14:22; II Timothy 2:12).

There is a further thought to stress as we come to the conclusion of our meditation on the *Parable of the Wheat and Tares,* namely, we still live in an age of grace when *tares* can become wheat, or sinners can be fashioned into saints. The parable does not exclude such a change before "the end of the age" is reached. From other words of Jesus we learn that by His power, the enemy can be defeated, and his slaves made servants of God. Children of the devil, they can yet become children of the Kingdom, and thus be saved from the final, terrible judgment of the wicked. Counterfeit members in the Church can be changed into genuine and profitable members. Then is there not a personal application to bear in mind? Jesus told Peter that he was *wheat* and that as such he was to be sifted by Satan, and that in the sifting the chaff, or tares, would disappear (Luke 22:31). Have we reason to search the field of our heart to discover whether the enemy has sown any tares therein? The more the Lord has of our heart, the less the devil will have.

# The Parable of the Mustard Tree and Birds
## (Matthew 13:31-32)

We can call this parable, and the following one, "The Parable of the Leaven," *Sandwich Parables,* seeing they are both placed between recital and the explanation of the previous parable of "The Wheat and Tares" (Matthew 13:13-18). Both of these parables, *The Mustard Seed* and *The Leaven,* and the six following ones, are left without interpretation on the part of Jesus, "as though to train the disciples in the art of interpreting for themselves." But, alas, as

we are to see, *The Mustard Seed Parable* along with other parables have suffered much mis-interpretation from the hands of expositors. What must not be forgotten is the fact that all the parables of Matthew 13 have to do with *our* age, and that by them our Lord was *not* teaching the complete and ultimate success of His Kingdom in this age which extends from His first advent right over to His second advent to earth.

Further, in these prophetic parables our Lord was not illustrating *the true nature* of His Kingdom. He surveyed the age and looked toward its consummation and described the mixed conditions that would prevail until His return as King of kings, when uniformity will prevail. In none of these parables is He found "revealing the *inward nature* of the Kingdom, except at the beginning when He showed that the Kingdom principles are found in the Word of God, as it is embodied in the lives of Christian men and women. That of course includes everything, but there is no detailed reference to it in interpretation. The ethics of the Kingdom are not found here in detail. These are found in the Sermon on the Mount." This, we feel, is the key opening to us the full significance of these peerless parables.

There are also other important factors to bear in mind as we come to consider these parables "depicting Kingdom processes during *our* age of divine procedure."

1. In our Lord's connected, prophetic forecast of the course of events in the whole realm of Christian profession up to the time of His return, He gives us *two* views of the one subject; namely, the *outward* aspect, shown to the people; the *inward* aspect, as revealed to His disciples.

2. The teaching of our Lord's parables is progressive. He sows only good seed — bad seed, sown among the good is sown by an enemy; the vision of outward growth — the vision of inward influence; the individual aspect of the subject — the collective aspect of the

subject; opposite results at the end of the age. Attention to these facts will make for clarity and correctness of interpretation.

3. Distinction must be maintained between *Interpretation* and *Application*. Too often the two are confused. In the parable of *The Mustard Seed,* opposite interpretations are held and applications made. As we shall more fully discover, there are many expositors who hold that this brief parable forecasts the amazing growth of the Christian Church according to divine design. Other expositors, however, hold that the parable is an unfolding of the abnormal and unnatural extension of the nominal church, contrary to divine design. Both of these interpretations cannot be right.

4. Each of these Kingdom parables must be interpreted within its imposed limits, namely, this present age. Their prophetic teaching is seen in historical fulfilment. Often, in an attempt to understand these parables, there is a misinterpretation of history.

5. As *The Truth,* our Lord is consistent and uniform in His teaching. He never makes one parable contradict the teaching of another. He is never found using one figure of speech in two different senses. Throughout all of His parables there is perfect harmony in conception and teaching. Thus, comparing what He had to say in other discourses about things waxing worse and worse as the age draws near its consummation, with the common idea that the Gospel is to be preached until all the world becomes Christian, we see that such an idea is a mistaken one.

6. A peril to avoid is that of popularity of interpretation. Warning against the reliance on the general consensus of expository opinion, Campbell Morgan says that, "The acceptance of popular interpretation of Scripture led to the crucifixion of Jesus. . . . Whatever the popular interpretation may be, it is not therefore necessarily the correct one. It may be correct, but popularity is not any guarantee of accuracy." With this observation in mind, the student of parabolic literature will find that the majority of expositors follow the same line in the interpretation of *The Mustard Seed,* namely, that in it our Lord predicted the great, complete and ultimate success of His Kingdom in this age. But His consistent teaching denies such a success. Here is a synopsis of our search of the popular yet mistaken interpretation of this parable.

The idea of the Kingdom's growth from very small beginnings to ultimate universality is expressed in the following ways:

*Arnot* describes the parable as "The progress of the Kingdom under the idea of a living growth."

*Lange* writes, "The grain of mustard seed — so small and despised in the outward appearance of Him who bore the form of a servant, or rather, in that of His disciples—shoots up, and the smallest of seeds grows into a huge bark, so even to resemble a tree. But in consequence of this very growth, the birds of the air mistake the bark for a tree and seek to make a lodgment in its branches."

*Alford* says that "We must beware of imagining that the *outward church-forms* in this Kingdom . . . The parable reveals the inherent *self-developing power* of the Kingdom of Heaven as a seed containing in itself the principle of expansion — the penetrating of the *whole mass of humanity,* by degrees, by the influence of the Spirit of God."

*Leslie D. Weatherhead,* whose modernistic treatment of the Bible has brought him much notoriety, is also adverse to the interpretation that this parable portrays the abortive growth of religious organization, in the sphere of Christian profession. In his volume, *In Quest of the Kingdom,* he summarizes what a score of other writers say of *The Mustard Seed Parables:* "Behold how vast a tree has grown from so small a seed. A despised Rabbi in a despised corner of the Roman Empire, coming from despised Nazareth, sowed the seed

Himself and entrusted it to a dozen untrained, non-university men of lowly birth and little influence — and the world-wide Church is the result." Well, this may be attractive and appealing writing, but it is not *truth*. Had Christianity continued humble and unpretentious, its ministry would never have been sought as a *profession*, with many unclean birds lodging in the topmost branches of the great mustard tree.

*Fairbairn,* in his *Imperial Bible Encyclopedia,* expresses the same general interpretation of the parable thus: "A little germ and a large result; an obscure commencement and a surprising progress; 'the least of all seeds' and 'the greatest of herbs' — are the avowed contrast of the parable, and the resemblance of this to the Kingdom of God is the declared lesson of the Lord." What Fairbairn and so many others fail to distinguish, is the distinction between the inward and outward aspects of the Kingdom or between its divine conception and human development.

As our understanding of the parable hinges upon a correct interpretation of its three central elements, namely, The Seed, The Great Tree, and The Birds of the Air, let us now examine these in detail.

*The Grain of Mustard Seed.* What we know as *mustard,* does not grow into anything that can be called a tree. While there are several kinds of mustard seed, botanists suggest that the species spoken of in the parable is *The Khardah,* Arabic for "mustard." Because of the minuteness of a grain, the seed came to symbolize small beginnings, and denotes the smallest weight or measure. It is tantamount to a particle, "ever so little." Because of its hot, fiery vigor, and giving only its best virtues when bruised, it is therefore attractive to the taste of birds who are drawn to the herb for food and shelter. In the parable, the small seed is not so much the Word as in *The Parable of the Sower,* as a genuine Christian society, the Church which appeared as the first-fruits of the Word.

The identity of the male sower is not given, as in *The Sower,* just as the female mixer in the next parable of *The Leaven* is anonymous. But without doubt the Man sowing the grain of mustard was "the Son of Man," as in the case of *The Sower,* for He it was who had a most insignificant entrance into the world and founded His Church (which He called a "little flock" — small in appearance and unbecoming of it to make a spectacle of its virtue).

While Matthew says this seed was sown in a "field," Mark says it was sown in the earth (Mark 4:30-32), and Luke, in "his garden" (Luke 13:18,19). Regarding these differences in detail, G. H. Lang says that they illustrate the fact that "details must not be pressed to yield different specific meanings; and also that differences may not be contradictions; for any soil is earth, and a garden may be a corner of a field." The "field" in our parable is "the field of the world" in a previous one. The seed, then, sown in the world on the Day of Pentecost was small and insignificant — "about an hundred and twenty" (Acts 1:15-26).

*The Great Tree.* Matthew describes the rapid growth of the seed into a "great herb" as a tree; Luke says the seed "grew and waxed a great tree." *Herbs,* even though they may grow into a tree-like appearance, are an entirely different specie than *trees.* The growth of trees is slow, but that of a herb, like mustard seed, is abnormal, developing without the strong wood-issue of a tree, and living only long enough to develop flowers and seed. Thus a *herb* becoming a *tree* suggests an expansion entirely foreign to its very nature and constitution. How could this condition of things possibly describe the true Church of Jesus Christ? In a matter of months *The Khardal* can grow into a tree-like shrub between ten and twenty feet high, and with a wide coverage of fan-like branches.

Because the grain of mustard seed grows into a "great tree" suggesting loftiness, expansion and prominence, many expositors err in using this botanical detail to announce the rapid spread of the Gospel and the expansion of Christianity throughout the World. The organized Church has wrongly changed the emphasis from *seed-sowing* to *tree growing.* Instead of scattering the seed in all lowliness, the Church became more concerned with building larger denominations, institutions and orders. The great ecclesiastical systems, including the great religious-political Roman Catholic system representing Christianity do not appear in the New Testament. The Founder of Christianity never meant to use the mustard-seed taking root deeper and deeper in the earth, to describe His Church, whose hope, calling and citizenship is in heaven. Did He not say that His own are not of this world, even as He is not of this world?

The field is where the seed is sown in *the world*–sphere in which the flesh and the devil are united in opposition to all that concerns Christ and His Church. A godless world, while a necessary place to some seeds of godliness, does not offer a congenial soil for the expansion of Christianity. There is continuous harmony running through the parables of Matthew 13. Thus, in *The Sower* the seed did not take root and flourish in every part of the field, only a fourth of it. In the *Parable of the Wheat and Tares,* we have the continuance and consequences of Satan's work, which positively forbids the expectation of a world won for Christ in this present age. Therefore, the *Parable of the Mustard Seed* cannot teach that which is adverse to the previous parables, namely, a whole field containing *all* good seed, and in which *wheat* alone grows. The ultimate universality of the Gospel before Christ returns is foreign to His teaching.

Before we summarize the difference between Christianity and Christendom (the insignificant "garden shrub outdoing itself," a condition speaking of abnormality) let us briefly consider the significance of:

*The Birds of the Air.* By comparing Scripture with Scripture we find that the birds, or fowls, of the air symbolize Satan and his subtle forces. Used in a former parable in this sense, they must have the same significance in this parable. Matthew identifies "the birds of the air" as "the wicked one." Mark speaks of them as symbolizing satanic activity. Luke links the "fowls of the air" to the devil. Fowls came down on the carcasses of the bodies of sacrifices, and Abraham drove them away (Genesis 15:11; Deuteronomy 28:16). Toward the end of the Gentile Age, Babylon becomes "the habitation of demons, and the hold of every foul spirit and a cage of every unclean and hateful bird." We believe that our Lord had this symbolic significance in mind when, describing the amplitude of "the great tree," He said the birds of the air would lodge in its branches.

Many expositors, however, agreeing that the *Mustard Seed Parable* teaches the speedy and ultimate triumph of the Gospel, use the figure of "the birds of the air" in a good sense. Thus Ellicott says that these birds are "no longer, as before the emblems of evil but refer to the systems of thought, institutions, and the like, of other races — finding refuge under the protection of the tree." Others wrongly suggest that "the birds" typify young converts flocking to the Church. Trench, in spite of his admirable treatise on *The Parables,* seems to have missed the prophetic aspect of many of them. Of "the birds," this renowned expositor says, "They are a prophecy of the refuge and defence that should be for all men in the church." Stier has a similar interpretation of "the birds" and asks, "What then are the birds but, in the first place, the many men and nations who are brought beneath the shelter of this protecting structure?"

If the above interpreters mean unconverted men and nations, surely such birds could only defile the tree, and if they mean converted men and nations, this would be the expansion of the tree itself. A tree does not grow by birds lodging in its branches, and Jesus could never have expressed such a jumble of ideas as the Church increasing by the addition of something foreign to its nature. We hold that "the birds of the air" do not represent men and nations, but the wicked one, Satan, the prince of the power of the air, who has watched the spread of the Kingdom in mystery from its small beginning to the great extent, and has ever sought to find a shelter in it, as he quickly did in those false brethren who became a part of the Church unawares.

Our Lord in this parable states the fact that, however rapid and vast the expansion of His cause during His absence, it would be befouled by the presence and plots of the prince of darkness. Those who reject this interpretation argue that it represents the devil as lodging in the Kingdom of Heaven, which they regard as being equivalent to the Church Jesus came to establish. But history proves that the outward growth of the Church sheltered evil, and today it shelters many cults and organizations foreign to its true nature. Another undeniable fact is that as God permitted Satan to tempt Job to the extremest limit, and to sift Peter as wheat, in His providence He permits tares to grow alongside of wheat, and evil birds to lodge in the branches of the tree.

We now approach a matter of vital importance in an effort to rightly interpret our Lord's Parable at this stage in His ministry, namely, the distinction between Christianity, or the true Church — and Christendom. Too often, we lose sight of the difference between the Church as an *organism* and as an *organization*. A person may be in the *organism* and not in the *organization* and *vice versa*.

Nebuchadnezzar is a key to the parable of "a great tree" which was a figure of his mighty and earthly empire (Daniel 4:10-12; 20-22). Samuel likened the proud Assyrian to a giant cedar tree which symbolized Assyria's earthly greatness and worldly prominence, giving shelter to surrounding nations. Christianity started with Christ, and *is* Christ, and with a few loyal followers which He called a "little flock." After His Ascension, the Church was founded in many parts but soon experienced, to its full force, satanic antagonism. It is reckoned that all the Apostles except John were martyred. Then Satan turned from fierce persecution and, changing his tactics, worked from within the Church. Truth and error were mixed. Satan's fowls of the air snatched away the seed.

The *Parable of the Mustard Seed* corresponds in point of time with the era marked by the letter to the Church in Pergamos (Revelation 2), when the Church, at first planted in lowliness and humility, assumed the appearance of worldly greatness, and passed from under the persecuting power of Imperial Rome, to be the subject of its patronage in the reign of Constantine the Great. Now the tree, with its lofty height and wide-spreading branches, became the emblem of earthly dignity and greatness. Princes of the Gentiles commenced to exercise dominion in Church affairs (Matthew 20:25-28). The Church was corrupted from her simplicity in Christ (II Corinthians 11:2,3). She became great in the earth and thus contrary to her original character and design, and so unlike her Head who was meek and lowly in heart.

As the professed church passed from an *organism* to an *organization,* there developed the passion for prominence, power and position. Men, actuated by worldly principles, sought supremacy in the church. Thus, Emperor Constantine, after his defeat of the heathen Licinius, 328 A.D., "set Christianity upon the throne of the Caesars," and princes took upon themselves the title of "high priest." Dr. Campbell Morgan gives us the following excellent summary of the abnormal growth of the Church as the result of Constantine's espousal of Christianity: "That was the darkest day that dawned in all history of the Church. His espousal of Christianity was an astute and clever political move and he grafted upon Christianity much of paganism, and elevated it to a position of worldly power; and in that hour the whole Church passed under the blight from which it has never completely escaped. That is the whole sin and wrong of Papacy, domination done in the name of Christ, the claiming of power to rule over kings, emperors, and rulers and dictate terms to them; a great tree, spreading its branches. That spirit remains in every attempt even today, to realize the divine purpose by high organization, vested power. It is not a good thing. It is an abnormal growth." Such a speedy but unsubstantial, unreliable and abortive growth of Christian profession was not in keeping with the teaching of the Founder of Christianity. Baptismal regeneration, a deadly heresy in which Constantine firmly believed, became a firmly rooted doctrine in the Church. Mary, the mother of our Lord, became the Queen of Heaven in lieu of the old Babylonian goddess of that title (Jeremiah 45:17-19). The use of incense, holy water, candles, gorgeous vestments, and worship of saints were introduced and became as "the fowls of the air. . . . lodging in the branches" of this religious "tree." Satan had obtained a secure dwelling place in the professing Church of Christ, that he was now in the position to produce his first great travesty of God's truth, a prophetic intimation of which our Lord gave in the *Parable of the Leaven,* namely, catholicity, no longer the characteristic of the *true* Church of Christ, but appertaining to the *false* church.

Much could be written on the development of falsehood in Christendom — the emergence through the centuries of false religious systems and cults, all owning the right to the title of *Christian,* such as "Christian Science," which is neither Christian nor scientific. Then we have the union between Church and State; the proposal of the union of so-called branches of the Christian Church into one universal Church. Regeneration is absolutely essential for inclusion with the Church, which is the Lord's body, but today church membership is wide open and the mass of church-goers have had no experience of the new birth and faith in the fundamentals is no longer necessary. Christendom is so top-heavy because too many "fowls of the air" lodge in the branches of its tree.

Reporting on the enthronement of Michael Ramsey, son of a non-conformist, as Archbishop of Canterbury, June, 1961, the Bishop of Southwark, describing the gorgeous scene at Canterbury Cathedral, remarked: "Hundreds of the people were in top hats and swallow coats. But I didn't run into a single working-class person. I sometimes wonder what the Carpenter of Nazareth must think about His Church. And I wonder whether He would have been admitted to the enthronement; probably not." Describing the end-time period of the Church, Jesus Himself has told us what He thinks about it in language, not at all complimentary: "I will spue thee out of My mouth" (Revelation 3).

As those who distinguish between Christianity and Christendom, between the true, invisible Church and the false, visible church, we have the Master's own assurance that if our faith is only as "a grain of mustard seed," we shall prevail and remove mountains. Ours is not the task to Christianize society and assist in the development of a great tree springing out of the least of all seeds. Grace must be ours to keep out of our life that which is contrary to the purpose and spirit of the Master. Loftiness, pride, mastery, love of prominence and position are adverse to the character of Him who humbled Himself. The fowls of the air must not be given lodgment in the tree of our life.

# The Parable of the Leaven and Meal

## (Matthew 13:33-35)

In this brief (only 24 words) *sandwich parable,* which Luke also mentions (13:20-21), Christ continues and develops His teaching of the previous parable sandwiched in between the proclamation and explanation of the *Parable of the Sower and the Soils.* In *The Mustard Seed,* our Lord foretold the appearance of professed Christianity in its outward, worldly form. Here, in the *Parable of the Leaven,* He foreshows its internal doctrinal corruption. Many expositors, however, in their effort to *expound* this parable have only *confounded* its true significance in affirming that it teaches how the Gospel, slowly but surely, is to permeate society until the whole world is converted by, and to, Christ.

In the four parables which are in two pairs, the truth all four teach is consistent and progressive:

> In *The Sower,* we have the rejection of the Divine *Word.*
> In *The Wheat and Tares,* there is opposition to the Divine *Work.*
> In *The Mustard Seed,* there is abortion of the Divine *Design.*
> In *The Leaven and Meal,* there is corruption of the Divine *Agency.*

To understand what our Lord meant when He uttered the latter parable, it is essential to examine its three component parts: The Woman; The Leaven; The Meal. Here again we recognize "the rule of three." The un-Scriptural use of these figures of speech has resulted in the misinterpretation of the parable. It will be found that the popular interpretation of it is on the side of *mis*-interpretation, as we hope to show.

*The Leaven.* We commence with this disturbing and descriptive element because *leaven,* when used figuratively, as here in the parable, consistently means something bad. To affirm that the simile can mean either good or bad, is to violate its symbolic usage by the Holy Spirit in the Bible. Therefore, because *leaven* is invariably used to signify that which is bad, corrupt, unsound, how can it mean otherwise in the parable we are now considering? If types are "as rigid as mathematics," then the typical meaning of *leaven* here must be in full harmony with its usage elsewhere in Scripture.

Interpreters, in their attempt to square this parable with what they thought was the Christianizing of the world, have made it a more disputed parable. Briefly, the opposing schools of interpretation are these:

That the *leaven* alone in the parable is a type of the conquering power of the Gospel. Thus many stop at our Lord's first phrase, "The kingdom of heaven is like unto leaven," and affirm that the figure typifies something good, and therefore represents the completely victorious influence of Christ in this wicked world. While this is the popular and generally accepted interpretation, it is not necessarily correct. In fact, as we shall see, it contradicts the whole symbolic use of *leaven* in Scripture. Further, the view contradicts the teaching of the other parables of our Lord, and also His description of the process of this age, in all of which He speaks of the mixture of good and bad, of holiness and corruption.

Then those who treat this parable thus violate a most important principle. Jesus did not stop at, "The kingdom of heaven is like unto leaven," but is "like unto leaven, which a woman took, and hid in three measures of meal, till it was all leavened." It was not the *leaven* alone that illustrated the kingdom of heaven, but the *whole* of the parable. Other parables speak of mixture, but if this one of the leaven is taken as being good, and the *whole* becomes *leavened* or made good, then there is no mixture at all, which is contrary to the teaching of other parables. The leaven was hidden in the meal, and as a type of evil, represents the way in which Satan's subtle forces militate against the truth. *Leaven* is uniformly symbolic of that which disintegrates, breaks up, corrupts, as the following biblical usage proves.

The leaven which came to play a great part in Israel's bread-making, their law and ritual, and their religious teaching, possibly consisted of "a piece of fermented dough kept over from a former baking." The lump of dough thus preserved was either dissolved in water in the kneading-trough before the flour was added, or was "hid" in the flour and kneaded along with it. The bread thus made was known as "leavened," as distinguished from "unleavened bread."

The first time that *leaven* in its negative form, occurs in the Bible is in Genesis 19:3 where we are told that Lot "did bake *un*-leavened bread" for the angels and that "they did eat," which shows most plainly that *leaven*, a common commodity, was the appropriate food for doomed, wicked Sodom. Why did not righteous Lot place *leavened* bread before the angels? Because he knew better. "Nothing common or unclean" could pass their lips. Food for angels must have no semblance of evil in it. Are we as careful as we should be about our *soul-food* provided by the pulpit?

The next reference to *leaven* is in connection with Egypt, with the blood-bought Israelites, who, on the eve of their departure from the land of bondage, received this divine command: "Seven days shall ye eat unleavened bread; even the first day ye shall put away leaven out of your houses; for whosoever eateth leavened bread from the first day until the seventh day, that soul shall be cut off from Israel" (Exodus 12:15-20). Why, if *leaven* is a type of that which is good, were the Israelites told to rigidly purge their houses of it at the Passover season? It is somewhat significant that the origin of this common Scripture symbol of evil, traced to Sodom and Egypt, comes into view again in the last days during the culminating evil of the Anti-christ (Revelation 11:8).

*Leaven* is used as a type of sin in its essence in the further Mosaic legislation. "Thou shalt not offer the blood of my sacrifice with leaven" (Exodus 34:25).

The reason why leaven was excluded from any sacrifice made by fire unto the Lord, was because these were typical of the offering up of the *sinless* sacrifice of Jesus Christ Himself.

"Ye shall burn no *leaven,* nor any honey, in any offering of Jehovah made by fire" (Leviticus 2:11; see 6:14-18; Exodus 12:8,15,19,20).

A natural reason for this prohibition is sought on the ground that fermentation implied a process of corruption. *Honey* was excluded from the sacrifice because this was a type of men seeking their own glory (Proverb 25:27). Christ could assert, "I seek not mine own glory" (John 6:38; 7:18; 8:50). Thus what was sour and also sweet was prohibited in the meal offering.

Then cakes made from flour without leaven, were the only kind allowed on the altar of Jehovah. These were named "unleavened cakes" (Leviticus 10:12; 23:17,18). It is said that the injunction about "leavened bread" (Leviticus 7:13), is an exception to the rule of leaven symbolising evil. But this is not so. Every act of man's worship must necessarily to some extent have sin mixed up with it. If iniquity is in the heart, the Lord will not hear us. The two loaves presented unto the Lord at the Feast of Weeks were baked "with leaven." This event foreshadowed Pentecost (Acts 2), where the "first fruits" of this dispensation of Grace are seen. The *two loaves* prefigured saved Jews and Gentiles, in whom a good deal of the old nature remained, as is seen in Ananias and Sapphira. Typical bread, representing Christ, had to be unleavened, but where bread typifies His people it is leavened bread.

The reference of Amos regarding offering, "a sacrifice of thanksgiving with leaven" (Amos 4:5), was a message of irony, meaning the very opposite of what was said, as the previous verse reveals. The context suggests a gross infraction of the law. The use and non-use of leaven by the Israelites is summed up in the deep and searching word: "The iniquity of the holy things the children of Israel shall hallow in all their holy gifts" (Exodus 28:38).

To the Jews, then, leaven was a symbol of evil. The words, *leaven* and *unleavened,* occur 71 times in the Old Testament, and 17 times in the New, the leaven in every instance denoting that which is evil. The only solitary exception is our Lord's use of *leaven* in this parable. Yet knowing of its Old Testament typical significance, He used the word in the same way both here and elsewhere, as we are to see.

Lightfoot remarks that rabbinical writers regularly used *leaven* as a symbol of evil. One of the rabbis said, "Trust not a proselyte till twenty-four generations, for he holds his leaven."

The Talmud used it to signify, "Evil affections and the naughtiness of the heart." Plutarch, the Greek historian, voiced the ancient conception of leaven when he said of it, "Leaven is both itself generated by corruption, and also corrupts the mass with which it is mingled." The figurative uses of leaven in the New Testament reflect and confirm the ancient view of it as "corrupt and corrupting." For instance, as used by Christ, leaven is a type of bad, corrupt, unsound doctrine: "Beware ye of the leaven of the Pharisees, which is hypocrisy" (Luke 12:1). He here warned His disciples of the false doctrine of the Pharisees as is manifest from the parallel passage Mark cites, with the addition, "the leaven of Herod," which was worldliness (Mark 8:14,15). "The leaven of the Pharisees and Sadducees," was infidelity, which Jesus rebuked His own for not detecting (Matthew 16:6, 12; see 22:23,29; Acts 23:8). How could Jesus, using *leaven* as a type of *evil,* deliberately confuse His disciples by using it as the figure of good in the parable before us?

The leaven of the *Pharisees* was hypocritical formality, or religiousness,

a blinding externalism in religion, and it is so today in the church's legalism.

The leaven of the *Sadducees,* scepticism, or rationalism, is a denial of the supernatural, so common today among evolutionists.

The leaven of *Herod* was that of a debasing sensualism, the fruit of the two former. Departure from God and His Word results in secularism and indulgence in worldly lusts, the calamity of this hour. Herod's leaven consisted in power and greatness based upon the possession of material things. Is this not the sin of nations and men today?

Coming to the teaching of Paul we find him using leaven in the accustomed way, and as a type of sin in its development. "A little leaven leaveneth the whole lump. Purge out therefore the old leaven, that ye may be a new lump, as ye are unleavened . . . the leaven of malice and wickedness . . . the unleavened bread of sincerity and truth" (I Corinthians 5:6-8). Paul's reference to the sinless sacrifice of Christ, and his statement that believers, as such, are *unleavened,* settles the whole question of the typical significance of leaven, and that the popular interpretation of it is erroneous. In the "little leaven leavening the whole lump" Paul was referring to the casting out of the incestuous man because of the spreading or diffusive quality of his sin if allowed to remain unjudged. There was no need to purge out that which was good.

The last passage in which *leaven* is mentioned is Galatians 5:7-9, where the Apostle is concerned with the spreading or diffusive quality of false doctrine. In the previous passage, *leaven* is associated with an evil walk, the corrupting power of a bad example. Here the simile is used to describe the harmful effects of false doctrine, the twofold aspect being summed up by the Apostle in his warning against "filthiness of the flesh and of the spirit" (II Corinthians 7:1). The *leaven* which legalizers were trying to spread among Galatian believers, was that of the Pharisees, even a formal keeping of the Law as to circumcision being made needful unto salvation.

It is interesting to note three things in Paul's use of *leaven:*

1. It is called a "persuasion," something which exerts a powerful and moving influence.

2. It hinders men from "obeying the truth."

3. It is expressly said to be, "not from Him which calleth you."

Pink remarks that "it is remarkable that the word *leaven* occurs just *thirteen* times in the New Testament, a number always associated with evil and the work of Satan. Thus, as we have seen, that which is a thing of fermentation (really, incipient putrifaction) is, throughout Scripture, uniformly a figure of corruption — evil." Yet in spite of this evident fact many expositors, ancient and modern, persist in using *leaven* in the parable as an emblem of the good and beneficial influences of the Gospel in the world.

Martin Luther, in his *Exposition,* says of the *leaven* in the parable, "Our Lord wishes to comfort us with this similitude, and gives us to understand that, when the Gospel, as a piece of new leaven, has once mixed itself with the human race, which is the dough, it will never cease till the end of the world, but will make its way through the whole mass of those who are to be saved, despite of all the gates of Hell. Just as it is impossible for the sourness, when it has once mingled itself with the dough, ever again to be separated from it, because it has changed the nature of the dough, so is it also impossible for Christians to be ever torn from Christ. For Christ, as a piece of leaven, is so incorporated with them that they form with Him one body, one mass . . . leaven is also the Word which renews men." Expositors, through the years, have followed the Reformer's false reasoning.

Straton thinks that we have an excellent illustration of the originality of Jesus in His use of leaven. "In the think-ing of His hearers, leaven had always stood for the infective power of evil; yet here Jesus applies it to the transforming power of God, making what was in all probability an entirely new use of it." But surely the Lord, as a deep student of the Old Testament, would not go contrary to the inspired, ancient typical significance of leaven?

A. B. Bruce, who provides us with a rich study in his *Parabolic Teaching of Christ,* unites three symbols, "Ye are the salt"; "Ye are the light"; "Ye are the leaven of the World." But Jesus said that the leaven had to be *hid* in the meal. So from Bruce's application, Christians are to hide themselves in the world and not openly confess the Master. Butterick says that leaven, ordinarily used, even by Jesus, "as a symbol of evil influence need not debar us from the interpretation which is explicit in this parable — The Kingdom of God is a permeating and transforming influence; it conquers the life of mankind as leaven subdues dough." All we can say is that after almost 2,000 years of Christianity, there is a terrible mass of dough in the world to subdue. Lange speaks of leaven as "the transforming power on the whole mass of humanity, and on the whole being of individuals."

Even dear Alexander Maclaren subscribed to the popular interpretation of the *leaven.* "Now, of course, leaven is generally taken as a symbol of evil or corruption . . . But fermentation works ennobling as well as corrupting, and our Lord lays hold upon the other possible use of the metaphor. The parable teaches us that the effect of the Gospel, as ministered by, and residing in, the society of men, in whom the will of God is supreme, is to change the heavy lump of dough into light, nutritious bread." But we feel this learned expositor failed to realize that leavened meal could not possibly represent both the spread of good *and* the spread of evil. The fact remains that if leaven be good, the world is today less leavened than it has ever been. Did not our Lord Himself say,

"When the Son of Man cometh, shall He find faith on the earth?" (Luke 18:8).

The appalling fact is the world is living in blackest darkness. Speaking generally, the Gospel is today neither believed nor wanted. Paganism has increased enormously during the last decade. So far from the world being converted, the church is being corrupted. If the *meal* is the world, and the *leaven,* the Gospel, then the whole design has miscarried. The solemn declarations of Jesus regarding the course of this age, as well as those of the Apostles, cannot be true if the world is getting better through the diffusing quality of the Gospel (See Luke 17:26-30; Matthew 24:1-14; I Thessalonians 5:3; II Thessalonians 2:1-12; II Timothy 2:1-5; II Peter 3:3,4; Jude 18; Revelations 3:16; 17:1-6).

*The Woman.* Who, or what, are we to understand by the figure of the woman in the parable? Is she only *incidental,* or is she *essential* to the parable? The majority of expositors seem to neglect her presence and part. Perhaps they feel that her inclusion is natural because as sowing seed in a field is a man's work, so bread-making at home is a woman's task. But there is far more to what the woman does in the parable, as Jesus, in uttering it, turned from the agricultural realm to the domestic. Often He had watched Mary, His mother, knead the dough and bake the bread, and now uses the homely illustration to great effect. Further, there was no need of any explanation of the parable on Christ's part. Those listening to Him did so from "the Hebrew standpoint, and with their knowledge of the Hebrew writings, and of the symbolism of Hebrew figures of speech," as well as the process of bread-making, they understood, undoubtedly, the significance of the parable.

The Bible uses the figure of a *"woman,"* symbolically, in a three-fold way:

1. *As a Kingdom*
 "Sit thou silent, and get thee into darkness, O daughter of the Chal-

dees: for thou shalt no more be called the lady of kingdoms" (Isaiah 47:5).

2. *As a City*
 "I have likened the daughter of Zion to a comely and delicate woman" (Jeremiah 6:2; see Isaiah 3:26; 51:17, 18; Ezekiel 24:6,7).

3. *As a Church*
 TRUE—"Jerusalem, which above is free, which is the Mother of us all" (Galatians 4:26; see Psalm 45:10,13; Isaiah 54:1, 6; Revelation 12:1,6,17.)

 FALSE—"Come hither: I will shew unto thee the judgment of the great whore that sitteth upon many waters" (Zechariah 5:7; Revelation 2:20).

Several Bible scholars identify the "woman" in this parable as the apostate Church of Rome, who represents a *city,* a *kingdom* and a *church.* Campbell Morgan comments, "The woman represented authority and management in the hospitality of a home . . . We speak of the Church as a mother. The great Roman system ever speaks of Mother Church." Newberry says that this parable of the Woman, Leaven and Meal corresponds in chronological order with the letter addressed to the fourth Church, the Church in Thyatira (Revelation 2:18), and that the historical type is found in the account of the reign of Ahab, with his wife Jezebel: "There was none like unto Ahab, which did see himself to work wickedness in the sight of Jehovah, whom Jezebel, his wife, stirred up" (I Kings 21:25). When Jesus came to address the Church in Thyatira, He had this severe condemnation for its fellowship: "Notwithstanding I have a few things against thee, because thou sufferest that woman Jezebel, which calleth herself a prophetess, to teach and to seduce my servants to commit fornication, and to eat things sacrified unto idols" (Revelation 2:20). Newberry says, "It is the Papal system represented by the woman Jezebel, through her dogma, 'Hear the Church,' which has corrupted Christian doctrine and by that means has leavened the Church wherever that doctrine prevails. Thus, it is that the Papal system corresponds with the woman that puts the leaven into the meal." Rome does not want God to speak directly to man through His Word, and so the personal possession and perusal of the Bible is discountenanced. Roman Catholics are instructed that the Scriptures are only to be received on Rome's authority and as explained by her.

Our Lord declared that the woman Jezebel, posing as a prophetess, taught and seduced His servants. Paul wrote: "I suffer not a woman to teach, nor to usurp authority over the man, but to be in silence" (I Timothy 2:12). "As the church is subject unto Christ, so let the wives be" (Ephesians 5:24).

In the parable the "Woman" hid the leaven in the meal. The Lord, however, did not commit His Gospel into the hands of *women* of whom there were none among the Twelve, nor among the Seventy which He commissioned and sent forth. Certainly, regenerated women have their part to play in the furtherance of His cause. Scofield has the note that, "A woman, in the bad ethical sense, always symbolizes something out of place religiously" (Revelation 2:20; 17:1-6). It is somewhat significant that women have had much to do with the founding of false religious cults like Christian Science, Theosophy, Spiritism, Unity, Seventh Day Adventism, etc. Then, has not the modern church been somewhat feminized? Whether by women, personally, or as a woman symbolizing an apostate church, souls have been corrupted from the simplicity that is in Christ, and the whole system of revealed truth has been vitiated by her.

The particular action of the woman is noticeable. She *hid* the leaven in the meal. This is a feature we cannot pass over lightly. If the *leaven* in the parable represents something *good,* why *hide* it? The woman *took* the leaven — she did not *receive* it. Is this the way Christ's servants preach His Gospel? Do they whisper in secret and act stealthily? Did not the Master instruct His own to preach from the housetop (Matthew 11:27)? *Hiding* is never predicated in the Bible of the preaching of the Word: but the reverse (Psalm 40:9,10). Jesus Himself spoke *openly* unto the world (John 18:19-21), and His followers are to do the same (Mark 16:15). Divine messengers are exhorted to lift up their voices like a trumpet and speak out boldly (Isaiah 58:1; Acts 19:8; II Corinthians 5:20).

Secret hiding and the scattering of false doctrine go together. False doctrine was brought into the Early Church by false brethren unawares (Galatians 2:4). False teachers brought in their damnable heresies *privily* (II Peter 2:11,12). Jude speaks of those who crept in unawares to corrupt the saints (Jude 4:5). Silly women are led astray by those who *creep into houses* (II Timothy 2:6,7; II Thessalonians 2:7). Thus, in the parable the woman acted dishonestly and deceitfully. Her object in stealthily introducing a foreign and corrupting element into the meal was to effect its deterioration. It is thus that apostate Rome works so secretly and subtly to achieve her purpose.

*Three Measures of Meal.* Many fanciful interpretations of this amount of meal have been given. Post-millennialians say the "three measures of meal" represent the human race among whom the Gospel is working. As "the whole world lieth in the wicked one" (John 5:19), this makes the "meal" a figure of that which is evil, sinful, depraved. Others say that the "meal" stands for God's elect in their natural state, but the analogy of Scripture is against such a view. One commentator has the suggestion that the woman passed a portion of leaven in each measure of meal until all *three* were leavened, and that these *three* correspond to faith, hope and love (I Corinthians 13:13), each of which Rome has corrupted. Trench, usually conservative in his treatment, follows Jerome in suggesting that symbolically the "three measures of meal" mean the three parts of the ancient world, or body, soul and spirit — the three elements of human life; or the race descended from the three sons of Noah.

But when Jesus employed the phrase, "three measures of meal," He did not employ mere figurative, occasional language, but used a Bible phrase that had a definite meaning and value for the Hebrew mind. In the interpretation of Scripture "the law of first mention" is highly important. The first allusion to "three measures of meal" is when Abraham prepared a meal for the Lord (Genesis 18:6). This was a meal of fellowship, of hospitality, prepared for the supernatural Visitor, and a meal over which host and Guest communed. The smallest amount that might be offered as a meal-offering according to the Law was an omer, the tenth part of an ephah (Exodus 16:36). Three-tenths was the uual offering, and is seven times mentioned (Numbers 15:9; 28:12,20, 28; 29:3,9,14).

The "measure" in the parable was the third part of an ephah, and therefore three measures were equal to an ephah — the same amount offered as a meal-offering by Gideon and Hannah (Judges 6:18, 19; I Samuel 1:24), and likewise the quantity commanded for meal-offerings by Ezekiel (45:24; 46:5,7,11). Therefore there is distinct relationship between the "three measures of meal" and the meal (or meat) offering of which it is distinctly commanded, "No meat-offering which ye shall bring unto the Lord shall be made with leaven" (Leviticus 2:11). Thus, when the woman *hid* the *leaven* in the *meal,* she was doing something God prohibited. She mingled a foreign element with the meal.

The meal-offering typifies "the hospitality of the soul to God, and the hospitality of God to the soul." Christ is the Food of His people, of which they partake in communion with God. Christ is the Bread of Life, and His doctrine is the Church's most precious deposit. The maintenance of such doctrine in purity is her great responsibility. Alas, she has adulterated it with leaven!

The *meal* may also be looked upon as the Church herself. Christ, as the corn of wheat falling into the ground and dying, brought forth a harvest of His own. Meal comes from wheat, and Paul speaks of the true Church as "one loaf" (I Corinthians 10:17). Ordinarily, when leaven is mixed with meal it causes the dough to swell; it becomes *puffed up.* This is not what the Gospel does when it enters the human heart. The opposite effect is produced, for the convicted sinner is humbled and abased. Simply put, the *Parable of the Leaven* represents degeneracy in power, a breaking in upon divinely ordered fellowship, the corrupting influences of apostasy.

With this parable Jesus concluded His instructions to the multitude. Since they failed to receive Him as their King, He addressed them in parables in which He "spoke of things that supposed His rejection, and an aspect of the Kingdom unknown to the revelations of the Old Testament, which have in view either the Kingdom in power, or a little remnant receiving, amid sufferings, the word of the Prophet-King who had been rejected."

## The Parable of the Treasure and the Field
### (Matthew 13:44)

Our Lord is no longer with the multitude at the seaside, a place suited to the position in which He stood toward the people after the testimony borne at the end of chapter 12, and whither He had repaired on quitting the house. Now He re-enters the house with His disciples. He "sent the multitude away" (the *outside* "world, which lieth in the wicked one") seeing they were not able to receive the *inner* aspect of His message. Within the house, His disciples came unto Him for an *inner* expositon of all things (Matthew 13:10,17; I John 5:19).

In the four parables now to be given, Jesus having spoken to "men of sight" now speaks to "men of faith." To the men of sight among the multitude He spoke of the outer aspects, patent and self-evident of the course of the age. Now He turns to assure the men of faith, His disciples who had received Him as the Christ, and instructs them in the divine thought and method and purpose concerning the course and consummation of the age. He was soon to leave His own, and thus revealed that which characterizes His Kingdom to the spiritual man, and what he is to understand as to the true mind of God with regard to the Kingdom. The inner secrets of God could not be discerned by sight. As Campbell Morgan expresses it, "They constitute the secrets of God, but they are revealed to men of faith, knowing which, and understanding which, they will be strengthened and heartened and equipped for all their service. That is the character of the four parables to which we now come."

To those understanding the purpose of God, two parables were given which form a pair, *The Treasure* and *The Pearl*. These two parables constitute together but one text and teach the same general lesson, namely, the incomparable worth and the ultimate triumph of the Kingdom of God. Butterick says of these two brief Parables: "The stories of the Treasure and the Pearl are twin parables with likenesses so evident that they cannot deny the blood bond. Yet, as with twin children, each is markedly individual. The resemblances and the differences can be best shown as they are considered in company. . . . These two stress the worth of the Kingdom to the individual."

Trench has a similar observation of the two parables: "The two are each the complement of the other: so that under one or the other, as finders either of the pearl or hid treasure, may be ranged all who become partakers of the rich treasures of the Gospel of Christ."

Comparing and contrasting the *Treasure* and the *Pearl*, Habershon says we have first *God's view* and then *faith's view*, which is by-and-by to be recognized by all the Universe: "The hidden treasure possibly suggests a look into the past, and shows how its preciousness was discovered by Him even when the treasure was hidden in the field. The priceless value of the pearl when exhibited would be acknowledged by all, and it seems to look onwards to the time when He will come to be admired in all them that believe, and when the gem He has won from the ocean of the world shall be the wonder of the Universe."

Further, in this first pair of parables there is this distinction to observe: *The Treasure,* though collective, would be made up of *units* of precious things, such as coins and gems of various kinds. In *The Pearl,* however, there is but *one* object. This use of double symbolism was explained by Joseph long before Christ's day (Genesis 41:32). These two pictures together then, seem as though they represent different aspects of the same truth. But both of these short parables stop at the same point, namely, the completion of the purchase. Together, they emphasize twin truths: the costliness of the Treasure or Pearl, and the delight of the purchaser.

The closely related parables we are now to consider serve another purpose. If we had only the preceding parables of *The Sower, The Wheat and Tares, The Mustard Seed,* and *The Leaven,* with their gloomy, pessimistic outlook we might have been tempted to ask: "Is the divine purpose to end in failure? Is the enemy to triumph?" But *within* the house any fears the disciples may have had as to final victory were silenced. "When I thought to know this, it was too painful for me, until I went into the sanctuary of God; then understood I" (Psalm 73:17).

As we look around at the terrible condition of the world, and the impoverished, divided condition of the Church in Christendom, despondency may be ours. Many ask, "Has Christianity failed?" But as those who believe in the ever-victorious Lord, we must share His optimism expressed *within* the house, an optimism based on the hidden and mysterious workings of God even in a devil-driven and discouraging age. God's mills may appear to grind slowly, but they grind exceeding sure.

Propounding His parables, Jesus asked the men of faith, "Have ye understood all these things?" They answered, "Yea, Lord." He had satisfactorily settled any problems they may have had in this three-fold way:

In *The Treasure,* He allayed the suspicion that this little earth is a hopeless prodigal in an otherwise benevolent universe. Hendrik Van Loon wrote of this world, "Ours is a fifth-rate planet revolving around a tenth-rate sun in the forgotten corner of the universe." But Jesus assures us that this world is the object of His concern, and one which He purchased for the manifestation of His glory.

*The Pearl* reveals God's ultimate victory in the presence of man's failure. As we shall see, when considering this parable in detail, the One who purchased the Pearl discloses "the glorious transmuting of the murderous hate of sinful humanity into redemption by the love of God."

In The Dragnet, the Lord gave His own the assurance that complete justice will be executed. Presently, much sowing of seed seems to be wasted: tares dominate the field of wheat, the mustard seed is perverted, leaven corrupts the meal, but the time is coming when the Lord will effect an uncompromising separation of good and evil. His ultimate program for a sinning, corrupt world is universal purification.

Turning now to the first parable, *The Treasure,* there are two figures in it already used in previous parables and carrying the same connotation.

*The Field.* Jesus said that, "The kingdom of heaven is like unto treasure hidden in the field." Earlier He had declared, "The field is the world." By "the world" we understand this habitable globe on which we live and dwell. The "treasure," whatever it is, is hidden in *this* field. Trench's interpretation differs: "To me," says this expositor, "the field rather represents the outer visible Church, as contra-distinguished from the inward spiritual, with which the treasure would then agree."

*A Man.* In earlier parables the "man," sowing seed in the field was identified by our Lord as being Himself, "the Son of Man." That He is the "man" here secreting and securing the Treasure is clearly evident because in the parable Christ gives us a picture of the world and of His relationship to it.

When it comes to the interpretation of the parable as a whole, how confused we are by the different expositions given. Wordsworth and a score of other writers of parabolic literature would have us believe that "Christ is the treasure hid in the field; He is hid in the field of Holy Scripture, where He is presignified by types and parables." While we agree with the latter part of this assertion, we reject the former as being utterly unScriptural. How could He be the purchaser of the field, the owner of the treasure, and the treasure itself?

Then there are others who see in "the treasure hid in the field" a figure of Israel, particularly the so-called lost Ten Tribes. From earliest times redeemed Israel is spoken of as God's "peculiar treasure," as "a special people unto Himself," as "a royal diadem" (Exodus 19:5; Deuteronomy 7:6; 14:2; Psalm 135:4; Isaiah 62:1-4; Jeremiah 31:1-3). Those who hold that Israel is the treasure, affirm that it was for her sake God bought the world, as the theater on which to display among the nations the greatness of His unchangeable love for

His hidden, ancient people. The contention is that God has two bodies of elect people through whom He purposes to reveal the riches of His grace and glory in the two provinces of His empire — the world and the heavens. One of these is *Israel* presented in the parable of *The Hid Treasure;* the other is the *Church* as set forth in the parable of *The Pearl.* But while we believe that the Jew is one of God's treasures, we are not satisfied that "the treasure" is the Jew exclusively.

That the true Church is the treasure Christ found hidden in the field (and then gave His all to acquire the field and its buried treasure) is hard to reconcile with the fact that the Church of God was chosen before the world began and that Christ was associated with such a choice (Ephesians 1:4). Existing already in His and the Father's joint counsels, how could He be ignorant of its existence? (Job 17:6). Newberry says that "this parable corresponds chronologically with the address to the Church in Sardis (Revelation 3:2-6), which Church is symbolic of the period of the Reformation, the historical type of which is found in the history of Jehu (II Kings 9: 10), which was a time of outward reformation. In the *Parable of the Wheat and Tares,* 'the good seed are the children of the kingdom' mingled together with mere professors, so as with difficulty to be distinguished from them. Here the same children of the kingdom are looked at as treasure hid in the world; among the mass of mankind."

G. H. Lang sees in "the treasure" the present aspect of the Kingdom of God and heaven which is the realm of existence in which the authority of God is owned and the holiness and happiness of heaven are enjoyed. Lang then goes on to cite the spiritual experience of Abraham, Moses, the apostles, Paul and Martin Luther, who when they became the recipients of an hitherto hidden revelation of the reality and glory of the Kingdom of God, were willing to sacrifice all things in order to appreciate fully their discovered spiritual wealth. A price has to be paid for God's hidden treasure.

Whatever "the treasure" may be, it, and not the field, was the man's object. Then in order to possess the hidden treasure He purchased the field. Whether we believe with Darby that the treasure represents God's people, "the Church looked at, not in its moral and in a certain sense divine beauty, but as the special object of the desires and of the sacrifice of the Lord"; or with Morgan that "the treasure is the Kingdom of God hidden in the world, the divine government, in its principles, its order, and its exceeding beauty," this we do believe that Christ not only sold all that He had for our salvation, but likewise bought the world. Thus, it is His in a double sense. He created it, and then redeemed it — and what a price He paid!

Christ redeemed both the world in which men live and men in the world "not with silver and gold," the coinage of commercialism, but with "the precious blood of Christ, as a Lamb, without blemish." The mystery of Deity is agony. Thus, both the Church and the world are His property. The world was purchased, not so much for its own sake, but because of the treasure it contained. Does not Paul teach us that through the blood of the cross peace is the possession of ransomed souls and that also by the same cross all things, whether on earth or in heaven, have been reconciled unto God (Colossians 1:20).

When David went up by divine command to erect an altar to Jehovah in Ornan's threshing floor, in order that the sword of the angel executing judgment might be put up again in its sheath, David purchased not only the threshing-floor as the site of the altar for 50 shekels of silver, the redemption price for 100 souls, but he also purchased "the place," the surrounding field, for another 600 shekels of gold, whereon the temple was to be erected to Jehovah's praise (I Chronicles 21:25). The whole creation, redeemed at infinite cost, awaits the time of the perfect realization of His ultimate purpose. Presently the world is sin-cursed, blood-soaked and godless, yet it is His world, and will yet be filled with His glory at a time when all flesh shall see it together. The time is coming when the tabernacle of God shall be with men, and His redeemed world, the center of His glorious universe.

## The Parable of the Merchantman and the Pearl
(Matthew 13:45,46)

While this charming parable is similar in many ways to the previous one, there is one marked difference to note. In the former parable, the man discovered by accident the treasure of the field. He was not engaged in the search for it, nor was he even thinking of it. Occupied with other things, he stumbled upon the treasure quite unexpectedly. But in the *Parable of the Pearl* the situation is different. The merchantman was seriously and deliberately searching for goodly pearls, the very business of his life. In order to secure the costliest gems he would travel far, and was prepared to secure them no matter what the cost. Thus, in one we have a man who appears to be aimless, while in the other we have a merchant of earnest purpose and lofty aim, a man who, because he was able to appreciate the best when he saw it, cared only for pearls of real worth. The personal application of this difference is clearly evident. The best comes to those who are sincere in their search for truth.

As with other parables, *The Pearl* also has suffered much at the hands of well-meaning expositors. The most popular and general interpretation of this parable is that the *Pearl* is Christ Himself. While it does not follow that all that is popular is wrong, or what is traditional is false, we feel that the general interpretation of this parable is both wrong and false. This particular view has been expressed in a hymn otherwise beautiful, but in words untrue to the teaching of the parable —

I've found the Pearl of greatest price,
  My heart doth sing for joy;
And sing I must, for Christ I have —
  Oh, what a Christ have I.

But such an interpretation is open to serious objection for two reasons:

1. It puts the parable entirely out of harmony with the teaching of its context. The *sower,* the *man,* the *merchantman* are the one person — The Master Himself.

2. It represents the sinner as sacrificing his all in order to acquire Christ. The parable, however, is not a picture of a sinner seeking Christ, but of Christ seeking His Church.

Paul declares that "there is none that seeketh after God" (Romans 3:11). It is Christ who seeks the sinner. "The Son of Man is come to seek and to save the lost" (Luke 19:10). The Shepherd seeks the sheep, not the sheep the Shepherd. Further, Christ cannot be purchased. He is God's unspeakable gift. "The gift of God is eternal life" (Romans 6:23), and a *gift* cannot be bought, sold or bartered. Scripture represents the sinner having "nothing to pay" (Luke 7:42). Then having nothing but "filthy rags" (Isaiah 64:6), he has nothing to sell in order to buy Christ. So this popular view of the parable turns God's truth upside down, for He declares that salvation is without money and without price (Isaiah 53:1). To *buy* or *get* Christ violates the clear teaching of Scripture. The sinner is not the *active* agent in choosing Christ (John 15:16).

G. H. Lang rejects that which we believe to be the correct view of the parable, namely, that Christ is the Merchant, the Pearl the Church, and that Calvary was the price paid for the Pearl. Lang rejects this as an erroneous view which, along with the others, are "excluded by the fact that the parable does not say that the Kingdom of Heaven is like a *pearl,* let alone that the Church is like a pearl; it says that the Kingdom of Heaven is like a merchant." Then this expositor, who in *The Parable of the Leaven* seeks to prove that believers when they die do not go straight to heaven and glory, but to "Abraham's bosom," looks upon "the pearl of great price" as the deep truths of God for which we must search, and the possession of which will cost all we have. In support of his theory Lang quotes Tersteegen:

"I searched for truth, I found but
doubt;
I wandered far abroad:
I hail the truth already found
Within the heart of God."

A. B. Bruce held a similar view and wrote of the *Pearl* as the truth of the Kingdom which must be sought at all hazards: "This is the law by which the true citizen of the Kingdom is guided. . . . In acting on such a law a Christian exposes himself to a charge of folly. What a fool was the man who parted with all to obtain a single pearl, which he must keep in his possession. It was the act of one who had a craze, who had gone mad in the pursuit of a hobby. True, yet such folly is characteristic of the seekers after God. It is the folly of the wise." Against this untenable interpretation is the fact that pearl-seeking was not a mad hobby of the merchant, but a sane and serious business.

Believing as we do, that the description given of the Pearl, its cost and buyer, offers an appropriate and striking figure of the Church, we now purpose to expound the parable along these lines. Recognizing the fact that a good deal of confusion exists as to the difference between the Kingdom and the Church, it is our contention that the Kingdom of Heaven in mystery is equivalent to the present Christian dispensation with its partial success, and with the continued presence, until the end of the age, of the wheat side by side with the tares.

"Christ also loved the Church, and gave Himself for it" (Ephesians 5:25-27), and she will ever be the object of His desire. This same Church is *one* pearl, one body though composed of many members; one habitation of God, through the Spirit, though builded of many stones; one, as the purchase of Christ's all-atoning blood; one, as the workmanship of the Eternal Spirit whose ministry it is to fashion the Church into one body. This Church Jesus said He would build, is composed of all regenerated Jews and Gentiles from Pentecost till the return of Christ as the Bridegroom for His Bride — The Church of the living God.

1. *The Merchantman.* As the two conspicuous features of the parable are the Pearl and its Purchaser, we look first at the person Jesus called the *merchantman.* The term used here had the primary meaning of one who goes on a ship as a passenger. It is used in this way in Revelation 18:3,11,15,23. Then it came to signify a *wholesale* dealer, as distinguished from a *retail* dealer (who made voyages and imported goods to himself), a description which could not in *any* sense be applied to the sinner some expositors say is symbolized by the merchantman. The one Jesus portrayed was a connoisseur and knew all about pearls. He had discernment and knowledge, as to their real worth, and could not be deceived by any sham production. Assessing their value, he paid the price and never regretted his purchase.

Our Lord, so conspicuous for His use of figurative speech, never used a simile, metaphor, or parable without a complete understanding of all the figure of speech implied. It is more than likely that as a boy, He had often seen merchantmen with their caravans passing through His home town, exhibiting their precious stones. As these men had traveled far, their presence created great interest. The merchantman in the parable was *seeking* goodly pearls. The word for *seeking* implies leaving "one place to go to another." The Greek verb, scholars tell us, means, literally, to go away, depart from, implying an actual *departure* from one place and an actual *arrival* at another, a particular meaning which answers to Jesus who left heaven for earth that by His blood He might buy the precious pearl of His Church. Viewing the parable, then, from the heavenly standard, we believe it presents a beautiful picture of the purchase of the Church of God. The "man" who sowed the good seed, and the "merchantman," are one and the same, the Lord Jesus Christ.

As to the "merchantman" in the parable, we are told that desiring goodly pearls, he sought them. Finding one pearl of great price he sold all that he had to purchase it. Does it not pass our comprehension to realize that Christ's desire was toward us and that even when we were His enemies He died to possess us? His desire was towards us (Psalm 45:11). In the previous parable, the treasure was *found:* in this case the pearl was *sought.* Then the merchantman, knowing pearls as he did, deemed this one to be a pearl of "great price." No wonder C. H. Spurgeon thought that "such language could never be true of poor sinners on earth, that it could only be appropriate of the Christ of God." Yet the renowned preacher was wrong, for those redeemed by precious blood are precious in His sight, and His delights are with the regenerated sons of men.

Further, seeking and finding the valuable pearl, the merchant man "sold all that he had" to possess it. No sacrifice was great enough to have that lustrous pearl in the palm of his hand, as his very own. We will never know all that it cost Jesus to bring the Church into being. None of the ransomed will ever know all that was involved in the price He paid to have a redeemed people as His "pearl." Though He was rich, yet to purchase us, He became poor. This heavenly Merchantman had no money or possessions to barter for the pearl. He gave one's most precious possession — His life. "With his own blood He bought her." The preciousness of this "one pearl" consists, not so much in its own intrinsic value, as the price paid for its possession. Whether we deem the "goodly pearls" to represent *individual*

believers in Him, and the "one pearl" as the Church *collectively,* matters little. What we do know is that His Church is "one body" and we are "all one in Christ Jesus" (John 17:21; I Corinthians 13:12). The price paid for the creation of a glorious Church was the death of the cross.

Before leaving the *Merchantman* we might ask the question, Why did he seek goodly pearls, and buy one at infinite cost? Did he seek, and sacrifice to secure them merely for himself? One expositor says, "Pearls in so far as their value was known then, were specifically and particularly for the adornment of kings. The man who was seeking them was doing so in order to provide that embellishment, that symbol of glory, for other than himself. The merchantman was seeking for pearls, not to hoard them, or to possess them, but for some other." But with our heavenly Merchantman it is different. He purchased us that He might eternally possess us. As His Church, we are His very own, and one day when glorified, He is to present to Himself such a pearl without spot or blemish. The very word "pearl" is derived from a Sanscrit word meaning, *pure.*

2. *The Pearl.* Using this expressive parabolic illustration, Jesus knew all about the history of a "pearl" — where it came from, how it was formed, and its real value. Pearls were not counted precious by the Jews and are never mentioned in the Old Testament. Recent investigations have unearthed the regalia of kings in which actual pearls were found. Pearls, however, are frequently mentioned in the New Testament, and during our Lord's time were most highly prized as an ornament. All are familiar with the story of the dissolute Cleopatra, who at a supper with Antony, snatched from her ear one of a pair of pearls valued at £80,000 and having dissolved it in vinegar, swallowed the costly draught in honor of the equally licentious Roman. Thus the poor disciples must have opened their eyes in surprise

when Jesus spoke of Himself as the Merchantman seeking "goodly pearls." There are many aspects of a "pearl" which we can apply to Christ and His Church.

One of the facts about a real pearl is that it is a product of a living organism, which is not true of any other precious stone, whether sapphires, diamonds, rubies or emeralds. The pearl is produced as the result of an injury suffered by a living organism, such as an oyster. The immediate occasion of the pearl's production is the presence of some extraneous substance, such as a grain of sand, an egg either of the *Mollusc,* or some parasitic intruder. Calcareous matter in thin layers is spread over the intruding object until ultimately it assumes a pearly luster. Thus in the process of its making, the living organism surrounds the tormented and unperceived thing with mother-of-pearl, with nacre, until gradually the pearl is formed. Out of much suffering, an object of beauty is produced. The offending particle becomes a pearl of great worth. How accurate is this fact of the Church which came out of the wounded side of Christ! Greater than the mystery and the wonder of the creation of a pearl in an oyster shell, is the marvel of Him who, through the travail and pain our sin caused Him, covered us over and transformed the thing of injury to the desired thing. As the little grain of sand is ultimately clothed with a beauty not its own, so we are covered with a comeliness of Him who suffered on our behalf.

Habershon suggests the following contrast between the Mustard Seed and the Pearl. "Both grow from something small: the shrub from the little mustard-seed, and the pearl from the tiny bit of sand that has come inside the shell of the oyster. But what a different result. The pearl never assumes very large dimensions, but its value may be almost priceless, and the two parables together teach us that *size* is not everything. The value is not to be estimated thus."

Another resemblance between a pearl and the Church may be drawn from the fact that the pearl is formed slowly and gradually. Behind its production is a tedious process of waiting while the pearl is being secretly and surely formed. Is it not thus with the formation of the Church which Christ's death made *possible,* and which the Holy Spirit through more than nineteen centuries has been making *actual?* "Just as the oyster covering the wound in its side and that which pierced it with one layer after another of the beautiful nacre, constantly repeating the process, so out of each generation of men on earth God has called a few and added them to that Church which He is now building." When Christ returns His Church will be ready as His pearl.

Another comparison we may make is that of the pearl being at first embedded in a mass of living but corruptible flesh, then separated and cleansed from its surroundings in order that it might appear in its purity as well as its beauty, a fit gem for the imperial diadem. Is it not thus with the Church? The triumphant Church in heaven is saved to sin no more. But the militant Church on earth is still surrounded with a mass of corruptible flesh, and it would seem as if the professed Church is deeply embedded in worldly things. The Lord, however, by His Spirit is occupied with the purification of His own, and will ultimately present the whole Church to Himself, "a glorious Church, not having spot, or wrinkle, or any such thing" (Ephesians 5:26,27). Then He will be admired in all them that believe (II Thessalonians 1:10).

There is a further comparison to observe, namely, the lowly origin of the beautiful pearl. Originally, its home was in the depths of the sea, among the mire and scavengers of the depths. In Scripture, the sea is the well-known type of the godless peoples, nations and tongues, out of which the Church is taken. The oyster out of which the pearl is taken is not sightly. By nature, our origin was in the filth and mire and ruin of the fall (Ephesians 2:11,12). May we never forget the pit from which we were dug! The *treasure* was buried in the earth; the Pearl was sunk at the bottom of the ocean. The miracle of grace, however, is the truth that Jesus descended into the deep to extricate the pearl of its surroundings and fashion it as a pearl fit to be placed on His royal diadem. As a diver descends into the ocean, at no little risk detaches the rough oyster shell from its rocky bed and brings it up to the light, so Jesus went down at the sacrifice of His life in order to bring us up from the depths of sin into the light of life. Do we not bless Him for drawing us out of many waters (Psalm 18:4-6,15,16; Romans 7:9)?

Then it must not be forgotten that the formation of the pearl is a secret one. None but the eye of God watches the oyster transforming an intrusion into a pearl of intrinsic beauty and great worth. Is it not so with the Church which Christ is now forming? Unknown and unseen His pearl is being fashioned. Certainly we can see the organized, visible church. Churches of wood, stone and cement we can see, both plain and ornamental, but no man can see the Church of the living God. Behind the scaffolding with which we concern ourselves there is the Church, which is His body, growing up into a holy temple in, and for, the Lord. Our life is *hid* with Christ in God (Colossians 3:3).

Last of all, *the* Church, an object of value and beauty, presently hid from the eyes of men, has the prospect of an honorable and exalted future. As pearls adorn the crowns of monarchs, so in the ages to come Christ will display His own and in them "show the exceeding riches of His grace" (Ephesians 2:7). The world may not count us worthy, but dignity, honor and glory are to be ours when He displays His glorified Church to a wondering universe. Many "goodly pearls" will be His, Old Testament and tribulation saints, but all in Christ are one (Galatians 3:28) and will forever be His one pearl of great price. To all the ages, His Church will be the revealer of His infinite grace.

> He found the pearl of greatest price,
> My heart doth sing for joy;
> And sing I must, for I am His,
> And He is mine for aye.

# The Parable of the Good and Bad Fish
## (Matthew 13:47-50)

This solemn parable is paired with the similar one of *The Wheat and the Tares.* Both of these parables show *good* and *bad,* side by side at first, then divided; both were explained by Jesus in the words, "So shall it be at the end of the age." Both describe the work of the angels in separating the wicked from the just; both describe the doom of the wicked, and "fire" where there shall be "the wailing and the gnashing of teeth." Each parable, then, has this one central and distinguishing fact, so much so that we might have expected Matthew to place them together, as he did *The Mustard Seed* and *The Leaven, The Treasure* and *The Pearl.* There are differences, however, to be noted between *The Wheat and Tares* and *The Dragnet.* In the former there is an earth scene; in the latter, a sea scene, but in both cases the world is implied. Taken together these two parables teach two outstanding truths, namely, that in the professed Church good and evil are intermingled; and, further, that a time of separation has been set. Thus the good may rejoice because of their bright, eternal future. The bad should mourn, for if they die in their sin they are eternally doomed.

It may be that *The Dragnet* is given the last place in a series of seven parables because it fixes attention upon the end of the age of grace, the final consummation and judgment. Emphasis in this parable is not upon the use and haul of the net, but on "the consummation of the age." After relating the parable in terms so familiar to His fishermen-disciples, Jesus said that the Kingdom of Heaven is like such in its consummation when the net will be drawn in and separation undertaken. As with the three previous parables, this seventh one was given to men of faith whom the Lord initiated into the internal and hidden aspects of His Kingdom — truth, not as seen by men but from the standpoint of God's counsels. We can analyze the parable thus: the net, the sea, the fishermen, the fish, the angels.

1. *The Net.* The word Jesus used for *net,* singularly appropriate for the parable was spoken by the Sea of Galilee, implies a dragnet, a large, hauling net of great length, weighted by lead and made to sweep the bottom of the sea and gather fish in masses. It is called a drag or draw net because it drags along the bottom of the water and gathers fish of every kind into its mesh. The symbolism of the net is plain to all. It represents the proclamation and presentation of the Gospel of redeeming grace to the responsibility of men. The wide-sweeping, all embracing net illustrates the wide reach and effectual operation of the Gospel whereby men are drawn into the profession of Christianity and into the fellowship of the visible Church of Christ. For interesting references to the *net* see Job 19:6; Psalm 66:11; Ecclesiastes 9:12. Says Cumming: "The ordinances, the preaching of the Gospel, its ministrations, its means of grace, are the outspread and comprehensive net . . . none are so deep that it does not descend to them, none so high that it does not reach them, none so bad that they are cast out, none so good that they are passed by; it collects good and bad." Thus the kind of net indicates the sweep of the Kingdom of God in its present work. It brings into view God's providence sweeping across the entire dispensation, through the whole course of the intervening time, until the eternal separation of the wicked from among the just. The present dispensation of Grace, beginning with Pentecost and terminating with Christ's Second Advent is frequently described as "the Kingdom of Heaven" (Matthew 11:12). The gospel net is flung on a wide sea without regard to condition, clime, caste or creed. In this age "God is no respecter of persons" (Acts 10:34,35).

2. *The Sea.* The *sea* in the parable represents the whole mass of fallen humanity. "The wicked are like the troubled sea, when it cannot rest, whose waters cast up mire and dirt" (Isaiah 57:20,21; see Daniel 7:3; Revelation 13:1). What a dark abyss of sin, error, and ignorance men live in, yet they can be drawn out of it by the Spirit of God, as the terms of the Gospel are accepted. Arthur Pink affirms that the *sea* stands for the Gentile nations, because in this present dispensation God's mercy is turned to the Gentile. But the world God loves includes all souls, whether Jew or Gentile, for both form the sea of the world. Without doubt the greatest number of fish caught in the net are *Gentiles.* In comparison, few Jews are saved. *The Wheat* or *The Good Fish* are made up of both regenerated Gentiles and Jews. In Christ, there is neither Jew or Gentile. Both are one.

The *net,* we are told, when cast *into the sea,* did not enclose *all* the fish in the sea, but *gathered* out of it *some* only *of every kind.* Thus the parable teaches that although such a glorious Gospel is preached it does not have the effect of bringing all who hear it into the professing Church of Christ. There is a *gathering* together of *some* out "of *every* kindred, and tongue, and people, and nations" (Revelation 5:9). The word *gather* is applied in the Bible to both *good* and *bad.* Of the *good* it is said, "He shall gather his lambs" (Isaiah 40:11). "With great mercies will I gather thee" (Isaiah 54:7). "Gather together in one the children of God" (John 11:51,52). "Gather my saints together unto me" (Psalm 50:5). Of the *bad* it is said, "Gather not my soul with sinners" (Psalm 26:9). "Men gather them . . . they are burned" (John 15:6). "Gather the nations . . . for judgment" (Joel 3:1-16).

3. *The Fishermen.* The disciples listening to Jesus fully understood the implication of this parable. When He found many of them they were casting or mending their nets, for "they were fishers." Then, in His call to service, did He not say, "I will make you to become fishers of men"? Plying the sea with the gospel net, they were to catch men alive. Is this not the obligation of all who have experienced the saving power of God? Taken out of the sea of sin, theirs is the privileged task of trying to rescue others. All who have been *forgiven* should be fishers. Soul-winners are God's fishers. "Behold, I will send for many fishers, saith the Lord, and they shall fish them" (Isaiah 19:8). "It shall come to pass, that the fishers shall stand upon it from Engedi even unto Eneglaim" (Ezekiel 47:10). "From henceforth thou shalt catch men" (Luke 5:10).

In the previous parable Jesus is before us as the Merchantman, seeking goodly pearls. He is the principle Worker in the gathering out of the saints during this dispensation, but the parable before us teaches the truth that in His condescending grace He does not work alone. While it is perfectly true that Christ alone can save souls, He never saves them *alone.* He uses the saved to save more. This is why in this Dragnet Parable, the pronoun is changed. Hitherto it had been "He," "The Son of Man," "The Merchantman," now it is not *He* but *they.* "*They* drew to shore." This is the first time we have *they* in the parables. Are we not privileged to be workers together with Him? In the miracle of the water turned to wine, He said to the *servants,* "Fill the waterpots"; "draw it forth." Feeding the hungry Jesus did not hand the bread *directly* to the crowd. He first gave it to His disciples and then said, "Give ye them to eat." In like manner, His consecrated servants are the *fishermen* He uses to catch fish. May we not fail Him!

We cannot fail to be impressed with the inconspicuousness of the fishermen.

Jesus does not mention them by name but simply refers to them as *they.* Those who have a part in casting the net into the sea are hidden from view. What a rebuke this is to the preacher-worship of the day! (I Corinthians 3:4). "Neither is he that planteth *anything,* neither he that watereth." The instrument is nothing. He is everything. His treasure is in earthen vessels that all the glory might be his. John the Baptist exemplified this trait when he said of Jesus, "He must increase, I must decrease."

A further characteristic of these fishermen is that although they knew the net would gather in "of every kind," they separated the good from the bad. It was no reflection upon their skill that they had a mixed haul. Once the result of their fishing was secured, we read that they "sat down" on the shore, which indicates that the work of sorting out and separating the good fish from the bad required time, care and deliberation. Then all that was bad they cast away, while the good fish were placed in vessels. Surely the application of all this is not hard to seek. While we are to preach the Gospel to every creature, it is God's purpose that we should seek good fish. As the result of an evangelistic effort there may be a mixed profession, yet the Spirit-guided soul-winner will be able to detect the good fish and guide same into vessels, which can represent Christian fellowship. While selection is necessary, such as in the building up of a center of worship, ministry and fellowship, judgment is not passed upon the *bad.* We are only responsible for *separation,* not judgment, which is future and of God.

4. *The Fish.* The parable says that the fish were of "every kind," "good" and "bad." Habakkuk must have had such a mixed catch in mind when he said of the wicked and the many oppressed ones more righteous than himself, "He taketh up *all* of them with the angle, he rejoiceth and is glad. Therefore he sacrificeth unto his net, and burneth incense unto

his drag; because by them his portion is fat, and his meat plenteous" (Habakkuk 1:15-17). The fishermen, of course, could not estimate the kind of haul made until the net was drawn to the shore and the fish were sorted.

*Good* and *bad* in the net, takes us back to the wheat and tares growing and mingling together. As these parables symbolize the visible church, the mixture of saved and unsaved in Christian profession, those who seek a perfect visible church are doomed to disappointment. There was a *Ham* in the Ark, a *Judas* among the Apostles; *Esau* and *Jacob* still struggle together in the womb of the visible church of Christ. They are not all Israelites who are of Israel. Many say they are Christians but are not. Belonging to a visible church does not necessarily include membership in the true Church. People may be religious yet not regenerated, baptized yet never washed in the blood of Christ; professors yet not possessors (see Matthew 7:21). In spite of religious affiliations and desires, if the heart is destitute of the Grace of God, then the soul is lost. There are only two kinds of fish: *good* or *bad*. If we are not God's *wheat* then we must be Satan's *tares*.

By the *good* fish, we are to understand those that were sound and salable, and spiritually represent those who belong to the good Lord, and who, in turn, are good and do good. By the *bad* fish, we can visualize putrid, dead fish; being corrupt they were unfit for food. Being offensive and worthless, they were cast away. The oft-used expression in Scripture, "cast away" or "cast out," denotes a state of condemnation. "Cast out from the presence of God" is expressive of an amount of suffering, sorrow and separation, which nothing else may adequately embody. Of the quality of the *good* fish an ancient poet wrote:

"Fisher of mortal men,
 Those that the saved are,
 Ever the holy fish
 From the wild ocean
 Of the world's sea of sin

By thy sweet life Thou enticest
 away."

5. *The Angels.* Throughout this dispensation of grace, the Holy Spirit is actively forming the true Church, the Bride of Christ, and His own, as fishermen, are occupied with the gospel net. But at the close of this dispensation, which will terminate with the return of Christ to receive His own, He will take to Himself all the *good* fish, or *wheat,* and leave all the *bad* fish, the *tares* behind. Then when He appears on the earth as its rightful Lord and King, angelic ministry will operate and the action will be totally the reverse. Instead of the good taken and the bad left, it will be the wicked taken out and the just left for the enjoyment of our Lord's millennial reign.

The declaration of the execution of a complete, final and everlasting judgment makes solemn reading: "The Son of Man will thoroughly purge his floor and burn up the chaff with fire unquenchable" (Matthew 3:12). When the separation between the precious and the vile takes place and the vile are cast into the furnace of fire, where there is wailing and gnashing of teeth, how dreadful will be the lot of the wicked.

Chrysostom spoke of *The Dragnet* as "a terrible parable." Gregory the Great said of it that it was "rather to be trembled at than expounded." If only this terrible prospect were as vivid to us as it was to our Lord surely ours would be a more urgent desire to warn the wicked to flee from the wrath to come. It is to be regretted that we are not impressed sufficiently with the fact of the coming complete separation of the saved from the lost. Of this, we are assured that the scrutiny will be exact. The angels will not mistake any of the good for the bad: "He will take out of His kingdom all things that offend, and them which do iniquity. Then shall the righteous shine forth as the sun in the kingdom of their father" (Matthew 13:41, 42; see Daniel 12:3).

Such discriminative judgment, which

many of the parables vividly depict, and which was always in the mind of Christ, receives a most emphatic and sevenfold repetition, a repetition signifying that such a matter is "established by God, and God will shortly bring it to pass" (Genesis 41:32).

> In *The Parable of the Tares* the separation is between wheat and tares.
>
> In *The Parable of the Dragnet,* the separation is between good and bad fish.
>
> In *The Parable of the Marriage Feast,* the separation is between guests with and without a wedding garment.
>
> In *The Parable of the Household,* the separation is between good and evil servants.
>
> In *The Parable of the Ten Virgins,* the separation is between wise and foolish virgins.
>
> In *The Parable of the Talents,* the separation is between profitable and unprofitable servants.
>
> In *The Parable of the Sheep and Goats* the separation is between them.

It must be borne in mind that the final separation between the *good* and the *bad* did not take place on the shore. The tares are left bound on the field, the bad fish are cast out of the net and left on the shore. Separation is now necessary, but not enforced as it should be. Execution of final separation and judgment is another matter. The fishermen have nothing to do with this. At the end of the age, the Angels are to come forth and sever the wicked from among the just, not the good from the bad as the fishermen did. The Angels in *The Parable of the Wheat and Tares* and *The Parable of the Dragnet* are occupied only with the wicked.

We do not dwell sufficiently upon the biblical revelation of angelic agency, a treatment of which may be found in the author's volume on *The Mystery and Ministry of Angels*. While this is the Age of the Spirit, when He is active in the Divine Agent, nevertheless "there are angels hovering round," and at the end of the age they will once more intervene in human affairs, even as they have in the past. Presently, the angels minister to the heirs of salvation, but the day is coming when they will carry out the grim task of severing the wicked from the just, and casting the wicked into the furnace of fire. Thus, as Butterick expresses it, "The spectrum of His teaching has colors dark and bright." So the issue is plain. Angels are to be the agents of final separation. Now, as fishermen we spread the net; the Angels are to make the distinction. We gather all, and invite all to come, good and bad; the Angels, according to Christ's word, are to separate the bad from the good, the tares from the wheat.

In the ultimate issue, the Lord alone pronounces doom. Presently, as fishermen, our office is not judicial but declarative. We are to proclaim Christ and His salvation and beckon all sorts to His cross. At the same time we are to warn sinners of the Great White Throne which will determine the lot and eternal condition of the lost. Then no net will be spread from the shore of the Judgment Day. This is the day of grace when the lost can be saved, but the last assize is the time for the ratification of condemnation already pronounced. May the Lord enable us to spread the net of salvation, and inviting all men to repent and believe, leave Him as the Judge of all the earth justly to separate the good from the bad at the time determined!

## The Parable of the Scribe and Householder

### (Matthew 13:51,52)

This last and eighth parable of this great parabolic chapter seems to be the unwanted orphan by many writers on the parables of our Lord. Expositors like Trench, Goebel, Marcus Dods, Arnot, Cummings, Taylor, C. Dodd, Guthrie, Scofield and other less known names, make no mention whatever of this most important, climactic parable.

Evidently it is reckoned as not belonging to those parables which open up and explain the nature of the Kingdom of Heaven. Yet surely it belongs to such parables for in this concluding parable, Jesus directs His own on how they must conduct themselves as teachers in that heavenly Kingdom. It is therefore a definite parable and not a mere analogy.

The boundaries of that parabolic day in our Lord's teaching are clearly defined. As He was about to discourse on the eight parables, it is said, "He spake to them many things in parables." At the completion of the octave we read, "When Jesus had finished these parables (which included the one we are now considering), He departed thence." But ere He departed He gave His disciples this great final parable, so suggestive of application to them and to us, and of their and our responsibility.

Then, further, this brief parable must be studied in the setting of the question and answer surrounding it. Jesus asked His disciples in privacy: "Have ye understood all these things?" They answered, "Yea." Whether they fully understood all the implications of His teaching in the seven previous parables is to be doubted. Later events proved that they had not grasped the over-all significance of all He had taught, but taking them at their own valuation and reply, He immediately commenced this parable with a significant "Therefore." Asserting that they had received His instruction, and had understood His message, now as disciples to the Kingdom of Heaven, they must bring forth from such a treasure, spiritual riches for the spiritual enrichment of others. Taught of Him, they must now go forth to teach others.

As we read *The Acts* and *The Epistles* it is evident that the Apostles had grasped, at least, the dominant message of the Lord's parables. Peter knew that it was not his ministry to convert the world, but to urge men to save themselves from a "crooked generation" (Acts 2:40). James believed that the work of God through the Apostles was to "take out a people for His name," or to separate the wheat from the tares. Jude, remembering the words of the Lord Jesus that in the last days (in the consummation of the age He spoke of), re-affirmed that there would be mockers, walking after their own ungodly lusts (Jude 17,18). Can we say that we have understood *"all* these things," meaning, the parables as a whole in their inter-relationship?

Interesting comparisons have been made between the first parable, *The Sower,* and the eighth, *The Householder.* Says Habershon, "The eighth parable in the thirteenth of Matthew is very like the octave in musical harmony. It is the complement of the first note of the scale, and as we listen to it thus, we hear how it repeats it." By way of comparison and contrast the parable of *The Householder* returns to the parable of *The Sower.* Both parables speak of the treatment of God's Word by the individual recipient. Had the sowing of the seed failed altogether, the other parables would never have been spoken. Note these features as you study the first and eighth parables:

In the *first,* the Word of God is *received* into the heart and allowed to bear varying degrees of fruit. In the eighth, the Word of God is *imparted* to others. Here the heart is not like *soil* but a *treasury,* out of which stores are produced for the benefit of others. The *first* speaks of something *put in;* the eighth, of something *brought out.*

The *first* tells of *fruit* for God, a Godward aspect; the eighth speaks of *good* for men. A household speaks of the use of supplies. Thus, the two together speak of *keeping* what we get, yet of *giving* what we have. In *The Sower,* fruit-bearing is shown to be understanding, receiving and keeping the Word. In *The Householder* we are taught that the best way of keeping the Word is to transmit it to others.

The *first* represents the *evangelist,* who as the sower, sows in the field of the world. The eighth pictures the work of the *teacher,* who as instructed Scribe feeds the household of faith. Is this not the true order of the ministry? We cannot teach what we fail to understand. Thus, as Habershon says, "Neither the *first* parable nor the *eighth* in the chapter commences with the words, 'The kingdom of heaven is like,' but they are both connected with the kingdom. That of the sower is the key to the understanding of the mysteries of the kingdom, that of the householder shows the use that is to be made of the mysteries when they are thus understood."

1. *The Scribe.* The Greek term our Lord used for "scribe," *gramma,* is the source of our English word, *grammar.* Originally, "scribes" were men of letters, teachers of the Law, and therefore qualified to teach in the Synagogues (Mark 1:22). Like Ezra, they were originally taken from the priests and Levites. By New Testament times the Scribes had become a party, and instead of teaching, developing and applying the Law, they surrounded it with their own traditions and precepts, teaching these instead of the Law, which had been designed to help the spiritual and moral life of the people, but which became an instrument for preventing true access to God (Luke 11:52). Consequently, the Scribes earned Christ's stern denunciation, not only for the perversion of their responsibility, but because they were ambitious for honor which they demanded from the pupils and people generally.

Ezra is the outstanding example of a good "scribe," who from a raised pulpit of wood read the Law correctly and with clear articulation, and then gave the sense, or explained and expounded what he read. Thus the Scribes, who came into being during the revival of the reading of the first five books of the Bible, stood out as moral and official interpreters of the Law. But, as we have indicated, by our Lord's time the Scribes had fenced the Law around and commanded the people to approach it through their manufactured traditions rather than go to the Law direct. Jesus set His seal upon the direct interpretation of the Law, but because the recognized teachers had failed, He now transfers the responsibility of teaching divine truth to His disciples.

Naming those He had called to follow Him as *Scribes,* He commissioned these representative men to go out and interpret the mystery and message of the Kingdom of Heaven to an ignorant world. "In so doing, He transferred the fulfilment of an office from men who had failed to men who were to succeed them. In order to achieve the fulfilment of responsibility, therefore, there must be understanding of the King's teaching concerning the Kingdom in this age." Although those first disciples had not the teaching of rabbinical schools (unlearned), they had three years in the school of Christ. Like Mary, they studied in *The College of the Feet* (Luke 10:39), and were thus well qualified, with the Spirit's enduement, to interpret their Lord's teaching (Acts 1:1; Galatians 6:6; II Timothy 2:2).

Christ was, and is, the Chief Scribe. Truth received from His Father (John 17:14) was transmitted to His disciples. Out of the divine treasure He brought forth "things new and old." Knowing that Scribes are "a perpetual need of the people of God and a perpetual gift to them," Christ concentrated His tuition upon His disciples and before His Ascension, commissioned them to go out into the world and unfold His teaching which had become part and parcel of their own lives. In this age of grace, all God's people should be taught of the Spirit and seek from Him spiritual perception and increase in the knowledge of God (Colossians 1:9; II Peter 3:18; I John 2:20). In His goodness, the Lord raises up those He blesses with special gifts who are "apt to teach," and who are to "labour in the world and teaching" (I Corinthians 16:15,16; Ephesians 3:2-5; 4:11-13; I Timothy 3:2;

5:17). The Church's greatest need today is that of heaven-sent and heaven-instructed scribes.

Paul understood the Lord's simile of the *scribe*. Describing "the ministers of Christ," he said that they were to function as "stewards of the mysteries of God" (I Corinthians 4:1). A "steward" is equivalent to a "scribe" instructed in the mysteries of the Kingdom. From other parables we learn that a faithful steward is one who uses his master's goods aright and for the best advantage, while the unjust steward is one who fails to use his master's possessions for the benefit of others. May we share Paul's ambition to be judged faithful by the Master Himself!

2. *The Disciple.* Our Lord uses three terms in this parable to describe those who were to impart to others the truths they had learned from His lips: *scribes, disciples, householder.* A *disciple* means a "learner," or one who follows another's teaching, and who is not only a pupil, but an adherent and imitator of his teacher (John 8:31; 15:8). By imparting to others the divine knowledge received from Christ, those who were first adherents became "disciples unto the Kingdom of Heaven." Understanding and experiencing the truth, in their declaration of it they were to make other disciples (Matthew 28:19,20). To Christ, *scribe* and *disciple* were synonymous terms. Made *disciples* of the Kingdom, the Apostles exercised the spiritual and moral authority which true scribes by their office represented. Says Campbell Morgan, "Disciples of Jesus are those seen as the true rulers of the age, as they correctly interpret the Kingdom and represent Him in it. They have access to the eternal treasure-house, and in that treasure-house there are things new and old."

3. *The Householder.* This further description of a teacher of the Word has more than one meaning. With us, a householder is one who owns and occupies a house. But as used by our Lord, a *householder* was a "house-despot," a master of his house, or "goodman of the house." In these days, when an evil despotism is all too common, we may shrink from using the word *despot,* yet it is a term representing tremendous authority. "It is a picture of a shepherd, father and king, all of which phases are merged into one personality, one head of affairs. . . . That word *householder* was on the lips of Jesus some ten or twelve times, and almost invariably He used it of Himself. It is the word that marks authority. The disciples were to be scribes, authoritative interpreters of the Law."

A householder, then, was the head of his house, with real and acknowledged authority, who controlled his treasured store, and "who brought forth the right kind of food at the right time, suiting meals to eaters, not giving new when he ought to give old, and not giving only new or only old." He gave to all in his household "meat in due season." Those who are called to feed the flock of God must act precisely as a householder with a house full of goods, able and ready to serve up both what he himself needs and what others require.

4. *The Treasure.* Martin Luther in his Exposition of this parable says that "the treasure, or rich supply of knowledge, is nothing else than the knowledge of the Law and the Gospel. For in these two the whole wisdom of God is enclosed and comprised as in a brief extract" (Matthew 5:17; Acts 26:22). As used by our Lord in speaking to His disciples, the "treasure" had in mind that which through knowledge and experience had become theirs. Two different words are used for "treasure" in the New Testament. The one means to lay up and keep. The other word implies that which is spent. The first suggests a miser, the second, a spendthrift. As householders, we have vast treasures in the Scriptures. What are we to do with them? We are not only to hide them within our heart but scatter them lavish-

ly. We have been made the recipients of truth, and this must be bountifully shared with others. And the paradox is that as we share we save, as we remit we retain.

"There was a man some thought him mad,
    The more he gave, the more he had."

The treasury in the parable is the heart of the true scribe, disciple, householder. Did not Jesus Himself say? "A good man out of the good treasure of his heart bringeth forth that which is good. . . . . . for out of the abundance of the heart his mouth speaketh" (Luke 6:45). C. H. Spurgeon says, "That which lies in the well of your thought will come up in the bucket of your speech."

Then our Lord explicitly states what is to be brought out of the treasury, namely, "things new and old." We can take this to mean all that He had taught in the seven preceding parables, in which the mysteries of the Kingdom contained prophecies of the old with added new significance. The disciples were shown how to throw new light on Old Scriptures, which, as instructed Scribes it is our duty to do. Under the guidance of the heavenly Teacher, His scholars were taught to connect new meanings to old truths. The one eternal, unchangeable, truth of divine love and righteousness, old as a past eternity, was announced in a more fresh and agreeable form. The *new,* the Gospel Jesus made possible by His death and resurrection, came as the fulfilment of the promise of the *old.*

It will be noted that Jesus did not say that His instructed Scribes were to bring forth from the treasury new things and old things. There were not two orders of things, for the two are one in essence. The *Law* is old, and the *Gospel* is new, yet the latter came as the development of the former. Old truths are eternal, but there must be new applications of eternal truths to the passing phases of changing times. "The new which contradicts the old is always false: and the old which has no new is dead and useless." The root is old; the fruit is new.

The Kingship of God is as eternal as God Himself, but it has ever new manifestations and applications.

The foregoing parables contain "things new and old." The teaching of the Kingdom, for instance, was a well-known doctrine taught by the prophets of old, but it was quite new that the Kingdom should take the form described by Christ. Now the Kingdom embraces the whole world, and the people of God draw their existence, not from Abraham, but from the Word of God. The Jewish rulers prided themselves on the privilege of natural birth, but Jesus taught that the children of His Kingdom are born of His Word. If the old tree grows no new leaves, it dies. Butterick observes, "It is only the scribe, filled with the spirit of the Kingdom, which is love and peace and righteousness, who can interpret the old to the new, and the new to the old and clothe the eternal verities in fresh and appropriate time vesture." Alfred Tennyson, in *The Passing of Arthur,* has given us the lines: —

"The old order changeth, yielding
    place to new,
And God fulfils Himself in many
    ways,
Lest one good custom should cor-
    rupt the world."

John Robinson, puritan of the seventeenth century, was persuaded that "the Lord had yet more light and truth to break forth from His holy Word." The divine revelation is *old,* but the apprehension and experience of it is *new.* Divine principles are *old,* the practice of them is *new.* It is this fact that makes the Bible so fascinating to disciples of the Kingdom. Its truths are so old, yet they are ever new, fresh, flashing with new glory, pulsating with new life. To all those who are new creatures in Christ Jesus "old things are become new." Have we understood "these things," not only His superb parables, but other aspects of Divine truth? If so, ours is the solemn responsibility of sharing the spiritual treasure with others. "Give, and it shall be given you."

# Precious Parabolic Pictures
## (Matthew 15-18)

Before we take up the next recognized parable, there are several parables in germ (minor Parables) which we can group together from the above three chapters and briefly consider. All parables and parabolic illustrations must be dealt with in the light of their immediate context.

*The Parable on Purity.* As Jesus ended the central period of His public ministry, hostility toward Him became more intense. The religious leaders, stung by His authoritative teaching and the result of that teaching as manifested in the lives of His disciples, sought to entangle Him in His utterances. With blunt ruthlessness He strove to rid God's ancient Law of the manifold traditions that had gathered around it, but the traditionalists fought hard for their traditionalism, to which many had become slaves. The multiplicity of traditions proved how the Pharisees and Scribes had miserably failed as interpreters of the Law. One of these useless traditions concerned the eating of food with unwashed hands, hence the question, "Why do thy disciples transgress the traditions of the Elders when they eat bread?" The form of such a question shows how they were alarmed, not at any non-compliance with the original Law of God, but with disobedience to their own manufactured traditions. The Elders were taken up, not so much with any law regarding cleanliness, but with external ritual. One foolish tradition was that a demon known as *Shibta* sat upon the hands of men as they slept, and ceremonial washing was necessary, or food eaten by demon-visited hands would be contaminated. Like a sharp arrow came the condemnation of Jesus, "Ye have made void the word of God because of your tradition . . . ye hypocrites." Having administered this deserved rebuke to His critics and foes, Jesus turned to the crowd and uttered a brief parable characterized by the greatest simplicity and one which the simplest in the audience could understand.

How authoritative was His call, "Hear and understand!" Then He told the people that physical organism deals with physical ailment, and that it has no reference to moral cleanness or defilement. "Not that which goeth into the mouth defileth a man; but that which cometh out of the mouth, this defileth a man." After Jesus gave two further parabolic illustrations, Peter, speaking for himself and others, asked for an understanding of the parable. Then in Matthew 15:16-20, we have the Lord's explanation and exposition, the sum of which is that food eaten with unwashed hands does not defile the body, but that false thinking and evil imagination defile not so much the body, but the soul. Richard Glover remarks that "the Saviour attributes more importance to words than we do (Matthew 12:37), and that all the evils named usually employ the mouth —

*Thoughts* are hardened by being uttered;
*Murders* are plotted through lips;
*Adulteries* and Fornication employ the seductive influences of flattery;
*Theft* lies to hide its fault;
*False witness* and *blasphemies* are pre-eminently sins of the mouth."

The food we eat, whether with washed or unwashed hands, goes not into the heart, but the belly; and anything in it unfit to build up the body is ejected. Such food may infect the body with disease, but cannot affect the soul. Sin is the polluting power of the heart. The unregenerate heart is the spring of evil thoughts. Seekers after a clean heart will not be negligent regarding the possession of a clean body. Such cleanliness is one of the by-products of godliness.

# The Parable of the Uprooted Plant
## (Matthew 15:12,13)

It would seem as if the disciples felt

that the Master has gone just a little too far in His rebuke of the Pharisees for their empty and dangerous ritualism. "The Pharisees were offended, after they heard this saying," and Jesus meant them to be. Pharisees were, and still are, offended at true doctrine. The disciples, however, had to guard against giving too much heed to the popularity or unpopularity of truth. By "every plant" we are to understand, not the Pharisees, but their self-conceived doctrines. Jesus is here teaching in parabolic form that "every error that obscures the truth of God and hurts the soul of man, will be rooted up." We may feel that errors and evils are most firmly rooted and most enduring, but God works in His own way and time uprooting every evil plant.

## The Parable of Blind Leaders
### (Matthew 15:14)

Are you not impressed with the wide variety of our Lord's illustrations? How apt and striking they are! Here, for example, He uses the power of the body to reject its waste, rooting up trees, and a proverb to enforce His message. With the critical, traditional Pharisees in mind Jesus said, "Let them alone," meaning, leave them unheeded, or to themselves, for theirs is teaching that blinds and blunts the heart and following it ends in disaster.

The Master's use of this phase of human affliction and accident must have impressed the disciples. "Leaders of the blind" was a phrase in common use to describe the ideal of a Rabbi's calling. Paul speaks of those teachers in Israel as "A guide of the blind, a light of them which are in darkness" (Romans 2:19). But Jesus exposed the state of recognized teachers as being the very reverse of the ideal, and their spiritual blindness was exaggerated by the fact that it was self-chosen. "Their eyes have they closed" (Matthew 13:15). Worse still, unconscious of their blindness, they boasted that they saw. "We see" (John 9:41). How often we say that "there are none so blind, as those who won't see."

As for the blind leading the blind, and both falling into a ditch, our Lord was here employing a well-known proverb giving it the character of a prophecy: "He spake a parable (proverb) unto them, Can the blind lead the blind? shall they not both fall into the ditch?" (Luke 6:39). The *ditch,* as applied to the fate of the prejudice-blinded Pharisees, was an expressive simile of the tragedy overtaking them and those they had deluded, prior to, and during, the terrible destruction of Jerusalem. "Bitter sectarianism, and wild dreams, and baseless hopes, and maddened zeal, and rejection of the truth which alone had power to save them, this was the issue which teachers and people alike were preparing for themselves, and from which there was no escape."

As with Israel of old, so with the Church today. Preachers, blinded by modernism, lead those who are blinded by the god of this world. There is nothing so pathetic in the physical realm as to see a man who is actually blind trying to lead another blind man. But in the religious realm it is tragic when those who profess to see the truth are blind to its realities, and with their vaunted wisdom, impress other spiritually-darkened minds with a perverted message.

## The Parable of the Puppies
### (Matthew 15:21-28)

For the *miracle* Jesus accomplished for the woman of Canaan, see the author's volume *All the Miracles of the Bible.* All we are concerned with in this cameo is our Lord's parabolic use of "dogs." Contrary to the instructions given to His disciples not to go "into the way of Gentiles," Jesus is here found taking them in the direction of heathen Tyre. As yet, they had not received the commission to go into all the world and preach the Gospel, but Jesus journeys outside the Holy Land for a simple deed of mercy. Perhaps He went into a house for privacy and rest (Mark 7:24), but both were soon invaded for "He could not be hid." Who can hide the fragrance of a rose? The Gentile woman beseeching Christ's help for her demon-possessed daughter is described as a "Canaanite," "Syro-Phoenician," "Greek." As such, she had been an idolater, for the Phoenicians worshiped *Ashtoreth,* the queen of heaven. But because her cries to her heathen god had failed she now turns to the Christ of heaven for her dear daughter's relief.

It would seem, however, that she knocked in vain at heaven's door, for Jesus told His disciples to inform the anxious woman that He was sent to the lost sheep of Israel, and not to the Gentiles who were known as "dogs," and that bread for the children (Israel) should not be cast to dogs (Gentiles). But the woman was not deterred by the Master's reply. Hope within her was not destroyed. She owned that she and her people were dogs, outside of the commonwealth, and with no claim. Dogs, however, get scraps, and what she wanted would not impoverish the children, while it would enrich herself. She wanted mercy for her afflicted daughter, but not others' mercy.

It is interesting to note the uncommon word used only here for "dogs." It is in the diminutive form and means "little dogs" or *puppies.* Outside the house were the dogs, wild and half-wolfish, but in homes there were the small domestic dogs, pets of the children, who waited around the table for scraps of food. All the desperate woman wanted was a crumb of mercy for her "puppy," her dear small daughter. Her faith and persistence prevailed. She received her crumb, and more besides, the testimony of the Lord to the greatness of her faith.

## The Parable of Weather Forecasting
### (Matthew 16:1-4)

*Television* has helped to educate us in the intricacies of weather forecasting, but over 1900 years ago Jesus knew all about this art and employed it to illustrate and illumine His answer to the Pharisees and Sadducees as they tempted

Him for heavenly signs as to His claims to deity. Evidently the sign they had just witnessed in the miraculous feeding of the multitudes was too *earthly* for them. Wanting something from the skies as confirmation of a divine testimony, they were blind that in the Christ who stood before them was Heaven's Greatest Sign.

Reproving His tempters for their ignorance and wickedness Jesus said they ought to be able to discern the signs of the times as easily as those of the weather. They should have known that God's signs are always simple to read, and that their abounding sin was a sign of approaching doom. Quoting from commonplace speech, Jesus said, "When it is evening, ye say, Fair weather . . . in the morning, Foul weather today." Think the old adage: "A red morning is a shepherd's warning; a red night is a shepherd's delight." With great force Jesus applied His illustration to those who as they watched the sky, were clever in surface observation, yet were not able to discern the signs of the time. They were correct in weather forecasting, but were blind to the meaning of events crowding in upon them. They wanted a sign and Jesus gave them one, namely, that of Jonah, whose three days and three nights in the great fish were the type of His coming death and resurrection, the greatest sign of His authority as the One co-equal with God.

## The Parable of the One Leaven
### (Matthew 16:6-12)

Already reference has been made to the figure of the *leaven.* Here we note that Phariseeism and Sadduceeism have the same essential fault, namely, intense earthiness. They were *one* leaven, not two. The policies of the Pharisees and Sadducees were based upon a materialistic and naturalistic conception of life, and not the spiritual conceptions of Jesus. *Leaven* represents that which destroys, breaks up, ferments. Working quietly, insidiously and persistently, leaven is here used as a type of the teaching and influence of ritualistic and rationalistic teachings. False teachings form the leaven that forever destroys. The two aspects of error represented by the Pharisees and the Sadducees sprang from one serious fault — unbelief (of heart) in God.

## The Parable of the Rock and the Keys
### (Matthew 16:15-19)

While those outside the immediate circle of *The Twelve* had different views of Christ, He questioned His own as to what they thought of Him, and Peter, ever the spokesman of the apostolic band, said, "Thou art the Christ, the Son of the living God." Such an astounding confession from a Jew whose creed had been *The Unity of God,* thrilled the heart of Jesus and resulted in a most remarkable benediction for Peter. To him had been granted a special revelation from God. Peter had received an insight into His Lord's Messiahship: "Thou art the Christ," and also of His deity: "Thou art the Son of the living God."

As the result of Peter's confession of Christ, Christ had a confession of Peter to make, "Thou art Peter, and upon this rock I will build my Church." The name *Peter* means a small rock, a piece of stone, *Petros;* but the word Jesus used for "rock" was *Petra,* meaning the essential rock. Rome wrongly teaches that the Church is built on Peter — the so-called first Pope. But what Jesus implied was that He would build His Church, not on a fallible, impulsive disciple but upon what he had confessed to, namely, His own deity, or Himself. He alone is "the Church's One Foundation" (I Corinthians 3:10). *The Rock* is only used figuratively in the Old Testament of God. "Their rock is not as our *Rock.*"

Swiftly Jesus changed the figure of speech from *rock* to *gates,* from foundation to foe. "The gates of hell shall not prevail against it." The gate in every city was the spot where rulers exercised judgment and took counsel. Gates also guarded a city from enemy attack.

*Gates,* as used by our Lord, meant "powers of Hell." His true Church is invincible against attack. *Communism* seeks to destroy her, but built on "The Rock," she is invulnerable. Discouraged child of God, banish any fear you may have that the powers of hell will prevail. No one and nothing can destroy those whose life is hid with Christ in God.

Changing to another figure, Jesus promised Peter the possession of *keys* to His Kingdom. *Keys* were symbols of authority (Revelations 1:18) and indicated that Peter, and all like him who were Christ's, would exercise spiritual authority. The scribes of old looked upon *Keys* as the insignia of their particular office as interpreters of the moral law. Peter first used the *Keys* when, on the Day of Pentecost, he preached to the multitudes gathered together and opened the Kingdom to about 3,000 who believed. At Antioch, Peter was the first to open the door of the church to Gentiles. All who have been saved by grace, and have a passion for the salvation of the lost, are those who have the keys to open doors for those willing to enter the Kingdom of God. As to *the binding* and *the loosing,* to which Rome lays false claims, the promise of such is for all true believers to claim. "*Binding* seems to mean binding sin to the conscience in words of reproof, calls to repentance, and warnings. *Loosing* means to comfort the conscience, assuring it of forgiveness." The Church of Jesus Christ is in the world to enforce laws, in the sense of moral standards — "*to bind,* to declare that which is obligatory; *to loose,* to declare that which is voluntary."

## The Parable of the Grain of Mustard Seed
### (Matthew 17:19-21)

The necessity of grasping the chief lesson Jesus teaches in any parable or parabolic picture He used, is most important. Such an effort saves us from taking a parable out of its context and misinterpreting its original intention.

We say that "a text out of the context is a pretext." The same is true of a parable out of its context. In our study of the *Parable of the Mustard Seed,* we saw how the phrase Jesus used was a recognized proverb of the infinitely little. The question is, Why did He use it here, and what did He intend to illustrate by its use? The background of the narrative where the illustration is found is that of the failure of His disciples to do anything for the demoniac boy. Why had they failed? The answer to Jesus was brief and explicit. "Because of your unbelief." Then illuminating His answer, He said, "If ye have faith as a grain of mustard seed . . . nothing shall be impossible unto you." A seed, no matter how small, contains the life principle, and faith of this nature is vital in operation. When Jesus rebuked His disciples, and said, "Because of your little faith," He did not refer to quantity. Neither was an increase of quantity in the prayer of the disciples, "Lord, increase our faith." The thought implied is a change of *quality,* not *quantity.* The quality of faith, no matter how small, is life, and such a living faith moving in harmony with the will of God can accomplish mighty things. Mountains cannot stand before it.

## The Parable of the Millstone and Lost Sheep
### (Matthew 18:1-14)

The illustrations of the millstone, cutting off a limb or plucking out an eye, and the straying sheep all occur in the narrative dealing with our Lord's reply to the disciples' question as to who was greatest in the Kingdom. This chapter may be rightly called *The Chapter of the Child,* for Jesus taking a child and placing it in the midst of His disciples taught them the necessary lesson of humility. In their quest for greatness they had to be reminded that ambition can be an impatient thing and can trample upon others in order to reach the top. The wrong kind of ambition can

sink men to perdition and make them sink others with them. So, as Richard Glover puts it so forcibly: "The *hand* of ambitious rudeness should be *cut* off; The *eye* of ambitious coveting should be *plucked* out; The *foot* of ambitious wilfulness should be *cut* off." Our Lord's most descriptive language prescribes proper treatment for all fleshly ambitions: they are to be starved, slain. Unless we are as simple and emptied of all pride as a little child we are not fit for the Master's use. Using the illustration of the lost sheep, Jesus showed the value of a child who is a type of greatness in His Kingdom. And children, because they are *children,* are not to be neglected or despised because it is not the Father's will that one little one should perish. The value of children by eternal standards is indicated by the fact that the Father, and the Son, and the angels are associated with them. Their *angels* always behold the face of the Father, and they have constant access to God on behalf of the children of whom they are guardians; the *Son,* who is the Good Shepherd, ever seeks the young; the *Father* is unwilling that one of them should perish. Those who have the spiritual welfare of children at heart should note these truths as they seek to win the young for Christ.

## The Parable of Forgiveness and the Unmerciful Servant
### (Matthew 18:21-35)

In this generally acknowledged parable of Christ, He is found illustrating the matter of forgiveness, not God's forgiveness of man (although this is in the background by suggestion) but of man's forgiveness of man. Strife among brethren is a grave thing and may easily become an "offence," which causes one to stumble and prevents further progress in the path of holiness. Our Lord is explicit as to the treatment that injuries, those who injure, and the injured should receive. Beginning with the *commendation* of the child-like spirit, He now advances to the *commendation* of the forgiving spirit and the *condemnation* of the opposite.

Christ taught that the more innocent we are in the confessed wrong, the more power we have to heal the variance, and the more responsible we are for doing so. The *doer* and the *sufferer* of wrong must seek to end the quarrel. First of all, Jesus says we are to act with *privacy*. "Between thee and him alone." If others are communicated with first, it is harder for the two concerned to meet. In case the breach is not healed, the mutual friends of both parties are to be consulted, and if their efforts fail, the local church to which the injured one and the injurer belong must be consulted. But if the transgressor fails to respond to the discipline of the church, he is to be treated as "an heathen man and a publican," meaning, as one who has put himself outside the circle of Christian fellowship. We are warned, however, not to allow such separation to become hatred (See I Corinthians 5:11; II Corinthians 2:7).

This parable of *The Unmerciful Servant*, which can be coupled with that of *The Two Debtors*, seeing the same symbolism recurs either in the main subject or in the details (Luke 7:41-43), came as our Lord's reply to Peter's question regarding the frequency of forgiveness. Peter knew that in the past forgiveness was on a three-fold basis, "For three transgressions of Israel . . . I will not turn away punishment" (Amos 2:6), but now a disciple of Jesus, he feels he should be more generous. So he goes from *three* to *seven*. But he was to learn that forgiveness is "not a question of celestial arithmetic, but of conduct," and that divine forgiveness, which is to be emulated, is unlimited. When Jesus said, "seventy times seven" did He have in mind, God's word of old, "If Cain shall be avenged sevenfold, truly Lamech seventy and sevenfold" (Genesis 4:24)? What a gospel of forgiveness that was to proclaim in the dim era of revelation!

The truth unfolded in the parable, then, is that forgiveness must be, as it is with God, a constant attitude. "There *is* forgiveness with Thee, that Thou mayest be feared." The word *forgive* actually means, "forth-give," that is, to dismiss absolutely from thought. When God forgives, He forgets: "Your sins and iniquities will I remember no more," and our Lord's striking parable illustrates this divine trait. As in His previous parables, we are given portraits of Himself, so here in *a certain king* we have His first appearance as King in His parabolic teaching, and we are His servants with whom He takes account. How bankrupt before Him we are! Truly, we are nothing else but His bond-servants, so deep in His debt.

Whichever way we look at the debt of the bondservant who, apart from his enormous debt, was a "wicked servant," the "ten thousand talents" represented an enormous sum. If a "talent" be taken as a talent of silver then according to the *Roman* calculation, "ten thousand talents" would amount to over one million pounds, or to some three million dollars. "This may be regarded as the *human* estimate; such an estimate as civilized and educated man might form of sin." If the "talent" is according to the *Jewish* calculation, then the "ten thousand talents" would represent well over three million pounds, or about ten million dollars. "This may be regarded as the *legal* estimate: such as the Jew under law might form of sin against his God." But if the "talent" be taken to mean a talent of gold, then the "ten thousand talents" would mean upwards of fifty million pounds, or over 150 million dollars, a colossal sum! "This can be made to represent the divine estimate, or sin judged of in the presence of God, and secret sins in the light of His countenance."

But the servant with such a tremendous debt had no assets, so his lord commanded all that he had to be sold, even to his wife and children. Such a mode of exacting payment was in accordance with ancient customs (II Kings

4:1; Nehemiah 5:8). Realizing the poverty-stricken condition of the debtor, his lord was moved with compassion, so much so that he wiped out the entire debt (Matthew 18:25-27). What a glimpse our King here gives of the mercy and compassion of the divine heart! Mercy alone can meet our case, for we have nothing to pay toward our indebtedness. Even if we could atone for our sin by the payment of money, monetary exchange "would not be acceptable seeing salvation is 'without money and without price.' " It is solely on the ground of the finished work of Christ, the crucified King, that God can meet our bankrupt state and abolish our debt. "He forgave him the debt."

The next phase of the parable reveals the heartlessness of the forgiven one, and also the utter disregard of his obligation to emulate the noble example of his lord. Forgiven, he should have forgiven. But see what happened. One of his fellow-servants owed him only "three hundred pence," around four pounds, or twelve dollars, a sum out of all proportion to the very heavy debt which had been graciously wiped out. The lord had dealt with his servant in a most compassionate way, but when he in turn tried to extract a mere pittance from his companion, there was no love, no compassion, only hard-heartedness. "He took him by the throat and said, Pay me that thou owest." Himself so freely and fully forgiven, he forgot that grace bestowed lays the receiver under an obligation to manifest the same grace (Ephesians 4:32). "Forgiving . . . even as God for Christ's sake hath forgiven you."

The lord, learning of the violent, ungrateful attitude of his forgiven servant, was angry, and delivered him up to the tormentors (it was customary to use torture to extract payments and confessions) till he should pay all, meaning, the "ten thousand talents" originally owed (Matthew 18:28-35). The king's compassion had been forfeited, and his greed, anger, lack of compassion lost

everything for the heartless servant. The parable then was designed to teach a Christian how to forgive. The Lord freely forgives all. "Seventy times seven" is the pattern of Divine forgiveness.

"Unwearied is forgiveness still
His heart could only love."

Do we forgive as we have been forgiven? If God treated us for our debts, as we treat others, what desolation would be ours. In the prayer Jesus taught His own to pray He says, "If ye forgive men their trespasses, your heavenly Father will also forgive you; but if ye forgive not men their trespasses, neither will your Father forgive your trespasses" (Matthew 6:14,15). Solemn words these that must not be watered down. If ours has been a mere intellectual acceptance of the doctrine of the forgiveness of sin, but conduct and character remained unchanged and our heart is hard toward others, the Lord will deliver us to the tormentors. He will leave us to the upbraidings of our conscience, or the assaults of Satan, until we are brought to act in conformity with His will and example. We are to behave toward others as God behaves toward us. If we claim to be His, then we must have His disposition to forgive, even our enemies. Thus merciful, we can expect to obtain mercy (Matthew 5:7). O for grace to be unlimited in our forgiveness of others!

## The Parable of a Camel and a Rich man
### (Matthew 19:16-26)

It was the refusal of the rich young ruler to surrender his much-loved possessions and follow Christ that gave birth to this arrestive figure of speech, of a camel trying to work its way through the eye of a needle. By this parabolic picture Jesus sought to teach His own the blighting influence of wealth on personality. It must be borne in mind that Jesus did *not* say that rich men cannot enter the Kingdom of God, but that because of the way their riches dominate them it is hard and difficult for them to enter. Christ then used His somewhat impossible illustration (see also Mark 10:17-31; Luke 18:18-30).

It is said that our Lord employed a proverbial expression which denoted literally a thing impossible, but figuratively, very difficult (a difficulty so great as to be comparable to a camel going through a needle's eye). This touch of humor must have brought a smile to the faces of the disciples. It has been explained that "the needle's eye" referred to a gate with the smaller arch, through which no camel could pass except unladen. But it is more natural to assume that our Lord coined the illustration to prove how hard it is for the rich in goods but poor in grace to enter His Kingdom. The disciples may have thought that rich men had fewer temptations, but Jesus said they have more. Men should be more afraid of wealth, less afraid of poverty. Wealth tends to pride, indulgence and selfish power. The young ruler had wealth, but not everything. He lacked the most essential possession — eternal life. The rich man in another parable did not go to hell because he was rich, but because he had neglected his soul's salvation.

Amazed, the disciples asked through Peter, "We have forsaken all and followed thee; what shall we have therefore?" They wanted some recompence of reward for the voluntary life of poverty. But it is wrong and perilous to look at our sacrifice and inquire about the payment we should receive. "Love neither urges claims nor asks wages — especially when it owes infinitely more than it has earned." The glory of life is not to get, but to give. Yet Jesus assures us that no surrender for His sake will pass unrewarded.

## The Parable of the Householder and His Servants
### (Matthew 20:1-16)

Actually, this parable is connected directly with the last four verses of the previous chapter and provides an answer for the question, "What shall we have therefore?" (Matthew 19:27) It is also related to relative position, standing at the commencement and the close of the two narratives (Matthew 19:30; 20:16). "Many that are first shall be last; and the last first." The disciples were not to despise the rich young ruler and all like him: if they repent, then far from being last, they may become first.

Again, we are introduced to the Householder, the house-despot, who is Christ Himself. Before sunrise He is afoot, and there is no hour of the day when He is not at work. "Man may waste brief time till the eleventh hour surprises him idle still in the marketplace. The Householder, however, is never found standing idle, and wherever He can find those who are willing to work diligently in His vineyard, He hires them. At various hours of life's day we can begin to work for Him, and demanding the longest day of service we can render, He promises us wages."

The parable teaches that if we start at the eleventh hour we shall receive more than we ever hoped. Starting under a fearful disadvantage, eleven-twelfths of the day gone, yet we can be made equal with those who started at sunrise. "The parable cannot indicate the secret, but it names the fact, that often those repenting late may overtake those who started long before in goodness and service." It is not the length of service that tells, but the quality of it. Discontent, however, seems to be the essential difficulty of the parable. The discontent of those who had labored long yet received no more wages than those who started late seems incompatible with rendering service and inconceivable in presence of great reward. The mood which says, "We have left all — what therefore shall we receive?" is the mood which mars discipleship with discontent. The Householder, being just, knows what each laborer of His is worth, and therefore discontent at His rewards for service is unwarranted. All who enter His service must enter with the full persuasion that their labor for Him will not be in vain.

When it comes to the distribution of rewards for service, there will be the manifestation of three great and glorious principles, Newberry says: *justice, sovereignty, grace.*

*As the Householder* (Matthew 20:1), He promises, "Whatsoever is just, that shall ye receive." As His laborers we are guaranteed a full and just remuneration for our service whether long or brief. Each will receive the due recompense of the reward.

*As the Lord of the Vineyard* (Matthew 20:15), He claims the sovereign right to do what He wills in His own affairs. It is not for us to question His choice of laborers, nor their respective reward. Because of who and what He is, He cannot act unfairly. With our finite understanding we may question His ways. At the end, however, as the Interpreter, He will make any seeming inconsistency plain. Till then, let us rest in His word, "Whatsoever is right, that shall ye receive."

*As the Goodman of the House* (Matthew 20:11), He retains to Himself "the privilege, the exercise of His goodness and grace, whatever might be thought of His generosity. *Sovereignty* will not be exercised at the expense of *justice* or of *grace;* whilst the magnificence of *grace* is manifested in the far more exceeding and eternal weight of glory, the recompense for light and temporary affliction and service, will be for the honour of the *justice,* and the glory of the *sovereignty* displayed. So, then, if the last are first, and the first last, and some are chosen to especial services, and others chosen to peculiar privilege, and will be alike the subjects of *divine justice, sovereignty* and *grace;* and the language of each and all will be, "Not unto us, O Jehovah, not unto us, but unto Thy name give glory, for Thy loving kindness, and for Thy truth's sake!"

Because the divine vineyard requires *laborers,* not *loiterers,* may we be saved from one of the sins of Sodom, which was that of *idleness,* the forerunner of temporal and eternal ruin. As laborers may we ever remember that *motive* gives character to service, and that acceptable service is determined, not by duration, but by its spirit.

# The Parable of the Fig Tree and Faith

(Matthew 21:17-22)

Although actually we have a *miracle* in this narrative, and have dealt thus with it in *All the Miracles of the Bible,* it was also a *parable of judgment.* This aspect we are now to consider. This parable, and the remainder of our Lord's parabolic teaching in Matthew, was given during His last days before Calvary, and now becomes largely denunciatory with His administrative actions. As He gathered His own around Him for final teaching, His manner was one of a full and supreme authority, as the purging of the Temple proves.

In the city, Jesus found hatred and plots to kill Him by those He wished to save. So He left Jerusalem for Bethany where He found loving fellowship, gratitude and peace. Having spent the night in such a quiet sphere, He returned to Jerusalem and on the way cursed and destroyed the fig-tree. This parabolic act, our Lord fully explained, was His only miracle of judgment, and that against a barren tree. The destruction of the swine at Gadara did not have the objective of judgment, but the delivery of a demon-tormented man. With the withering up of the fig-tree He exhibited His power to blast, not bless. But behind the mere destruction of the tree there was a parabolic significance.

Difficulties have been raised regarding our Lord's unique action. Some say that it was an act of injustice, seeing it was not "the season of figs." Why should He expect fruit when it was not the season? But although the usual time of figs was about June, it was in the month of April the tree was cursed. There was, however, a kind of first ripe fig, before the time of the full harvest of figs, found on certain trees, as Isaiah points out (Isaiah 28:4). This was a fact of nature known by all of those with Jesus. Whenever such first ripe figs appeared, they did so before the leaves appeared. Jesus, knowing that this tree was one producing figs before leaves, saw nothing but leaves where there should have been no leaves at all. Leaves suggest fruitfulness, but fruit was lacking which indicated a false development of show and appearance. The tree had failed in its purpose and was therefore smitten with destruction.

Further, our Lord's action was not one of anger. We sometimes say that "a hungry man is an angry man." But Jesus, as a Man, was not angry, although hungry. When righteous indignation was necessary, He manifested it, but in this miracle-parable there is not the least sign of personal vindictiveness. Because the tree was faulty, a failure, its judgment was swift — a speed which surprised the disciples, who came to see that although their Master was meek and lowly, He could be majestic in His wrath.

The meaning of the parabolic action is not hard to find. Christ's physical hunger was a symbol of a deeper hunger possessing Him. Israel is pictured as a *fig-tree,* and He came to the nation, His nation, expecting fruit. Leaves of religious formalism He found in abundance but the fruit of holiness was lacking. He was hungry for the salvation of the people but crucifying Him, they told Him to save Himself. Thus in His "strange act" (Isaiah 28:21), He rejected the tree, emblem of the nation. Cursing the fig-tree was the forerunner of the national judgment which the next two parables cover.

The disciples, over-awed by our Lord's display of miraculous power, asked not *how* He had destroyed the tree but *why.* He then gave them a sermonette on the power of faith, showing the connection between His destructive act and believing prayer. The tree was now blighted, and there it stood a symbol of that which was untrue to reality. Why had the nation it symbolized failed — because it lacked faith in God, a fruit-bearing faith. In spite of the outward appearance of life, Israel was spiritually dead. Fruit was professed but not possessed. But all who have faith, born of God, can cooperate with Him in the manifestation of His power. Such faith laughs at impossibilities and cries, "It must be done." May we be spared from disappointing the Master! Through faith and obedience, the fruit of the Spirit may be ours, and such fruit ever gladdens the heart of Him whose life was ever pleasing to God.

## The Parable of the Two Sons and Vineyard
(Matthew 21:28-32)

This parable, and the next dealing with *The Husbandman,* are often grouped together, seeing their subject is one. Both parables are based on *The Song of the Vineyard* we dealt with in our study of the parabolic in Isaiah (5:1-7). As all who listened to Jesus were familiar with that old-time song, all should listen to His two parables with deep interest. In the parable before us, Jesus is found condemning the *method* of the religious leaders rejecting His witness; and in the next parable (Matthew 21:33-46), He administers a condemnation of their *motives.* The key to both parables is found in the words, "When the chief priests and the Pharisees had heard His parables, they perceived that He spake of them" (Matthew 21:45). His foes felt the power of His truth and beheld His mercy, yet they plotted to kill Him.

The Jewish rulers had challenged Christ's authority. His question about John's baptism and mission having the sanction of heaven or not, or being merely of men, put them on the horns of a dilemma. They halted between expediency and convenience and had no answer to His question. These rulers had utterly failed in the plan of God, and to lead them to pass a verdict on their own conduct, Jesus resorted to the simple method of telling stories. With a master hand He reached into the defects of these self-exposed religious leaders and made them feel that He was talking about them. Thus these two parables must be interpreted in the light of the occasion which called them forth.

The contrast between the self-righteous and sinners occurs in other parables; for instance, in *The Parable of the Pharisee and the Publican.* Religious professors rejected the Word of God, but the outcasts accepted it. The priests and elders were unmoved at the stern preaching of John the Baptist, but great and notorious sinners repented as they listened. The son who said, "I go, Sir, and went not," was a portrait of the Pharisees, while the other son who said, "I will not: but afterwards he repented, and went," represented penitent sinners like the publicans and harlots. While this is the direct interpretation of the parable, the application is general. Whenever and wherever the Gospel is preached in the power of the Spirit there are still sinners who repent and turn to the Saviour, and alongside of them those answering to the Jewish priests and elders, religious, yet not willing to confess they are likewise sinners and are as lost in God's sight as the most profligate alive. Clinging to their self-righteousness and false obedience, they see no need of a Saviour.

Previous parables provide us with several portraits of Jesus. Here, we are introduced to another person, for the "certain man" was the "father" of the two sons. Is this a portrait of God, such as we also find in *The Parable of the Prodigal Son?* Some expositors say that God, as the *Father,* is the principle figure in the parable, and that His *sons* may be divided into the obedient and the disobedient. Perhaps, in a creative sense, God is the Father of all, just as Job speaks of Him as the Father of the "rain." *Son,* however, is a term implying a birth-relationship — a relationship which regeneration alone can bring

about. Unless we have received the spirit of adoption we have no right to call God, *Father* (Galatians 4:5).

Further, God does not ask service from those who are not His. *Saved,* we serve, and the "vineyard" is the sphere in which we serve Him. For every "son" there is a vine to care for, and if he neglects it, no one else will care for it. For each He has a specific task, which must be accomplished while it is "today." Now let us consider the two distinct and opposite answers, and also the two distinct and opposite acts given in the parable:

*The Two Sons.* Both sons in the parable heard the father's command. One refused to obey but afterwards repented; the other promised obedience but failed to render it. "The latter is just as disobedient as if he had refused from the first, and though his promise of doing his father's will might deceive those who heard it and make them think him a dutiful son, the father could not be satisfied with conduct which so entirely contradicted the promise." Receiving their father's direction to work in his vineyard, the one son point-blank declined to obey, but soon repented his refusal and obeyed, the other deferentially promised obedience but actually did not obey.

The *first* son said, "I will not." This was an evil answer flowing from its native spring in an evil heart. He rudely refused to obey his father and meant what he said. This disobedient son represents those who have neither the profession nor the practice of pure religion. They neither fear God nor pretend to fear Him. There is no hypocrisy about them. They are not consistent. They know they are sinners and plainly say so.

The *second* son said, "I go, Sir; and went not." He said one thing and then acted in the opposite direction. He was not consistent. There was a contradiction between his word and work, his promise and performance. While his father was present he concealed his determination not to obey. His smooth language was a lie. His brother said, "No," but then repented and went, but there was no repentance on the part of this one. Professing obedience, he had no intention of obeying and was therefore a hypocrite. He said, "Lord, Lord," but was not willing to accomplish his father's will.

Both sons were in a false and unsafe position. Their characters were opposite; they differed in thought and word, but their different answers only indicated varieties of sin. The *first* son was bold and guilty of unblushing rebellion; the character of the *second* son was cowardly, false. The one son neither promised nor meant to obey; the other promised obedience but intended not to keep his word. There is no ground for preferring the one to the other. It is in their ultimate *act* that they were different, for the *first,* after a blunt refusal, repented of his sin and went out to labor for his father. The other son promptly promised but failed to perform. His brother changed from bad to good, but this son was not changed from good to bad. His attitude was pre-determined. He had no intention of changing.

*The Two Classes.* These *two* sons were meant to illustrate *two* different types of people. The first son represented the publicans and sinners and harlots. Under the preaching of John the Baptist these profligates, who were rebellious and defied God, repented and obeyed and became the sons of God. They had made no profession of obedience. They lived in open sin and were not surprised when men denounced them as hopelessly corrupt. "Publicans (tax-gatherers) and harlots" was a by-word for the wicked of that time. These people were sinners, and knew it. But under John's Spirit-inspired preaching, the miracle happened. The message of sin and repentance went to their heart, and repenting of their sin, they found a way to God and to service in His vineyard.

The second son represented the Pharisees, Sadducees and Scribes, who wore the robes and livery of religion, but who were as far from God as the outcasts. Professing to be the Lord's they were yet "disobedient and rebellious in all the deep facts of their life." These religionists should have exemplified the best in possession and profession, but they lacked the possession of the true life of God. They were outwardly correct and righteous, and were ever ready with a deferential, "I go, sir," but were destitute of the desire and will to obey. They typified Israel of old who said, "All that the Lord hath spoken we will do," but subsequent history shows how they failed. Israel was like the son who said to his father, "I go, sir, and went not."

After uttering His simple, telling story, Jesus pressed for a verdict from the Pharisees and chief priests. This was immediately forthcoming and was a verdict upon themselves: "Whether of the twain did the will of his father? They say unto Him, the first." Then Jesus drove home the application to those who failed to repent as the result of His words and works: "Verily I say unto you, That the publican and the harlots go into the kingdom before you." There is more hope of those who are consciously wicked than of the self-satisfied. Those who feel that they are "rich, and increased with goods, and in need of nothing," fail to realize how spiritually bankrupt and impoverished they are. If religiously respectable, they have been deluded by Satan into believing that their own righteousness will prevail. But failing to see that Jesus died to save sinners, and that if they die without Him as a personal Saviour, they die lost forevermore, they continue to live outside the Kingdom.

Yet Jesus did not fail to leave the door open for those self-righteous Pharisees. There is a Gospel for them in the Master's declaration. He did not say, "The publicans and the harlots go into the kingdom *instead of you,"* but *"before you,"* in front of you. Does not this suggest that all of them could, and some of them would, follow after the saved sinners into the kingdom? Was not Saul of Tarsus, who became Paul the Apostle, one of such? Linking His parable to John's mighty work in bringing sinners to God, Jesus claims greater authority to give men His commands, obedience to which results in eternal life.

# The Parable of the Householder and the Heir

### (Matthew 21:33-46)

Was there a touch of satire in our Lord's request, "Hear another parable"? *Another* parable! Had the Jewish rulers not heard enough to expose and anger them? Why give the sword a turn in the wound? Doubtless those ecclesiastical dignitaries felt they had heard enough for one day. Their prestige was suffering in the eyes of the crowd and they could see that Christ had turned the tables against them, yet here was Jesus rubbing salt into their sorely stricken reputation. He had already shown up the Pharisees as men who were hollow shams, and now a more condemning parable exposes them as murderers.

*Another* parable, and what a great one it was, remarkable in itself and its occasion. The Scribes and Pharisees had tried to impeach the Saviour, only to find themselves in turn impeached of Him. They had discounted Him as the Son of God having all authority. He now, in a further condemnatory parable sets forth who He is, who sent Him, and the death He is to die at the hands of His foes. Mercilessly, He exposed a breach of sacred trust in a parabolic presentation of Israel's past history, and of the future punishment for the betrayal of such a trust. This parable is found in the first three gospels (Mark 12:1-12; Luke 20:9-19), with Luke adding that it was addressed to the people as well as to the chief priests and elders.

First of all, we think of the privileges conferred on Israel by God, here likened to a *householder, a father, Lord of the vineyard*. Jesus used language well-known to His Jewish hearers, describing the complete and perfect equipment of a vineyard. Frequently, we read of Israel, endowed with peculiar privileges, compared to a vine or the aggregate of vines in a vineyard (See Psalm 80:8-15; Isaiah 5:1-7; Ezekiel 15:2-5). The vine was the noblest of all plants, needing the utmost care, but repaying it most richly. Israel, as an honored vine, was hedged round about by its Owner, which can be looked upon as the Law with all its ordinances. Through such (Deuteronomy 7:8; Ephesians 2:14), the Jewish nation was separated from other nations because of the peculiar mission she was to exercise. The digging of the press, referring to the provision made to receive the juices of the grape as it flowed out in rich abundance, can illustrate the true fruits of piety through the Law.

As for the *tower,* it was a necessary erection for guards to dwell in when the fruit was ripe, and the danger of losing it was considerable. From the watchtower, the whole vineyard could be observed, symbolic of the way in which the Divine Householder, the Lord of the Vineyard, guarded, preserved and watched over His ancient people. In all of these features we have the proprietor's perfect promise made for fruit to be gathered from his vineyard.

This "vineyard," however, was rented out to husbandmen, and the "householder went into a far country." These "husbandmen" were the Chiefs and Princes of Israel (Jeremiah 33:18; Ezekiel 34:2; Malachi 2:7; Matthew 23:2,3), who were placed in a rich vineyard of divine promises, the Temple, and great examples. Although they represented and were responsible to the Householder, they persistently betrayed their trust. Having made them answerable to Himself, He went into "a far country," leaving them apparently to themselves. After the first planting of His vineyard, and after the deliverance out of Egypt, the giving of the Law, and the possession of Canaan, Israel did not have extraordinary manifestation of the presence of God (Deuteronomy 34:10-12). They had to walk by faith and sight.

When the time of fruit drew near, the owner sent his servants to collect what was due, the rent being paid in kind. Such a return was equitable and reasonable. We believe the "servants" to be the noble array of prophets, who, as ambassadors of God, had a special commission to remind the nation of its obligations and to call the people and rulers alike to the subjection that was due. Describing the treatment the prophets received, Jesus Himself claimed to have sent those divinely inspired men, "Behold *I* send unto you the prophets" (Matthew 23:34).

But the privileged "husbandmen" abused their privileges. Jewish rulers became wayward, selfish, unscrupulous, and turned against the prophets because of the way their God-inspired ministry disturbed the rulers' conscience and robbed them of the respect of the people. Isaiah was sawn asunder; Jeremiah was stoned; Amos was murdered with a club; John the Baptist was beheaded; Stephen was stoned to death (See I Kings 18:13; 22:24; II Kings 6:31; 22; Jeremiah 20:1,2; Matthew 23:29-37; Acts 7:5; Hebrews 11:36-38). The treatment of the "servants" of the husbandmen" proves that the worst crimes are often perpetrated by the most highly privileged. "It cannot be that a prophet perish out of Jerusalem."

The "householder" was slow to deal with the hopeless evil of the "husbandmen." How patient he was! Israel proved so wayward, yet God expended more and more labor and patience to win her for Himself. At last, He sent His Son, His Heir. The contrast between the Old Testament prophets and Christ is marked: the former were God's *servants*. Christ was His *Son* and *Heir*. "Last of all He sent His Son." The sending of Christ was the last trial of divine mercy with His covenant-people, as such. In Mark's report of the parable,

Christ's pre-existence as the Son of the Father is most emphatic. "He *had* yet one, a beloved Son." "He did not become the Son of the Owner by being sent: rather was He sent because He was the Son."

Then there came the decision to kill the heir. "Let us kill him, and let us seize on his inheritance . . . and they slew him." After the utmost forbearance on the part of the Owner, and His solicitude to obtain the tribute which the people owed, He risked His Son, concluding they would have respect for Him and yield Him His deserved homage. But they filled up the measure of their iniquity by basely putting Him to death. Afterwards, Peter charged the Jewish rulers with the murder of Jesus (Acts 2:23). How brave and fearless it was of Jesus to confront His foes and predict that they would kill Him, and try to seize the vineyard (Acts 4:25,27). The term, "inheritance," expresses the full title to lordship, and His murderers thought that with Him dead, they might be able to constrain the Divine Law to subserve their own interests and ambition, and regain their lost honor and influence as the result of Christ's exposure. They set a watch upon His sepulchre, in case He should rise again as He said He would, and exert still greater authority.

Then Jesus went on to ask the question, "When the lord of the vineyard cometh, what will he do unto those husbandmen?" Passing a righteous sentence on themselves, the Pharisees said, "He will miserably destroy those wicked men" — a sentence executed when the Romans destroyed Jerusalem, and the people were cut off from the privileges which for thousands of years they had possessed. Caught in the grip of the depravity of their own hearts those rulers saw themselves as being *wicked,* a word the dictionary describes as being "evil in principle and practice: deviating from, or contrary to, the moral or divine law, or to morality, or religion, addicted to vice, or sin, vicious; sinful; depraved."

How true such a designation was of those who crucified the Lord of Glory!

Because God never leaves His vineyards in wicked hands, there came the transference of His "vineyard" to others. "He will let out His vineyard unto other husbandmen." The Pharisees, without knowing it, passed judgment on themselves and are now informed, not only of their fate, but of the cessation of their privileges. The kingdom of God was to be taken from them, and from the nation they represented, and given to another nation, which the Lord of the harvest hoped would prove to be more fruitful. Did not our Lord forecast here the casting off of the Jews, which Paul refers to in Romans 11:15-23? Prophecy teaches that the vineyard will be once again entrusted to Israel. What was the other "nation" to which authority over God's interests passed? Was it not the Church which Peter describes as "a holy nation" and John speaks of as "a kingdom"? (I Peter 2:9; Revelation 1:6). This "nation" consists of all regenerated persons and is constituted on a different principle and held together by different bonds. It is not after the flesh, but after the Spirit that citizenship is obtained in this Christian commonwealth, in which saved Jews and Gentiles are one. Yet the Church, more highly privileged than Israel, must beware lest she forfeit her position. How solemn is the warning, "I will move thy lampstand out of its place" (Revelation 2:5; 3:16).

Declaring the doom of those about to kill Him, Jesus said that a "Stone" would grind them to powder. Was He not the great "Corner-stone" whose very greatness and majesty caused the evil craftsmen to refuse? In stern language, using prophecies of old, He declares His own kingly judgment (Isaiah 8:14-15). His foes and rejectors were to be broken and ground to powder, as the crushing of Gentile monarchies Daniel foretold (Daniel 2:34,35). The nation's doom is set forth with the fearful sublimity of a poetic utterance —

Did ye never read in the Scriptures;
"The stone which the builders rejected
The same is become the head of the corner:
This is the work of the Lord,
And wonderful in our eyes"?

Therefore I say unto you;
The Kingdom of God shall be taken from you;
And given to a nation bringing forth the fruits thereof.
And whosoever shall fall against this stone shall be bruised:
And on whomsoever it shall fall, it will grind him to powder.

Israel fell on the *Stone* and was broken, and ere long the same *Stone* will fall on a hypocritical and apostate Christendom and break the image in pieces. After listening to their pronounced doom, the Pharisees, perceiving that Jesus had revealed their horrible guilt, would have laid hands on Him there and then and killed Him, but they feared the reaction of the multitude who had come to take Him as a Prophet. Was He not the Prophet raised up of Jehovah (Exodus 20:9), and who is known revealing His authority, not only as a Prophet but as God's Son and Heir? Thus, as Campbell Morgan says, this parable, and others to follow reveal His authority: "That authority is demonstrated by the line of His accomplishment, of the revelation of truth, His recognition of the divine rights, His restoration of a lost order. This was the purpose of His presence in the world."

## The Parable of the Marriage Feast and Garment

### (Matthew 22:1-14)

There is a vital connection between the previous parable and this one, as can be seen by linking Matthew 21:43 with 22:2. Both parables set forth that combination of mercy and justice which is the glory of God. In the former parable Jesus "showed His hearers their neglect to calls of duty, and the judgment overtaking their abuse of such privilege. This parable points out their neglect of calls to mercy, and the judgment that overtakes abuse of these higher privileges still." Richard Glover goes on to say that "the great teaching here given is such as only the Saviour has ventured to impart. None but He has dared to represent divine mercy as so sublime, and none but He has represented human guilt as so wicked."

Many expositors confuse this parable with a similar one in Luke 14:16-24. Both parables use the illustration of a festival to which guests are invited, some refusing the invitation and some accepting, but here the similarity ends. The two parables are not different accounts of the same discourse Jesus delivered. On *external* and *internal* grounds, the two parables are quite different from and independent of each other, as the full discussion of this matter by Trench clearly proves. They were given on different occasions: Luke's *Great Supper* was given at a meal in the house of a Pharisee; Matthew's *Marriage Feast* was a parable uttered in the Temple (Luke 14:1; Matthew 21:13). Then, both parables belong to different periods of Christ's ministry. Luke's parable was delivered by Jesus before His last journey to Jerusalem, in Peraea; the one here recorded by Matthew was uttered in the Temple at Jerusalem, before the high priests and elders of the people (Matthew 22:23). In the former the Pharisees had not openly broken with Jesus, but in the latter their enmity had reached the highest pitch and they were bent on murdering Him. Luke's festival was ordinary entertainment provided by a private host whose invitation was contemptuously set aside. Matthew's festival was given by a king as a celebration of the marriage of his son. In Luke, the guests were discourteous; in Matthew they are rebels. In Luke, the invited were merely shut out of the festival; in Matthew, they are destroyed and their city burned. As Trench says, "In the higher dignity of the person inviting, in the greater solemnity of the occasion, there are manifest aggravations of the guilt of the despiser. And as the offence

is thus heavier, so is the doom more dreadful."

The contention that both parables form the same discourse by Jesus rests upon the assumption that He never repeated with variations in one place the substance of a lesson which He had given in another. Jesus, however, often repeated the same material on different occasions. As Arnot expresses it, "This 'Teacher sent from God' was wont in later lessons to walk sometimes over His own former footsteps, as far as that track best suited His purpose, and to diverge into a new path at that point where a diversity in the circumstances demanded a variety in the treatment. This is the method both in nature and revelation — the method both of God and man."

Examining the features of *The Royal Marriage Feast,* we have, first of all, the royal state of the father, and the specific designation of the festival as the nuptial feast of his son. The father is described as "a certain king," and, without doubt, this was our Lord's description of His Father. In the previous parable God was the *Householder,* here He is *King.* In the former, Christ was the Son and Heir; here He is the King's Son (Psalm 72:1). The dignity of His descent, and the royalty and nobility of His Person, are herewith implied. Scripture also makes it plain that He is also *King,* as well as the King's *Son* (Psalm 2:6). Martin Luther comments: "The king who made the marriage feast is our heavenly Father; the bridegroom is His Son, our Lord Jesus Christ; the bride is the Christian Church, we and all the world, so far as it believes." Some expositors affirm that a feast such as Jesus describes, was wont to be given at the commencement of a king's reign, who then married himself, as it were, to his people (I Kings 1:5,9; I Chronicles 29:24). Christ was about to come into union with His redeemed people. His soon-coming death and resurrection would give the Church her historical birth, from which both would be eternally united. The *Bride, as such,* does not figure in the parable; everything is ordered for the pleasure of the Son. Habershon suggests that all the three Persons of the Trinity are represented by the King, the King's Son, and the Servant, who compels the guests to come in to the feast.

By the "marriage" we are not to understand "the Marriage of the Lamb" (Revelation 19), although the festival here will result in that thrilling union taking place when Christ presents His true Church to Himself. All that we presently experience and enjoy is a "dinner," but the "supper," the last festival, is yet future. Trench remarks that the idea of a feast "unites the two favorite images under which the Prophets of the Old Covenant set forth the blessings of the New, and of all near communion with God . . . that of a festival and that of a marriage."

Earlier, John the Baptist had referred to Jesus as a "Bridegroom" (John 3:29), a designation He, Himself, confirmed. All through the Old Testament the union between God and Israel is spoken of under the figure of the marriage covenant, and in the parable before us there is a hint broadly stated by Paul when he speaks of the Church as the "Wife" of Christ; and by John when he calls her, "The bride, the Lamb's wife." But here the marriage idea drops almost entirely out of sight, and the feast is prominent because it was the main purpose of Christ to illustrate the full benefits of His Gospel under the similitude of a banquet, or a feast "excellent in quality, abundant in quantity, and varied in character, in the enjoyment of which a multitude of guests have great fellowship and happiness." In short, we have here a fitting description of the spiritual banquet set before men in the blessings of the Gospel, "a feast of fat things" (Isaiah 25:6). The glorious feast He has spread includes pardon of sin, favor with God, peace of conscience, the exceeding great and precious promises, access to the Throne of Grace, the com-

forts of the Spirit, the well-grounded assurance of eternal life. What a wealth of gospel mercy is at the disposal of every sinner! A feast of inconceivable delights is accessible to every soul. To all who avail themselves of such a bountiful provision there is the culminating feast, "The marriage supper of the Lamb."

The tragedy unfolded in the parable is the strange refusal of the invited guests to attend the royal celebrations. The king, it would seem, sent forth three invitations, yet all were rejected. The repeated word *bidden* is interesting and speaks of the divine desire to have men participate in the feast of divine mercy. All men are "bidden." Israel had been "bidden" by long prophetic intimations of the approach of salvation. Since Pentecost, the Spirit has "bidden" men to come to the gospel feast. Fereday suggests that in the first two invitations absolutely refused there may be a reference to the two distinct missions to Israel: one before, and one after, the cross of Calvary. But let us distinguish between the three invitations sent out by the king and delivered by his servants.

In the *first* invitation (Matthew 22:1-3), those invited "would not come." The invitation was not repudiated or rejected, but returned. They were honored by the royal request but treated it somewhat indifferently. It is said that in the East, it is the fashion to give a preliminary invitation to a feast, somewhat indefinite as to day and hour, then follow it up with definite invitation when the feast is actually ready. But those in the parable receiving the first invitation decided to abstain from attending before the second one reached them.

The *second* invitation was more explicit and urgent (Matthew 22:4-7). The dinner was prepared, and all things were ready for the marriage celebrations. The further group of servants, however, were not more successful than the first. This time the importunate kindness of the king was met with contemptuous mockery. Indifference became scorn.

"They made light of it, and went their ways." Their business interests meant more to them than any obligation to attend a marriage festival as the king's guests. Some of these who spurned the invitation carried their opposition beyond supercilious neglect into bloodthirsty enmity: "the remnant took his servants and entreated them spitefully and slew them." What a strange response to infinite mercy! Acting thus, they had sinned against the king, his son, his servants, and themselves.

These two invitations typify the two-fold attempt of the Lord to win Israel. There was His own mission, for He was among men, not only as the King's Son, but as the Servant inviting men to come unto Him. Often He would have gathered them into the feast, but they would not. Soon He was to die, and all things would be prepared and ready, so another invitation goes forth in the apostolic age, but His servants experienced great cruelty, Stephen and James being murdered. What was the reaction of the slighted, insulted King! "He was wroth, and sent forth his armies and destroyed those murderers, and burned up their city." The light refusal of the invited, leading to the more grievous sin of murder, resulted in unexpected judgment. The prophetic aspect of this parable was fulfilled in the destruction of Jerusalem, in the year 70 A.D., when the armies of Titus ransacked and burnt up the city (Matthew 23:34; Luke 21:20-24). This parable, then, was distinctively one of *judgment*. Those armies, made up of Roman soldiers, were *"His* armies" carrying out His pronounced sentence upon a nation utterly rejecting both His Son and His Servants. Those armies were "the rod of God's anger" scattering the people who were spared over the face of the earth.

The *third* invitation reveals divine mercy seeking other objects (Matthew 22:8-10). But those who were bidden "were not worthy." The king's goodness was not quenched by the ingratitude and evil of the previously invited guests. The grace of God had been scornfully rejected by the Jews; now the invitation goes out to the Gentiles, who were deemed unworthy of any of the theocratic privileges of Israel. Deemed as "heathen," the Gentiles responded to the great gospel cry of "Whosoever." The king's servants were to go into the highways, or "the parting of the highways," as Campbell Morgan suggests. The Roman world was celebrated for its highways, all of which led back to Rome. The king's servants were to overleap mere geographical boundaries, which they did as *The Acts* clearly show.

The wedding was to be furnished with guests "both bad and good." The servants were to gather together as many as were willing to attend the feast. Who were those described as *bad* and *good?* In every section of society two classes are found distinguished by their moral character, described in ordinary language, the good and the bad, the virtuous and the vicious. If the servants came across men on the highways who had no character, no moral standing, who were *bad,* and knew it, they were to be invited to the marriage. If others were contacted who were *good* by worldly standards, who were true to the light in them, whose goodness aspired after unknown higher heights, they, too, were to be invited. Once in the Kingdom, moral conduct or standing is essential, but before entrance no matter who we are, or what we are, we are sinners and need to repent of our sin and accept the Saviour. In His sight, "there is none good, no not one." All have sinned, and there is only one way to be saved. Human goodness cannot recommend us to God's favor, and the worst, like the best, are only welcome through the blood of Christ. Once guests of the King, all are admitted to all the great privileges of the Kingdom of God.

We now come to the necessity of the bad and the good, made guests, to wear the wedding garment (Matthew 22:11-14). This latter part of the parable has been dealt with as a separate parable.

But it is, in fact, an integral part of the parable — an episode of it. Arnot says the *Wedding Garment* is another, though connected, parable. A. B. Bruce thinks the two stories were originally joined by Jesus. But the phrase, "When the king came to see his guests," is dead against this paragraph being another and distinct story. Neither is it "hung as a pendant to the story of the Great Feast," as Butterick suggests. The imagery of the feast and its requirements are preserved throughout the first fourteen verses of the chapter. It would be natural for the king to visit the banquet hall and welcome the guests who had come, and rejoice with them.

But the guests who came did not enter the great hall immediately. Opportunity was given them to array themselves in appropriate garments provided by the king. Those gathered from the highways would be poor and poorly clad. Trench gives us quotations showing that it was the custom in some parts of the East to supply royal guests with some simple robe, securing the uniformity of all present. Campbell Morgan has a most illuminating comment on the little word *not*. The king saw there a man which had *not* on a wedding garment. Then the king said to him, "Friend, how camest thou in thither *not* having a wedding garment?" Morgan says: "The little word *not* appears twice over, but it is not the same word on those two occasions. The first word for 'not' is *Ou,* and simply marks a fact — he had not it on. But when the king asked him the reason, Jesus used a slightly different word for 'not': *Me,* which suggested not merely the fact that he lacked the wedding garment, but that he did so definitely, of his own thought, of his own will, and intention. When the man came in not having a wedding garment, and the king talked to him, he said, 'It is not only a fact that you have not a wedding garment; you do not intend having one. Your "not" is the not of definite willing. You are determined *not* to have it on. Your presence in here is the supreme sign of your rebellion against the order set up of which this marriage feast is the great symbol.' *And he was speechless* — he had nothing to say."

The wedding garment then was something conspicuous and distinctive. This was why the king quickly spotted the un-robed man. The garment was not a part of the man's ordinary clothing, but rather a significant badge of his loyalty. To come to the feast without it was a decisive mark of disloyalty. Without it, he endorsed substantially the act of those who had proudly refused to comply with the king's invitation. Realizing his sin in refusing the king's order, he was speechless and silent as his judgment was pronounced.

There is much of solemn import in the judgment given. The man was to be bound and taken away from the light and joy of the feast and cast into the darkness outside. The phrase, "weeping and gnashing of teeth," is of solemn import. What did Jesus mean by this terrible pronouncement? Butterick says that, "Insincerity is robbed of all disguise when the king enters. It has no haven save the poor haven of outer darkness. It is cast forth from the brightness and warmth of the banquet hall where Jesus plights His troth with those who would sincerely love Him. It is flung into the street which has no light." We do not know all that is implied by "outer darkness," or the darkness of the outside. We cannot see through the veil and penetrate the darkness, and tell of the sufferings within it. Our Lord has told us that it is *outer* darkness, but He has covered it from our sight. Particulars of the torments of the wicked are not revealed. The only safety from them is to hide in His bosom.

What is the symbolic significance of the wedding garment? What application has it to our hearts in this age of grace? Does it not imply the laying aside of the garment of sin and self-righteousness, and clothing ourselves with penitence and divine righteousness? Says a writer of a past century: "The wedding garment is essentially a habit of holiness and righteousness. I repeat it: inward, spiritual happiness, developed by the presence of God, and the consciousness of heaven, into visible manifestation — this is the wedding garment which Christ beholds and approves in the saved."

How many there are who want a place in the Church without regeneration and obedience, or salvation, without giving Christ true acknowledgement and service! Is it not the sin of *presumption* to take, without salvation, the title and hopes of the saved? Every sinner must comply with the King's terms, if they are to experience the King's grace. The man without the wedding garment seems to say, "I am my own master, and I shall work my own way to heaven." But the man wearing the provided garment has a different confession: "I am not my own; I have been bought with a price; my righteousnesses are as filthy rags, but the Lord is my righteousness." Yet the garment, as a symbol of Christ's all-perfect righteousness, had an added significance, for Paul exhorts us to "put on the Lord Jesus Christ." The garment, therefore, represents a Christ-covered life, and as a result, a character consistent with the Gospel we profess.

If men die without such a garment, then they can never participate in "the marriage supper of the Lamb" which is only for saints, or saved sinners. For all who die without Christ as their covering, there is the doom of "the blackness of darkness for ever." What a terrible sentence is here pronounced! In concluding His parable Jesus said, "Many are called, but few are chosen" (Matthew 20:16; 22:14), or "few are choice," as D. L. Moody expresses it. Those who are called, but fail to accept Christ, will die in their sin. But those who are called and receive Christ, become His choice ones, and guests in the King's festive house. God's chosen ones are those who received His Son as Saviour and whom He justified. These are the blessed ones, "Chosen in Him before the foundation of the world."

# Prophetic and Parabolic Pictures
### (Matthew 23:24)

We have now reached a most important phase of Christ's oral ministry, the chief design of which was to enforce the lesson of constant watchfulness in view of His second advent. He spoke most unqualifiedly of the certainty of His return and repeatedly warned His own that He would return and take the world by surprise, and that therefore His followers should be ready to meet Him at any time. The main proposition of His return, the time of which no one has any knowledge, is presented under different aspects, but always with the emphasis of readiness for such an event.

Later on, we have the three-fold repetition of the statement, "But of that day and hour knoweth no one, not even the angels in heaven, but the Father only" (Matthew 24:43,44; 25:13). Always in the background of this fact is the plea for the conscientious discharge of our solemn task as His representatives, and that of unfailing preparation because of the uncertainty of the time of His return. In the eschatological discourses before us we cannot but be impressed by the solemnity of the occasion, namely, Christ's last hours in the Temple, which He was to leave, never to again enter. He had called it "God's house," "the house of prayer," but now it is *"your* house." No longer God's but *theirs.* *"Your* house is left unto you desolate." God, in Christ, was to utterly forsake it. Thus, as Campbell Morgan so forcefully expresses it: "He left the Temple to go back no more. His word had excommunicated the Hebrew people, not from salvation, or the possibility of it, but from the office they held by divine appointment, of being the instrument through which the kingdom of God was to be proclaimed and revealed among men. He had uttered His final, kingly, divine word of excommunication when He said to the nation through its rulers, 'The Kingdom of God shall be taken from you, and shall be given to a nation bringing forth the fruits thereof.' "

The discourse containing the six parabolic pictures in this chapter was a continuous one and fell into three distinct parts. *First,* Jesus addressed the multitudes round about Him, and the disciples who were nearest to Him (Matthew 23:1-12). *Second,* although the crowd and His own are still there, He spoke directly to the rulers, and those in authority, whom He did not spare in His condemnatory message (Matthew 23:13-26). How full of terror were His words to those in authority! *Third,* He spoke of His aching heart to the city of Jerusalem, represented by the rulers. He addressed the city, built around the Temple, as the mother of the nation (Matthew 23:37-39).

It will be found that Jesus uttered an eightfold *Woe,* as He pronounced judgment upon the Scribes and Pharisees. As He commenced His public ministry He delivered His great ethic in the Sermon on the Mount with an eightfold *Beatitude,* now for those who rejected His witness and whose hostility toward Him had now reached its climax. He pronounces His eight woes. Take the eight Beatitudes and Woes, and they stand over against each other; and we can see how they answered each other in the most wonderful way.

We now come to the prophetic and parabolic illustrations Jesus made use of, not only to denounce His foes thirsting for His blood, but to unveil the deep feelings of His own grieved and disappointed heart. Although brief in themselves, these illustrations, or figures of speech, are "graphic beyond degree, and as a clear and sharp lightning flash they lit up the things He was saying." They also reveal our Lord's familiarity with life and how gifted He was in drawing from the most ordinary objects and incidents in the lives of people.

## The Parable of the Overladen Beasts of Burden
(Matthew 23:1-4)

In unmasking the cold, heartless treatment of the Jewish people by their rulers, Jesus likened the latter to cruel men who overloaded their beasts of burden with loads too heavy to carry. Our Lord's phrase, "They bind heavy burdens," presents a picture of a beast of burden so weighted down that it sinks beneath its load. Applying this expressive figure of speech, Jesus told those rulers that this was the sin of which they were guilty. They, themselves, carried few burdens and would not move a finger to assist those they burdened (Luke 11:46). They "touched them not," which refers, not so much to the irksomeness of the imposed legal rites, though they were irksome enough (Acts 15:10), as to the heartless rigor with the most striking pictures of great truths which they were enforced, by those men of shameless inconsistency.

The rulers overloaded the people with severe traditions and rules and thus abused their authority by such calculated inconsiderateness. Sitting in "Moses' Seat," the seat of authority, usurped authority, they crushed the soul by their multiplication of do's and don't's which resulted in the people being driven both from the Law and from God. Thus, some seven times Jesus called these heartless rulers *Hypocrites* because they were false interpreters of the ancient Law.

## The Parable of the Blind Guides
(Matthew 23:16,24)

Already we have considered the force of this illustration and the utter absurdity and futility of a blind man trying to lead another blind man, and of the result of such an effort. Its further double use here (Matthew 23:16,24) gains added emphasis. *Blind guides.* Here we have one fatal result of their erroneous teaching. Not only were they blind, they blinded others. These supposed spiritual guides, who should have known the way and led others along it, could not see. Destitute of the spiritual vision of relative values, their teaching was blurred and false. If guides are blind, how can they guide?

## The Parable of the Gnat and Camel

### (Matthew 23:24)

Can you not imagine the people laughing at such a grotesque idea? To expose the glaring inconsistency of the religious leaders, Jesus intended His simile to be absurd. The word "strain" means to "strain out" a gnat. Trench says that it was the custom of the stricter Jews to strain their wine, vinegar and other potables through linen or gauze, lest unawares they should drink down some unclean insect therein and thus transgress (Leviticus 11:20,23,41,42), just as Buddhists do in Ceylon and Hindustan. The "camel" was the largest animal known to the Jew, and the "gnat," the smallest insect, both being by the law unclean. The Pharisees were guilty of magnifying non-essentials and neglecting essential values.

## The Parable of the Cup and Platter

### (Matthew 23:25,26)

Luke adds, "Ye fools, did not He that made that which is without make that which is within also?" (Luke 11:40), which implies, "He to whom belongs the outer life, and of right demands its subjection to Himself, is the inner man less His?" Campbell Morgan calls the figure of speech Jesus uses here, "graphically disgusting," and goes on to say that, "certainly nothing could be more loathsome than a dirty cup inside, when the outside was clean. But Jesus used the figure intelligently. It *was* disgusting."

Luke's addition is of immense value, "But rather give alms of such things as ye have, and behold, all things are clean unto you" (Matthew 11:41). The Pharisees were meticulous about external cleanliness, but their hearts were the habitation of every form of corruption and evil. They had clean bodies but corrupt hearts. Greed was one of the most conspicuous features of their character (Luke 16:14), and our Lord challenged them to exemplify the opposite character, and then "their *outside,* ruled by this, would be beautiful in the eye of God, and their meals would be eaten with clean hands, though never so fouled with the business of this working world" (Ecclesiastes 9:7). Those hypocrites had no compunction of conscience when filling the platter by means of extortion and fraud, or to take the cup so often to their lips and drink to excess. So the Master counsels them to make the inside clean with equity and moderation, then it will be of little matter what is the state of the outside.

## The Parable of Whited Sepulchres

### (Matthew 23:27-32)

What a gruesome illustration our Lord used to expose an hypocrisy so particular about externals and yet so negligent of the internal! Lightfoot reminds us that the process of white-washing sepulchres was undertaken on a certain day every year, not for ceremonial cleansing, but, as the language of Jesus implies, to beautify them. Such beauty, however, only hid corruption, so we have the appalling contrast — sepulchres with their attractive, clean exterior, but full of dead men's bones! People attracted by the white appearance of the burial places were capable of inhaling the deadly germs of corrupting bodies. Was there not a powerful way of showing that the Pharisees with all their fair show yet had hearts full of corruption (Psalm 5:9; Romans 8:13)? These hypocrites were concerned with a clean, external appearance which veiled an inward corruption. Horror is added to this illustration by the fact that many of the sepulchres the rulers pretended to honor and respect were filled with the decaying bones of the prophets they themselves had killed. "Ye are children of them which killed the prophets." Now they were about to kill the greatest Prophet of all.

## The Parable of the Vipers
### (Matthew 23:33)

We considered the significance of "the vipers" when dealing with the parables of John the Baptist. Here our Lord uses with stinging effect the same figure at the end of His ministry, as John had used at the beginning of his. It would seem as if Jesus intimates that the only difference between John's condemnation of the corrupt leaders and His, was that now they were ripe for doom, which they were not in John's day. The picture of a spawn of serpents with their keen eye, subtle movements and poisonous bite was terrible yet true. Jesus gave His reasons for describing the Pharisees in this way. Doom would be theirs for the iniquitous treatment of God-sent messengers.

## The Parable of the Hen and Chickens
### (Matthew 23:37-39)

How ineffably grand, melting and simple is Christ's word of pity! The glaring sins of the Pharisees had elicited the "woes" of the Saviour, but those sins could not destroy His love. To the last He pitied and mourned over the fate the sins of the people necessitated. It was the expression of a Divine love so loathe to let the sinner go. Well might we ask, "Was ever imagery so homely inverted with such grace and such sublimity as this?" Heart-broken over the long-continued and obstinate rebellion of the people, Jesus speaks of His longing to overshadow and preserve defenseless souls with the kindly wing of a mother-bird. "Under His great mediatorial wing

would He have *gathered* Israel" (Deuteronomy 32:10-12; Ruth 2:12; Psalm 17:8; Isaiah 31:5; Malachi 4:2). But there came the sob of unwanted love. "And ye would not." What an awful gift free-will is when it is used to frustrate the Saviour's will to save! Here we witness not only the mystery of the liberty of self-undoing but also the mystery of the patient love of Christ. Refusing "the wings of the Shekinah," the glory departed from them. "Ye shall not see Me henceforth." Thus a nation so divinely privileged sealed its own fate. Yet amid the terrible gloom of desolation there shone a light that spoke of a time of restoration for a deserted and scattered people, "Blessed is he that cometh in the name of the Lord." Denouncing hypocrisy, as He alone could, we observe all through His passion for righteousness, and we find in the unveiling of His heart His compassion for the worst. "His passion for righteousness never destroys His compassion; but His compassion never destroys His passion for righteousness."

## The Parable of the Lightning
### (Matthew 24:27)

As we consider the parabolic references in this chapter, it is essential to carry with us an understanding of their setting. After His parables of judgment and denunciation against Jewish rulers, Jesus is now with His own. Sitting at the Mount of Olives, He answers the three questions presented by the disciples —

"Tell us, when shall these things be . . .
What shall be the sign of thy coming . . .
The end of the age?"

The first question referred to the destruction of the Temple, which Jesus had just predicted. This happened around 70 A.D. when Titus ransacked the city. The second and third questions are those around which the parables and parabolic material now gather. As to the second question, the only aspect of Christ's second advent the disciples understood at that time was His return to earth.

*The Rapture* was a truth they later grasped. They still had visions of a material Kingdom to be set up after the conquest of Roman power, and of the Messiah reigning in Jerusalem. The third question, as to when the end of the age could be expected, gives us a key to the unlocking of Christ's teaching from now on. In this chapter and the following one, the consummation of the Gentile Age is before us, coupled as it is with the necessity of being prepared against such an event. Christ's remarkable Olivet discourse, then, moved wholly within the realm of prophecy.

The first illustration is of the lightning coming from the east and seen even unto the west. Lightning is seen by all, being self-evident. It is also sudden and unexpected and awesome in appearance. Jesus said that His return to earth will be the same. When He appears to consummate the age, His coming will be sudden, self-evident and universal. "Every eye shall see Him." His return for His Church, however, as indicated by Paul, will likewise be sudden but not universally discerned. He will appear for those who look for Him, and who love such an appearing.

## The Parable of Carcase and Eagles
### (Matthew 24:28)

Here our Lord is describing finality of judgment, which no sinner will be able to elude. As eagles, or vultures, as the term implies, settle on a carcase, so deserved judgment comes to sin. This figure of speech is associated with the previous one but with a judgment application. As a flash of lightning the Son of Man will appear, and what effect will His coming have? Why, judgment to the full for the godless. Carrion and swift birds, like vultures, instinctively detecting the presence of a dead person or animal, swoop down upon it for its complete annihilation. That many will be involved in the last processes of divine

judgment represented by the vultures is evidenced by the fact that when Christ returns, there is little faith on the earth. "The world in its final outworking of its choices and inspiration is looked upon as dead."

## The Parable of the Fig Tree
### (Matthew 24:29-36)

The disciples asked for a "sign" of Christ's return to earth. Here He gives them a sign — it is *Himself*. "The sign of the Son of Man in heaven" (Matthew 24:30). The awesome language He used is found related to prophesied national judgments (Isaiah 13:9-13; 34:8-10; Ezekiel 32:7,8; Psalm 18:7-15 etc.), which are precursors of "that day" when the described judgment will have its final and most awful fulfilment. Appalling portents seen in the past will be analogous to those experienced when Christ returns to earth as its Universal Ruler.

The fig-leaf, telling that summer is nigh, provides another parable-sign. The variety of illustrations our Lord uses reveals His ability of fastening on matters of common knowledge and interest, employing them as the media of instruction. Here He takes the "fig-tree," the significance of which we have previously considered, to assure His own that "summer is nigh." This simple illustration from Nature assured His Jewish disciples that after their Nation's "winter of discontent" there would be a summer of national blessing. Israel shall yet become His glory. Luke, however, adds four words to the parable "and *all* the trees." With Israel's present resurgence, there is the manifestation of Nationalism the world over. Peoples long unidentified as nations are now claiming and receiving national independence. But with Christ's return to earth all Gentile nations, once purged, will participate in the benefit of His reign. When all the kingdoms of the world become His world-kingdom *all* trees will flourish.

## The Parable of the Thief
(Matthew 24:35-44)

Christ's reference to the Ark suggests that while its associated judgment was meant as a symbol of mercy, it yet resulted in a surprising calamity for the heedless multitudes. Then the righteous (only eight in number) were mixed with the godless, but judgment separated them. It will be so with those taken, and others left behind when Jesus returns. In the illustration He uses of a "thief" Jesus is stressing *preparation* not *expectation*. We do not *look* for thieves but by every precaution we are prepared against their coming. With His own people in view, He urges vigilance, alertness, and wakefulness on their part. In this illustration of contrast, Jesus speaks of Himself as a "thief." Thieves, however, break into houses to steal. Plunder is their aim. We are not to think of Christ in this way. Had the goodman of the house known a thief was coming, he would have prevented him breaking into his house. We know that Christ is coming, but when is not revealed. We must "pray that we may ever put upon the things of God the measurements of His own outlook, in which there was an utter absence of dates, or of the fixing of an hour. Processes, events are marked, the consummation is revealed: but there are no dates from first to last." Because He may come at any season, there is the necessity of constant watchfulness.

## The Parable of the Faithful and Wise Servant
(Matthew 24:45-51)

In this paragraph the Master has an exhortation for all His servants. The Pharisees had failed as servants, now true spiritual guides are described. They must be *faithful,* living and laboring in the Master's absence in exactly the same way as if beneath His eye. Then they must be *wise,* skilled to deal with fellow-servants in a way that will encourage the timid and reprove the forward. They must be *rulers,* both in and out of their own households. To rule aright means to unite and inspire others, leading them in right ways. If fully subject to their heavenly Ruler, they will lead others to be subject to Him and feed them with truth, example and sympathy. For those who serve the Master thus, there will be higher duties and immortal dignities when He comes.

In His added warning against unfaithfulness, Christ links belief to behavior. If we believe in His coming, we must behave accordingly. We cannot live as we like, if we truly believe that He may come at any moment. Advent truth should regulate our home life and preserve us from giving way to riotous excess of living. God-honoring service, true fellowship, holiness of life, watchfulness will be ours if we allow the thought of the Master's return to dominate every part of our lives. For those *evil* servants who scorn the truth of His coming and arrogantly smite others and indulge with the gluttonous, there is a judgment, sudden and swift. For them there is no reward — only a portion with the hypocrites. The weeping and gnashing of teeth expresses the utmost degree of their shame. May grace be ours so to live that we shall not be ashamed before Him at His coming!

## The Parable of the Ten Virgins
(Matthew 25:1-13)

We are still dealing with the unbroken discourse which Jesus delivered to His disciples. Great, predictive truths continue to be fittingly illustrated by the master Storyteller. In this parable, He continues the solemn declaration of the uncertainty of the time of His return and of the necessity of being ready for such an event. This is why the opening word *Then* is important in a two-fold way. First, it is a link binding the previous chapter and this one together. There was no break in our Lord's discourse. The word *Then* also provides the key to the interpretation. When will the Kingdom of Heaven be like ten virgins? Why, when He comes at the consummation of the age. The previous parable of the householder and servants, this one of *The Virgins* and the next one of *The Talents,* all belong to the same period. All three parables speak of an absent Lord, but in each case He returns to deal aright with those who, during His absence, were left with certain responsibilities. In the first parable we have our *communal* responsibility. In the second, the responsibility of our *individual* life. In the third, our responsibility in relation to our *imperial* matters, or trading for Him during His absence.

The emphasis in the parable before us is on *life* rather than on our *labor,* with the whole parable leading up to the final injunction — *Watch!* There is not the sense of comparison in the phrase, "Then shall the kingdom of heaven be *like."* It implies, "shall become like," suggesting that when the hour of Christ's advent is near, "a development shall take place in the sphere of the kingdom of heaven, resembling the occurrences of the following narrative of the ten virgins." Then what are we to understand by "the kingdom of heaven," or "heavens," as it should read? The terms "Kingdom of God" and "Kingdom of the heavens" correspond with what Daniel says about "the God of heaven setting up a kingdom" (Daniel 2:44). Christianity is a heavenly order of things. Newberry's explanation is clear on this matter: "It is the kingdom of God in contrast with the rule of man, and the kingdom of the heavens contrasted with mere earthly kingdoms. 'The Most High ruleth in the kingdom of men' (Daniel 4:25). This is the kingdom of God. 'The heavens do rule' (Daniel 4:26). This is 'the kingdom of the heavens' — which term is peculiar to Matthew, and connects the saints of the heavenlies with the exercise of rule. 'The saints of the Most High (high places, or heavenlies) shall take the kingdom.' "

Jesus has not yet taken His own throne (Revelation 3:21). When He does, His saints will reign with Him.

Meanwhile, as the parables of Matthew reveal, the kingdom of the heavens takes on a peculiar character. Here, such a kingdom in its final phase will resemble *Ten Virgins.* Of the parable as a whole, Professor Salmond says that "No parable surpasses this one in beauty or in a pathos which becomes tragic. Nor in any is there a greater contrast between the simple and familiar things which makes its story and the magnitude of the truths illustrated." It is one of the larger pictures of the gallery of parables, sublime in its ample outline, exquisitely tender in its details, and charged with many precious lessons which flow at the gentlest touch. It is a parable over which much controversy has raged. There are those who apply it entirely to this present age, others who reject this interpretation and apply it to the time when the true Church has been raptured and the believing Jewish remnant await the Coming of the Messiah. Perhaps the parable has a double application, namely, the need of watchfulness on the part of believers as they await their Lord from heaven, yet also a reference to a future period in Israel's history, for Israel, as well as the Church, is likened unto a "virgin" (Isaiah 23:12; 37:22; Jeremiah 14:17). Cosmo Lang says, "We take the virgins to represent simply our human nature awaiting its true consummation."

The persons referred to in the parable are the "Bridegroom," also addressed as "Lord," who is none other than Christ Himself. Then we have "the ten virgins" Goebel describes as "the complete virgin-choir that is to receive the bridegroom and take part in the marriage." We also have those who sold oil for lamps. The Bride is not mentioned. Why? Several expositors affirm that the figure of the Bride represents the Church, and the Church is not here seen in its entirety as the Bride because the mystery of the Church as such was not yet fully known (Ephesians 3:3-5). Here, believers are regarded individually and collectively as "virgins" expecting the Bridegroom. But as the Bible clearly teaches that all born-again believers form the Bride, the Church, how can they be the *bridesmaids* and the *bride* at the same time?

It is true that Paul contemplated the Church at Corinth in this virgin character. "I have espoused you to one husband, that I may present you as a chaste virgin to Christ" (II Corinthians 11:2). But there is a difference between one virgin and *ten* of them. Some writers say that the five *wise* virgins represent the true Church, while the five *foolish* illustrate professors but not possessors of Christ. Another explanation given is that it takes many illustrations to set forth all the aspects of the Second Advent. In the *Parable of the Marriage Feast,* no bride nor bridesmaids are mentioned. Apart from the King and His Son, there were "guests," and these are the same as "virgins" in this parable, namely, the Church. Trench and other expositors interpret the whole parable as referring to the homecoming of the Bridegroom with His bride. Then again it may imply the Bridegroom coming for his bride. Amid all these conflicting views can we not appreciate the sentiment of Arnot: "It is cruel to put the parable to the torture and compel it to give meanings which it never received from its Author"?

Granted that there may be some elasticity in Oriental manners, what was the prevailing marriage custom at that time? While in the parable the bride is not mentioned, but the bridegroom and virgins hold forth all the intended instruction, is not the presence of the bride implied? Marriage usages of Eastern lands require the bridegroom to go to the house of the bride and fetch her back to his own. Then as he returns with his bride, at various points on the route friends of the bride and bridegroom join the procession, and "go in" to the marriage feast. Thus as Moffat translates the first verse of the parable, "Then shall the realm of heaven be compared to ten maidens who took their lamps and went

out to meet the bridegroom *and* the bride." Then Moffat gives us this interesting footnote to the verse: "The words 'and the bride' are added, in the Latin and Syrian versions, etc. Their omission may have been due to the feeling of the later Church that Jesus as the Bridegroom ought alone to be mentioned." It would seem, therefore, that the bride is not mentioned in our version because she was already with the Bridegroom. The Psalmist speaks of the virgins as "companions" that follow the bride (Psalm 45:14). G. H. Lang remarks, "Virgins invited to a wedding feast were an incongruous simile for the bride without whom a wedding feast could not be held at all, whereas five of the virgins miss the feast. Will anyone hold that half the bride will do so?"

As the "virgins" dominate the parable, let us look closely at what is said of them. First of all: they are all described as "virgins" or "maidens," as Moffat gives it. *The New Bible* has the word "girls." Young, chaste, and unmarried women are implied and as Arnot says, "The structure of the parable required virgins in this place, in order that the picture might be true to nature; as the customs apparently of all times and all countries, this position at a marriage feast is assigned to young unmarried women." In biblical symbolic usage a "virgin" represents an undefiled male or female (II Corinthians 11:2; Revelation 11:2). There are those who say that the five *foolish* virgins typify the lost, those whose hearts are destitute of divine grace, but "virgin" is not an appropriate figure of speech of an unregenerate sinner, nor of a Christian guilty of committing spiritual adultery with the world (James 4:4). Says Lisco, "We would not include in these two classes of wise and foolish virgins, those who revile and persecute the Gospel, for such are not good enough to be named even among the foolish virgins."

Then, in the next place, there were *ten* virgins. Why this specific number? As *seven* among the Jews denoted perfection, so *ten* was the number that made a thing *complete*. A company was considered complete if *ten* were present. In seeking to comfort his childless wife Elkanah said, "Am I not better to thee than ten sons?" There was an ancient Jewish law that wherever there were ten Jews, there a synagogue could be built. How wonderfully condescending is the Master who said, "Wheresoever (not, as in the old law, ten Jews, are met together, there shall be a synagogue but wheresoever) *two* or *three* are met together in my name, there am I in the midst of them." *Ten,* then, is the number of completeness and as used here implies as Goebel puts it, " . . . a complete virgin-choir . . . with each individual virgin sharing in the duty and the hope as belonging to this complete choir. But nevertheless they bring their *own* lamps to receive the bridegroom."

Further, all *ten* took their lamps and went forth to meet the bridegroom coming with, or for, his bride. These lamps were the personal property of the virgins, so that each one was responsible for the due preparation of her own lamp. Lamps, in this case, were simple vessels fixed at the top of a pole, holding only a small quantity of oil, with a protruding wick or rag of some kind. These lamps were necessary to have in the dark, unlighted Eastern streets. All ten alike wanted to share in the bliss of welcoming the bridal pair. To those virgins their lamps meant guidance for they showed the way to the bridegroom's house in the gathering darkness of the night. In the moral and spiritual darkness of the world's Saturday night, we have the divine lamp to guide us aright (Psalm 119:105; II Peter 1:19).

Another feature is: They were divided into two groups — five were wise; five were foolish. The virgins were all alike in that they responded to the call to meet the bridal party and go to the bridal feast; they were all dressed alike in the same virgin garb, and they all carried the same kind of lamp. Yet they differed deeply. They were all alike in their knowledge of and regard for the bridegroom and the bride. They all had lamps which at the moment were burning, and as the bridal pair were delayed, all the virgins, quite naturally, nodded off to sleep. They all were roused to action at the cry, "Behold, the bridegroom cometh." But it was at this point that the difference between the virgins was revealed.

It is essential to a right understanding of the parable to settle plainly what is meant by the presence of oil for five virgins, which made them *wise,* and the absence of oil which made the other five *foolish.* Alike in *outward* things, the wise and foolish were unlike in an *internal* necessity, the lack of oil. The wise were *wise* because they knew what to expect and therefore made every preparation for future needs. The foolish were *foolish* in that they acted without inward reasons. They failed in the provision of necessary supplies and resources.

The majority of expositors take the "oil" to be a symbol of the Holy Spirit, and believe that the wise, having oil, represent the truly regenerated. "If any man have not the spirit of Christ he is none of His." Absence of oil indicates the lack of salvation, a Christian profession without possession. All *ten* virgins had some oil, otherwise their lamps would not be spoken of as "going out." The wisdom of five of them consisted in the provision in advance of a supply of oil necessary to replenish their lamps. This division of *wise* and *foolish* cuts deeply. How many there are who, like the foolish virgins, see a lamp is needed and get one and light it and profess to belong to Christ's festal party, but have no divine resource within, or as the *Parable of the Sower* expresses the same lack, "no root."

With the advent of the bridegroom, *"all"* those virgins arose, and trimmed their lamps," but the foolish discovering they had no oil besought the five wise girls to share what they had. Condemning differences are revealed. Five lamps glowed brightly, because of added oil;

five lamps flickered out for lack of supply. The request for oil was refused in words that seem to be selfish, "Not so, lest there be not enough for us and you: but go ye rather to them that sell, and buy for yourselves." Unreadiness was the height of folly. Had the wise shared what they had with the foolish, all ten of the virgins would have been left in darkness. In the realm of grace, no true Christian can share his salvation with another. Each must go to God's market and buy, without money and without price, the necessary oil.

The foolish hurried away to buy oil, but whether they secured it or not, we are not told. What is recorded is that while they were away, the bridal party arrived and the five virgins with their bright, swinging lamps, went into the festal hall with the rest of the procession. "And the door was shut." What a solemn note there is in this phrase! That shut door meant the *inclusion* of the wise but the *exclusion* of the foolish. Ultimately, returning from the oil-seller, the five foolish knocked on the shut door and begged for admission, but they were met with the lordly bridegroom's answer, "I know you not." He disowned their connection with himself and with those within. Writing of the mystic oil creating light, Campbell Morgan makes this application of the separation when the door shut: "Then those who had the oil went into the marriage feast, a picture of the sifting of Christendom at the conclusion of the age; an hour when profession, with its symbols and ritual, devoid of oil and light and power, will have no avail: an hour when if there have been similar provision, similar symbols, plus the oil that keeps the flame burning, these will be the password, and the passport to the marriage feast."

> "No light! so late, and dark and chill the night!
> Oh, let us in, that we may find the light!"
> "Oh, no! too late! ye cannot enter now."

The broad warning of the parable is not to be confused by seeking too many spiritual meanings of the *oil,* the *sleep,* the *vessels,* and the *lamps.* The parable's burden is that of readiness for the Bridegroom's coming. Thus our Lord brings His parable to a climax in the warning, "Watch therefore, for ye know not the day nor the hour wherein the Son of Man cometh." Marcus Dods says: "The parable is not addressed to those who have never made any preparation for Christ's coming, but to those who have not made sufficient preparation. It reminds us that all who may at one time show similar preparedness for Christ's presence do not in the end show the same." Origen, great father of the early Church, said that *oil* consisted of good works. Martin Luther said the *oil* is the Spirit's symbol. Some modern teachers imply that the parable teaches, not the *rapture* of the Church as a whole when the Bridegroom returns, but its *rupture.* Only those Christians who are fully sanctified and baptized by the Spirit will be taken; others, less holy, although regenerated, will be left. Amid conflicting interpretations of the parables our personal responsibility is to "Watch," for watching implies a constant supply of oil. Amid the world's gathering darkness our lamp must shine, and "in the supply of the Spirit of God, and the life yielded to the Spirit, and dominated by that Spirit, there is always the oil which provides the light." The question for each heart to answer is, Will I be ready when the Bridegroom comes?

## The Parable of the Talents and Rewards

(Matthew 25:14-30)

There was no break between the utterance of the previous parable and this. Jesus, continuing His last words to His own, added this parable of *The Talents* as a needful complement to that of *The Virgins.* The phrase, "The kingdom of heaven is," is in italics, meaning that it is not in the original, but was added by the translators for the sake of smoothness. Thus verses thirteen and fourteen are one, and should read: "Wherein the Son of Man cometh, for He is as a Man," etc. This complementary parable proves that He was not one-sided in His teaching. If He stressed a particular quality in one parable, He guarded His hearers from supposing that nothing else was needed. Thus in the presentation of truth, Jesus was well-rounded. In *The Virgins,* He revealed the necessity of attending to *inward* character, but here in *The Talents* He combined that necessity with a strong enforcement of outward exertion.

Nehemiah's builders combined vigilance and activity. "The builders every one had his sword girded by his side, and so builded, and he that sounded by the trumpet was by me" (Nehemiah 4:18). Is not the same combination supplied by these two parables? *The Virgins* teach us the need of *watchfulness; The Talents,* the duty of *work. Looking* for Christ's return, we must *labor* in the light of it. Paul had to write in strong terms to those who thought that because Christ was at hand they should cease working, thereby causing great disorder and reducing themselves to dependence upon the charity of others for their daily food. With prophetic foresight Jesus foresaw this peril and so exhorted His own not only to watch in readiness for His return but to work in earnestness toward it.

In his introduction to this parable Trench says: "While the Virgins were represented as *waiting* for their Lord, we have here the servants *working* for Him: there is the *inward* spiritual life of the faithful described, here his *external* activity . . . It is not, therefore, without good reason that they appear in the actual order, that of the Virgins first, and of the Talents following, since it is the sole condition of a profitable *outward activity* for the Kingdom of God, that the life of God be diligently maintained *within* the heart."

As this parable of *The Talents* has been confused with that of *The Pounds* which Luke gives us (19:12-36), it might be as well to consider the two parables at this juncture. In some respects both are similar. For instance, both parables describe a rich man going to a distant country and committing a sum of money to his servants to invest for him. In both there is the promise of the traveler that when he returns he will deal with his servants according to the use they have made of the money entrusted to them — reward for the faithful, punishment for the negligent. But here, it would seem, the resemblance ends. Here are the important features of difference between the parables, marking them out as being separate:

In *The Talents,* Jesus addressed His own while at the Mount of Olives; In *The Pounds,* He is speaking to the multitude at Jericho.

In *The Talents,* variety of stewardship is dealt with. We differ from each other in the amount of gifts received. In *The Pounds,* all are alike responsible. The servants differed from each other in the diligence they displayed.

In *The Talents,* the servants receive a different number of talents, according to personal ability. The use of the talents by two servants was equal and therefore their reward was equal also. In *The Pounds,* the amount given to each is the same, but the servants made different use of the money and were therefore differently rewarded.

While both parables exhibit the grand cardinal distinction between the faithful and the faithless, the reward of diligence and the condemnation of unprofitableness, yet both view responsibility from opposites. The one supplies what the other omits.

First of all, let us look at the main lines of the parable, noting their implications for the members and citizens of the heavenly Kingdom. Wm. M. Taylor says of the parable that it is true to the Oriental life of our Lord's time: "When a wealthy man was leaving his home for a while, two courses were open to him for the arrangement of his affairs. Either he might make his confidential slaves his agents, committing to them the tilling of his land and giving to them his money, to be used by them in trade; or he might take advantage of the money-changing and money-lending system which had been introduced by the Phoenicians, and which was at that time in full operation throughout the Roman Empire. In the present use the Lord adopted the former of these courses; and there was at least a tacit understanding, if no formal contract, that the servants would be rewarded for their fidelity."

The main lines of interpretation are not difficult to follow. The wealthy master referred to as "Lord" by his servants is "the Son of Man," the Lord Jesus Christ. The journey into the far country refers to His departure into heaven after His Ascension. The servants, or bond-servants, or slaves were, in the first instance, the twelve disciples to whom Jesus addressed the parable, and then in a broader sense all born-again believers. By the talents we are to understand the spiritual gifts Jesus received for His servants and which He dispenses to them. The lord, absent from his home, suggests the withdrawal of Christ's visible presence from the earth; while his return is equivalent to the Master's promised return. The trading of the servants during their master's absence indicates the faithful use the Lord's people should make of spiritual gifts and opportunities for service. The commendation of the servants by their master on his return sets forth what can be expected at the Judgment Seat of Christ, when our service is to be reviewed. The judgment upon the one servant who failed in his trust is a warning against the non-use or mis-use of Heaven's gifts. Now let us look at the parable more particularly.

1. *The Nature and Number of Talents.* What are we to understand by *talent?* Today, we use the word in a different sense and speak of a person as being "talented," meaning, he has some outstanding natural ability in one direction or another. But here, the word

means something different. The original word *"talantos"* is a noun rather of quantity, not a revelation of quality. "Talent," as used by Jesus, does not mean something we possess, but which He possesses and loans to His servants. All the talents in the parable belonged to the lord and were handed over by him to his servants to be used in trade. In money, a *talent* represented about 350 pounds or over a 1000 dollars (a large sum for those days) and, in the case of the servant who received five talents, a considerable amount. In the *Parable of the Pounds,* the "pound" would be about three and a half pounds in English money. All three servants, even the one who received only one talent, were amply furnished for trading, with purchasing power more favorable than it is today.

What is the spiritual significance of these talents of which Jesus spoke as the master's *goods?* What magnificent merchandise is ours to trade with! The complete revelation of God Himself as given in the Bible; the glorious Gospel of redeeming love and grace; the spiritual gifts to the church Paul wrote about; the faith committed to the saints; the gift and graces of the Holy Spirit: these are among "His goods." Pertaining to Him, they are *His* and not natural endowments. Thus, what we trade with in our Lord's absence, belongs to Him. It is not our merchandise. Our "goods" are of little value and hardly worth investing. Spiritual wealth, secured at the infinite cost of Calvary, is what is offered us to enrich the World. Such wealth beyond compare is committed to our hands to invest. The "goods," then, are not a question of our possessions or fitness, but are the unsearchable riches of His grace, provided for an impoverished humanity in quantity.

As to the distribution of the talents, the master gave one servant "five," another "two," and the third "one." Does this not teach that God's gifts accomplish much more through some than through others? The whole truth of God is of equal value, and every servant of Christ owns the whole revelation, but the fact remains that different servants receive from the Lord differing measures of spiritual understanding. We do not receive more from Him than we can understand and use. The qualifying clause in the use of talents is, "to every man according to his several ability." G. H. Lang says that "God does not attempt to put a lake in a bucket. The man with larger capacity for knowledge has larger privilege of service, heavier responsibility to be faithful, with richer reward if he wins."

Because God's servants differ in capacity, so the Spirit bestows His gifts to each servant as He pleases (I Corinthians 12:11). *Talent* and *ability* do not mean the same thing. The master in the parable knew the trading capacity of the servants chosen and distributed his talents accordingly. *Talents* are the spiritual gifts of the Master; *ability* is our own natural fitness and personality. A person may have great natural ability, yet no spiritual gifts. Natural ability, however, which is also one of God's gifts, is necessary for the reception of supernatural gifts. This is no reflection on the third servant because he only received one talent. He was not able to handle more. Among the great gifts to and for the Church, Paul mentions *helps,* just "helps," but these are in no sense inferior to the other gifts mentioned. Each servant of the Lord receives for his service all that he needs and can use (Romans 12:4-9; I Corinthians 12:4-30).

The unequal distribution of the talents teaches us many important truths. A few are privileged to employ *five* talents in the Master's service. They are conspicuous as preachers, expositors, evangelists, missionaries. Because of their deep knowledge of spiritual truths and power to make them known they carry great responsibilities, and more is expected of them than others less gifted of the Lord. A larger number have *two* talents. They do not have any conspicuous distinction. They are not clever. Their capacity is limited. But the servant with the *one* talent describes the vast majority of us. We are among the rank and file in the Lord's service. Yet those of us who have least are bound to serve the Lord with what we have, and if we serve Him faithfully with the little He has given us, honor and reward will be ours.

The sovereignty of the Lord is seen in the allocation of His gifts. Appollos was not so richly endowed as Paul, but both were equally responsible to use to the utmost what they had. We must never bemoan the smallness of His gifts to us, "for if there be first the willing mind, it is accepted according to that a man hath, and not according to that he hath not." If ours is not the *first* place, we must glory in the *second* or even the *third* place. The true art of life is to accept our limitations by divine appointment and not struggle against them nor grumble about them. There must be no resentment or jealousy on the part of the servant with only *two* talents, toward the one with five; or the *one*-talent servant against his fellow-servant with *two* talents. It is better to have the last place in God's service with faithfulness than the first place with unfaithfulness. Remember that more is expected from the five-talent servant than the two, or three-talent servant. The psalmist scaled the heights of Christian philosophy when he said that he would sooner be a doorkeeper in the house of the Lord.

If we have only *one* talent we must use it to gain *one* more. The fact of our limitation should act as an incentive to spiritual and moral activity and persistence. In the long run what God commends and rewards is not genius, brilliancy, or popularity, but faithfulness and devotion to Him without human recognition or applause. If we cannot be a Moses we can be as Aaron or a loyal lesser Levite. If we cannot be a Paul, we can be among those unknown saints who ministered unto the Apostle of their substance. Joseph was content to ride in the second chariot after Pharaoh. If yours is not the first place here, if faithful to Christ, you will have the first place at His side when He returns to reward His own.

2. *The Use and Abuse of the Talents.* When the servant received the five talents, and the second servant his two talents, we read that both of them went "straightway" (Matthew 25:16,17 R.V.) and traded with same. What great force there is in this word, "straightway," meaning immediately! There was no delay. They knew not how long their master would be absent, so as soon as he left they started to trade. "What thy hand findeth to do, do it with thy might." They traded, or bartered until they doubled what they had. The one with five talents made other five — 100%. The servant with *two* talents was just as successful, for his gain, too, was 100%. In each case, original capital was doubled. Had the man with only *one* talent traded with it, his gain would have been the same.

Are grace and power ours to double our original, spiritual capital? Having received grace, has growth been ours *in* grace? Has desire for prayer been intensified? Is our hope more firm and real? Have earlier aspirations ripened? Have our spiritual influence and results in service multiplied? The true motive for service, and constant fruitfulness in it, is affection for the Master. Pious deeds can accomplish nothing if our dedication to Him is not complete. While the first servant received more than the second, both were equally diligent and faithful according to their deposit. Are we spiritually prosperous in trading with the Master's goods? Are we using to the full, the spiritual talents entrusted to us, not to hoard up, but trade with for the joy and honor of Him who is the Giver of every good gift?

The tragedy of the story is that the man with only one talent failed to trade with it and multiply it. Digging a hole in the earth, he wrapped the talent in a handkerchief and hid his lord's money.

Note, it was not *his* money, but his lord's. Perhaps he dreaded losing the money, and so buried it for protection. How pathetic it is when men are in fear of losing what they will not use. Some are afraid of losing their spiritual gifts and refuse to employ these gifts. We never lose what we use. While his two fellow-servants were active trading their talents, this third servant was idle. Not only so, he was disobedient in not following his master's instructions. His disobedience was not active but passive. He did not positively injure his master's property; he simply failed to turn it to profitable account. Rather than exert himself to improve what he had received, he went and buried it. The foolish virgins suffered because they neglected to make preparation, and this servant likewise suffered because he did nothing with his talent. Does not this servant represent many nominal Christians today who have all the outward privileges of the Gospel, but who never think of using and improving their opportunities of sharing these privileges with others? Any talent they have is buried. The mercy of God is rendered of no effect. There is little desire for growth in spiritual things, for the Word of God, and for the soul-saving witness. Any light they have is hid under a bushel.

3. *The Return and Reward of the Talents.* The phrase, "after a long time the Lord of those servants cometh," does not imply that Jesus meant to teach that His second advent was not to be expected for centuries. He never set a time for His coming, seeing He may come at any time. This we know, there is always time enough before He comes for "diligent servants to double the capital entrusted to them." What a reckoning there was when the servants appeared before their lord! The first and second servants proudly related their success in trading, and gave their master back his own with double interest. Both were rewarded in exactly the same way. Both received the praise: "Well done!" Both received the promise: "I will make you

ruler." Both received glory: "Enter thou into the joy of thy lord." "The joy of the Lord" is a full joy: the joy, faithful service brings Him, the joy of His approval, the joy of seeing others in heaven because of our faithfulness. These two servants were unlike in the talents received, but they were alike in obedience to their master, in diligence and faithfulness, and so received a like reward. Not *fame* but *fidelity* will win the Master's approval when He returns to reward His own.

What a solemn judgment fell upon the servant who buried his talent! As the faithful are rewarded according to the intrinsic value of their service, so there is condemnation for the non-use of Christ's trust. At the Judgment Seat of Christ many will be commended, but others will be condemned. For those who have honored Him there is a *crown* (II Timothy 4:8): a *throne* (Revelation 3:21): a *kingdom* (Matthew 25:34). Will ours be a full reward, or shall we be among those "saved yet so as by fire"? A saved soul, but a lost life and forfeited reward.

How the true character of this third servant comes out in his reply, and in his lord's condemnation of his failure. First of all, he had a false estimate of his master which he used as an excuse for the failure of his trust. He had lied about his lord as being a hard man, reaping what he had not sown, and now repeats this lie to his master's face. Why was he afraid to face his master, while the other two servants were ready and jubilant over seeing him return? This in *defence* was an *offence*. To his idleness, he added injustice. His master said he had proved himself to be a *wicked* and *slothful* servant (note, he was still a servant), wicked because he thought his master was hard and unfair, and slothful because he had failed to use his talent.

Silenced and condemned, the master commanded the servant's one talent to be taken and given to the servant who had the ten talents. He thus lost what he had so carefully kept. The lesson

here seems to be, *use* it or *lose* it. The gainer keeps increasing his gain — the non-gainer keeps losing his store. Saul lost his crown to David. "From him that hath not shall be taken away even that which he hath"; "Unto everyone that hath shall be given, and he shall have abundance." As an unprofitable trader, the servant was cast out in darkness. The Bible does not reveal all that is implied by the term, "outer darkness," which seems to imply a "darkness outside some region of light." Campbell Morgan speaks of it as "the darkness that is outside the Kingdom of responsibility." This servant did not bury his talent because he only had *one,* but because he was a wicked and slothful servant. As those who claim to be the servants of the Lord, may we be found serving Him to the limit of our ability and capacity, so that when He returns, His reward will be ours.

## The Parable of the Sheep and Goats
(Matthew 25:31-46)

Several expositors, not accepting this narrative as a parable, fail to deal with it in their collection of parables. We feel, however, that it should be included among them because of its description of the same events and the figurative language linking it with *The Parable of the Shepherd*. While what we have is the portrayal of an actual scene, the language used is parabolic, "As a shepherd divided his sheep from the goats."

Among the many judgments of the Bible there are three, often confused, which must be kept distinct.

1. There is the Judgment Seat of Christ, which will take place when the Lord returns to the air. This judgment is related to the true Church—the saved only being present for the review and reward of faithful service (Romans 14:10; II Corinthians 5:10).

2. There is the Judgment of the Living Nations (the parable before us) which will take place when Christ returns to earth to usher in His reign. At

this assize all righteous and unrighteous nations will be assembled, and both rewards and rejections will be announced.

3. There is the Judgment of the Great White Throne taking place at the end of time, after the Millennial Reign of Christ and the last rebellion of Satan (Revelation 20:11). All lost souls will be arraigned at this dread judgment to hear the pronouncement of their doom.

Thus it will be seen that the Bible knows nothing about a general judgment at which all the saved and lost will appear, and when the Judge will separate them, parting them right and left. If we are at the first judgment, we shall not be at the third. If missing from the first, we must appear before the second, if alive when Christ returns to earth, but most certainly at the third for the ratification of our condemnation. Our coming judgment depends upon our relationship to Jesus Christ. If we are in Him we shall never hear the terrible pronouncement, "Depart from me, ye cursed, for I never knew you." The judgment of all nations we are now about to consider is almost incredible in its consolation; and awful in its terrors. The opening word *but,* which is in the original, distinguishes and contrasts the scene to follow, from those preceding it.

I. THE JUDGE. Our blessed Lord is to be the august Judge at this great international judgment. Since His Ascension, He has been sitting upon the throne of His glory, on "the right hand of the majesty on high" (Hebrews 1:3), waiting till His enemies be made His footstool (Psalm 110). Here He comes, with clouds descending as the true Solomon in all His glory, to judge the earth and to establish His millennial reign in righteousness and peace. Think of the usual and also parabolic titles He uses of Himself. First of all, when He appears, it will be as —

*The Son of Man.* Some eighty times He thus designated Himself and this familiar title was a racial one as the representative Man (I Corinthians 15:45-47). It was as "the Son of Man" that

He was soon to stand at the bar of Pilate to be condemned. Here, as the same Son of Man who was judged and killed, He appears to pass judgment on all living men (this is not a judgment of "the quick and the dead." No resurrection is associated with this judgment). This expressive title speaks of His humanity, and of His degradation when men treated Him as "a worm, and no man, a reproach of men and despised of the people" (Psalm 22:6). But the once-rejected Son of Man will appear in power and great glory surrounded by heaven's angelic host to administer righteous judgment among all men.

As "the Son of Man," all authority to judge was committed unto Him by His Father. "Who judgeth no man, but hath committed all judgment unto the Son." God gave Him "authority to execute judgment also because He is *the Son of Man*" (John 5:22-27). In the narrative His just judgment (John 5:30) is related to those in the grave who hear His voice, but the judgment in the parable before us is that of *living* nations. It will be noted that the future tense is not employed here. Jesus did not say, "The Father *will* commit," but *"hath* committed." Assuming humanity's flesh, Jesus was invested with a judging power, and because of all that He was in Himself and by His words, works and looks, men were conscious of being judged by Him. There was something about Him that made those who surrounded Him conscious of their sin. Then among men there was a constant division because of Him. We speak of the *last* judgment, but for the *first* judgment we go back to His life among men only to discover that His *last* judgment is but the consummation of His *first.*

Christ had already definitely told His disciples that as "the Son of Man" He would "come in the glory of His Father with His angels," and that as "the Son of Man" He would "sit in the throne of His glory" (Matthew 16:27; 19:28). The Judgment of the Sheep and Goats is the opening incident in the great, prophesied administration. This will be the "appointed" day for Him, as "that man to judge the world in righteousness" (Acts 17:31).

*A Shepherd.* Exercising His knowledge and insight in this capacity, Christ is to separate the sheep from the goats. In David we have an illustration of a shepherd who reigns, yet shepherds at the same time. It is as "the chief Shepherd" that Jesus is to appear, and it is in this way He will function at this royal assize. While on earth He saw men as "sheep having no shepherd," but when He returns as the Shepherd, His sheep will be eternally cared for. Because of the many points of similarity between sheep and goats of a Syrian flock, it takes the practiced eye of the shepherd to distinguish one from the other. The Divine Shepherd whose eyes are "in every place keeping watch upon the evil and the good" (Proverbs 15:3), will make no mistake when He comes to judge the doings of nations. We look on the outward appearance and too often mistake the form of godliness for its reality and the profession of faith for true loyalty; but He who ever looketh on the heart is never deceived.

*The King.* Twice over Jesus referred to Himself as "King." The judged ones call Him, "Lord." While in veiled, parabolic form He had spoken of Himself as "King," this is the first and only time in which He directly assumed the title. How marvelous it is that three days before men crucified Him as a criminal He speaks of Himself as "The King" of all men, whose judgment was to decide the everlasting destinies of nations. Addressing heirs of His Kingdom, Jesus assured them that He would return in all His regal majesty. As a King, He must have a throne, so He refers to "the throne of His glory," that is, the throne of His judicial authority as King. He will be seen in His own glory, which is His personal, moral and eternal glory. Then the government shall be upon His royal shoulder (Isaiah 9:6). As the King, He will have the right and

power to tell "the sheep" to inherit the Kingdom prepared for them in a past eternity.

It is somewhat significant that this Judge is spoken of as "King of Nations" (Revelation 15:3), which competent authorities affirm is how it should be read, and not "King of saints." He is described as the "King of Israel, King of the earth, King of kings, and here 'King of nations' but never as the 'King of saints,' although in the truest sense He is our King seeing we have been translated into His Kingdom" (Colossians 1). His saints in the present dispensation have kingly rule and authority conferred upon them (I Corinthians 4:8; 6:2,3; Revelation 1:6); its exercise is yet future. We shall reign *with* Him (II Timothy 2:12).

The nations, about to come under His judgment, reveal the appropriateness of His title "King of nations" (Jeremiah 10:7). Exercising His power as such, He will break the iron will of the peoples, and all will be made to bow before Him and acknowledge His supreme sovereignty.

Turning from His manifold titles and His throne, we think of His train of attendants. The angelic train filling His Temple will accompany Him to earth — "all the holy angels with Him." *All* the angels are to assist Him in His judgment of *all* the nations (see Deuteronomy 33:2; Daniel 7:9,10; Jude 14; Hebrews 1:6; I Peter 3:22; Revelation 19:11-16). All heaven attends as all the earth stands to be judged. The angels who are to be present as witnesses of the Lord's righteous judgment are likewise administrators of His just decrees. Paul speaks of a "general festal assembly of myriads of angels" (Hebrews 12:22,23). Such a glorious retinue are to gather the elect, bundle the tares, witness the glory of saints, and look upon the misery of sinners (Matthew 13:39-42; 24:31; Luke 12:8; Revelation 14:10-13).

It would also seem as if the Church, Christ's blood-bought Bride, will join the angels, although she is not introduced into this parable. As the glorified redeemed are to share with Him His Kingdom, it can be safely assumed that they will be present with the angels to witness the just administration of judgment of the nations by their Redeemer as He takes unto Himself His power to reign as the King of kings.

II. THE JUDGMENT. While the scene of this judgment is the earth, particularly the part of it known as *The Holy Land,* because when Christ returns to the earth His feet are to stand upon the Mount of Olives (Zechariah 14:4), the recipients of the judgment are international in character. "Before Him shall be gathered all the nations, or all the Gentiles." When the plural is used in the Bible, it represents all the heathen or Gentile nations of the world as distinguished from the Jewish nation (Romans 15:11, 12; Ephesians 2:11). Joel describes this great gathering of the nations for judgment — "I will sit to judge all the nations round about" (Joel 3:1,2,11,12; Zechariah 14:2).

It would seem as if the nations will not be so populous then, as they are now, or will be when God's King and Judge returns to intervene in the desperate condition of international affairs. Universal desolations and death are pictured by the Prophets (Psalm 46:6-9; Ezekiel 38; 39). John describes how the vast population of the earth will be reduced to a minimum as the result of divine visitations (Revelation 6:8; 8:9,11; 15:18). Of Israel herself there will be left at that time but "a very small remnant" (Isaiah 1:9; Zechariah 13:8,9). The *sheep* nations judged righteous will enter the Millennium Age with the King. This gathering of the nations, then, will form the earthly counterpart of the heavenly myriads surrounding the Judge. "I saw Jehovah sitting on His throne, and all the host of heaven standing by Him on His right hand and on His left" (I Kings 22:19).

More than one expositor suggests that all the nations gathered around the Throne of Glory does not necessarily mean that *all* the people of all the world are to be gathered together at one spot. "The King is seen calling together every nation, possibly through its representatives . . . to obliterate old national lines." Nations, as such, do not visit the sick or prisoners, but their representatives do. We speak of the United Nations Organization with headquarters in New York. This does not mean that all forming the nations of the world are in New York. Large as it is, this great city could never hold the 3000 million souls, the nations represent. At the U.N.O. the authorized representatives of almost all the nations of the world are gathered together to deal with national and international affairs. A ruler of a country influences his people for good or ill. With his advisers, he directs the life of his nation and is responsible for its character. At the judgment of the living nations then, it would seem as if they will be separated and judged in the persons of their rulers and representatives.

There now comes the separating of the nations by the Shepherd-Judge into two groups. The *sheep* nations are set on His right hand, the position of favor and honor; the *goat* nations are placed at His left hand, the position of shame and dishonor. Then, as now, there are only two classes, and into one or other of them all men go. Judgment is according to character, and the two-fold, differing character and disposition is cited under the similes of *Sheep* and *Goats*.

*Sheep* have ever been considered an emblem of mildness, simplicity, innocence, patience and usefulness. The peoples chosen as *sheep* nations will be those who were beneficent and capable of unconscious and unaffected goodness. Innately kind and outwardly practical because of inward faith, these peoples are rewarded by the King.

*Goats* are naturally quarrelsome, lascivious, excessively ill-scented and are therefore considered a symbol of riotous, profane and impure men. Innately and unconsciously selfish, they will represent those nations given up to their own passions and lusts, and who, consequently, fail to see the needs of others. They had no heart of compassion constraining them to alleviate the need of others.

Our Lord mentions another group, the treatment of which decides the respective future of the above two groups, namely:

*My Brethren.* Who did Jesus have in mind when He described these people as "my brethren"? Was He referring to the Jewish nation of which He formed a part? Several writers affirm that these are the believing remnant of Israel who will preach the Gospel of the Kingdom for a witness to all nations during the last dread crisis (Micah 5:3; Matthew 24:14). The Great Tribulation will be a time of severe trial for the Jewish remnant and for sharing their possessions with and caring for those made destitute by the Antichrist, they are now honored by being named as Christ's *brethren.* But surely the designation has a wider application than this! Did the Lord not say that *all,* whether Jews or Gentiles, who obeyed His will and word were His brethren (Matthew 12:46-49). Did He not also say "One is your Master, and ye are all brethren" (Matthew 23:8)? When He uttered this parable He was looking down this whole Gentile Age, which is to culminate with His return to the earth, and was thinking of His own (regenerated Jews and Gentiles) from the standpoint of their responsibility as His spiritual brethren, acting as He would in a world of need because He was acting through them.

What is to be the basis of judgment? What is to determine the national division with the *sheep* or *righteous* people entering upon age-abiding life, and the *goats* or wicked people going out into age-abiding fire? Campbell Morgan suggests that Pilate's question is to be asked over again from the national standpoint, "What shall I do with Jesus?" This is to be the question for the nations. "What are they doing with Jesus? What are they doing with His message? What are they doing with His

messengers? What are they doing with all the spiritual forces and moral powers that He has set at liberty, and which are to work through His people in the age? Upon the basis of that, His judgment will be found for, or against them."

The underlying principle our Lord enunciates is that He is coming to "gather out of His Kingdom all things that cause stumbling, and them that do iniquity," and inaugurate the new era in which the righteous shall shine forth as the sun in the Kingdom of His Father. What terrible doom is pronounced upon those who failed Christ! "Everlasting fire" was prepared for the devil and the angels he seduced because they were first in transgression. But the unrighteous are to share the same doom because with the devil and his host they represent one unholy character. Those departing from Christ were negative and selfish in life. If the righteous knew not their good, the wicked knew not their evil. Their sins against the *brethren* had been against the Master Himself (Acts 9:4), and despair is theirs as they go away from Christ into an eternity of woe. Is it not solemn to realize that the last word of His public ministry before the Cross was — "These shall go away into everlasting punishment: But the righteous into life eternal" (Matthew 26:46)?

Ellicott says that "the solemnity of the words at the close of this great prophecy of judgment tends obviously to the conclusion that our Lord meant His disciples, and through them His people in all ages, to dwell upon the division which was involved in the very idea of judgment, as one which was not to be changed. Men must reap as they have sown, and the consequences of evil deeds, or of failure to perform good deeds, must, in the nature of the case, work out their retribution, so far as we can see, with no assignable limit."

How impressive is the sequel to our Lord's parabolic discourse on the Mount of Olives! "It came to pass, when Jesus had finished all these sayings, He said to His disciples: Ye know that after two days is the Passover, and the Son of Man is betrayed to be crucified" (Matthew 26:1-2). Was it not wonderful for Him with calm dignity to step down, as it were, from "the Throne of His glory" and proceed to Gethsemane and Calvary, there to finish the work His Father had given Him to do? For the joy set before Him He endured the Cross. During those days of anguish and shame He turned His back upon the glory and majesty of His coming Kingdom which He had described on the Mount of Olives, and went out to die a terrible death for our salvation. "Hallelujah! What a Saviour!"

# THE PARABLES OF OUR LORD (in Mark)

## The Parable of the Growing Seed and Harvest
### (Mark 4:26-29)

It will be recalled that we are not dealing with the parables in groups, but singly as they appear in the four gospels. The method adopted is that of taking each parable and parabolic picture, allowing it to tell its own story, "just as a gem, while forming part of a glittering tiara, sheds forth its individual lustre." As already hinted, the value of group-study may be seen in the treatment of the parables by Butterick, Kirk and Straton.

While some writers affirm that there are only *four* parables in Mark, if by a "parable" we mean a *comparison,* then it would seem as if there are eighteen parables in all. Even a "proverb" is often a "concentrated parable." Mark uses the word "parable" twelve times ( 3:23; 4:2,10,11,13,33,34; 7:17; 12:1,12; 13:28). Ten of the parables also appear in Matthew and Luke, another five in Matthew, a further one in Luke. Two are peculiar to Mark, the one before us, and that of *The Porter* (Mark 13:34-37).

This parable is given by Mark alone and is the only one peculiar to him. Evidently it escaped the notice of Matthew and Luke in their eagerness to gather up all that they could find of our Lord's teachings. Because this is the only parable not recorded elsewhere, attempts have been made to show that it must only be a modification of some other parable, such as that of *The Tares* or *The Sower.* But we believe the parable to be distinct from all others, bearing "the undeniable stamp of originality, both in its matter and form." Without doubt, it can be regarded as supplementary to the parable of *The Sower,* being designed to complete the history of the growth of the good seed which fell on the good ground. It is one of the three parables which reveal the mysteries of the Kingdom of God in terms of a sower's work.

Campbell Morgan suggests that the parable was given by Jesus on the first day of His parabolic discourse as He commenced to speak unto His disciples in parables. "It is possible that the little parable was spoken on that self-same day. It is even possible that it was spoken on the first day of parabolic discourse between others that are closely related to it, possibly after the parable of *The Sower* that went forth to sow, and before the parable of *The Wheat and Darnel,* showing the two sowings going forward, and so leading on to that of the *Mustard Seed,* which Mark also records."

Like many other parables, this one by Mark has received varied interpretations. Some writers say that the analogy of growth is designed to show the growth and progress belonging to Christian character, which Paul spoke of when he said that when he was a child he acted as a child, but when he became a man he put away childish things. From the seed to the full corn in the ear, we have growth in grace. Peter tells us to "grow *in* grace" (II Peter 3:18) — not *into* grace. We can no more grow *into* grace, than we can swim *into* the sea. Once we are *in* the sea we may swim in it — and once *in* grace, we may grow in it. Such a growth implies increase in a spirit of conformity to the will of God and to govern our life more and more by divine principles.

Others, like Straton, accepting the unproven theory of evolution, see in this parable of gradual growth an application to the development of the world and also to man. From the *seed,* the protoplasm, there evolved a full harvest. Needless to say, we have no sympathy with such an interpretation or application of Mark's parable.

Further, there are those like Ellicott who speak of the parable as symbolizing three stages in the growth of the Church of Christ in the field of the world; or of three stages representing the influence of new truth on thoughts, acts, purposes, in the individual soul. While these are profitable applications of the parable, we feel its chief design was to teach the progressive revelation of the divine purpose. Introducing the parable, Jesus said that the Kingdom of God could be compared to the man who sowed his seed and waited patiently for it to grow to maturity. Thus we must look for its interpretation in the analogous phenomena of the growth of the Kingdom, the affairs of which go on though unperceived by man.

*The Kingdom of God,* in contrast to kingdoms ruled by men, represents His rule, His reign, His triumph over all human affairs. But for the bringing in of His harvest, the seed must first be sown. Because of the eschatological aspect of the parable, its prophetic interpretation which so many seem to miss

but which provides the key to the glorious, ultimate purposes of God, is clearly evident. Our Lord was directing His disciples to the three stages of *The Kingdom of God*.

1. The *Blade,* or the Kingdom in mystery, the Church Age during which the Holy Spirit is active completing "the mystery hid from ages," namely, the Church of the living God.

2. The *Ear,* or the Kingdom in manifestation, which will be experienced during the Millennial Reign of Christ, which was the main theme of Old Testament Prophets. "Thy Kingdom come."

3. The *Full Corn,* suggests the Kingdom in all its majestic perfection, the New Heavens and New Earth when God will be all in all. This will be the "Kingdom Ultimate," The Eternal Ages: the "Dispensation of the fulness of times" about which Paul wrote (Ephesians 1:10).

Let us now look at the parable itself and endeavor to understand its component parts. First of all, there is —

*The Sower*. Who is the man described in the parable? Some say that it is Christ Himself, the Son of Man of other parables. But what is said of the sower here cannot be applied to Christ. He does not sleep or rise night and day as the man in the parable. He neither slumbers nor sleeps. Ever awake, He watches over His affairs, as well as over His own. Then it is said of the man, he did not know how the seed grew up. It cannot be affirmed of Christ, who overrules in the sowing and growth of the seed, that He knoweth not how. As "the Author and Finisher of our faith," He is the *Alpha* and *Omega* of the divine purpose, and is active in its completion.

The man casting the seed is representative of all those God uses in the establishment of His Kingdom within the hearts of men, and in the world. Presently, He uses all those redeemed by the blood to fulfil His redemptive work. During the Great Tribulation,

He will use the believing Jewish remnant to proclaim the Gospel of His Kingdom. During the Millennium, the saints are to assist the King in His governmental control of all things.

*The Seed.* This can be no other than the Word of God, the secret, invisible energy of which can make men "children of the Kingdom." This is "the incorruptible seed" Peter says brings men to a spiritual birth. The Bible was first a *blade,* the Pentateuch; the *ear,* the Old Testament; the *full corn* in the ear, the New Testament making the complete revelation of the mind of God to the people of God. All the truths of the Word are used by God in the formation and fruition of His Kingdom.

*The Ground.* Here the soil is the same as in *The Sower,* namely, the human heart. A "kingdom" implies *subjects* as well as the King, and *subjects* become so through obedience to the Word of the King sown within the heart. The ground cannot sow, and it cannot reap, but it can receive and nurture the seed, supplying it with all its own nutritious qualities until at last there is a harvest. The starting place of the Kingdom of God is in the heart He captivates.

*The Mystery of Growth.* What a human touch we have in the sower, who after sowing the seed, sleeps, rises night and day, and knows not how the seed springs and grows up. After the single act of casting the seed into the ground, there came the repeated, continual sleeping and rising while the seed was growing. Two periods are given, "night and day": night for sleeping, day for rising. After he had sown his seed, the man went about his ordinary life. He can do no more now, but wait and watch. Going about the customary routine, he contentedly sleeps and rises, making no attempt to hasten the growth of the seed which he has left to the natural operation of forces hidden in the soil.

The phrase, "he knoweth not how," implies that the seed grows, the sower not knowing how. But he takes his rest and carries out other duties for he can do nothing to hurry on the harvest. He is not guilty of over-anxiety, but patiently waits for the evidence of an imperceptible growth. He knows that without any interference on his part, all unknown to him the seed will pass through all the stages of its natural development. The mysterious workings of God may be beyond our understanding but in this we rest — that although He often hides Himself, His purposes are ripening. The deep mysteries of His Kingdom have a way of unfolding themselves to His loving, obedient subjects. Then, describing the bursting forth of the seed, Jesus said that "the earth bringeth forth fruit of herself."

The phrase, "of herself" or "of itself," implies self-acting, and is a word only used here and in Acts 12:10, where the city gate opened of its *own accord.* In the original, the word is *automate,* from which we have *automatic.* In spite of demons and men, the affairs of the Kingdom of God go on. Uninterruptedly, God continues His activities, even as the forces of nature go on automatically. "The earth beareth fruit spontaneously" —automatically.

Says Ellicott, "It is not well in the spiritual husbandry, either of the nations of the world or of individual souls, to be taking up the seeds to see whether they are growing. It is wiser to sow the seed, and to believe that sun and rain will quicken it" (Ecclesiastes 11:6). So we come to the spontaneity and gradualness of growth indicated by the three stages: first —

*The Blade.* Applying the parable of the individual, one expositor suggests that the three successive stages of progress correspond to John's beautiful appeal to *children, young men and fathers,* not according to natural age but spiritual life. But as already indicated, we believe the three stages are related to the different manifestations of the Kingdom of God. When good seed falls into good ground it begins at once to work toward its designed purpose, namely, to bear fruit. It is thus with the engrafted Word of the Kingdom.

*The Ear.* The plant assumes shape, puts out its branches and leaves, and fruit begins to take form, but it is not yet ripe. Even the Millennium, although so manifestedly the Kingdom in visible operation, will not be perfect, as the universal revolt at its end proves.

*The Full Corn in the Ear.* At last maturity has been attained and the only process left is that of ripening and harvesting. When the fruit is ripe the sower immediately puts in the sickle and reaps his harvest. "Putteth in" is the same phrase used of sending forth the Apostles to reap a harvest of souls, "I sent you to reap" (John 4:38). Growth is a process after the crisis of seed-sowing. The ultimate harvest, however, is determined by ripeness, "not by calendar or clock." There comes the definite season when action is taken to secure the harvest.

That there is a divine purpose of the ages is evident from the teaching of Christ and His Apostles. Here in the parable, the "harvest" can be looked upon as the consummation of all things when God will be "all in all" (Ephesians 3:10,11; II Corinthians 5:19; Matthew 13:39,40,49; Revelation 14:14-18). "The harvest is the end of each man's life, and the sickle is in the hands of the Angel of Death." There is to be a dread harvest of doom for "the tares," for all who die out of Christ. There is to be a harvest of reward for all those who are faithful unto death. But here "the harvest" is related to the consummation of the Kingdom of God, the most glorious consummation when with the final forever vanquished, and sin completely destroyed, and the emergence of a new heaven and a new earth, Jesus will surrender all things to the Father.

If these lines are being read by one who is ripe for heaven, having matured in godliness, fear not, the gracious Sower, whose loving hand holds the

sickle, knows when to gather His precious grain. As you await His moment of reaping may you abound in hope as you contemplate the joy of harvest in the heavenly fields above.

## The Parable of the Lamp and Light
(Mark 4:21,22; Luke 8:16,17)

In the section dealing with the parables in Matthew, we gave consideration to a similar simile Mark here uses, as well as Luke. A further word, however, is necessary, seeing that Mark omits all the other parables that follow this one of *The Lamp* (Matthew 5:15), and "connects it with that of *The Sower,* sayings more or less proverbial which in Matthew appear in a different context." That Mark's use of *The Lamp* was different from that in Matthew is suggested by Ellicott who comments, "Looking at our Lord's method of teaching by the repetition of proverbs under different aspects and on different occasions, it is not unlikely that this of the candle was actually spoken in the connection in which we find it here. Their (the disciples) knowledge of the meaning of the parable was not given them for themselves alone, but was to shine forth to others (Luke 8:16). We probably owe to the saying so uttered the record of this parable given in three out of the four gospels." The reason for teaching in parables is given (Mark 4:10-12). Truth is hidden in parables in order that it may be revealed (Mark 4:21-25). This important principle is further enunciated in the phrase, "The measure you give will be the measure you get" (Mark 4:24. R.S.V.).

This parable follows on that of *The Sower,* and related to it, teaches them at least two great truths.

1. The light of divine truth is given, not to be obscured by the believer's commercial affairs, *the bushel,* or by his domestic responsibilities, *the bed,* but to be manifested before all.

2. The primary obscuration in the parabolic form of teaching was gradually to give way to full illumination. "Now we see through a glass darkly: then face to face." Our Lord promised His own the Divine Spirit, who, when He came, would take of the things of Christ and reveal them unto their minds. This meant that He would unfold the inner, spiritual significance not only of all the parables, but of *all* the truth He had declared while in their midst. The full revelation once grasped was not hid but published abroad.

## The Parable of the Master and the Porter
### (Mark 13:34-36)

It would appear as if this was an abbreviated form of the *Parable of the Talents* (Matthew 25:14-30). Ellicott suggests that we might have here an imperfect fragmentary report, as from a note taken at that time, of that which appears in a developed form in *The Talents*. There are one or two added aspects, however, that seem to suggest that this brief parable, while resembling *The Talents,* is yet distinct from it and was one which like the *Parable of the Growing Seed* Mark observed and records. The chief design of this parable is, of course, similar to *The Talents,* namely, the promotion of watchfulness on the part of the Lord's people during His absence.

The *Man* taking the far journey is Christ, the Son of Man, who at His Ascension, left His own, giving them all authority to witness for Him. The added feature here is the phrase, "and commanded the porter to watch." Who are we to understand by "the porter," a figure and feature unique in our Lord's parables? The "servants" we accept at once as *The Twelve* and then the wider

application to all His disciples. "What I say unto *you*" — those first disciples Jesus was speaking to in private — "I say unto *all*" — all who since those first disciples have become servants of the Lord.

But who, specifically, was "the porter" or "gate-keeper" who was likewise commanded to watch? Our Lord used the same figure of speech in His parable of *The Shepherd and his Fold* (John 10:3). Several writers feel that Peter answers to the description of "the gate-keeper" because of the promise made him of having the keys of the Kingdom (Matthew 16:19). It was the Apostle's work to open the door of that Kingdom wide both to Jews and Gentiles and to declare the necessity of being ready for the Lord's return. In a wider sense it is the solemn and privileged task of all ministers of the Word to act as porters and warn God's people of approaching crises.

"The master, or lord, of the house" is the Master Himself, who will return as suddenly as He disappeared. An allusion to the four Roman watches of the night, beginning at 9 P.M., 12 midnight, 3 A.M., 6 A.M., may be found in *even, midnight, cockcrowing* and *morning.* Each of the seasons named has had its counterpart, we may well believe, embracing many centuries of the world's history. The *sudden* return of the master of the house is a kind of echo of the two parables — *The Talents* and *The Wise and Foolish Virgins.* At this end-time period of the Age of Grace it is more imperative than ever to *watch* and to function as true *porters.* As we look out upon the disordered condition of the world it would appear that the day cannot be far distant when He who promised to return will come and not tarry. Can we say that we are ready to hail Him?

# THE PARABLES OF OUR LORD (in Luke)

## The Parable of the Creditor and Two Debtors
### (Luke 7:41-43)

The gospel of Luke, like that of Matthew, is rich in its parabolic material. Luke, "the most versatile of all the New Testament writers," lists thirty-five parables, nineteen of which are to be found only in Luke. The other sixteen parables are to be found in one or more of the other gospels. For instance, *The Bride and the Bridegroom* (Luke 5:34, 35; Matthew 9; Mark 2). How much we should have lost if Luke's series of parables had not been preserved! Those he records are known as *intermediate parables,* or *Parables of the Second Period* of our Lord's ministry.

As we shall see, these parables peculiar to Luke are characteristic in that they are taken up with the great truths of love, grace, forgiveness and condescension. While many of the parables already considered set forth the general effects of the message on the Kingdom, Luke's parables seem to concentrate upon the specific effects of the reception of such a message. Dr. Salmond, writing on the delight of *all* the Evangelists in reporting Christ's words and works of grace, says of Luke: "It is most distinctive of him to select for his narrative those incidents and discourses which speak most eloquently of Jesus as the Friend of all sinners, even the most depraved, the Associate and Healer of all souls even the most sick and wounded . . . It is Luke, above all others, who represents the Son of Man as the Physician whose joy it is to give access to Himself to the most diseased and sunken that He may do the physician's work among them. So it is among the parables peculiar to the third gospel that we find those which best deserve to be described as 'the very poetry and quintessence of the Gospel of pardon and of Divine love' (Bruce). And the grace of their form matches the grace of their contents. They are of inimitable simplicity, tenderness and beauty."

The setting of this first of Luke's own parables, namely, what took place in the house of Simon the Pharisee, must not be confused with a similar scene recorded in the other three gospels (Matthew 21:7; Mark 14:3; John 12:3). The recurrence of the name Simon is of no consequence, seeing it was one of the most common names among the Jews. The incident which Luke gives us occurred in Nain, while the other took place in Bethany. The woman Luke depicts could not have been Mary, the sister of Lazarus, a member of the holy family of Bethany. The Pharisee called this woman a "sinner," one notoriously wicked, a prostitute. Equally without reason has Mary Magdalene been confounded with this woman. The profligate woman in Luke's parable is unnamed. Jamieson says that it is a great wrong to Mary Magdalene to identify her with the dissolute character in this parable and to call all such female penitents, *Magdalenes.* In Luke's scene, objection to the anointing of Jesus came from the host, in the other, from the guests. In the former, the woman had not been invited, in the latter, Mary was a guest. Then Luke alone adds the parable to the occasion, which although similar to the other, is definitely distinct from it.

The parable before us, which is a parable of *grace* in a supreme sense, its only rivals being the three Luke also gives us (chapter 15), is another illustration of "the rule of three" in the Parables. Actually, Luke gives a triad of groups, with each group presenting a triad. For instance, we have the group made up of three actual persons: The Saviour of sinners, Simon the Pharisee, and The sinner whom the Saviour forgave. Then in the peerless parable itself, we have three fictitious persons:

The creditor, The man who owed 500 pence, and The man who owed 50 pence. Both of these groups merge, the one illustrating the other, for:

The Saviour is the forgiving creditor.

Simon, the professedly righteous man, was the one owing 50 pence,

The woman who was a sinner, was the person owing the 500 pence.

Further, there is the Group of three questions around which the parable proper revolves, namely:

"Which of them will love Him the most?"

"Seest thou this woman?"

"Who is this that forgiveth sins also?"

First of all, let us look at Simon the Pharisee whose Pharisaic properties were altogether shocked by the sinner's action, and not less by Christ's attitude to her. How self-complacent and coldly respectful he was. Look at him as he wrapped himself around with the mantle of self-righteousness: satisfied with his own goodness, dignity and importance. While he had invited Jesus to eat at his house, it was not with any desire to hear Him teach, for he was already satisfied with his knowledge of the Law. Nor had he any peculiar desire to honor Jesus because he highly esteemed Him. In rebuking him, Jesus reminded Simon of his negligence of ordinary Jewish civility.

Jesus had entered his house as an invited guest, yet Simon did not extend to Him the usual water for His feet, a custom that went back to Abraham's days, "Let a little water be fetched, I pray you, and wash your feet."

Simon offered no anointing oil for the head, nor kiss of salutation, friendship, and peace. Such a kiss, even among heathen, was a token of reverence and subjection. All these things were of common courtesy in an Eastern home, but Simon was lacking in courtesy. There was no cordiality in his invitation to

Jesus, who was simply asked to come in and sit down to meat.

Now look at the uninvited guest, "the woman of the city, which was a sinner." Although she was a woman of shame, Luke, with fine delicacy uses the phrase, "a woman . . . a sinner." It was the custom then for a person to enter a house uninvited as a spectator. All through the incident this woman never uttered a single word but her actions were louder than words. Knowing that Jesus was present she came as a penitent and burst in upon the guests, and in a passion of contrite, thankful, reverent feeling, took her place behind Jesus as He reclined at the table. She had not come to eat at that table. Hers was a deeper hunger of the soul for she was a transgressor, and she knew and felt it. No wonder she wept, but hers were tears of repentance, joy, love and gratitude.

She washed the feet of Jesus with her warm, copious tears. The phrase, "began to wash," really means "to water with a shower." Simon had denied those sacred yet soiled feet of Jesus the necessary water, but this unnamed woman poured down a flood of involuntary tears upon His naked feet. Then perhaps deeming she had rather fouled than washed those feet, she hastened to wipe them off with the only towel she had, the long tresses of her own hair "with which slaves were wont to wash their master's feet." When Hannibal threatened Rome with his army, the Roman ladies flew to the temples and altars and washed the floors of the temples with their hair.

Then she kissed those cleansed feet, and here again the word *kissed* is suggestive. It means "to kiss fondly, to caress" or "to kiss again and again." She did not *cease* to kiss His feet. There was much love, springing from a sense of much forgiveness. Then she anointed the feet of Jesus, not with the common olive oil Simon would have used had he been courteous enough, but with the costliest and finest aromatic balsam. She felt that nothing was too good for Him who had made her the recipient of the immeasurable gift of cleansing and forgiveness. Had He not turned back the current of her miserable sinful life? Thus, in these surpassing yet most artless ways, her whole soul went out to Him who had pardoned her guilty soul.

The third and dominant Figure in the group is Jesus, the Son of God, the Omniscient One who could read the inner thoughts of both Simon and the penitent sinner. Had He not come to save sinners, and did He not eat with "publicans and sinners"? Did He not invite guilty sinners to come to Him for rest? Did He not utter this parable to "correct the hard judgment of one who mistook at once the grace of a penitent's act and the grace of the Saviour's condescension"? Contact with a sinner no more contaminated Him than the sun is fouled as it shines on a dung heap.

Simon, cold and dispassionate, moral, upright and conceited had no need to be afraid of a woman like this sinner coming near him, but when he saw how she treated Jesus he was perplexed. Simon knew all about the disreputable character of this woman, and when Jesus accepted her evidences of affection and devotion, he wondered what kind of a Prophet Jesus was. Had He been the right kind of Prophet, then knowing what kind of woman was at His feet, He should have shunned her. That was his outlook. But Jesus *did know* the woman. He saw what Simon had failed to see, a yearning to be free from the past with all its sin and shame, and accepted the actions of the woman because of what He knew of her. As Jesus unfolded His parable, He made Simon feel that all his boasted morality was as coarse as sackcloth alongside the fine-spun silk of the woman's penitence and devotion.

Having considered the setting of the parable, we now come to the parable itself, and the subject it was intended to illustrate. In this second group we have another three persons: A certain creditor, or money-lender, who loaned money to those in need. Here our Lord uses a commercial figure to illustrate His lesson. There were money-lenders then, as now. Evidently, this creditor was a kind-hearted one as we shall presently see. By implication, Jesus pictured Himself in this way, and is He not the Divine Creditor? We have nothing apart from His gifts, and all of us are deeply, so very deeply, in His debt. "I am debtor" (Romans 1:14).

The one debtor owed 500 pence (about 18 pounds or some $50.00), a debt somewhat modest alongside the great sums referred to in *The Parable of the Unmerciful Servant*. Jesus, knowing the working of Simon's mind and that he thought of the woman as being the 500 pence debtor, aptly applied the figure of speech. Simon felt she was ten times the sinner he was. He would admit he was a sinner but not such a vile one as the woman.

The other debtor owed only 50 pence (almost 2 pounds or around $6.00), a small sum hardly worth mentioning as a debt, being ten times less than the former. In this estimate, Jesus accepted Simon's valuation of his own degree of guilt at 50 pence. Actually, of course, there are no such degrees in sin. Any sin, or number of sins, form rebellion against God, whether the sin is that of a hypocrite like Simon or that of the fallen woman.

Then Jesus introduced a most unusual, extraordinary note in His parable. The money-lender, knowing that neither debtor had anything to pay, forgave them both. This cancelled obligation in both cases was "a purely gratuitous act on the part of the creditor, on the ground only of the bankruptcy of the debtors." How astonished Simon must have been as Jesus described the generosity of the money-lender. Both were debtors and equally insolvent, and both are equally forgiven. Then Jesus, concealing His home-thrust under the veil of a parable, made His discourteous host pronounce upon the case, which brings us to the third group, namely, that of three questions.

The first was: "Which of them will love him the most?" How else could Simon answer, somewhat reluctantly, "I suppose that he, to whom he forgave most"? He admitted that the man to whom most is forgiven will feel the greatest degree of obligation, that he who was forgiven most should love most. Thus Jesus made Simon "pronounce judgment at once on his misapprehension of the woman's act, his doubt of Christ Himself, and the stinted honour he did his Guest." The sins of the woman were many, and she knew it. So did Christ, but He here proclaimed in naked terms the forgiveness of all her sin. Her sins were many but a full pardon brought forth great love. "To whom little is forgiven, *the same* loveth little." The woman was not forgiven because she loved, but loved because she was forgiven. While both debtors in the parable were forgiven, and Christ was as willing to forgive Simon as He did the sinful woman, there is no evidence that Simon repented of his sin and experienced the joy of sins forgiven.

"Simon, seest thou *this* woman?" The emphasis here is on two words, *thou* and *this*. Jesus knew the thoughts in Simon's mind. "He knew what was in man." The inmost thoughts are known to Him. *"This* woman." Simon saw her as she was known to be — a profligate, abandoned soul. Then Jesus with "delicate politeness, as if hurt at the inattentions of His host; which though not *invariably* shown to guests, were the customary marks of studied respect and regard," laid bare the cold, loveless, disrespectful treatment of Simon. Our Lord's remark, "She loved much, but to whom little is forgiven, the same loveth little," is the key to the parable.

"Who is this that forgiveth sins?" We can imagine how startled the guests of Simon were as they heard One who was reclining at the same couch, and partaking of the same hospitalities, assuming the divine prerogative of forgiving sins. "Who can forgive sins but God only?" Jesus did not deny or soften down such

a claim, but enforced it. He was either, then, a blaspheming deceiver or God manifest in the flesh, and being the latter, He exercised the prerogative of granting a double assurance of forgiveness. He announced what was the one secret of the full and free forgiveness the woman had received, and which carried salvation in its bosom: it was her faith, not her tears, kisses and ointment, but her faith in Christ's love and compassion. Thus she became a woman "nobly born, because she was born again." Then there came that glorious dismissal of the woman in that "peace" which she had already felt surging through her saved soul. Christ's last word to her was "Go in peace," or "Go into peace." Peace had become hers, and she receives the Master's full warrant to enjoy that peace and live in the full realization of the peace passing all understanding.

The lessons of the parable for our hearts are obvious. We are all bankrupts, debtors, in the sight of our heavenly Creditor. "All have sinned." Then the best of us, like the worst of us, have nothing wherewith to discharge our debt. But through His willingness to take our debt and make it His own, Christ can now forgive all who truly repent of their sin and turn to Him in faith. If forgiven, then love and devotion to the One who forgave us should be ours. Freed from the burdensome debt of our sin, our gratitude must be manifested in a life of holiness and of service for the bringing of other sinners to Him who alone can save them.

## The Parable of the Neighbor and the Good Samaritan
### (Luke 10:25-37)

H. T. Sell, in his introduction to this story of all times, wrote of it as a "wonderful apologue true in every age and clime. The circumstances in which it is set, the human types it introduces, the conditions it describes, find place in the annals of all sorts and conditions of men. As a narrative — considered quite apart from its moral significance—it will never become stale, never superseded, never grow old. And this, simply because it is composed of the elements of eternal truth, and, in classic form, epitomizes the whole economy of human conduct."

There are those writers who say that what we have in this portion is not exactly a parable. The mode of pictorial representation is not as in the parables already considered, that of symbolic clothing, but simply that of exhibiting a concrete example. Goebel's view, which Salmond mentions, is that "it is the first *typical* parable in distinction from the *symbolic,* which here meets us, for it illustrates its subject not, as most of the other parables of Jesus, by means of symbol, but simply by means of example." Jesus did not use symbols taken from the realm of nature or from custom but from actual occurrences. While this may be so we feel that the narrative was conceived by Jesus to set forth a particular truth. We agree with Cosmo Lang that it is "one of our Lord's greatest and most typical parables. It is so simple that a child can read its meaning; yet it is in truth a treatise of practical ethics more profound and more powerful in effect than any other in the world. . . . Our very familiarity with the parable blinds us to the greatness of its mingled simplicity and depth and — let us add — to the greatness of the claim which it makes upon us." As we are to discover, each figure in the story does not represent a spiritual analogue. The whole is simply an illustrative example of the working of benevolence as contrasted with that of selfishness.

Our Lord's conversation with the lawyer, which gave rise to the parable, must not be confused with His contact with another lawyer (Matthew 19:16; 22:35-40; Mark 12:28-34; Luke 18:18). In the seemingly parallel occasion in Mark 12:28,34, our Lord joined two famous Old Testament passages together in His answer to the lawyer's question (Deuteronomy 6:4; Leviticus 19:18), and Straton says that "Luke begins his story where Mark

leaves off." But the lawyer in this parable asked more pointed questions than his fellow scribe. "Logically," says Arnot, "this parable may be conveniently associated with that of *The Unmerciful Servant*. They constitute a pair; that teaches us to forgive the injurer; and this to help the injured."

It will be noted that the narrative commences with the exclamation, *Behold!* These "Beholds" of Scripture demand notice wherever they occur; "they call special attention to what follows as containing truth not always apparent on the surface, but requiring careful investigation and prayerful pondering, truths to be sought for as for hid treasure." This "behold" forces us to consider, first of all:

*The Purpose of the Parable.* "A certain lawyer" tested the knowledge and authority of Jesus with two questions. By profession, a "lawyer" was one occupied with the Mosaic Law. It was his official business to interpret the Law and guide people on how to relate their life to it. If a Jew had a difficulty, he would consult a lawyer or scribe, to find out what the Law said on the matter of behavior troubling him. Confronting Jesus, this lawyer said, "What shall I *do* to inherit eternal life?" He wanted Him, the Great Teacher, to give him instruction on how to obtain life in its fulness — life, full-orbed and perfect.

How skilful was the reply of Jesus! Employing a technical term, constantly used by the scribes or lawyers who, when they consulted one another about some matter of the Law would say, "How readest thou?" Jesus said, "What is written in the law, how readest thou?" The man was thrown back upon himself, and upon what he already knew of the Law's requirements, and gave the only right and complete answer he could, namely, the necessity of loving God and also his neighbor. Jesus, commending him for his answer, said, "Thou hast answered right. This do, and thou shalt live." The lawyer then, sincerely desiring further instruction, asked, "And who is my neighbour?" He fastened upon the second part of his own answer. He was in no doubt as to God's reality and of the necessity of loving Him with heart, soul, strength and mind. What troubled him was the identity of the neighbor he must love. As a lawyer, he belonged to a class of teachers declaring that no Gentile was a neighbor. For him as a Jew, neighborliness belonged within the covenant people. We are told that the lawyer asked this second question about his neighbor to justify himself. *Justify himself with whom?* Not with the crowd around him, but with his own conscience. In his own mind, there lurked the suspicion that the rejection of a Gentile, simply because he was a *Gentile,* was not right and dodging the issue, he sought to throw the onus on Jesus, who answered the lawyer in the beautiful, enchanting story we call *The Good Samaritan.* Having considered the setting, or purpose of this parable, let us now look at the picture growing before us.

*The Personalities in the Parable.* Along a road over which many travelers journey, and certain events happen thereon, our Lord depicts the traveling man going "down from Jerusalem to Jericho." In this geographical accuracy, for the road did go, and still goes, down, we have the two boundaries: Jerusalem and Jericho.

*Jerusalem,* meaning "the vision of peace," was the seat of blessing, of history, of religion, of privilege. This was the City where God had chosen to place His name, the center of worship and communion with Himself.

*Jericho* was the city of curse (Joshua 6:26), but yet a city beautiful for its situation and its palm trees. But this city that had been under a curse for centuries had become by this time, a priestly city where priests lived when not fulfilling their courses in Jerusalem, some fifteen miles from Jericho.

The road between the two cities, a rocky and dangerous gorge, was a road haunted by marauding robbers and therefore unsafe for travelers. Priests and Levites, because of their religious calling, were never molested by the thieves who, because of their deeds of violence, earned for this untenanted part of the wilderness, the name of *Adummim* (Joshua 15:7; 18:7) or *The Pass of Blood.* Josephus tells us that Herod had dismissed 40 thousand workmen from the Temple, shortly before Christ's recital of this parable, and that a large part of them became vicious highway robbers, who were aided in their diabolical plunder by the hiding places and sharp turnings on the road.

It was along this thief-infested road that "a certain man" was traveling down from Jerusalem to Jericho. Who he was we are not told. Probably he was a Jewish merchant. Perhaps there had been a recent outrage of this kind, and our Lord with knowledge of it, uses the incident with great effect. There is also the probability that the robbers watched the ways of the traveler, and knowing of his business transactions, and the likelihood that he carried money on his person, waylaid him as they did, stripping, wounding him, and leaving him half dead. There was the utter, reckless plunder of what the man had and wore. But this was only the least injury done the man by the thieves. They inflicted heavy blows upon him, and left him exhausted and half-dead to perish in the lonely wilderness. Those brutal robbers never expected another traveler to pass that spot on the dangerous, unfrequented road in time to save the half-murdered victim.

It is here that the Master Storyteller introduces a delightful touch: "By chance there came down a certain priest that way." *By chance.* Did chance or fate represent the abandoned half-dead traveler's view of the case? Do you not think that he felt God had something to do with the weaving of human events and knew how to guide relief his way? The word used here for "chance" is *coincidence.* It was no idle chance that the Priest, the Levite, and the Samaritan, came to the spot where the bleeding sufferer lay. They came that way by a specific arrangement and in exact fulfilment of a plan, the plan of God. As the Omniscient Designer He knows how to bring about a necessary meeting between man and man. "Many good opportunities are concealed under those events which appear to be *fortuitous.*"

In the Providence of God, or in the arrangements of the Gospel, there is no such thing as *chance.* The priest passing that way was one event falling in with another. He could not avoid meeting the man who needed help. The priest, however, did not look upon it as a happy coincidence, a God-planned opportunity to help a needy soul. He saw the beaten, bleeding traveler, but passed by on the other side.

*The Priest.* This hale, comfortable priest was a servant of the Law which enjoined mercy even to a beast (Exodus 23:4-5). Here was a man, professedly consecrated to God, and even now on his way home after his turn of office in the Temple. Surely after his prayers and oblations, he will show mercy to the man who sorely needed it. But this spiritual leader, one of the 12,000 priests living in Jericho at that time, had evidently left God back in the Temple and had neither time nor compassion for his unfortunate fellow Jew. Perhaps, he was in too much of a hurry to get home and to other affairs. Like the lawyer to whom Jesus uttered this parable, this Priest knew the Law with its enactment about loving God *and* his neighbors, but if anyone was his neighbor, surely it was the helpless, half-naked, bleeding man at his feet. Alas, heartlessly he passed by on the other side!

*The Levite.* Along came another traveler, and with the tread of his footstep, the hopes of the half-dead man would rise again. The Levite was of the same tribe as the Pharisee, but of one of the inferior branches. He was a servant of the Temple and as a minister of religious worship and an interpreter of the Law should have been eager to assist the dis-tressed soul he *looked on* yet left unaided. These two spiritual leaders should have been the first to translate their faith in God into concern for the battered body of the traveler.

Why did Jesus bring the Priest and the Levite into the parable? Was it not to rebuke an unreal, heartless, compassionless, formal, organized religion and to reveal in the Samaritan the real, essential spirit of religion? Jesus loyally conformed to the religion of the Jews, but chose the Samaritan in order to strengthen His rebuke of the Priest and Levite who had failed in their solemn obligation, just as the Church forgets her primary duty when wealth, comfort, ease and pride enfeeble the energy of her compassion.

*The Samaritan.* Samaritans were half-caste, a mixture of Jew and Gentile, therefore hated by the full-blooded Jew. Jews would have no dealings with the Samaritans, treating them as outcasts. Although the Jews and Samaritans were locally closest neighbors, they were morally most unneighborly. Therefore, the lawyer must have been amazed when Jesus introduced a *Samaritan* as the only one on that lonely, dangerous Jericho road willing to befriend a helpless *Jew.* The very man from whom no needy Jew could expect the least relief, was the one who gave it.

It must be clearly understood that by His description of the heartlessness of the Priest and the Levite, and the opposite treatment of the Samaritan, that all religious representatives were cruel, and all Samaritans were tender-hearted. Without any doubt there were many benevolent priests and Levites and contrariwise many unkind Samaritans. They were Samaritans who would not permit Jesus and His disciples, when they were weary and in need of rest and refreshment, to pass the night in their village (Luke 9:53). It is a Levite, Barnabas, who was named *Son of Consolation,* and sold all that he had for the relief of poorer brethren (Acts 4:36).

Our Lord's parable was addressed to

a Jew and was so designed as Arnot reminds us "to smite one blow at the two poles on which a vain Jewish life in that day turned": *They trusted in themselves that they were righteous, and despised others.* Having no respect of persons, Christ would not overlook kindness in the one, nor sanction cruelty in the other. Thus, His parable was so constructed as to humble the lawyer's self-righteous trust in his birthright as a Jew, and at the same time take the mean position of a Samaritan in the lawyer's estimate and exalt him for his compassion. Like the leper-stricken Samaritan, who was the only one out of the ten (the other nine were Jews) this Samaritan paused to praise the Lord for healing. Here, a Samaritan is represented as being more beneficent to the needy, whose expressions of painstaking compassion were enumerated by Jesus. What a beautiful cameo He gives us of the Samaritan's kindness. "He came where he was, he had compassion on him, and went to him, and bound up his wounds, pouring in oil and wine, and set him on his own beast, and brought him to an inn, and took care of him. And on the morrow when he departed, he took out two pence, and gave them to the host, and said unto him, Take care of him; and whatsover thou spendest more, when I come again, I will repay thee."

How concise yet comprehensive is this description of Christ's parabolic interpretation of the brotherhood of man seen in the brotherhood of need! Priest and Levite passed by the half-dead man, but the Samaritan came *to* him, and seeing his battered, blood-spattered body, had compassion on him and rendered quick and effectual help. Wisely the Samaritan provided for his journey through hostile country, and so as part of his outfit he carried bandages, oil and wine. *Oil* was widely used by the ancients as an external remedy to assuage the pain of open wounds (Isaiah 1:6). The use of *wine* was also an external remedy for wounds and bruises. Having cleansed the wounds and staunched the blood,

after this essential relief the kind Samaritan proceeded unweariedly in the rendering of help. He lifted the half-dead man up on to his own beast. There is no reference to the mule of the priest or that of the Levite, seeing there was no occasion for making mention of such. The Samaritan renounced the use of his own beast and walking, led the beast and its burden to an inn on the road. The Samaritan stayed the night with the rescued traveler, paid for his care, and promised to return and reimburse the host for further food and shelter the sufferer required.

The usual trio should have been *Priest, Levite, Jew,* or Israelite, but "the substitution of a Samaritan was a masterstroke," and Jesus having told His superb story asked a direct question of the lawyer in reply to his question, "Who is my neighbour?" In effect, Jesus gave the lawyer his question back again, calling upon him to decide who was the true neighbor to the man who fell among thieves. What else could the lawyer say but, "He that showed mercy of him"? Then Jesus drove home the application, "Go, and do thou also likewise," which in effect meant, "Do thou in like manner show mercy, and thou too wilt by this means become neighbour to him whom thou showest it." This sequel to and moral of the parable was to show that the divine command of loving our neighbor as ourself is fulfilled by the assiduous endeavor to help the needy, without asking first who he is, and in what relation he stands to us. The Samaritan proved himself to be neighborly for true neighborliness reveals itself in mercy.

The deep principle of human conduct, or philosophy of life, which this parable contains for us is the same question of the lawyer, "Who is my neighbour?" How are we to distinguish our neighbor? Cosmo Lang says, "Be in your spirit neighbourly, and then every man will be your neighbour." Without distinction of race or religion that man is our neighbor who has need of us. "It is not place but love that makes neighborhood." The question is not so much, "Who is my neighbor?" but, "Am I neighborly?"

We look upon our neighbors as those who live next door to us. But we, or they, may be most unneighborly, and we find it easier to love and help those at a distance, than one's actual neighbor. Yet these are our neighbors. In connection with the keeping of the Passover is the enactment, "If the household be too little for the lamb, let him and his neighbour *next unto his house* take it according to the number of souls" (Exodus 12:4). Says Habershon, "Our neighbor is one with whom we may share the Lamb. We have neighbors on both sides, those who are saved, those who are unsaved — those to whom we can offer succor, those with whom we can hold fellowship."

But the teaching of our Lord's parable is that "nearness does not make neighborliness," as Butterick expresses it. "The Priest and Levite were near both by race and by office, and the Samaritan by race and office was remote. People may live divided only by a narrow wall, and yet not be neighbors. People may live with no intervening wall, and yet not be neighbors. Only the eyes and the spirit of the Samaritan make neighborliness." As we take our journey through life, those we come upon "by chance," who are in dire need of help (spiritual, physical, material), these are our neighbors, the Great Good Samaritan Himself would have us assist.

A final word is necessary regarding the various applications of this choice parable. In our introductory section on *The Interpretation of Parables,* we mentioned the most fanciful treatment of the parable by Augustine, one which is extended somewhat by Keach. But apart from far-fetched allegorical interpretations, there is a legitimate *application* of the parable. Did not God make humanity His neighbor? Seeing a world of sinners robbed of their true nature, stripped of divine ideals, wounded by sins, unable to rise, God came down in the Incarnation to where the sinner was and gave the world a corresponding example *in act* of the merciful Samaritan. Christ, through His death and resurrection, covers our nakedness, binds up our wounds and heals them with a balm extracted from His own broken heart. Not only so, but He puts us in a place of safety, provides for our needs, and has promised to return and take us to Himself. Thus the parable is radiant with the beauty of the Gospel of Christ who, in His life and death kept all the injunctions given in this peerless parable.

# The Parable of the Friends at Midnight
### (Luke 11:1-10)

In this great "prayer" chapter there are three parabolic pictures which, although separate, are yet connected by the same theme. The illustration of *The Father and the Child* which Matthew also records, dwells on the same theme as that of *The Friends at Midnight,* namely, "Prayer." Then the *Parable of the Strong Man* (Matthew 12:29), here given with greater detail, presents the praying, Spirit-filled Christ as the One stronger than Satan, the strong one. By His death, Jesus defeated the enemy and took his goods. If we would be overcomers we, too, must seek by prayer the continual infilling of the Spirit of power.

In prayer, as in every other phase of His ministry, Jesus taught His disciples by performance as well as precept. It was the Lord's praying that led to *The Lord's Prayer.* As His disciples heard Him praying in a certain place they held their breath till His intercession was finished, then asked, "Lord, teach us to pray." Complying with their request, He gave them that wonderful model-prayer "which serves at once as the first lesson for babes beginning, and the fullest exercise of strong men's powers." Then, after having taught His disciples to pray by example and by precept, Jesus gave them a parable-lesson on importunity and perseverance in praying, which we now consider.

Actually, there are three friends in this parable. A friend had a friend who was in need of bread and he went to another friend for a loan of the bread required. Christ is the fourth Friend, a Friend above all friends, who loves us at all times and "sticketh closer than a brother." We say that "A friend in need, is a friend indeed"—and Christ, beyond all others, is this unfailing Friend.

The dramatic force of many of our Lord's parables is seen in this parable of *The Three Friends,* the story of which has its approach to a crisis of interest. "The training of The Twelve was advanced through the dramatic setting of this dramatic, parabolic method of instruction."

1. *The Visiting Friend.* This benighted traveler, journeying in the coolness of the night to escape the fierce heat of the day, threaded his way to a friend's house where he knew food and shelter would be offered him. After many hours of travel, he arrived footsore and weary around midnight, and hearing his knock and recognizing his voice, the friend opened the door to receive the tired traveler with the accustomed Eastern hospitality. "To every true Jew the law of hospitality is sacred, sees nothing for it but to go, late as it is, to the house of a friend."

2. *The Importunate Friend.* With the late arrival of the traveler, his friend realized his difficulty. After his household had satisfied their wants for the day, there was no bread left over and all retired to rest. More bread would be baked in the morning for the needs of another day. To have no food for a visitor was an insufferable reproach to an Oriental. Thus, late as it was, the host went to his other friend's house nearby to ask him to lend him three loaves—sufficient for the amount necessary for the intended meal to feed the hungry guest. Those who attempt to give each detail in a parable some symbolic significance, see in "the three loaves" a figurative description of three particular spiritual gifts. All this action is meant to convey is the fact that this friend would not be found inhospitable, and so at the midnight hour he knocked on his friend's door, just as the traveler had knocked upon his.

3. *The Unwilling Friend.* The sleeping friend who was aroused by his friend, who had just been aroused by the traveler, was not at all pleased at being disturbed at so late an hour and met the request for bread with a polite but peremptory refusal. His wife and children were asleep and unwonted movements would awaken and alarm them. Better that one person should fast until morning than that a whole family should be disturbed at midnight! But the suppliant at the door would not take *No* for an answer. He would not listen to a refusal, and so continued to knock and plead. The aroused friend, seeking to shield his own sleeping family from disturbance, realizes that the method he was adopting to preserve the seemly stillness of the night was the surest way of disturbing it. Persistent knocking and shouting would arouse not only his family but the neighborhood, so he got out of bed and gave his friend the bread he required: mark, he did not give from friendship, he gave in to importunity. Butterick's description at this point is appealing, "No chance to sleep with such a racket! There was the shuffle of feet in the cottage, a fumbling with the latch, a hand thrust through the partly opened door: 'Here! Take your bread and be off!' Surely Jesus' eyes twinkled as He said, 'I say unto you, though he will not rise and give unto him because he is his friend (!), yet because of his shamelessness, he will arise and give him anything he asks for.' "

Butterick goes on to say that the story is true to life and perhaps it was an incident Jesus recalled of His early days, as He listened with eyes wide open in the darkness, while Joseph, His foster-father, held gruff converse with a neighbor banging on their cottage door for something.

The word *importunity* is an interesting one. Campbell Morgan says that this is the only place in the New Testament where it occurs, and is from the Latin *importunas,* meaning troublesome or impudence. "The Greek means 'shamelessness'." Goebel uses the word *impudence* for "importunity" and says: "By the natural conduct of the petitioner the intentionally strong expression signalizes the element which ensures his final success — the importunity that knows no shame; for this importunity must in the course of time become more irksome to the petitioned than the slight trouble of rising up. And having once risen, he gave without stint, as much as was needed for only thus will he be quickly rid of his importunity." Arnot comments that the term translated "importunity," signifies freedom from the bashfulness which cannot ask a second time.

In the succeeding verses (Luke 11:11-13), Jesus unfolds the chief purpose of His homely parable. God is the Householder and is more willing to give than we are to receive. He never sleeps and therefore is never disturbed when we approach Him. James speaks of Him as "The Giving God" (1:5), and satisfying our needs is one of His delights. We must, however, pray perseveringly for "the spirit of successful prayer is the spirit of persevering prayer." If urgent continuous asking prevailed with a selfish, indolent, churlish man, how much more must prayer prevail with God, who cares for us with a Father's love!

What we must guard ourselves against is reading into the parable more than Jesus intended. The friend who was aroused had to be badgered into lending the necessary bread. But God neither slumbers nor sleeps, and we do not have to force Him into giving, and He never gives what we seek reluctantly. If He does not appear to answer we must be tireless in our approach to the Mercy Seat. Those who have been mighty in prayer have been those who, like Jacob, have wrestled and cried, "I will not let thee go, except thou bless me" (Genesis

32:26). Arnot has this precious comment, "Sweet to the Angel of the Covenant was the persistent struggle of the believing man, and sweet to the same Lord today is the pressure which an eager suppliant applies to his heart and his hand. . . . The Lord loves to be pressed; let us therefore press, assured by His own word that the Hearer of prayer never takes urgency ill." Says Butterick, "The strong souls of mankind have been under necessity of proving to God that their prayer was the plea of their all-controlling desire."

Such intensity in prayer is indicated by the Lord's exhortation: *Ask, Seek, Knock,* the last two imperatives repeat the meaning of the first in figurative form and give expression to what is implied in the parable. As Goebel expresses it, "Not every asking, but only a patient, persevering one can be figuratively called a 'seeking'; and in the same way, not any asking whatever, but an energetic, persistent one, is denoted by 'knock', which, standing thus absolutely and independently, cannot mean a timid tapping, but only a vigorous knocking. . . . The threefold utterance of the exhortation is in itself a demand for an ever-repeated, unwearied asking." By parable and precept Christ exhorts us to persevering, persistent prayer. If the friend who sought bread for his friend was not discouraged by a refusal, but continued to ask in ever increasing earnestness for what he needed, how much more does it become us, whom Jesus called His "friends," never to grow weary in presenting our petitions to God, whose fatherly love does not need, like man's precarious friendship, to be reluctantly constrained, but willingly and gladly lets itself be compelled? God does not answer our oft praying to get rid of us, but because He loves us.

## The Parable of the Rich Fool
### (Luke 12:13-21)

This further parable peculiar to Luke, "almost startling in its clarity and supreme in the light it throws upon life," must have made a profound impression on those who heard it. While speaking to the multitude around, including His disciples, Jesus was interrupted by a listener who presented a most inappropriate demand: "Master, speak to my brother that he divide the inheritance with me." If disputed questions of property and possessions arose, the disputants sought the advice of the Scribes, the custodians of the Law, on such matters. Knowing that Jesus was a Rabbi sent from God, this man sought His verdict in the matter of the inheritance. But Jesus rejected the appeal because it was outside the sphere of His proper mission. He asked the question, "Who made me a Judge or a Divider over you?" He then warned "the petitioner against the covetous spirit which makes and maintains such disputes." Jesus went on to use the parabolic illustration of the rich fool to expose the folly of covetousness in any form and the error of thinking that a man's life consisted in the abundance of the things he possessed. To think of life only in terms of *things* is both foolish and fatal, because *life* is not held together by material possessions, even if they are abundant, but by things spiritual and eternal. Such is the background of the parable.

Now let us consider the brief and forceful parable itself. Jesus used a hard word to characterize the mistake of the man He described, possibly from His own personal observation and knowledge. He called him a *Fool* — a word meaning, without reason, want of mental sanity, lack of commonsense perception of the reality of things natural and spiritual. And that he was a *fool* is proven in various ways. He was a:

1. *Godless Fool.* David portrayed a *fool* as a man who affirms, "There is no God" (Psalm 14:1). The words, "There is," are in italics, added to carry the sense of the passage. *No God!* is the original expression, as if the fool is one who says, "No God for me!" This implies not actual atheism, the denial of God's existence, but a practical atheism, the denial of the moral government of God. This is why *fool* and *wicked* are sometimes treated as synonymous terms. A life lived without God is a God-*less* life. It may be a life full of "many things" but if it is minus God it is an empty life.

The man Jesus described may not have been a morally bad man. There is no evidence that he had added wealth to wealth by any fraudulent practices. He appears to have been a diligent, thoughtful sagacious man. His great folly was that he was ignorant of the divine hand supplying his multiplied prosperity. He was blind to the fact that man cannot live by bread *alone*. He forgot that back of the fruits, the corn, and all his possessions was *God,* the Giver of every good and of every perfect gift. He failed to see himself as God's steward of all with which He had enriched him. There was no grateful recognition of God as the Giver of the rain and the fruitful seasons, or any grateful return to Him from whom all blessings flow. How graphically the Psalmist of old depicted this rich fool and multitudes like him!: "They that trust in their wealth and boast themselves in the multitude of their riches, their inward thought is that their houses shall continue for ever, and their dwelling-places to all generations; they call their lands after their own names. Nevertheless, man being in honour, abideth not: he is like the beasts that perish. This their way is their folly, yet their posterity approve their sayings" (Psalm 49:6,11-13).

2. *The Rich Fool.* Jesus spoke of this most successful farmer as a *rich* man, but actually he was a *poor* rich man. Like the Laodician Church, he was rich, increased with goods, having need of nothing, yet poor and miserable. As his riches increased, he set his heart upon them rather than upon the One who gave him the ability to accumulate wealth. "All things come of thee, and of thine own have we given thee" (I Chronicles 29:14). In his passion to produce and hoard up mundane things,

the rich man had no thought of their divine source and the use of them for divine purposes.

Paul says that it is the *love* of money, not money itself, that is the root of all evil (I Timothy 6:10). Jesus never made any sweeping indictment of money itself. In some of His parables, He had a good deal to say about the use of riches, both spiritual and temporal, the one symbolizing the other. The Rich Fool and the other Rich Man contrasted with Lazarus (Luke 16:19-31), did not use their riches for others. "The deceitfulness of riches" choked any desire for God and His Word. In both cases the harvest of the field destroyed the true harvest of life. The one rich fool hoarded his possessions, while the other spent his wealth upon himself. In contrast to the misuse of riches, we have their right use in the good man and his treasure (Luke 6:45). The parables of *The Talents* and *The Pounds* reveal how God expects His servants to use what He has given them, with interest accruing to Himself as the Lender.

In the parable before us Jesus exposed the sin of the rich fool — he failed to be "rich toward God." This was not a tirade against riches as such, but a warning against the desire for their acquisition to dominate life and destroy all thought of and desire for God. Even if a person is a Christian, great possessions can prove a handicap in the race to heaven, which it has been said, "Is a place to which few kings and rich men come." But whether our possessions are many or meager we cannot be rich toward God until we are rich in grace, rich in faith, rich in good works. The only currency worth having is the gold tried in the fire, which the Lord offers to sell. Eternal wealth of this sort is within the reach of all. A person may be a millionaire, yet a spiritual bankrupt. Many merchant princes are paupers in the sight of Him who, although rich, for our sakes became poor, that we through His poverty might become truly rich.

Blessed be God, if we are poor, we can yet possess all things of abiding worth.

3. *The Self-Centered Fool.* How skilful Jesus was in the portrayal of the egotism of the rich fool! Examine the man's soliloquy and you will find six *I*'s, five *my*'s, and four *I Will*'s. How prominent are the pronouns of personal possession. In the presence of his multiplied and multiplying wealth we see this egotist rubbing his hands with glee and saying, *"My* fruit, *my* barns, *my* corn, *my* goods, *my* soul." God, who supplied them all, was not in his thoughts. "What hast thou, thou didst not receive?" The man's life was self-ruled, "Verily I thought within myself" (Acts 26:9). True, his ground had brought forth plentifully, but who provided the fertile soil, the rain, the sun, and all of nature's aids producing the harvests causing the barns to bulge?

This self-made farmer even called his soul his own, *"My* soul." But had not God said, "All souls are mine" (Ezekiel 18:4)? And because it was all *my* and no recognition of *"Thine,* O Lord is the glory," Jesus called him a *fool* — his foolishness consisting in his failure to recognize the Source of supply. Such a failure resulted in the loss of all.

4. *The Ambitious Fool.* In itself, *ambition* is commendable. Paul was very ambitious. Three times over he speaks of the Christian's ambition which each of us should manifest (Romans 15:20; II Corinthians 5:9; I Thessalonians 4:11 R.V.). The rich man's ambition was selfish and sensual. He was determined to build larger barns, not that he might have more to give away and with which to glorify God, but that his increased reserves might add to his own indulgences and indolences. His real aim in expansion was, as G. H. Lang summarizes it —

A. "Security for many years to come, a confession that he was not trusting God for the future;

B. A love of ease, in disregard for the will of God that, for his own good, he should toil (Genesis 3:17-19).

C. The desire to gratify the lusts of flesh by eating, drinking and foolish mirth."

5. *The Doomed Fool.* How solemn are the words, "Thou fool, this night thy soul shall be required of thee!" He had said to himself, "Soul, thou hast much goods laid up for *many years.*" But the God he forgot quickly reversed that proud boast by saying, *"This* night (the night of the very day he made his boast) thy soul shall be required of thee." Instead of barns, he had a burial; instead of anticipated luxurious living there came a call to account to God for his hoarded possessions. The original here is more emphatic, "They shall require thy soul of thee." Who were these strong executioners of the divine edict? They were death's angels who take no denial. The rich fool, in his shortsightedness, never thought of his mortality, and that his breath was only in his nostrils.

Habershon reminds us that in two of our Lord's parables there are pictures of rich men who had to leave everything behind them — The Rich Man and his barns (Luke 12:16-21), and Dives and Lazarus (Luke 16:19-31). "The one emphasizes the thought of what must be left behind, the other, what lies ahead. The parable of Dives carries the picture a stage further than the earlier one; it shows the man's condition after God has said, 'Thou fool! this night thy soul shall be required of thee.' " Both of these rich men went to Hell, not because they were rich, but because they had left God out of their life.

Jesus added the question, "Then whose shall these things be, which thou hast provided?" The rich fool could not take a grain of his loaded barns with him into Eternity. He must leave the world as empty-handed as he entered it. The Old Testament commentary of the folly of this rich farmer is striking — "As the partridge sitteth on eggs, and hatcheth them not, so he that gathereth riches, and not by right, shall leave them in the

midst of his days, and, at his end, shall be a fool" (Jeremiah 17:12). Is not this folly daily perpetrated in the world? Men sacrifice all legitimate pleasures and their deeper spiritual interests, to make money, and then die suddenly, leaving their hard-earned gains to be dissipated by indolent, pleasure-loving children. Butterick reminds us that, "The fact that wealth of a man's careful hoarding may be wasted riotously by his heirs, serves to emphasize the folly of living for wealth" (See Psalm 39:6; 49:6; Ecclesiastes 2:18-23; Job 27:17-27).

While this man had nothing to say to God, God had plenty to say to him and condemned him for making three mistakes. First of all, he mistook the purpose of his *life,* imagining that it consisted in the abundance of his material possessions. Paul could say, "To me to live is *Christ.*" But substituting human reason for divine direction, this fool of a man never gained happiness of life, nor the continuance of life on earth. Further, he mistook the right use of his *worldly means.* Choosing his own will rather than the will of God as to what should be done with his means, he hoarded them up when it would have been wiser and more profitable to use them for the good of others. He forgot, as Ambrose puts it, that the barns for his superfluity were "the bosoms of the needy, the houses of the widows, the mouths of orphans and children."

Perhaps this man's most glaring mistake was his *negligence of the future.* He preferred riches he could see and handle to the unseen and eternal treasures laid up in heaven. He presumed on length of days when the night of the day of his boast was to be his last. For the peril of greed, there came its retribution for the selfish use of his possessions. He lost his gathered substance — and his soul. What an ignoble end! No wonder our Lord, after uttering this parable, went on to teach by contrast a more excellent way of life. He told His disciples to consider the ravens, and the lilies, and the sparrows, His Father cares for, and that His only barn or storehouse is "in the heavens" (Luke 12:33). If God, and not our *goods,* be first, then whatever He permits us to have, whether much or little, will be used as unto Him.

## The Parable of the Watchful Servants
### (Luke 12:35-48)

While this parable in its fulness is peculiar to Luke, other parables move in the same realm (see Matthew 24; 25). Jamieson says that this portion presents "the germ of thought which was afterwards developed into The Parable of the Ten Virgins." The phrase, "the goodman of the house," is identical with that to be found in Matthew 24:43, 44. "Matthew recorded briefly this parable as our Lord uttered it in the Olivet prophecy," says Campbell. "Luke gives it as our Lord had uttered it in an earlier part of His ministry." The prominent idea in this parable, as in others, is that of preparedness for Christ's coming. All who are members of the household of faith, bond-slaves of the Master, stewards of the mysteries of grace, must be found serving each other in things of the Divine Kingdom, and together living and laboring as unto the King.

## The Parable of the Barren Fig Tree
### (Luke 13:6-9)

This parable must not be confused with the parabolic miracle of the fig tree which Jesus cursed (Matthew 21:18-22; Mark 11:12-25). The only common bond between the two parables is the fact that there were no figs on either tree. Jesus, as we know, made constant illustrative use of the fig tree (Matthew 24:32-33; Mark 13:28, 29; Luke 21:29-30). The reason for this parable, which Luke alone records, was to expand and enforce our Lord's declaration in the verses preceding the parable. There were those who came and

reported to Him the melancholy story, which Josephus enlarges on, that some of the hot-headed Galileans had been slain by Pilate who mingled their blood with the offered sacrifices.

Jesus detected in His pharisaical reporters the marks of a self-complacent spirit. If those guilty Galileans had been removed by a sudden death, surely the escape of those who deemed themselves worthy of God's favor could take their preservation from death as an indication of God's special approbation. They were blind to the fact that a particular calamity does not measure or prove the particular guilt of those who suffer in it. Note the reply of Jesus: "Think ye that these Galileans were sinners above all the Galileans because they have suffered these things?" If those to whom He was speaking imagined that such swift judgment was evidence of flagrant sin, they were made to realize that they had completely misunderstood the Providence of God and also life: "I tell you Nay: but except ye repent, ye shall all likewise perish."

The Galilean incident the news-letters reported to Jesus as evidence of aggravated wickedness in the case of the sufferers, He interpreted as a warning to the nation which prided itself on its exemplary holiness as a whole. When He told the people that unless they repented they should all *likewise* perish, He meant that they would die in like tragic manner as the Galileans. As Trench puts it: "The threat is, that they shall literally in like wise perish. Certainly the resemblance is more accidental between these two calamities here adduced, and the ultimate destruction which did overtake the rebellious Jews, as many refused to obey the Lord's bidding and to repent. As the Tower of Siloam fell, and crushed eighteen of the dwellers at Jerusalem, exactly so multitudes of its inhabitants were crushed beneath the ruins of their temple and their city; and during the last siege and assault of that city there were numbers also who were pierced through by Roman darts, or, more miserably yet, by those of their own frantic factions, in the courts of the Temple, in the very act of preparing their sacrifices, so that literally their blood, like that of those Galileans, was mingled with their sacrifices, one blood with another." After such a warning, Jesus, by means of a parable, enlarged the scope of His call to national repentance, and added to its solemn definiteness.

Passing from the context of the parable, we come to consider its clear, concise construction. In this simple and human illustration we have, first of all—

*The Design of the Proprietor.* The certain man whom Jesus portrayed, planted a fig tree in the vineyard he owned, and from his soil the fig tree could have derived all the resources necessary for fruitage. The tree had been *planted.* This was no foreign, forbidden tree from a seed planted in the vineyard (Deuteronomy 22:9). It had been deliberately planted in the vineyard to which it had no title, and grew in the corner where the soil was most favorable. The proprietor desired this particular tree, adapted by its nature to produce figs, and designed its position in a protected part of the vineyard where it could be skilfully cared for. The language, then, is precise. The fig tree had been planted within the vineyard, in a most favorable position, by a deliberate act of the owner, in order that he might ultimately enjoy its fruit.

The key of the parable is furnished for us by the occasion of the parable. The peculiar privilege of *the fig tree* illustrated the Jewish nation (Isaiah 5:1-7); and the *vineyard,* the enclosure of privilege, symbolized the nation secluded from all others, and especially honored by God with the light of a supernatural revelation through the Prophets, and all the influences of supernatural grace. A. B. Bruce indicates that a vine is a more winsome emblem of Jewish national life than a fig tree, and that Jesus employed the latter symbol for the purpose of lowering the pride of His hearers. The whole construction of the parable, however, suggests the special privilege of Israel, as God's chosen people.

*The Disappointment of the Proprietor.* One purpose dominated the mind of the "certain man" when he planted his fig tree in the vineyard and that was at the appointed time he might gather fruit. After all the care, time and money he had expended on his tree, he had every right to expect fruit. For three years successively he came looking anxiously for fruit, but disappointment overtook his natural and reasonable expectation. By the "three years," we are not to understand, as some writers suggest, that as a rule the tree bears fruit within three years of its being planted, but that the owner came the first year, the second and, then the third, and met with disappointment each time. "Three years" fruitlessness is proof of barrenness. Three fruitless years resulting in complete barrenness, hence the command to the vinedresser, "Cut it down!" The soil was too valuable to waste on a fruitless tree, so it must perish, and its room be given to another tree.

Entitled to expect fruit, the owner's just expectations were not realized. What is the interpretation of these three disappointing, fruitless years? Israel was the divine vineyard over which Jesus spent so much trouble during the "three years" of His earthly ministry. All through these years He had sought, by life, parable, miracle and discourse, to make Israel fruitful. Now and again there were signs of promise, but in the end there came His total rejection by the nation He had nurtured. But when He comes again the fig tree will blossom, and He will not be disappointed (Matthew 24:32, 33). Some writers interpret the "three years" as representing the whole course of Israel's history. Augustine reckoned that they stood respectively for the natural law, the written law, and grace. Theophylact hinted that these "three years" stood for Moses, the Prophets, Christ, or for childhood, manhood and old age in the individual. This we do know, Christ came expecting fruit from His own people and met with failure. He found corruption where He looked for holiness; contempt where He longed for reverence. The fig tree of Israel was willing to content itself with all the benefits of the sunshine and showers of divine privilege, but most unwilling to produce fruit for the Owner. So there came the command, "Cut it down!"

*The Delay Asked of the Proprietor.* Knowing that the owner of the vineyard had every reason to be disappointed over the progressively barren fig tree, the dresser or keeper of the vineyard begged for the tree's life. Interceding, he begged, "Lord, let it alone this year, till I shall dig about it, and dung it: and if it bear fruit, well: and if not, then after that thou shalt cut it down." *Let it alone this year also* — can we not feel "the throb of an intense emotion" in this plea? "Give me one year more," said the vine dresser, "to arrest this continual barrenness." He did not plead for the indefinite existence of a fruitless tree. He only asked for one more year in which to adopt the most stringent measures for stimulating the barren tree into fruitfulness. If under further treatment it bears fruit, then the vine dresser knew that the owner would gladly permit the tree to retain its privileged position; but if it persisted in its barrenness, then he would abandon it to its deserved fate. All that was asked for was a respite or postponement.

In the intercessory plea of the vine dresser we have an illustration of the reluctance of Jesus to let Israel go. On the cross He prayed for the fruitless nation rejecting Him, "Father, forgive them; for they know not what they do." In answer to this prayer, Peter and the other Apostles were sent with another opportunity of repentance and, as Habershon states it, "The book of Acts gives the history of 'this year also,' not a literal year, but an 'acceptable year of the Lord,' which was granted the fig

tree in answer to the prayer of the dresser of the vineyard." But such an extended period of grace was without avail, and rejection of the Jewish nation followed.

Can we not see in the dialogue of this short parable, a revelation of Jesus as the Intercessor? The owner of the vineyard wanted to destroy the tree, but the vine-dresser prayed for its continued life for another year. We must not stress this dialogue too far, making it represent God as the Owner full of wrath, and Jesus pleading with Him to turn from His anger. The Father and the Son are equally angry at sin, and both are alike full of love to the sinner. Thus any thoughts Christ had toward Israel were also the thoughts of the Father. Christ is an Intercessor who cares for man and prevails with God. His first plea is, *Spare.* Yet longsuffering as He is, Christ agrees with the Owner of the vineyard in cutting down the tree if the offer of further grace is rejected. The Son never denies the right of the Father to destroy. Both concur in offering salvation to the sinner, and in his judgment, if such a blood-bought salvation is finally refused.

*The Destruction Ordered by the Proprietor.* Because the vineyard and the tree planted in it belonged to the owner, and he had the moral and absolute right of expectation of fruit, he likewise had the punitive right of, as the owner, destroying anything barren and useless on his soil. How terrible is the decision coming from the Intercessor's life, "Thou shalt cut it down." If men let the day of grace run waste, even Jesus on the morrow of judgment will not plead for them any more. "There remaineth no more sacrifice for sin."

The divine fiat, *Cut it down,* was carried out in the decree for " the destruction of Jerusalem, and the removal of the Jews from their vineyard privileges, preparatory to, and in order to, the calling of the Gentiles." The stroke of justice was arrested for a season, for divine love was loath to let it fall upon the guilty. Perhaps the people interpreted the respite as an evidence that judgment would not fall upon them. "Because sentence against an evil work is not executed speedily, the hearts of the children of men are fully set in them to do evil" (Ecclesiastes 8:2; II Peter 3:3-10). The wilfully and finally unrepentant are suddenly destroyed, and that without remedy (Proverbs 29:1). For Israel ultimately the axe was laid at the root of the tree and it was hewn down and cast into the fire.

*Cut it down!* Such was the end of divine cultivation, divine expectation and divine disappointment. Such a sentence was a righteous one, for Israel, in spite of all her privileges, was a fruitless tree; and a fruitless tree was useless. It cumbered the ground, occupying room where another tree might have grown fruit abundant. Is there not in this parable a solemn warning for the Church, as well as for each professed member of it? Says Habershon, "The barren fig tree is a warning to a fruitless world, a fruitless sinner, a fruitless Church, or a fruitless believer." Because this is still the day of grace, sinners must be warned although they are spared from judgment. This year also, the sentence still hangs over them, *Cut it down!* In the light of this parable all who resolutely reject the overtures of divine mercy will be cut down as cumberers of the ground, and how terrible will be the doom of the Christless!

> But if we still His call refuse
>   And all His wondrous love abuse;
> Soon must He sadly from us turn,
>   Our bitter prayer for pardon spurn.
> Too late, too late, will be the cry,
> When Jesus of Nazareth has passed by.

# The Parable of the Ambitious Guest
## (Luke 14:1-11)

This remarkable chapter, containing as it does the incomparable "Table-Talk" of Jesus, while eating bread on the Sabbath Day, is conspicuous for its parabolic nature. Altogether it contains six parables, five of which are peculiar to Luke:

The Parable of the Ambitious Guest (14:1-11)
The Parable of the Feast (14:12-14)
The Parable of the Great Supper (14:15-24; see Matthew 22:1-14)
The Parable of the Tower (14:25-30)
The Parable of the King At War (14:31-33)
The Parable of the Savourless Salt (14:34-35. Matthew 5:13); Mark 9:50)

Several expositors dealing with *The Parable of the Great Supper,* employ the first two parables — *The Guest* and *The Feast* as part of same. But although all three were spoken at the same time in the same house, our Lord described three different occasions, namely: a wedding, a feast, a great supper. While it is evident that His conversation was all of one piece, and contained one main theme, we yet feel that distinction should be drawn between the figures of speech the Master skilfully used.

On the Sunday, perhaps the last one before Jesus died at Calvary, He went on invitation to the house of a Pharisee of high position. Sunday hospitality, as Campbell Morgan suggests, was one mark of degeneracy of the Hebrew people, and is "a mark of degeneracy today, very often, in the Christian Church. Our Lord went to this house. We can go to such gatherings, too, if we do what He did there." But Jesus was not invited to eat bread because His company was sincerely desired. He was offered hospitality that He might be watched by critical, cynical eyes. "They watched Him." The ulterior motive behind the invitation was what Jesus would do about the healing of the dropsical man on the Sabbath. Then the Pharisee and his crowd wanted to hear, at close quarters, what He could add to the after-noon table-conversation.

To all points and purposes, our Lord was there on exhibition. Neither the Pharisaical host nor his guests regarded

Him as one of themselves. It is not at all pleasant to be asked to a specially assembled company to be put on probation, to have one's every action and word weighed. But what those prejudice-blinded people forgot was that the One invited to partake of their hospitality was the omniscient Lord, and as such had a distinct advantage over them. They could not read *His* thoughts, but He could read *theirs,* and in the parables of this chapter He revealed the thoughts of their minds, and the sinister significance of their actions. That memorable Sunday afternoon, He dominated the company — *it* did not dominate Him. Permitting Himself to become the prey of the passing hour, He did not lower His ideals nor abandon His principles in order to sit "in well" with the rest. Invited as a Guest, He proved to be most unconventional in that He became the outspoken critic of the bad manners of host and guests alike.

After silencing His "watchers" on the matter of Sabbath Day healing, He uttered the parable about a wedding and of the right and wrong ways of inviting people to same. The word "marked" is an interesting one. The people watched Jesus, but He *marked* or watched how the bidden guests sought out the best position at the wedding. There was the struggle for precedence, prominence for oneself, rivalry for chief seats, thereby making secondary the proper purpose and pleasure of social intercourse. In His parable, in conjunction with what He had previously said about the Pharisees loving the uppermost seats in the synagogue (11:43), our Lord made clear that "self-emptying is the true secret of exaltation. Office seekers were excluded; those wanting the chief places were dismissed. Those not seeking were to have the chief places in social life."

Ellicott observes that our Lord's rebuke is hardly "a parable in our modern sense of the term, but is so called as being something more than a precept, and as illustrated by a half dramatic dialogue." Yet the Bible calls it a "para-

ble," and it must have proved itself a most effective one in that it revealed the difference between the *acquisition* of seats, and their *relegation.* It would seem as if it was the common practice for guests to seat themselves, hence, the scramble for the best ones. Turning to the guests of the wedding, Jesus, in exposing the false principles they acted on, said, "Lest a more honourable man than thou be bidden of him." Jesus was the most honorable Man at that Sunday afternoon gathering, and doubtless took the lowest place in the room thus illustrating, by action, the lesson of His parable, "Whosoever exalteth himself shall be abased, and he that humbleth himself shall be exalted" (see Philippians 2:9; I Peter 5:5). Our highest place is lying low at our Redeemer's feet (Proverbs 25:6, 7).

## The Parable of the Feast
### (Luke 14:12-14)

Here Jesus addresses Himself particularly to the host "that bade Him." While this paragraph was a continuation of our Lord's conversation on correct social manners, it stands out distinctly as a further parabolic illustration. Because it is a link in the chain of connected lessons, we cannot agree with Arnot that the previous parable, and the brief one before, are unnecessary to elucidate the significance of the greater parable of *The Supper* which follows. All three parables deal with the general theme of *hospitality.* In this parable of *The Feast,* which could have been a "dinner or a supper," (two words used respectively for the noon and the evening meal), Jesus gave his host a lesson on who to invite to a meal, namely, those poor folks who were not in a position to invite him back. The key of the parable is in the line, "Lest they also bid thee again, and a recompense be made thee." If the host invited only his rich friends, of course, he would expect them to offer him a like hospitality, but when people act on this basis they cut the nerve of true hospitality.

Looking over the guests that afternoon, Jesus quickly sensed the ostentatious hospitality, calculating on a return in kind. If any host desired to be blest and to be recompensed not here, but at "the resurrection of the just" (the first occurrence of the word *resurrection* in our Lord's teaching), then the gates of hospitality must be widened to admit those who, because of their poverty and physical disabilities, needed the feast, but who had nothing to offer in return save their sincere gratitude. Commenting on our Lord's pronouncement of blessing for those thus benevolent, Ellicott says, "On this point our Lord, while rebuking the pride and hypocrisy of the Pharisees, accepted the fundamental doctrine of their system (resurrection); and so furnished a precedent for Paul's conduct in Acts 23:6."

## The Parable of the Great Supper

(Luke 14:15-24)

This further parable, suggested by the meal at the Pharisee's house, is termed *great* because of the many invited and also because of the greatness of the One symbolized by the lord providing the supper. The parable itself arose out of the exclamation of one of the guests who listened to Christ's previous illustrations, "Blessed is he that shall eat bread in the kingdom of God." Expositors are divided as to what this exclamation really meant, and the spirit in which it was uttered. Some say that it was a genuine exclamation of admiration. Understanding the simple, yet searching, admonitions of Jesus, one of the company realizing the blessedness of those who practiced a hospitality destitute of self-exaltation and self-seeking, spoke as he did. He saw the beauty of a social order by the principles Jesus enunciated.

Other writers, however, reckon that the speaker betrayed a superficial idea of the Kingdom, his Pharisaic thought of it being a privilege only such as he could secure. His was a Pharisaic ignorance of the moral conditions of inherit-

ing the Kingdom and in His reply, Christ laid bare in the pungent story of the great banquet, the folly of the Pharisaic attitude toward the Kingdom of God. Wm. M. Taylor speaks of this man's fervent ejaculation as "holy humbug, absolute cant. The man was talking about that of which he knew nothing." But whether the man's outburst of a beatitude was sincere or supercilious, it furnished the occasion for Christ's matchless prophetic parable, which bears a strong resemblance to *The Parable of the Royal Marriage Feast* (Matthew 22:2) but which is clearly distinct and peculiar to Luke.

While both parables are symbolic of a *feast* to which men are invited, and from which they rudely absent themselves, the differences between the two are apparent. For instance:

*The Royal Marriage Feast* was spoken at an early date in our Lord's ministry; *The Great Supper,* at the end of His ministry during the Passion Week. The *former* was addressed to the multitude in the Temple; the *latter* to the guests in a private house. The *former* displays messengers treated with violence; the *latter* shows them receiving excuses. In the *former,* the invited are destroyed and their city burned; in the *latter,* despisers of the invitation are merely excluded. In the *former,* antagonism to Christ was mild; in the *latter,* it was more expressive and murderous. Then the episode of the guest without a wedding garment has no place in the parable of the Great Supper.

*The Provision of the Supper.* Men of rank and affluence in the East sent out two calls to a planned feast; the first was a preliminary one conveying the invitation and a hint to make all necessary preparation for accepting the invitation, and was received with satisfaction; the second call came later and intimated that the feast was now ready and that the invited should give up what they were engaged with and act upon the host's grace. In this parable, the second call was declined with sundry apologies.

Our Lord depicted a feast on a scale of great magnificence, provided by a person of wealth with the purpose of bringing people together for a season of mutual, agreeable and social fellowship. The provision was abundant, and the banquet was not for solitary pleasure. It was a *feast,* not a *funeral.* Giver and guests were to rejoice together. Has not God thus provided for mankind on a more magnificent scale, "a feast of fat things," at which all man's personal, social and spiritual necessities can be satisfied? God as our Host has provided, as a gift of His love and grace, the feast of His Kingdom for all who respond to His invitation.

*The Persons Invited to the Supper.* Who were the *many* invited by the Master of the house to the supper? Without doubt, the primary application of the call is to the Jewish people. The servant who went out with the first call symbolizes those God commissioned to call the Jews to prepare for the coming of the Messiah. Old Testament Prophets, and John the Baptist, pleaded with the officials of Israel to prepare for the coming feast, but such an invitation was ignored. Then the offer went out to the Gentiles with a great response, as *The Book of Acts* reveals. Like *The Parable of the Fig Tree,* this parable of *The Great Supper* was a parable of solemn judgment on God's chosen Nation. In the *former* parable, judgment was in the form of the destruction of Israel's national existence and predicted a doom which genuine repentance alone could avert. In the latter parable, judgment is in the form of exclusion from the blessings of Messianic grace, without any hope being offered of a place in the Kingdom. So, as Professor Salmond puts it: "The Supper is a figure of the rich grace which was to come to men by Christ. The Jews are those whom God designed to be its first participants. The first call is the earnest which the Jews had under the Old Testament, in contrast with the Gentiles, outside the theocracy, of the coming grace; and this

they used only as a thing of privilege, a note of superiority. The second call is the token of the realization of that grace and of Christ's actual invitation of the Kingdom which is not of this world; and this they put away from them because of its demands of repentance, faith, unworldliness and consecration. The place in the promised Kingdom of God, therefore, which they refuse, passes from them and . . . goes to others, even to the outcasts of the Gentiles."

*The Pretexts Given for Refusing to Attend the Supper. All* receiving the first invitation to the supper begged to be excused. The word *consent* is in italics which means that it is not in the original but was supplied by the translators to carry the sense of the passage. We can read it, "They were one in the excuse they made," with all three excuses being one in spirit and essence. All the invited were "animated by one spirit, moved by one impulse, under the influence of the same disposition." They had no intention of going to the supper. One writer suggests that in the refusal is the implication of hostility toward the host on the part of those who were bidden. Not liking the host inviting them, they made up excuses for refusing.

Let us examine the three excuses Jesus spoke of, which were taken from things lawful in themselves and in their own place. All three excuses were *pretexts.* With a little forethought, each person could have made arrangements that would have enabled him to go. But the real truth was, they did not want to go. They typify those Jews Jesus spoke of, "Ye *will* not come unto me, that ye might have life." The self-delusion of the trio was all the more insidious because the things they presented as excuses were proper in themselves, when kept in their own place.

*Excuse Number One.* "I have bought a piece of ground, and I must needs go and see it." As the man Jesus depicted was a Jew, we can hardly conceive of a *Jew* buying anything before seeing it. Surely, he would be the last person to buy "a pig in a poke." Further, if he had bought the ground without seeing it, how could he see what it was like in the *dark?* Seeing he was invited to a *supper,* which is a meal taken at night, daylight would be the best time to view his land. Not only so, having already bought it, he could wait until the next morning to examine it. Ground cannot run away. But the probability is that this man saw the land *before* he bought it and was more concerned about his investment than an invitation to a supper. He, therefore, remains a type of those whose large possessions necessitate all their attention, robbing them, thereby, of spiritual wealth. "How hardly shall they that have riches enter the kingdom."

*Excuse Number Two.* "I have bought five yoke of oxen, and I go to prove them." While the note of necessity is missing from this excuse, its tone is definite and final. Without any apology for refusing the invitation, this man announces his intention, "assuming there to be no doubt as to its validity and propriety." No explanation is forthcoming. He feels his oxen come first and assures himself that the host inviting him has no claim upon his time. Does he not represent those who are so absorbed in their occupations as to leave no leisure or opportunity for concerns of the soul? How tragic it is when affairs mercantile, agricultural, financial, clerical, or industrial leave us no time for God!

*Excuse Number Three.* "I have married a wife, and therefore I cannot come." The hollowness of this excuse is proved by the fact that it was no "stag party" to which the man had been invited. The host would know of the man's recent marriage and therefore included his wife in the invitation. Had he not been so selfish, he would have gone to the feast with his wife, giving her a pleasant night out. But no, he sent a paltry excuse couched in terse, harsh and rude language. This third man stands for those domestic cares and responsibilities controlling so much of our time

and thought. But marital union and family obligations, if rightfully and righteously undertaken, never keep us from God or from fellowship with His saints. The precious relationships of home are dearer and sweeter when the Lord is its Head.

In each case there was a secret unwillingness to partake of the feast. Neither of the parties had any desire to accept the invitation. Had they wanted to go, in spite of their respective obligations they would have said, "Yes, we'll come," for "Where there's a will there's a way." But the three excuses are species of the thorns that grow up and choke the Word. The excuses may differ in terms, as the things differ which engross the men for the time, in field, or mart, or house, with the last of the three being more blunt and rude than the others, but all three express the same satisfied immersion in worldly interests, the same preference of these to the host's grace. Multitudes today are invited to the gospel feast, but respond in the same way to the invitation as those Jesus described almost two millenniums ago. What those of our time fail to realize is that the invitation is from the King of kings to His royal table, and that the rejection of same constitutes the most aggravated form of disobedience.

*The Punishment for Refusal to Attend the Supper.* The master of the house was naturally wroth when the refusals were brought to him and resolved that others more responsive should take the places of those who had treated him so disrespectfully. "None of those men which were bidden shall taste of my supper." Those first invited guests represent the general rejection of Israel. There remained, however, "the remnant according to the election of grace" (Romans 11:5), treated differently by the Host. Although after seating the second group of guests there was yet room for more, the master, in his just indignation would not re-invite the first group who had dealt so discourteously with his warm invitations. They were exluded for no other reason than their own refusal to attend the Supper.

The element of righteous indignation is more strongly emphasized in the sister parable of the king's marriage feast for his son (Matthew 22:6, 7), "where the mere apathy of those who were invited passes into scornful outrage." If, in "the master of the house being angry," we have a reminder of God's displeasure over those who offer insult rather than gratitude, then how solemnized we ought to be over the fearfulness of falling into the hands of a living God. Sinners, who persistently and blatantly continue to reject the overtures of divine mercy, will tremble too late when they find themselves in the hands of an angry God. Once the doors of the gospel banquet are closed, Christ's rejectors will clamor in vain for admission.

*The Promise of Provision for the Needy at the Supper.* In the first parable of this chapter we thought of those self-seeking guests who selected their own places at the feast; here we have illustrated the choice of God in the kind of guests He desires at His table. In the first call, which was rejected, the simple invitation was *Come* (Luke 14:17). Now assistance is needed, so we read, *"Bring in"* (Luke 14:21). Then, for the third group it is, *"Compel* them to come in" (Luke 14:23).

*The first call* represents salvation offered to the Jew, and his rejection of the Saviour. *The second call* to the poor, maimed, halt and blind, symbolizes the Gentile sinners and harlots who warmly welcomed the King's Son and pressed eagerly into His Kingdom. *The third call* was to a yet lower class, tramps and squatters whose only home was the highways and hedges, who represent the wanderers of the outlying Gentile world, the world's "broken earthenware," upon whom moral compulsion has to be used. This is the constraint, equivalent to the love of Christ, which Paul brought to bear upon men (II Corinthians 5:14). Thank God, there is room for the worst! None are too bad to sit at the royal table.

But whether good or bad, the only right of entrance to the feast is that of grace. Gate-crashers cannot enter God's banquet hall. What a motley crowd the redeemed of all ages represents! Millions of them, spiritually impoverished and disabled, accepted the royal invitation, "Come unto Me," and are now eating bread in the Kingdom of God. Wonderful though, is it not, that although myriads of needy souls have entered the banqueting house, "yet there is room" for more? Would that multitudes more could be seen availing themselves of the gracious opportunity of sitting down with the Master of the house! On the part of those of us who are in, there must be the exercise of every form of persuasion, and of sanctified force to bring the outcasts into the feast where the Master's provision is "enough for each, enough for all, enough for evermore."

# The Parable of the Tower Builder
## (Luke 14:25-30)

The setting of this brief yet arresting parable is to be found in our Lord's teaching of self-renunciation as the one indispensable condition of discipleship. All who taste of His supper (Luke 14:24), must count the cost of full fellowship with Him. The demand for our whole heart is in stronger form than in a similar, previous appeal (Matthew 10:37-39), and is here addressed not only to His disciples, but to the great multitudes of eager would-be followers. As the bearing of His own cross was becoming every day "more clear and terrible in its growing nearness," His appeal to all who desired to follow Him to bear *their* cross, took on a deeper significance.

Actually, the three parables and an exhortation found in verses 25-35 form a connected whole. "They follow in natural order and sequence," says H. T. Sell, "and are dovetailed, the one into the other, with rare artistry and unerring craftsmanship." All through this portion, the same, main lesson is emphasized, namely, the nature and influence of true discipleship. This is why three times over we have the authoritative pronouncement, "cannot be my disciple" (Luke 14:26, 27, 33). Christ's demand is far-reaching. Those who would follow Him all the way must be prepared to *hate,* or love less, "father, and mother, and wife, and children, and brethren, and sisters, yea, and his own life also." Loyalty to our Lord must be above the highest and finest and noblest loyalties of earthly love. All natural loves and the love of self, and of life, must be subordinate to our love to Him who must be first in our life.

To enforce His demand, Christ gave the two forceful Parables of a Building and a Battle. In a telling fashion Campbell Morgan compares and contrasts, and develops the idea that building a Tower is *constructive* work — fighting a battle is *destructive* work. Separating the two parables, let us endeavor to understand the symbolic significance of the tower-builder. If you are a preacher of the Gospel be sure to read C. H. Spurgeon's masterly sermon on this parable in which he deals at some length with these three main points:

1. True Religion Is a Costly Thing;
2. Wisdom Suggests That Before We Enter Upon It We Should Estimate the Cost;
3. Cost What It May, It Is Worth the Cost.

In his introduction to this sermon on *Counting the Cost,* this famous gospel preacher, discussing our Lord's winnowing out process, says that "The Master was far too wise to pride Himself upon the number of His converts; He cared rather for quality than quantity. He rejoiced over one sinner that repented, but ten thousand sinners who merely professed would have given Him no joy whatever. His heart longed after the real, He loathed the counterfeit; He panted after the substance, and the shadow did not content Him."

With His knowledge of local matters, it is quite likely that Christ's parable of the Tower was suggested by a recent fact. Pilate, perhaps, began to build an aqueduct, or tower of some sort, but he had not been able to finish. Failing to count the cost and not being able to use money from the Temple treasury, Pilate may have been at the end of his resources, and the building project probably had to be abandoned. How often this folly has been repeated by those who had not the wisdom to calculate all that would be necessary for the completion of a project! History can point to many unfinished towers, startling monuments to the folly of unpreparedness.

The application of the parable is not hard to find. An unfinished life is a more tragic spectacle than a cement foundation without a building. Too many are like John Bunyan's *Pliable* who turned back, and who, like the builder in the parable, failed to count the cost before he started to lay the foundation, and was ridiculed for his shameful failure. Paul had to rebuke those in the Galatian Church who began in the Spirit and ended up in the flesh. "Ye did run well, who did hinder you?" Failure to adequately count the cost of following Christ results in an unfinished life.

That which costs nothing is worth nothing. The discipleship to which Christ calls us means a life in which His claims must have the pre-eminence. If He is not Lord *of* all, then He is not Lord *at* all. But if we count the cost of a full surrender to His royal claims we may count, also, on all the grace, aid and succor our complete identification with Him will necessitate. In all this costliness of devotion to the divine will and purpose, Jesus left us an example that we should follow His steps. He never asks of us what He has not done Himself. He has every right to ask us to leave our father — He left His own Father, and the Father's house, when He came from Heaven to earth. His earthly mother, Mary, had a secondary place in His concern. Did He not rebuke her with the question, "Wist ye not that I must be about My Father's business?"

He knew all about the shame, contempt, humiliation, and anguish associated with a life lived in the will of God.

Why did He leave His Father's abode? Was it not to build the tower of His Church, the plans of which were designed in a past eternity? But both the Father and the Son counted the cost of building such a tower, which the gates of hell could not destroy. The gigantic cost was the voluntary humiliation and atoning death of the Son. Such a cost was settled upon before Jesus took upon Himself the likeness of our flesh, because when He came, it was as the Lamb slain from before the foundation of the world. Thus over the road of true discipleship we can see the blood-marks of Him who calls us to follow Him, even as He followed the Father. Then in the matter of completion He is our Exemplar. He knew all about the task He had been sent into the world to accomplish, and in spite of demons and men, fulfilled it. With what triumph He could cry with a loud voice, "It is finished!" and pray, "Father, I have finished the work Thou gavest me to do." Today, if we desire His best, we can have it on the terms stated in this parable. For the kind of *disciples* He must have, there are no bargain prices.

## The Parable of the King Going to War
(Luke 14:31, 32)

This parable continues the theme of the previous one, namely, counting the cost. The motto of Von Moltke, the great military strategist was, "First weigh, then venture," which is the policy both builder and king must pursue. With the man building the tower, the cost is reckoned in money; with the king, the cost covers the men required to conquer his foes. The first represents deliberation and adequate preparation; the second calls for stamina and fighting strength to face a foe with twice the strength we possess. The king whom Jesus depicted was going to make war with another king against tremendous

odds. Would he be able to meet the "twenty thousand" coming against him with his "ten thousand"? The king had to give much thought whether his every soldier would be equal to two of the enemy. If he does not have men of quality to overcome superior forces, before long there will be an embassage from the other side coming to the king, with conditions of a peaceful surrender.

As a King, Jesus looked out on the crowd of would-be soldiers and tested them as to their quality. Would they know how to appropriate the mighty spiritual resources enabling them to win His battles? As the Son of God, He was going forth to war against Satan and his legions; would these around Him be fit enough to follow in His train? Do you never wonder how many responded to His vibrant challenge, "He that hath ears to hear, let him hear"? As soldiers of the King we are not to be discouraged by the mighty foes before us. Heaven is not always on the side of big battalions. One *with* God is always in the majority.

But we must not lose sight of the fact that the central thought in this parable is not the heroism implied in the king's proposal to fight a superior force. The issue at stake is not the outcome of the battle, whether victory or defeat, but the willingness and deliberation to *count the cost*. Such a venture must not be undertaken in hot blood, rashly, or with inconsiderate haste. If it is, then there will be disaster, and all will be lost. Are we, as Christian soldiers marching to war, cognizant of what such a war means? Our enemies — the world, the flesh, the devil — are too strong for us, but not for the King beneath whose banner we fight. Through Him, we are more than conquerors. "So fight I," said Paul, "not as one that beateth the air." The life to which Christ calls us is not one of slippered ease. The good fight of faith must be fought against principalities and powers. Hardness must be endured as valiant soldiers of Jesus Christ. All that true discipleship entails must be accepted. Its guerdon must be faced with due regard to the battle and the toil. Then when the King comes back, His chaplet of reward will be ours (Revelation 2:10).

## The Parable of Lost Possessions
(Luke 15)

Usually this renowned chapter of the Bible is broken up by writers and preachers, and dealt with as containing three precious distinct parables: *The Lost Sheep* (1-7), *The Lost Silver* (8-10), *The Lost Son* (11-32). Actually, however, the whole chapter is but *one* parable having three pictures. There is no break in the verses. One illustration flows into the other. So when we read, "He spake this parable unto them" (Luke 15:3), the singular form *"this* parable" means that the entire chapter constitutes the particular parable. While there are succeeding stages in the parable, there is no break in it. The illustrations Jesus used in it merge and blend.

F. W. Boreham, in his delightful small volume on the immortal story of *The Prodigal Son,* has an enlightening chapter dealing with "The Trilogy of Jesus" in which he says that the three incomparable parables in this chapter are not isolated drawings but three panels of one picture. What we have here are not so much as three parables, but one parable with three aspects. By means of this triune parable, Jesus set forth the supreme and sublime fact that as the Son of Man He came into the world to seek and save the lost. Usually, the parables of Jesus were simple sketches, each standing out with their own distinctness. Here we have His notable triad presenting a fascinating study in values.

Charles H. Spurgeon in his great, evangelistic *Sermons* on Luke 15, expresses a similar thought as to the unity of this chapter, so full of grace and truth. He says: "The three parables recorded in this chapter are not repetitions; they all declare the same main truth, but each one reveals a different phase of it. The three parables are three sides of a pyramid of gospel doctrine, but there is a different inscription upon each. Not only in the similitude, but also in the teaching covered by the similitude, there is variety, progress, enlargement, discrimination. We need only to read attentively to discover that in this trinity of Parables, we have at once unity of essential truth and distinctness of description. Each one of the parables is needful to the other, and when combined they present us with a far more complete exposition of their doctrine than could have been conveyed by any one of them."

Before taking up a study of these three pictures separately, noting the special features of each, let us deal with them collectively for an understanding of the repetition of the same doctrine taught under different metaphors. Concern over something lost, and joy at the recovery of that which was lost, is the prominent note of each simile our Lord used. At the heart of this masterpiece of parabolic literature, the sheep, the coin, the son were all lost and all worth saving. It was serious to lose a sheep, worse to lose money, and worst of all to lose a son. A sheep is valuable, money more valuable, but man is the most valuable of all.

*The sheep* was lost and likely knew it was lost. It had a vague idea that it was without companionship and the care of the shepherd. Because of curiosity it strayed. Seeing a gap in the hedge it wandered from the rest, or nibbling away at the pasture, it drifted aimlessly in the opposite direction and became separated from the shepherd and the other sheep. Such a sheep represents the stupid, foolish, unthinking kind of wanderer from God. Happily it was overtaken by the seeking shepherd and brought back to the fold.

*The coin* was lost, but being without life, had no consciousness or sensation of being lost. Further, its lost condition occasioned neither discomfort or anxiety. The silver piece was lost, not because of any inferiority in its composition or mintage. It was lost either because it was badly handled or unconsciously dropped. We have here symbolized those lost sinners who are largely ignorant of themselves and passive in the hands of those with whom they associate. Such are easily handled by stronger personalities. The coin remained stationary until found where it had been dropped.

*The son* was lost, deliberately, wilfully and consciously, and the loss of a man is "the dizziest pinnacle of tragedy." The prodigal was guilty of an inexcusable waywardness. His departure from his father and home was self-determined and daring. But father and prodigal moved toward each other and found each other again.

Essayist Boreham remarks that *Mathematics* are cold and unconvincing and cannot explain everything.

The lost sheep represented 1%
    loss — one out of a hundred
The lost silver meant a 10% loss—
    one out of ten
The lost son was a 50% loss —
    one out of two.

But the shepherd sought his lost sheep, as if it had been the only one he possessed. The other ninety and nine sheep were left behind as if they did not matter.

The woman felt the loss of her coin as if she had no other silver piece. It was no comfort telling her that she still had the other nine pieces safe. Since she was poor, much depended on finding the lost coin and so she searched diligently for it.

The father was heart-broken over the loss of his younger son. It was not enough to tell him that he still had another son with no desire at all to leave home. His father's heart went out to the missing one in spite of his wilfulness and wickedness.

Further, as Spurgeon, Habershon and other writers remind us, the three Persons of the blessed Trinity are linked together in the recovery of the lost. In the *first* picture we have Christ, as the Good Shepherd, laying down His life to save lost sheep. In the *second* picture, the woman sweeping the house for her lost coin, is an illustration of the Holy Spirit working through His Church (the saved) to save others. The Spirit's work naturally follows the Shepherd's task. In the *third* picture, God is suggested by the father seeking his lost child. Here the Divine Father is before us in all His abundant love to seek and save the lost.

Thus all three pictures are needed and are complementary. Spurgeon has the illuminating comment: "We have sometimes heard it said—here is the prodigal received as soon as he comes back, no mention being made of a Saviour who seeks and saves him. Is it possible to teach all truths in one single parable? Does not the first one speak of the shepherd seeking the lost sheep? Why repeat that which has been said before? There is no hint of the operation of a superior power upon the prodigal's heart. Of his own free will, he said, 'I will arise, and go unto my father.' But the Holy Spirit's work had been clearly described in the second parable, and needed not to be introduced again."

Looking, then, at the three pictures set out before us, they symbolize the whole compass of salvation, but each one apart sets forth the work in reference to one or other of the Divine Persons of the Trinity —

*The shepherd,* with much pain and
    self-sacrifice, seeks the reckless,
    wandering sheep.
*The woman* diligently searches for the
    insensible, but lost, piece of silver.
*The father* receives his wandering, re-
    turning son with the kiss of recon-
    ciliation.

Thus, "the three life-sketches are one, and one truth is taught by the whole three, yet each one is distinct from the other and by itself instructive. What God hath joined together let no man put asunder."

An understanding of the occasion of this matchless, three-tier parable will enable us to appreciate its central message. An old divine has said that the key of the parable hangs on the front door, meaning that the contemptuous remark, "This man receiveth sinners, and eateth with them" (15:2), supplies us with the reason for the parable. As Jesus neared the end of His public ministry, "publicans and sinners" were drawn to Him, and He to them. His just, indignant treatment of the hypocritical Pharisees gave the outcasts more courage to approach Him. Since they were sincere in their desire to follow Him, Jesus freely identified Himself with them. Unlike the Pharisees, the sinners knew they were *sinners* and needed to be saved. So, in response to the Pharisaical taunt about receiving sinners, Jesus portrayed in His parable the effort of the Trinity to seek and to save them.

By the parable, the Pharisees themselves stood condemned. Supposedly spiritual interpreters of the Old Testament, with all its prophecies of a Messiah who would come into the world to save sinners, the Pharisees found fault with such a blessed task they saw Jesus accomplishing. In the parabolic illustration of the self-righteous, coldhearted elder brother, Jesus exposed the utter lack of love and compassion of the Pharisee toward those whose sin was conspicuous, and who, therefore, needed tender dealing and forgiving grace.

### The Shepherd and the Lost Sheep.

The first part of our Lord's parable must not be confused with *The Parable of the Lost Sheep* already considered (Matthew 18:12-14), even though the two are told in similar vein. In each case, the connection is different, as is the purpose. In Matthew, Jesus described God's care over the least, the little ones. Here in Luke, He magnifies divine grace to the lost and that their recovery is the desire of the Trinity. The sympathy of heaven with the love that seeks and recovers the lost was Christ's last rebuke of the murmurings of the Pharisees, and the highest vindication of His grace to

the outcast. Thus, all three stories "were addressed to those censorious representatives of official Jewish religionism."

We cannot agree with S. H. Lang that the three pictures of this chapter contain no features that are true of the unregenerate sinner. "Primarily therefore the picture is of a backslider and his restoration." In support of his theory, Lang quotes Isaiah 53:6, "*All* we, like sheep, have gone astray," and also Psalm 119:176; Romans 3:10 etc. "Sinners are not the Lord's possession." But seeing He created sinners they are His. "*All* souls are mine." While the writer in question is justified in making any application he deems fit, the fact remains that the parable was uttered by our Lord to reveal the divine heart toward "publicans and sinners" (Luke 15:1, 2), and not toward the regenerated, although, of course, these have become recipients of divine grace.

Hillyer H. Straton says that we might name the three stories of this chapter, "The Parables of the Four Verbs — *Lose, Seek, Found, Rejoice.*" These four verbs certainly summarize for us the illustration of the sacrificial Shepherd. Those who heard Jesus use this figure of speech both of Himself, and of His great work were conversant with the Old Testament usage of the figure. Moses and David were shepherds by occupation and also functioned in the same capacity as leaders of God's flock. Then there were the many prophetic references to One who would appear as the Ideal Shepherd, and who would look out upon the lost multitudes as sheep having no shepherd (Psalm 23:1; Ezekiel 3:4; Zechariah 11:16, 17, etc.).

When the Lord appeared among men, He claimed for Himself the title of the Good Shepherd. Here in Luke He *seeks* the lost sheep; in John 10, He *dies* for them. The lost sheep in question are not regenerate backsliders, as Lang affirms, but unregenerate sinners seeing that the Good Shepherd gave His life for the *ungodly.* He came to save those who were lost in sin. Those described as straying sheep by Isaiah (53:6), were those who had hid their faces from the Lord, despised and rejected Him and for whose iniquities the Shepherd was to be smitten of God and afflicted.

What are we to understand by the reference to "the ninety and nine" left behind? Jesus could not have had in mind the self-righteous Pharisees when He spoke of "the ninety and nine" for of these He said that they were *just* and had *no need* of *repentance* (Luke 15:7). But the Pharisees were far from being *just,* and because of their hatred of Christ they certainly had need to repent. Is there not a hint here of our Lord's descent from heaven, when He left behind the angelic host who had kept their first estate, and who ceaselessly served God before His Throne, and who, therefore, had no need of repentance? This world, "a world of sinners lost and ruined by the fall," was the one sheep necessitating the incarnation and death of the Shepherd.

Further, as joy of grace is one of the keynotes of the chapter, the question might be asked, "Why should there be *more* joy over the repenting sinner than over the legions of unfallen angels?" The answer is evident. The Shepherd never shed His blood for angels. Having never sinned, they had no need of the sacrificial work of the cross. To the angelic host, the life and death of Jesus form one of the solemn mysteries of the Godhead upon which they meditate with reverence. But repenting sinners represent the reward of the Shepherd's compassion, love and sacrifice. In their recovery, He sees of the travail of His soul and is satisfied, and because He is satisfied the angels rejoice with Him as sinners are saved. As to the "friends and neighbors" rejoicing with the Shepherd, these may symbolize "the spirits of the just made perfect," as well as the saved in any assembly of the Lord's people whose joy is unbounded when sinners turn to Him in penitence and faith. May we know what it is to share the Shepherd's concern for the lost! If we faith-fully assist Him in their recovery, then when He comes as the Chief Shepherd, reward will be ours.

## The Woman and the Lost Coin
### (Luke 15:8-10)

In these next three verses Jesus addresses a second question to His hearers, and the simple word *either,* or, as Goebels translates it, *or,* connects the two sections or pictures, the second one being a continuation of the central truth declared in the picture of the shepherd. The shepherd seeking his sheep symbolizes divine *tenderness;* the humble woman searching for her silver piece with much diligence and painstaking portrays divine *earnestness.*

After using the illustration of a *man* who had lost one of his sheep, Jesus now turns to a *woman* who seeks her lost possession. There may be something in the suggestion that the variation was made to interest a different class of hearers, namely, the women who were listening attentively to Jesus, and who had little experience in going after the sheep that were lost. Then, as He was dealing with the solemn task of rescuing the lost, we can see in His use of the woman, the way in which her "feminine virtues and graces are needed for the deliverance of souls that have fallen — patience, and diligence, and minute observation — not less than what we think of as the more manly qualities of courage, and enterprise, and endurance."

Further, it is far more natural to a woman than a man to search for something lost in the house. If she was a poor woman, having to live frugally and eke out her housekeeping money, one silver piece out of ten would constitute a considerable loss. Hence her concern about finding the lost coin.

There is another explanation for the woman's earnest search, however. Campbell Morgan hints at it. As the piece of silver in question represents less than a shilling in English money, or an American *quarter,* it does not seem feasible that the woman should search so diligently for such a small amount. The somewhat impressive explanation Morgan gives is this: "The women of that time often wore upon their brow a frontlet that was called *semedi*. It was made up of coins, in themselves largely valueless . . . But it was a coin that had stamped upon it the image of authority. The frontlet signified betrothal or the marriage relationship. Whether it was of little monetary value or not, it was of priceless value to the woman who wore it. This is evidenced by the fact that she sought it diligently, sweeping the house until she found it." Because the coin had sentimental value, and was an article of charm, and adornment, the woman's search for it was earnest and thorough. She was anxious to recover that which perfected the symbolism of her frontlet.

As the special features of the shepherd seeking the lost sheep have a spiritual significance, so here with the woman and her coin. While the outstanding lesson may be the same in each parable, there is not mere repetition which would be superfluous. Essentially new features are added under another figure, with our Lord giving more than a mere ornamental variation of imagery. For instance, the sheep strayed from the *fold* and was lost in the *wilderness;* the coin was lost in the *house* and lost, not by its own volition, but through the carelessness or inattentiveness of the owner. *Lost at home!* Does this not imply the possibility of the soul, precious in God's sight, being lost even though in a Christian home, or in a visible Christian Church? Are there those living where we do, and attending the Church we do, who are not saved, who continue lost because of indifference on our part? Have we not need to emulate the diligence of the woman in the parable and seek more earnestly the salvation of the lost who are nearest to us where we live and labor? As Jesus was illustrating His own saving ministry among men, He tried to make those heartless Pharisees see that if a woman could exert all possible care in finding a coin of little worth,

was He not justified in taking all possible care in winning back to Himself lost sinners whose souls were worth more than silver? Further, if the woman was so elated over the recovery of the coin she herself had lost, as to call in her neighbors and friends to rejoice with her, had not Jesus every right to ask us to rejoice with Him, and with the angels, over the restoration of those repenting of their sin?

## The Father and the Lost Son
(Luke 15:11-32)

Luke makes an easy transition from the second parable to the third with the words, "And He said." Although independent of the first two parables, this third one does not interrupt the continuous flow. All three were spoken to the same persons on the same occasion and emphasize the same central message, namely, the dispensation of divine grace and mercy. The sheep is wandering, the silver is lost, the prodigal is perishing. The first two parables are in question form; this one is in a positive narrative form, with our Lord relating an incident from common daily life. He might have had in mind a father and his two sons, of whom He knew only too well.

This third picture has been described in many commendatory ways as the "crown and pearl of all parables," as "the Gospel within the Gospel." George Murray said of this parable, which remains without equal in all literature, that it is "the most divinely tender and most humanly touching story ever told on earth." Charles Dickens described it as "the finest short story ever written." Of this mighty spiritual figure Cosmo Lang wrote, "Regarded as a mere fragment of human literature, it is an incomparable expression of the patience and generosity with which human love bears with and triumphs over human wilfulness and folly." Arnot says of it, "Among the parables, that of the Prodigal is remarkable for the grandeur of the whole, and the exquisite beauty of the parts." A.

R. Bond suggests that it might be called "The Parable of the Bereaved Father — it is unequalled in literature for its tenderness, grace and pathos. Jesus knew how to touch the heart-strings." At the outset, let us note that the Bible does not call the son who left home a *prodigal*.

The two-fold purpose of this parable, "standing unique, towering in magnificence and beauty above all human composition, ancient or modern," is hinted at in the first two verses of the chapter, namely, Christ's love and compassion for lost sinners, and His rebuke of the Pharisees for their censoriousness toward sinners. The parable opens with a reference to *two* sons, who were not twins, and certainly not a pair. John and Judas were two of the disciples, but not a pair as David and Jonathan were. The younger son, the prodigal, will always describe those in disgrace, just as the elder son will always remain a pattern of propriety.

Broadly speaking, the parable is in three stages: the rejection of home; the return to home; the reception at home. An old writer puts it — *at home; away from home; back home.* We see the prodigal sick of home, homesick, home bent. His two vastly different requests were *Give me — Make me.* Let us take the first request for his portion of his father's goods, which he knew was his in virtue of the Law (Deuteronomy 21:17). According to this ancient Jewish Law of Inheritance, if there were but two sons, the elder would receive two portions, the younger the third of all movable property. A man could, during his life time, dispose of all his property by gift if he chose. If the share of the younger children was to be diminished by gift or taken away, the disposition must be made by a person presumably near death. No one in good health could diminish, except by gift, the legal portion of the younger son. In the parable, the younger son was thus entitled by law to his share, though he had no right to claim it during his father's lifetime.

Thus, as Edersheim expresses it, "The request must be regarded as asking a favour," which the father granted, with both sons receiving their lawful portion.

With a craving for false independence, the younger son took his portion and went abroad. The publican and sinners *drew near* to Jesus but the rebellious young man deliberately went into a far country and became a prodigal. The "far country," Augustine tersely said, "is forgetfulness of God." It represents that state of being Paul described as "alienated from the life of God." All the dissatisfied young man wanted to do was to fill his belly and live for the satisfaction of his sensual and sexual desires. He "devoured his living with harlots." But with the loss of all he had, there was the loss of so-called friends, for "no man gave unto him." He had spent plenty on them, but they forsook him in his dire need. How true this feature is to life! Reduced to poverty, he was forced to seek work and found it in the piggery of an alien. The Jews listening to Jesus must have shuddered at these words, "to feed swine," for to a Jew, there could not be a greater depth of debasement. Yielding to his baser appetites brought the prodigal so low that he felt like satisfying his hunger by eating the husks, or bean-like pods of the carob-tree, on which the swine fed.

When men — and women — identify themselves with brute appetites, and like beasts, feed upon the world's garbage, how depraved they become! Happily the story changes, and the prodigal "came to himself," and then "came to his father." Perishing with hunger, the young fellow thought of home with all its comforts and well-filled larder. Extreme hardness induced reflection. Vincent in his *Word Studies* says that "this striking expression — came to himself — puts the state of rebellion against God as a kind of madness. It is a wonderful stroke of art, to represent the beginning of repentance as the return of a sound consciousness." Wretchedness stirred reason, and a sinner is half way on the road to salvation when he comes to himself. There is an old Jewish saying to the effect that "when Israel is reduced to the carob-tree, they become repentant."

The resolve of the deluded, beggared youth to return home brings us to his next request, *"Make me."* Preparing his plea, he arose and came to his father, who must have been watching for the return of his prodigal boy, for "when he was yet a great way off, his father saw him," which seems to imply that he saw his son, before he saw his father. What a precious touch Jesus gave to the narrative when He said that the excited father *ran* to meet his hungry, ragged, footsore boy! So weary, the prodigal could not run, but his aging father forgot his age and dignity and ran to meet the wanderer. *Compassion* here, means, his vitals moved; the father's heart beat quickly. What a glimpse we have here into the heart of God! In His eagerness to welcome the returning, repentant sinner He goes more than half way to meet him.

The prodigal was not able to express all the plea he had prepared to present on meeting his father. His kisses smothered the lips of the prodigal, who was back home, and that was all that mattered. The original implies that the father "covered him with kisses." Often he had looked out along the road for this moment, and now his outgushing pity and unrestrained, overflowing manifestation of tender fatherly embrace were proofs of his unextinguished love for his lost son. How suggestive this is of God's welcome for the penitent sinner! Once enfolded in His fatherly arms, there is no casting up of sins. God "kisses the past into forgetfulness."

After the disillusionment, destitution, and degradation of the far country, the prodigal felt he was no longer worthy to be called a son and made up his mind to ask his father to make him as one of his hired servants. But his speech of contrition was never completed. The father never received that part of the plea, and as soon as his son was safe home, he re-instated him into full sonship. His rags were removed, and he was given "the best robe," or "the *first* robe" — symbolic of the vesture of righteousness which the repentant, believing sinner receives from God. This best robe in the house meant that the son was re-instated to his original position and rights. Do you recall the lines of George Macdonald in his *Masterpieces of Religious Verse?*

> My Lord, I have no clothes to come to thee;
> My shoes are pierced and broken with the road;
> I am torn and weathered, wounded with the goad,
> And soiled with tugging at my weary load.
> And more I need Thee. A very prodigal
> I stagger into Thy presence, Lord of me.

The signet-ring, symbol of the union of heart father and son experienced, was placed on the finger; and shoes adorned his almost naked feet. Only members of the household wore shoes — slaves were barefooted. Thus, these were the signs of the prodigal's restoration to the standing of a son. Then the calf, fattened for some special feast of joy, was brought forth. Jesus, knowing rural manners, used this feature to describe the father's joy over his son's recovery. Commentators describe the spiritual significance of these details in different ways. The robe — the righteousness of Christ. The ring — the token of authority and assurance. The shoes — the badge of sonship. The feast — the Lord's Supper. Of the feast, Arnot says, "It indicates the joy of a forgiving God over a forgiven man, and the joy of a forgiven man in a forgiving God."

The announcement of welcome, so full of wonderful pathos, is full of the moral significance of the son's return. He came back another person from what he was when he left home. Imagine the joy of the father in receiving him now, indeed a son, once dead, now alive; once lost to heaven and himself, but now found alike by both the heavenly Father and the earthly one. Says Goebels, "In all three parables a moral state is *symbol-ized* by being lost, and a moral conversion by being found; and this is especially conspicuous in the third parable, where the being lost is identical with the departure from the father into the strange country by the son's own choice, and the being found with the return to the father by his own resolve."

Because of the son's self-chosen alienation and shame, his father thought of him as "dead." Perhaps his physical death would have been easier to bear. In the realm of grace, repentance means the passing from the death of sin to the life of righteousness. "Lost" and "found," common to all three pictures, are likewise expressive of the sinner's abandonment of the far country of sin for the Father's home. Butterick says that his word *lost* "recurs like a ball to warn and plead . . . Jesus seldom called people *sinners;* He called them *lost"* (Matthew 10:6; 15:24; 18:11; John 17:12). Countless multitudes are still lost in sin, but our God is the God of the lost, and longs for their return.

The merriment of those at home, symbolic of those outward signs of gladness in the hearts of God's children, when sinners are saved, aroused the curiosity of the elder brother as he was returning from the fields. This last picture Jesus added was directed against the Pharisees and Scribes, the cold-hearted ritualists who criticized His sympathy for sinners. The two sons referred to at the beginning of the parable (Luke 15:11), now reappear, and what a contrast in character they present. Into the merry, jubilant harmony of the household because of a loved one restored to virtue, home and blessedness, comes the jarring discord caused by the grating notes of fiendish pride and jealousy. We might feel that such a sour ending should have been left out of such a lovely story.

This story of the prodigal begins with the younger son away from home, and his elder brother staying at home (although he was never "at home"), but it ends with the younger son home, and

the elder one refusing to enter the home. Actually, the latter was as much a prodigal as his brother. The younger son came back from a far country to a father's heart and home. The elder went out into the far country of smug self-satisfaction and sullen resentment. The Bible says that "he would not go in"; it does not say whether he ultimately repented of his attitude and went in to complete a happy family circle.

The contempt this elder son felt is seen in the fact that he never came into the house to ask his father what all the merriment was about but accosted "one of the servants." That the joy of the household was alien and indeed repellent to the elder son is exhibited in his treatment of his brother. Twice over, the happy father said, "Thy brother." *Brother,* this harlot-loving prodigal, my brother — never! So in a churlish, contemptuous way, he said to his father, "This *thy* son." Scorn, bitterness, and bitter sarcasm are packed into the elder brother's recall of his brother's sin in its coarsest and darkest colors. Says Ellicott: "the very turn of the phrase, 'this thy son,' speaks of a concentrated malignity."

The father wanted his older boy to receive the prodigal back as a "brother," just as he had taken him back to his heart as a "son." How touching is the final entreaty of the father, in which he assured the older boy who had never caught the spirit of his father or his father's house, "Son, thou art ever with me, and all that I have is thine," or more literally, "All mine is thine." But the Bible is silent as to whether the tender appeal for brotherly love succeeded.

There is no doubt that Jesus meant His Pharisaic murmurers to see in the sketch He gave of this *elder brother,* "the unloveliness of their hard, unfilial spirit," as Salmond expresses it. "If the former parables show them how they ought to have acted, this one shows them, it is rightly observed, how they had acted." In the whole range of literature there can be found no exhibition of stern, but courteous rebuke, at once so simple and effective, as the portrayal of the proud, sullen, cold, self-righteous attitude of the Scribes and Pharisees in the figure of the elder brother. As Arnot puts it: "All the excesses of the prodigal will not shut him out of heaven, for he came repenting to his father: but all the virtues of the elder brother will not let him into heaven, for he cherished pride in his heart, and taunted his father for overlooking his worth." This parable clearly teaches that the Saviour calls sinners and not the self-righteous to repentance — although the latter need to repent as much, if not more so, than the former. Summarizing the important lessons of *The Parable of the Prodigal Son* (which has done more to win the prodigals and down-and-outs of human society, more than any other part of the Bible) we ask three questions.

*Who Is the Father in the Story?* Do we not see in the tender, forgiving father our Father in heaven, whose love is broader than the measure of man's mind? Do we not have here the most winsome and attractive picture of a forgiving God ever drawn on earth? What a Gospel this is to preach that we have a loving God eager to forgive utterly, and to restore sinners to fellowship with Himself — to take prodigals from the dunghill and place them among princes!

*Who Is the Prodigal in the Story?* All who reject a Father's love and waste their God-given substance in riotous living are *prodigals*. People do not have to be dressed in rags to qualify as prodigals. They are often found among those who can afford silks and satins, but whose heart and ways are given over to gross fleshliness. As Butterick reminds us, "The far country is far in many directions; it is far in motives rather than in miles. Even a church-man may be an exile from his Father's house."

The self-righteous are as lost in God's sight as the worse profligates alive. In the chapter in which we have considered the word *lost* in each parable, it is not so much related to the condition of what

is lost, as to the agony upon the heart of the one who has lost. The shepherd suffered more than the straying sheep; the woman suffered more than her silver which was destitute of life and feeling; the father had a depth of agony either of his sons could not share. It is thus with God, whose loving heart is moved with deep compassion over those who are lost in sin, and who fail to understand the anguish of His heart.

*Who Is the Elder Brother in the Story?* He certainly represented the Pharisees who resented Christ's interest in sinners, and those in the early Church who looked askance at the Gentile's inclusion within it. There were those disciples at Jerusalem who immediately after Paul's conversion were "afraid of him, and believed not that he was a disciple" (Acts 9:26). Among ourselves, the elder brothers are those who, in self-conceit think they are good enough to enter the Father's home, and have no need of being "found," or "made alive again." To them, soul-saving activities are most distasteful. It is hard for them to realize that all their self-righteousnesses are but the filthy rags of a prodigal in God's sight.

Multitudes of saved sinners in heaven and on earth bless God for the matchless parable of the prodigal, resplendent with all the glories of divine grace and love. With its message of hope and call to faith may it still be used to woo and win myriads of wanderers back to the Father's heart and home.

## The Parable of the Unrighteous Steward
### (Luke 16:1-13)

This further parable, peculiar to Luke, is still a part of that memorable Sunday afternoon conversation in the house of a Pharisee, which covers chapters 14 through 17:10. The simple word, *also* (16:1), indicates that the parable before us was addressed, particularly to Christ's disciples. Its message was also meant for the rich among the Scribes and Pharisees, as well as among the publicans and sinners who had chosen to become disciples. That the parable stung the conscience of the money-loving Pharisees is evident from their reaction to it. "The Pharisees also, who were covetous, heard all these things, and derided Him" (16:14). The word *covetous* used here and by Paul (II Timothy 3:2), literally means "lovers of money." Those Pharisees felt the force of Christ's parable and showed visible signs of scorn which He met with a forceful rebuke. "A little grain of conscience made them sour." Love of money, and not money itself, is the root of all kinds of evil and was the motive actuating the Pharisees. Christ's parable exposed such a motive.

Because of its unusualness, this parable has been subjected more than any other to various and discordant interpretations and explanations. Excessive literalism has turned the parable into a maze of subtleties. Fantastic theories have been extorted out of every clause, leaving behind a pathetic record of wasted ingenuity — pathetic because many of these interpretations represent a pitiable abuse of the right reverence due to all the words of Christ. By His use of this parable He was condoning a fraudulent transaction. As the personification of Truth, Honesty and Righteousness, He could not use a rogue, as the unjust steward was, to "point a moral and adorn a tale." Christ did not commend the cunning deceit, but the *astuteness* of this steward. Butterick says that our Lord used this man as an "example in resource, not as an example in point of corruption . . . He crowded His canvas with a motley array of types, not all of them unsmirched. An earthly story even for the purpose of a heavenly meaning must use earthly people, and earthly people are not paragons."

The gist of the parable is that a rich man, perhaps one of whom Jesus had heard in ordinary conversation, was a shrewd man who paid close attention to his affairs and kept his agents under vigilant control. The unfaithful were promptly dismissed, and commendation was forthcoming for the shrewdness of villainy, without very severe reprehension. The steward was one who looked out for himself, for he was wise in his generation. The debtors fell in with his cunning arrangements, helping thereby, their own purses. The simplest explanation of such a parable is that Jesus used it to describe worldly astuteness, and to teach a lesson of spiritual prudence. As to the details of the steward's clever fraud, they are of no intrinsic importance. All Jesus did was to take this man's foresight and promptitude — wicked as they were in their application — as an illustration of qualities which have a necessary place in the life of true disciples.

The figure of a *steward,* previously used by Jesus (Luke 12:42), is used to describe the office of the Apostles, and of all who are called to minister the Word of God. All such are "stewards of the mysteries of God" and must be found faithful (I Corinthians 4:1,2). The Pharisees, as official interpreters of the Law, were supposed to be *stewards,* and all true disciples must function as such in this capacity. The Master's goods must not be wasted. While perhaps the Pharisees had not "wasted their substance in riotous living," they are here shown that the "goods" committed to them could be wasted in other ways than in association with "harlots."

Breaking down the parable then, we find our Lord condemning the Pharisees for their misuse of God-given responsibilities. They were guilty of the same sin as the prodigal in proportion as they had failed to use what He had entrusted them with for His glory and the good of men. As stewards, not only of the mysteries, but of money and the privileges and opportunities material goods bring, they must give an account to God hereafter. Further, in the first section of the parable (vs. 1-4), our Lord teaches that wealth and influence may be so employed that, should reverses come and poverty ensue, those helped in days of prosperity will act as friends in the time of adversity. God requires truth and uprightness in all the dealings of His stewards and servants. It is only thus that reward can be theirs when the final account is rendered.

The transaction of the steward with his master's debtors revealed his true character. He was destitute of integrity and fidelity in office. Seeking to redeem himself from the shame of dismissal, he sought to ingratiate himself with the debtors by lowering the debts they owed his master. This wise steward had no regard to the interests of his master, or of his just claims on the debtors (vs. 5-8). It must not be forgotten that it was not Jesus who commended the steward's fraudulent act, but the lord mentioned in the parable. The Lord Jesus cannot condone any practice contrary to His holy and righteous ways. Today men are guilty of lowering the claims of God in regard to holiness and truth, by their assertion of a false estimate of divine requirements. Men may praise us when we do well to ourselves, but what the world may highly esteem may be an abomination in God's sight because of the lack of righteous principle.

In our Lord's application of the parable to His disciples, He told them to learn a lesson from the prudence and foresight often exercised by successful men of the world. At the same time, however, they must constantly avoid acting upon any shady principle of conduct. "Make to yourselves friends of the mammon of unrighteousness, that, when ye fail, they may receive you into everlasting habitations" (Luke 16:9). What, exactly, is meant by *mammon?* In the Syriac Version, the word means "money" or "riches," and is used to contrast the service or worship of money with that which is due to God (Matthew 6:24). Mammon, the symbol of wealth, was that possessed by the rich man in the parable, but "mammon of unrighteousness (unrighteousness being the absence of goodness) is neither moral or immoral but non-moral. Here, Jesus is not telling His disciples to make friends

of material wealth, but to make friends by means of it. They were to so use money, not for themselves alone, but to gather friends to themselves. Then, looking beyond this world, in which men can accumulate wealth, if they lose same, the friends they made by use of it shall receive them into the eternal tabernacles. Those whose lives had been enriched by the prudent use of wealth, would greet the giver on the other side. Many rich men would not *leave* so much behind, if only they had made more friends with their money.

The lesson at this point, then, is clear. The possession of wealth, influence, position, leisure, or opportunity are so to be used here on earth as never to be forgotten in the eternal state. God's bountiful stewards will never lose their reward. Friends for eternity will be theirs because of the wise use of their temporal means in the spirit of Christian love. Primarily, we are responsible to our divine Lord for whatever gifts, whether temporal or spiritual, He has committed to our stewardship. Campbell Morgan relates an experience he once had while staying in the home of a wealthy Christian. One morning at family prayers, this devoted church member eloquently and tenderly prayed for the salvation of the heathen and for the missionaries. When prayers were finished, the father was startled beyond measure when one of his boys, a lad of ten, said to his father:

"Dad, I like to hear you pray for the missionaries." The pleased father replied, "I am glad you do, my boy." Then the boy replied, somewhat to the chagrin of his father, "But do you know what I was thinking when you were praying? If I had your bank book, I would answer half your prayers."

Our choice is between two motives — love of possessions for their own sake, which is love of self and results in the forgetfulness of others; or the use of possessions as a trust from God for the benefit of others, and for the glory of the Giver of all good gifts. Too many fail to enjoy their Mammon because their service of it is spoiled by the scruples and rebukes of conscience. These people also fail to enjoy God because their visible service for Him is spoiled by their indulgence of alien desire.

Our Lord's final lesson is that the manifestation of common-sense or prudence is the test of faithfulness. If what we have, whether much or little, is faithfully used as a servant, and as a discipline of fidelity, then it is capable of providing us with resources of eternal value. Faithfulness is to be the basis of reward in eternity (Revelation 2:10). Our Lord commends fidelity, seeing it produces and directs prudence. Disciples are to act at all times as under a responsibility to a divine Master in the little things as well as in the greater, both in temporal affairs and in regard to spiritual gifts. Then in eternity, those who benefited through their ministry or money, or both, will form their joy and crown of rejoicing. "They that be wise (astute as the steward) shall shine as the brightness of the firmament, and they that turn many to righteousness, as the stars for ever" (Daniel 12:3). Gifts and graces used as unto God, bring a present satisfaction and go to build a memorial in the ages to come.

## The Parable of Dives and Lazarus
### (Luke 16:19-31)

This most solemn parable was born of the sneers of the Pharisees over the teaching of the parable they had just heard from the lips of Jesus (Luke 16:14). These religious leaders who fared sumptuously, living in the love of money, and of the enjoyments which money purchased, only mocked at the counsel of using their wealth for the benefit of others in a way to earn them eternal rewards. Their money was theirs, and they wanted no advice from Jesus as to its right use. Then came this parable, teaching, as it does, the terrible end of those who live only for the gratification of their own sinful and selfish desires. Their "good things" (Luke 16:25)

might have done much good in the world, but trust was betrayed and hell came at the end of a mis-used life.

At the outset, let it be noted that "this parable was not intended, primarily," says Sell, "to emphasize the dire consequences following the abuse of wealth and hard-hearted contempt of the poor, but to declare that men cannot arrange and reconcile, to their own satisfaction, their professed reverence for God and their love of self-gratification — that externals are not infallible indexes to character — that God's appraisals are just and (most important of all, perhaps) that long-continued habits result in fixity of character, for good or ill, in time and eternity."

There are some writers who do not regard this narrative, peculiar to Luke, as a *parable*. Their contention is that it is not called a "parable" and that names are introduced. In all other parables of our Lord names are never given. It wasn't His custom to introduce names into His parabolic instruction. The rich man and Lazarus were actual characters, possibly known to Christ, and their history both in this world and the world to come is solemnly traced by Jesus for the moral profit of men everywhere. Abraham, Moses and hades are realities, not figures of speech. But if the narrative was real history, the facts are presented in symbolic form and the "symbols are the flung shadows of realities."

Before we consider the series of tremendous contrasts, with the practical application of them, it must be affirmed that the rich man did not go to hell because he was rich, and Lazarus to Abraham's bosom because he was poor. There are multitudes of one-time rich persons in heaven, just as there are myriads of one-time poor people in hell. Neither affluence nor poverty determines the eternal state. Our relationship to Jesus Christ alone decides our eternal bliss or woe.

*The Contrast in Life.* What extremes of social life our Lord brings together in this parable! The "certain rich man" is known as *Dives,* which is the Latin term for "rich man." Tradition has given him the name of *Ninevis,* and his contrast to Lazarus is the chief feature of the narrative. This unnamed man, as far as the Bible is concerned, was wealthy, and was one of a wealthy family. Doubtless his five brothers, as rich as he, all formed one of the great magnates of the neighborhood. Because of his riches, Dives was able to dress in the best and to eat and drink sumptuously every day.

Although the rich man, along with his family, was godless, nothing is said about him being positively vicious. He is not described as being guilty of any glaring sin, or a monstrous member of society. He is not before us as a tyrant or an oppressor of the poor. Had he been notoriously selfish or uncharitable, he would not have allowed Lazarus to lie at his gate, day after day, beseeching alms. Without doubt, he lived a luxurious self-indulgent life, but he was not arbitrarily condemned because of his wealth. He went to hell because he failed to realize that he was God's trustee, with wealth and influence that could have been used for God's glory, and for the spiritual and material benefit of his fellow-men. Thus it was his wickedness and not his wealth that brought him eternal misery. His selfishness, not his sensuality (not any conspicuous evil deeds, but his failure to have God at the center of his whole life) brought him under the condemnation of Him to whom he owed all that he possessed. No vices or crimes are laid to his charge. His sin was that he lived only for the present.

Coming to Lazarus, he is conspicuous in that this is the only instance where Jesus gives a name to a parabolic character. Even in a parable admission may be given to a proper name (see Ezekiel 23:4). He might have been an actual beggar known to Jesus, the disciples and the Pharisees, but the significance of his name suggests that he was meant to symbolize the outward wretchedness of one who had no other help but God. *Lazarus* means, "God has helped," or "God is

the helper." The word *beggar* conveys the idea of poverty rather than of begging. In contrast to the rich man, he was poor and destitute; the rich man was clothed in purple and fine linen, the beggar, in rags; the rich man lived in a stately mansion; the beggar was laid by sympathetic friends at the gate of the mansion; the rich man had a healthy, well-nourished body; the beggar was full of sores; the rich man fared sumptuously *every* day; the beggar lived on crumbs from his table; the rich man had physicians to care for him; dogs licked the sores of Lazarus.

Yet the merit of Lazarus was not found in the sad fact that he was poor, helpless and diseased. A beggar may be as vile and filthy in heart as he may be in body. No, the precious thought is that while lying at the rich man's gate, hungrily eyeing the pieces brought him, he learned contentment. As a son of Abraham, he found his help in God. As a pensioner upon divine bounty, he knew his bread and water would be sure. Ultimately he went to Paradise not because he was poor and diseased but because, in spite of his pitiful condition, he had served God, finding his constant help in Him. We are left with the mystery why a good man like Lazarus was allowed to be so destitute and diseased. If God was his helper, why was he not relieved of his misery? Then why was a self-centered, self-indulgent person like the rich man allowed to possess such wealth? These questions were not answered by Jesus who, in the parable, sought to focus the attention of His hearers upon the solemn lesson that the life we live on the earth determines our eternal status.

*The Contrast in Death.* The two men Jesus portrayed were as opposite in death as they had been in life. As the beggar's death comes first in the narrative, we think of it first. All Jesus said of him was, "the beggar died." Nothing is said about his burial. Being so destitute, he was not able to leave anything for a decent burial. Then did he have a burial or was his diseased and emaciated corpse hurried away roughly and unfeelingly by the city officials to the potter's field? In the words of the song, did they:

"Rattle his bones
Over the stones,
He's but a pauper
Whom nobody owns."

Campbell Morgan says that beggars of the type of Lazarus were not buried. "Almost inevitably the cleaners passed the dead body, unknown, unclean, and hurried it away in the early dawn until they came to Tophet, Gehenna, the rubbish and refuse heap of fire, where they flung the body in. That is a known fact of the time, and the very fact we are not told Lazarus was buried, leads us to suppose such an end for him." But although his body had an ignominious end, the angels came and carried Lazarus himself into Paradise. These angelic guardians of the righteous escorted the spirit of Lazarus to the realms of bliss, for they knew the route to such.

But with the rich man it was different. He died, as all must die, whether rich or poor, but he "was buried," and doubtless had a stately burial, with hired mourners and all the pageantry of woe, the rich could afford. Yet though his body was conveyed to an ornate tomb with all due honors, his soul on departing from earth was solitary. No angelic convoy appeared to escort him to the regions of the blest. He went straight to hell, there to endure torment. For him as a Jew, there was no height of seraphic bliss, a resting place in Abraham's bosom. All the ostentatious splendor of the rich man could not buy off the rider of the pale horse, or secure for him eternal happiness beyond the grave. In his death, the rich man was more of a pauper than Lazarus had ever been. He went into eternity stripped bare of all he had possessed and with the terrible realization that an eternal inheritance would never be his. How different it would have been if God, and not gold, had been first in his life!

*The Contrast in Eternity.* Having come from eternity there was no one more competent than the Eternal Son to draw aside the veil which separates this present world from the unseen. With divine knowledge, He could speak with authority of the life to come. What, then, was implied in His use of the Jewish figure of speech, *hades,* which is the Greek word for "hell"? The word meant the place of departed spirits, the unseen world of the dead, both good and bad. This one great realm was divided into two spheres — Abraham's bosom, or Paradise for the righteous; and "hell," the abode of the unrighteous. When Christ rose again, having come forth from Paradise and ascended on high, He carried captivity captive, meaning that He emptied Paradise taking all prisoners of hope with Him to the Father's house. Now, when a believer dies—absent from the body, he is present with the Lord!

The other sphere, hades — hell — remains and is the temporary abode of lost souls. Hell, however, is to give place to the Lake of Fire as the final depository of all who died outside of Christ (Revelation 20:14). To be in "Abraham's bosom" means to be near the holy patriarch, sharing his blessedness. As a son of Abraham, Lazarus now enjoys nearness to him as a fellow-heir and companion of Abraham. The rich man had considered him an outcast from God, but in the unseen world he is highly honored as a friend of the father of faith, whom God called His "friend."

What cannot be gainsaid as we read our Lord's description of the after life is that this is a state of conscious existence with the continued use of our faculties. To Lazarus, Paradise was a place and state of highest joy and heavenly communion. For the rich man, hell was the place and condition of remorse, suffering and woe. Evidently in hades, as it existed at the time Jesus uttered this parable, there was close proximity between the two divided spheres because the rich man could see Abraham afar off and Lazarus near his side.

The contrast between the two departed souls is given by Jesus, "Lazarus is comforted, and thou art tormented." The word for *comfort* is *parakaleo,* the word from which we have Paraclete, the designation used of the Holy Spirit, the Divine Comforter. The word means, "to call near," and Lazarus had been called near to Abraham's side and to the God he had trusted. The rich man was tormented and begged Abraham to send Lazarus with relief for his anguish. This means that over the gulf dividing the two spheres, voices could be distinctly heard. With perfect spiritual intelligence Abraham knew all about the prosperity of the rich man, as well as the penury of Lazarus, and told the rich man to remember the past. He was remembering — and such a memory constituted his hell and was the flame tormenting him. Then our Lord went on to make Abraham's bosom explain the fixity of character, and the impossibility of lost souls going to heaven, or of the saved to visit hell. The great gulf was *fixed.*

Conscious of his doom, the rich man prayed that Lazarus might be liberated for a season to act as an evangelist to his five brothers who were on their way to the same place of torment. He could not bear the thought of a re-union in hell. But Lazarus, the one-time beggar, now companion of Abraham, would have had no success. Later on, another Lazarus was raised from the dead. What effect did his resurrection have upon the wealthy, self-satisfied Pharisees? Why, they tried to kill him. Finally Jesus died and rose again, with what result? Why, these same people were unchanged in their attitude to Christ, as their endeavor to put to death all who followed him clearly proved.

"They have Moses and the prophets," let your brothers hear them. Nothing spectacular or miraculous can have any effect upon the life of men, if the Word of God is not believed and obeyed. We have no light beyond the revelation of God. The rich man thought that something sensational would appeal to the consciences of his five lost brothers. But

nothing could prevent them from sharing their brother's doom apart from the revelation given in Old Testament Scriptures. If the Parables of Luke 15 speak of the mercy and compassion of God toward the penitent, the parable just considered presents in the clearest light the righteousness and righteous indignation toward those who died impenitent (Romans 1:18). The solemn lessons we are left with should be seriously considered by all:

Man cannot serve two masters. If he gains the world, and loses his soul, his loss will be eternal.

The choice made on earth determines the life to come, and such a choice is final. The grave can work no miracle.

In the future, personality continues — feeling, knowing, seeing, reasoning and remembering. Are these faculties to aid our bliss, or add to our torment?

Heaven and hell are realities, and our eternal destiny depends, not upon wealth or poverty, but upon our relationship to Jesus Christ, who came as prophesied by Moses and the prophets as the Saviour of the world.

## The Parable of the Seed and Unprofitable Servants
### (Luke 17:1-10)

It is somewhat surprising to find that some of the best expository volumes, such as Goebel's on *The Parables of Our Lord,* entirely omit any reference to this short yet significant parable. Kirk, G. H. Lang, Newberry, Keach, Sell and others pass over it. Trench, however, has a most helpful study of it. Perhaps it is felt that, in comparison with many other parables, it cannot rank as one of the most important. But if the parable was meant to be a caution to the disciples, lest they should presume upon their possession of the power of faith (Luke 17: 6), then surely it is an important parable to study. Doubtless many of the other parables have a superior attractiveness, and this one is neglected by some writers because its lessons are not so palatable as can be gathered from the Master's other allegories, or because of a difficulty in the parable's interpretation. Godet and Bruce dismiss this portion in Luke as "a remnant scrap at the bottom of the portfolio."

Although the parabolic illustration of the "mustard seed" was used by Jesus before, it is repeated here in a new and distinct discourse to His own, which brings us to the connection between the parable and the conversation preceding it. Usually, there is some event, question, or circumstance leading to a parable. Here, there is not only a connection between the parable and its antecedent instruction, but an absolute union. The lesson of verses 1 through 6, pass into the parable, verses 7 to 10. Jesus had spoken to His disciples of the inevitable offences in the shape of wicked and malicious opposition of the world to His Gospel and to those who proclaimed it, but made clear the guilt of those responsible for such offences (1-2). Then He admonished them to cherish a loving and forgiving disposition, ready to pardon however often injured.

But the Apostles, conscious of the difficulty of the human heart to fulfil such a command, asked, "Lord, increase our faith." The hardship of the warfare to be maintained, and a desire for future rest and reward, might have possessed the minds of the disciples: hence this parable on the obligation of serving the Master without thought of release or reward. No matter what trials faced them, His followers must render complete obedience to Him, and like Him, conquer by suffering.

In His further use of the parabolic illustration of the mustard seed (see our exposition of Matthew 13:31-33), our Lord emphasizes the kind of faith His disciples would need to endure coming trials, and to obey His commands. They wanted more faith so as to be equal to all demands, but Jesus saw that it was not *quantity* they needed but *quality*. Not an increase of faith that would bring some reward following the results of its exercise, but a faith which like a grain of mustard seed had the principle of life in making it mightier than any other force. Such a living faith is convinced of the fact of God, conscious of an experience of relationship with God, concerned about absolute submission to the will of God. Proceeding from His teaching regarding the quality of faith enabling one to do the seemingly impossible, He introduced His parable with the phrase, "But who is there of you."

If His disciples received more faith what result would it have upon them? Would they pride themselves on the victories of faith, or allow such conquests to make them, more than ever, the Master's bondslaves? When He sent them out upon a mission, they came back rejoicing and exultingly said, "Even the demons are subject unto us." They glorified in their accomplishment, not in the One who had made it possible. Thus, the Lord rebuked them, telling them not to rejoice over demon-submission but over the fact that they were "the burgesses of heaven from where Satan had already fallen."

The parable, then, was designed to guard against the subtle peril of satisfaction in service, and the expectation that service shall be recognized with reward. In the four verses forming the parable Jesus impressed upon His own the arduous and unceasing nature of the service required of them, and the spirit and temper in which such service should be rendered.

Concerning the parabolical representation succeeding our Lord's lesson on the right quality of faith, Calvin says: "The sum of this parable is, that since God can by an absolute right challenge every thing to Himself, and hold us for His property, however jealously we may apply to any duty, we cannot bind Him to us by the obligation of our merits, because since we are His, He can be in nothing indebted to us . . . All are condemned of sinful arrogance; who imagine that they deserve something at the hands of God, as if they laid Him under contribution to themselves."

The only way of attaining, or obtaining, increased faith is for the working servant to manifest an unmoved, persevering obedience, grounded upon humility (Luke 17:9,10). Through humility and obedience the twin virtues developed in the parable, a mighty faith is begotten. Let us now take the four verses and trace the necessity of these virtues:

1. *In all matters, as servants, we must be subject to God* (Luke 17:7). The word for "servant" and "servants" means a bondslave. Repeatedly in His parables, our Lord used the term "servant" implying a bondslave, which also was the favorite designation of himself Paul used when he wrote of himself as "the bondslave of the Lord Jesus Christ." As servants we are not our own. We belong to Him who bought us with the price of His blood. Because we are "the possession of God's purchase," we have no title to ownership of anything we possess. God has every title to all a Christian is and has, and can do. As His, we must hold ourselves absolutely at the Master's disposal. All our time is His, and there are no days off or holidays in His service. As Christians we must be *Christians,* so long as life lasts. He demands our *all* and at *all* times. "God has given all, owns all, has a right to all." We are His by right of Creation, by Redemption and by the surrender of our lives to Him.

"Ploughing or feeding cattle," are parabolic images of the spiritual labor, to which Christ had called His own (John 21:16; Acts 20:28; I Peter 5:2). Having ploughed the fields or fed the cattle is no warrant for an immediate refreshment and recompense. Before the servant sat down to eat, he must take up another task and prepare his master's meal. A slave's work is never done. He must keep himself always at the call of His Master. Although weary he is still under the obligation to serve.

2. *All our powers must be employed in His service* (Luke 17:8). The master properly regarded all the servant had already accomplished as a matter of obligation, and now demands from him further obedience and additional service. The master's needs must first be satisfied; then, in due course, the slave can eat. "Gird thyself, and serve me, till I have eaten and drunken; and afterwards thou shalt eat and drink." It has been suggested that this presentation of the haughty bearing of the master toward his tired and hungry slave and the seemingly unappreciative spirit in which he received the services rendered, is inconsistent with our general teaching. How can this kind of a master be a representative of God? Taylor says that this portion of the parable, telling of "the gruffness and thanklessness of the master belongs to what may be called, 'the blind side' of the parable. It belongs to what may be styled the drapery of the parable, and is not to be pressed into significance."

The somewhat harsh words take on a fresh significance when compared to the heavenly side Jesus previously presented, whereas the Master would gird Himself and minister to His disciples (Luke 12:35-37). The parable before us reveals the Christian toiling on earth, giving the Master the meat and drink of seeing His Father's will accomplished here below (John 4:32-34). In heaven, faithful servants will be sharers of His joy (Revelation 3:20). What a feast He will spread! Presently, we are under obligation to our Lord, and "without haste" but also "without rest," we must hold ourselves absolutely at the Master's disposal. When we reach heaven, the Master, in gratitude and affection, will care for us.

3. *We have no claims for any special praise or recompense from obedience* (Luke 17:9). "The only limit to the servant's duty," says Cosmo Lang, "is his master's will; there is no point at which he can choose for himself to claim that he has done enough and is entitled to ease; that the servant is always a debtor of service, the master is never a debtor of reward." The man who makes

duty his idol, might be satisfied when his duty is accomplished, and expect the praise of others, but slaves have no claim to thanks. Was our Lord here seeking to counteract the subtle poison of self-righteousness creeping into the hearts of His disciples? They had asked Him, "What shall we have therefore?" and requested high places in His coming Kingdom (Matthew 19:19,21).

While rewards are promised us, we do not labor for the Master simply to receive His recompense. As slaves, we serve Him, because we are His and because we love Him. But as the One who has every right to our service, He is under no obligation to thank us for our obedience. It takes much grace to sing—

"We will ask for no reward,
Except to serve Thee still."

4. *An unpretending humility is demanded of us* (Luke 17:10). Our Lord now applies the parable to His disciples. "There was among the Apostles an overweening regard to the obedience they had hitherto rendered, strengthened by what they saw of the shameful obstinacy of others (16:16); the Lord here calls them away from such a line of reflection." If we have yielded a perfect obedience to the Master, the highest fidelity is nothing but obligation. Because there is no such thing as a surplus of merit in a Christian, after having served his best, he is still an unprofitable servant. After the perfect performance of duty, we are still destitute of merit before God, who deals with us, not on the ground of merit, but of grace. Tennyson has the couplet —

"For merit lives from man to man
And not from man, O Lord, to Thee."

We can build nothing on our worth or work. When slaves have given everything because they are slaves, they deserve nothing. The most devoted Christian is an unprofitable servant in that he has not loved and trusted God, as he should have done. If we expect thanks for having done our duty, that shows our hearts were not in the duty. Our Master expects every servant of His to do their

duty in a union of mind and will with His. In view of all He accomplished for us, and has treasured up for us, our impression must be in spite of our most arduous service and costly sacrifices, "We are unprofitable servants."

"Unprofitable servant though I be,
Gladly or sadly let me follow Thee."

We cannot conclude our meditation on this parable in a better way than to quote the summary Wm. M. Taylor gives us: "Although the parable at first sight may seem to present God to us in a repulsive light, as a mere slave-master, we see, now that we have got to the end of it, that we can comply with its requirements only when we attain to the apprehension of His love. Thus the allegory has as its unseen foundation, all the while, the very grace which it appears to ignore. I cannot say, 'I am an unprofitable servant,' until I am a redeemed man; and when a redeemed man, I am no longer a mere servant, but a son, working for love, and not simply from a sense of duty. The Christian calling requires that we shall do more than others; but then it gives us, in the love of Christ, a motive which will not allow us to be content with doing just what others do."

# The Parable of the Unrighteous Judge
(Luke 18:1-8)

Paired with *The Parable of the Friend at Midnight* (Luke 11:5-13), this one likewise teaches the necessity of patient, persistent and persevering prayer. Both parables agree in design, although delivered under different circumstances. In both there is an argument founded on the complete and infinite contrast between God and man, and the evidence that God yields to the saint's argument and persuasion. The two parables are, therefore, closely akin in that they make the same comparison and contrast between what we expect of human nature even in unworthy types and what we may expect of God. In both there is the same inference that God will not fail us as friends sometimes do.

Dispensationally the parable before us is connected with the last days (Luke 17) and the final great crisis and painful circumstances the godly remnant of Israel must face at that time. In these dark days of anti-Christian apostasy, when Christendom and Judaism will combine in the basest iniquity, those who remain true to God will have no resource but prayer, hence, the appeal of this prayer parable. God will assuredly avenge the wrongs of the godly remnant and judge their oppressors, but as they await deliverance, persevering prayer will be their refuge and resource of patience.

A further distinction this parable shares with the one that follows it on *The Pharisee and the Publican,* is the distinctness with which their object is announced at the beginning, and the principle of interpretation at the close. Why did Jesus tell these striking parables, the only two recorded parables in which the reason for giving them is stated? Both parables are related to prayer. That of *The Unjust Judge* is a revelation of the attitude of God towards human prayer. Thus, at its outset we read, "He spake a parable unto them to this end, that men ought always to pray, and not to faint." The next parable provides a revelation of man in prayer, and so commences, "He spake also this parable unto certain which trusted in themselves that they were righteous, and set all others at naught" (Luke 18:9).

The object of *The Parable of the Judge* was to teach perseverance in prayer. God will certainly answer though He may seem for a time to disregard our petition. Two features are to be noted about the kind of earnest prayer we are to pray. First of all, it must be *always,* which means "continually." We are to be "instant in prayer." Too many of our prayers are like naughty boys' runaway knocks — given and the giver is away before the door can be opened. But we are not only to

ask, but to keep on asking, seeking and knocking until the door of heaven opens. In our continual praying we are to be specific as the widow was who day after day, approached the judge with the same petition. Often our prayers are too general and aimless.

Then praying, we are "not to faint." If prayer is not immediately answered, we must not be discouraged. If dangers threaten us, our spirit must not flag or sink, if help seems to be deferred. Prayer, which the Lord inspires, must be answered by Him. Truehearted souls are frequently tried by divine delay in answer to prayer and are tempted to give up the praying attitude. To all such this parable speaks with an encouraging voice.

In the parable of the hard-hearted, unfeeling judge, he is before us as a man of no principle. He had no fear of God, or regard for man. A widow of the same town as the judge had been ill-treated by an adversary and came to the judge for justice. Although her cause was just, he paid no attention to her case. But she persisted in coming with the same plea until at last the judge, not because he cared for justice but simply to get rid of the widow pestering him, decided to see her case righted. No better motive prompted him. What contrasts this parable presents! Extreme arrogancy and extreme impotency — yet in the end, impotency won. Seeking to divide the parable we have —

The Importunate Widow,
The Unjust Judge,
The Divine, Righteous Judge.

*The Importunate Widow.* Widows have a prominent place in the Bible. In our Lord's time widows were somewhat despised and a prey for any unprincipled man. Poor, they had no one to protect and deliver them. Their only hope was resort to the dispensers of justice for intervention on their behalf. Widows, nearly always an object of pity, had their helplessness mercifully recognized by the Jewish Law. "Ye shall not afflict any widow" (Exodus 22:22-24; Deuteronomy 10:18; 24:17). Pure religion includes caring for widows in their affliction (James 1:27).

We are not told what her urgent cause was. She had been wronged and needed simple justice in the matter of her adversary. The judge was callous and dead to pity, yet the widow came "oft unto him"—it was a "continual coming" (Luke 18:6), as ours must be to the Throne of Grace, if our original request is not answered. So persistent was her approach that at last the heartless judge gave in and offered to redress her wrong "lest she weary me." The disciples must have smiled at this humorous touch. "Weary me" means "to wear out," to come to blows, to strike under the eyes, to bruise me. Literally the phrase means, "Come to blows and give me a pair of black eyes." Well, her persistency prevailed, and in the end she got from the reluctant judge the justice she needed and deserved.

*The Unjust Judge.* The conduct of this judge testifies to "the general disorganization and corruption of justice which prevailed under the then government of Galilee and Peraea." Doubtless the case Jesus portrayed was an extreme one. Nevertheless, there were those representatives of the law in whom conscience was dead. The one before us was a godless man. He was not religious or even humanitarian. God and man never concerned him. He cared only for himself. As a Jew, he acted contrary to the Law which decreed the appointment of judges in the cities through all the tribes, and strictly forbade the wresting of judgment, respect of persons, or taking bribes (Deuteronomy 16:8-10). This judge was shamelessly corrupt. He only vindicated the widow because she pestered him, and he was afraid of bodily harm.

The remarkable feature of the parable at this point is that the judge came to see himself as Christ saw him. Christ said of him, "a judge, which feared not God, neither regarded man." Stirred to action through the widow's persistency,

the judge said "within himself, Though I fear not God, nor regard man." Within himself! This unjust judge was not thinking of God, or of the widow — only of himself, as one not to be compelled to do anything. This man had prostituted a privileged position.

*The Divine, Righteous Judge.* Coming to our Lord's application of His parable it may be surprising to find that He compares the dealings of God with those, not of a good man, but of a bad, godless man, and this feature but adds force to the parable. What a contrast between all the judge was, and God is not. All that God is, the judge was not. God is exactly the opposite to all the judge was in character. Taking the application in sections, we have, first of all, God's willingness to hear and answer the pleadings of His own. "Shall not God avenge his own elect, which cry day and night unto him, though he bear long with him?" Because of all He is in Himself, God must answer those prayers offered in accordance with His own will. He is bound by "the sanctions of His own being and by the sanctions of human necessity" to hear and answer prayer. The word "avenge" used of the unrighteous judge, and here of God, means, the working out of His vengeance, not in the sense of *retaliation,* but of *vindication* or *justice.* His elect, if wrongly treated, can be sure of His vindication.

"Crying day and night," expresses the same idea as our Lord's injunction that "men ought always to pray." If the unjust judge at length responded to the widow's cry merely to rid himself of her, shall not God, the all-righteous One, answer the prayers of His own who labor under injustice and oppression? If a mere selfish feeling prevailed with the bad man, how much more the saints can expect from God. If the importunity and perseverance of the widow at last prevailed, how much more will these virtues prevail with God. If we are on right terms with God, then we know that as He elects, He will avenge and answer us. We can expect better treatment from a God of love than a heartless judge.

"Though he bear long with them." The unjust judge bore long with the persistent widow, and God may seem to be as indifferent to our cry. George Müller prayed some fifty years for the conversion of a friend before that man turned to the Lord. Too often human interference is the greatest hindrance to unanswered prayer. Then, one purpose of delayed answer to prayer is the strengthening of our faith and patience. This we do know, prayer He inspires will be answered in His own way and time. "He will act" (Psalm 37:5). God does not have to be aroused from slumber as the friend at midnight, neither is He One who, when He answers, gives grudgingly of His help and abundance. When He appears to withhold the help for which His children plead, He acts with wisdom and love combined.

"Nevertheless when the Son of Man cometh, shall He find faith on the earth?" Here our Lord goes back to the prophetic angle of the previous chapter. When He comes to break in on all the godlessness of earth, shall He find faith on it? Yes, there will be plenty of faith in false objects. The margin reads, "*the* faith," and "the faith" delivered unto the saints will be a scarce commodity. Our solemn charge, in spite of avowed opposition and trials, is to keep the faith — "the faith of God" (Mark 11:22-24 R.V.).

Our parting word is that the widow did not prevail because of her eloquence or elaborate plea. Her words were few, eight only, "I pray thee avenge me of mine adversary." Her cry was short and explicit. She had nothing to say about her widowhood, her family, or divine judgment upon unjust judges. All she wanted was one thing — justice meted out to her adversary. J. D. Drysdale has the pertinent thought, "Words are cumbersome in prayer. It often happens that an abundance of words reveals a scarcity of desires. Verbiage in public prayer is generally nothing better than a miserable fig-leaf with which to cover up the nakedness of an unawakened soul. Let us keep our long prayers for the secret place, and our short ones for the public gallery, lest we come under the condemnation of the man who stood and prayed thus with himself!"

God has assured us that He hears and answers prayer, and this should induce us to continue asking. The links of the chain reaching from earth to heaven, and which draws heaven down to earth, are links resulting in effectual prayer:

A sense of continual, personal need

An unfailing desire to receive what God sees I need

An unshaken faith that He has what I need in store

A consciousness that though He withholds awhile, He loves to be asked, and asked again

A firm belief that if I ask, believing, I shall receive.

# The Parable of the Pharisee and the Publican
(Luke 18:9-14)

As indicated in our introduction to the previous parable, the purpose of this parable was to expose those who trusted in themselves that they were righteous, and despised others. By the "certain" we understand not only the self-righteous Pharisees, against whom the parable was particularly directed, but also "the disciples in whom the Pharisee temper was gaining the mastery." The word "despise" as used by our Lord, describes the religious egotism the Pharisees personified in a most repulsive form. The term literally means, "to count as nothing," a term Paul frequently employed (Romans 14:3, 16; I Corinthians 16:11 etc.). The best of us have to guard against the depreciation of others. We have to guard against thinking of ourselves more highly than we ought to think. Calvin, writing on this short yet most searching parable, said: "Christ reproves and condemns two sins — improper confidence in ourselves, and pride in despising others — the one which springs from the other; for whoever deceives himself by a false confidence, cannot fail to magnify himself above others. Nor is it wonderful that he should despise his equals, who deals proudly toward God Himself. But everyone, who is puffed up by such self-confidence, avowedly wars with God Himself, as His favour can not otherwise be gained, than by an entire renunciation of ourselves, and a simple dependence upon His mercy."

Before taking up the Pharisee and the publican, separately, let us compare and contrast them together as our Lord portrays them in this well-known parable, which Luke alone records. It is interesting to note, as Campbell Morgan points out, that the parables which have generally taken hold more profoundly upon the heart of man, are those found in Luke's gospel, the chronicle of God's second Man, and the last Adam. As a Greek writer, Luke portrays Jesus in all the perfection of His human nature. That may account for this appeal of some of his parables to the human heart.

The two men who went up into the outer temple to pray, are different in character, creed and self-examination. Both presented themselves before the same thrice holy God but with what a different attitude of mind. Here are two individuals widely apart from each other, as well in their manner of life, and in the opinion publicly entertained of them. The two are the representatives of the two classes — of the self-applauding, arrogant law-keeper, and the abased lawbreaker. The two characters are presented in deep relief, without confusion or ambiguity. Each is portrayed in his own color with the one sharply distinguished from the other. Yet all their features are not diverse. Points of likeness as well as of difference can be observed. One was not good and the other bad — both were alike, and at the beginning of the parable, equally sinners. While the outward form of their sin was opposite, the essential character

of sinfulness was the same. Arnot, who reminds us of a strong resemblance between the two men and the two sons who were severally asked by their father to work in his vineyard (Matthew 21:28-32), says that: "The Pharisee said and did not; the publican neither said or did. The Pharisee pretended to a righteousness which he did not possess; the publican neither professed righteousness nor possessed. While one maintained the form of godliness, but denied the power, the other denied both the form and the power of godliness. . . . The one was a hypocrite, the other a worldling. . . . Both go at the same time to the same place to pray, and both adopt in the main the same attitude in this exercise; they stood while they prayed. . . . Both alike look into their own hearts and lives; and both permit the judgment thus formed to determine the form and matter of their prayer. Both addressed themselves to the work of self-examination, and the prayers that follow are the fruits of their research. . . . One found in himself only good, the other found in himself only evil."

1. *The Attitude and Prayer of the Pharisee.* How different in spirit and in the object of prayer are these two men! In the temple, one flattered himself, and was full of self-commendation; the other sought mercy, and was honest in his self-condemnation. What a study in pride and humility the two men offer! The first thing we notice about the Pharisee's prayer, prayed in the forecourt of the temple at the usual fixed hour of prayer, is his proud posture. He took his "stand apart, and prayed thus." If he had noticed the publican enter the temple at the same time, the Pharisee quickly assumed a distinctly separate position. He not only stood with himself, but prayed with himself, or to himself. A prayer like this, drenched with self-pride, could never reach the ear of God.

He stood by himself because he was not the kind of man to mingle with the common herd of worshipers who were not fit to be in his company. The publican prayed alone because he considered himself unworthy to associate with others: the Pharisee prayed, or spoke, to or toward himself. Pride was the god he worshiped, as the words of his prayer reveal. Two words are used for the one English word, *stood*. The one Jesus used of the Pharisee standing (taking up his position ostentatiously) suggests in itself a static and upright position of perfect security and self-satisfaction. With the publican, "stood" means he stood with a bowed head and sorrowful countenance — the crest-fallen attitude of contrition. Praying with himself, the Pharisee used thirty-four words to the publican's seven words — almost seven times as long a prayer. It was also a prayer conspicuous for its five big *I*'s. Thus it was a prayer of self-congratulation, full of "self-righteousness which is as noxious a sin as penitent humility is an essential grace," and rose no higher than the beautiful roof of the temple in which it was prayed.

The frame of the prayer shows how the Pharisee relied on his negative morality for justification. He moved in a circle, the center and circumference of which was *self*. Ignorant of divine righteousness, he established his own righteousness and could plead only what he was not, what he did, and how much better he was than others. Look how he paraded his merits in the divine presence! Listing his abstentions from evil, and informing heaven of his virtues, he proceeded, "God, I thank thee that I am not as other men are."

There was no lowly feeling of what he owed God, no thanksgiving for what God had done for him, or given him, no word of praise for divine goodness. His thanksgiving was in the form of self-gratification. What a spectacle is here! A man praying, yet no gratitude to, or adoration for God. He asked for nothing, confessed nothing, and received nothing. There is a tradition to the effect that every true Pharisee ought to thank God every day of his life for three things:

1. That he was not created a Gentile.
2. That he was not a plebeian, or ordinary Roman citizen.
3. That he was not born a woman.

"Not as other men." This proud boast actually means "the rest of mankind." The Pharisee did not compare his own imperfections with the infinite perfections of the Eternal, but with the imagined greater imperfections of the rest of his fellow-men. He looked with pride, not pity, on the majority of men who were sinners, and knew it. Paul, a one-time Pharisee of the Pharisees, confessed himself to be the chief of sinners. In his effort to set forth his own fancied purity, the Pharisee enumerated three articulate and manifest forms of wickedness. He was not an —

"Extortioner," an official having a right to something, who unjustly forced from the oppressed more than was due.

"Unjust," like those who ought to have acted justly but dealt unfairly in the ordinary intercourse of life.

"Adulterer," the deepest and most daring transgressor of laws, both divine and human — the sin associated above all others with shame. There is nothing in the parable to suggest that the Pharisee was guilty of any of these vices. As he confessed, he was probably free of these sins. But by way of purging himself from sin in the lump, the Pharisee went on to thank God in a contemptuous tone that he was not —

"Even as this publican." The Pharisee may have known the publican, and cognizant of his character, knew he was guilty of all three sins, and therefore not to be thought of as being in his class. But the Pharisee erred in that it is not the office of one sinner to judge and condemn another, which he did when he dragged the publican into his make-believe prayer to furnish the dark background on which the bright colors of his own virtues could be more gloriously displayed. Can we not see the sneer on his face as he said, "Even as this publican"? Augustine says, "This is no longer to exult, it is to insult."

Then from the negative, he went to the postive, "I fast twice in the week." The Law required only one fast in a year, that on the great day of Atonement (Leviticus 16:29; Numbers 29:7). But this supposedly devout Jew fasted every Monday and Thursday during the weeks between the Passover and Pentecost, and again between the Feast of Tabernacles and that of the Dedication of the Temple.

"I give tithes of all that I possess." The Law only required the Israelite to tithe on his gains, his annual increase, not on his possessions (Genesis 28:22; Deuteronomy 14:22; Leviticus 27:30). This Pharisee tithed *all* that came his way (Matthew 23:23; Luke 11:42). Parading these virtues, he sought to make God his debtor. The very precepts which should have awakened the sense of inward poverty and need, only ministered to self-conceit and pride. His prayer, then, was an address of congratulation to himself, having no acknowledgement of God or of his need, or any confession of sin.

One of the terrible possibilities suggested by the Pharisee's attitude and prayer is that a man's religion may be his ruin. The very strictness of life may result in perdition, simply because the religious man priding himself on his religiosity and morality becomes utterly blinded to the fact of his real sinnership before a holy God (Roman 9:30 — 10:4). Before Paul had a revelation of the glorified Christ, he pursued righteousness on the principle of works instead of the acceptance of divine righteousness by faith (Philippians 3:4-9). Once Paul became the Lord's, he realized that he had absolutely nothing in himself to glory about. "God forbid that I should glory, save in the cross" (Galatians 6:14).

2. *The Attitude and Prayer of the Publican*. As the narrative passes from the Pharisee to the publican how different and more wholesome the atmosphere. The Pharisee stood apart from the crowd of worshipers, feeling that he was holier than any of them. Pride kept him apart from the rest. The publican, however, stood afar off because he felt himself unworthy to unite with the rest of the worshipers at the temple. His was a timid, humble position, with the thought of no other, only his sinful self. Painfully conscious of his guilt, he stood shamefacedly alone.

Who, or what, was a *publican?* He was a renegade Jew who worked as an under-collector of Roman taxes. Chief collectors, like Levi, who became Matthew, and Zaccheus, who also became a disciple, were men of wealth and political influence, but a corrupt and hated class who helped forward the oppression of God's suffering people. The publicans were despised by the good Jews, who would not allow them to enter the temple or the synagogue, or give testimony in a court of justice. This publican now in the presence of God feels deeply the sacredness of the temple and his own unfitness to be in it. Trench quotes the following verse from Crashaw's *Divine Epigrams:*

"Two went to pray; O! rather say,
One went to brag: th'other to pray.
One stands up close, and treads on high
Where th'other dares not send his eye.
One nearer to God's altar trod,
The other to the altar's God."

The Pharisee cast a haughty look heavenward but the publican would not lift up his eyes unto heaven. His downcast look stands in contrast to the supercilious expression of the Pharisee. The publican blushed to lift up his face to God (Ezra 9:6). His was the manifestation of deep humility and of contrition for he "smote upon his breast," the indication of his keen remorse and melting of heart because of sin. How different was the cold, static attitude of the Pharisee whose prayer was pride-ridden! In all humility and penitence the publican prayed, "God, be merciful to me a sinner." Only a seven-word prayer, yet it reached the ear of God because it emphasized three features:

I am a great sinner;

I am liable to, and deserve punishment;

I beg for pardon of sin, mercy, and remission of deserved punishment.

Literally it reads, "the sinner." Perhaps the Pharisee was not a sinner, but he, the publican, certainly was. He singled out his guilt as being exceptional and like another penitent thought himself to be "the chief of sinners" (I Timothy 1:15). How true is the sentiment expressed by Butterick, "Every stroke in the picture of the publican deepens the impression of humility." This is seen in that he pleads for *mercy*. The Pharisee was puffed up with his *merit* but the publican cried for *mercy*. Taking the place of a sinner, he utters a sinner's cry and sues for God's mercy, who can only save sinners "according to His mercy" (Titus 3:5).

> Mercy, good Lord! mercy I crave,
> This is the total sum;
> For mercy, Lord, is all my suit;
> Lord, let Thy mercy come.

The term rendered "be merciful," however, is related to atonement for it actually means "be propitiated" (Romans 3:25; I John 2:2). Through grace, mercy may be extended to the sinner without derogating from justice. Through Christ's propitiation mercy can glory against justice (James 2:13). Heaven bends low to a sinner feeling his need and sense of inferiority, and pleading the atoning work of the Saviour. Casting himself on divine mercy and grace, the publican obtained favor with God.

One lesson we cannot fail to learn from the publican's confession is that one of the foundations of character is a personal sense of sin. Sin means separation from God, and to confess our sin, to be penitent, to be concerned about deliverance from it, is not morbid or unreal, but essential both for the life that now is and the life to come. It is related that Wm. E. Gladstone, was once asked what was the great lack of modern life. He replied slowly and reflectively, "Ah,

a sense of sin; that is the great lack of modern life."

What two different end products there were! Said Jesus, "This man went down to his house justified rather than the other." Both men went home justified but with a different kind of justification. The Pharisee went to his house wrapped in the same garment of self-justification he wore into the temple. Justifying himself, he was unaccepted and unapproved. But the publican went home divinely justified. Self-condemned, he received a righteousness apart from works and thus went home with the joy of sins forgiven (Romans 3:24, 25; 4:5-6; 5:9).

The parable fitly concludes with words Jesus had used before (Luke 14:11), but which well bear repetition: "Every one that exalteth himself shall be abased; and he that humbleth himself shall be exalted." The final word is in praise of *humility,* which is not a mistaken sense of inferiority. Jesus set great store by this virtue and demanded it of His followers. Humility is the absolute hall-mark of the sterling of Christian mintage. Without this virtue, a Christian is either altogether counterfeit or below the standard of assay. The impeccable trait of Jesus still stands, "He that humbleth himself shall be exalted." Haughtiness, God abominates; humility, He asks for and rewards with true exaltation. We are wise when we learn that the only way *up* is *down.*

# The Parable of the Pounds
## (Luke 19:11-17)

The previous parable had many repercussions. Doubtless, by way of the grape-vine among the publicans, word of the Lord's gracious treatment of the penitent publican was warmly received, and brought hope to those in such a despised fraternity. Among these was Zacchaeus, who, as chief among the publicans, would be the first to receive the story of *The Pharisee and the Publican.* Thus, when Jesus on His journey to Jerusalem passed through Jericho, Zacchaeus living here, was determined to see this Teacher so compassionate toward his class, and who, as the Miracle-Worker, had given sight to a blind man at the entrance to Jericho.

The occasion of *The Parable of the Pounds* was the conversion of Zacchaeus. "As they heard these things, he added and spake a parable." "These things," were the animated crowds following Jesus, the rich publican's ingenuity to catch a glimpse of the passing Teacher, Christ's inviting of Himself to the home of Zacchaeus and of his conversion, and of Christ's declaration of the nature of His mission that as the Son of Man, He had come to seek and to save the lost. With this background of the parable before us, we have His reason for its utterance, "Because he was nigh to Jerusalem, and because they thought that the kingdom of God should immediately appear."

The purpose of the parable, then, was to correct the mistaken idea of the immediate manifestation of the Kingdom. The disciples entertained high hopes of the Master's visit to the city of the King. In their belief that He should redeem Israel, eager anticipation was likely theirs that in Jerusalem, He would unfurl His standard, deliver the chosen people from foreign servitude, and usher in the Kingdom of David in all its ancient glory. To the disciples, the Kingdom was not a spiritual reign, but a spectacular temporal dominion. As the people were willing to acclaim Jesus King, perhaps on reaching Jerusalem, His Kingdom could immediately appear. Alas, the moral necessity of the cross had not gripped their minds! They failed to understand the truth at that point that as the result of the death and resurrection of Christ, the Church could be brought into being, and that His Kingdom could not be ushered in until His return to earth as its rightful King.

The exciting events of those days, the crowds and miracle at Jericho, stimulated the idea of Christ's Kingship, but the parable was designed to correct such a false expectation. In it, He intimated His approaching departure from the earth, the trial-time between His ascension and His return, the necessity of fidelity on the part of His servants during His absence, and the hostility of His rejectors. We have here another of those prophetic parables, this one being prophetic of His treatment of servants and rejectors alike on His return. As Godet in his volume on *Luke* expresses it: "The dominant idea of this parable is of a time of trial which must needs come between the departure and return of the Lord to prepare the judgment which shall fix the position of every man in the state of things which shall follow the Coming."

Akin to *The Parable of the Talents* (Matthew 25:14-36), the parable before us has decisive differences. We disassociate ourselves from the idea that Matthew has the parable in its simple form, and that Luke has by a sort of incongruous mixture joined to it another parable, spoken at another time, and for another purpose. *The Parable of the Pounds* is distinct from that of *The Talents* in that it gives us the testament of Jesus wherein He reveals, not only the nature of His coming Kingdom, but His intervening death, resurrection, ascension and glory. Comparing the features of both parables, we note these likenesses and differences:

Both teach that the Lord bestows privileges on His servants and demands faithfulness in return, and rewards at His coming.

Both deal with privileges, but in different aspects. *The Talents* presents the bestowal of *unequal* privileges, with the teaching that when unequal gifts are used with equal diligence, the reward is equal in the day of rewards. *The Pounds* reveals the reception of *equal* privileges, and the fact that those who are faithful may yet be unequal as to the amount of their success.

Both parables alike exhibit the cardinal distinction between the faithful and the faithless. While *The Talents* teach that Christians differ from each other in the amount of gifts received, *The Pounds* teach that we differ from each other in the diligence displayed.

*1. The Nobleman.* Here our Lord describes Himself as a Man of a noble family with rights to a Kingdom, "A nobleman, to whom the kingdom among his citizens was, by birthright, due." Our study of the parables reveals the wonderful variety of illustrations Jesus used of Himself and others, and how often He laid hold of things near at hand, or incidents and persons to illustrate His message. This parable of the nobleman going away to receive a Kingdom, leaving his interests in the charge of bond-slaves and of those citizens who, on his return would not own his Kingship, recalled an incident familiar to the people at that time. The historic background, then, may have been that of Archelaus, whose palace was at Jericho. Having gone to Rome, he left the interests of his kingdom to his servants with money to trade with while he was away. While he was absent, a deputation of fifty Jews was dispatched to him with a protest against his kingship and they were so successful that Archelaus never received the coveted title of king. Returning to another tetrarchy, he called for an account of the use of money while he was absent.

Laying hold on this incident Jesus applied it to Himself. Correcting the error that He would immediately establish His Kingdom, He told those around Him that He was going away to receive a kingdom, and that His servants would have the responsibility of caring for His interests while He was absent and that on His return He would reward all who had been faithful and deal drastically with all those rejecting His rule. He was the noblest Nobleman, who came of noble birth, of earth's best blood. The Son of Abraham, the Son of David, the eternal and only-begotten Son of God (Matthew 1:1; John 1:1).

As the Nobleman, Jesus went into the far country to receive a kingdom. On His ascension, He sat at the right hand of the Majesty on high (Hebrews 1:3), and from there He exercises power (Philippians 2:9-11; Ephesians 1:17, 20-22). Presently, His Kingdom is an invisible one and consists in the execution of the great plan of redemption, translating those in sin's bondage into His Kingdom of light and liberty (Colossians 1:13). In the far country, heaven, all power in heaven and on earth was granted to Jesus, and He received an investiture of a present spiritual Kingdom, and the right to rule as the supreme King in His coming visible Kingdom (Daniel 7:18,22,27; Hebrews 12:28).

*2. The Servants.* Rich noblemen had a retinue of servants or bond-slaves among whom there were those who, because of their integrity and resourcefulness, could be trusted to care for their master's interests in his absence. These privileged bondsmen might have been noblemen in their own right but did not have their master's rights of absolute ownership of property. The parable speaks of *ten* servants, another *ten* as in *The Parable of the Virgins.* As *ten* is one of the perfect numbers of Scripture, suggesting the completion of the divine order, the figure as used here by our Lord represents not only the disciples of His time who were singled out for service during His earthly ministry, but all the saved whom He expects to serve Him faithfully until He returns.

*3. The Pounds.* The nobleman distributed ten pounds to his ten servants, a pound a piece. The *pound* represents over three pounds in English money, or some nine dollars. In *The Talents,* the sums mentioned are far greater, as we saw when considering this parable in which each servant received according to his ability, and the amounts were unequal. Here, each servant received alike. The whole ten started on an equal footing.

What do the *pounds* signify? Certainly not any natural or imparted gifts to trade with. During our Lord's absence these *pounds* represent the Gospel with all its privileges conferred alike on all those saved by grace. The pound, is "the faith once for all delivered to the saints" (Jude 3). This is our deposit on trust with which we are to trade until Christ returns. We are to witness to this faith in a world hostile to the claims of our King. Says Ellicott of the *Pound,* which all disciples of Christ have in common, "It represents their knowledge of the Truth and their membership in the Kingdom, and not the offices and positions that vary in degree."

With these "ten pounds," the ten servants were to occupy until the nobleman's return. This particular word for "occupy," occurring only here in the New Testament, means, "to do business with," or to "gain by trading" (Ezekiel 27:9,16,21,22). The nobleman was the owner of the money but the servants had to trade with it. But the end contemplated by the nobleman was not so much "money-making as character-making," as A. B. Bruce puts it, "the development in his servants of a hardihood of temper and a firmness of will which can be turned to good account when the obscure traders shall have been transformed into distinguished rulers."

What are we doing with the *pound?* Are we using to the full all the privileges of the Gospel? Are we successful traders with eternal truths? Trench cites one of the great religious poets of the East who has given us this same image of life, with all its powers and privileges as a sum of money to be laid out for God:

> "Thee thy Lord gave, thy faithfulness prove,
> The sum of life, as capital in hand.
> Hast thou forgotten thine entrusted pound?
> Dazed with the market's hubbub dost thou stand?
> Instead of dreaming, up and purchase good;
> By precious stones, exchange not gold for sand."

*4. The Citizens.* As already remarked, our Lord may have had in mind the recent incident of Archelaus whom the Jews rejected, and whose complaints to the Emperor brought about his deposition and banishment to Gaul. This feature of the parable laid bare the animosity of the Jewish rulers and their determination to kill Christ. But there is a wider application. All are His enemies who willingly reject His claims and refuse to accept His sovereignty. The Jews were especially Christ's fellow-*citizens* for like them He, too, was of the seed of Abraham, a Jew (Romans 9:3; John 4:22). Yet they hated Him, plotted His death, and continued their hatred of Him by persecuting His servants who witnessed for Him after His ascension. Those Jewish rulers would recognize no king but Caesar (John 19:21; Acts 17:7).

During the Great Tribulation multitudes of Jews and Gentiles alike will be the rebellious citizens casting off all divine restraints (II Thessalonians 2:1-10; Revelation 13:5-6; Psalm 2:2). The final manifestation of rebellion to His claims will be after His millennial reign with terrible results to the rebels. This final judgment will be executed on all His enemies (Proverbs 20:8; Revelation 20:11). All adversaries are to be punished. How many there are, all around us, who will not have this Man to reign over them. Both men and governments will not acknowledge Christ's sovereign rights. But He is patient amid all antagonism to His claims and when He returns to earth to establish His Kingdom, all rebels will be drastically dealt with.

*5. The Returning and Rewarding Lord.* What a pleasant transition it is from rebels to good and faithful servants! Here our Lord emphasized the fact of His return. "When he was returned, having received the kingdom." All regal rights have been granted Christ by the Father, and when He returns to earth, having already virtually received the Kingdom, He will establish it among men. "Thine is the Kingdom." In the rule of such a Kingdom, the King must have trusted servants to assist Him in the government and control of all things.

Do we not have the promise that if we suffer for Him now, we are to reign with Him?

The nobleman commanded his servants to appear before him to give an account of what they gained through trading with the deposit during his absence. There is a suggestive thought in the phrase, "that he might know." Our returning, heavenly Nobleman as the Omniscient One, knows all things. The lesson here is that our conduct as *servants* and *citizens* alike must be made known before others when He comes to reward and punish.

The first servant with all humility said, "Lord, thy pound hath gained ten pounds." Note, he did not say *I* have gained ten pounds, but *"thy pound* hath gained ten pounds." The pound, the Gospel of the Grace of God, has within itself the power of increase. The servant, however, fulfilled his responsibility and traded with the pound. Buying up every opportunity, he increased his deposit tenfold and was made a ruler of ten cities — full fidelity brought with it fuller responsibility. The second servant had not been so diligent and ambitious. His pound brought a return of five. His success was partial yet increased responsibility became his — a ruler of five cities. Greater responsibilities were proportioned to the fidelity and capacity of the servants. Do we realize the necessity of preparing ourselves for coming, greater responsibilities in the Kingdom? The Lord we serve notices both the quantity and the quality of what is done for Him (Luke 19:15; I Corinthians 3:13). Persis labored *much* in the Lord (Romans 16:12).

The third servant could not report any gain. He hid his pound in a handkerchief. Asked why he had not traded with his pound, he confessed to an entirely wrong conception of his lord. Out of his own mouth he was condemned and his pound was taken from him and given to the servant who had been most successful. Having failed to increase his deposit, he lost any further opportunity of serving the lord. Straton says of this servant, he was guilty of "the sin of omission." "Here is where good people often err gravely, for there is *a sin in not doing.*" Our churches are full of those guilty of this sin. They seem to have no desire to serve the Saviour. They have the pound to trade, but it is buried in a napkin.

There is an ominous silence as to the other seven servants, each of whom had received a pound with which to trade. Only three are singled out as representatives of classes (Luke 14:18-20). The rest are passed over. Whether they were successful, or did nothing with their deposit, we are not told. Ambrose said, "There is no word as to the others, who, like prodigal debtors, had wasted what they had received." May we be found faithful, true to the trust the Master left us! Then when He returns His "Well done!" will be ours!

> "Thou at the hours of His return
> will see
> Thy Monarch set, with open book
> in hand.
> What thou from Him receivedst
> He will bring
> To strict account, and reckoning
> demand:
> And a large blessing, or a curse
> from Him
> Thy faith or sloth will then command."

# THE ABSENCE OF PARABOLIC MATERIAL IN JOHN

After the abundant parabolic material of the first three gospels, it is somewhat surprising to come to John and find that there are no parables such as we have in the Synoptic Gospels, where Christ's parabolic method is adequately illustrated. Just as John never used the word *miracle,* but used *sign* to indicate the value of the miracle, so he never used the word *parable.* The word we have for *parable* in the phrase, "This *parable* spake Jesus unto them" (John 10:6) is *proverb,* and in the same word used in two other places as *proverb* (John 16: 25,29). In all three places the term is not *parabolic* but *paroimia,* meaning "a wayside discourse." The first word from which we have "parable" implies "to set by the side of," or "drawn together," the similarity shown by an illustration by its side. The second word from which we have "proverb" means to "make something like something else." Here the idea is that of similitude, whether of a picture, story, or saying.

While the entire omission of all the synoptic parables in John is conspicuous, yet this fourth gospel is by no means devoid of rich symbolism. "The whole gospel from end to end is, penetrated with the spirit of symbolical representation." Dean Farrar says that, "The arrangement of the book is throughout constructed with direct reference to the sacred numbers three and seven." Thus, by seven symbols we shall presently discuss, Christ shows what He *is* to His believing people. John records more of the actual words of Jesus than the other three evangelists, and among His discussions we have some fourteen parables in germ.

While John, like the rest of the gospels, proclaims Christ as the promised Redeemer of a lost race, John is different from the other synoptic writers in that he gives prominence to the deity of the Saviour (John 1:1-3). In order to grasp the perspective of this fourth gospel it is essential to bear in mind that John only describes some twenty days out of the Lord's public ministry of three years. Out of the many miracles He performed, John selected only eight as being sufficient for his purpose. Then Christ's discourses, some of which are peculiar to John, are grouped around the eight great I Am's. The last tragic week of Christ before His death takes up two fifths of the entire gospel.

The first three gospels are called *synoptic* because they survey the life and labors of Christ from a common viewpoint. John's category is all his own and because he pre-supposed all that the other three had recorded, he set out to record that which the synoptists omit. This fact accounts for the absence of parables. Yet the precious allegories, similes and symbols John gives us, add to the rich store of figurative speech the Bible contains. John lived nearer to his Lord than the other Apostles and seemed to understand the inner significance of His messages more than the others, and supplies us with the suggestive imagery He used in His discourses.

## The Parable of the Word
### (John 1:1-14)

Without any introduction of himself, or of his gospel, John, with singular abruptness, plunges right into his description of the Lord he dearly loved. He repeats the expressive figure of speech, as he declares the deity of Christ, namely, *The Word.* What parabolic instruction there is in such a phrase! What are words? Are they not garments for our thoughts? Thoughts cannot exist without words. Thus, spoken words are the manifestation of our thoughts.

Christ, says John, came as the *Word* and as the *Word* became flesh, all of which means that He came as the revelation of the mind of God. By His life, works, and teaching, Jesus revealed the thoughts of God toward us. Further, such a designation is symbolic of His eternal ministry, "His name is called the Word of God" (Revelation 19:13). It is wonderful to know that as "the Word" He *created* flesh and *pities* flesh — "the frail and transitory fabric woven from the dust," but it is beyond our comprehension to realize all that is wrapped up in the mystery of His *becoming* flesh. He became God in human form, in order that God might become more real to us humans. Yet through His mortal body, and even through His garments, His majesty and glory shone. Nothing could hide His glory as the only-begotten of the Father.

## The Parable of the Light
### (John 1:3,9)

As the *Word,* Jesus clothing Himself with our flesh became, not only our *life,* but also our *light.* He had proclaimed Himself as "The Light of the World," and as such lighted every man coming into the world. But John gives us a most pregnant phrase, "The *life* was the *light,*" and true life is always luminous. The life He imparts never fails to illuminate. Is your *life* a *light,* making bright the pathway of souls lost in the darkness of sin? When Christ as the Word became incarnate, He flooded the world with the light of heaven. He came as the *Dayspring* from on high.

The tragedy is that such divine light shone amid blind and darkened hearts which could not comprehend His effulgence. Their senseless minds were darkened (Romans 1:21). He came as the Light of His chosen people, but they received Him not. Because of their evil deeds, they preferred darkness to light. John preceded Him as a "burning and shining light" and his witness to *The Light* was likewise rejected. Through all the Apostles, the Word of God spoke, and the true light shone, but they suffered the same rejection as the Master. Yet for all those who received, and receive the true Light there are the privileges and position of sonship.

## The Parable of the Voice
### (John 1:23,29,37)

The religious leaders, whose heartless ritualism John the Baptist exposed, were compelled to take action against John's mighty preaching of repentance and of the coming Kingdom. To their questions as to who John was, he answered with brevity that he was not the prophet whom Moses prophesied about, neither was he the Messiah that should come. In true self-abnegation, he said that he was only a *Voice* crying amid the uninhabited places of the wilderness, "Prepare a way for the King." With sublime humility, so characteristic of John, though he was the greatest of woman-born, he confessed that he was "Not the *Light,* but sent to bear witness of it; Not the *Sun,* but the star that announces the dawn, and wanes in its growing light; Not the *Bridegroom,* but the Bridegroom's friend; Not the *Shepherd,* but the porter to open the door into the fold" (John 3:27-30).

Here, he speaks of himself as a *Voice,* not the Word of God, but only a voice, divinely used to declare the Word. What victories were his as a *Voice,* simply a human voice. This Baptist did not want his unique and rugged personality to obtrude itself and make prominent its presence. He wanted to function only as a voice, whose tones and utterances were Godgiven and concerned with the glory of the Messiah whose way he prepared.

Yet although John the Baptist was only the voice of one that cried in the desert (Isaiah 40:3), it was yet a distinct and individual voice, and no mere echo of another's voice. His voice had a clear accent of its own, which those who listened to it could not mistake. Other prophets had preceded John, the voices of whom were unmistakably theirs, but the Baptist did not catch up and reiterate what other voices had thundered forth. His voice was vibrant with its own definite, clear and penetrating message because behind it was the Voice with the music and power of many waters. May grace be ours to be content with being simply a voice uttering those truths, carrying with them divine authority.

"Take my voice . . . Take my lips,
    Let them be
Filled with messages from Thee."

## The Parable of the Dove
(John 1:32)

Before Jesus went into the wilderness of temptation (where for forty days He had no companionship save that of the wild beasts, and the threefold approach of him whom Peter described as "a roaring lion"), he made His way to Jordan to be baptized of John. Countless numbers had passed through his hands, but what a memorable moment that must have been when Jesus sought baptism from John who felt he had more need to be baptized as a sinner, than administer the baptism of repentance to One who was thrice holy. But Jesus silenced John by saying that He had come to fulfill all righteousness. By His baptism, He identified Himself with the sinful race He came to save.

As Jesus emerged from the water, the long-expected sign was given — The Holy Spirit descended on Him from heaven like a dove, and with Him came the Father's benediction. Before the battle in the wilderness, there came this wonderful benediction at Jordan. The symbol of the dove spoke of the nature and mission of Him on whom the dove rested. As the love-bird, the dove is the symbol of *peace*. Had not Jesus come as the personification of peace? Did not Paul write, "He is our peace"? Twice over we read that as the dove, the Spirit "abode on Him." This was no transient baptism, as that with water was. The baptism with the Spirit was no fitful enduement but an abiding unction.

Then as John saw a flock of lambs being led to slaughter for the forthcoming Passover, with the Voice he gave utterance to the symbolic truth of Jesus as *the* Lamb of God, who was to die for the sin of the world. Immersed, as John was in Isaiah's prophecies, he knew that the One he had baptized and on whom the dove rested, was the Lamb who would be led to the slaughter for our iniquity.

## The Parable of the Angels and the Ladder
(John 1:47-51)

The formula of double words, "Verily, verily," which John alone uses, is found here for the first time, and introduces us to the angelic ministry exercised on Christ's behalf. This revelation, coming at the end of the chapter taken up with the call of His disciples, was given to Nathanael, an Israelite who knew no guile. In this chapter, Jesus used an expressive figure of speech in the call of Peter. "Thou shalt be called Cephas, meaning a *stone*" (John 1:42). A rock is the symbol of strength, of durability, and after a good deal of chiseling the rock-like character of Peter appeared. What confidence Christ must have had in this disciple who was to deny Him, to say, "Thou shalt be a Rock-man" (see Matthew 16:17).

Jesus not only addressed Nathanael, but all those first disciples when He spoke of the angels ascending and descending upon Him. Jacob had a vision of that *ladder* centuries before Christ's day (Genesis 28:12,13). Used parabolically, the *ladder* from earth to heaven was "the Word made flesh." Heaven was opened at His incarnation and from then on, messengers have been going backward and forward between humanity and its God. This *ladder* goes down to the very depths of man's wretchedness and sin, and reaches up to the throne of His glory.

This great chapter abounds in striking names and titles for our Lord, and they make a striking study in themselves — The Word; The Light; The Life of Men; The only-begotten of the Father; The Christ; The Lamb of God; The Master; The Son of God; The King of Israel.

Then we have Christ's favorite designation of Himself, *The Son of Man*. With only one exception (John 12:34), it was His own title for Himself. Nathanael had said, "Thou art the Son of God," but He Himself said of Himself, "I am the Son of Man." And He was both. He had perfect humanity, perfect deity, and perfectly united both humanity and deity in His Person.

The order of the traveling angels is worthy of note, "ascending and descending upon the Son of Man." It is not descending from heaven to earth, then ascending from earth to heaven, but ascending first. This means, does it not, that the angels are here around us, as they were with Christ while on earth? As ministering spirits, the angels were sent forth to do service for those inheriting salvation. There is the old gospel hymn about "Angels hovering round," which is true. They ascend to God with our penitence, prayers and praise, and then descend from heaven to us to carry out divine errands for the welfare of the redeemed. Jesus knew that angels encamped around Him, seeing he feared God.

## The Parable of the Temple
### (John 2:13-22)

Among all the parabolic sayings Jesus used of Himself, none is so significant and sacred as this one in which He spoke of His body as a Temple. By His use of it, He predicted His resurrection from the dead, as He did when He took Jonah as a sign (Matthew 12:38). The double sense in which He employed the word, "Temple," was not understood by the Jewish rulers — custodians of the temple. Thus, when they asked for a sign of His authority to purge the outer courts of the material sanctuary, His "Father's house," He gave them the sign of His coming resurrection, a sign, the disciples only fully understood when Jesus was raised from the dead (John 2:22).

Those mystic words, "Destroy this temple, and in six days I will raise it up," formed His answer to the question regarding His usurpation of the three-fold office of prophet, priest and king, who alone had the right to interfere and suspend the orderly and permitted arrangements of the Temple which was the center of Jewish national and religious life. Standing within the Temple with a heart grieved over the pollution of its holy precincts, Jesus, burning with righteous indignation, purged them. The Jews, thinking that Jesus meant the destruction of the whole Temple, when He said if you "Destroy this temple," ridiculed Him by saying that it was utterly impossible for Him to build in three days what it took them forty-six years to build. But two words are used for "Temple." The one the Jews used, *Hieron,* meant the whole of the building—Outer Courts, Holy Place, Holy of Holies. The word, however, Jesus used was *naos,* meaning the Holy of Holies, the inner sanctuary, the sacred center of everything related to the Temple.

When Jesus spake of the Temple of His body He was therein emphasizing the solemn truth that "the true shrine of deity was the body of the Incarnate Word. The Temple of wood and stone was but the representative of the Divine Presence. That Presence was then actually in their midst." As the ornate Temple was meant to be God's dwelling place, the medium of divine revelation, and the center where God and man could meet by divine appointment, so Christ, in and through Himself, was to become the true and only meeting place of worship.

The two-fold imperative Jesus employed speaks of His death and resurrection, *Destroy this temple*. Note, that He did not say, as He was wrongly accused at His trial of saying, "I will destroy this temple," but *destroy,* that is, you destroy it! Christ knew that the hostility of the Temple hierarchy would end in His death. So He challenged them to do their worst, "Destroy My body." Then the second imperative carried with it divine authority, *In three days I will raise it up*. These two great central truths of His death and resurrection constitute the infallible sign of His authority, not only to purge a desecrated Temple, but to build a spiritual Temple in the world which He is doing on the basis of His death and resurrection. Material shrines can be easily destroyed, but no power can destroy the mystic fabric of the Temple of His Church which He is building. "Ye are God's building" (I Corinthians 3:16,17).

As Jesus spake of the Temple of His body, so Paul used the same figure, so full of spiritual significance of the body of the believer (I Corinthians 6:19; II Corinthians 6:16). In his introduction to an impressive study on *The Temple of His Body,* F. B. Meyer writes: "What is your body? An inn, thronged with busy traffic! A library, whose shelves are being gradually filled with the gathering stores of knowledge! A country-house, dedicated to money-making, in which the amassing of wealth, or the maintenance of a competence is the one and all important object! A playhouse, used for no higher purpose than pleasure-seeking! A stye, where swinish passions revel!" Because the Lord has made our bodies His dwelling place, may they be constantly presented to Him as a living sacrifice. Having Him as a personal Saviour of the soul, may we at all times recognize Him as "the Saviour of the body."

# The Parable of the Water and Wind
### (John 3:1-13)

For the miraculous aspect of "The New Birth," the reader is directed to the full treatment given in the author's *All the Miracles of the Bible.* All we are dealing with at this point is the significance of the parabolic language used to describe the work of the Holy Spirit in the regeneration of a soul. The chapter before us is a continuation of what goes before and not a separate narrative. The word *But,* which should introduce the chapter, is a conjunction connecting the visit of Nicodemus to what happened at the Passover when many believed in His name, when they saw the miracles which Jesus did (John 2:23). Doubtless Nicodemus was one of these, for when alone with Jesus he said, "No man can do these miracles that thou doest, except God be with him" (John 3:2). And because He knew what was in man (John 2:25), He had no need that any should tell him what was in the mind of the man of the Pharisees who came to Jesus that night for spiritual instruction.

The three figures of speech Jesus used were — birth, water and wind. First of all, the *birth* is described in different ways which, in their totality, indicate its exact nature:

"Born again" or "born from above," or "born afresh," or "anew."

"Born of water and of the Spirit," or "the wind."

"Born of the Spirit."

Every man enters the world, born of the flesh — flesh being used in its widest and special sense as the realm of the physical. In an impressive repetition Jesus told Nicodemus that he needed, in spite of the fact that he was deeply religious and highly educated, to be born a second time, a simile Nicodemus thought referred to a second physical birth. But Jesus was teaching the teacher in Israel that as there is no entrance into the kingdom of the flesh-life save by a natural birth, so there can be no entrance into the kingdom of the spirit-life, save by a spiritual birth.

As the result of a physical birth we are brought into an earthly family and assume human relationship, so through a spiritual birth we are introduced into a heavenly family, even the Kingdom of God with all its holy relationships. Through the first birth we enter the world, a new and distinct personality. Through the second birth we become a new creation, the same personality but transformed by the Spirit. But although our first birth was the gate into life, we were not asked to be born, or of whom we would be born. With the second birth it is different, for this new birth cannot take place apart from our own volition, *"Ye* must be born anew." And when Christ uses the imperative mood, He means it. The sinner *must* be born from above, if he is to go above at death. This new birth can only take place as the repentant, believing sinner wills it.

Coming to the second figure of speech, What exactly did Jesus mean by being *born of water?* One writer ingenuously connects it with the cradle of water surrounding the unborn babe within the womb, and which assists in its birth. Many other writers affirm that *water* refers to the baptismal waters, which Nicodemus as a Jew would know about in connection with John the Baptist's ministry. The Baptist proclaimed that Jews and Gentiles must repent and be baptized if they would become new-born babes in the Kingdom. To such, *baptism* would become an outward sign of inward grace, a public profession in the presence of witnesses, and an open loyalty to the new King and His Kingdom.

There are other expositors who look upon the simile of *water* as referring to the Spirit whose varied ministry our Lord likened unto "rivers of living water." Then there are those who take the *water* as the emblem of the Word. Jesus said, "Now are ye clean through the word I have spoken unto you (John 15:3). Both David and Paul speak of the cleansing effect of the Bible as *water* (Psalm 119:9; Ephesians 5:26). Perhaps a combination of the two may be nearer the thought Jesus had in mind. It is as the Spirit operates through the Word, that sinners are born anew. "Faith cometh by hearing, and hearing by the Word of God" (Romans 10:17).

Coming to the third figure Jesus used, namely *Wind,* we have a forcible illustration of the mysterious operations of the Spirit in His work of conviction and regeneration. If the conversation between Jesus and Nicodemus took place on the house-top, or in the garden, perhaps as they were speaking, a gentle breeze arose, and Jesus in His usual, unique way seized on the passing inci-

dent to elucidate and impress His meaning. The word Jesus used for *wind* was not the ordinary one, *"anemos,"* but *"pneuma,"* meaning "breath" or "breeze." *The wind bloweth where it listeth* — not the whistling wind, but the gentle breeze that rises and falls, comes and goes, one knows not how.

The *wind* is uncertain and variable and mysterious in its operation — "it bloweth where it listeth." It moves where it wills or pleases, is not subject to our order or command. Thus it is with the Spirit's work. "The things of God knoweth no man, but the Spirit of God" (I Corinthians 2:11-16). Saul of Tarsus had no knowledge that day he set out to murder those defenseless Christians that at its noon-hour, he would be caught by a breeze from heaven. The Spirit disperses His gifts and influences where and when, on whom, and in what measure and manner He pleases. He divideth to everyone severally as He will (I Corinthians 12:11).

Further, although the wind is invisible we can yet trace its course in the changes it produces and often stand in awe at its effects. "Thou hearest the sound thereof." When the soft winds blow in spring, what an awakening it produces in creation. Is it not thus when the heavenly Wind blows over the souls of men, arousing them from spiritual death to life for ever more? "Thou canst not tell whence it cometh" — *its origin;* "and whither it goeth" — *its destination.* It gathers its strength and then uses and spends its strength. It is thus with the working of the Spirit, who, as the Quickening One, is eternal in His origin and life-giving in His operation. How blessed we are if our sails are set to catch this heavenly Breeze! It would seem as if Nicodemus came to fully understand the import of our Lord's parabolic language, and through the water or His Word and by the wind of the Spirit, became a child of God. He became a friend of Jesus, defending Him when He was falsely accused (John 7:50), and with Joseph of Arimathaea took Christ's dead body and buried it with a rich offering of love (John 19:39).

Because Christ was born of a woman to give man "second birth," the question of paramount importance is, Have *you* experienced this second birth? Your first birth, whether in affluent or poor circumstances, is of no criterion. "*Ye* must be born anew." Such a spiritual birth is equivalent to the reception of Christ as Saviour. "To as many as received Him, to them He gave the power, or right, or authority, to become the children of God" (John 1:12,13).

## The Parable of the Serpent on the Pole
### (John 3:14-17)

The conjunction, "And," proves that the picture from Jewish history Jesus used was still a part of His conversation with Nicodemus, who asked two questions of Jesus:

"How can a man be born when he is old?" (3:4).

"How can these things be?" (3:9).

The first question was asked in all sincerity. Nicodemus, understanding the phraseology of being born anew, mistakenly considered the change of personality from the physical standpoint. But Jesus answered this question by saying that the laws governing the flesh and governing the Spirit are not the same. "That which is born of the flesh is flesh," but entrance into the realm of the Spirit is never after the flesh. There is a pathetic note in the question, "How can a man be born when he is *old?*" If this implies that when he asked it, Nicodemus was an aged man, deeply set in his religious, traditional ways, then we can understand his problem about changing his entire outlook and entering into a higher realm of life and personality. The tragedy is that few old people become born-again believers. Thank God, some do!

The second question is related to the basis upon which the Holy Spirit can bring about the new birth. Then Jesus, answering the well-known teacher of Israel, reminded him that as a renowned instructor of Old Testament Scriptures, he should have known the spiritual truth He was expounding. Jesus then recited an historical event Nicodemus knew only too well, and applying it, revealed that *redemption* is the basis of *regeneration*. "How can these things be?" How can a man be born anew? How can he become a new creation, only through faith in the uplifted Saviour? Nicodemus asked for heavenly secrets and Jesus after using the illustrations of water and wind from the realm of natural phenomena, now comes to the realm of historic record, which Nicodemus knew by heart. Why was the serpent lifted up on a pole? (Numbers 21:8,9) It was because of the murmurings of the Israelites against God and His ways. Notwithstanding all His goodness toward them, they became a stiff-necked people.

Because of their wickedness, God sent fiery flying serpents to destroy them. God miraculously increased the number of serpents with which the wilderness was infested, and being of a very malignant nature, their bite resulted in a fatal inflammation from which the bitten people died. But Moses interceded for the afflicted murmurers, and God appointed them an easy remedy, the use of which healed their wounds and removed calamity. God ordered that a brazen serpent, a replica of the live serpents but without their deadly venom, be erected on a pole in the midst of the camp, and all the serpent-smitten people had to do to escape death, was to look at the serpent. And all who looked, lived.

Showing Nicodemus how "heavenly activity creates the opportunity for earthly activity, and that when the heavenly activity and the earthly come into touch with each other, there is the way of life," Jesus used those two little words so common to Scripture — as and so. "*As* Moses lifted up the serpent in the wilderness, even *so* must the Son of Man be lifted up; that whosoever believeth in him should not perish but have eternal life." Nicodemus was brought face to face with the cross as the only way by which old things can pass away and a new life become a reality. As the mercy of God provided a way of healing for the Israelites that their bodies need not die, so His grace provided the cross by which all who are dead in sin can possess life eternal and experience healing of the soul. Now all the sinner has to do in order to become a child of God, is to look by faith to the crucified One. "*Look* unto me, and be ye saved, all the ends of the earth; for I am God, and there is none else" (Isaiah 45:22).

## The Parable of the Living Water

### (John 4:14; 4:1-42)

How varied and apt was the earthly ministry of our Lord! No matter where He was, or with whom He conversed, His technique of approach was perfect. After His nine months' successful tour in Judea, a success that engendered the hatred of the Pharisees, Jesus leaves the city for the country. His ministrations were transferred to Galilee, "where the authority of the Sanhedrin was less rigorous, and the people were liberalized by the larger admixture of Gentile residents." There were two roads from Jerusalem to Galilee — the roundabout one along the Jordan valley which orthodox Jews always took so as not to contact the despised Samaritans in Samaria, and the more direct one through Samaria to Galilee. Jesus chose "the latter road for reasons which dated from the council-chamber of Eternity." He knew what was in woman, as well as man (John 2:25), and in Samaria was a woman of sin and shame who needed His grace. Therefore, although He was a Jew, with a love independent of race, religious bigotry, and human need, He took the despised road to the heart of a Samaritan woman whose degraded life was to be transformed by His message and power.

Leaving Nicodemus and coming to the woman at the well, Jesus used it as a pulpit to plead with all who wearily seek after life, satisfaction and blessedness to come unto Him. We cannot but be impressed with His art as a soul-winner. What extremes and contrasts are presented between the teacher in Israel, and the female slave drawing water from Sychar's well. The one was at the top of the social ladder; the other at the bottom. The one was highly respected, cultured, religious; the other a woman of passion, ignorant, debauched and godless.

Then in His dealing with these opposite characters, it would seem as if Jesus had His lines crossed. What He said about the necessity of being born anew was surely the message the Samaritan woman needed most — and the teaching regarding inner spirituality and spiritual worship was more suited to Nicodemus, the religious instructor, and also for Christ's more advanced disciples, than for the piece of earth's "broken-earthenware" which He found at the well. But He never made a mistake in His approach to those in need of His saving touch. He knew that deep down in the underworld of this wretched woman's life there were yearnings Godward. True, as a Samaritan she was reckoned to be outside the Covenant of Israel, and because she was that kind of woman she was fit only to be left to rot in her sin.

We thus come to the beautiful setting of the meeting of the Saviour and the sinner. Jesus, weary with His journey, sat on the edge of the well. What an encouraging touch John gives us! The Apostle reveals Him as the One who, being perfectly human, was so weary with the walk from Judea to Samaria that He needed a rest by the way. But often weary *in* His mission, Christ was never weary *of* it. He was never weary *in* well-doing. Then He was not only weary but *thirsty,* and said to the woman, "Give me to drink."

Not knowing who the stranger was, only that He was a Jew, the woman was amazed that a Jew begged a drink from her, a detested Samaritan. Reading between the lines it would seem as if Jesus forgot His weary, thirsty condition, for here was a soul weary of her sin, and thirsty for soul-satisfaction. Thus, following the method characterizing His teaching, Jesus used what was at hand to illustrate His message. The woman was a drawer of water, and in a simple, natural and exemplary way Jesus led the woman from the natural to the spiritual, from the water in Jacob's Well to the unfailing source of life and satisfaction to be found in Himself.

In his illuminating study of the chapter before us, Campbell Morgan points out that two entirely different words for our English word *well* are used in the context. In speaking of the well at Sychar, the woman said, "The well is deep . . . our father Jacob gave us the well" (John 4:11,12). Here, the word for "well" is *phear,* meaning a hole, or cistern, containing an amount of accumulated water. But the word John employed when he said "Jacob's well was there" and "Jesus sat by the well"; and then the word Jesus Himself used when He spoke of "a well of water" (4:6,14), was not the same word *phear,* but a word meaning a spring of water, a springing or leaping up of water. This particular word occurs only here and twice in the Acts (3:8; 14:10), where it is used of the lame man at the Beautiful Gate "leaping."

The woman called it a *well.* Jesus spoke of it as a *spring.* Knowing the deep thirst of the woman's life, He used the term illustrating the source of the water the well supplied. The difference was between an accumulation of water (water gathered up and retained) and living, flowing water. When Isaac's servants digged in the valley they "found there a well of springing water" (Genesis 26:32). The woman came to draw collected water, and stored water soon becomes stagnant water. Jesus offered the thirsty soul at Sychar's well, springing, living water to satisfy her deepest need. The well of water springing, bubbling up, perennially full and fresh, was His parabolic illustration of all that He can supply a parched, thirsty and feverish humanity. The water from the world's broken cisterns fails, but as we drink from the life-giving stream in Him we can sing —

"My thirst was quenched, my soul
    revived,
And now I live in Him."

From the riven side of Jesus on the cross, blood and *water* flowed forth. A fountain was opened adequate to banish thirst from those who come to God. The woman at the well drank and lived, and was the means of leading many other spiritually thirsty souls to the Source of satisfaction. She left her *waterpot* and went into the city and told the Samaritans of the springing well she had found and they, too, came to believe on Jesus as "the Christ, the Saviour of the world" (John 4:42), the Giver of the living water. Would that multitudes of thirst-stricken souls today could be found taking of this water of life *freely* (Revelation 21:6; 22:17)!

# The Parable of the Bread
# of Life
(John 6:35-38)

Comparing our Lord's teaching here with that of His conversation with the woman of Samaria, we discover a similar thought expressed. The woman came to draw water, and the Lord offered her Himself as a well of water springing up. In the narrative we are now considering the people desired bread, and He offered Himself as the Bread of Life from heaven. This chapter as a whole can be fitly termed "The Bread Chapter," seeing *bread* occurs some 21 times, and Christ's parabolic illustration of bread is full of spiritual instruction.

The day before this discourse, Christ had supernaturally fed the hungry with literal, physical bread, as we have shown in *All the Miracles of the Bible.* But the loaves out of the lad's five small loaves were not sufficient for another day's need, so the people returned to our Lord, hoping for another manifestation of His power to satisfy their hunger. They only thought of the material, being ignorant of the spiritual satisfaction which the miracle of the multiplied bread was meant to signify. All the people wanted was full bellies. They sought and labored for the food that perished. Jesus came to give them *Bread* that could supply them with life eternal, just as He gave the woman a life-giving *Spring* banishing her spiritual thirst. The pivot around which our Lord's teaching about Himself as living Bread revolves is to be found in His words: "He that eateth me, even he shall live by me" (John 6:57). After announcing Himself as "The Bread of Life," He glided from a deep into a deeper revelation. "The bread that I will give is my flesh, which I give for the life of the world" (John 6:51-53).

The three great essentials to physical life are *breath, water* and *food*. Man can live only a few minutes without breath, only a week without water, and some forty days without food. In John's *gospel,* Jesus offers to meet these three essentials in the spiritual life.

In the third chapter, He spoke of the breath or wind of the Spirit, without which man cannot have spiritual, eternal life.

In the fourth chapter, He told the woman of the living water by which she could live forevermore.

In this sixth chapter, He offers Himself as the food so essential to life here and hereafter. Man's deepest hunger is spiritual, and Jesus is the only One able to satisfy such hunger. As Bread, He meets our deepest hunger seeing He came as the Bread of God, or the Bread who is God. As Man, He knows every human need; as God, He is able to meet every one of them. Was it not fitting that Jesus was born in *Bethlehem* which means, "the house of bread"? He was born to be the "bread of God" (John 16:32,33), "the Bread of Life" (John 6:35,48), "the Bread from Heaven" (John 6:33,50,51,58). Do not these designations declare His antiquity, abil-

ity and authority? As "The Life" (John 14:6), He can impart and sustain life. Deep beneath all other needs, is man's spiritual hunger, which Christ alone can satisfy; and which, when He satisfies it, helps to eliminate lesser needs.

In the East, bread as we understand the term, made of meal, was the primary, principal food of people, their general source of sustenance. When God said to Adam, "In the sweat of thy face shalt thou eat bread" (Genesis 3:10), the word for bread did not merely imply a meal made up of barley or wheat, but food in general. To the Eastern mind, bread always represented hospitality and fellowship. Meeting together, friends would break bread with one another as a token of unity in fellowship. Our natural life depends upon the eating of suitable, nourishing food. Ordinary bread cannot beget or impart physical life. It can, however, if thoroughly digested, impart energy and strength fitting us for the daily task and common round. Christ offers Himself as life-giving Food, and it is only as we appropriate and assimilate what He is in Himself that we can be vitalized or quickened.

While Bread does not beget life, it contains life-germs, so necessary for the maintenance of our physical well-being and vitality. With august majesty Jesus declared Himself to be "The Bread of Life," "The Living Bread." Unlike natural bread, He is able to supply life as well as sustain it. Those wonderful eight *I Am's* of Jesus contain significant claims. The great name of God revealed to Moses at the bush, reasserts itself in august and dreadful majesty in these *I am's* — "I am, that I am." When Jesus said, "I am the Bread of Life," He meant that He was able to communicate life and continue it. Did He not say, "As the Father hath life in Himself, He gave to the Son to have life in Himself"? Thus He brought with Him, this infinite and ever-blessed life of the Eternal. He came as the Bread from Heaven, that man through Him might go to heaven.

The manna He uses in the narrative as a parabolic illustration of Himself, although miraculous in its origin, was yet material in its nature. But Jesus came as "the true Manna" — *true*, in that the old manna ceased. Jesus was, and is, miraculous, both in origin and nature, and therefore, all-sufficient for life. As the bread we eat contains in itself many of the elements needed for nutrition, so in Christ we have all that is necessary for our spiritual and eternal life.

"Bread of Heaven, Bread of Heaven
Feed me till I want no more."

But what is the bread we daily eat? Is it not bruised corn? Says the prophet, "Bread corn is bruised" (Isaiah 28:28), which reminds us that our spiritual sustenance comes as the result of His sufferings. At Calvary, the Bread from Heaven was bruised and broken for our iniquity. Now, we have life through His death.

"Bread of the world, in mercy broken;
Wine of the soul, in mercy shed."

Bread, however, is only nourishing and sustaining as it is appropriated and assimilated. This is why Jesus went on to utter those mystic words, which the Romish Church falsely interprets, about eating His flesh and drinking His blood. His "real Presence" is not in the so-called "mass" but in the heart of those quickened by His Spirit. Our Lord's use of the parabolic illustration of "flesh and blood" must be taken in a spiritual sense (6:55,57; see Jeremiah 15:26; Ezekiel 2:8; 3:4; Revelation 10:6,7). At His incarnation, He became flesh, and at Calvary His blood, or life, was liberated through death. Thus eating His flesh and drinking His blood represents our appropriation by faith of all that His life and death made possible. Did not the Israelites of old eat spiritual food (I Corinthians 10:3,4)? When Christ enters the believing sinner and incorporates Himself within his life, He becomes the Source of spiritual vigor and victory, of energy and expansion, of strength and sustenance. Eating of Him, we have life forever (John 6:51).

The practical side of the parable before us must not be forgotten. Jesus, as the Bread of God, does not satisfy us merely for our own personal relief. Once He becomes our Life, He wants to feed other hungry hearts, through our lives and lips. "Give ye them to eat." The bread Jesus broke for the multitudes was passed to them through the hands of the disciples who thus had a share in His glorious task. Shame on us, if we are content to feast our souls on Him, neglectful of the cries of myriads who are perishing with hunger. We dare not surfeit ourselves and leave others without a crumb. Saved, we must become the means of saving others. Strength derived through feasting on Him must be used to His service for the leading of those who are spiritually starved to the Bread of God from heaven, so that they, too, can be made partakers of His nature.

## The Parable of Living Waters
### (John 7:37-39)

From the spring of water Jesus spoke of to the woman at the well, we now come to the parabolic figure of *rivers*. Not a spring, or a brook, or even a river, but *rivers*, the plural suggesting the plenteousness of provision in and through Him, who spoke of the Spirit. Before we come to the significance of the incident when Jesus stood and cried, "If any man thirst, let him come unto me and drink," it may prove profitable to point out the three-fold aspect of the Spirit's ministry in connection with the walk and witness of the believer. In the third of John, we have the incoming of the Spirit (John 3:7). In the fourth of John, His upspringing (John 4:14). In the seventh of John, His outflowing (John 7:37-39). Thus, the life-giving Spirit *regenerates*, then *permeates*, and through the life He permeates, He seeks to *irrigate* the dry, barren wilderness around. He flows *in*, then *through*, and finally *out*. These three aspects of the Spirit's work are likewise associated with our *salvation, sanctification* and *service.*

The immediate setting of our Lord's impressive illustration of rivers of living water flowing from the believer, was the last day, the great day of the Feast of Tabernacles which lasted for eight days (Deuteronomy 16:13; Numbers 29:12, 35; Leviticus 23:36; Nehemiah 8:18). Every day during this Feast, there was a procession of priests who, with empty, golden vessels from the Temple on their shoulders, marched through the streets, singing parts of *The Great Hallel,* or Psalms 113-118, accompanied with cymbals and trumpets. The sacrifice over, priests and people found their way to the fountain at Siloam, where the vessels were filled and the joyful procession wended its way back to the Temple, where in the presence of the assembled host, the leading priest went up to the altar of burnt-offering, and the people cried out to him, "Lift up thy hand!" and he made the libation, turning the golden vessel to the West, and to the East a cup filled with wine from two silver vases pierced with holes. Then during the libation, the people sang, always to the sound of cymbals and trumpets, "Ye shall draw water with joy out of the well of salvation" (Isaiah 12:3). These words, the Jews of old believed, were heavy with Messianic significance.

Campbell Morgan points out that by our Lord's time many items had been added to the ritual of the ancient Feast. and that on its *eighth* day, there was no procession of priests and carrying of water. It was on this "last and good day" of the Feast that Jesus, the Great High Priest, applied to Himself "one of the most striking Messianic symbols among all those which the national history contained." From Rabbinical literature we gather that the rites were emblems recalling to mind one of the great theocratic miracles wrought in the wilderness, namely, the pouring forth of water out of the rock smitten by Moses and the continuance of the water

through the wilderness pilgrimage. Reaching Canaan, the supernatural supply was no longer necessary, because there were springs and rivers everywhere in the Land of Promise. The Jewish leaders affirmed that the ritual of the Feast also symbolized the recognition of those promises and prophecies of a time when new fertilizing powers would come to the Nation and the land. The absence of priests on the eighth day signified there was no need of a supernatural supply of water; and also that "the long hoped-for promise of the new dispensation of fruitfulness and re-dedication had not dawned."

The pregnant phrase, "As the Scripture saith," reveals not only Christ's intimate knowledge of Old Testament Scripture, but also His authoritative seal to their divine inspiration and veracity. Here, in John's gospel, He seems to have lived in the past seeing in many of its miracles, parables of His own life and work.

> In chapter 2, He presented Himself as the true Temple.
> In chapter 3, He is the One lifted up on a pole.
> In chapter 8, He is the *Shekinah,* the true luminous cloud.
> In chapter 19, He speaks of Himself as the Paschal Lamb.

And here, in chapter 7, He is the true Rock, from which rivers of living water are to flow. As multitudes quenched their thirst from the water flowing from the rock which Moses smote, so once Christ, as the Rock, is smitten at Calvary, there will be liberated the life-giving water of the Spirit. As the waters came "from within" the interior cavity of the rock at Horeb (Exodus 17:6; Number 20:11), so out of Jesus there was to flow those rivers of the Spirit's presence and power, and streams of new life and spiritual gifts so necessary for the spiritual quickening and refreshment of all believers.

Usually Jesus uttered His parables while seated. Here, we read that He *stood,* a fitting posture seeing that the priest stood as he poured out the water from the golden vessel. That the rivers of living water were parabolic of the Spirit's prophesied effusion is proved by John's specific announcement regarding Christ's utterance and action, "This He spake of the Spirit . . . who was not yet, because Jesus was not yet glorified." While the translators of the A.V. fittingly added "given," the actual text reads, "The Spirit was not yet," and refers to the new and fuller bestowal of the Spirit which was granted at Pentecost after Christ's ascension to heaven and glorification there. In the Old Testament, there was only a dim conception of the Spirit as a *Person*. Then He was looked upon more or less as a Divine *Power* coming upon men to equip them for a special task as in the case of Bezeleel, and when the task was completed, the Power was withdrawn. Now Jesus promises the Spirit in *Person* to dwell with believers. He was to come and take up His abode in them. But such an advent of the Third Person of the blessed Trinity was contingent upon the going of the Second Person to Heaven. "If I go not away, the Paraclete will not come unto you" (John 16:7).

Christ's glorification came as the result of His death, resurrection, and ascension to the right hand of the Majesty on high, and once He was seated as the glorified Son of Man, the Holy Spirit came in all the plenitude of His power and gifts for believers. In the Acts, from Pentecost on, we have the outflowing of the mighty, life-giving rivers of the Spirit, with everything made to live whithersoever these rivers flowed. Thereafter, He became the perennial sower of spiritual life and the perfect satisfaction of this life for the true Church in all ages.

The parable has its personal and spiritual counterpart, for as the Spirit's coming was consequent upon the glorification of Jesus, now the Spirit can only bestow His fulness upon those hearts, glorifying Jesus by giving Him the place of pre-eminence in their life. There must be an ascension and enthronement within, with all things put under His feet, if the Spirit is to infill us with successive waves of power. All who have a thirst for the Lord, who come to Him by faith and drink of the waters out of the Rock, are eligible to become channels of blessing to the thirsty around. Can we say that rivers of blessing issue from under the sanctuary of our life? Are we transmitting to others the refreshing benefits of divine grace? Is your life comparable to a river, nay, to many rivers of holy influence?

If the *rivers* Jesus spoke of are suggestive of life in a two-fold way, namely, "the satisfaction of life in its thirst; and secondly, the fructifying of all life, that it may bring forth a harvest," then experiencing the first aspect of having our thirst quenched and our soul revived, are we through the Spirit-possessed life producing a harvest of souls for the Lord's glory? If we are not fully satisfied, how can we lead others away from the broken cisterns of the world to Him who is the Life-giving Stream? One asks, "Are we satisfied? Because unless we are, no rivers are flowing from our lives. We may be good men and women doing good things, but the running rivers are not there. The influence we are exerting is not that of the Spirit because the effluence, the incoming of the Spirit, has not been what it ought to be. No rivers run from thirsty souls. . . . There is no thirst when the rivers are running. No rivers if we are still thirsty. No thirst? Then the rivers are running."

Channels only, blessed Master,
And with all Thy wondrous power;
Flowing through us, Thou canst use us.
Every day and every hour.

## The Parable of the World's Light
(John 8:12-30)

In this second great I Am of Jesus, we have a parabolic illustration in His direct, stupendous claim, "I am the Light of the World." The One who came as the revelation of God, full of grace and truth (John 1:1,14) now proclaims Himself to be this dark world's *Light*. Having claimed to quench the thirst of humanity, He now proclaims Himself to be the only One able to illuminate the sin-darkened minds of men. The common word Jesus used for "light" was well-known to all who heard Him. It is *Phos,* meaning, "to shine, in order to make manifest." God said, "Let there be light," and light became, shone.

> All our knowledge, sense and sight
> Lie in deepest darkness shrouded,
> Till God's brightness breaks our night
> By the beams of truth unclouded.

As the celebration of the Feast of Tabernacles suggested the parable of "the rivers of living water" to Jesus, what prompted Him to designate Himself "the Light of the world" (*world,* meaning "cosmos," the sum total of humanity? Many writers have thought that He was alluding to the brightness which was shed forth by the two seven-pronged candelabras which were lighted at evening during the Feast, the light of which, the Rabbis said, shone over the whole of Jerusalem. But Jesus came not only as the Life (John 7:31). He offers Himself as the Light emanating from Life, and as the Light, not only for a city but as the Light of, and for, the world.

Nothing is so pure as light. Snow is pure but is soon polluted. Not so with Light, which man's hand cannot soil or corrupt. Nothing can defile its rays or pollute its beams. Although, as the Light, Jesus took upon Himself the form of sinful flesh, He was born, and lived, without sin. "He was holy, harmless, undefiled, separate from sinners." Light is also as bright as it is pure. The day, and our homes, are bright in proportion as they are full of the sun's light. As the Light, Jesus came as "the brightness of the Father's glory," and His office is to dispense brightness wherever sin's darkness prevails. Light, too, is free, free as the air we breathe, and shines equally on prince and pauper. Without money and

without price, light shines upon both slums and palaces. Christ, as Heaven's Light, is offered equally freely and on the same terms of grace to Jews and Gentiles alike. He is the true Light, ready to lighten every man that cometh into the world. *Revelation* is another quality pertaining to the nature of light. Darkness obscures, but light reveals. It is thus as the Light that Christ functions. In the spiritual world, He is the great Revealer. As the Light, He throws light into "the darkened cells, where passion reigns supreme," and reveals our true selves in His sight.

Last of all, light is life-giving. Without the sun, and the myriads of stars, this world would die. "It is the warming light of spring that starts the dormant germs, that swells the buds, that clothes the vineyards, the field and the woods with vegetation, fragrance and plenty." It is so with Christ as the Light. Hearts into which He has not shone are spiritually dead. If destitute of the warm rays of His grace, then we live in a condition of spiritual winter. If, as the Light, all His benefits are to be enjoyed, He must first of all be received. As a fresh day dawns, we draw the curtains, that the morning light may flood the house. It is thus with man, who must open the shutters of his heart for "the Lord God, who is a Sun" to dispel all darkness with His radiant beams.

As "the Living Water" is for all who are athirst, so "the Light" is for those who are willing to walk in it, and if we walk in the light as He is in the light, and is *the Light* then we walk no longer in the darkness of sin, but become reflectors of the Light. This brings us to the challenging word, "As He is, so are we in this world." Jesus said of Himself, "I am the light of the world," and of those who are His, "Ye are the light of the world." But are we light-dispensing orbs? Are we shining as bright lights amid the world's gathering darkness? Our light is to shine before men, that seeing our good works, the Lord is glorified thereby.

Let the lower lights be burning,
Send a gleam across the waves.
Some poor fainting, struggling seaman,
You may rescue, you may save.

# The Parable of
# Day and Night
## (John 9:4)

Wrapped up with the miracle of the man blind from his birth made to see, is the parabolic illustration Jesus used of the works of God which He was sent to accomplish: "I must work the work of him who sent me, while it is *day*; The *night* comes, in which no man can work." Godet says that the contrast of *day* and night, "cannot denote that of opportunity and inopportunity, or that of the moment of grace and the hour when it can no longer be obtained; it can be here only the contrast between the time of *working* during the day, and that of *rest* when once the night is come. There is therefore nothing sinister in this figure: night."

But does not Paul speak of this span of life, as "the day of salvation," and as the time of man's acceptance of Christ as his Light (II Corinthians 6:2)? It may be that on the same great day of the Feast, as the sun was sinking to the west, that Jesus was reminded that His day of service was fast ending. He went on to say, "As long as I am in the world," but the night of His death was not far distant when His own human activity on earth would cease. As natural night does not come until its appointed hour, so Jesus knew that the day of His life was marked by limits no less sure (John 11:9). But while it was yet full day He must do the work appointed of the Father.

This season of grace, when Christ's Church is continuing His work under the guidance of the Spirit, is our day of opportunity, and its hours must be filled with Spirit-inspired activity. This is the day of soul-winning, a holy ministry which the night of death ends. The ungodly must be warned that this is the day of grace when they can be emancipated from the guilt and burden of their sin, but that if this day of opportunity is finally spurned, it will pass, never to return.

Work for the night is coming!
Work through the sunny noon:
Fill the bright hours with labour,
Rest comes sure and soon.
Give to each flying minute
Something to keep in store:
Work for the night is coming,
When man works no more.

# The Parable of the Door
# and the Porter
## (John 10:1-3,9)

Although the bulk of this renowned chapter is taken up with the parable of Jesus as *The Good Shepherd*, within it we have parabolic illustrations that may be distinguished, like The Porter, The Door, Thieves and Robbers, Hirelings, all of which are part of the imagery of the Shepherd and the Sheep, but which like them, are used in a spiritual sense.

The opening formula, "Verily, verily," which John alone gives Jesus as using in His teaching, and which occurs some 25 times in his gospel, proves that he was an acute listener. The double affirmation actually means, *Amen, Amen,* and introduces truth of tremendous importance and urgency. Usually, the formula occurs in the midst of other statements and was resorted to by Jesus to re-arrest and focus attention on the new aspect of truth about to be expounded. Here, "Verily, verily" (John 10:1), does not commence a fresh discourse, but acts as a development of our Lord's deeper teaching (John 1:51). The chapter before us is an extension of His teaching commenced in the previous chapter (John 9:35), which arose out of the miracle of the blind man, a miracle which caused the Pharisees to realize their spiritual blindness. Jesus follows on to describe them as thieves, robbers, and hirelings, much to their anger (John 10:21).

*The Door.* The common figure of a "door" is not only used literally (Matthew 6:6; 27:60), but in various metaphorical ways as W. E. Vine indicates:

Of faith, by acceptance of the Gospel of grace (Acts 14:2)

Of openings for the ministry of the Word of God (I Corinthians 16:9; II Corinthians 2:12; Colossians 4:3; Revelation 3:8)

Of entrance into the Kingdom of God (Matthew 25:10; Luke 13:24,25)

Of Christ's entrance into a repentant believer's heart (Revelation 3:20)

Of the nearness of Christ's Second Advent (Matthew 24:33; Mark 13:29; James 5:9)

Of access to behold visions relative to the purposes of God (Revelation 4:1)

Of Christ as the One through which we enter into grace (John 10:7,9)

By the *door* into the sheepfold through which the shepherd enters, we are to understand a door *to* the sheep, not *for* them. Jesus takes up this material provision for the shepherd and applies it to Himself: "*I am the* Door." What impressive thoughts are connected with this further I Am of Jesus! A door has a two-fold function — it admits and excludes; it can shut in all who are welcome and shut out those whose company is not desired. When the door was shut at the Marriage Feast (Matthew 25:10), it shut in the five wise virgins and shut out the five foolish ones.

Christ is the Door, and as we enter in, we are saved. It is only through Him that we have access unto the Father (Ephesians 2:18). The figure of the Door is parallel to that of "the strait gate" and "the narrow way" (Matthew 7:13,14; see Romans 5:2). We cannot narrow the Door to the fold, nor yet may we widen it. Christ is the Door for all those excommunicated by the religious authority of the Pharisees. The man who had received his sight, was cast out, and Jesus asked him, "Dost thou believe on the Son of God?" The man replied, "Who is He, Lord, that I may believe?" Then Jesus offered Himself as the Door into a new life when He said, "He it is that speaketh with thee"; and receiving Him, the once-blind man found through Him the entrance into an entirely new realm. When Jesus addressed the religious rulers who cast out the man whose sight He restored, He condemned them for being excommunicators. "Woe unto you lawyers! for ye took away the key of knowledge; ye entered not yourselves and them that were entering in ye hindered." They had failed as doors through whom others could enter into the true knowledge of God, now He offers Himself as the Door.

With Eastern shepherds the door was not actually a door with hinges as we understand the term, but an opening in the fold which was an opening in the walled enclosure or palisade. Into this somewhat high enclosure, the sheep were taken in the evening and the porter took over the watch and was responsible for the safety of the sheep. There were thieves bent on stealing the sheep, and robbers out to slaughter the sheep, and if the porter at the door of the fold was not alert the thieves and robbers could climb over the wall and take the sheep. These *thieves* and *robbers* who preceded Christ, "All that ever came before me," cannot apply to Old Testament prophets and teachers who faithfully witnessed to Jesus as the true Door. He was figuratively representing the priestly caste which emerged in the Old Testament. These religious teachers usurped the place of the true prophetic schools and claimed for themselves the position of door to the Kingdom of God. But by their self-made additions to the Law, and their traditions, these exclusionists closed the true door and plundered and oppressed those whom they kept outside. These were the thieves and robbers, and wolves in sheep's clothing, stealing into the flock of Christ and rending those who were true sheep (Acts 20:29; I Peter 5:2).

Campbell Morgan often told the illustration of the Door which had a profound effect upon him when it was related to him by Sir George Adam Smith. It seems that during one of his many

Atlantic crossings, Dr. Morgan had as his fellow-traveler, the renowned theologian. One day, while musing over the things of God, Sir George told Dr. Morgan of a visit he paid to the Far East. While touring he came to one of those folds or enclosures with its opening in the wall. As a shepherd was nearby, Sir George asked him —

"Is that a fold for the sheep?"

"Oh yes," the shepherd replied.

"I see only one way in," said Sir George.

"Yes, there it is, there is the door," replied the shepherd, pointing to the opening in the wall.

"But there is no door there," said Sir George. Although the two were not talking of the *Parable of the Good Shepherd,* or of Christian truth at all, Sir George was amazed when the shepherd said,

"Oh, I am the door."

The great theologian's mind went back to this tenth chapter of John and he asked the shepherd:

"What do you mean by calling yourself the door?"

To which, quite naturally the shepherd replied,

"The sheep go inside, and I come there and lie down across the threshold, and no sheep can get out except over my body, and no wolf can get in except over me."

How rich in spiritual suggestion is this telling illustration. Christ is the Door, and we cannot go out except across His body, and no ravening wolf can reach those sheep except across His body. None can pluck us out of His hands (Luke 10:28, 29). As the Door, Jesus Himself preserves and protects His sheep, and they can go in and out and find pasture. *In* and *out.* Entering through Christ, we find Salvation, Service and Sustenance. Godet reminds us that *To go in and go out* is an expression frequently employed in the Bible to designate the free use of a house, into which one goes or from which one departs unceremoniously, because one belongs to the family of the house, because one is *at home* in it (Deuteronomy 28:6; Jeremiah 37:4; Acts 1:21).

*To go in* expresses the free satisfaction of the need of rest, the possession of a safe retreat.

*To go out* suggests the free satisfaction of the need of nourishment, the easy enjoyment of a rich pasturage (Psalm 23:-2, 5). This is the reason why the words, "shall go out," are immediately followed by the words which explain it, *and shall find pasture.* We go *in* for salvation, and go *out* to serve the One who saved us.

As Jesus is the Door, on which side are you? Are you *in* or *out?* "In Christ" or "without Christ" — saved or lost? What a solemn reminder we have in that simple children's chorus —

> One door, and only one
> Yet its sides are two.
> Inside and Outside —
> Which side are you?

*The Porter.* While this person may not be an essential part of the allegory, yet he has his place in it and was used by Jesus to apply to those specially related to Himself as the Shepherd, and also to the sheep. Actually the word *porter* means "door-keeper," or "guardian of the door," and is used of males and females (Mark 13:14; John 18:16, 17). In pastoral life, the porter was an undershepherd, to whose charge the sheep were committed after they had been folded for the night, and who opened the door on the arrival of the shepherd in the morning.

To our minds, a *porter* suggests a twofold office. One who carries bags, or parcels, like the willing porters at railway stations. The word also describes those at large business establishments and hotels who open the door for those entering or leaving. The latter office is the one indicated by the porter Jesus spoke of, and who, in the spiritual fold, is the one who opens doors for the Shepherd. As the forerunner of Jesus, John the Baptist was the outstanding porter who opened the door for Him whose way he prepared. And when Jesus, as the *Door* appeared, John felt that as he was only a porter, he should retire into the background in order that *The Door* could be clearly seen and entered. "He must increase," the porter said of the Door, "I must decrease." Paul had in mind the Holy Spirit as a Divine Doorkeeper when he wrote about doors of service being opened for him. At Ephesus, "a great and effectual door was opened unto him" (I Corinthians 16:9). At Troas, to which Paul came to preach Christ's Gospel, "a door was opened unto him of the Lord" (II Corinthians 2:12). The Colossians were urged to pray that " a door of the Word may be opened, to speak the mystery of Christ" (Colossians 4:3). Then Paul reported to the brethren that "God had opened the door of faith unto the Gentiles" (Acts 14:-27). Having received the keys from Jesus, Peter, on the Day of Pentecost opened the door of the Gospel to the multitudes gathered together.

A *porter* — door-keeper and door-opener! All who belong to the Good Shepherd should be spiritual porters, guarding the Door or lovingly defending the faith, and also active, opening doors for the Lord to enter. In the spiritual realm, door-openers are soul-winners. As a Christian, are you functioning in a double sense as a Porter? Are you helping to carry the burdens of others? "Bear ye one another's burden." Then are you always on the watch to open a door for the Saviour? If you have never opened a door for Him, or in other words, never won a soul for Him, yours is not the abundant life of which He speaks in this parable.

# The Parable of the Good Shepherd
## (John 10:1-18)

Among the features of John's peculiar style is the repetition of a word or sentence, which serves to underline the thought he endeavors to communicate. Double mention means divine emphasis. Twice over, in the same verse, John records Jesus as saying: "I am the Good Shepherd; the Good Shepherd giveth his life for the sheep" (10:11). The minds of men had been prepared for the conception of Christ as the Shepherd. He was prophesied as the Shepherd (Psalm 23; Isaiah 40:11; Ezekiel 34:11-16, 23; 37:24). The first to receive announcement of His wondrous birth were the lowly shepherds, which was fitting, seeing that the One born in the manger would feed His flock like a shepherd.

As the *Good* Shepherd, He died for the sinful of earth who, as sheep had gone astray (John 10:10, 15).

As the *Great* Shepherd, He rose again, and ascended on high, there to intercede for His sheep (Hebrews 13:20).

As the *Chief* Shepherd, He will return to reward His under-shepherds who were faithful in their care of the flock (I Peter 2:25).

*Good,* as used here, means not only in the possession of goodness, in a physical sense that which is in its own nature excellent, but that which, in a moral sense, is beautiful, noble and true. As used by Christ, the word implies that the perfection of all attributes are His. In Him, they *merge* and from Him *emerge.* As Ellicott expresses it: "He is the Shepherd who is ideally good, fulfilling every thought of guidance, support, self-sacrifice that had ever gathered round the shepherd's name. No image of Christ has so deeply impressed itself upon the mind of the Church as this has. . . . The pastoral staff is the fit emblem of the bishop's work, and the pastor is the name by which the humble wayside flock thinks of him who in Christ's name is appointed to be their guide" (Ephesians 4:11).

Passing from the figure of Christ as the *Door,* let us discover all He is as the *Shepherd* who came to "gather together into one the children of God that were scattered abroad" (John 11:52), and to die for those who were not of this flock. It has been suggested that "the shepherd was always the symbol of the king." Homer once said, "All kings are shepherds of their people." What a different world ours would have been if all sovereigns and rulers had been true shepherds of the people they governed! When we think of Israel's kings and prophets, it is interesting to enumerate how many began as shepherds.

Jesus did not mix His metaphors when He exhorted His disciples to be of good courage, "Fear not, little flock; for it is your Father's good pleasure to give you the kingdom." *Flock, Father, Kingdom,* these three figures of speech merge and constitute the ideal kingship recognized in the East. The ideal *King* was the *Shepherd* of his flock, the *Father* of his family, and authoritative *Ruler* over his nation. When Jesus, with august majesty and dignity, advanced His claim, "I am the good Shepherd," all the above implications of the term were merged in Him.

As "the shepherd and bishop of our souls" (I Peter 2:5), Jesus assumed such a mission, first of all:

*By the Father's appointment.* He knew His beloved Son, as the true Shepherd in contrast to those who were merely hirelings. Did not God speak of Him as, "My Shepherd, the Man that is My Fellow" (Zechariah 13:7)? When Jesus came in the flesh He emphasized the fact that He had been sent by the Father and His mediatorial authority, offices, mission and power were received from His Father.

*By His own voluntary choice.* Although *sent* by the Father, the Son did not come unwillingly. Delighting to do God's will, Jesus heartily conformed to all that was involved. Both Father and Son were one in their love for a lost world, and the Son freely came to seek and to save lost sheep. As we are to see, His death and resurrection, that perishing and self-destroyed souls might be ransomed out of the hand of the enemy, were of His own choice and doing (John 10:15, 17). Let us now seek to identify the blessed relationship existing between the Good Shepherd and His Sheep.

*He owns the Sheep.* Jesus used the pronoun of personal possession when speaking of the Sheep. "His own sheep"

(v. 4), "My sheep" (v. 14), "Other sheep I have" (v. 16). By virtue of creation and redemption, all souls are His, but become His in the truest and deepest sense through the surrender of heart and life to His claims. Those who enter Him as *The Door* can say with David, "The Lord is *my* shepherd" (Psalm 23:1), and of them the Shepherd says, "I know *my* sheep" (John 10:14). Mountain shepherds and their trained dogs know a single sheep among many others, and there is nothing more strange in the sheep being trained to know its own name and its shepherd's voice. If you are the property of the Divine Shepherd, then He knows your name and address and is ready to meet your need as it arises.

*He knows the sheep.* Jesus said that *this* knowledge is mutual: "I know My sheep, and am known of mine" (John 10:14,27). Three times over He speaks of Himself as "the Good Shepherd," twice in connection with His death for the sheep (John 10:11), and here where the designation is repeated to express the closest union and communion between the shepherd and the sheep. Known by Him, and knowing Him, implies more than knowing His voice. It implies that we are partakers of His nature. We are one with Him, even as He could say, "My Father and I are one" (John 10:15,30). We are fully recognized by Him. Bearing the mark of divine ownership, His own are known by the Lord.

An Eastern shepherd knew all the particulars of each of his sheep — history, defects, temper, and tastes — some of which were embodied in the name he gave the sheep. The Father knew all about the One who stood in so peculiar relationship to Himself, "The Father knoweth me, and I know the Father." Perfect knowledge existed between Father and Son. In the same way the Shepherd has a comprehensive and perfect knowledge of each of His sheep. Nothing is hid from Him. "There is not a word on our tongue, but Thou, O

Lord, knowest it altogether." Godet observes: "The word *to know* does not mean: I distinguish them from the rest of the Jews. The import of this word is much more profound, and the meaning *distinguish* is not suitable in the three following sayings. Jesus penetrates with the eye of His loving knowledge the entire interior being of each of the sheep, and perfectly discerns all which He possesses in them. For there is a close relation between this verb, '*I know*' and the possessive, '*my* sheep.' This knowledge is reciprocal. The believers also know what their shepherd is, all that He feels and all that He is willing to do for them. From this intimate relation between Him and His sheep, Jesus goes back to that which is at once the model and source of it: His relation to God."

*He leads the sheep.* With us, the shepherd follows on behind his sheep, driving, prodding and urging them forward, but Eastern shepherds led their sheep. "He goeth before them, and the sheep follow him, for they know his voice" (John 10:4). "The Lord is my Shepherd. . . . He leadeth me" (Psalm 23:1,2). Sheep seldom find their way safely. Other animals may do so, but sheep go astray and their guidance and safety are secured by following the shepherd whose voice is known and is the prime essential for the sheep. "Hear His voice," expresses "the familiar knowledge which the little flock has of the voice of their own shepherd who leads them day by day."

Strangers, thieves or robbers may call the sheep by name and try to imitate their shepherd's voice, but through long usage and intimacy, they can discern a strange voice and are therefore afraid. If we seek to live in full harmony with the will of our heavenly Shepherd, His unerring guidance and direction will be ours because He always leads His sheep in "paths of righteousness for His name's sake" (Psalm 23:3). And trained by the Spirit to know the Shepherd's voice as He speaks to us through His Word, we immediately discern and turn from

a strange voice, even if it is a religious one. The Scribes and Pharisees were imitators of shepherds, and their voice confused and misled the sheep. Because these false leaders failed to understand the parable Jesus was uttering, He reiterated its significance (John 10:6,7). The word "parable" is used here in its widest sense and includes every kind of figurative and proverbial instruction, and every kind of speech. We have already remarked upon John's omission of parables as found in the other gospels.

*He gives His life for the sheep.* Twice over we have the phrase, "I lay down my life for the sheep" (John 10:15, 17); and twice the sentence, "I lay it down" (John 10:18), and twice over the words, "I have power to take it again" (10:17,18). Of His own will, the good Shepherd gave Himself up to die. His life was not taken from Him by Roman crucifiers; His life was willingly given. His death was absolutely self-determined and voluntary. At the final moment, He dismissed His spirit (Luke 23:46). He *gave* His life for the sheep (John 10:11). At Calvary, the sword awoke against the Shepherd, but not against His sovereign will (Zechariah 13:7). Vincent in his *Word Studies* says that "The phrase, 'Giveth His life,' is peculiar to John, occurring only in his Gospel and First Epistle, and can be explained in two ways: either

1. *As laying down as a pledge,* or *paying a price,* according to the classical usage of the word for 'give.' Or —

2. *To lay aside* His life like a garment. 'He laid aside His garments' (13:4). The latter seems preferable. As He cried, 'It is finished,' He laid aside His earthly life as a garment, which, at Bethlehem He took voluntarily upon Himself."

Jesus thus died and rose again by His own volition. He gave His life as a ransom for sinners and triumphed over death on their behalf. While "*My* sheep" applies to believers only, yet when He died it was as "the Propitiation, not for our sins only, but for those of the whole world" (I John 2:2). There is no contradiction between, "The Spirit which raised up Jesus from the dead" (Romans 8:11), and "I have power to take it again." Says Godet, "If it is in the Father that the power lies which gives Jesus life, it is Himself who by His own free will and His prayer calls upon His person the display of this power . . . God neither imposes on Him death nor resurrection." Jesus had no obligation to die. Since He had never sinned, death had no dominion. Further, as He was led out to die, He could have commanded twelve legions of angels to deliver Him from His crucifiers, but the glory of the Gospel is that Christ, of His own free will, went out to die for sinners.

*He gives life and satisfaction to His sheep.* Having given His life *for* the sheep, He is able to give life, and life more abundant, *to* His sheep. Because of the sacrifice of His life, He can offer eternal life to all who believe. "I give unto (my sheep) eternal life" (John 10:28). Entering Him as the Door, we are saved and blessed with supreme, unfailing satisfaction. Both pardon and pasture become ours, for the Shepherd not only saves but satisfies. He also provides eternal security for His own. The life He gives cannot be "eternal" if we receive it one day and lose it another. Jesus declared that no man can pluck His sheep out of His mighty hand, nor out of His Father's hand. Thus the double grip is ours. We have been collected, folded, preserved here, and are to be glorified hereafter. He has called us unto His eternal Kingdom and glory. It is His will that we may behold His glory (John 17:24).

*He protects His sheep.* Hirelings, or tramp-laborers, secured to help with the sheep, have no heart interest in them, and if danger threatens the flock, these hirelings flee and leave the sheep to the mercy of thieves, robbers, and wolves. Want of any concern about the protection of the sheep is implied in the double statement, *not the shepherd* and *whose own the sheep are not.* While the hirelings are not as destructive as thieves and robbers, nevertheless, in leaving the sheep in time of peril, they assist in the plunder or death of the helpless animals. The Pharisees who listened to our Lord's description of the cowardly guardians of the sheep, must have had disturbed consciences. Instinctively they felt that *hirelings* fittingly portrayed their love of money and ease and position, and their lack of any deep interest in the spiritual welfare of those for whom they were supposed to care. No wonder they took up stones to kill Jesus (John 10:31) after hearing themselves styled as *thieves, robbers* and *hirelings* (Ezekiel 34:2). Ministers of religion whose hearts are destitute of divine grace, or who boast of being the way of salvation and the gate to heaven, or who deny the glorious fundamentals of the Christian faith, come under the same three-fold category.

Who, or what, are we to understand by the *wolf* catching and scattering the sheep? Thieves, robbers and hirelings are human foes of the sheep, but the wolf is the animal (nature's enemy making havoc in the flock). The word Jesus used of the true shepherd who *seeth* the wolf coming is a somewhat graphic one. It implies "a gaze fixed with the fascination of terror on the approaching wolf." Expositors differ as to the typical significance of the wolf. Here are a few interpretations. The *wolf* is the person who is the personification of hostility to the Kingdom of God, the devil, acting by means of all the adversaries of the Church (Jesus completely identified Pharisaism with the diabolic principle, John 8). The wolf was the great Roman power; the figure of the wolf may be applied to all anti-Messianic power, including Pharisaism; the wolf represents the future hirelings in the midst of the Christian Church. Godet's interpretation is concise: "The wolf represents the principle positively hostile to the Kingdom of God and to the Messiah—the Pharisees; and the hireling, the legitimate, accredited and paid functionaries who by their station were called to fulfil the task which Jesus accomplished by voluntary self-devotion, the Priests and Levites, accredited doctors of the law." All spiritual foes bent on destroying the Church of Christ are wolves. Jesus spoke of "false prophets" as "ravening wolves" (Matthew 7:15). He sent forth The Twelve "as sheep in the midst of wolves" (Matthew 10:16); and The Seventy were as "lambs among wolves" (Luke 10:3). Paul predicted that wolves would try to destroy the flock of God (Acts 20:29). All these wolves are related to the *wolf*, the devil, who waits to snatch and devour the sheep.

But over against the ferocious wolf there is the faithful, all-powerful Shepherd protecting His sheep. Throughout His ministry, Jesus was in conflict with the satanic wolf who tried to harm and kill Him. At Calvary, He grappled with the wolf, and although Jesus was bruised and torn by the encounter, and died, He was not killed by the wolf. Such a grim contest ended in victory, for by "dying, death He slew." His conception of good shepherdhood meant killing the wolf, then rising again to make His sheep the sharers of His invincible life. Now the believer's security is inviolable, for with the cross behind him, he knows that no enemy can destroy him. None can pluck him out of the mighty Victor's hand. His preservation is guaranteed. He shall never perish. Once the life the Shepherd offers comes to indwell the believer's heart it must remain.

*He desires one flock.* Our last word is about the Divine Shepherd's all-embracive purpose and passion, indicated in His statement, "Other sheep I have, which are not of this fold; them also I must bring, and they shall hear my voice. And there shall be one fold, and one shepherd" (John 10:16; Ezekiel 37:22). The word for *fold* in the text is different from the one used at the beginning of the parable—sheep*fold*. There it means an inanimate object, the walled enclosure, the sheep rested in. Here, in the verse before us, the word is *flock,* not "fold" (see Matthew 26:31; Luke 2:8; I Corinthians 9:7).

A shepherd with a large number of sheep may have many folds for them, but they are all his sheep, or one flock. Such a "unity was not created by the fold, or folds, but by the nature of the sheep, and their relationship to the shepherd." In the next chapter we have the pronouncement of Caiaphas when he defended Christ against His enemies. "He prophesied that Jesus should die for the nation; and not for the nation only, but that He might gather together into one the children of God that are scattered abroad." The Jews formed one fold, and the Gentiles another fold, Jesus died to gather both into a single *flock*. Gentiles were not to be incorporated within the ancient Jewish fold, but regenerated Jews and Gentiles brought a unity consisting of a common relation to the Saviour. The grand consummation of His redemptive work is that multitudes, saved by grace, gathered from all generations and all nations, peoples and tongues, should form His flock, His Church having present and celestial pastures. For the present, "The Lord is my shepherd, I shall not want." For the future, when His flock arrives in the heavenly fold, "The Lamb which is in the midst of the throne shall feed them" (Psalm 23:1; Revelation 7:17). The visible Church on earth may consist of many denominational folds, but all who are one in Christ Jesus, form one flock. Living unity with the Good, Great Shepherd, makes His sheep one vast flock.

If we are His sheep, awaiting the eternal pastures of unfailing verdure and waters of unruffled rest within the heavenly fold, may we be found cultivating both the *ear* mark and the *foot* mark:

"My sheep *hear* my voice."
"My sheep *follow* me."

Surrounded as we are by thieves, robbers, and wolves, may grace be ours to hear, believe, follow and obey the Shepherd as He leads the way.

# The Parable of Death As Sleep

(John 11:11-15, 23-26)

With the miracle of the resurrection of Lazarus we are not immediately concerned. The reader can find an exposition of Christ's display of miraculous power at Bethany in our volume, *All the Miracles of the Bible*. All that presently concerns us is the expressive simile Christ used for *death*. Four days after the death of Lazarus from sickness, He said, "Our friend Lazarus sleepeth: but I go, that I may awake him out of sleep." Among biblical parabolic illustrations of "death," *sleep* appears to be the favorite one. Daniel wrote of those who were physically dead, as sleeping in the dust of the earth (Daniel 12:2). Jesus had a fondness for this figure of speech. Of the ruler's daughter, He said, "The maid is not dead, but sleepeth" (Matthew 9:24). Death, of course, was real to Him, but He knew it only applied to the body. In the calmness of conscious deity, He bade the people withdraw from the death chamber that He might awaken the damsel out of sleep, that is, bring her conscious life back into her unconscious body.

Our Lord had a similar thought in mind when He answered the hostile Pharisees: "If a man keep my saying, he shall never see death." As a believer, he possesses the true spiritual life which can see, or experience, death — a life passing into a fuller spiritual and glorified life hereafter. Death attacks the body, making it lifeless until its resurrection at Christ's return, but the person within the body does not die, but lives with Him who is "The Resurrection and the Life." When Jesus rose again from the grave and ascended on high, He became the firstfruits of those whose bodies sleep (I Corinthians 15:20). When He returns, the spirits of those bodies that sleep return with Him and will experience "the redemption of the body" (I Thessalonians 4:13-18).

*Sleep* as an image of death is common in secular literature from earliest times. Pagan writers, as well as Jewish writers, used the illustration. From Homer on, poets have spoken of sleep and death as twin sisters. For instance, look at these quotations:

Samuel Daniel (sixteenth century) in his *Defence of Rhyme* wrote:

"Care-charmer, son of the sable Night,
Brother to Death, in silent darkness born."

Fletcher and Beaumont, of the same period, had a similar couplet,

"Care-charmer Sleep, thou easer of all woes,
Brother to Death . . . Thou son of the Night."

Lord Byron, in *And Thou Art Dead,* speaks of,

"The silence of that dreamless sleep I envy now too much to weep."

Phineas Fletcher, 1582-1650 wrote,

"Sleep's but a short death; death's but a longer sleep."

John Milton, the blind poet, in *Paradise Regained,* put it thus,

"A deathlike sleep,
A gentle wafting to immortal life."

Shakespeare, in *Hamlet,* has the impressive lines,

"For in that sleep of death what dreams may come,
When we have shuffled off this mortal coil."

From various sources we string these further quotations together —

"Sleep is fine so like Death, I dare not trust it with prayers."

"And Sleep, Death's brother, yet a friend to life,
Gave wearied Nature a restorative."

"O Sleep, thou ape of Death."

"How wonderful is Death
Death, and his brother Sleep."

"Sleep, Death's allay."

"There will be sleeping enough in the grave."

"Peace, rest and sleep are all we
know of death,
And all we dream of comfort."

With this universal conception of
Death we come to our Lord's comforting
word to the disciples, "Our friend
Lazarus sleepeth, but I go, that I may
awake him out of sleep." Misunderstanding His parabolic description of
Death, the disciples said, "Lord, if he
sleep, he shall do well." If Lazarus was
only sleeping, naturally there was no use
of Jesus going to Bethany, because sleep
indicated that Lazarus was beyond the
crisis of his sickness. Sleep was looked
upon as one of the six favorable symptoms that fever or disease, was passing.
Peter, James and John who were among
the disciples who thought Jesus was
speaking of dead Lazarus as taking rest
in natural sleep, should have remembered how He had applied the word
"sleep" to death before (Matthew
9:24). Then Jesus answered them
plainly: "Lazarus is dead." The words
of deeper truth, "Our friend Lazarus is
fallen asleep," conveyed no true significance to their minds. *Dead* was the
only word they understood, even as they
came to look upon the lifeless body of
Lazarus.

Why did Jesus use this appropriate
metaphor of "sleep" when, speaking of
the dead? He knew, and we do, the
similarity in appearance between a sleeping body and a dead body; restfulness
and peace normally characterize both
as the above quotations illustrate. Vine
in his *Dictionary of New Testament
Words,* says: "The whole object of the
metaphor is to suggest that, as the
sleeper does not cease to exist while his
body sleeps, so the dead person continues to exist despite his absence from
the region in which those who remain
can communicate with him, and that, as
sleep is known to be temporary, so the
death of the body will be found to be."

It is in this sense that "sleep" is used
of saints who died before Christ came
(Matthew 27:52; Acts 13:36); of believers since His Ascension (I Thessalonians 4:13-18; Acts 7:60; I Corinthians 7:39; 11:30; 15:6,18,51; II
Peter 3:4), as well as of Lazarus. An
aspect, however, that must be stressed is
that "sleep" is used of the *body* alone:
and that "resurrection" is likewise used
of the body *alone.* To quote Vine again,
"When the physical frame of the Christian (the earthly house of our tabernacle
— II Corinthians 5:1) is dissolved and
returns to the dust, the spiritual part of
his highly complex being, the seat of
personality, departs to be with Christ
(Philippians 1:23). And since that
state in which the believer, absent from
the body, is at home with the Lord (II
Corinthians 5:6-9), is described as 'very
far better' than the present state of joy
in communion with God and of happy
activity in His service, everywhere reflected in Paul's writings, it is evident
the word 'sleep,' where applied to the
departed Christians, is not intended to
convey the idea that the spirit is unconscious." There is no confirmation
whatever for the "soul-sleep" theory
taught by a few cults. The other Lazarus, who went to Abraham's bosom
(Luke 16), was alive and conscious,
just as Dives was. It is interesting to
observe that the early Christians used a
word for the place of burial meaning a
"resting-house." Our English word
*cemetery* is from the same source and
means "the sleeping place."

At night, when we go to sleep, it does
not mean that we ourselves cease to be
in sleep, but that mysteriously the cur-
tain falls and we become unconscious of
surrounding things, and sleep becomes
the equivalent of repose. The disciples
thought of sleep as "Nature's sweet restorer, balmy sleep," or as Shakespeare
expresses it:

. . . In innocent sleep:
Sleep that knits up the ravelled sleave
of care,
The death of each day's life, sore
labour's bath,
Balm of hurt minds, great Nature's
second course,
Chief nourisher in life's feast.

The famous bard also gives us this further ode to the beneficial qualities of natural sleep:

> O sleep! O gentle sleep!
> Nature's soft nurse, how often have I frighted thee,
> That thou no more wilt weigh mine eyelids down,
> And steep my senses in forgetfulness.

Once in the presence of death, the disciples realized the fact of it, as Jesus had done for four days, but He thought of the fact of it in a different light. The disciples only saw the immediate, the corpse of Lazarus; Jesus looked beyond and knew that that sleeping body would awake. All Mary and Martha saw was the dead form of the brother they loved, but Jesus saw where Lazarus himself was and how unconscious he was of the world he had just left. *Lazarus* was not dead, so Jesus brought him back to his body, back from the unconsciousness of earthly things to a consciousness of them.

There is a legend to the effect that the early Christians never said, "Good-by" but "Good-night," as they parted with their dying friends. They knew that although their bodies slept, that they would awaken on the resurrection morning. Living in the heavenly realm where the voice of Jesus is heard and obeyed, those early saints knew that their happy dead did not cease to be, but that they would come forth to the resurrection of life. The blessed hope is that all who sleep in Jesus will God bring through Him. We do not sorrow as those who have no hope, for we know that the conscious spirit will meet the unconscious, or sleeping dust, on that glorious resurrection day.

> Sleep on, beloved, sleep, and take thy rest;
> Lay down thy head upon the Saviour's breast;
> We love thee well; but Jesus loves thee best —
> Goodnight! Goodnight! Goodnight!

# The Parable of a Grain of Wheat
## (John 12:20-26)

As a young Christian over half a century ago, I heard the late Dr. F. B. Meyer preach a harvest festival sermon on this portion, and his message on the fruitfulness of the sacrificial life left an indelible impression on my mind. That renowned, eloquent and devotional preacher made it clear that —

> "The life of self is death,
> The death of self is life."

This twelfth of John marks the end of Christ's public ministry. In chapters thirteen through seventeen, He is alone with His disciples, and the world shut out. His parabolic illustration of "a grain of wheat" arose at the request of Greeks, or Gentiles, who desired to "see Jesus." They came, quite naturally, to Philip and Andrew, who alone among the Apostles bore Gentile names. Jesus, seeing the approach of these men outside the limits of Judaism, announced that "the hour marked out in the counsels of God, and ever present in His own thought, had now come." Had He not spoken of laying down His life for His sheep, and the *other* sheep, a death for Jew and Gentile alike (John 10:16-19)? These seeking Greeks were "the first-fruits of the great flocks of humanity, and their presence is as the first stroke of the bell which sounds the fatal but glorious hour."

But if the single grain of wheat is to produce a bountiful harvest it must fall into the ground and die. Thus Jesus passes on to His mystic word with a usual and solemn, "Verily, verily." By itself, a grain of wheat remains a single grain, but if dropped into the earth, Nature multiplies. Out of death comes life. A harvest comes from a grain. Jesus used this analogy of a natural law to illustrate what happens in the moral and spiritual worlds alike. Only as single grains are buried in the earth can the life-germs within burst forth producing the blade, stalk and ear of corn. Death results in the true life, for "it released the inner life-power which the husk before held captive, and this life-power multiplying itself in successive grains would clothe the whole field with a harvest of fruit."

Jesus, first of all, applied this law of life out of death to the moral world. If life is loved simply for itself, it is lost. But if it is lost in the well-being of others, then by such a loss life is saved and kept. The self-life dies hard, and martyrdom is hard for the flesh to face. Self-seeking and self-loving never result in a harvest of divine blessing. All self-sacrifice, however, whether in the daily round of service for others, or as the devotion of all we are and have to God, reaps a bountiful harvest of reward.

But in the phrases, "The hour is come"; "Now is my soul troubled; and what shall I say, Father save me from this hour?"; "I if I be lifted up from the earth, will draw all men unto me," point to Calvary when Jesus as God's grain of wheat fell into the ground and died for Jews and Gentiles alike who had been subjects of the prince of this world (John 8:44; Romans 2). He knew that through that dreaded death (Matthew 26:39), He would be able to draw *all* men unto Himself. He regarded His own death as the dark path which must needs be trodden before the multitudes no man can now number could tread the path of glory. While Jesus was still on earth He was as a grain of wheat having life for all in its germs. But through His death and resurrection there was a bursting forth and an immediate harvest, as the 3,000 saved on the Day of Pentecost proves. Thereafter the harvest multiplied, as the Acts, and the history of the Christian Church clearly reveals. In every newly born-again life, He sees of the travail of His soul and is satisfied.

Are we prepared to follow the Master in self-sacrifice? If we —
"Live for self we live in vain — but if we —
Live for Christ we live again."

Years ago I came across this slogan over a "Cleaners and Dyers" establishment, and it greatly intrigued me —
"We live to dye,
We dye to live."
By altering the 'y' to an 'i' we have a deep spiritual truth to keep before our minds. The selfish life, with self as its center and circumference, is a useless, isolated life; but the sacrificial life, with God and others as the center and circumference of life and labors, means the multiplication of our influence, and a harvest of souls to greet us at the Judgment Seat of Christ (I Thessalonians 2:19,20).

## The Parable of Feet-Washing
(John 13:1-11)

Here we have one of our Lord's acted parables. While no figurative language was used by Him, because of the truth He was illustrating, He gave us a parable by way of example as He was alone with The Twelve. But shortly after this parabolic action, Judas excluded himself from the group, going out to sell His Lord for thirty pieces of silver. Omniscient, Jesus knew that His hour had come to depart out of the world and go unto His Father. His constant reference to His death frightened and saddened the disciples, who did not realize its import until after His Ascension. But although He discoursed upon His death and resurrection, He also prophesied and portrayed His Coming Kingdom.

With the Kingdom in mind there was "strife among them which of them should be the greatest" (Luke 12). All the disciples thought of was their own pre-eminence, their own position of power. They were blind to the fact that humility is the pathway to honor. To enforce this truth Jesus illustrated it by taking the place of the slave, whose duty it was to wash the feet of those who entered the house. Jesus laid aside His garments, the outer ones which would impede the action of washing feet. Do we not have here a parabolic illustration of what happened at His incarnation, when He laid aside the garment of His eternal glory and wrapped Himself around with the garment of our humanity?

Assuming the slave's task, He took a towel, and pouring water into a basin, washed the disciples' feet, and then dried them with the long towel He had knotted around His waist. Perhaps John, being nearest the Master, had his feet washed first, then came Peter, who remonstrated with Jesus saying, "Lord, dost *Thou* wash my feet?" Such an act was regarded as one from an inferior to a superior, but here was the Master washing the feet of a servant. Such an act was beyond Peter's comprehension hence Christ's reply. "What I do thou knowest not now; but thou shalt know hereafter." Both Peter and John came to know and declare hereafter the symbolic significance of their Lord's self-emptying action. Peter, reminding them that the towel was the badge of slavery, urged the saints to be girded with humility, or as Phillips interprets it, "Put on the apron of humility" (I Peter 5:5). By the Spirit's illumination, Peter came to see the manifestation of divine grace in his Master's action. John, too, came to see that his Lord's humiliation led to His glorious exaltation; that the badge of slavery became the girdle of kingship. In the revelation of His glory, John saw Him "girt about the breasts with a golden girdle." The old sackcloth of the slave was transmuted into the glory and purple of sovereignty.

What particularly interests us in this acted parable is our Lord's reply to Peter's wish to be washed all over, "Not my feet only, but also my hands and my head." Jesus said, "He that is washed (bathed all over) needeth not save to wash his feet, but is clean every whit: and ye are clean, but not all." It would seem as if the latter part of His reply had particular reference to Judas. All Twelve had been called as His disciples, but one who had been bathed, cleansed and made Christ's by His word, had allowed evil to enter his heart and pollute it. "For him cleansing had been neglected," comments Ellicott, "and the daily corruption of the world remained; evil thoughts had been harboured until at length they had made corrupt the whole man." Failing to abide in the vine, Judas was cast forth as a useless branch (John 15:4).

There is, however, the wider application of Christ's figurative language. The word used for "washed" or "bathed" means to bathe the whole person. So what Jesus said to Peter was, "He that is bathed only needs to wash his feet." Jesus, familiar with Eastern habits, had in mind a man who had been to a local "bath-house," and having completely washed himself, wended his way homeward. As he returned a good deal of the dust of the highway covered his half-bare feet, and reaching home he had to cleanse his feet from defilement contracted by the way. He had no need to take another bath, but only wash the dust-covered part of his body, associated with his walk.

Charles Wesley, in one of his great hymns, urges us to pray for cleansing from sin's "guilt and power." What does this double cleansing imply? Once a sinner repents of his sin and, by faith, accepts Christ as a personal Saviour, he is washed in the blood, once and for all, from the past guilt and penalty of his sin. But as a saved sinner, he has a daily need of washing from the defiling influences of sin. John uses the present tense when he speaks of the cleansing blood of Jesus, "which cleanseth (keeps on cleansing) us from sin" (I John 1:7). Our *standing* before God is secure, but often our *state* here below is not in harmony with our *standing*. We contract defilement in our daily walk and need to be washed.

The last thought is that of example, for Jesus said, "I have given you an example, that ye should do as I have done to you." There are many devout souls in a certain denomination who take these words literally, and who periodically have a "Feet-Washing Ceremony" in their churches, when the brothers wash each other's feet, and the sisters, each other's feet. But surely our Lord meant us to practice what He was illustrating by His parabolic action, namely, meekness and lowliness of heart, and not necessarily to repeat the action itself. Spiritual "feet-washing" is what Paul referred to when in writing to the Church at Galatia he said, "Brethren, even if a man be overtaken in any trespass, ye which are spiritual, restore such an one in a spirit of meekness, lest ye also be tempted" (Galatians 6:1). Even cleansed men will contract defilement by the way, and when they do, we are not to draw attention to their lapse, and in a holier-than-thou attitude spurn them. Our obligation (if our own feet are clean) is to restore such, in the spirit of meekness. Among distinctions and orders people covet, there is one sadly neglected and yet one all of us can qualify to possess. It is *The Order of the Towel*. All belonging to this highest of all "Orders," seek to be like the One who initiated the "Order," meek and lowly in heart, and clothed with the apron of humility. The glory of divine grace is manifested in and through seed. Like the Master, they show forth "the transfiguration of service at the lowest to sovereignty at the highest."

# The Parable of the Many Mansions

## (John 14:1-6)

The precious words of the first half of this portion, revered by the saints of all ages, were spoken by Jesus while still in conversation with His disciples in the final and intimate days before the cross. Judas the traitor had left the group, hence the significance of the singular Jesus used, although He was speaking to eleven men. "Let not your *heart* be troubled." With Judas away, there was unity among the rest, making them as *one* heart.

The constant announcement and near approach of Jesus' death greatly disturbed the loving disciples. They could not bear to think of the future without this One who had become the center and circumference of all things in their lives. Now He was going to leave them, and the future was dark and foreboding. Often He had spoken of going away. Where and why was He going? Then He told them, "Whither I go, ye cannot come." But the promise was that ultimately they would follow Him and be with Him where He was, "That where I am, there ye may be also." Four of the perplexed disciples spoke, and in the course of Christ's replies, He gave them (and the Church of all time) the most heart-warming parabolic promise of heaven:

*Peter* said, "Where art Thou going?"

*Thomas* asked, "We do not know where Thou art going, how can we know the way?"

*Philip* demanded, "Show us the Father, and it sufficeth us."

*Jude*'s query was, "What is come to pass that Thou wilt manifest Thyself unto us, and not unto the world?"

These four representative men, greatly troubled over Christ's near departure, approached such a dreaded hour from different angles.

Peter had known for many months that Jesus was going to die. His question goes beyond the Tomb. What he wanted to know was something about the mysterious beyond. Where was Jesus going?

Thomas was more perplexed about the way to the future abode Jesus was going away to prepare for His saints. If he did not know where Jesus was going, how could he follow Him?

Philip, in his characteristic, quiet way, was taken up with the profound truth of divine manifestation. His ultimate was not so much the abode but the august One whose presence filled it. "Shew us the Father, and it sufficeth us." Jesus, in His answer, claimed to be the manifestation of the Father. "He that hath seen me, hath seen the Father." He was the culmination of the revelation of the

Father. If men wanted to know what God was like, all they had to do was to think of His Son's works, words, and ways.

Jude, in a practical way, taken up with the present, wanted to know if the revelation granted to the disciples could be shared by the world, once Jesus had left them. It was out of all these questionings, reflecting general sorrow, that Jesus gave utterance to a three-fold cure for the troubled hearts of His own.

First, there was faith in Christ Himself. "Believe *also* in me." The disciples, as Jews, had believed all along in the covenant-keeping God, but somehow Jesus was beginning to disappoint their hearts. An echo of this deep disappointment is heard on the Emmaus Road, "We thought it had been He who would have redeemed Israel" (Luke 24). They had looked for a powerful Messiah to deliver them from the tyranny and oppression of the Roman Government, and here was this Messiah going out to die as a felon on a wooden gibbet. So Christ urges His own not to lose faith in Him because His glorious resurrection would prove the validity of His claims.

In the second place, He called for faith in the future, in the spacious Father's abode where there would be a prepared place for His own, a prepared place for a prepared people. Christ's parabolic illustration in the second verse conveys the idea of spaciousness and of unlimited accommodation. Godet in his exposition at this point says, "The image is derived from those immense oriental palaces in which there is an apartment, not only for the sovereign and for the heir to the throne, but for all the king's sons however numerous they may be." Homer's description of Priam's palace expresses this idea of roominess:

"A palace built with gracious portieres,
 And fifty chambers near each other . . ."

We feel, however, that Jesus was using the *Temple* (which He had called,

"the Father's house. . . . the house of God," and "my house" and which He ultimately forsook, leaving it desolate) as the background of His illustration of the Father's House above. That Temple, almost fifty years in creation, was a masterpiece of construction having numerous parts. The Temple was a massive house, not only of worship, but of living quarters. Sir George Adam-Smith in his exposition, *Jerusalem,* describes it thus: "Herod's temple consisted of a house divided like its predecessor into the Holy of Holies, and the Holy Place; a porch; an immediate forecourt with an altar of burnt offering; a court of Israel; in front of this a Court of Women; and round the whole of the preceding a Court of Gentiles . . . Chambers for officials, and a meeting place for the Sanhedrin. Against the walls were built side-chambers, about 38 in all." Thus the Temple was made up of many sections and places, each having their own value, but all part of the Temple. Westcott and Hort give us *home* for "house," and "In My Father's home" has a warmer and loving air about it. The word used by Jesus means an "abode," a dwelling place, while "mansions" mean resting or abiding places. Christ's present ministry in the heavenly spacious abode is the preparation of a place in it for His true Church. "I go to prepare a place for *you*" — the disciples were the Church in representation.

In reply to Philip's desire for information about the way to the eternal, abiding place, Jesus said that He was the only *way* to it, the full *truth* concerning it, and the *life* of it (John 14:6). He never lifted the veil too high. How we would like to know more about the locality of heaven and of its contents and occupants. This we know that wherever it is, Jesus abides and to be with Him will be heaven in itself. For the millions of the ransomed there is ample space. Cramped conditions will not prevail in the King's palace. Let us make more of heaven than we do. Who knows, we may be nearer the abode of eternal rest than we realize!

The third cure for their distressed hearts which Jesus gave His disciples was faith in His return. "I will come again and receive you unto myself, that where I am, there ye may be also." Once the place is complete for His Church, and the Church is complete to be raptured, Christ is coming from heaven to take her there. If He does not return, personally, as He said He would, then He is not *The Truth,* as He declared Himself to be. But He was not a man that He should lie. He will come, as He promised, and when He does appear in the earth, the saints presently in heaven with Him but who return with Him, and the saints on earth, are to be caught up *together* — one, complete body.

"With such a blessed hope in view,
  We would more holy be;
  More like our gracious, glorious Lord,
  Whose face we soon shall see."

# The Parable of the True Vine
## (John 15)

These further last words of Jesus are full of deepest meaning for all our hearts. The beautiful allegory of The Vine is introduced suddenly, with nothing in the context to lead up to it. The natural explanation of this complete discourse, which reaches into the next chapter, is that the allegory was suggested by an external object catching the eye of Jesus as He left the upper chamber to go to Gethsemane. On His way through the vineyards of Kedron, with its fruit-covered vines, and the fires burning along the sides of the valley consuming the vine cuttings, there would come to the Saviour's mind the familiar Old Testament symbolism of the Vineyard and the Vine (Psalm 80; Isaiah 5:1-7; Jeremiah 2:21; Ezekiel 19:10) and so this striking, matchless discourse was born.

When Jesus, using another of His great *I Am's,* called Himself "the true vine," or "the vine, the true." He was

not contrasting Himself with something false. He was not "the true light," or "the true Vine" as opposed to the untrue, but "true" as answering to "the perfect ideal, and as opposed to all more or less imperfect representations." He was ideally true. Ideal truth, of which the natural vine is a figure, was fulfilled in Him. The Vine was a symbol of divinely chosen Israel (Hosea 10:1; Matthew 21:33; Luke 13:6), but she came far short of the ideal. She became an empty vine, bringing forth fruit to herself. But Jesus came as the true, gracious Vine, answering to the perfect ideal.

Then when Jesus said, "I am the Vine, ye are the branches," He did not imply that the one was separate from the other. Vine is a comprehensive term, implying unity in diversity, for root, stem, branches, leaves, tendrils and grapes are all of the vine. Christ is all and in all. He is everything, and we are parts of Him, vitally connected to Him as branches are to the vine. Severed from Him we are useless. The vine exists for fruit-bearing, and to this end the vital sap is so necessary. Can it be that that Holy Spirit (about whom Jesus has so much to say in this portion) is the Divine Sap making possible the fruit of the Vine? The various parts forming the vine as a whole speak of union and interdependence. The root is no use without the stem, and the stem without the branches, and the branches without the fruit. The binding and producing is the live sap flowing through all. Ours is a living union with Jesus Christ through the indwelling Holy Spirit, who produces fruit in life and service. Different from the vine, we do not produce fruit, we only *bear* it. Fruit is the Spirit's (Galatians 5:22).

Four conditions of the fruitful life are set forth by Jesus in the narrative. We have:

1. *Union.* "Every branch in Me." *In* Christ, His life through us producing fruit unto holiness (Romans 6:22). If we have the appearance of branches

(profession but not possession) then we are not a part of the true Vine, and fit only to be taken away.

2. *Purging.* Three degrees of fruit are spoken of: fruit; more, or better fruit; much and remaining fruit (John 15:2, 5,8,16). Fruit is the outstanding evidence of life, and so God, the Husbandman, "cleans every branch which does not bear fruit, to make it bear better fruit" (John 15:2, Moffat). We may shrink from the purging, cleansing process, but how necessary it is if we are to function as fruitful branches of the Vine (Matthew 5:6).

3. *Abiding* (v. 4). Branches cannot bear fruit of themselves. They must be in union with the main stem of the vine, constantly receiving the flowing sap, if they are to bear fruit. Abiding requires no effort; it is being at rest. Resting in the Lord, and living in unbroken fellowship with Him, we become fruit-bearing branches. Knowing His commandments, we obey them and thus abide. We abide by obedience to Him who calls us to follow Him all the way. To obey Him is to abide in Him. To abide in Him is to obey.

4. *Asking* (v. 5,7). "If ye abide . . . ask what ye will." Actually, there is no conflict between "abiding" and "asking." As the branch abides in the vine, it keeps asking for the sap, the life-element it needs to fulfil its purpose. If we could hear a branch speak we would find it saying, "Every moment I must have sap or die." Does not the hymn remind us that "moment by moment we've life from above"? Abiding, we ask aright and receive because the indwelling Spirit prompts us to ask for those things in harmony with the Divine Will.

For the preacher a message on the whole chapter may be developed along these lines:

1. Our Relation to Christ — union and fruitfulness (John 15:1-11; Colossians 1:20-23)

2. Our Relation to Christians — love and fellowship (John 15:12-17; Ephesians 4:25-32)

3. Our Relation to a Christless World — hostility and faithfulness (John 15:18-27; 17:6-18).

We *come* to Jesus as the *Saviour;*
We *learn* of Jesus as the *Teacher;*
We *follow* Jesus as the *Master;*
We *abide* in Jesus as the *Life*.

# The Parable of
# the Travailing Woman
(John 16:20-22)

This is the last of the parabolic illustrations from the Gospels we are to consider, and among the one hundred or more we have dealt with, this final one is the most delicate and sacred. Campbell Morgan calls it a "superlative final illustration" and one "demanding most reverent consideration." The importance of our Lord's statement is proven by His special seal of verity, the two-fold "Verily, verily," or "Amen, amen"; and the seal of authority, "I — *I am, that I am* — say to you" (John 16:20).

The impressive feature of the brief portion before us is the clarity that views the coming dark hours and days as though they were already past. It was the sorrowful days ahead that gave rise to the *sorrow* and *joy* conversation and illustration. The disciples knew about the road of suffering and death before the Master, and He knew that they would sob, with unrestrained weeping and wailing, as those who moan for the dead. Their Lord and Lover would die a malefactor's death, but while they would be overwhelmed with sorrow, the godless world would rejoice. The world, wreaking its murderous will upon Him, was to jubilate in unholy glee.

Jesus did not soften His statement but told them of the excessive grief into which they would be plunged. He also assured them that suddenly their sorrow would become joy. After the dark clouds the sun would shine. After a "little while, ye shall see Me," which does not refer to His second advent, but to the Holy Spirit who would come as the Comforter to console their sad hearts and cause them to rejoice. Then to enforce His teaching, Jesus came to His arresting and final figure of speech, which was common in Old Testament literature as an image of sorrow issuing in joy (Isaiah 21:3; 26:17; Hosea 13:13; Micah 4:9,10). As we shall point out when we come to the epistles, Paul follows Christ in the application of the same maternal illustration. The simple interpretation means that the joy of motherhood swallows up the pangs of child-birth. The travail pangs cease, but the joy continues. The joyful mother forgets the one in the fulness of the other. She has passed from extreme pain to extreme joy. The moment between the most painful anguish and the most abounding joy is short.

Our Lord applies the profound figure of sorrow of a woman going down under the whelming floods into darkness, agony, and possible death, but whose sorrow passes when her child, a life won out of death, is safe in her arms, to the sorrow-stricken disciples. Great grief over the Master's death would fill their hearts, and severe trials and tribulations would beset them in their witness for Him, but compensation is promised them for all their suffering. Out of their travail many children would be born into the Kingdom. Fellowship with Christ in His sufferings would result in a crown of eternal joy. The hour of the disciples' travail pangs (the word used for their sorrow is the same as that describing the woman's travail) was at hand, but it would pass away and the fulness of joy would be theirs in the abiding presence of Jesus in the Holy Spirit, whom He would send to comfort their hearts. The present hour is one of sore travail for many dear saints, especially those in communist countries, and missionaries in those lands where there is so much strife and bloodshed; but their anguish is only temporary. Jesus is coming again, and when He does appear He will grant them beauty for ashes, the oil of joy for mourning, and the garment of praise for their heaviness. Then they will have a joy no man will be able to take from them.

# PARABOLIC INSTRUCTION IN THE ACTS

While the miraculous permeates this fifth book of the New Testament (which has been called "The Gospel of the Holy Spirit"), *Parables* such as the gospels present are not to be found in the Acts. Hillyer H. Straton rightly observes that it is ". . . a striking fact that outside of the gospels there are no parables in the New Testament. The disciples of Jesus were loyal to their Lord, they could interpret His mission to men, they could preserve His matchless teaching, including this remarkable body of stories, they could witness to the world even to the point of death as to what God in Christ had done for them and for all who believed, they could establish a Church to be a living and continuous witness to their faith in Jesus as God's Messiah and the world's Saviour. Yet not once, even with the form before them in the gospel parables, did they produce a single parable. This is true even though there were many circumstances in the life of the Early Church in which a fresh parable would have helped greatly."

Perhaps the nearest approach to a "parable" is the miracle of the sheet let down from heaven (Acts 1:9—11:18). This parabolic-miracle delivered Peter from his religious isolationism and brought him into harmony with God's embracive purpose. Through this parable of grace, the Apostle came to see that the salvation Christ purchased with His blood was for all men. At last he perceived that God was no respecter of persons, that Jews and Gentiles alike could become recipients of God's saving power.

Listening, as we read the book, to all the notes of the glorious Christian Gospel, as they peal forth in rapturous harmony for both the Jewish and the Roman worlds to hear, it is apparent that the Apostles did not follow their Master's method of parabolic teaching. Their Spirit-inspired messages were unadorned. Their words so plain and pointed were devoid of imagery yet weighted with power to convict. Their ministry was largely of a miraculous nature, with their miracles establishing their authority as Apostles, and also confirming the Church as a divine institution. It is not difficult, however, to imagine that when Paul taught the people out of the Law and Prophets, and preached the Kingdom as those concerning the Lord Jesus Christ (Acts 28:24, 25,31), that he drew attention to the significance of the Kingdom parables. After the Apostles, some of the Early Church Fathers constructed Parables for the setting forth of spiritual mysteries. Trench gives several samples of these parables.

In his *Dedication,* so to speak, of the Acts to his intimate friend, Theophilus, Luke used his characteristic word "began," the verb which occurs some 31 times in his "gospel." Its occurrence here (Acts 1:1) is a proof of the identity of authorship. All Christ began to do (His works) and teach (His words) in the days of His flesh, as recorded in the four gospels, He here continues through His Apostles in the Acts. After His resurrection Christ spent 40 days, continuously or at intervals, with His own. What days they must have been! Now on the victory side of the cross, fresh light would be focused upon all Jesus had taught them while He was among them. Parables would be reiterated seeing He further instructed them in "things pertaining to the kingdom" (1:3).

In the light of His previous teaching regarding the true interpretation of the admission of the Gentile world into the Kingdom (Matthew 28:19), Jesus' parables like *The Sower,* with the broadcasting of the seed, and *The Feast,* with the universal invitation sent out to the highways and hedges of Gentile peoples, took on added meaning. The parables became "the bridge which joins the two dispensations." Then the book, as a whole, illustrates the second opportunity given to Israel in the parable of *The Barren Fig Tree.* "This year also," was not a literal year, but an "acceptable year of the Lord," which the book of Acts covers. The delayed judgment on the tree resulted in multitudes of Jews turning to the Saviour. By parable and precept, He had taught His own that His provision was for all men, and in the Acts the one message was for all places — Jerusalem, Judea, Samaria, and the uttermost parts of the earth. Out went the Apostles to preach the Gospel to every creature but not "adapt the Gospel to every century."

Although, as we have indicated, there are no recognized parables in this dynamic book, yet this "fifth gospel," as it has been named, contains many expressive figures of speech. We herewith enumerate the majority of these parabolic germs for the guidance of the reader.

*Baptism.* When Luke uses the term "baptism" in connection with the Holy Spirit, he takes a visible rite to illustrate an inward experience. "Ye shall be baptized with the Holy Spirit" (Acts 1:5,8) means, "Ye shall be immersed in spiritual power, which shall cover you as well as fill you and flow out from you." The Bible nowhere speaks of "the baptism *of* the Holy Spirit." He is not the Baptizer, but the element into which we are baptized or immersed.

*Pentecost.* The miraculous aspect of this historic day is dealt with in *All the Miracles of the Bible.* At this point we are only concerned with the symbolic aspect of the manifestation of the Spirit's presence and power (Acts 2:2). "The rushing mighty wind" is a figure of speech describing the supernatural in-breathing and irresistible force of the Spirit, of which those covered in the upper chamber were conscious. "Cloven tongues like as of fire" (Acts 2:3), that is, tongues of fire distributed among the Apostles, illustrated the burning message they were to proclaim. How the sermon of Peter burned its way into the con-sciences of those who heard him declare the truth of the Gospel in their language. Those who listened were divided in their response to the Word. Some mocked, saying, "These men are full of new wine." The Apostles were God-intoxi-cated men. There was a certain appear-ance of holy excitement in their tone, manner, and words. Some of the people thought of this as drunkenness. Peter, however, with his new tongue boldness quickly dispelled this explanation of their demeanor (Acts 2:15).

*The Prophecy of Joel.* The prophet by divine inspiration not only spoke to his own age (Acts 2:28,31), but set forth a judgment-parable related to the far-off future. His descriptive language of the promised Spirit had a partial fulfilment at Pentecost. The full and final fulfil-ment, however, is yet future (Acts 2:20).

*The Divine Footstool.* The quotation Peter uses from Psalm 110 is parabolic of Christ's supreme conquest of His foes. Having them as His *footstool* (Acts 2:35) implies His absolute sovereignty. Being at the right hand of God, the posi-tion of authority and privilege, all power is His to subjugate His enemies and reign supreme.

*The Rejected Stone.* Not only are certain elements, such as fire, wind and water, used of the Lord; things pertain-ing to earth likewise symbolize all He is in Himself. He is a *Stone* (Psalm 118:22; Matthew 21:42; Acts 4:11; I Peter 2:7). He is also a *Corner-Stone* (Ephesians 2:20,21), a *foundation* and *stumbling stone* (Isaiah 8:14; 28:16; Zechariah 3:9; Luke 2:34; Romans 9:32,33; I Peter 2:4,6,7,8), a *Rock*

(Deuteronomy 32:31; Psalm 18:2,3; 31:2,3,4; 42:9; Isaiah 73:26 margin). *The builders* were the leaders of Israel, and the *Stone* they rejected was Christ, whom God had chosen to be the chief corner-stone — "the Stone on which the two walls of Jew and Gentile met and were bonded together" (Ephesians 2:20). Thirty years after Peter thus spoke, Christ was still to him as "the head of the corner." The Holy Spirit illuminated his mind as to the true sig-nificance of His Lord's use of the simile (Matthew 21:42-44).

*The Temple.* Stephen's illustrative use both of the Tabernacle and Temple of old (Acts 7:46-50) recalls our Lord's conversation with the woman at the well (John 4:21-23), and of the application of the Temple to Himself, as the incarna-tion of the divine presence. It is inter-esting to observe that Paul reproduces the thought, which, when he was the persecutor, he heard from the lips of the martyr Stephen (Acts 17:24-25). We are prone to be taken up with the *sphere* of worship. What matters most is the *spirit* of worship. They that worship God, whether in a barn or a cathedral, must worship Him in spirit and in truth.

*The Gall and the Bond.* Peter repels with horror the thought of Simon Magus that the gift of the Spirit could be pur-chased with money. *Gall* used in its literal sense in the gospels (Matthew 27:34) is now used by Peter figuratively of Simon's extreme moral depravity. (Romans 3:14; Ephesians 4:31). "The bond of iniquity," speaks of the strong chains of evil habits from which he could not free himself. Simon, however, seemed to be more concerned about a future penalty for his sins, than for a present deliverance from them.

*The Vessel.* While we have many parabolic terms describing those who are elected of God to serve Him, none is so arrestive as that of a *vessel* (Acts 9:15), which has a wide range of mean-ing in the Bible (see Genesis 27:3 — of arms; Deuteronomy 22:5 — of gar-ments; Genesis 31:56 — of household goods). The whole body of the believer, or members of his body, are spoken of as a "vessel," or a "tool" (Matthew 12:29: Luke 8:16; John 19:29; Romans 9:22; II Corinthians 4:7). Paul was one of God's chosen tools to work out His gracious purpose in the bringing of the Gentiles into the Church. Our solemn responsibility is to see that the vessel, although an earthen one, is clean enough for the Master of the House to use.

*A Light.* Through the Spirit's tuition, Paul came to see that Old Testament references to Christ as a "Light," and His own use of the symbol as illustrative of His mission, was now being fulfilled in the unfolding of the divine purpose of love toward the whole Gentile world. Paul knew that he himself was as a "light" shining amid its darkness.

*The Dust of Their Feet.* The Scribes taught that the dust of Gentile lands caused defilement. The shaking of the dust of the feet was, therefore, symbolic of the tradition that although the place might be in Israel, it was as though it were a heathen and profane and defiled place (Acts 13:51). Paul, of course, would have in mind our Lord's use of such a parabolic action (Matthew 10:14; Mark 6:11; Luke 9:5; John 13:16).

*The Opened Door.* Paul, knowing of our Lord's use of the simile of the *Door* (John 10), made it one of his favorite figures of speech (Acts 14:27; see I Corinthians 16:19; II Corinthians 2:12; Colossians 4:3). Through grace, the Door into the Father's house was now opened wider than it had ever been before. "Whosoever will," can enter through the Door while it stands ajar. No man can shut this Door (Revelation 3:8; Galatians 2:9). He who opened it, will shut it, and when He does, it will be bliss for those on its right side, but woe for all those shut out. "The ascribing directly to God of such access to the Gentiles is to be noted."

*A Yoke on the Neck.* Paul's exhortation to the Jewish Council and his use of heavy yokes (Acts 15:10), reveals how familiar he was with Christ's parabolic language and was able to weave it into his own discourses. Here he reproduced the "heavy burdens" of Pharisaic traditions (Matthew 23:4), and the Master's "easy yoke" (Matthew 11:30). When we come to Paul's epistles we shall find him using the same figure of speech again (Galatians 5:1). The yoke of burdensome ceremonies, earnest and spiritual men found impossible to fulfill.

*The Shaking of Raiment.* The shaking off of dust from the feet, and the shaking off of a garment, were parabolic actions common in ancient times, both among Jews and Gentiles (Matthew 10:14; 27:24). By such actions, those performing them vividly shook themselves from all *connection* with others, and all *responsibility* for the guilt of rejecting them and their message (Acts 18:6). As a Jew to Jews, no words and no act could so well express Paul's indignant protest against the rejection of his ministry. "It was the last resource of one who found appeals to reason and conscience powerless, and was met by brute violence and clamour."

*The Shorn Head.* In connection with the vow of a temporary Nazarite, the cutting off of the hair implied a separation from the world and common life. While under the vow the man who had taken it was to drink no wine or strong drink, and to let no razor pass over his head or face (Numbers 6:1-21). Jamieson says that it is unlikely that Paul practiced this particular vow (Acts 18:18). "It was probably one made in one of his seasons of difficulty or danger, in prosecution of which he cuts off his hair and hastens to Jerusalem to offer the requisite sacrifice within the prescribed thirty days." Paul, as we know, condemned long hair on a man as effeminate (I Corinthians 11:14). Gratitude for deliverance from danger often gave birth to a solemn vow, and Paul's vow may have been one of renewed consecration to a life of fuller devotion. The Apostle had not learned to despise or condemn such expressions of devout feeling.

*The Grievous Wolves.* Paul warned the Church at Ephesus of two classes of enemies that would seek to destroy the flock: the one class, wolves, more external to themselves; the other class bred in the bosom of their own community — "of your own selves." Both groups were to be teachers — the grievous wolves would make a prey of the folk: the other group would be perverters of the truth, dividing the flock by their heresy (Acts 20:2,9,30; see I Timothy 1:15-20; II Timothy 2:17; 3:8,13). Here the Apostle adopts some of the figurative language our Lord used of the flock, and of its open enemies. Wolves in sheep's clothing were the false prophets, usurpers of authority, leaders of divisive parties within the Church (Matthew 7:15; John 10:12).

*The Girdle.* The dramatic action of Agabus in taking Paul's girdle to announce an important event recalls how the prophets of old symbolized their predictions. In the Old Testament section of our study we dealt with this prophetic manner of predicting by symbolic acts (See Isaiah 20:34; Jeremiah 13:1-11; 27-2; Ezekiel 4:1-3; 5:1-4). Agabus (Acts 11:27; 21:10-13), forseeing the danger to which the Apostle would be exposed, sought to warn him by means of a parabolic illustration, of the plot of the Jews to deliver Paul up to the Gentiles. Deep emotion was his at parting with the saints at Ephesus, but he was ready, not only to be bound, as the girdle-action represented, but to die for his Lord.

*The Whited Wall.* Probably with Christ's condemnation of the Pharisees as "whitened sepulchres" (Matthew 23:27; Luke 11:44) in mind, Paul used a similar expression to the high priest Ananias who had commanded those who stood by to smite Paul on the mouth — a method common in the East

of silencing a speaker. Paul hastily said, "God shall smite thee, thou whited wall" (Acts 23:2,3), which He did some years later when during the Jewish War Ananias was killed by an assassin. In true gentlemanly fashion, Paul apologized for addressing the high priest as he did. Recognition that "the powers that be are ordained of God," was the ruling principle of Paul's conduct (Romans 13:1-6).

*Ears and Eyes.* In this last glimpse of the Apostle we see him with "a patience almost exhausted by the long contest with prejudice and unbelief" (Acts 28:26-28). After his exposition of the Kingdom of God, as it concerned Jesus, "some believed the things which were spoken, and some believed not." The former were among the faithful remnant, and the latter the hardened (Romans 11:7-25). "Blindness in part had happened unto Israel." Following the track of the Master's teaching, Paul used language illustrative of wilful blindness and deafness to those truths which should have produced repentance and faith (Matthew 13:13; Mark 4:12; John 12:40; see Acts 20:35). It was Paul's heart's desire and prayer that Israel might be saved. Great heaviness and continual sorrow were his over Israel's hardness of heart (Romans 9:2; 10:1). Therefore, it must have been with much pain that he delivered this last, stern condemnation to those who heard with their ears his message, yet heard it not; and who read the truth with their eyes yet saw it not. Alas, multitudes are still spiritually deaf and blind!

Of Paul's oral ministry as a whole Ellicott says, "He spoke, not with the rhetorical cadences in which Greek rhetoricians delighted, but with words that went home like an arrow to the mark, and pierced men's hearts. The voice was perhaps untuneable, but the words were full of life" (II Corinthians 10:10; 11:25; I Corinthians 14:25).

# PARABOLIC INSTRUCTION IN THE PAULINE EPISTLES

Fourteen of the epistles, including *Hebrews,* which we ascribe to Paul, are known as *The Pauline Epistles* and the remaining seven, as *The General Epistles,* seeing they came from James, Peter, John and Jude. As a whole, all of the epistles offer the student a rich vein of illustrative material. Paul, in particular, seemed to revel in the use of parabolic language in his presentation of the truth. While it is true, as Hillyer Straton suggests, that Jesus had the parabolic mind, thinking and speaking in terms of dramatic images, and that "His use of the parable is one of the finest incidental proofs we have of the historicity of Jesus of Nazareth," it is likewise true to say that Paul had a symbolic mind. While he did not create parables equal to those of the Master he dearly loved, his writings present many striking allegories. Paul was grateful for the incomparable aid that Christ's parables gave, and with matchless skill he wove their teaching into the texture of his own.

Because of the many links between the parables of the Gospels and the epistles, it is essential to study the parables in the light of the epistles, and also to note how the epistles should be read as sequels to the parables. In her chapter, "The Parables and the Epistles," Ada R. Habershon deals in a most comprehensive way with the association between the two: "The parables explain the writing of the epistles. They tell us how it was that Greeks and Romans were now addressed instead of only Jews. It is true that the parables do not fully reveal the position of the Church in this dispensation, but they explain the causes which brought about a condition of privilege for the Gentiles; trace the steps which led up to it; and prepare the way for the revelation made to Paul. The Church Epistles are but the result of the broadcasting of the Seed, foretold in the Parable of the Sower . . . . We also see that the epistles are the *sequels* or supplements of the parables. The Lord told His disciples that He had yet many things to say unto them, but they were not able to bear them. . . . In many cases, as we shall see, the Apostle used the same symbolism to teach further lessons. . . . Another important fact to be learned especially from the epistles, is that Israel's history is *typical.* . . . It is Paul who so clearly opens to us a large field of study." With these practical observations in mind let us examine some of the parabolic illustrations and instructions Paul has for us in his precious epistles.

*The First Figure.* When Paul wrote, "Adam . . . who is the figure of Him that was to come" (Romans 5:14-20), he gave us the earliest of all types. In time, this type comes first; in position, it lies deepest. There is none before it, none beneath it. Says Arnot, "Bowing down from heaven in love, God the Spirit grasps the first fact of man's history, and therewith points the lesson of man's redemption. There was no delay, for the King's matter required haste. The Giver was prompt and eager; the receivers have been indolent and slow." As with a seal and its impression, so with a type and its antitypes, there are at once likeness and diversity; they are the same yet opposite.

Adam and Christ were the true sources or federal heads of their respective families. The first Adam stood as the head and representative of the human race, and when he fell, he brought all down with him. The Last Adam also stands at the head of a great multitude which no man can number. As soon as the First Head sinned, the Second Head was promised as the Saviour from sin. The seed of the First Head derive from him sin and death; the seed of the Second Head derive from Him righteousness and life. The first

346

seed includes the whole of the human race. The seed of the second, although contained within the first, is a "little flock."

The word Paul uses for "figure" is *type,* or "likeness." But having spoken of the similarity between Adam and Christ, Paul immediately proceeds to set forth the dissimilarity between them. The contrast, or points of difference, are thrown into relief by the points of resemblance in this way:

| | One man *Adam* | One Man, Christ |
|---|---|---|
| The Actors | One man *Adam* | One Man, Christ |
| The Action | One act of trespass | One act of obedience |
| The Character of the action viewed in its relation to the Fall and Salvation | The great initial trespass or breach of the law of God. | The great accomplished work of grace, or the gift of righteousness. |
| Persons afflicted by the action | All mankind | All mankind |
| Proximate effect of the action | Influx of many transgressions | Clearing away of many transgressions |
| Ulterior effect of the action | Loss Death | Gain Life |

Paul graphically portrays sin and death, grace and life as opposing sovereigns. He speaks of death reigning and of grace and righteousness as reigning (Romans 15:14,17). Man is controlled by the one Sovereign or the other. When God fashioned the heart of man He made it as a throne capable of holding only one sovereign at a time. Who and what reigns in your life? That Old Testament Scriptures were written with a view to New Testament readers is proved by the Apostle's three-fold assertion:

*Genesis* was "for us" (Romans 4:23,24)

*Deuteronomy* was "for our sakes" (I Corinthians 9:9,10)

*Exodus* and *Numbers* were "for our admonition" (I Corinthians 10:10)

*The Marriage Bond.* Discussing the obligations of true union with Christ, and the precise nature of Christian freedom, Paul borrows an illustration from the estate of marriage to expand his teaching that we are not under the law but under grace (Romans 6:14,15). Having worked out "the conclusion of the Christian to sin, so now he works out that of his death to the Law."

In a marriage-contract, the bond is dissolved by the death of one of the parties to it. In like manner the identification of the Christian with Christ in His death, releases him from his obligation to the Law, and brings him into a new and spiritual union with Christ (Romans 7:1-6). Now married to Him, such a mystical and eternal union with Him is productive of fruit in holiness and service.

*The Olive Tree.* The parable of the *Engrafted and the Wild Olive Branches* contained in Romans eleven makes it one of the most important in Jewish history. Paul uses a familiar symbol of Israel, to describe the change of dispensation under the figure of the breaking off of the natural branches of the olive tree, and the grafting in of the Gentiles. This engrafting, as Paul shows, brought the Gentiles into possession of many of the blessings and privileges of Israel, including their responsibilities as witnessbearers, and thus the olive of the Old Testament changes to the olive of the New. With the setting aside of Israel the mercy of God was extended to all men, and the symbolism Paul uses proves that believing Gentiles come by faith into the system of blessing indicated by God with Abraham. As Israel, a branch broken off, so Gentiles, as engrafted branches, must take heed lest, through sin, they are cast off as worthless branches (John 15). "If He spared not the natural branches, neither will He spare thee."

*The Builders.* Similes our Lord used

concerning Himself in His parables are applied to His servants also. He is the Builder of the Temple, His Church (Matthew 16:18), and we, too, are builders with the responsibility of using the right kind of materials (I Corinthians 3:9-15). The other parable of *The Wise and Foolish Builders* — one house on rock, the other on sand, can be compared to Paul's parabolic teaching about building. Paul makes use of the same double symbolism which the Gospel presents — of God as the *Husbandman* and as the *Builder*. In both respects "we are labourers together with God." "Ye are God's husbandry, ye are God's building." Paul compares himself to a husbandman in planting and watering (I Corinthians 3:6), and to a master-builder who lays a good foundation for another to build on (I Corinthians 3:10). In the Apostle's *Parable of the Bema* (I Corinthians 3:10-15), the builders are all saved ones, are all on the foundation, but also build with different materials. In *The Parable of the Two Builders* (Matthew 7:25-27; Luke 6:48,49), both saved and lost are represented, the difference being in the foundation: rock and sand. May our works stand the test of the fire!

*The Temple.* Jesus spoke of His physical body as a *Temple* (Mark 14:58) and Paul uses the same figure of speech to describe the Church at Corinth (I Corinthians 3:16,17). As punishment befell those who defiled the ancient Temple (Exodus 28:43; Leviticus 16:2), for it was made holy because of the indwelling Divine Presence, so believers indwelt by the Spirit are holy unto the Lord, and will not go unpunished if they defile the spiritual temple. Individual believers, as well as the Church as a collective body, are spoken of as a Temple (I Corinthians 6:19; II Corinthians 6:16). Other expressive figures of speech for the reader to develop are minister, stewards, kings (I Corinthians 4:1,8), a theatre (I Corinthians 4:9 margin), tools (I Corinthians 4:10).

*The Leaven.* Twice over Paul uses the pregnant expression, "A little leaven leaveneth the whole lump" (I Corinthians 5:6; Galatians 5:9). In the first instance, Paul is referring to evil deeds; and in the second reference, he is speaking of evil doctrine contrary to nature, and commands the purging out of the leaven. It is not possible in actual fact to take away leaven from the meal (Matthew 13:33), but in spiritual things the only way of preventing the leaven of evil deeds and evil doctrines from spreading is to remove them. Paul told the Church at Corinth that until the leaven (the sinning member in the Church) had been purged out, the Church could not keep the Feast with the unleavened bread of sincerity and truth. Both the Corinthians and the Galatians had to learn that a holy God cannot tolerate evil whether in deed or doctrine.

*The Sower.* The echo of the Master's parable of *The Sower* is heard again and again in the epistles, both Pauline and general. The Lord and His servants are sowers of the seed of the Word. Paul, quoting Isaiah, says, "How beautiful are the feet of them that preach the Gospel of peace" (Isaiah 52:7), and all heralds of the cross are sowers of the seed (II Corinthians 9:6,10). While the narrative is taken up with the receiving and giving of temporal things, the same truth applies to the receiving and sowing of the Word of God. "We must sow that which has already fed our own souls; and the harvest will be in proportion to the amount of the seed sown." The sowing and harvest correspond (II Corinthians 9:6). Paul also tells us that the harvest will not only depend on the *quantity* of the seed sown, but on the *quality* of the seed. "We reap *what* we sow" (Galatians 6:7-9). We can read *The Parable of the Tares* alongside of Paul's solemn warning.

The Apostle also uses the figure of sowing and reaping in his great Resurrection chapter, which has been called "The Magna Charta of Resurrection" (I Corinthians 15). The dead body placed in the grave is to take on a more glorious form when Jesus comes (I Corinthians 15:37,38). As with the seed in our Lord's parable (Mark 4), when the harvest is come, the seed will be found to have grown, we know not how.

Closely linked to sowing and reaping is that of fruit-bearing, just as there is a vital connection between *The Sower* and *The Vine.* Paul, more than any other apostle, clearly defines the fruit-bearing branch (Galatians 5:22,23). The cluster of precious fruit which Paul describes consists rather of *life* than of *service. Living* is not the same as *service,* although both are associated with fruit-bearing, and the two should always harmonize. We are to be fruitful in every good work. Sometimes, however, a believer, because of physical disability, cannot serve although suffering may yet be passively fruit-bearing.

In *The Parable of the Vine,* the Father is the Husbandman who is glorified as the Branches bear much fruit (John 15). Paul re-echoes this same truth in his second letter to young Timothy, "The husbandman that laboureth must first be partaker of the fruits" (II Timothy 2:6), which has a double application: the Divine Husbandman and His under-husbandman. This whole chapter offers several expressive similes. The key-verse of the chapter is, "Remember Jesus Christ" (II Timothy 2:8), around which the Apostle gathers various figures of speech illustrating our relationship to Jesus Christ:

> We are soldiers — He is the Divine Captain (v. 4)
> We are athletes — He is the Umpire with rewards (v. 5)
> We are workmen — He is the Master we serve (v. 15)
> We are vessels — He is the Owner using us (v. 21)
> We are the fruit — He is the Husbandman refreshed by the fruit (v. 6).

In his parabolic illustrations Paul often uses *pairs.* Plants and buildings, for example, are coupled as similes of saints:

> *"Rooted* and *built* up in Him" (Colossians 2:7)
> *"Rooted* and *grounded* in love" (Ephesians 3:17)
> "Ye are God's husbandry, ye are God's building" (I Corinthians 3:9)

The Apostle thus followed the Master in the use of the same double symbolism. The leaders of Israel were compared to husbandmen and to builders. Israel and the Church are spoken of as a Vine and a Flock (Psalm 80; John 10:15).

*The Coming Night.* Another connection between the parables of the *gospels* and the parabolic illustrations in the *epistles,* is that of our Lord's Second Advent. The Holy Spirit was promised as the Enlightener of future events. "He shall show you things to come," and it is Paul who by the Spirit unfolds the truth of the Lord's Return for His Church. In his writings, Paul is prominent as "The Apostle of the Rapture," employing many striking similes of such a blessed hope.

As with our Lord so with Paul, *night watching* is emphasized. This age is the world's dark night, but for the believer "the day is at hand." We must not sleep as did the virgins, but casting off the works of darkness, clad ourselves with the armor of light, even with Him who is *The Light* (Romans 13:11-14). Because the dawn of the glorious morn is near, we must live as those who are ready. We are not to sleep like those who belong to the world's night season. We must be alert and ready to hail Christ at His coming (I Thessalonians 4:13 — 5:10).

Lingering amid the gathering shadows, Paul reminds us in graphic language of our responsibility to Him who is returning for His own. Awaiting His coming, we are to function as "ambassadors for Christ" (II Corinthians 5:20) — an ambassador being equivalent to the messengers sent forth in the gospel parables to invite guests to the feast. As the day of grace continues, we are to beseech men to be reconciled to

God. Then Paul follows Christ in the simile of the "steward" to illustrate the kind of service we are to render as we await His return from "the far country." As His *ministers* and *stewards* of His mysteries (I Corinthians 4; Matthew 13), we are to be faithful in the use of the Master's goods, and not to waste them as the unjust steward did (Luke 16). If the service to which He appoints us seems to be hard, unattractive and not likely to yield results, we are not to rebel. Under the figure of the ox, Paul stresses the necessity of obedience to the will of God (I Corinthians 9:9,10).

## Military and Athletic Metaphors

Prominent among the figures of speech Paul employs are those associated with the customs of the Romans and Greeks which are not found in our Lord's parables because of their inappropriateness to His audience. Writing to the Romans and Greeks, Paul used those illustrations with which the people were familiar. We have:

The figure of the soldier in complete armour (Ephesians 6)

Soldiers, who have Christ as their Captain (II Timothy 2:3,4; 4:7; Hebrews 2:10)

Warriors who must fight a good fight (Joshua 11:18; II Timothy 4)

Victors who triumph over sin and Satan (II Corinthians 2:14; 10:5)

Athletes who win and wear the crown (I Corinthians 9:24-27; II Timothy 2:5; 4:7; Hebrews 12:1-3)

*The Two Women.* Dealing with the typical significance of Israel's past history, Paul shows that the story of Hagar and Ishmael was allegorical and declares that all the events of the wilderness journeyings happened to the people for types and were written for our ad-

monition as we journey from the Egypt of this world to the heavenly Canaan (John 3:14; I Corinthians 10:11). In his allegory on slavery or liberty (Galatians 4:25 — 5:1), Paul, adopting the plan of duality, enumerates these opposite and opposing features:

The Two Women — Hagar, the slave; Sarah, the free-born.

The Two Sons — Ishmael, son of the slave; Isaac, son of promise.

The Two Mountains—Sinai, scene of Divine Law; Jerusalem, sphere of Divine Grace.

The Two Covenants—with Moses; with Abraham.

The Two Generating Powers — the flesh, Ishmael thus born; the promise, Isaac thus born.

The Two Actions — the flesh, persecuting; the spiritual, enduring by faith.

The Two Results — flesh disinherited; grace inheriting.

These two sets of irreconcilable conditions and circumstances are before Paul, particularly in *Romans, Galatians* and *Hebrews,* in which he contrasts *law* with *grace* and clearly teaches that if we are children of God through faith in Christ's finished work, then we are free from the dominion of the Law.

*Living Epistles.* From the example of His Lord, Paul acquired the habit in his exposition of the truth of gliding softly and quickly from a common object of nature to the deep things of grace. As Jesus could take the water of Jacob's well as an illustration of the Water of Life, so Paul could make any common topic a stepping-stone over which he carried his hearers into the more serious matters of the Kingdom of God. The practice of carrying letters of commendation was introduced at an early period into the Christian Church. There were those of doubtful character who carried a letter signed by worthy names. Some of these recommended workers had been spoiling Paul's efforts at Corinth. When challenged to produce his own letter of recommendation, Paul said to the Elders, "Ye are our epistle" (II Corinthians 3:2,3). The great results of his labor were proof enough of his divine call.

Believers, then, are open letters for all to read. Christ is the Author, and the writing is not by pen and ink but by the Holy Spirit. Paul speaks of himself as the scribe, and the material on which the writing was inscribed was not a wax tablet but living personalities. While it is a great privilege to carry Christ's message by lip and literature to others, it is much more important that the *life* should be His message.

In a natural way, Paul goes from a written letter or epistle, to Christians as letters to be known and read of all men. What an expressive figure of speech this is! The reeds, leaves, or skins used by the ancients all needed preparation before they could be written upon, just as rags today, the raw material of paper, must be processed before the paper can be written on. How illustrative this is of our new creation! Black, because of our sin, the precious blood made us white as wool. Further, over against legible writing on paper, we have Christ written in our hearts, and as a letter can reveal character, as epistles or letters we must have conduct corresponding to character. What we believe must be reflected in behavior. Can those around read the life of Jesus in our actions? Writing on letters may be erased or fade, but "the epistles of Christ" have durable writing which time cannot erase or fade. The Holy Spirit is the Divine Penman and what He writes, abides. He also writes in the plainest letters for all to see.

For those who are physically blind, we have the remarkable *Braille System,* whereby dots and letters instead of appealing to the eye, are raised from the surface so as to be sensible to the touch of the blind reader. It should be thus with the writing of Christ's mind on our heart and life. The writing should be in characters raised and sharp and high, so that those who are still blinded by sin, as they read us day by day, may realize that Christ dwells in our hearts by faith.

*The Shipwreck.* While it would be profitable to have a complete list of *all* the similes and metaphors Paul uses in his matchless epistles, we conclude with this one of the shipwreck of faith (I Timothy 1:19). There is a vital connection between faith and a good conscience. The former results in the latter, but when a man surrenders faith he soon begets a bad conscience, and a shipwrecked life follows. Without the anchor of faith, which pleases God, we drift and sink as a ship does when it dashes against the rock that should have been avoided. Upon the sea of life, there are many wrecks. I think of young men with simple faith in divine verities, who, desiring to be well-educated for the ministry, went to a modernistic college and received their degrees but lost their convictions. We have too many of these theological wrecks floating around in the ministry. May grace be ours to remain anchored to Christ and to the infallible Word of God!

Space fails us to dwell upon the multiplied metaphors Paul uses in all of his epistles. How full his pastoral, prison and prophetic Letters are of figures of speech taken from many realms of life! To dwell on these with the aid of the lists E. W. Bullinger gives in the index of his monumental work on *Figures of Speech,* opens up a vast field of profitable exposition for the preacher. As an example, take *Ephesians,* where the illustrations of riches, inheritance, seal, earnest, children, workmanship, wall, foreigners, citizens, household, temple, corner stone, heirs, prisoner, body, savor, fruit, light, armour, and other similes are used with great effect by the Apostle. Such an array of telling illustrations, proves how they are as windows for the heavenly light to shine through.

# PARABOLIC INSTRUCTION IN THE GENERAL EPISTLES

James, Peter, John and Jude, all alike, familiar with Christ's symbolic teaching through contact with Him, employ the same method if only in a somewhat limited degree.

## Parabolic Material in James

First of all, let us glance at the epistle of James. As "the Lord's brother," he would not be ignorant of the illustrative way Jesus had of presenting His message. Thus, in his epistle, written to his own countrymen scattered over the earth, James uses striking similes in writing of practical Christian living to his Christian brethren. His denunciations, rebukes and warnings are couched in appealing imagery, making his epistle not "worthless as one of straw," as Martin Luther called it, one of sterling worth to every believer. Here is a brief summary of the figures of speech James employs:

*Waves.* Those who waver in faith and are doubleminded, are compared to a "wave of the sea driven with the wind and tossed" (James 1:5-8). Yet the One who walked the troubled sea is near the storm-tossed soul to console and deliver.

*Grass.* The rich, exhorted to manifest lowly-mindedness, are reminded that in spite of all their possessions they must pass away as "the flower of the grass" (James 1:9-11; Isaiah 40:6-8). What a simple yet forceful simile of human instability and vanity is here presented!

*Drawn and Dragged.* Those who yield to temptation are described as being "drawn and dragged" by their lust (James 1:12-15). The striking figures "drawn . . . enticed" reveal the sad process of temptation yielded to. Arnot has this comment on verse 14: "The first expression does not yet mean drawn *by* the hook; it means rather drawn *to* the hook. There are two successive drawings, very diverse in character. In classic

Greek, the first term is indifferently applied to both; but in this case the circumstances confine it to one. The first is a *drawing* towards the hook, and the second is a *dragging* by the hook. The first drawing is an invisible power, the second is a rude and cruel physical constraint. The first is a secret enticement of the will, the second is an open and outrageous oppression by a superior force, binding the slave and destroying him." How imperative it is to discern the subtle, satanic hook, or to follow the exhortation of the Master, to watch and pray lest we *enter* into temptation! Once hooked, the way of the transgressor becomes hard.

*The Looking Glass.* James, in his warning as to self-deception, urges us to have a true knowledge of ourselves. We must be *doers* of the Word, not *hearers* only. The man who only hears, but fails to act upon what he hears, is like "a man beholding his natural face in a glass" (James 1:22-25). The glass, or mirror, is God's infallible Word, a true mirror of the soul. Alas, too many look into the mirror and see themselves as they actually are in God's most holy presence, but the vision is only superficial or momentary, for they continue to live unto themselves. If we are honest with what the mirror reveals and obey the light, then there comes a transformation of heart and life. "Beholding as in a mirror the glory of the Lord, we are changed into the same image" (II Corinthians 3).

*The Bridle, Bit, Rudder, Fire.* It is James, above all other Bible writers, who gives us much practical and parabolic advice on the power of the tongue. If "slow to speak," then our testimony will not be spoiled by letting the tongue loose in untruth, unkindness, or damning speech. Grace must be ours to proximate, "He hath not slipped with his tongue" (Ecclesiastes 15:8). Sins of the tongue, and warnings and examples of uncontrolled speech, are given in plenty (James 1:26; 3:1-12). If speech is not to be offensive, it must be governed. Moses, the meekest of men, failed once in speaking inadvisedly with his lips (Psalm 39:1). Five comparisons of the tongue are introduced by James:

*The Bridle.* If the most unruly member of the body, the tongue, is in subjection to Him into whose lips grace was poured, then the whole body will be controlled.

*The Bit.* By means of the *bit,* the wildest of horses may be tamed. Mastery is gained by discipline. If we allow Christ to set a watch over our lips, then our whole life will be directed by His will.

*The Rudder.* "The very small helm," or tiny rudder of a mighty ship, helps to direct its course. The tongue is only a little member, but is often boastful of what it can do. The tongue directs the ship either on the right course, or on a disastrous one.

*The Fire.* The smallest spark may kindle a forest fire resulting in colossal damage. In fact, James had in mind "the picture of the wrapping of some vast forest in a flame, by the falling of a single spark." Then he applies the illustration, "the tongue is a fire . . . that world of iniquity." How we need to exhibit the godly discipline of silence and thus escape the damaging effects of an uncurbed tongue.

God promised that all kinds of beasts would be mastered (Genesis 1:26-28). The most untamed creature can be won by kindness, patience and gratitude. But the tongue, James says, no man can tame. What is not possible with man, however, is possible with God.

*The Fountain.* Both sweet and bitter water cannot issue from the same fountain. It must be one kind or the other. Thus is it with the tongue. From it comes evil or good, poison or healing-balm, cursing or blessing, wild berries or figs, salt water or fresh. If we would be wise then we must trust the Lord to control our tongue, making possible thereby, "a good conversation" coupled "with works of meekness and wisdom, gentleness and peace" (James 3:13-18). What need we have to pray Job's practical prayer, "Teach me, and I will hold my tongue" (Job 6)!

*A Vapour.* To all those who are abandoned to pleasure, or absorbed in the quest of gain or material advancement, James has a warning as to the uncertainty of the future as well as the brevity of life. This practical Apostle asks, "What is your life?", and then goes on to say, "This is your life. It is even a vapour, that appeareth for a little, and then vanisheth away" (James 4:13-17). Man counts on the morrow, but it may never come. All he has lived for may pass away as a breath. "Dust we are, and a shadow." Because the future is in the hand of God, His will is best. Possessions and time must be under the control of One supremely wise and living Will. Our attitude at all times must be "If the Lord will" (I Corinthians 4:19).

*The Husbandman.* James, who has much to say about the grace of patience, urges the saints to be patient in the light of the Lord's return as the Husbandman to gather His precious fruit (James 5:7-11). When James used this simile did he have in mind his illustrious Brother's parable of Himself as the Husbandman, who, at His return from a far country would gather His harvest? Impatience, on our part, is a sign of weakness. We must emulate the patience of Him who has waited so long for a great ingathering.

# Parabolic Writing in the Epistles of Peter

The epistles of Peter are characterized by the use of vigorous, gripping metaphors and illustrations, some of which are indeed terrible when Peter comes to describe false teachers and scoffers. It is a most profitable exercise to search for those germs of all the doctrines in our Lord's teaching, which the Apostles subsequently repeated and expanded. Peter, remembering the words of the Lord Jesus regarding readiness for His return (Luke 12:35), exhorts the saints to "gird up the loins" of their minds. This metaphor was taken from persons gathering up the flowing Oriental dress (let down for repose but gathered together for energetic action and an immediate journey, I Kings 18:46).

In his exhortation to holiness of life, Peter reminds us that we have been redeemed at infinite cost (I Peter 1:15-20). To redeem a person meant to ransom him, to deliver him out of slavery or captivity by paying a ransom (Matthew 20:28; Mark 10:25; I Timothy 2:6). Christ as the Lamb gave His life a ransom, and by His death and resurrection delivers us from all our foes. What a beautiful and articulate symbol of true redemption Peter provides us! A blood-bought emancipation from the bondage of the vain and vicious habits of sin is ours through the blood of the Redeemer.

Then it is Peter who gives us one of the most expressive similes of the Word of God. He calls it the *incorruptible* seed (I Peter 1:23). "The corruptible seed" refers to Abraham. But salvation could not come from Abrahamic descent. Man can only be saved through the revelation of a spiritual regeneration as the Bible unfolds (John 3:5-7). The Word of God is Christ Himself (John 1:1), and He alone can save.

When Peter says that *all flesh is as grass* (I Peter 1:24-25), he borrows the parabolic illustration Isaiah used to describe the temporary nature of life (Isaiah 40:6-8). Man is here today — gone tomorrow. The analogy used is as exact as it is beautiful. First, there is the simple and comprehensive intimation, "All flesh is as grass." Then we have a more special analogy rising out of it, "The glory of man is as the flower of grass." Man himself is like the grass — his glory like its flower. Life is short, and the period of its perfect develop-

ment is shorter still. No matter how fragrant and attractive the flower of humanity, it is short and withers and dies.

Discussing those elements of disunion, tending to separate those who were recently incorporated into a new life in Christ, Peter goes to the nursery for two illustrations of spiritual immaturity. "As newborn *babes*," those who were still far from maturity in Christ, were exhorted to "desire the sincere *milk* of the Word" (I Peter 1:23). Paul likewise used the metaphor of *milk* (I Corinthians 3:2). Infants, while such, thrive on milk, and "the sincere milk of the Word" refers to those simplicities of the Gospel so easy for young Christians to understand. As with children, so with believers, as they grow and develop, more nourishing body-building food is required (Hebrews 5:14).

*A Blood-Treasure.* After dealing with those who blatantly rejected Christ, Peter turns to the privileges and position of those who embraced Him as their Messiah-Saviour. The divine estimation of their new life (I Peter 2:5; Colossians 3:3,5), must now be lived out. All the glorious titles of the old Israel belong in a fuller sense to those who are now the true Israel of God.

1. *A Chosen Generation.* The redeemed were chosen in and by God before the foundation of the world. The spring of our choice and redemption were in the Father's purpose. "Thine they were." But the new race or generation is not one of common physical descent. We are a new creation in Christ Jesus.

2. *A Royal Priesthood.* Because of our relationship to the King who was crucified, we are "a kingdom of priests." Through grace, we are made "kings and priests unto God" (Revelation 1:6).

3. *An Holy Nation.* The world has no "holy nation." Of old, Israel was a holy nation when beneath Mount Sinai, but she prostituted her privileges and became a degraded and divided nation.

Through Christ's redeeming work, all the saints form His consecrated nation or people.

4. *A Peculiar People.* This word "peculiar" does not carry with it its present connotation of being "odd" or out of the ordinary. It means a people for His own possession, or for His special reservation (Exodus 20:5). "Peculiar," actually means "over and above," and was common to the secular life of the Romans. Law and custom permitted a slave to acquire private property through his own skill and industry. If he accumulated a considerable sum he could purchase his liberty and thereby raise himself to a high position. The savings of such a slave were called his *peculium,* his very own property, with the law protecting his right to his own. The figure of speech as used by Peter indicates the kind of ownership God is pleased to claim in those won back to Himself after they had been the slaves of sin. All, saved by His grace, are His own cherished treasure.

Further parabolic germs received from the Master which Peter develops are those of Christ as a *Stone,* and His Church as a *Temple,* or Spiritual House (I Peter 2:4-8). And Peter, as we can see, had a fondness for explaining his figures of speech which proves how closely he walked in Christ's footsteps. *The Stone* we come to is not a dead one but a *living* one, even Him who spoke of Himself as "The Stone." All who are His become "living stones," polished after the similitude of a palace (Psalm 144:12; I Corinthians 3:9). Together the living stones form a "Spiritual House," an edifice time cannot decay or destroy.

*Strangers and Pilgrims.* Dealing with the arena of conflict, Peter describes the fighters waging the war through life against multiform sin as *strangers and pilgrims* (I Peter 2:11). What is the difference between a "stranger" and a "pilgrim"? A stranger is a person *away* from home; a pilgrim one who is on his *way* home. Are we not both away from

our heavenly home, yet on our way to such a blissful home?

When Peter penned this simile he had in mind those military monarchies whose policy it was to employ soldiers away from home, or who had not a home to care for, and who were thus more completely at the disposal of their commanders. As soldiers of Jesus Christ, we should not be at home in the world. Because our citizenship is in heaven, we ought not to mind earthly things (Philippians 2:18-30). The more loosely connected our hearts are to things on earth, the more firm will be the anchor of our souls on high.

Urging us to follow the steps of the Master, Peter uses a curious word for "example," found nowhere else in the New Testament (I Peter 2:21-25). It means the *copy book* which the child must write from, or a *plan* suggested for carrying out in detail, a *sketch* to be filled in. We are to copy the way Jesus endured suffering and thereby "follow His steps." The day was when Peter was called to follow those steps, and he did so literally (Matthew 4:19). As our *Shepherd* and *Bishop* we are to follow Him. With his acquaintance with the *Parable of the Good Shepherd* (John 10), it was natural for Peter to use the simile of the *Shepherd.*

When he comes to deal with the subjection of wives to husbands, Peter ventures upon the theme of the most fitting *adornment* for wives (I Peter 3:1-7). In these days when colossal sums are spent on hair styles, jewelry and fashionable clothes, it is necessary to turn to the Bible for advice about these trifles. Here we have a portion dealing with female adorning and others condemning one style of adorning and commending another. The God who fashioned our bodies tells us what style of apparel makes His children beautiful. It is not physical beauty but spiritual holiness, not costly jewels but the possession of the more precious promises, not the costliest and most fashionable clothes but the ornament of a meek and quiet spirit. Grace in "the hidden man of the heart" is the most suitable adornment. The best of apparel and ornaments are perishable, but the spiritual adornment is imperishable. Ordinarily a woman's ornaments are worn to be seen and admired, but the ornament of great price in God's sight is hidden within, yet is seen in a life of holiness. Concerning the duty of husbands toward their wives, Peter says that honor is to be given to wives, as weaker *vessels* (I Peter 3:7). Vessel is used of the body (I Thessalonians 4:4), and here refers to female physical frailty. Men, built for rougher tasks, are by implication less delicate vessels.

In his exhortation to the elders, Peter returns to the parabolic teaching of the Master, and to His final commission. Before He left Peter, Christ enjoined him to "feed my sheep." Taking up the same simile, Peter urges the Elders to *feed the flock* of God without any thought of personal gain or superiority (I Peter 5:1-4). If they function as faithful, humble, under-shepherds, then when Christ, who as the *Good Shepherd* died for the sheep, returns as the *Chief Shepherd,* He will reward them with the unfading crown of glory.

As shepherds have to be vigilant, preserving the flocks while drowsy, from a prowling lion, so we must be alert seeing that the devil as *a roaring lion* (I Peter 5:8) is always prowling about seeking to devour "the little flock." Says Ellicott, "Satan is eyeing all the Christians in turn to see which he has the best chance of, not merely stalking forth vaguely to look for prey."

When Peter came to speak of his immediate death, he referred to it as the putting off of a *tabernacle* (II Peter 1:14, 15). Christ had foretold that Peter's death would be a violent one (John 21:18), and so he knew that no ordinary death-bed would be his. The phrase, "the putting off of my tabernacle," involves "a mixture of metaphors; we have a similar mixture in Colossians 5:1-4. The word for 'putting

off' occurs nowhere but here and I Peter 3:21."

Dealing with the prophetic Word, Peter strings several metaphors together. The more sure word of prophecy is a *"light* that shineth in a dark place, until the day dawn, and the day star arise in your hearts" (II Peter 1:19,20). The Prophetic Scriptures, like John the Baptist, are as a "lamp that is lighted and shineth," preparatory to the Light. *Dawn* can mean two things:

1. The clearer vision of the purified believer, whose eye is single and whose body is full of light (I John 2:8).

2. The return of Christ in glory to illumine the darkness of the world and show the way through its obscurities. *Day star* occurs nowhere else in the New Testament. Christ speaks of Himself as "the bright morning star" (Revelation 22:16).

Describing God's judgment upon false teachers and those who are corrupt and presumptuous, Peter employs some striking epigrammatic descriptions. He calls them *natural brute beasts,* fit only for destruction because of their corrupt influence (II Peter 2:12-13). Because of their luxurious living, they are as *spots* and *blemishes* (II Peter 2:13-14) in contrast to those godly souls "without spot and without blemish" (I Peter 1:19). Of these adulterous, covetous, self-indulgent sinners, Peter says they are "cursed children" and *wells without water* — dried up, not able to refresh the thirsty, and *clouds carried away with a tempest* — mists promising refreshment but so flimsy as to be blown away by the wind. It is thus that false teachers deceive those thirsting for true knowledge (II Peter 2:17). The parable describing these wicked men will be realized, "The *dog* is turned to his own vomit again; and the *sow* that was washed to her wallowing in the mire" (II Peter 2:22. See Proverbs 26:11). What abandonment to abomination is here figuratively depicted!

Discoursing on the longsuffering of God, who is not slack concerning the redemption of any of His promises, Peter, using Old Testament language, says that "One day is with the Lord as a thousand years, and a thousand years as one day" (II Peter 3:8,9; Psalm 90:4). This means that according to divine reckoning it is not quite two days since Jesus died. Then dealing with "the Day of the Lord," not "the Day of Christ," which is related to His return for His own, but "the Day of the Lord," which is associated with judgment, Peter, employing language he had heard the Master use, adopts the figure of *the thief* coming at night (II Peter 3:10; see Matthew 24:43; Mark 13:3; I Thessalonians 5:2).

Coming to the epistles of John, it is not surprising to discover how almost devoid they are of symbolic illustrations. His gospel, as we have seen, uses the word "proverb" for "parables," and while rich in its allegorical material, does not mention our Lord's parables. It is evident that the words of the Master made a deep impression on John's mind. In after years, as he meditated upon them, he reproduced them rather than his own thoughts and words. Thus, in his epistles he writes with "the most commanding authority and the most loving tenderness," in simple, clear and calm language, unadorned by imagery. Contrasts are marked — light and darkness, life and death, Truth and lying, holiness and sin, loving and hating, love of the Father and love of the world, children of God and children of the devil, the Spirit of Truth and the spirit of error: *Light and Darkness* (I John 1:5-7; 2:10,11) are about the only similes John uses and are reminiscent of the Apostle's previous language (John 1:5; 12:35). The parallels between John's gospel and first epistle of John, as tabulated by Ellicott, will be found profitable for the student to explore.

The concluding brief, poetic and vivid epistle of Jude, has a graphic style all its own — "broken and rugged, bold and picturesque, energetic, vehement, glowing with the fires of passion . . . it has at the same time a considerable command of strong, varied, and expressive terms." The reader should note Jude's fondness for triplets, of which there are some twelve groups in the twenty-five verses of his epistle. Then there is also the matter to consider of similarity between II Peter and Jude.

In his endeavor to urge the saints to contend for the faith in an age of deepening apostasy, Jude exposes and denounces evil-doers and false teachers in a series of striking symbolic terms. Nowhere else in the Bible can we find so many arresting declarations and figures of speech crowded together in so small a space. An early Church Father, Origen, referred to the epistle of Jude as, "an epistle of few lines, but one filled full of strong words of heavenly grace."

*Everlasting Chains.* The angels who rebelled with Lucifer before man was placed on this earth were by divine judgment condemned to bonds of darkness to await the greater judgment of The Great White Throne (Jude 6; II Peter 2:4; Revelation 6:7; 16:14; 20:10). These bound angels are different from those who have freedom and activity but who are as apostate as the former (Luke 22:31; I Peter 5:8; Ephesians 6:12).

*Filthy Dreamers.* Those, like the Sodomites, who defile the flesh, libertines who provoke God, are described in a series of arrestive similes. While the word "filthy" is not in the original, it is used in the same sense of the next clause, "*defile* the flesh." *Dreamers* cover those who "defile the flesh, despise dominion, and speak evil of dignities." All of these ungodly men are deep in the slumber of sin, and are like dogs who, when they dream, make a noise in their sleep (Jude 8; Romans 13:11; Isaiah 56:10). As a dream is somewhat empty, "dreamers" may refer to the empty speculations of those Jude vividly described.

*Brute Beasts.* When men by grave irreverence abuse what they do not know and cannot know, and by gross licentiousness, abuse what they know, and cannot help knowing, they become both brutal and bestial (Jude 10; Romans 1-3). Such corrupt men work their own ruin — present and eternal.

*Spotted Feasts.* "The rocks in your feasts of charity" (Jude 12) may refer to those practices wrecking the love-feasts. In a scandalous way the libertines gorged themselves first instead of feeding the poor which was one great purpose of the love-feast (I Corinthians 11:21; Isaiah 56:11). While Peter uses the word "spots" (II Peter 2:13), seeing he dwells on the sensuality of sinners, the word Jude uses has the significance of rocks in his analogy between Cain and the evil-doers. "These libertines, like Cain, turned the ordinances of religion into selfishness and sin; both, like sunken rocks, destroyed those who unsuspectedly approached them."

*Clouds Without Water.* Empty clouds are easily carried about, or driven out of their course, by winds. How empty and flimsy the sinner is! Lacking stability of character, he is easily swayed by any wind of passion. How disappointing it is when clouds giving promise to the farmer, prove to be without water! (Jude 12).

*Trees With Withered Fruit.* What a contrast we have here to those good men who meditate upon the Word of God and are like trees planted by the rivers of water, bringing forth fruit in their season! (Psalm 1). Believers are branches of the Vine and should bring forth much fruit. Jude piles metaphor upon metaphor in an effort to express his indignation and abhorrence over those who are so destitute of godliness. They have only barrenness where there should have been fruit. They are "twice dead," that is, utterly dead. After a profession of faith, they returned to the death of sin, and being barren and completely dead, they

are fit only to be plucked up by the roots and cast out into the fire (Jude 12; II Peter 1:5-8).

*Raging Waves.* What a symbol this is of those who possess no stability, but are easily swayed by every wind of doctrine, and whose life produces nothing but vanishing foam! Jude uses the plural, *shames,* meaning, their shameful acts. These wicked people are "like the troubled sea, whose waters cast up mire and dirt" (Isaiah 57:20). How different is the epithet of those who are built upon the firm "Rock of Ages," and whose life and witness are consistent and established! (Jude 13).

*Wandering Stars.* The ungodly, Jude depicts, are unlike the planets, moving in their regular orbits with mathematical precision and order because of their subservience to the laws of their Creator. They resemble those erratic meteors or comets that flash in the heavens for a brief while then wander away into sunless gloom and darkness forever (Jude 13).

*Pulling Them Out of the Fire.* Before Jude closes his epistle with a wonderful benediction he has a solemn exhortation for all those who are built on the Rock, pray in the Spirit, keep themselves in the love of God, and look for the mercy of our Lord Jesus Christ unto eternal life. There must be a deep compassion for the lost, an endeavor to win those who are separated from us because of their sin. Having a hatred for garments spotted by the flesh, and trusting Him who is able to keep us from falling, we must yet exhibit deep concern for those who are altogether spotted by the flesh. We are to pull them out of the fire — out of the fire of their own sins enveloping them, and out of the coming fire of judgment (Jude 22-25).

# PARABOLIC INSTRUCTION IN THE REVELATION

What a marked contrast in style there is between John's epistles and the Revelation, which he also wrote! The former are unadorned as far as imagery is concerned, while the latter book is parabolic throughout. In symbolic and apocalyptic language, John was inspired of the Spirit "to encourage and stimulate the people in times of national distress by the assurance of a glorious future in the triumph of Israel's long-wished-for Deliverer." But when Christ appears to reign, it will not only be as Israel's Deliverer. He is to govern as "the Prince of the kings of the earth" (Revelation 1:5).

We have also a contrast in tone and temper between John's epistles and the Revelation. Yet both *thunder* and *tenderness* were in the Apostle's make-up (Mark 3:17). The former books display his *thunder* (I John 2:22; 5:16; II John 10; III John 9; 10), while the Revelation is eloquent with *tenderness,* as well as the thunder of judgment (Revelation 1:9; 7:14-17; 21:3,4). The symbolism John uses was not of his own creation, but simply a new combination of ancient Hebrew symbols, almost all of which are traceable in the Old Testament. Dr. Scroggie affirms that "every figure in *Revelation* is drawn from the Old Testament. Of its 404 verses, 265 contain Old Testament language, and there are about 550 references to Old Testament passages. But for the Old Testament this book would remain an utter enigma."

While this last book of the Bible is related, both by contrast and comparison, to its first book, yet, in the main, Revelation, because of its prophetic content, is more related to Daniel than to any other Old Testament book. While Daniel outlines Gentile history during the succeeding Empires — Babylonian, Medo-Persian, Grecian and Roman — John deals only with the last phase of Roman history. Daniel presents the whole course of the Roman Empire. Revelation is a book of consummations, just as Genesis is a book of commencements.

Our present purpose is to show that John's prophetic book (Revelation 1:3; 22:7,10,18,19), revealing as it does so many future events, is written largely in symbolic or parabolic language. Hence the statement in its prologue, "He sent and *signified* it by His angel unto John." The word "signified" means "*sign-ified*," or given in *signs* and *symbols* of which there are more here than in any other book of the Bible. Many neglect revelation because of its highly symbolic character, not knowing that the symbols, if not explained in the book itself are explained in some other part of the Bible. Daniel was told to "seal up" the words of his prophecy until the "Time of the End" — not the end of time — but the end of the "Times of the Gentiles." John, writing of such a time being at hand (Revelation 22:10), was instructed to "seal not" the sayings of the book.

The expressive symbolism of Revelation is related to Christ and His Church, at the beginning of the book; to Israel, in the middle; to the Nations, at the end. In the construction of the Holy City, the New Jerusalem, the Church is the foundation represented by the names of the Twelve Apostles; Israel is the gates with the names of the Twelve Tribes written over them; the saved nations are the *streets,* where they walk in the light of the City's Glory.

To fully expound all the figures of speech in Revelation would mean an exposition of this fascinating book as a whole — a task which has been admirably accomplished by Walter Scott in *The Exposition of Revelation.* All that we can do is to list the symbols with a brief comment on their respective significance, thereby completing our study on the parabolic in Scripture. In consecutive order we have:

# 1. Symbols of the Glorified Son of Man in Vision

(Revelation 1:1-20)

A feature giving this book supreme value is the fact stated at the beginning, namely, that it is *The Revelation of Jesus Christ*. Such a symbolic unveiling covers our Lord's —

*Nature:* He is Alpha and Omega, Lord, Word, Jesus, Christ, King, Master, Lamb, Lion, Bridegroom, Morning Star.

*Activities:* He chastens the Church; restores the Jews; judges the world, Satan and his hosts, the wicked; reigns as King.

*Relations:* To the Father, the Spirit, the angels, saints, sinners, heaven, earth and hell.

Habershon observes that John's 'preface' "establishes a link between the *Apocalypse* and the *Parables* for they, too, were a revelation first from God Himself to the Lord Jesus Christ, and then from the Lord to His servants, of things which would shortly come to pass. Matthew was not the composer of the parables recorded by him, and John did not originate the visions which he then described. The Lord Himself being the Author alike of the Apocalypse and parable, we shall expect to find the same symbolism in both. He presents Himself in the Revelation as in the parables as King, Master, Owner of a Vineyard, Husband, Shepherd, Conqueror and Judge; while men are spoken of as subjects, sheep, fruit of the earth, virgins, and corporately under the figure of a woman and a bride."

The *visions* John saw were largely the continuation of the picture stories he had heard from the lips of Jesus on whose bosom he leaned. John had seen his Lord in humiliation; now he sees Him in glory. As the Apostle's "hearing ear" listened to the Master's parables, so now his "seeing eye" gazes on visions of His majesty and conquering power.

The *salutation* (1:4-6) was not only from John to the Churches but also from "the seven Spirits, which are before His throne." There are not seven "Holy Spirits." By the seven here we are to understand the sevenfold manifestation of the Spirit of God (see Isaiah 11). Then the spiritual mind can discern precious truth in Christ as the *Prince,* and in ourselves as *kings* and *priests*.

Coming to the Vision, "a great voice, as of a *trumpet*," said, "I am *Alpha* and *Omega,* the first and the last." These two names are the first and last letters of the Greek alphabet and declare that Jesus is the Beginning and the Ending, and all in between. Then we have a seven-fold description of Christ, in His judicial and kingly capacity, as He stands among the seven golden candlesticks: "His head and his hairs were white like wool, as white as snow."

This beautiful language is akin to Daniel's vision of the "Ancient of Days, whose garment was white as snow, and the hair of his head like the pure wool" (Daniel 7:9). As a color, *white* is symbolic of "purity"; and when applied to hair denotes old age. Unflecked holiness characterized Christ's life among men. "Which of you convinceth me of sin?" (John 8:46). Here, His *white hair* refers to His antiquity, to His patriarchal dignity, the venerableness of His character. As the Eternal One, He never grows old, and therefore does not have hair white by age.

"His eyes were a flame of fire." In Scripture, *fire* is expressive of divine holiness and justice. The eyes of Jesus had looked in anger upon those rejecting His claims, and had often been stained with tears as He wept with the sorrowing, and also over the sinning. Now His eyes burn with an "omniscient flame." When He comes to judge the earth, all things will be open and naked before His searching gaze.

"His feet like fine brass, as if they burned in a furnace." *Brass* is symbolic of deserved judgment, as the Brazen Serpent on the pole (John 3:14) indicates. The feet of Jesus, still bearing their nail-marks, will be as "incandescent brass" when He descends to tread and crush the Antichrist and also Satan in wrath of Almighty God" (Revelation 19:15).

"His voice as the sound of many waters." This figurative expression is capable of several interpretations, just as the movements of waters are manifold. We have the melodious or musical babbling brook, or the thunderous rush of a cataract over the falls. When He comes in power and glory His own will be consoled with the note of tenderness in His voice, but how fearful will His words be when, as the Judge of all the earth He passes sentence upon the doomed and the devil (Matthew 25:41)?

"In His right hand seven stars." In biblical usage, *the right hand* illustrates the place of position, authority, responsibility. *The Seven Stars* are equivalent to the *angels* of the Seven Churches to whom Jesus wrote. *Angels* describe not only angelic messengers, or ministers, but human ones as well. Here the representative leaders of the Church are described as receiving their office and power from Him who holds them in His right hand. As *stars,* they are to reflect His glory.

"Out of his mouth went a sharp two-edged sword." The *sword* is an emblem of the Word of God (Ephesians 6:17; Hebrews 4:12). Being two-edged it can cut both ways. If the Word does not save, it slays. It will function as a destroyer of Christ's enemies, when He comes to smite the nations (Revelation 19:11-15).

"His countenance was as the sun shineth in his strength." Glory and majesty shone from His face at the Transfiguration (Matthew 17:2). When He returns as "the Sun of Righteousness" (Malachi 4:2), a seven-fold glory will radiate from His strong and radiant countenance. Such radiance will supply all necessary illumination for the New Jerusalem (Revelation 21:23).

## 2. Symbols Related to the Seven Churches
### (Revelation 2; 3)

The letters constituting these two chapters were not only sent to seven churches in existence in John's day. The churches were representative churches and typical of seven well defined periods in Church history from its inception at Pentecost right on to the Rapture. These churches are spoken of as *Candlesticks,* or "Light-holders," meaning that the church's function is to shine for Jesus amid the darkness of the world.

To the *church at Ephesus* (Revelation 2:1-7), the message went that the Builder of the church walked in the midst of it. If, however, the church failed to walk with Him and return to its first love, then as a *candlestick* it would be taken out of its place. Those who within this backsliding church remained true to their Lord, would eat of "the *tree* of life," the promise of a restored Paradise (Genesis 3:8; I John 1:3). This boon of immortality is Christ's own gift to overcomers.

To the *church at Smyrna,* Christ reveals Himself as "the first and the last," and all in between (Revelation 2:8-11). Religious hypocrites are described as forming "the *synagogue* of Satan." As to the "ten days," they symbolize, "The Ten Great Persecutions under the cruel Roman Emperors. *Smyrna,* meaning 'bitterness,' is associated with *myrrh,* an ointment associated with death." The promised reward for martyrdom was "a *crown* of life."

To the *church at Pergamos,* Christ speaks of Himself as having a "sharp sword with two edges." This figurative language describes the power of His Word to save or slay. Pergamos is referred to as Satan's *seat,* that is, his center of operation, and from which he inspired Constantine to inaugurate his Christian commonwealth. It was also at this time that Roman Catholicism commenced to flourish. Against all apostates and errors the Lord said He would fight with "the sword of my mouth." To those remaining true to Him in such a degenerate age, there was the promise of *hidden manna,* a *white stone,* and a *new name.*

To the *church at Thyatira,* the Lord reveals His eyes as a *flame* of *fire,* and feet of *fine brass* — symbols found in John's vision of the Lord (Revelation 1:19-26). The *Jezebel* of the Old Testament (I Kings 16:19-33), caused all Israel to sin after the sin of Jeroboam the son of Nebat. Whether the *Jezebel* Christ refers to in His letter was a real person or not, is hard to determine. What is evident is that she typified an evil system responsible for pernicious doctrines, seduction and idolatrous worship. A careful study of the development of the papal system with its paganizing of Christian rites, corresponds to the *Jezebelism* of the church at Thyatira. To those resisting the false claims of such a system there is the promise of power to rule the nations with a *rod of iron,* and the possession of the *Morning Star.* These figures of speech represent the overcomer's coming authority and glory.

To the *church at Sardis* (Revelation 3:1-16), the Lord describes Himself as possessing the *Seven Spirits of God* and the *Seven Stars.* Such parabolic language, slightly different from that previously used (1:4), implies that the Lord is not only the Sender of the Holy Spirit, but also His Owner or Possessor, and that He alone can make the messengers of His Church shine as stars. To those in the formalistic, spiritually-dead church at Sardis, who sought to stem the tide of ritualism, the Lord promises clothing of *white raiment* and everlasting remembrance in *the book of life.* Walking with Him in the robe of the lustrous white of glory, will be the eternal reward of faithful witness. His coming *as a thief* takes us back to the parabolic teaching of the Gospels (Matthew 24:42,43; Luke 12:39,40).

To the *church at Philadelphia* (Revelation 3:7-13) Christ speaks of Himself not only as the Holy and True One, but also as having *the Key of David* (Isaiah 22:22; Hebrews 3:2,5,6). The recognized teachers of the Law had failed to use the key of knowledge aright (Luke 11:52). Christ is the true Steward of the House of David. If this Philadelphian church represents the revival of the church in the seventeenth century, after the dead period of the Dark Ages, then through the revivals of Whitefield and the Wesleys, and the missionary work of William Carey, the door of grace was opened to multitudes. Here, overcomers are referred to as receiving a *crown,* becoming a *pillar* in the divine Temple, and bearing the signet of *Christ's New Name.* Behind these expressive symbols is the prospect and possession of reward for keeping the Word of His patience.

To the *church at Laodicea* (Revelation 3:14-22), a Church for which He had no commendation whatever, but only complaint, Christ provided a magnificent cameo of Himself. He is "The Amen, the Faithful and True Witness, the beginning of the Creation of God." These titles are symbolic of His unchangeableness, custodianship, and headship. How full of expressive symbols is this letter of severe rebuke! The self-righteous, self-contented and affluent church in Laodicea was neither *cold* nor *hot,* but *lukewarm,* and because of its tepid condition, nauseating to Christ, He said that He would *spue* it out of His mouth. Here we have a parable of the rejection of the apostate organized church at His return for His true church.

For its cankered or ill-gotten gold, the church was counseled to buy of the Lord, *"gold* tried in the fire," heavenly untainted riches; for the spiritual blindness to the Saviour's claims and worth, *"eye-salve"* that they might see. Merchants with their ointments and herbs of healing value could not supply any salve able to restore impaired spiritual vision. Only the Divine Unction can do this. For their spiritual nakedness the church members were urged to purchase of

Christ *"white raiment"* without which no one can stand in His presence. For their inclusion of all but exclusion of Him within the precincts of the church, individuals were lovingly asked to open the *door* and let Him in. What a contradiction of terms is a *Christless church!* Only to those who open the *door* to Him, will there be a *door* opened in heaven (Revelation 4:1).

## 3. Symbols Associated With the Seven-Sealed Book
### (Revelation 4-8:1)

From now on, the Apocalypse John received is permeated with impressive parabolic illustrations. They seem to fall thick and fast. *Thrones, rainbows, precious stones, lamp of fire, sea of glass, crowns of gold, living creatures, a seven-sealed book* with its descriptions of different *horses* are all marshalled to illustrate the bliss of the faithful, the sorrows and terrors of the godless, as well as Christ's governmental control of all things. All right is His, as the slain *Lamb,* to break the seals of judgment upon a guilty, godless world. Those unprotected by His *sealing* must certainly perish. The seventh *seal of silence* (Revelation 8:1) indicates a lull before the storm. The silence in heaven will be intense as God's terrible judgments burst forth on the earth under the *trumpets* and *vials.*

## 4. Symbols Connected With the Seven Trumpets
### (Revelation 8:1-11:15)

Following the awesome silence in heaven, seven angels with seven trumpets appear, and an eighth angel is seen having an incense-filled golden censer in his hand. Prayers of the saints ascended to the *altar* as pure incense, then the censer was filled with the fire of judgment as vengeance upon their enemies. *Thunderings, lightnings, earthquakes, hail, fire, seas* turned into *blood, locusts,* cavalry of *scorpion locusts, beasts* out of the *bottomless pit,* are all

harnessed to prepare the way for the coming of "the King everlasting" to fashion the rebellious kingdoms of earth into His own world-kingdom. Great events, the most remarkable and momentous that has ever happened on this earth, will be encountered by those who are alive as they occur.

## 5. Symbols Introducing the Seven Personages
### (Revelation 12-13:18)

The *first* personage in this section is the "woman clothed with the sun and the moon under feet, and upon her head a crown of twelve stars: and she being with child cried, travailing in birth, and pain to be delivered" (Revelation 12:1-2). This highly parabolic portion has been variously interpreted. The Old Testament presents *Israel* as a *woman,* and a married one (Isaiah 54:10). Sun-clothed and star-crowned takes us back to Joseph's dream of the sun, moon and eleven stars, Joseph himself being the twelfth star (Genesis 37:9). Such symbolic language describes the privileges and blessings which Israel as a nation received from God (Romans 9:4-5). Then it was from Israel that Christ came. As the promised seed He came from the tribe of Judah.

The *second* personage, *the dragon,* was another "wonder" appearing in heaven (Revelation 12:3-4). Characteristics of the dragon can be identified in the following ways:

As the *dragon,* "the old serpent, the devil," is the fierce, destructive enemy. As the *great dragon,* he is the *prince* of darkness and death, and as the *red* one he is depicted as a murderer (John 8:44), *red* being the color of blood.

*His seven heads, ten horns, seven crowns,* typify the universality of Satan's dominion and the seven-fold perfection of his power as the god of this world, and as the prince of the powers of the air (Ephesians 6:12; John 12:31; 14:30; 16:11).

*The third part of the star of heaven* cast down to earth by the dragon's tail is emblematic of the expulsion from heaven of the angels (referred to as stars in Job 38:7) who followed Satan in his rebellion; and also of their share in increased Satanic activity before Satan's imprisonment for one thousand years.

*The Child,* about to be delivered, which the dragon waits to devour as soon as it is born, is no other than the "man-child," the Lord Jesus Christ. From the first announcement of Christ as the coming seed of the woman (Genesis 3:15), Satan set out to destroy the royal seed from which the Saviour was to come, and almost succeeded. Then he tried to prevent the birth of Christ, and having failed, sought to kill Him when the edict went forth to slay all innocent male-babes. Foiled again, the dragon endeavored to kill Christ before He reached the cross to secure man's redemption.

This parabolic sketch of the dragon may be linked to the Parable of the Widow who cried continually to the judge, "Avenge me of mine adversary." The dragon is the great adversary behind all the other enemies of Israel. Here in symbolic language John describes Satan's last attempt to persecute and destroy God's chosen people. But crying "day and night" for deliverance God will avenge them speedily.

The *third* personage (Revelation 12:5-6), *The Man-Child,* is spoken of as having power and authority "to rule all nations with a rod of *iron.*" Christ, who came as the Seed of the woman, is the One to be endowed with universal dominion. He is to break the godless nations with a rod of iron and dash them in pieces as a potter's vessel (Psalm 2). At His Ascension, Christ was "caught up" unto God and was seated at the right hand of the Father's throne (Hebrews 1:3). While His rule will be autocratic, it will not be tyrannical. He will rule and reign in righteousness.

The *fourth* personage, the *Archangel* (Revelation 12:7-12), declares "war in heaven." Opposing armies are set for a grim and final conquest. Michael and his angels face the great dragon, the Serpent, called the devil and Satan, and his angels, and the true angelic host prevail. Satan, the accuser, is cast down as "the celestial potentate," as the prince of the powers of darkness in the heavenlies (Ephesians 6:12), to the earth, and woe be to the inhabitants of the earth! Knowing that the time is short before his millennial imprisonment, he will be filled with, and manifest, great wrath. Grace will be granted *the brethren* to overcome the devil through the shed blood of the Redeemer, and through their own Spirit-inspired testimony. Divine coverage will also be granted to the "sun-clothed woman," Israel, during Satan's fierce antagonism. God will be their "City of Refuge."

The *fifth* personage is *the remnant* of the woman's seed (Revelation 12:17). By the remnant we understand the believing remnant of Israel, who refuse to bow the knee to the "image of the beast." Inspired by Satan, the Antichrist will wage a remorseless war of persecution against godly Jews, and many of them will die a martyr's death. The last half of "The Great Tribulation" is spoken of as "the time of Jacob's trouble," but God will be a present help in such a time of anguish (Psalm 46:1).

The *sixth* personage, *the beast out of the sea* (Revelation 13:1-10), will be the incarnation of the dragon, the Antichrist. How vivid is the parabolic presentation of his power, authority and cruelty! Out of the *sea* means, he is to emerge from the restless nations. *Beast* fittingly describes the character of this wicked one, the son of perdition and wilful king (II Thessalonians 2:3-8; Daniel 11:36). The seven heads and ten-crowned horns symbolize the beast's empire in which "the great whore" will play a prominent part. This satanically-controlled empire will include all the four characteristics of the four empires Daniel described. The *beast* is the Roman Empire; the *lion,* Babylon; *the leopard,* Greece; the *bear,* Medo-Persia. What deserved destruction will be meted out to this blasphemous beast as Christ returns to earth (II Thessalonians 2:3-10).

The *seventh* personage, *the Beast out of the earth* (Revelation 13:11-18), is the companion of the previous beast. The *first* beast is to head up everything in the political realm, and the *second* beast, everything in the religious sphere. Lamb-like, this second beast has *two horns* and is called *The False Prophet* three times (Revelation 16:13; 19:20; 20:10). His association with the dragon and the beast out of the sea brands him an evil person. The satanic trinity will be composed of the dragon, the beast and the false prophet. In some mysterious way the false prophet will be a miracle-worker causing fire to fall from heaven. His task will be to command the people to make an image of the beast and worship it. All will be forced to bear "the mark of the beast." Those refusing this "brand of hell" will be starved to death or killed.

## 6. Symbols Illustrating the Seven Vial Judgments
### (Revelation 15-16)

Before the emptying out of the wrath of God upon the godless we have the Lamb on Mount Zion with the 144,000 saved and sealed ones who sing a new song accompanied by the heavenly harpists (Revelation 14:1-5). This great host of saved singers is Israel — 12,000 from each tribe (Revelation 7:3-8; 15:2-4). Then we have three angel messengers. The *first* angel proclaims "the everlasting Gospel," and the hour of divine judgment (Revelation 14:6-7). The *second* angel announces the fall of Babylon and the merited judgment of its people (Revelation 14:8). The *third* angel declares the doom of the followers of the Antichrist (Revelation 14:9-11); and also the eternal blessedness of those who die in the Lord (Revelation 14:12-13).

The parabolic illustration of the harvest and the vintage (Revelation 14:14-20) reminds us of *The Parable of the Tares,* and the binding up of the tares for burning (see Isaiah 63; Joel 3:12, 13). The seven golden vials containing the seven plagues represent the perfection and completion of divine judgment upon a guilty earth. Seven angels, beautifully adorned from the temple of the tabernacle of testimony (Revelation 15:5-8), received the seven vials which were full of the wrath of God.

From the *first vial* there was poured out upon those who bore the mark of the beast and worshiped his image (Revelation 16:1,2) "a noisome and grievous sore." This is a repetition of the plague of boils that came upon the Egyptians for their idolatry (Exodus 9:8-12). As with such a plague, so with this vial, hearts were hardened and those afflicted refused to repent (Revelation 15:9).

From the *second vial,* an unmentioned substance was poured upon the sea making it as the blood of a dead man, with all life in and on the sea becoming dead (Revelation 16:3; see 8:8-9). As the restless *sea* is used as a symbol of the masses of men revolutionary in character, *the sea* becoming blood points symbolically to a scene of *moral death.* Jude speaks of those who are *twice dead* although physically alive. Universal moral corruption is deserving of judgment, as in the days of the flood.

From the *third vial,* judgment fell upon the rivers and fountains of waters changing them into blood. Those causing the blood of martyrs to be shed were given blood to drink (Revelation 16:4-7). This terrible vial recalls the first Egyptian plague when the sacred waters of the Nile were turned into blood and all fish died (Exodus 7:19-24). The phrase, "angel of the waters," indicates that certain divisions of nature are controlled by angels. "Thou art righteous," proves angelic acquiescence in divine judgment. Walter Scott, dealing with the symbolism at this point, says, "the national corruption is of a deeper kind — moral death and complete alienation from God are the results. The 'rivers,' the ordinary life of a nation characterized by known and accepted principles of government, social and political, its life-breath so to speak, as also 'fountains of waters,' the sources of prosperity and well-being, are all turned to blood, symbolically of course . . . *Blood* is the witness of death. In retributive justice, in holy righteousness, God judicially gives over the persecutors of His people to drink blood, to realize in their own souls and consciences *death* . . . an installment and foretaste of the horrors of the Lake of Fire."

From the *fourth vial,* power came to the sun to scorch men with fire and with great heat (Revelation 16:8,9; see 8:12). By angelic action, the heat of the sun is so intensified that men's bodies are seared with terrific heat and "burn as an oven" (Malachi 4:1-2). Because of the parabolic nature of the language used, by *the sun,* we understand the supreme governing authority, extending to the bounds of Christendom. Such a great governing power is to become the cause of intense and frightful anguish to those deluded by the Antichrist. Burnt, or scorched, naturally conveys the anguish arising from the increasing severity of God's judgments (Deuteronomy 32:24; Malachi 4:1). But so thoroughly corrupt will man be that the storm of divine wrath will not bring forth the fruits of repentance. Blasphemy of the divine name is to be the response to deserved chastisement.

From the *fifth vial,* wrath descends upon the throne of the beast and thick darkness upon his kingdom. How graphic is the description of those who suffer. "They gnawed their tongues for pain, and blasphemed the God of heaven because of their pains and sores, and repented not of their deeds" (Revelation 16:10-11). The ninth Egyptian plague of darkness offers a parallel to this vial of darkness (Exodus 10:21-23). This is the day of darkness which both Joel and Christ foretold (Joel 2:1-2; Mark 13:24). As this vial of dark-

ness follows the one of scorching heat it would seem as if God in mercy hides the sun-rays so hard to bear. John leaves us in no doubt as to the specific subject, namely, the center and seat of the beast's power and dominion. The executive of the kingdom receives the stroke of divine judgment — a forerunner of the darkness and blackness forever (Matthew 25:30). Wm. Ramsay says of the phrase, "They gnawed their tongues with distress," that it is "the only expression of its kind we have in all the Word of God, and it indicates the most intense and excruciating agony." So morally dark, hearts fail to bow in penitence.

From the *sixth vial,* there comes power to dry up the literal "great river Euphrates" (Revelation 16:12). The reason for such an action is stated, namely that the kings from the East with their armies may cross over and assemble for the Battle of Armageddon (Isaiah 11:15-16). Such a drying up of the waters will also enable the remnant of Israel to journey from Assyria to Palestine. What righteous retribution is to overtake the vast assemblage of opposing forces! The *three unclean spirits,* likened unto *frogs,* symbolize the trinity of evil, the dragon, the beast and the false prophet — a combination of direct satanic power and apostate brute force — who are to aid the massing of the most gigantic combination of opposing forces ever witnessed. But they, along with those they deceived, are doomed to destruction.

From the *seventh vial* (Revelation 16:17-21), there come thunders, lightnings, a great earthquake, great hail, every stone about the weight of 100 pounds. Hail has ever been one of God's engines of destruction (Exodus 9:13-35; Joshua 10:11). How fearful and awesome is the unleashing and intensification of the powers of nature! A voice from the Throne says, *It is done.* As Christ expired on the cross He cried, *It is finished,* which was the accomplishment of salvation for a sinning race.

Here, *It is done* announces the completion of the wrath of God upon a godless world.

## 7. Symbols Depicting the Seven Dooms
### (Revelation 17-20)

The graphic contents of these four chapters are indeed most solemn, presenting as they do in striking parabolic form, not only many startling events, but God's final judgment on an apostate Christendom, upon godless rulers, Satan and his evil hosts and also the wicked dead.

The *first* doom is taken up with *ecclesiastical Babylon* (Revelation 17:1-18). An angelic messenger revealed to John the judgment of *the great whore.* What is the significance of the vivid aspects of this foul creature? A *whore* is a woman who prostitutes the natural function of her body, and as used here the figure of speech represents a church far removed from its divine purpose, a false Church guilty of spiritual whoredom. This condemned church will be the satanic counterfeit of Christ's true Church. As Satan is the ape of God, so the bride of the Antichrist will be the ape of the Bride of Christ.

Paul speaks of the Church of the living God as a *mystery* (Ephesians 3:1-21), a designation taken over to describe, "Babylon the Great." It is not unusual for *bride* to be used of a *city* (Psalm 46:5; Revelation 21:9-10). Here the *city* represents, not a literal city, but an apostate religious system, a system composed of a rejected organized religion (Revelation 3:16), heathen religions and the Papal Church with the latter dominating such a renegade system. The religion of Babylon is that foreshadowed in the church of Thyatira, which represents the Papal Era in Church testimony.

The whore's fornication with the kings of the earth portrays her unholy association and traffic with the ungodly rulers of the earth — the culminating of the marriage of the Church and the State

in Constantine's reign. The *beast,* on which the whore rides, is the Antichrist, while the *seven heads* and *ten horns* represent those ruling authorities holding allegiance to the beast. The whorish woman arrayed in *purple* and *scarlet* and bedecked with *gold, precious stones* and *pearls,* is most suggestive, seeing that *scarlet* and *purple* are the present colors of the Papacy, and the Pope's mitre is studded with pearls, gold and precious stones. As for *the golden cup,* this is filled not with the blood of Christ, which priests declare they drink every time Mass is performed, but with abominations and fornications, and with the blood of martyred saints. The history of the persecutions of early Christians, the terrible story of "The Inquisition" in lands controlled by Roman Catholicism, as well as massacres in England, brand the Papal Church as a murderess, drunk with the blood of saints.

But John describes how the federated kingdoms under the beast, finding their power curtailed by a professed ecclesiastical system with supreme power, will hate such a "whore," strip her of her gorgeous apparel, confiscate her enormous wealth, and burn her churches of idolatrous worship (Revelation 17:16). What a terribly solemn occasion it will be when all tares will be separated from the wheat, and all leaven from the meal!

The *second* doom brings us to the destruction of commercial Babylon (Revelation 18:1-24). That the *woman* and the *city* do not symbolize the same thing is apparent. The *woman* is destroyed by the *ten kings,* while the *city* is destroyed by a mighty earthquake and fire, which occurs, it would seem, three and a half years after the end of the *woman,* the mystical Babylon of the previous chapter. The judgment of the magnificent city, as wicked as it is wealthy, takes place in "one hour," which is illustrative of the suddenness and completeness of a perverted civilization once the mighty angel takes up *the great millstone* and casts it into the sea. Fire also is to help in the obliteration of the city which "shall be found no more at all" (Revelation 18:21; see Jeremiah 50:40). Such drastic treatment will be necessary to purge a city allowing itself to become the habitation of devils, the hold of every foul spirit, and the cage of every unclean bird. Before such a sudden and total destruction overtakes the city, God will mercifully deliver those who remained true to Him in spite of such a polluted environment: "Come out of her, my people, that ye be not partakers of her sins, and that ye receive not her plagues."

An interval between this doom and the next is taken up with the great, heavenly *Hallelujah Chorus* (Revelation 19:1-7). All heaven concedes that the judgments overtaking both mystical and commercial Babylon were deserved. The cry of victory, a fourfold *Hallelujah* or its Greek form *Alleluia,* is ascribed to the omnipotent Lord God. There also takes place in this interval "The Marriage of the Lamb" (Revelation 19:8-10), of which the parables of the marriage feast and the great supper were forecasts. Now the Christ and His true Church are openly united, the Bride and the Bridegroom become One. The Church is now ready to assist her Lord in the governmental control of the earth during His millennial reign (Revelation 20:1-7).

Then we have a parabolic presentation of Christ as the Conqueror, who is depicted as returning to conquer all His foes, riding on a *white horse,* His eyes as a *flame* of *fire, many diadems* on His head, vesture *dipped in blood,* a *sharp sword* in His mouth, a *rod of iron* in His hand, and feet treading the *winepress of the fierceness and wrath of Almighty God.* The *armies* of heaven accompany Him riding upon *white horses,* clothed in *fine linen and clean.* The fowls of the air are invited to the *supper of the great God* to feast upon the flesh of the alien armies and their horses (Revelation 19:11-19).

The "White Horse Rider" herewith described is not to be confused with the one John presents in a previous chapter (Revelation 6:2). There the rider is the Antichrist with a bow in his hand, but his name is not given. Here the Rider is Christ, the Word of God, and He has not *a crown,* but *many crowns;* and uses not a bow, but a sharp sword. While on earth, Christ rode on an ass (Zechariah 9:9; Matthew 21:4-11); here He sits astride a magnificent white charger, which language is figurative of our Lord as He comes forth as a Conqueror (II Kings 2:11; 6:13-17), with 10,000 of His saints (Jude 14).

The fearful Battle of Armageddon will be the day of vengeance as foretold by the prophets (Isaiah 63:1-6). The pouring out of *the vials* (Revelation 14:14-20) was a prophetic foreview of the time Isaiah speaks of when the land shall be "soaked with blood" (Isaiah 34:1-8; Zechariah 14:1-3). Are you not relieved to know that through grace you will not be on the earth when its harvest of judgment will be ripe (Revelation 14:15), to be caught up in its terrible slaughter? All who are Christ's will form His armies of heaven, and sing in triumph:

Lo, He Comes! from Heaven descending,
Once for favoured sinners slain:
Thousand thousand saints attending,
Swell the triumph of His train!
Hallelujah!
Jesus comes, and comes to reign.

The *third* doom reveals the absolute victory of the White Horse Rider and His armies. The issue of the battle will never be in doubt. Christ is destined to make His enemies His footstool. *The beast,* or the Antichrist, and the miracle-working *false prophet,* responsible for deceiving many people, are both to be taken captive and cast *alive* into a lake of fire burning with brimstone (Revelation 19:20). As Enoch and Elijah were caught up to heaven without dying, so these two foul creatures are cast into hell without dying, and will still be there and alive when their hellish master, Satan, joins them a thousand years later. The language John uses proves that *the beast* and the *false prophet* are not "systems" but "persons," persons responsible for the creation of a system of anarchy and rebellion designed to rob God of His power and glory.

The *fourth* doom brings us to the destruction of antichristian nations (Revelation 19:17,18,21; see Ezekiel 39:1-12; Matthew 24:27,28). So great will be the slaughter that the occupants of Palestine will be seven months burying the bones of the dead. God will prepare for the aftermath of such carnage. In advance, provision will be made for it lest the stench of the unburied dead should breed pestilence. His hordes of feathered scavengers will be on hand to fill themselves with the flesh of the slain (Revelation 19:21). For the supernatural aspect of the destruction of a great army by means of great hail, the reader is directed to *All the Miracles of the Bible.*

Before the pronouncement of the next doom we have the binding of Satan for a thousand years (Revelation 20:1-3). The four names used — *dragon, old serpent, Devil* and *Satan* — as well as the fact that he is to be *bound* proves him to be a person and not an influence or principle of evil. The *great chain, bottomless pit,* shutting up and sealing, are all symbolic of Satan's impotence to escape from his captivity (II Peter 2:4; Jude 6). The "star angel" (Revelation 9:12), will be the custodian of the "key" of the "pit." Nothing is said of the binding of other evil agents during the millennium. Doubtless with their master in captivity, and Christ in control of all things, they, too, will be rendered powerless during the period. As the Omnipotent One, He can cause the Devil and his hosts to cease their activities when He is ready. After the thousand years of our Lord's princely rule, a rule shared by the Church, and the martyred saints of the Great Tribulation (Revelation 20:4-6), Satan is to be loosed for a little season (Revelation 20:7-8). Embittered by his long imprisonment and burning with hatred against God and

His people, the devil will try to lead a universal rebellion against them.

The *fifth* doom describes the fatal result of Satanic deception. Fire from God out of heaven destroys Gog and Magog (Revelation 20:7-8). This will be the last war this earth shall ever see, and it will be bloodless. Having promised Noah that He would never again destroy the earth with another universal flood (Genesis 9:11), God will purge it by fire (II Peter 3:7).

The *sixth* doom declares the banishment of the deceiving devil to eternal captivity. *The lake of fire* was prepared for him and his angels (Matthew 25:41), as the place of their eternal punishment. Whether or not the *fire* and *brimstone* are literal or only symbolic, this we do know, the actual experience will be more terrible than any figurative speech.

As *the Revelation* is the only book in the Bible recording the final perdition of the devil and his dupes, we can understand why he hates this book, confuses the issues it presents, and strives to keep people from reading it. It is hurtful to his satanic pride to have the world know what a terrible humiliating end awaits him. How Christ, the Seed of the woman, is to triumph gloriously over him!

The *seventh* doom provides us with a solemn symbolic presentation of the last judgment, *The Great White Throne* (Revelation 20:11-15). This "Judgment of the Great Day" (Jude 6) will be *great* seeing it will eclipse all other judgments in respect to its place, basis of judgment and result, and the Judge Himself. It will be *white* because of the purity of the judgment rendered. As the Judge of all the earth, He will do what is right and just. He cannot act contrary to His character. The *throne* speaks of His supreme power. At this final assize the wicked dead will be raised for the ratification of their condemnation. The books of every person's life kept by the recording angel, and the Book of God, will be opened and the record against them used to indict them. Raised from hell, their temporary abode since death, the doomed are cast into the lake of fire forever — hell itself will be destroyed.

# 8. Symbols Portraying Seven New Things

(Revelation 21-22)

Immediately after the destruction of Satan and his armies, and the judgment of the Great White Throne, John saw the earth and the heaven flee away, and the appearance of a new heaven and a new earth (Revelation 20:11; 21:1). Peter foretold the destruction of the heavens and earth by fire, and the emergence of new heavens and earth wherein dwelleth righteousness (II Peter 3:7-13). The language used implies that our present earth with its surrounding aerial heavens are to be completely renovated.

There is to be a *new heaven* (Revelation 21:1). As the singular number, heaven, is used, this last creative act refers to a new atmosphere for the new earth. As the prince of the power of the *air* (air here meaning the lower atmosphere), his long sojourn in this sphere of his satanic operations has polluted it, hence the need of a purified atmosphere and one conditioned to an eternal state. When we read that "the first heaven and the first earth were passed away" (Revelation 21:1), the term *passed away* does not mean the cessation of existence or annihilation but "the passing from one condition of existence to another." Their "departing as a scroll" does not mean a total disappearance, for afterwards John saw "the New Jerusalem coming down out of heaven, and nations living and walking in the light of it on the earth" (Revelation 21:2,24; see Ecclesiastes 1:4; I Corinthians 15:24-28).

There is to be a *new earth* because this present one bears the curse pronounced on sin, and is blood-soaked and tear-stained. It also witnessed the rejection and cruel death of its Creator and must therefore be transformed. Cleansed or renovated by fire, the new earth will exist as a pure one forever.

Already our old earth carries at its heart a reservoir of fierce fire presently held in check for its purification. Then the new earth will have *no sea*. The great oceans symbolizing mystery, sorrow and separation will have no place when earth puts on its original beauty and glory.

There is to be a *new city,* mighty and magnificent (Revelation 21:9-23).

Instead of John seeing the *Bride, the Lamb's Wife,* he saw, by the Spirit, a *Great City, The Holy Jerusalem,* and it is clear that the *Bride* and the *City* are identical. Inhabitants, and not merely buildings and parks, make up a city. The New Jerusalem is *The Bride,* as well as her residence. In highly symbolical language John describes this surpassingly grand and celestial residence the Divine Architect is preparing for His Church.

With its wall of *jasper,* and foundations of all manner of precious stones, and its pyramidal top crowned with the light of *The glory of God* (Revelation 21:23,25), this city will present a glorious spectacle, made up, as it will be, of *pure gold, like unto clear glass.*

"What we in glory soon shall be,
    It doth not yet appear."

There are to be *new nations* composed only of those who are saved and who walk in the light of the magnificent City (Revelation 21:24-27). Outside of the new, beautiful City, spread over the surface of the new earth, nations shall dwell whose kings shall bring their glory and honor into the City, and worship the King of kings, whose government shall know no end (Isaiah 9:7; 66:22). Nothing that defiles will appear on this new earth.

There is to be a *new river,* clear as crystal, proceeding out of the Divine Throne (Revelation 22:1). Earthly rivers are not crystal clear. Many of them are contaminated with factory outlets and with sewerage. Natural streams have their source in mountain springs, but the *River of the Water of Life* has its source in the Throne of God. Such an expressive parabolic illustration, recalling our Lord's use of same in connection with the ministry of the Holy Spirit (John 7:37-39), reveals Him as the unfailing eternal source of life and refreshment.

There is to be a new *tree of life* (Revelation 22:2,7). The Bible commences with a garden and ends with one (Genesis 3:22-24). But with Satan in his eternal prison, there will be no fear of this garden, with its *tree of life,* being contaminated with his evil presence. Beautiful fruit trees are for the health, not the healing, of the nations. Then there will be no sickness to heal. Perhaps if Adam had eaten of the Tree of Life in the Garden of Eden he would have been preserved in health. Death came through eating the forbidden fruit.

There is to be a *new throne,* from which God and the Lamb will reign (Revelation 22:3-4). The new earth is to become the residence of the Trinity. The Divine Tabernacle shall be with men, and the Godhead shall dwell with them. Then John mixes positives and negatives in his description of all that awaits us. On the positive side we are to serve the Lord, see His face, have His name in our foreheads, which means that we are to be branded as His forever. How different this will be from the mark of the beast! Then John gives us a few "no mores." The eternal abode is described by what it will *not* have, rather than by what it will possess. No more *tears,* no more *death,* no more *sorrow,* no more *pain.* All former things springing from sin are to pass away. Behold, all things are to be new in the eternity awaiting those who belong to Him who is *Alpha* and *Omega,* the beginning and the end.

Now that we have reached the end of our revealing and rewarding study, what else can we do but praise God for the revelation of Himself, His Word affords! What attractive variety there is in the truth it presents! "Variety," we say, "is the spice of life." Well, the many facets of the divine message the Bible exhibits add great zest to our meditation on its sacred pages. With such abundant presentation before us, we should never be guilty of clinging to any given, solitary expression of truth. Parables, metaphors, symbols, emblems, figures, types, stories, illustrations and interrogations — it takes them all, and more beside, to declare God's unsearchableness. Human language at its best cannot possibly express all the glory and grace of Him whose ways are past finding out. We trust, however, that the reader has found our attempt to set forth the parabolic aspect of Holy Writ both informative and inspiring.

# BIBLIOGRAPHY

The following commentaries were consulted on parabolic teaching in general, as well as on the parables indicated in our *Contents* and *Index*.

*The International Standard Bible Encyclopaedia;* Wm. B. Eerdmans, Grand Rapids, 1939.

*Expository Outlines on the Whole Bible;* Zondervan Publishing House, Grand Rapids, 1956.

*Commentary on the Whole Bible;* Charles H. Ellicott, Zondervan Publishing House, Grand Rapids, 1951.

*Imperial Standard Bible Encyclopaedia;* Patrick Fairbairn, Zondervan Publishing House, Grand Rapids, n.d.

*The Biblical Expositor;* Carl F. H. Henry, Pickering and Inglis, London, 1960.

*Commentary on the Whole Bible;* Jamieson, Fausett, Brown, Zondervan Publishing House, Grand Rapids, n.d.

*A Guide to the Gospels;* W. Graham Scroggie, Pickering and Inglis, London, 1948.

*A Key to Open Scripture Metaphors, An Exposition of the Parables;* Benjamin Keach, City Press, London, 1856.

*Figures of Speech in the Bible;* E. H. Bullinger, The Lamp Press, Old Town, London, 1890.

*The Dictionary of the Bible;* James Hastings, T. and T. Clark, Edinburgh, 1909.

*The Bible Student's Companion,* Wm. Nicolson, Pickering and Inglis, London, n.d.

*The Bible Handbook;* Walter Scott, G. Moorish, London, n.d.

*Knowing the Scriptures;* A. T. Pierson, James Nisbet, London, 1910.

For those desiring to study the parabolic in Scripture more extensively, the list of older British and European writers Lisco cites might be available for consultation from a long established Theological College library. Trench, in an *Appendix* to his renowned work on *The Parables,* gives us the fullest list of the more important works on this subject than any other writer. Both British and European authors are named, and Trench divides their books into three sections:

1. Works Introductory to the Study of the Parables.

2. Works on the Parables in General.

3. Works on Particular Parables.

Being called to task for mentioning books in a previous work of mine (books I had not read but knew of as being reliable), I was interested to find in Trench's paragraph prefacing his list of books, this sentence: "I have here set down only such works as I know, or have reason to suppose, possess some value. Most, *but not all,* of those named have come under my own eye." Lisco also quotes a few works to which, as he says, "I have not had access." In his *Guide to the Gospels,* Dr. Graham Scroggie mentions several works "I did not have access to, and consequently are not included in the following list." Goebel, in the "Preface" to his volume on *The Parables of Jesus,* gives us a list of old writers, principally German, on the same subject.

Archibald M. Hunter. *Interpreting the Parables.* Westminster Press, Philadelphia, 1960.

Cosmo Gordon Lang. *The Parables of Jesus.* Pitman and Son, London, 1906.

G. Campbell Morgan. *The Parables of the Kingdom.* Hodder and Soughton, London, 1960.

Geo. A. Butterick. *The Parables of Jesus.* Harper and Brothers. New York, 1928.

W. W. Fereday. *Our Lord's Parables.* John Ritchie, Kilmarnoch, Scotland, n.d.

C. H. Dodd. *The Parables of the Kingdom.* Nisbet and Co. London, 1955.

Siegfried Goebel. *The Parables of Jesus.* T. and T. Clark, Edinburgh, 1883.

Wm. M. Taylor. *The Parables of Our Saviour.* Doubleday, Doran Co., New York, 1886.

Hillyer H. Straton. *A Guide to the Parables of Jesus.* Wm. B. Eerdmans, Grand Rapids, 1959.

G. H. Lang. *Pictures and Parables.* The Paternoster Press, London, 1955.

Ada R. Habershon. *The Study of Parables.* Pickering and Inglis, London, n.d.

A. B. Bruce. *The Parabolic Teaching of Christ.* T. and T. Clark. Edinburgh, 1900.

F. G. Lisco. *The Parables of Jesus.* Daniels and Smith. Philadelphia, 1850.

Principal Salmond. *The Parables of Our Lord.* T. and T. Clark. Edinburgh, 1893.

R. C. Trench. *The Parables of Our Lord.* Kegan Paul, Trench and Co., London, 1889.

H. T Sell. *Studies of the Parables of Our Lord.* Fleming H. Revell. New York, n.d.

Thomas Guthrie. *Parables of Christ.* G. B. Treat and Co. London, n.d.

J. D. Drysdale. *Holiness in the Parables.* Oliphant's Ltd., London, 1952.

G. Campbell Morgan. *The Parables and Metaphors of Our Lord.* Fleming H. Revell. New York, n.d.

L. B. Buchheimer. *Emblems in the Gospels.* E. Kaufman Ltd., Chicago, 1946.

Thomas Newberry. *The Parables of the Lord Jesus Christ.* Pickering and Inglis, London, n.d.

Wm. Arnot. *The Parables of Our Lord.* T. Nelson and Sons, New York, 1872.

Wm. Arnot. *Lesser Parables of Our Lord.* T. Nelson and Sons, New York, 1885.

Jabez Burns. *Sermons on the Parables.* Zon- dervan Publishing House, Grand Rapids, 1954.

John Cumming. *Lectures on the Parables.* Arthur Hull, Virtue and Co., London, 1852.

Edward N. Kirk. *Lectures on the Parables.* James Blackwood, London, 1850.

C. H. Spurgeon. *Sermons on the Parables.* Zondervan Publishing House, Grand Rapids, 1958.

Marcus Dods. *The Parables of Our Lord.* Fleming H. Revell, New York, n.d.

Wm. Ward Ayer, *Christ's Parables for Today.* Zondervan Publishing House, Grand Rapids, 1949.

# INDEX